Nick

Nick

MATH
6-B

Nick

PRENTICE HALL
MATHEMATICS
COURSE 1

Randall I. Charles

Mark Illingworth

Bonnie McNemar

Darwin Mills

Alma Ramirez

Andy Reeves

PEARSON

Prentice
Hall

Boston, Massachusetts
Upper Saddle River, New Jersey

Acknowledgments appear on p. 728, which constitutes an extension of this copyright page.

Dorling Kindersley (DK) is an international publishing company that specializes in the creation of high-quality, illustrated information books for children and adults. Dorling Kindersley's unique graphic presentation style is used in this program to motivate students in learning about real-world applications of mathematics. DK is part of the Pearson family of companies.

ISBN 0-13-133990-7
4 5 6 7 8 9 10   10 09

Authors

Series Author

Randall I. Charles, Ph.D., is Professor Emeritus in the Department of Mathematics and Computer Science at San Jose State University, San Jose, California. He began his career as a high school mathematics teacher, and he was a mathematics supervisor for five years. Dr. Charles has been a member of several NCTM committees and is the former Vice President of the National Council of Supervisors of Mathematics. Much of his writing and research has been in the area of problem solving. He has authored more than 75 mathematics textbooks for kindergarten through college. *Scott Foresman-Prentice Hall Mathematics Series Author Kindergarten through Algebra 2*

Program Authors

Mark Illingworth has taught in both elementary and high school math programs for more than twenty years. During this time, he received the Christa McAuliffe sabbatical to develop problem solving materials and projects for middle grades math students, and he was granted the Presidential Award for Excellence in Mathematics Teaching. Mr. Illingworth's specialty is in teaching mathematics through applications and problem solving. He has written two books on these subjects and has contributed to math and science textbooks at Prentice Hall.

Bonnie McNemar is a mathematics educator with more than 30 years' experience in Texas schools as a teacher, administrator, and consultant. She began her career as a middle school mathematics teacher and served as a supervisor at the district, county, and state levels. Ms. McNemar was the director of the Texas Mathematics Staff Development Program, now known as TEXTEAMS, for five years, and she was the first director of the Teachers Teaching with Technology (T^3) Program. She remains active in both of these organizations as well as in several local, state, and national mathematics organizations, including NCTM.

Darwin Mills, an administrator for the public school system in Newport News, Virginia, has been involved in secondary level mathematics education for more than fourteen years. Mr. Mills has served as a high school teacher, a community college adjunct professor, a department chair, and a district level mathematics supervisor. He has received numerous teaching awards, including teacher of the year for 1999–2000, and an Excellence in Teaching award from the College of Wooster, Ohio, in 2002. He is a frequent presenter at workshops and conferences. He believes that all students can learn mathematics if given the proper instruction.

Alma Ramirez is co-director of the Mathematics Case Project at WestEd, a nonprofit educational institute in Oakland, California. A former bilingual elementary and middle school teacher, Ms. Ramirez has considerable expertise in mathematics teaching and learning, second language acquisition, and professional development. She has served as a consultant on a variety of projects and has extensive experience as an author for elementary and middle grades texts. In addition, her work has appeared in the 2004 NCTM Yearbook. Ms. Ramirez is a frequent presenter at professional meetings and conferences.

Andy Reeves, Ph.D., teaches at the University of South Florida in St. Petersburg. His career in education spans 30 years and includes seven years as a middle grades teacher. He subsequently served as Florida's K–12 mathematics supervisor, and more recently he supervised the publication of The Mathematics Teacher, Mathematics Teaching in the Middle School, and Teaching Children Mathematics for NCTM. Prior to entering education, he worked as an engineer for Douglas Aircraft.

Contributing Author

Denisse R. Thompson, Ph.D., is a Professor of Mathematics Education at the University of South Florida. She has particular interests in the connections between literature and mathematics and in the teaching and learning of mathematics in the middle grades. Dr. Thompson contributed to the Guided Problem Solving features.

Reviewers

Course 1 Reviewers

Donna Anderson
Math Supervisor, 7–12
West Hartford Public Schools
West Hartford, Connecticut

Nancy L. Borchers
West Clermont Local Schools
Cincinnati, Ohio

Kathleen Chandler
Walnut Creek Middle School
Erie, Pennsylvania

Jane E. Damaske
Lakeshore Public Schools
Stevensville, Michigan

Frank Greco
Parkway South Middle School
Manchester, Missouri

Rebecca L. Jones
Odyssey Middle School
Orlando, Florida

Marylee R. Liebowitz
H. C. Crittenden Middle School
Armonk, New York

Kathy Litz
K. O. Knudson Middle School
Las Vegas, Nevada

Don McGurrin
Wake County Public School System
Raleigh, North Carolina

Ron Mezzadri
K–12 Mathematics Supervisor
Fair Lawn School District
Fair Lawn, New Jersey

Sylvia O. Reeder-Tucker
Prince George's County Math
    Department
Upper Marlboro, Maryland

Julie A. White
Allison Traditional Magnet Middle
    School
Wichita, Kansas

Charles Yochim
Bronxville Middle School
Bronxville, New York

Course 2 Reviewers

Cami Craig
Prince William County Public Schools
Marsteller Middle School
Bristow, Virginia

Donald O. Cram
Lincoln Middle School
Rio Rancho, New Mexico

Pat A. Davidson
Jacksonville Junior High School
Jacksonville, Arkansas

Yvette Drew
DeKalb County School System
Open Campus High School
Atlanta, Georgia

Robert S. Fair
K–12 District Mathematics Coordinator
Cherry Creek School District
Greenwood Village, Colorado

Michael A. Landry
Glastonbury Public Schools
Glastonbury, Connecticut

Nancy Ochoa
Weeden Middle School
Florence, Alabama

Charlotte J. Phillips
Wichita USD 259
Wichita, Kansas

Mary Lynn Raith
Mathematics Curriculum Specialist
Pittsburgh Public Schools
Pittsburgh, Pennsylvania

Tammy Rush
Consultant, Middle School
    Mathematics
Hillsborough County Schools
Tampa, Florida

Judith R. Russ
Prince George's County Public Schools
Capitol Heights, Maryland

Tim Tate
Math/Science Supervisor
Lafayette Parish School System
Lafayette, Louisiana

Dondi J. Thompson
Alcott Middle School
Norman, Oklahoma

Candace Yamagata
Hyde Park Middle School
Las Vegas, Nevada

Course 3 Reviewers

Linda E. Addington
Andrew Lewis Middle School
Salem, Virginia

Jeanne Arnold
Mead Junior High School
Schaumburg, Illinois

Sheila S. Brookshire
A. C. Reynolds Middle School
Asheville, North Carolina

Jennifer Clark
Mayfield Middle School
Putnam City Public Schools
Oklahoma City, Oklahoma

Nicole Dial
Chase Middle School
Topeka, Kansas

Christine Ferrell
Lorin Andrews Middle School
Massillon, Ohio

Virginia G. Harrell
Education Consultant
Hillsborough County, Florida

Jonita P. Howard
Mathematics Curriculum Specialist
Lauderdale Lakes Middle School
Lauderdale Lakes, Florida

Patricia Lemons
Rio Rancho Middle School
Rio Rancho, New Mexico

Susan Noce
Robert Frost Junior High School
Schaumburg, Illinois

Carla A. Siler
South Bend Community School Corp.
South Bend, Indiana

Kathryn E. Smith-Lance
West Genesee Middle School
Camillus, New York

Kathleen D. Tuffy
South Middle School
Braintree, Massachusetts

Patricia R. Wilson
Central Middle School
Murfreesboro, Tennessee

Patricia Young
Northwood Middle School
Pulaski County Special School District
North Little Rock, Arkansas

Content Consultants

Ann Bell
Mathematics
Prentice Hall Consultant
Franklin, Tennessee

Blanche Brownley
Mathematics
Prentice Hall Consultant
Olney, Maryland

Joe Brumfield
Mathematics
Prentice Hall Consultant
Altadena, California

Linda Buckhalt
Mathematics
Prentice Hall Consultant
Derwood, Maryland

Andrea Gordon
Mathematics
Prentice Hall Consultant
Atlanta, Georgia

Eleanor Lopes
Mathematics
Prentice Hall Consultant
New Castle, Delaware

Sally Marsh
Mathematics
Prentice Hall Consultant
Baltimore, Maryland

Bob Pacyga
Mathematics
Prentice Hall Consultant
Darien, Illinois

Judy Porter
Mathematics
Prentice Hall Consultant
Fuquay Varina, North Carolina

Rose Primiani
Mathematics
Prentice Hall Consultant
Harbor City, New Jersey

Jayne Radu
Mathematics
Prentice Hall Consultant
Scottsdale, Arizona

Pam Revels
Mathematics
Prentice Hall Consultant
Sarasota, Florida

Barbara Rogers
Mathematics
Prentice Hall Consultant
Raleigh, North Carolina

Michael Seals
Mathematics
Prentice Hall Consultant
Edmond, Oklahoma

Margaret Thomas
Mathematics
Prentice Hall Consultant
Indianapolis, Indiana

Dear Student,

We have designed this unique mathematics program with you in mind.
We hope that Prentice Hall Mathematics will help you make sense of the
mathematics you learn. We want to enable you to tap into the power of
mathematics.

Examples in each lesson are broken into steps to help you understand
how and why math works. Work the examples so that you understand
the concepts and the methods presented. Then do your homework.
Ask yourself how new concepts relate to old ones. Make connections!
As you practice the concepts presented in this text, they will become
part of your mathematical power.

The many real-world applications will let you see how you can use math in
your daily life and give you the foundation for the math you will need in
the future. The applications you will find in every lesson will help you see
why it is important to learn mathematics. In addition, the Dorling
Kindersley Real-World Snapshots will bring the world to your classroom.

This text will help you be successful on the tests you take in class and
on high-stakes tests required by your state. The practice in each lesson will
prepare you for the format as well as for the content of these tests.

Ask your teacher questions! Someone else in your class has the same
question in mind and will be grateful that you decided to ask it.

We wish you the best as you use this text. The mathematics you learn
this year will prepare you for your future as a student and your future
in our technological society.

Sincerely,

Randy Charles.   *Andy Reeves*

Darwin E. Mills   *Mark Illingworth*

Bonnie McNemar   *Alma Beatriz Ramirez*

Contents in Brief

CHAPTER 1

Whole Numbers and Decimals

Student Support

Assessment and Test Prep

CHAPTER 2

Data and Graphs

Student Support

Vocabulary

Assessment and Test Prep

Patterns and Variables

Algebra

Assessment and Test Prep

CHAPTER 4

Number Theory and Fractions

Assessment and Test Prep

CHAPTER 5

Adding and Subtracting Fractions

Student Support

Vocabulary

GO Online

GPS Guided Problem Solving

Assessment and Test Prep

Multiplying and Dividing Fractions

Student Support

Vocabulary 🔊

Vocabulary Review, 261, 266, 272, 276, 282, 288, 292
New Vocabulary, 272
Vocabulary Tip, 262, 290, 292
Exercises, 274

GO Online

Video Tutor Help, 272, 277
Active Math, 266, 276
Homework Video Tutor, 263, 269, 275, 279, 285, 291, 295
Lesson Quiz, 263, 269, 275, 279, 285, 291, 295
Vocabulary Quiz, 298
Chapter Test, 300

GPS Guided Problem Solving

Exercises, 263, 269, 274, 278, 284, 290, 294
Practice Solving Problems, 286
DK Applications: Applying Mixed Numbers, 302–303

Assessment and Test Prep

CHAPTER 7

Ratios, Proportions, and Percents

Student Support

Vocabulary 🔊

GO Online

GPS Guided Problem Solving

Assessment and Test Prep

Tools of Geometry

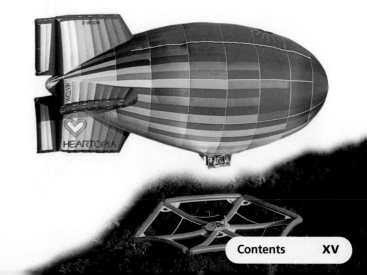
Student Support

Vocabulary 🔊

Vocabulary Review, 362, 367, 374, 380, 386, 392, 398, 402
New Vocabulary, 362, 367, 374, 380, 386, 392, 398, 402
Vocabulary Builder, 384
Vocabulary Tip, 362, 374, 403
Exercises, 364, 370, 376, 382, 389, 394, 399, 404

GO Online

Video Tutor Help, 368, 381
Active Math, 363, 387, 393
Homework Video Tutor, 365, 371, 377, 383, 390, 395, 401, 405
Lesson Quiz, 365, 371, 377, 383, 389, 395, 401, 405
Vocabulary Quiz, 408
Chapter Test, 410
Math at Work, 391

GPS Guided Problem Solving

Exercises, 364, 370, 376, 382, 389, 394, 400, 404
Practice Solving Problems, 396
DK Applications: Applying Geometry, 412–413

Assessment and Test Prep

Geometry and Measurement

Exploring Probability

Student Support

Vocabulary 🔊

Vocabulary Review, 476, 482, 488, 494, 500

New Vocabulary, 476, 482, 488, 494, 500

Vocabulary Builder, 493

Vocabulary Tip, 483, 486, 501

Exercises, 479, 484, 490, 495, 502

GO Online

Video Tutor Help, 483, 489

Active Math, 488, 501

Homework Video Tutor, 480, 486, 491, 496, 503

Lesson Quiz, 479, 485, 491, 497, 503

Vocabulary Quiz, 508

Chapter Test, 510

Math at Work, 487

GPS Guided Problem Solving

Exercises, 479, 485, 490, 496, 502

Practice Solving Problems, 505

DK Applications: Applying Probability, 512–513

CHAPTER 11

Integers

Student Support

Vocabulary 🔊

Vocabulary Review, 516, 520, 524, 530, 534, 540, 543, 548, 554, 558
New Vocabulary, 516, 548
Vocabulary Tip, 530, 548, 559
Exercises, 517, 550, 555, 561

GO Online

Video Tutor Help, 531, 535
Active Math, 521, 549, 559
Homework Video Tutor, 519, 522, 527, 532, 537, 542, 545, 551, 557, 561
Lesson Quiz, 519, 521, 527, 533, 537, 541, 545, 551, 557, 561
Vocabulary Quiz, 564
Chapter Test, 566
Math at Work, 552

GPS Guided Problem Solving

Exercises, 518, 522, 526, 532, 536, 542, 545, 550, 556, 561
Practice Solving Problems, 538
DK Applications: Applying Integers, 568–569

Assessment and Test Prep

CHAPTER 12

Equations and Inequalities

Student Support

Vocabulary

Vocabulary Review, 572, 578, 582, 587, 591
New Vocabulary, 572, 578, 587, 591
Vocabulary Tip, 588
Exercises, 574, 580, 589, 593

GO Online

Video Tutor Help, 592
Active Math, 573, 587, 591
Homework Video Tutor, 575, 581, 584, 590, 593
Lesson Quiz, 575, 581, 583, 589, 598
Vocabulary Quiz, 598
Chapter Test, 600

GPS Guided Problem Solving

Exercises, 575, 580, 584, 589, 594
Practice Solving Problems, 595
DK Applications: Applying Equations, 604–605

Assessment and Test Prep

• **Test-Taking Strategies:** Estimating the Answer, 597
• Chapter Review, 598
• Chapter Test, 600
• **Test Prep:** Cumulative Review, 601

Connect Your Learning
through problem solving, activities, and the Web

Applications: Real-World Applications

Applications: Math at Work

Applications: Interdisciplinary Connections

Activity Labs

Activity Labs: Hands On

Activity Labs: Technology

Activity Labs: Data Analysis

Activity Labs: Data Collection

Activity Labs: Algebra Thinking

Activity Labs: Chapter Projects

Problem Solving Strategies

Guided Problem Solving Features

Go Online

Throughout this book you will find links to the Prentice Hall Web site. Use the Web Codes provided with each link to gain direct access to online material. Here's how to *Go Online*:

1. **Go to PHSchool.com**
2. **Enter the Web Code**
3. **Click Go!**

Lesson Web Codes

Lesson Quiz Web Codes: There is an online quiz for every lesson. Access these quizzes with Web Codes aqa-0101 through aqa-1205 for Lesson 1-1 through Lesson 12-5. See page 19.

Homework Video Tutor Web Codes: For every lesson, there is additional support online to help students complete their homework. Access the Homework Video Tutors with Web Codes aqe-0101 through aqe-1205 for Lesson 1-1 through Lesson 12-5. See page 25.

Lesson Quizzes
Web Code format: aqa-0204
02 = Chapter 2   04 = Lesson 4

Homework Video Tutor
Web Code format: aqe-0605
06 = Chapter 6   05 = Lesson 5

Chapter Web Codes

Chapter	Vocabulary Quizzes	Chapter Tests	Chapter Projects
1	aqj-0151	aqa-0152	aqd-0161
2	aqj-0251	aqa-0252	aqd-0261
3	aqj-0351	aqa-0352	aqd-0361
4	aqj-0451	aqa-0452	aqd-0461
5	aqj-0551	aqa-0552	aqd-0561
6	aqj-0651	aqa-0652	aqd-0661
7	aqj-0751	aqa-0752	aqd-0761
8	aqj-0851	aqa-0852	aqd-0861
9	aqj-0951	aqa-0952	aqd-0961
10	aqj-1051	aqa-1052	aqd-1061
11	aqj-1151	aqa-1152	aqd-1161
12	aqj-1251	aqa-1252	aqd-1261
End-of-Course		aqa-1254	

Additional Web Codes

Video Tutor Help:
Use Web Code aqe-0775 to access engaging online instructional videos to help bring math concepts to life. See page 32.

Data Updates:
Use Web Code aqg-9041 to get up-to-date government data for use in examples and exercises. See page 35.

Math at Work:
For information about each Math at Work feature, use Web Code aqb-2031. See page 20.

Using Your Book for Success

Welcome to *Prentice Hall Course 1*. There are many features built into the daily lessons of this text that will help you learn the important skills and concepts you will need to be successful in this course. Look through the following pages for some study tips that you will find useful as you complete each lesson.

Getting Ready to Learn

Check Your Readiness

Complete the *Check Your Readiness* exercises to see what topics you may need to review before you begin the chapter.

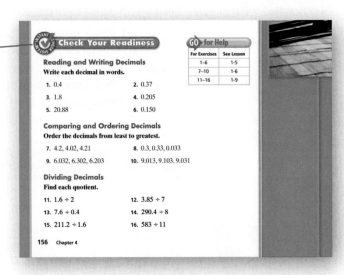

Check Skills You'll Need

Complete the *Check Skills You'll Need* exercises to make sure you have the skills needed to successfully learn the concepts in the lesson.

New Vocabulary

New Vocabulary is listed for each lesson, so you can pre-read the text. As each term is introduced, it is highlighted in yellow.

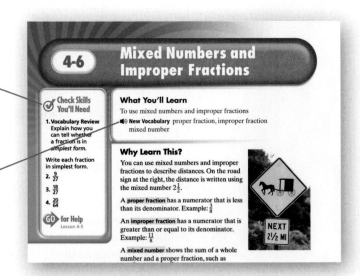

Built-In Help

Go for Help

Look for the green labels throughout your book that tell you where to "Go" for help. You'll see this built-in help in the lessons and in the homework exercises.

Video Tutor Help

Go online to see engaging videos to help you better understand important math concepts.

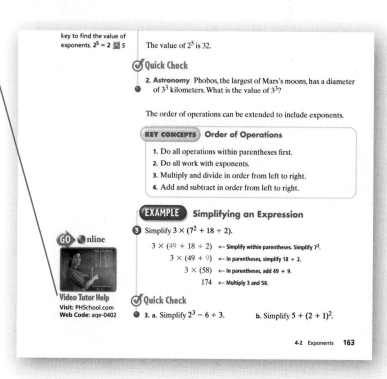

Understanding the Mathematics

Quick Check

Every lesson includes numerous examples, each followed by a *Quick Check* question that you can do on your own to see if you understand the skill being introduced. Check your progress with the answers at the back of the book.

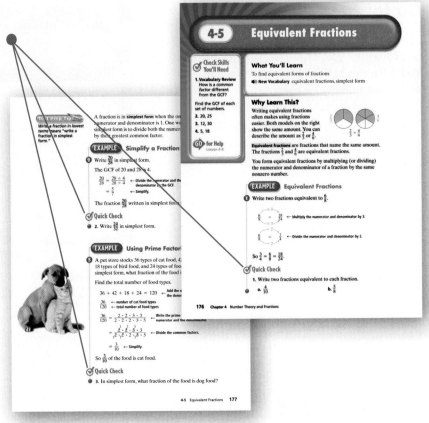

Understanding Key Concepts

Frequent *Key Concept* boxes summarize important definitions, formulas, and properties. Use these to review what you've learned.

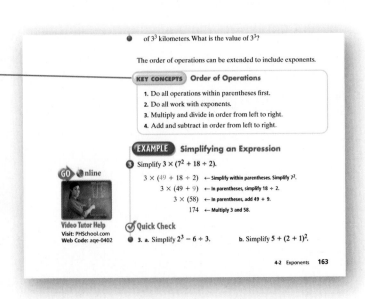

Online Active Math

Make math come alive with these online activities. Review and practice important math concepts with these engaging online tutorials.

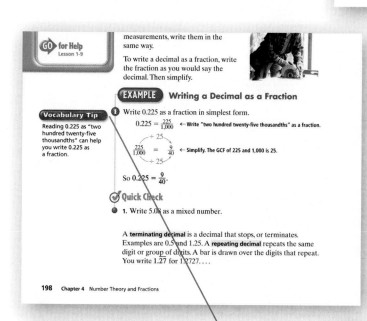

can use a division ladder or a factor tree to find the prime factorization of a number.

EXAMPLE Prime Factorization

3 Write the prime factorization of 84 using exponents.

Method 1 Use a division ladder.

2)84 ← Divide 84 by the prime number 2. Work down.
2)42 ← The result is 42. Since 42 is even, divide by 2 again.
3)21 ← The result is 21. Divide by the prime number 3.
7 ← The prime factorization is 2 × 2 × 3 × 7.

Method 2 Use a factor tree.

84 = 3 × 28 → ← Since the sum of the digits of 84 is 12, 84 is divisible by 3.

28 = 4 × 7 → ← Circle the prime numbers as you find them.

4 = 2 × 2 →

The prime factorization of 84 is 2 × 2 × 3 × 7, or $2^2 × 3 × 7$.

Quick Check

3. Find the prime factorization of 27.

4-3 Prime Numbers and Prime Factorization **167**

For: Prime Factorization Activity
Use: Interactive Textbook, 4-3

GO for Help
Lesson 1-9

measurements, write them in the same way.

To write a decimal as a fraction, write the fraction as you would say the decimal. Then simplify.

EXAMPLE Writing a Decimal as a Fraction

1 Write 0.225 as a fraction in simplest form.

$0.225 = \frac{225}{1,000}$ ← Write "two hundred twenty-five thousandths" as a fraction.

$\frac{225}{1,000} = \frac{9}{40}$ ← Simplify. The GCF of 225 and 1,000 is 25.

So $0.225 = \frac{9}{40}$.

Quick Check

1. Write 5.08 as a mixed number.

A **terminating decimal** is a decimal that stops, or terminates. Examples are 0.5 and 1.25. A **repeating decimal** repeats the same digit or group of digits. A bar is drawn over the digits that repeat. You write 1.27 for 1.2727. . . .

198 Chapter 4 Number Theory and Fractions

Vocabulary Tip

Reading 0.225 as "two hundred twenty-five thousandths" can help you write 0.225 as a fraction.

Vocabulary Support

Understanding mathematical vocabulary is an important part of studying mathematics. *Vocabulary Tips* and *Vocabulary Builders* throughout the book help focus on the language of math.

Vocabulary Builder

High-Use Academic Words

High-use academic words are words that you will see often in textbooks and on tests. These words are not math vocabulary terms, but knowing them will help you to succeed in mathematics.

Direction Words

Some words tell what to do in a problem. I need to understand what these words are asking so that I give the correct answer.

Word	Meaning
Identify	To show that you recognize something
List	To present information in order or to give examples
Justify	To give reasons supporting a decision or conclusion

Exercises

1. Identify each animal as a pet or a wild animal.
   a. kitten   b. elephant   c. dog   d. crocodile

Understanding the Mathematics

Guided Problem Solving

These features throughout your Student Edition provide practice in problem solving. Solved from a student's point of view, this feature focuses on the thinking and reasoning that goes into solving a problem.

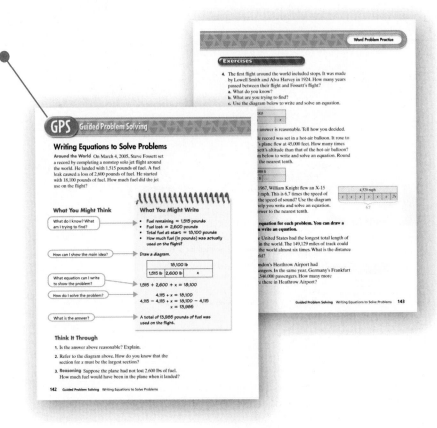

Activity Labs

Activity Labs throughout the book give you an opportunity to explore a concept. Apply the skills you've learned in these engaging activities.

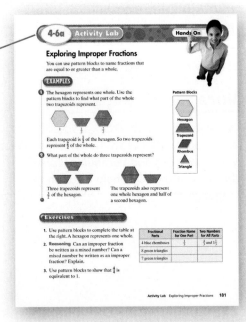

Practice What You've Learned

There are numerous exercises in each lesson that give you the practice you need to master the concepts in the lesson. The following exercises are included in each lesson.

Check Your Understanding

These exercises help you prepare for the Homework Exercises.

Practice by example

These exercises refer you back to the Examples in the lesson, in case you need help with completing these exercises.

Apply your skills

These exercises combine skills from earlier lessons to offer you richer skill exercises and multi-step application problems.

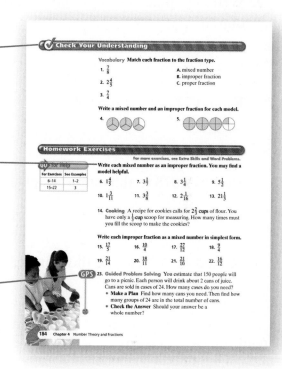

Homework Video Tutor

These interactive tutorials provide you with homework help for *every lesson*.

Challenge

This exercise gives you an opportunity to extend and stretch your thinking.

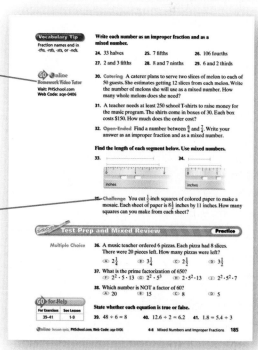

Beginning-of-Course Diagnostic Test

1. Write the place value of the underlined digit in 5_2_3,411,396.

2. Write the place value of the underlined digit in 40_2_,659.

3. Round 742 to the tens place.

4. Round 4,078 to the hundreds place.

5. Round 116,830 to the thousands place.

Add.

6. 4,208
  + 6,967

7. 591 + 79

8. 7,223
  + 4,279

9. 3,208 + 564

10. four thousand sixty-two plus nine hundred eighteen

Subtract.

11.   57
   − 42

12. 79 − 31

13.   8,841
   − 3,194

14.   116,493
   − 90,287

15. 2,051 − 988

16. nine thousand minus five hundred thirty eight

Multiply.

17. 594 × 8

18. $1{,}174 \times 6$

19. six thousand eighty-one times seven

20. 54×917

21. 806×255

22. one thousand sixty-nine times forty-eight

23. one hundred thirty-three times four thousand, two hundred eighty-six

Divide.

24. $6\overline{)822}$

25. $964 \div 6$

26. one thousand, two hundred eighty-seven divided by nine

27. $6{,}432 \div 24$

28. $504 \div 24$

29. $1{,}756 \div 29$

30. $5\overline{)1{,}016}$

Multiply using mental math.

31. $4{,}729 \times 10$

32. $462 \times 10{,}000$

33. $706{,}215 \times 100$

Divide using mental math.

34. $120 \div 10$

35. $17{,}000 \div 1{,}000$

36. $8{,}203{,}000 \div 100$

USING THE Problem Solving Plan

One of the most important skills you can have is the ability to solve problems. An integral part of learning mathematics is how adept you become at unraveling problems and looking back to see how you found the solution. Maybe you don't realize it, but you solve problems every day—some problems are easy to solve, and others are challenging and require a good plan of action. In this Problem Solving Handbook, you will learn how to work though mathematical problems using a simple four-step plan:

THE 4-STEP PLAN

1. **Understand** **Understand the problem.**
   Read the problem. Ask yourself, "What information is given? What is missing? What am I being asked to find or to do?"

2. **Plan** **Make a plan to solve the problem.**
   Choose a strategy. As you use problem solving strategies throughout this book, you will decide which one is best for the problem you are trying to solve.

3. **Carry Out** **Carry out the plan.**
   Solve the problem using your plan. Organize your work.

4. **Check** **Check the answer to be sure it is reasonable.**
   Look back at your work and compare it against the information and question(s) in the problem. Ask yourself, "Is my answer reasonable? Did I check my work?"

Problem Solving Strategies

Creating a good plan to solve a problem means that you will need to choose a strategy. What is the best way to solve that challenging problem? Perhaps drawing a diagram or making a table will lead to a solution. A problem may seem to have too many steps. Maybe working a simpler problem is the key. There are a number of strategies to choose from. You will decide which strategy is most effective.

As you work through this book, you will encounter many opportunities to improve your problem solving and reasoning skills. Working through mathematical problems using this four-step process will help you to organize your thoughts, develop your reasoning skills, and explain how you arrived at a particular solution.

Putting this problem solving plan to use will allow you to work through mathematical problems with confidence. Getting in the habit of planning and strategizing for problem solving will result in success in future math courses and high scores on those really important tests!

Good Luck!

THE STRATEGIES

Here are some examples of problem solving strategies. Which one will work best for the problem you are trying to solve?

- **Draw a Picture**
- **Look for a Pattern**
- **Systematic Guess and Check**
- **Act It Out**
- **Make a Table**
- **Work a Simpler Problem**
- **Work Backward**
- **Write an Equation**

Draw a Picture

When to Use This Strategy Drawing a picture can help you visualize and understand a word problem.

Volleyball A volleyball tournament will be held on a soccer field that is 110 yards long and 80 yards wide. Each volleyball court is 25 yd long by 15 yd wide. How many courts will fit on the field?

Understand The field is 110 yd by 80 yd. Each volleyball court is 25 yd by 15 yd. You are asked to find how many courts will fit on the field.

Plan To help decide, first *draw a picture* of the field. Then show how many courts will fit on the field.

Carry Out Mark off 7 courts along the length of the field and 3 courts along the width of the field. Since $3 \times 7 = 21$, you can fit 21 courts in the field.

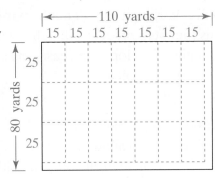

Check Check the answer by dividing the area of the field by the area of a court. Use the formula area = length × width.

$$\frac{\text{soccer field}}{\text{volleyball court}} \rightarrow \frac{110 \text{ yards} \times 80 \text{ yards}}{25 \text{ yards} \times 15 \text{ yards}} \rightarrow \frac{8{,}800 \text{ square yards}}{375 \text{ square yards}} \approx 23$$

So 21 courts is a reasonable answer.

● Practice

1. **Carpentry** A bookcase is made from wood that is 3 in. thick. The bookcase has four shelves, including the top. The space between shelves is 20 inches. Find the height of the bookcase.

2. **Lighting** Lights are placed every 2 feet along both sides of a 14-foot driveway. How many lights are needed?

3. **Gardening** A rectangular garden is 4 feet by 3 feet. A landscaper plants flowers 1 ft apart along the edges and corners. How many plants does the landscaper need?

Look for a Pattern

When to Use This Strategy In problems where more objects are added, you can *look for a pattern* to solve the problem.

Seating A rectangular table seats two people on each end and three on each side. How many seats are available if you push the ends of five tables together?

Understand There are five rectangular tables. Each table seats two people on each end and three on a side.

Plan To find the number of seats when five tables are pushed together, start by finding the number of seats when there are fewer tables.

Carry Out Start with 1, 2, and 3 tables.

1 table → 10 seats   2 tables → 16 seats   3 tables → 22 seats

Extend the pattern by adding six seats for each new table.

Number of Tables	1	2	3	4	5
Number of Seats	10	16	22	28	34

Check Five tables pushed together seat 5×6, or 30, people on the sides and 2 people on each end, or $30 + 2 + 2 = 34$.

● Practice

1. **Savings** A high school student has started a new job. He plans to save $1 in the first week, $2 in the second week, $4 in the third week, and $8 in the fourth week. If this pattern of savings could continue, how much would he save in the tenth week?

2. A rectangular table seats four people on each side and three on each end. How many seats are available if the ends of seven tables are pushed together?

3. Your younger brother is pulling a sled up a hill. Each minute he moves forward 20 feet but also slides back 3 feet. How long will it take him to pull his sled 130 feet up the hill?

Systematic Guess and Check

When to Use This Strategy Sometimes problems have a limited number of possible answers. Sometimes the solution to a problem involves several related numbers. Using *systematic guess and check* can get you closer to the right answer.

Movie tickets cost $10 for adults and $8 for children. On Friday the total sales from 120 tickets was $1,120. How many adult tickets were sold?

Understand Adult tickets cost $10. Children's tickets cost $8. The theater collected $1,120 by selling 120 tickets. You need to find how many adult tickets were sold.

Plan To find how many adult tickets were sold, make an initial guess, check the results, and then revise your guess.

Carry Out Try 40 adult tickets and 80 children's tickets. Organize the data in a table. If the total is too low, increase the number of expensive, adult, tickets. If the total is too high, decrease the number of adult tickets.

Adult Tickets	Children's Tickets	Total Sales
40 × $10 = $400	80 × $8 = $640	$400 + $640 = $1,040
50 × $10 = $500	70 × $8 = $560	$1,060
90 × $10 = $900	30 × $8 = $240	$1,140
80 × $10 = $800	40 × $8 = $320	$1,120

Check With 80 adult tickets and 40 children's tickets, the number of tickets sold is equal to 120, and the total sales are $1,120.

⬤ Practice

1. **Business** A vendor sells salads and juices. A salad costs $3.00 and a juice costs $2.50. The vendor earned $216 by selling 80 items. How many juices were sold?

2. **Pet Care** A rectangular turtle cage is made with 40 feet of wire fence. The length is 6 feet greater than the width. What are the length and width of the turtle cage?

Act It Out

When to Use This Strategy Sometimes the best way to solve a problem is to imitate the actions described in the problem.

Ten students stand in a circle. Starting with the first student, the teacher begins counting as follows: "One, two, three, four, five, six, out!" When a student is called out, he or she has to leave the circle. The teacher then continues until only one student is left. Which student is it?

Understand The teacher is counting out every seventh student as she goes around in a circle. The students are numbered 1 to 10. You need to find the number of the last student left in.

Plan Using 10 pennies you can *act out* the steps and see who wins.

Carry Out Arrange the pennies in a circle. Start counting, pointing at the pennies one at a time. Every time you reach seven, remove the penny you point to. When you are done counting, you are left with the ninth penny. The ninth student is left.

Check If you complete the table, you get the same result.

| | | | Student # | | | | | | |
1	2	3	4	5	6	7	8	9	10
1	2	3	4	5	6	X	1	2	3
4	5	6	X	1	2	X	3	4	5
6	X		X			X			
	X		X			X			
	X		X			X			

● Practice

1. If the teacher has 12 students and counts out every ninth student, which student will be left?

2. An uncle is giving some baseball cards away to five nieces and nephews. He decides the fairest way to do this is to give just one card to the first child, then two to the second, and so on. If everybody gets three turns, how many cards will each niece or nephew have?

3. Four robots stand in the corners of a four-by-four grid. All four robots are facing in the same direction. They move at the same time. If a robot sees another robot directly ahead, it takes one step forward, and if not, it stays in place but turns right. Where are the robots after three moves?

Make a Table

When to Use This Strategy Organizing data in a table can help you see connections.

Exercise Tara wants to walk in a charity event. In her first week of training, she walks three miles each day. Each week after that, she adds $\frac{3}{4}$ mile to her daily distance. In which week of training does Tara walk six miles per day?

Understand During the first week, Tara walks three miles each day. Each week, she walks an additional $\frac{3}{4}$ mile. You need to find the week in which her daily walk is six miles.

Plan *Make a table* that shows weeks and distance. Add rows until the distance reaches six miles.

Carry Out Label the first column Week and the second column Distance. Fill in the values for each week. Tara walks 6 miles during her fifth week of training.

Week	Distance (miles/day)
1	3
2	$3 + \frac{3}{4} = 3\frac{3}{4}$
3	$3\frac{3}{4} + \frac{3}{4} = 4\frac{1}{2}$
4	$4\frac{1}{2} + \frac{3}{4} = 5\frac{1}{4}$
5	$5\frac{1}{4} + \frac{3}{4} = 6$

Check You can check by working backward. In five weeks there were 4 increases of $\frac{3}{4}$ mile. $\frac{3}{4} + \frac{3}{4} + \frac{3}{4} + \frac{3}{4} = 3$. So the total increase was 3 miles. The 3 miles plus the original 3 miles per day is 6 miles.

● Practice

1. **Money** In how many ways can you make 25 cents using pennies, nickels, and dimes?

2. Find the smallest number that meets both of these conditions.
   - When you divide the number by 7, the remainder is 1.
   - When you divide the number by 9, the remainder is 7.

3. A certain farm has both chickens and goats. Each chicken has 2 legs. Each goat has 4 legs. There are 35 animals on the farm. All together the chickens and goats have 100 legs. How many chickens and how many goats does the farm have?

Work a Simpler Problem

When to Use This Strategy Using simpler numbers can sometimes help you solve a difficult problem.

Floor Tiles You tile a rectangular floor $17\frac{1}{2}$ ft by $13\frac{3}{4}$ ft. You are using square tiles that are $1\frac{1}{4}$ ft on each side. How many tiles do you need?

Understand The rectangular floor is $17\frac{1}{2}$ feet long and $13\frac{3}{4}$ feet wide. Each tile is a square with sides $1\frac{1}{4}$ feet long. You must find how many tiles are needed to cover the floor.

Plan First, *work a simpler problem*. Then use the same approach to solve the harder problem. Multiply each number by 4 to remove the fractions. Replace $17\frac{1}{2}$ with $17\frac{1}{2} \times 4 = 70$. Replace $13\frac{3}{4}$ with $13\frac{3}{4} \times 4 = 55$, and $1\frac{1}{4}$ with $1\frac{1}{4} \times 4 = 5$.

Simpler Problem A rectangular floor is 70 feet by 55 feet. How many 5 ft-by-5 ft tiles do you need to cover the floor?

Carry Out For one row of tiles to cover the length of the room, you need $70 \div 5$, or 14, tiles. For enough rows to cover the width of the room, you need $55 \div 5$, or 11, rows. So you need 14×11, or 154, tiles.

Now solve the original problem. For one row of tiles, you need $17\frac{1}{2} \div 1\frac{1}{4}$, or 14, tiles. For enough rows to cover the width, you need $13\frac{3}{4} \div 1\frac{1}{4}$, or 11, rows. So you need 14×11, or 154, tiles.

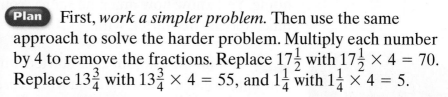

Check Because all the lengths in the simpler problem are four times as long, the answers to both problems should be the same. They are, so the answer checks.

● Practice

1. On a school day, José spends $5\frac{1}{4}$ hours in classes. Each class lasts $\frac{3}{4}$ hour. How many classes does José have?

2. Sewing A tailor has a section of material that is $28\frac{1}{2}$ feet long. He wants to cut it into pieces, each one $1\frac{1}{2}$ feet long. How many cuts will he have to make?

Work Backward

When to Use This Strategy Some problems involve a series of steps that lead to a final result. If you are asked to find the initial amount, you can *work backward* from the final result by using inverse operations.

Zoo Luis went to the zoo for a school trip. He paid $5 for admission. He spent $14 at the souvenir shop. When he got home, he had $18 left. How much money did he start with?

Understand You know how much money Luis had when he got home. You know how much he spent. You want to know how much money he started with.

Plan To find the amount Luis started with, begin with the amount he had at the end. Then *work backward*. To undo each operation, use its inverse.

Carry Out To undo the amounts Luis spent, add.

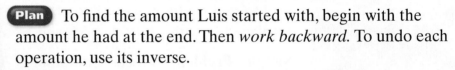

$18   ← Luis had $18 left at the end.

$18 + $14 = $32   ← He spent $14 at the souvenir shop. Add.

$32 + $5 = $37   ← He spent $5 on admission. Add.

Luis started with $37.

Check Read the problem again. Start with $37. Subtract the amounts as Luis spends money in the problem. $37 − $5 = $32. $32 − $14 = $18. The answer checks.

● Practice

1. You divide a number by 2, add 7, and then multiply by 5. The result is 50. What is the number?

2. **Shopping** Brenda spent half her money at a store in a mall. At another store, she spent half her remaining money and $6 more. She had $2 left. How much did Brenda have when she arrived at the mall?

3. **Hobbies** Kai sold half his baseball cards to Ana, half of the remaining cards to Joe, and the last 10 to Chip. How many cards did Kai sell in all?

Write an Equation

When to Use This Strategy To *write an equation* is one way of organizing the information needed to solve a problem.

Discount A bicycle is on sale for $139.93. This is 30% off the regular price. What is the regular price of the bicycle?

Understand The sale price of the bicycle, $139.93, is 30% off the regular price. You need to find the regular price.

Plan Translate the words into an equation. You will pay $100\% - 30\% = 70\%$ of the regular price.

Carry Out The percent you pay times the regular price equals the sale price.

Words | percent you pay | times | regular price | equals | sale price

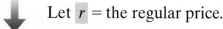 Let r = the regular price.

Equation | 70% | × | r | = | $139.93

$$0.7r = 139.93 \quad \leftarrow \text{Write 70\% as a decimal: 0.7.}$$

$$0.7r \div 0.7 = 139.93 \div 0.7 \quad \leftarrow \text{Divide each side by 0.7 to find } r.$$

$$r = \$199.90 \quad \leftarrow \text{Simplify.}$$

The regular price of the bicycle is $199.90.

Check The regular price is about $200. The sale price is about 70% of $200, or $140. This is close to the sale price.

● Practice

1. **Media** A magazine has 5,580,000 subscribers this year. This number is down 7% from last year. How many subscribers were there last year?

2. A "light" popcorn has 120 Calories per serving. This is 25% fewer Calories than a serving of regular popcorn. How many Calories does each serving of regular popcorn have?

3. The sign at the entrance of a store reads, "30% off all winter apparel! Discount given at the register." The price tag of a coat is missing. The register rings up a price before tax of $55.93. What is the regular price of the coat?

CHAPTER 1 Whole Numbers and Decimals

What You've Learned

- In a previous course, you compared and ordered whole numbers.
- You used addition, subtraction, multiplication, and division to solve problems involving whole numbers.
- You used rounding to estimate reasonable results for problems involving whole numbers.

 **Check Your Readiness**

GO for Help

For Exercises	See Skills Handbook
1–6	p. 637
7–12	p. 639
13–16	p. 640
17–20	p. 642

Rounding to the Nearest Ten
Round each number to the nearest ten.

1. 312 **2.** 7,525 **3.** 38

4. 55 **5.** 699 **6.** 1,989

Adding and Subtracting Whole Numbers
Add or subtract.

7. $59 + 116$ **8.** $182 - 37$ **9.** $8,745 + 5,447$

10. $4,823 - 1,796$ **11.** $9,004 + 996$ **12.** $2,049 - 657$

Multiplying Whole Numbers
Multiply.

13. 9×83 **14.** 64×71 **15.** 437×100 **16.** 33×14

Dividing Whole Numbers
Divide.

17. $50 \div 10$ **18.** $85 \div 5$ **19.** $256 \div 8$ **20.** $1,944 \div 27$

What You'll Learn Next

- In this chapter, you will learn how to compare and order decimals.

- You will use addition, subtraction, multiplication, and division to solve problems involving decimals.

- You will use rounding and compatible numbers to estimate reasonable results.

- You will use the order of operations to simplify numerical expressions.

 Problem Solving Application On pages 56 and 57, you will work an extended activity on order forms.

◀))) Key Vocabulary

- associative properties (pp. 12–13)
- commutative properties (pp. 12–13)
- compatible numbers (p. 9)
- expanded form (p. 23)
- expression (p. 16)
- front-end estimation (p. 32)
- identity properties (pp. 12–13)
- order of operations (p. 16)
- standard form (p. 4)

Understanding Whole Numbers

Check Skills You'll Need

1. **Vocabulary Review**
Give an example of a number that is a *whole number* and one that is not.

Write the value of the digit 2 in each number.

2. 28   **3.** 8,672

4. 12,980   **5.** 246

GO for Help
Skills Handbook p. 636

What You'll Learn

To write and compare whole numbers

🔊 **New Vocabulary** standard form

Why Learn This?

You can use the place and value of whole numbers to understand large numbers, such as the distance between stars.

The **standard form** of a number uses digits and place value. The *place* of the digit 5 in 254 is tens. The *value* of 5 is 5 tens, or 50.

EXAMPLE Writing Whole Numbers

1 In standard form, the number of meters light travels in one second is 299,792,458. Write the number in words.

Use a place value chart to identify the place value of each digit.

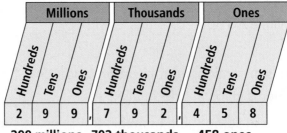

Millions			Thousands			Ones		
Hundreds	Tens	Ones	Hundreds	Tens	Ones	Hundreds	Tens	Ones
2	9	9	7	9	2	4	5	8

299 millions   792 thousands   458 ones

299,792,458 written in words is two hundred ninety-nine million, seven hundred ninety-two thousand, four hundred fifty-eight.

GO for Help

For help with identifying place value, go to Skills Handbook p. 636.

Quick Check

1. Write the value of $26,236,848,080 in words.

You can use place value or a number line to compare whole numbers. The numbers from left to right on a number line are in order from least to greatest.

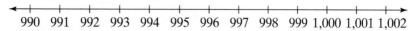

990   991   992   993   994   995   996   997   998   999   1,000   1,001   1,002

EXAMPLE   **Comparing Whole Numbers**

2 Use < or > to complete: 995 ■ 998.

Method 1 Use a number line.

On the number line above, 995 is to the left of 998. So 995 < 998.

Method 2 Use place value.

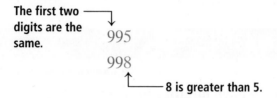

The first two digits are the same.

995

998

8 is greater than 5.

Since 8 is greater than 5 in the ones place, 995 < 998.

✓ Quick Check

● **2.** Use < or > to complete: 129,631 ■ 142,832.

To order whole numbers, start with the greatest place value and compare the digits. Do this for each place value. Then write the numbers in order from least to greatest.

EXAMPLE   **Ordering Whole Numbers**

3 Write in order from least to greatest: 12,875; 12,675; 12,695.

The first two digits are the same.

8 is greater than 6, so 12,875 is the greatest number.

12,875

12,675   ← Compare the tens digit in the remaining numbers. 9 is greater than 7, so 12,695 is the next greatest number.

12,695

The order from least to greatest is 12,675; 12,695; and 12,875.

✓ Quick Check

● **3.** Write in order from least to greatest: 9,897; 9,987; 978.

1. **Vocabulary** Write one thousand, two hundred seventy-three in standard form.

2. **Writing in Math** Explain how you know that $471 < 417$ is false.

Write each number in words.

3. 362: three __?__ sixty-__?__   4. 1,400: one __?__, four __?__

Use < or > to complete each statement.

5. 322 ■ 332   6. 745 ■ 739   7. 1,187 ■ 1,278

Homework Exercises

For more exercises, see Extra Skills and Word Problems.

For Exercises	See Example
8–14	1
15–20	2
21–24	3

GO for Help

Write each number in words.

8. 30,987   9. 145,675   10. 1,345,000

11. 7,347,200   12. 9,871,060,540   13. 63,380,509,710

14. **History** An estimate in A.D. 14 placed the population of the Roman empire at 4,937,000. Write the number in words.

Use < or > to complete each statement.

15. 366 ■ 36   16. 54,001 ■ 54,901   17. 8,801 ■ 810

18. 84,123 ■ 9,996   19. 29,286 ■ 29,826   20. 31,010 ■ 30,101

Write the numbers in order from least to greatest.

21. 910; 990; 901   22. 1,172; 1,472; 1,142; 1,572

23. 17,444; 17,671; 17,414   24. 20,403; 23,404; 23,040

GPS 25. **Guided Problem Solving** The average distance between Earth and the sun is one hundred forty-nine million, four hundred seventy-six thousand kilometers. Write the distance in standard form.

• Use a place value chart.

26. **Social Studies** The land area of Oklahoma is 68,667 square miles. Washington includes about 66,544 square miles and Missouri includes about 68,886 square miles. Order the three states from least to greatest number of square miles.

27. Order the apple types by number of cartons from least to greatest.

28. **Computers** There are 4,256 kilobytes of memory available on a digital music player. Is there enough space for a file that uses 4,290 kilobytes? Explain.

29. **Challenge** The sum of the digits of a two-digit number is 12. The tens digit is three times the ones digit. What is the number?

Yearly Apple Production in the United States

Type of Apple	Cartons
Ida Red	2,753,000
Empire	2,739,000
Braeburn	2,198,000
McIntosh	3,304,000
York	3,212,000

Source: U.S. Apple Association

Test Prep and Mixed Review

Practice

Multiple Choice

30. The six highest waterfalls in the world are listed below.

Waterfall	Country	Height (ft)
Angel	Venezuela	3,212
Mongefossen	Norway	2,540
Ostre Mandola Foss	Norway	2,152
Tugela	South Africa	2,800
Utigord	Norway	2,625
Yosemite	United States	2,425

Source: *The Top 10 of Everything*

Which statement is NOT supported by the data?
- Ⓐ The highest waterfall is Angel.
- Ⓑ The lowest waterfall is in Norway.
- Ⓒ The heights are in order from greatest to least.
- Ⓓ Three of the world's highest waterfalls are in Norway.

31. An auditorium has 10 rows with 22 seats in each row. There are 160 people seated. How many seats are empty?
- Ⓕ 100 seats
- Ⓗ 60 seats
- Ⓖ 80 seats
- Ⓙ 40 seats

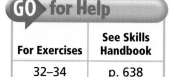

For Exercises	See Skills Handbook
32–34	p. 638

Find each sum.

32. 375 + 15

33. 1,820 + 309

34. 2,617 + 1,904

Estimating With Whole Numbers

What You'll Learn

To estimate with whole numbers by rounding and by using compatible numbers

◀)) **New Vocabulary** compatible numbers

Why Learn This?

When you buy materials such as fabric or wood, you can use estimation to decide how much material you need.

To estimate, you select numbers that are close to the exact numbers, but are easier to use for computing. Rounding is one method you use in estimation.

Round to the nearest   **Ten**   **Hundred**

Look at the value to the → 47   123   ← Look at the value to the
right of the tens place.   ↓   ↓   right of the hundreds place.
7 ≥ 5, so round up.   50   100   2 < 5, so round down.

To estimate sums and differences, round each number to the same place before you add or subtract.

Vocabulary Tip

When you *round* a number, you look for the nearest simpler number.

←— 43   47 —→
40   50

EXAMPLE   Estimating by Rounding

1 Estimate 37 + 62 + 48. First round each number to the nearest ten.

$$
\begin{array}{rll}
37 & 7 \geq 5, \text{ so round up.} \to & 40 \\
62 & 2 < 5, \text{ so round down.} \to & 60 \\
+\ 48 & 8 \geq 5, \text{ so round up.} \to & +\ 50 \\
\hline
& & 150
\end{array}
$$

So 37 + 62 + 48 ≈ 150.   ← The symbol ≈ means "is approximately equal to."

Quick Check

1. Estimate. First round each number to the nearest ten.
   a. 97 + 22 + 48   **b.** 94 − 32 − 41

Compatible numbers are numbers that are easy to compute mentally. They are particularly useful for estimating products and quotients.

$38 \div 6$
$\downarrow \quad \downarrow$
$36 \div 6$ ← Since you can divide 36 by 6 mentally, 36 and 6 are compatible.

6×78
$\downarrow \quad \downarrow$
5×80 ← 5 and 80 are compatible because 5 and 80 can be multiplied mentally.

EXAMPLE **Estimating With Compatible Numbers**

Test Prep Tip

When you are asked to find "about how many," you are being asked to estimate.

② Estimate $298 \div 16$ using compatible numbers.

$298 \div 16$
$\downarrow \quad\quad \downarrow$
$300 \div 16$ ← Change 298 to 300 because 300 is easier to use mentally.
$\downarrow \quad\quad \downarrow$
$300 \div 15 = 20$ ← Change 16 to 15 because 15 is compatible with 300.

So $298 \div 16 \approx 20$.

✓ **Quick Check**

2. Estimate using compatible numbers.
  a. 8×39 **b.** $672 \div 52$

EXAMPLE **Application: Food Drive**

③ **Multiple Choice** Northern Middle School had a food drive. Each of the 22 homerooms collected about 290 cans of food. About how many cans were collected in all?

  Ⓐ 400   Ⓑ 600   Ⓒ 4,000   Ⓓ 6,000

$$\begin{array}{r} 290 \\ \times 22 \\ \hline \end{array}$$
← 300 is easier to work with than 299. →
← 20 is easier to multiply by than 22. →
$$\begin{array}{r} 300 \\ \times 20 \\ \hline 6{,}000 \end{array}$$

So $290 \times 22 \approx 6{,}000$. The correct answer is choice D.

✓ **Quick Check**

3. You have 324 cards for a strategy game. To play the game, a person needs 12 cards. About how many different people can play using your set of cards?

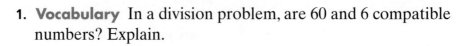

1. **Vocabulary** In a division problem, are 60 and 6 compatible numbers? Explain.

2. **Error Analysis** A classmate estimated that 29 + 42 + 37 is about 20 + 40 + 40, or 100. Explain your classmate's error.

GO for Help

For help with rounding numbers, go to Skills Handbook, p. 637.

Estimate. Round the underlined number first.

3. 70 − <u>29</u>   4. 200 + <u>812</u>   5. <u>87</u> − 20   6. <u>189</u> + 400

Estimate using compatible numbers.

7. $103 \div 11 \approx 100 \div \blacksquare$ 8. $52 \times 18 \approx \blacksquare \times 20$

9. $597 \div 31 \approx \blacksquare \div 30$ 10. $94 \times 13 \approx 90 \times \blacksquare$

Homework Exercises

For more exercises, see Extra Skills and Word Problems.

GO for Help

For Exercises	See Example
11–18	1
19–28	2–3

Estimate. Round each number first.

11. 47 + 228 + 23   12. 653 − 295   13. 34 + 68 + 93

14. 59 + 26 − 23   15. 6,963 − 3,098   16. 8,043 + 5,983

17. 42 + 86 + 51 + 38   18. 257 − 109 − 46 − 21

Estimate using compatible numbers.

19. $2 \times 3,978$ 20. $102 \div 25$ 21. $611 \div 58$

22. 997×5 23. $1,089 \div 521$ 24. $4,978 \div 983$

25. 48×41 26. $207 \div 51$ 27. $69 \div 7$

28. **World History** The Chinese kwan note was used in the 1300s. It was about 93 centimeters long. The United States dollar bill is almost 16 centimeters long. About how many times longer was the kwan note?

 29. **Guided Problem Solving** You need $78 to buy a new video game. You earn $9 one week and $22 the next week. About how much more do you need to earn to buy the game?
- Do you need to find an exact answer?
- About how much have you already earned?

30. Travel You are going on a vacation 1,038 miles away. The first day you travel 284 miles. The second day you travel 326 miles. About how much farther do you have to go?

31. Savings Suppose you saved $443 in one year.
   a. Estimate the average amount you saved each week.
   b. Reasoning Explain why you chose the method you used.

32. There are three small piñatas and two large piñatas at a festival. Each small piñata contains 85 prizes. Each large piñata contains 178 prizes. Estimate the total number of prizes.

Choose a Method Use either rounding or compatible numbers to estimate each answer.

33. $429 + 889$ **34.** $1,142 - 720$ **35.** $551 \div 86$

36. Writing in Math The cost of four copies of a book is $37. Estimate the cost of one book. Is your estimate higher or lower than the book's actual cost? Explain.

37. Challenge A ball has a mass of 238 grams. A box holds 9 balls. The total mass of the balls and the box is 2,437 grams. Estimate the mass of the box.

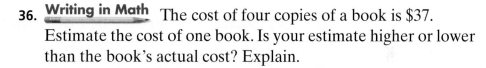

Test Prep and Mixed Review   Practice

Multiple Choice

38. A family of five went to pick berries. They filled 11 containers. Each container held about 18 ounces of berries. About many ounces of berries did the family pick?
   Ⓐ 100   Ⓒ 200
   Ⓑ 150   Ⓓ 300

39. A science teacher says that Jupiter's average distance from the sun is "seven hundred seventy-eight million, three hundred thousand kilometers." Susan is writing this distance in her notebook. Which number should she write?
   Ⓕ 78,030,000
   Ⓖ 78,300,000
   Ⓗ 778,300,000
   Ⓙ 778,300,000,000

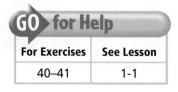

For Exercises	See Lesson
40–41	1-1

Write in order from least to greatest.

40. 287, 278, 275, 281   **41.** 4,567; 4,678; 4,687; 4,541

Properties of Numbers

What You'll Learn

To understand and use the properties of numbers

🔊 **New Vocabulary** commutative properties, associative properties, identity properties

Why Learn This?

The properties of numbers can help you do mental math.

KEY CONCEPTS Properties of Numbers

Commutative Property of Addition Changing the order of addends does not change the sum.
$$9 + 5 = 5 + 9$$

Associative Property of Addition Changing the grouping of addends does not change the sum.
$$(9 + 5) + 4 = 9 + (5 + 4)$$

Identity Property of Addition The sum of 0 and any number is that number.
$$0 + 9 = 9$$

You can simplify a mathematical phrase by replacing it with the simplest name for the value of the phrase. So to simplify $4 + 5$, you write 9 for its value.

EXAMPLE Using the Properties of Addition

1 **Field Trips** The table shows two groups of students who went on a field trip. Use mental math to find the total number of students.

Room	Number of Students
101	32
102	28

What you think

First I will think of 28 as $20 + 8$. Next, I will add $8 + 32$ to get 40. $40 + 20$ is 60. So $32 + 28 = 60$.

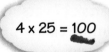

Vocabulary Tip

Parentheses ( ) indicate operations that you should do first.

Why it works

$32 + 28 = 32 + (20 + 8)$ ← **Rewrite 28 as 20 + 8.**

$= 32 + (8 + 20)$ ← **Use the Commutative Property of Addition.**

$= (32 + 8) + 20$ ← **Use the Associative Property of Addition.**

$= 40 + 20$ ← **Add inside the parentheses first.**

$= 60$ ← **Simplify.**

The total number of students is 60.

Quick Check

1. Mental Math Find $36 + 25 + 34$.

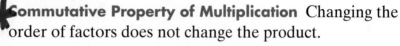

KEY CONCEPTS Properties of Numbers

Commutative Property of Multiplication Changing the order of factors does not change the product.

$4 \times 6 = 6 \times 4$

Associative Property of Multiplication Changing the grouping of factors does not change the product.

$(4 \times 6) \times 2 = 4 \times (6 \times 2)$

Identity Property of Multiplication The product of 1 and any number is that number.

$4 \times 1 = 4$

$4 \times 25 = 100$

EXAMPLE Using the Properties of Multiplication

2 Mental Math Find $4 \times 8 \times 25$.

What you think

First I will multiply 4 and 25. $4 \times 25 = 100$, and $8 \times 100 = 800$.

Why it works

$4 \times 8 \times 25 = 4 \times 25 \times 8$ ← **Commutative Property of Multiplication**

$= (4 \times 25) \times 8$ ← **Associative Property of Multiplication**

$= 100 \times 8$ ← **Multiply inside the parentheses.**

$= 800$ ← **Simplify.**

Quick Check

2. Mental Math Find $20 \times (6 \times 5)$.

1. **Vocabulary** Name the property used in this statement:
$25 + 27 + 15 = 25 + 15 + 27$.

2. Give a reason to justify each step.
$$(4 \times 9) \times 5 = (9 \times 4) \times 5 \qquad \underline{\quad ? \quad}$$
$$= 9 \times (4 \times 5) \qquad \underline{\quad ? \quad}$$
$$= 9 \times 20 \qquad \underline{\quad ? \quad}$$
$$= 180 \qquad \underline{\quad ? \quad}$$

3. **Writing in Math** Use mental math to find $(25 \times 9) \times 8$. Describe the steps you used.

Use mental math to find each sum or product.

4. $4 + 26$ 5. $33 + 0 + 17$ 6. $50 \times 7 \times 2$

Homework Exercises

For more exercises, see Extra Skills and Word Problems.

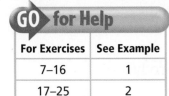

For Exercises	See Example
7–16	1
17–25	2

Use mental math to find each sum.

7. $0 + 57 + 4$ 8. $32 + 48$ 9. $18 + 6 + 42$

10. $(8 + 17) + 13$ 11. $81 + 23 + 19$ 12. $(17 + 24) + 183$

13. $837 + 14 + 26$ 14. $24 + 33 + 167$ 15. $160 + 0 + 2,740$

16. A train started a trip pulling 9 cars. At the first stop, 17 cars were added to the train. At the second stop, 11 more cars were added. How many cars was the train pulling then?

Use mental math to find each product.

17. $5 \times 47 \times 2$ 18. $70 \times 1 \times 4$ 19. $25 \times 13 \times 4$

20. $20 \times (19 \times 50)$ 21. $40 \times (33 \times 25)$ 22. $5 \times 683 \times 20$

23. $65 \times (100 \times 2)$ 24. $4 \times 20 \times 1,000$ 25. $5 \times 8 \times 25$

26. **Guided Problem Solving** Four running clubs raised money in a 24-hour relay race. Club A ran 183 miles, Club B ran 144 miles, Club C ran 117 miles, and Club D ran 146 miles. What was the total number of miles that all four clubs ran?
   • Which pairs of numbers can you add using mental math?
   • What is the sum of each of those pairs?

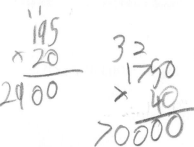

Use <, =, or > to complete each statement.

27. 41 + 29 ▪ 70

28. 737 + 373 ▪ 4 × 11 × 25

29. Modeling Draw a model to show the statement is true:
8 + 6 + 2 = (8 + 2) + 6.

30. Error Analysis Below is a friend's solution to a problem. Is your friend correct? Explain.

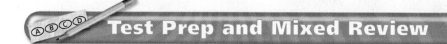

100 × (5 + 9) = (100 × 5) + 9 = 500 + 9 = 509

31. Choose a Method You plan to earn $15 per week for a charity. Will you use estimation, mental math, paper and pencil, or a calculator to determine how many weeks it will take you to earn $1,000? Explain why.

32. Art Class In a student art contest there are 14 drawings, 22 sculptures, and some paintings. There are 18 more paintings than sculptures. What is the total number of art pieces?

33. The monthly rate for a 3-year subscription to an online music service is $10. What is the total cost for 3 years?

34. Challenge Is subtraction commutative? Is division? Is either operation associative? Explain using examples.

Test Prep and Mixed Review   **Practice**

Multiple Choice

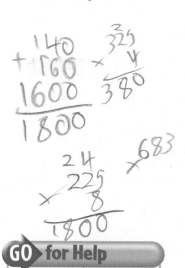

35. Gary is asked to find two whole numbers that have a sum of 9 and a product that is double the sum. He writes 7 and 2. Why is Gary's answer incorrect?
Ⓐ The sum of 7 and 2 is not 9.
Ⓑ The product of 7 and 2 is not double the sum.
Ⓒ The sum of 7 and 2 is 9.
Ⓓ The product of 7 and 2 is double the sum.

36. Last night Martha spent 29 minutes on social studies homework, 13 minutes on English, and 22 minutes on science. About how much time did she spend on all three subjects?
Ⓕ 40 minutes   Ⓗ 1 hour
Ⓖ 50 minutes   Ⓙ 1 hour and 10 minutes

Use < or > to complete each statement.

37. 98,410 ▪ 98,140   **38.** 78,296 ▪ 78,269   **39.** 40,000 ▪ 300,009

GO for Help

For Exercises	See Lesson
37–39	1-1

1-4 Order of Operations

Check Skills You'll Need

1. Vocabulary Review
Name the property that lets you write $35 + 5 = 5 + 35$.

Use mental math to find each sum.

2. $35 + 17 + 5$

3. $22 + 0 + 8$

4. $124 + (25 + 26)$

for Help
Lesson 1-2

What You'll Learn

To use the order of operations to simplify expressions and solve problems

◄))) **New Vocabulary** order of operations, expression

Why Learn This?

A problem such as $18 + 11 \times 6$ requires you to do more than one operation. To find the correct answer, you need to know which operation to do first. Should you add first, or multiply?

Diane's Work (addition first)

$$18 + 11 \times 6 \stackrel{?}{=} (18 + 11) \times 6$$
$$\stackrel{?}{=} 29 \times 6$$
$$\stackrel{?}{=} 174$$

Dana's Work (multiplication first)

$$18 + 11 \times 6 \stackrel{?}{=} 18 + (11 \times 6)$$
$$\stackrel{?}{=} 18 + 66$$
$$\stackrel{?}{=} 84$$

Only one answer is correct. To make sure everyone gets the same value, you use the **order of operations.**

KEY CONCEPTS **Order of Operations**

1. Do all operations within parentheses first.
2. Multiply and divide in order from left to right.
3. Add and subtract in order from left to right.

Players must put on soccer equipment— socks, shoes with cleats, and shin guards—in a certain order.

Based on the order of operations, you multiply before you add.

$$18 + 11 \times 6 = 18 + 66 = 84$$

So Dana's answer is correct.

An **expression** is a mathematical phrase that contains numbers and operation symbols. In the work above, $18 + 11 \times 6$ is an expression.

EXAMPLE Finding the Value of Expressions

1 Find the value of each expression.

a. $6 + 96 \div 3 = 6 + 32$ ← **Divide 96 by 3.**

$= 38$ ← **Add.**

b. $30 - (6 + 2) \times 3 = 30 - 8 \times 3$ ← **Add 6 and 2 within the parentheses.**

$= 30 - 24$ ← **Multiply 8 and 3.**

$= 6$ ← **Subtract 24 from 30.**

✓ Quick Check

1. Find the value of each expression.

a. $34 + 5 \times 2 - 17$ **b.** $(6 + 18) \div 3 \times 2$

EXAMPLE Using Expressions to Solve Problems

2 **Multiple Choice** Suppose you buy the items shown on the store receipt. What is the total cost of the items, including the tax?

Ⓐ $160   Ⓒ $190

Ⓑ $170   Ⓓ $1,570

You can write an expression to help you find the total cost.

CRAWFORD'S

ITEMS ORDERED

JEANS   3 @ $35.00 EACH
DISCOUNT   −$5.00
SHIRTS   4 @ $15.00 EACH

TAX $10.00
_____
TOTAL

Words	cost of jeans	−	discount	+	cost of shirts	+	tax
Expression	3 × $35	−	$5	+	4 × $15	+	$10
	$105	−	$5	+	$60	+	$10	← **Multiply.**
	$100			+	$60	+	$10	← **Subtract.**
						$170	← **Add.**

The total cost is $170. The correct answer is choice B.

✓ Quick Check

2. You are paid $7 per hour to rake leaves. Your brother is paid $5 per hour. You worked 4 hours and your brother worked 3 hours. How much did the two of you earn together?

Test Prep Tip Ⓐ Ⓑ Ⓒ Ⓓ
You can model a problem using words that describe the quantities in the problem.

1. **Vocabulary** A mathematical phrase that contains numbers and operation symbols is a(n) __?__.

2. **Error Analysis** A student says that the value of the expression $5 + 25 \div 5$ is 6. What error did the student make?

Which operation should you do first?

3. $6 - 2 \times 2$ 4. $33 - (4 + 6)$ 5. $6 \times (2 - 5)$ 6. $7 + 4 \times 3$

Use <, =, or > to complete each statement.

7. $(1 + 2) \times 2$ ■ $1 + 2 \times 2$ 8. $3 \times (4 - 2)$ ■ $3 \times 4 - 2$

Homework Exercises

For more exercises, see Extra Skills and Word Problems.

GO for Help

For Exercises	See Example
9–17	1
18–26	2

Find the value of each expression.

9. $450 \div 45 + 5$ 10. $29 - 4 \times 7$ 11. $16 + 36 \div 12$

12. $14 - (7 + 5) \div 2$ 13. $(13 + 21) \times 2$ 14. $400 \div (44 - 24)$

15. $16 - (2 + 4) \times 2$ 16. $26 + 5 - 4 \times 3$ 17. $13 + 5 \times 12 - 4$

18. $4 \times \$40 - \$5$ 19. $\$50 + \$20 \div 2$

20. $\$100 - 2 \times \$30$ 21. $\$35 \times 2 + \$42 \div 2$

22. $3(\$28 + \$32) - \$10$ 23. $\$15 \times 10 + \$30 \times 2$

24. $(\$45 \times 4 + \$125 \times 3) \div 5$ 25. $(\$75 \times 5) + (\$25 \times 6) - \$10$

26. **Marbles** You buy 2 red rainbow marbles for 50¢ each, 3 bumblebee marbles for 90¢ each, and 2 tricolor marbles for 65¢ each. Find the total cost of the marbles.

GPS 27. **Guided Problem Solving** A group of 25 students and 3 adults goes to an art museum. Admission costs $6 per student and $9 per adult. There is a $15 discount for groups of 20 or more. Find the total cost for the trip.
   • **Make a Plan** Write an expression for the cost of both the students and the adults. Next, find the total cost of the trip.
   • **Carry Out the Plan** An expression for the total cost for students and adults is $25 \times \$■ + 3 \times \$■ - ■$.

Reasoning Insert parentheses to make each statement true.

28. $11 - 7 \div 2 = 2$

29. $1 + 2 \times 15 - 4 = 33$

Nutrition Use the table to answer Exercises 30 and 31.

30. How many grams of protein are in 6 oz of chicken and 2 c of vegetables?

31. How many grams of protein are in 9 oz of chicken, 2 c of vegetables, and 1 c of rice?

Food	Serving Size	Protein
Chicken	3 oz	21 g
Vegetables	1 c	2 g
Rice	1 c	9 g

32. **Coins** There are 300 coins of the same type in two stacks. One stack is 380 millimeters tall. The other is 220 millimeters tall. Find the thickness of one coin.

33. **Writing in Math** Explain the steps you would use to find the value of the expression $8 \div 4 \times 6 + (7 - 5)$.

34. **Challenge** Copy the statement: $14 \blacksquare 7 \blacksquare 2 \blacksquare 3 = 7$. Insert operations symbols to make the statement true.

Careers Nutritionists help people plan their diets.

Test Prep and Mixed Review **Practice**

Multiple Choice

35. A group of 11 boys and 9 girls goes to a movie. Admission costs $7 per person. Which expression does NOT show the total amount the group will pay?
- Ⓐ $7 \times (11 + 9)$
- Ⓒ $(\$7 \times 11) + (\$7 \times 9)$
- Ⓑ $7 \times 11 \times 9$
- Ⓓ 7×20

36. There are 6 bike racks at a park. Each bike rack can hold 14 bikes. If there are 11 bikes, which method can be used to find the number of empty spaces in the bike racks?
- Ⓕ Add 6 to the product of 11 and 14.
- Ⓖ Subtract 6 from the product of 11 and 14.
- Ⓗ Add 11 to the product of 6 and 14.
- Ⓙ Subtract 11 from the product of 6 and 14.

37. For which sum is 2,200 a reasonable estimate?
- Ⓐ $422 + 1,085 + 897$
- Ⓒ $605 + 786 + 1,022$
- Ⓑ $280 + 1,375 + 466$
- Ⓓ $1,532 + 963 + 45$

GO for Help

For Exercises	See Lesson
38–40	1-2

Estimate using compatible numbers.

38. $57 \div 6$

39. 14×4

40. $627 \div 23$

Use < or > to complete each statement.

1. 455 ■ 45

2. 39,382 ■ 39,832

3. 21,040 ■ 20,401

Use rounding or compatible numbers to estimate each answer.

4. 553 − 385

5. 5,964 + 3,088

6. 1,085 ÷ 523

Use mental math to find each answer.

7. 19 + 7 + 31

8. (6 + 18) + 14

9. 25 × 10 × 4

Find the value of each expression.

10. 30 − 6 × 5

11. (12 + 23) × 2

12. $60 + $30 ÷ 3

13. The peregrine falcon can fly about 280 feet in one second. About how far can it fly in 4 seconds?

14. Jupiter has many satellites. Leda is 6,893,000 miles from Jupiter. Himalia is 7,134,000 miles from Jupiter. Lysithea is about 7,283,000 miles from Jupiter. Elara is 7,293,000 miles from Jupiter. Order the distances from least to greatest.

MATH AT WORK

Accountant

Accountants usually work in some area of finance. They must enjoy working with numbers and know how to budget money well.

They use mathematics to prepare and analyze financial reports, tax returns, and budgets. Accountants also help individuals and companies track financial history and plan for future growth.

Accountants' reports help people make good business decisions.

Go Online
PHSchool.com **For:** Information on accounting
Web Code: aqb-2031

Exploring Decimal Models

You can use grid models or base-ten pieces to represent decimals. For both types of models, the large square represents the whole.

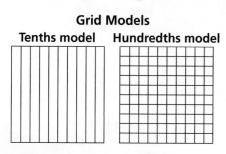

Grid Models

Tenths model Hundredths model

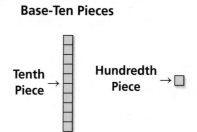

Base-Ten Pieces

Tenth Piece → Hundredth Piece →

EXAMPLE **Modeling Decimals**

Write the decimal for the model below, in words and in numerals.

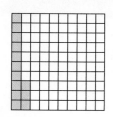

There are 100 squares. Thirteen squares are shaded.

Words   thirteen hundredths
↓   ↓
Numerals   0.13

Exercises

Write a decimal for each model.

1.
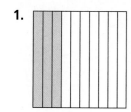

2.
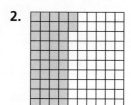

3.
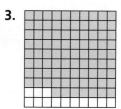

Model each decimal using a grid model or base-ten pieces.

4. two tenths

5. forty hundredths

6. eighty-five hundredths

7. a. Draw models for five tenths and for fifty hundredths.
   b. **Number Sense** Show that the decimals are equal.

1-5 Understanding Decimals

Check Skills You'll Need

1. **Vocabulary Review** Write one thousand, three hundred twenty-one in *standard form*.

Write each whole number in words.

2. 28   **3.** 8,672

4. 612,980 **5.** 58,026

 **for Help**
Lesson 1-1

What You'll Learn

To read, write, and round decimals

🔊 **New Vocabulary** expanded form

Why Learn This?

Decimal numbers allow you to write very precise values. In sports, the difference between first place and second place sometimes depends on decimal places.

You can extend the place value chart to include values for decimal places. When you read a decimal that is greater than 1, read the decimal point as "and."

EXAMPLE **Writing a Decimal in Words**

1 **Fuel** The price of a gallon of gasoline is $2.459. Write 2.459 in words.

Begin by writing 2.459 in a place value chart.

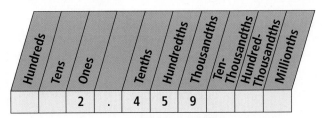

Hundreds	Tens	Ones		Tenths	Hundredths	Thousandths	Ten-Thousandths	Hundred-Thousandths	Millionths
		2	.	4	5	9			

2.459   ← **Three decimal places indicate thousandths.**

two **and** four hundred fifty-nine thousandths

✓ Quick Check

1. Write each decimal in words.
   a. 67.3   **b.** 6.734   **c.** 0.67

You can write decimals in both standard form and expanded form. **Expanded form** is a sum that shows the place and value of each digit of a number.

Standard Form		Expanded Form		
0.75	=	0.7	+	0.05
↑		↑		↑
seventy-five hundredths		seven tenths	+	five hundredths

EXAMPLE Standard Form and Expanded Form

2 **Sports** At a gymnastics meet, the best score on the pommel horse was nine and forty-two thousandths. Write the score in standard form and in expanded form.

9.   ← Write the whole number part. Place the decimal point.

9.■■■   ← Thousandths is three places to the right of the decimal point.

9.■42   ← Place 42 to the far right.

9.042   ← Insert a zero for tenths.

Standard form: 9.042   Expanded form: $9 + 0.04 + 0.002$

✓ Quick Check

2. The winning car in a race won by fifteen hundredths of a second. Write the decimal in standard and expanded forms.

Rounding decimals is similar to rounding whole numbers.

The value to the right of 3 → 0.32   0.36 ← The value to the right of 3
is < 5, so round down to   ↓   ↓   is ≥ 5. So round up.
nearest tenth.   0.3   0.4

EXAMPLE Rounding Decimals

3 Round 0.426 to the nearest hundredth.

0.426   ← Look at the digit to the right of the hundredths place.
 ↑
6 is ≥ 5, so round up.

So 0.426 rounded to the nearest hundredth is 0.43.

✓ Quick Check

3. Round each decimal to the underlined place.
  a. 2.3<u>4</u>28   **b.** 0.173<u>4</u>7   **c.** 9.<u>0</u>53

1. **Number Sense** In the number 12.057, which digit has the greater value, the 5 or the 7? Explain.

2. **Open-Ended** Write a decimal with 4 decimal places in words and in standard form. Then round the decimal to the nearest hundredth.

Find the value of the digit 3 in each number.

3. 0.3   4. 0.237   5. 7.553   6. 8.2103

Write each decimal in expanded form.

7. 1.2   8. 8.4   9. 7.52   10. 0.239

Homework Exercises

For more exercises, see Extra Skills and Word Problems.

GO for Help

For Exercises	See Example
11–20	1
21–25	2
26–33	3

Write each decimal in words.

11. 2.3   12. 6.02   13. 0.006   14. 2.061   15. 3.08

16. 0.40   17. 50.603   18. 1.28   19. 3.004   20. 0.23

Write each decimal in standard form and in expanded form.

21. forty and nine thousandths   22. sixty-four hundredths

23. seven hundred thousandths   24. nine and twenty hundredths

25. **Running** A marathon is twenty-six and two tenths miles long. Write the number in standard form and in expanded form.

Round each decimal to the underlined place.

26. 0.6_8_3   27. 2._7_248   28. 3.41_4_69   29. 10.9_5_6

30. 6.2_4_7   31. 0._5_54   32. 4.0_6_25   33. 4.8_9_6

34. **Guided Problem Solving** The diameter of a white blood cell is twelve ten-thousandths of a centimeter. Round the diameter to the nearest thousandth of a centimeter.
   • What is twelve ten-thousandths in standard form?
   • Is the digit to the right of the thousandths place *less than, greater than,* or *equal to* 5?

35. According to the bar graph, sales for Company A were 0.7 million dollars. As a whole number, this is written $700,000. Write the annual sales for each company as a decimal and as a whole number.

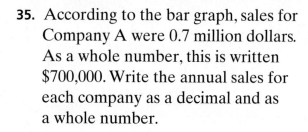

Annual Sales

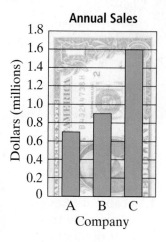

36. Money A mill is a unit of money sometimes used by state governments. One mill is equal to one thousandth of a dollar ($0.001). Write each amount as a decimal part of a dollar.

  a. 6 mills   **b.** 207 mills   **c.** 53 mills

Find the value of the digit 4 in each number.

37. 0.4   **38.** 42.3926   **39.** 17.55643

40. 1.2468   **41.** 121.004   **42.** 425.209

43. Artists use a ratio called the Golden Mean to describe a person's height. Your height from the floor to your waist is usually six hundred eighteen thousandths of your total height. Round this number to the nearest hundredth.

44. <u>**Writing in Math**</u> Describe how the values of the digit 2 in the number 22.222 change as you move from right to left.

45. Challenge Extend the place value chart to write 0.0000001 in words.

Test Prep and Mixed Review   **Practice**

Multiple Choice

46. At a sale, shirts were marked down $5 each. Lisa bought 3 shirts for $39. Find the price of each shirt before the sale.
  Ⓐ $7   Ⓑ $13   Ⓒ $18   Ⓓ $24

47. You and three friends bought a large pizza for $13.00. Each of you paid an equal share of the cost. Which method can be used to find the amount each person paid?
  Ⓕ Divide 13.00 by 3.   Ⓗ Divide 13.00 by 4.
  Ⓖ Multiply 13.00 by 4.   Ⓙ Multiply 13.00 by 3.

GO for Help

For Exercises	See Lesson
48–50	1-2

Mental Math **Use mental math to find each sum or product.**

48. $(20 \times 3) \times 5$ **49.** $70 + 0$ **50.** $2 \times (42 \times 5)$

Comparing and Ordering Decimals

 **1-6**

Check Skills You'll Need

1. **Vocabulary Review** Explain how to *order* numbers.

Use < or > to complete each statement.

2. 430 ■ 340

3. 2,005 ■ 2,050

 **GO for Help**
Lesson 1-1

What You'll Learn

To compare and order decimals using models and place value

Why Learn This?

Many measurements are recorded using decimals. You can use decimals to compare measurements in many applications, including construction and science.

You can use grid models and number lines to compare decimals.

EXAMPLE **Using Models to Compare Decimals**

① Use models to compare 0.4 and 0.36. Which number is greater?

Method 1 Use grid models.

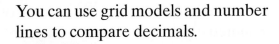

Use a tenths grid for 0.4. →   ← Use a hundredths grid for 0.36.

A greater area is shaded for 0.4 than for 0.36. So 0.4 is greater than 0.36.

Method 2 Use a number line.

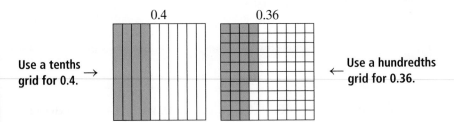

Make a number line showing hundredths.

Since 0.4 is to the right of 0.36, 0.4 is greater than 0.36.

GO for Help

For help using a number line, go to Lesson 1-1, Example 2.

✓ Quick Check

1. Use models to compare 0.59 and 0.6. Which number is greater?

EXAMPLE Comparing Decimals

2 Use <, =, or > to complete the statement 3.18 ■ 3.8.

Step 1 Line up the decimal points of the numbers.

3.18
3.80 ← Write a **zero** at the end of 3.8 so each number has two decimal places.

Test Prep Tip

You can write a zero at the end of a decimal without changing the value of the decimal.
0.7 = 0.70 = 0.700

Step 2 Compare the digits starting with the highest place value.

The ones digits are the same. ↓ ↓ The tenths digits are different. 1 is less than 8.

3.18
3.80

Since 1 tenth < 8 tenths, 3.18 < 3.8.

✓ Quick Check

2. Use <, =, or > to complete the statement 0.56 ■ 0.543.

You can also use a number line or place value to order decimals.

EXAMPLE Ordering Decimals

For: Ordering Decimals Activity
Use: Interactive Textbook, 1-6

3 **Science** Order these bodies of water from least to most salty.

Salt per Liter in Major Bodies of Water

Body of Water	Arctic Ocean	Dead Sea	Caspian Sea	Black Sea
Salt per Liter	0.032 kg	0.28 kg	0.013 kg	0.018 kg

SOURCE: *Natural Wonders of the World*

Compare the digits starting with the highest place values.

2 is the greatest tenths digit, so 0.280 is the greatest decimal.

0.032	0.032	← In the remaining numbers, 3 is the greatest hundredths digit. So 0.032 is the second-greatest decimal.
0.280	0.280	
0.013	0.013	
0.018	0.018	← 8 is the greatest thousandths digit. So 0.018 is the third-greatest decimal.

The decimals from least to greatest are 0.013, 0.018, 0.032, and 0.28. The bodies of water from least to most salty are the Caspian Sea, the Black Sea, the Arctic Ocean, and the Dead Sea.

✓ Quick Check

3. Order 3.059, 3.64, and 3.46 from least to greatest.

● More Than One Way

Nutrition Use the table at the right. Order the foods by sodium content from least to greatest.

Food	Sodium
Half of a bagel	0.19 g
1 corn tortilla	0.04 g
3 pieces of Melba toast	0.12 g
5 crackers	0.195 g
1 slice of wheat bread	0.132 g

Elena's Method

I can use mental math to order the decimals.

0.19   0.04   0.12   0.195   0.132

First, I compare the tenths place in all the numbers. $0 < 1$, so 0.04 is the least number.

Next, I compare the hundredths place in the remaining numbers. $2 < 3 < 9$, so $0.12 < 0.13 < 0.19$.

Finally, I compare 0.19 and 0.195. Since $0.19 = 0.190$ and $0 < 5$, $0.19 < 0.195$.

The correct order is 0.04, 0.12, 0.132, 0.19, and 0.195. The foods from least to greatest sodium content are corn tortilla, Melba toast, wheat bread, bagel, and crackers.

Leon's Method

I can order the decimals by graphing them on a number line.

I see that all the numbers are between 0 and 0.2. I will make a number line marked in hundredths.

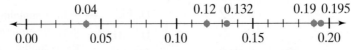

The decimals from least to greatest are 0.04, 0.12, 0.132, 0.19, and 0.195. The foods from least to greatest sodium content are corn tortilla, Melba toast, wheat bread, bagel, and crackers.

Choose a Method

Order the values 0.964, 0.26, 0.576, 0.059, 0.9, 0.96, and 0.264 from least to greatest. Describe your method and explain why you chose it.

1. **Reasoning** Explain how you can use place value to show that 1.679 > 1.697 is false.

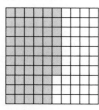

Two decimal models are shown at the left.

2. What decimal does each model represent?

3. Which decimal is greater?

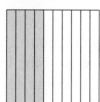

Select the value on the right that makes each statement true.

4. 2.37 > ■   2.74, 2.32, 2.38   5. 0.57 < ■   0.575, 0.502, 0.567

6. Order 1.2, 1.3, 0.9, and 0.8 from least to greatest.

Homework Exercises

For more exercises, see Extra Skills and Word Problems.

GO for Help

For Exercises	See Example
7–9	1
10–15	2
16–21	3

Use models to compare each pair of decimals. Which number is greater?

7. 0.4 and 0.5   8. 0.35 and 0.53   9. 0.2 and 0.02

Use <, =, or > to complete each statement.

10. 0.3 ■ 0.27   11. 5.7 ■ 5.70   12. 0.601 ■ 0.60

13. 0.4389 ■ 0.45   14. 0.36 ■ 0.365   15. 10.9 ■ 10.02

Order each set of decimals from least to greatest.

16. 0.5, 0.7, 0.65   17. 17.1, 17.7, 13.7

18. 0.503, 0.53, 0.529   19. 9.2, 9.02, 9.209, 9.024

20. 1.79, 1.991, 2.185, 1.979   21. 5.5506, 5.5660, 5.561, 5.58

 22. **Guided Problem Solving** The United States won the women's Olympic 100-meter run in all the years listed. What is the fastest time listed?
- Is the fastest time the least or the greatest time?
- What is the greatest place value in which the times differ?

Year	Time (seconds)
1984	10.97
1988	10.54
1992	10.82
1996	10.94
2000	10.75

Source: *The World Almanac*

709.52   952   370.973   031.02

398.9   944   398.2

23. **Choose a Method** The Dewey Decimal System assigns a number to every nonfiction book. The books at the left are in the correct order from left to right. Match each label to its book by ordering the labels from least to greatest.

Select the values on the right that make each statement true.

24. $4.18 < \blacksquare < 4.25$ $4.25, 4.17, 4.27, 4.2025, 4.319, 4.198$

25. $0.57 < \blacksquare < 0.67$ $0.6595, 0.5025, 0.6095, 0.62, 0.567$

26. **Open-Ended** Write six numbers between 2.2 and 2.222. Order the numbers from least to greatest.

GO Online
Homework Video Tutor
Visit: PHSchool.com
Web Code: aqe-0106

27. **Population** About 11.4 million people live in Jakarta, Indonesia. Roughly 13.0 million people live in Delhi, India. About 10.4 million people live in Karachi, Pakistan. Order the cities from least to greatest population.

28. **Writing in Math** Alia ran the 100-yard dash in 11.88 seconds. Patty ran it in 11.9 seconds. Who ran faster? Explain.

29. **Challenge** Estimate the decimals represented by A, B, and C.

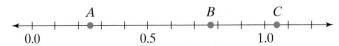

Test Prep and Mixed Review

Practice

Multiple Choice

30. Consuela measured the length of each finger on her hand. The table shows her data. Which list shows these measurements in order from least to greatest?

    Ⓐ 4.5 cm, 6.5 cm, 6.7 cm, 7.1 cm
    Ⓑ 7.1 cm, 6.7 cm, 6.5 cm, 4.5 cm
    Ⓒ 7.1 cm, 6.5 cm, 6.7 cm, 4.5 cm
    Ⓓ 4.5 cm, 6.7 cm, 6.5 cm, 7.1 cm

Length of Each Finger

Finger	Length (cm)
Index	6.5
Middle	7.1
Ring	6.7
Pinkie	4.5

31. Mrs. Xing drives at a constant speed of 60 miles per hour. How can you find how long it takes her to drive 420 miles?
    Ⓕ Multiply 60 by 420.   Ⓗ Divide 420 by 60.
    Ⓖ Subtract 60 from 420.   Ⓙ Add 420 to 60.

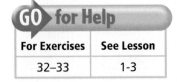
GO for Help

For Exercises	See Lesson
32–33	1-3

Find the value of each expression.

32. $(\$15 \times 4) - (\$5 \times 9)$

33. $15 + 4 \times 6 - 13$

Using Models

You can use models to add or subtract two decimals.

EXAMPLE **Modeling Decimal Sums**

1 Use a model to find 0.4 + 0.03.

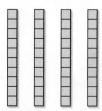

Start with four tenth pieces. **Add three hundredth pieces.** **Count the total number of hundredth pieces.**

There are a total of 43 hundredths pieces, so 0.4 + 0.03 = 0.43.

EXAMPLE **Modeling Decimal Differences**

2 Use a model to find 1.4 − 0.6.

Use two tenths grids. Shade ten tenths in one grid and four tenths in the other grid.

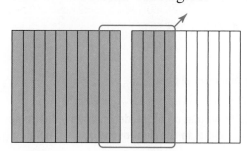

← **Remove six tenths from fourteen tenths.**

There are eight tenths left, so 1.4 − 0.6 = 0.8.

Exercises

Use a model to find each sum or difference.

1. 0.1 + 0.8   **2.** 1.5 − 1.2   **3.** 0.06 + 0.55   **4.** 1.54 − 0.72

5. a. Use a model to find 0.41 + 0.59.
   b. Number Sense Explain why there are no hundredths in the answer.

Adding and Subtracting Decimals

Check Skills You'll Need

1. Vocabulary Review
 _?_ is a method of estimation that compares a digit's value to 5.

Round each number to the underlined place.

2. 7<u>2</u>   **3.** 1<u>0</u>8

4. <u>1</u>49   **5.** 3,1<u>9</u>6

 **for Help**
Lesson 1-2

What You'll Learn

To add and subtract decimals and to solve problems involving decimals

◀)) **New Vocabulary** front-end estimation

Why Learn This?

To find the sum or difference of two amounts of money, you need to add or subtract decimals.

If you estimate before you add or subtract, you can tell whether your answer is reasonable. One way to estimate is to round.

GO ◉**nline**

Video Tutor Help
Visit: PHSchool.com
Web Code: aqe-0775

EXAMPLE Finding Decimal Sums

1 Find 3.026 + 14.7 + 1.38.

Step 1 Estimate.   3.026 + 14.7 + 1.38
                  ≈ 3   + 15   + 1, or 19

Step 2 Add.   ⌐———— Line up the decimal points.

$$
\begin{array}{r}
3.026 \\
14.700 \\
+\ 1.380 \\
\hline
19.106
\end{array}
$$

Write zeros so that all of the decimals have the same number of digits to the right of the decimal point.

Check for Reasonableness The sum 19.106 is reasonable, since it is close to 19.

✓ Quick Check

● **1.** Find 0.84 + 2.0 + 3.32. Estimate first.

In **front-end estimation,** you estimate by first adding the "front-end digits." Then you estimate the sum of the remaining digits. You adjust the sum of the front-end digits as necessary.

EXAMPLE Using Front-End Estimation

Popcorn
Small $3.98
Medium $6.49
Large $9.08
Junior $3.47

② **Food** Use front-end estimation to estimate the total cost of buying one of every size of popcorn shown at the left.

Step 1 Add the front-end digits. These are the dollar amounts.

$3.98
$6.49
$9.08
+ $3.47
$21

Step 2 Estimate the total cents. Then adjust the dollar amounts.

$3.98 → about $1
$6.49 ⎫
$9.08 ⎬ about $1
+ $3.47 ⎭
$21   about $2

The total cost is about $21 + $2, or $23.

✓ Quick Check

2. Use front-end estimation to estimate the total cost of one small popcorn and two large popcorns.

EXAMPLE Finding a Difference

③ A basketball hoop is 46 cm across. A basketball is 24.28 cm across. What is the difference between these measurements?

Estimate $46 - 24.28 \approx 46 - 24$, or 22

Write 46 with a decimal point and two zeros.	Rename 46 as 45 and 10 tenths.	Rename 10 tenths as 9 tenths and 10 hundredths.
46.00 − 24.28	45 10 46.00 − 24.28	9 45 10 10 46.00 − 24.28 = 21.72

The difference is 21.72 cm.

Check for Reasonableness 21.72 is close to 22, so the answer is reasonable.

✓ Quick Check

3. Use the graph at the right. How much greater is the women's record discus throw than the men's throw?

60 m   70 m   80 m
76.80 m
74.08 m
● Men's throw
● Women's throw

Check Your Understanding

1. **Error Analysis** Explain and correct the error in the work at the right.

$$\begin{array}{r} 5.8 \\ -\ 2 \\ \hline 5.6 \end{array}$$

Find each sum or difference.

2. $6.37 + 2.45$

$$\begin{array}{r} 6.3\,7 \\ +\ \blacksquare.\blacksquare\blacksquare \\ \hline \end{array}$$

3. $8.9 - 7.52$

$$\begin{array}{r} \blacksquare.\blacksquare\blacksquare \\ -\ 7.5\,2 \\ \hline \end{array}$$

4. $7.3 + 4$

$$\begin{array}{r} 7.3 \\ +\ \blacksquare.\blacksquare \\ \hline \end{array}$$

Use front-end estimation to estimate each sum.

5. $\$6.70 + \$2.40$

6. $\$8.92 + \$7.10$

7. $\$7.10 + \$4$

Homework Exercises

For more exercises, see Extra Skills and Word Problems.

GO for Help

For Exercises	See Example
8–13	1
14–17	2
18–27	3

First estimate. Then find each sum.

8. $0.6 + 3.4$

9. $6.2 + 0.444$

10. $8.001 + 0.77$

11. $7 + 11.436 + 3.08$

12. $0.445 + 8.99 + 3$

13. $0.33 + 1.11 + 3.2$

Use front-end estimation to estimate each sum.

14. $\$4.89 + \$3.97$

15. $\$6.15 + \$8.86$

16. $\$14.65 + \$27.29 + \$63.85$

17. $\$16.81 + \$19.94 + \$11.49$

First estimate. Then find each difference.

18. $22.2 - 4.3$

19. $8.91 - 6.08$

20. $9.45 - 3.76$

21. $9.1 - 6.05$

22. $0.8 - 0.126$

23. $4 - 1.29$

24. $60 - 2.037$

25. $9 - 0.45$

26. $6.72 - 2.45$

27. A digital camera costs $174.99 online. At a local store, the same camera costs $222.98. What is the difference in prices?

28. **Guided Problem Solving** Jonah had $340.87 in his checking account. He deposited $52 and wrote a check for $38.72. Find his new balance.
   - How did Jonah's balance change after he deposited $52?
   - How did the balance change after he wrote the check?

Use <, =, or > to complete each statement.

29. $0.041 + 0.009$ ▧ 0.5

30. $0.315 + 0.14 + 0.05$ ▧ 0.5

31. $669.583 + 204.222$ ▧ 873.8

32. $665.5 - 281.7$ ▧ 373.8

33. Population In 2000, the New England states had a total population of about 13.92 million. Find the population of Maine.

State	Population
Connecticut	3.41 million
Maine	▧
Massachusetts	6.35 million
New Hampshire	1.24 million
Rhode Island	1.05 million
Vermont	0.61 million

Source: U.S. Census Bureau.
Go to **www.PHSchool.com** for a data update.
Web Code: aqg-9041

34. A series of orders was placed with a clothing company. Using the prices at the left, estimate the total cost of each order.
  a. 2 XXL adult T-shirts and 1 child sweatshirt
  b. 3 XL adult sweatshirts and 4 child sweatshirts
  c. 3 child T-shirts, 2 XL adult T-shirts and 2 XXL adult T-shirts

35. Choose a Method A hot dog vendor receives a $20 bill for a $5.25 purchase. Is the vendor most likely to use estimation, mental math, or a calculator to find the amount of change? Explain.

36. Challenge Find the missing numbers.
  a. $1.2 \times$ ▧ $= 18$
  b. $2.5 \times$ ▧ $= 11.25$

T-Shirts and Sweatshirts For Sale

Adult T-shirt
(M-XL) $15.00
(XXL) $17.95

Adult Sweatshirt
(M-XL) $29.50
(XXL) $29.95

Child's T-shirt
$12.50

Child's Sweatshirt
$16.95

Test Prep and Mixed Review

Practice

Multiple Choice

37. At a baseball game, Ben ordered peanuts for $3.25. He paid with a $5 bill. How much change did Ben get?
  Ⓐ $1.25　　Ⓑ $1.75　　Ⓒ $2.25　　Ⓓ $2.75

38. Patrick spent $22 on a taxi ride, $48 on a theater ticket, and $31 on snacks. Which is closest to the total amount he spent?
  Ⓕ $90　　Ⓖ $100　　Ⓗ $110　　Ⓙ $120

39. Which statement about 11.924 and 11.942 is true?
  Ⓐ $11.924 > 11.942$　　　Ⓒ $11.942 > 11.924$
  Ⓑ $11.924 = 11.942$　　　Ⓓ $11.942 < 11.924$

Round each number to the nearest hundred.

40. 287　　**41.** 812　　**42.** 86　　**43.** 1,413　　**44.** 6,546

GO for Help

For Exercises	See Lesson
40–44	1-2

High-Use Academic Words

High-use academic words are words that you will
see often in textbooks and on tests. These words
are not math vocabulary terms, but knowing
them will help you to succeed in mathematics.

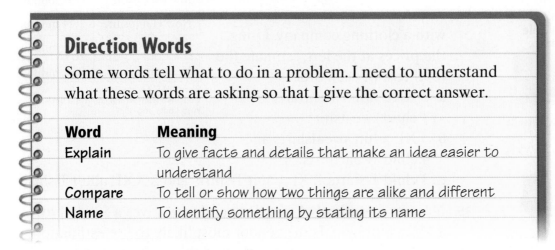

Direction Words

Some words tell what to do in a problem. I need to understand
what these words are asking so that I give the correct answer.

Word	Meaning
Explain	To give facts and details that make an idea easier to understand
Compare	To tell or show how two things are alike and different
Name	To identify something by stating its name

Exercises

1. Explain how to make a peanut butter and jelly sandwich.

2. Compare a peanut butter and jelly sandwich to a ham and cheese sandwich.

3. Name the ingredients in a peanut butter and jelly sandwich.

4. Explain how to order a group of numbers using a number line.

5. Compare 0.8 and 0.85.

6. Name the place and value of each digit in 10.92.

7. a. **Word Knowledge** Think about the word *reasonable*.
   Choose the letter that shows how well you know
   the word.
   A. I know its meaning.
   B. I have seen it, but I don't know its meaning.
   C. I don't know it.
   b. **Research** Look up and write the definition of *reasonable*.
   c. Use the word in a sentence involving mathematics.

Modeling Decimal Multiplication

A model can help you to multiply decimals.

EXAMPLES **Multiplying Decimals**

1 **Coin Collecting** A collector buys two 1942 Mercury dimes. Each coin costs $.92. Draw a model to find the total cost.

You want to find 0.92 + 0.92, or 2 × 0.92.

Shade 92 squares in each of two grids.

0.92   0.92

Move 8 hundredths to fill the first grid.

Miss Liberty's winged cap makes her look like the Roman god Mercury, so the coin was called the "Mercury" dime.

Count the shaded squares in the grids.

The shaded area is 1 whole and 84 hundredths, or 1.84. The total cost is $1.84.

2 Draw a model to find the product 0.5 × 0.4.

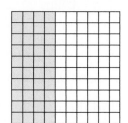 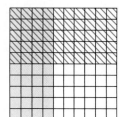

Shade 4 *columns* of a grid to represent 0.4.

Shade 5 *rows* to represent 0.5. Use a different color or style.

The shadings overlap in 20 squares, representing 20 hundredths, or 0.20. So 0.5 × 0.4 = 0.20.

Exercises

Draw a model to find each product.

1. 3 × 0.9   **2.** 2 × 0.61   **3.** 0.8 × 0.5   **4.** 0.7 × 0.2   **5.** 0.1 × 0.6

6. <u>**Writing in Math**</u> Explain how to use models to find 2.6 × 0.2.

Multiplying Decimals

Check Skills You'll Need

1. **Vocabulary Review** Are 130 and 5 *compatible* numbers when dividing 130 by 5? Explain.

Estimate using compatible numbers.

2. 21×29 **3.** 59×3

4. $498 \div 5$ **5.** $71 \div 7$

for Help
Lesson 1-2

What You'll Learn

To multiply decimals and to solve problems involving decimals

Why Learn This?

Understanding how much a plant will grow over time is important in gardening. You can multiply decimals to estimate how tall a flower or tree will grow.

The model below shows how to find 0.5×1.5. You are finding half of 1.5.

Shade 15 columns to represent 1.5.

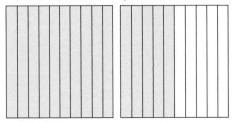

Shade 5 rows of each grid to represent 0.5.

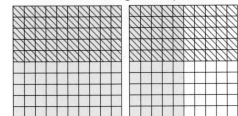

The shadings overlap in 75 squares, or 0.75. So $0.5 \times 1.5 = 0.75$.

The model shows a pattern. To find the number of decimal places in a product, add the number of decimal places in the factors.

EXAMPLE Multiplying by a Decimal

1 Find the product 0.47×8.

$$
\begin{array}{rl}
0.47 & \leftarrow \quad \text{2 decimal places} \\
\underline{\times \ 8} & \leftarrow + \text{ 0 decimal places} \\
3.76 & \leftarrow \quad \text{2 decimal places}
\end{array}
$$

Quick Check

1. a. Find 6×0.13. **b.** Find 4.37×5.

You can show multiplication in these three ways:

$$0.5 \times 1.5 \qquad 0.5 \cdot 1.5 \qquad 0.5(1.5)$$

Video Tutor Help

Visit: PHSchool.com
Web Code: aqe-0775

EXAMPLE **Multiplying Decimals**

2 Find the product $1.31 \cdot 2.4$.

$$\begin{array}{r} 1.31 \quad \leftarrow \textbf{2 decimal places} \\ \times\ 2.4 \quad \leftarrow \textbf{+ 1 decimal place} \\ \hline 524 \\ +\ 262 \\ \hline 3.144 \quad \leftarrow \textbf{3 decimal places} \end{array}$$

Check for Reasonableness It makes sense that a number slightly greater than 1 times a number slightly greater than 2 equals a product of about 3.

✓ Quick Check

2. Find each product.
  a. $0.3(0.2)$ **b.** $1.9 \cdot 5.32$ **c.** 0.9×0.14

You can also use compatible numbers to estimate with decimals.

EXAMPLE **Application: Predicting Growth**

3 A eucalyptus tree grows 5.45 meters in one year. At that rate, how much does the tree grow in 3.5 years?

Estimate $3.5 \times 5.45 \approx 4 \times 5$, or 20 $\leftarrow$ **4 and 5 are compatible numbers.**

$$\begin{array}{r} 5.45 \quad \leftarrow \textbf{2 decimal places} \\ \times\ 3.5 \quad \leftarrow \textbf{1 decimal place} \\ \hline 2725 \\ +\ 1635 \\ \hline 19.075 \quad \leftarrow \textbf{3 decimal places} \end{array}$$

At that rate, the tree grows about 19.075 meters in 3.5 years.

Check for Reasonableness 19.075 is close to 20, so the answer is reasonable.

The leaves and flowers of eucalyptus trees are the koala's main diet.

✓ Quick Check

3. One pound of tomatoes costs $1.29. To the nearest cent, how much do 2.75 pounds of tomatoes cost?

1. **Reasoning** You are multiplying 9.876 × 5.4321. How many decimal places does the answer have? Explain.

2. **Error Analysis** A student says 19.8 × 3.1 = 612.8. Is this answer correct? Explain how you know.

Number Sense Is the product *greater than, equal to,* or *less than* 1? Explain your reasoning.

3. 2 × 0.2   4. 2.2 × 0.7   5. 2 × 0.5

Copy each problem. Place the decimal point in the product.

6. $\begin{array}{r} 0.403 \\ \times\ \ 5 \\ \hline 2015 \end{array}$
7. $\begin{array}{r} 524 \\ \times\ 0.5 \\ \hline 2620 \end{array}$
8. $\begin{array}{r} 0.15 \\ \times\ 0.31 \\ \hline 465 \end{array}$
9. $\begin{array}{r} 8.42 \\ \times\ 6.7 \\ \hline 56414 \end{array}$

Homework Exercises

For more exercises, see Extra Skills and Word Problems.

GO for Help

For Exercises	See Example
10–17	1
18–34	2–3

Find each product.

10. $\begin{array}{r} 0.018 \\ \times\ \ 4 \end{array}$
11. $\begin{array}{r} 1.9 \\ \times\ 9 \end{array}$
12. $\begin{array}{r} 35 \\ \times\ 5.6 \end{array}$
13. $\begin{array}{r} 39 \\ \times\ 0.06 \end{array}$

14. $\begin{array}{r} 358 \\ \times\ 0.7 \end{array}$
15. $\begin{array}{r} 0.12 \\ \times\ 47 \end{array}$
16. $\begin{array}{r} 53 \\ \times\ 0.04 \end{array}$
17. $\begin{array}{r} 0.25 \\ \times\ 92 \end{array}$

18. $\begin{array}{r} 0.2 \\ \times\ 0.7 \end{array}$
19. $\begin{array}{r} 0.8 \\ \times\ 0.4 \end{array}$
20. $\begin{array}{r} 0.3 \\ \times\ 0.5 \end{array}$
21. $\begin{array}{r} 0.7 \\ \times\ 0.9 \end{array}$

22. 0.12(0.96)   23. 0.06(0.18)   24. 0.486 · 0.9   25. 0.03 · 0.574

26. 4.5(230)   27. 1.7 × 3.702   28. 3.2 · 4.5   29. 8.1 · 1.3

30. 3.3(420)   31. 3.2 · 15.5   32. 4.25 · 6.18   33. 1.2 × 2.065

34. A year on Mars is 1.88 times as long as a year on Earth. An Earth year lasts 365.3 days. Find the length of a year on Mars.

35. **Guided Problem Solving** Ham costs $8.79 per pound and turkey costs $9.48 per pound. What is the total cost of 2 pounds of ham and 1.5 pounds of turkey?
   • What is the cost of 2 pounds of ham? 1.5 pounds of turkey?

Hybrid car
58.0 miles per gallon

**Sport utility
vehicle (SUV)
13.5 miles per gallon**

36. Nutrition There is 0.2 gram of calcium in 1 serving of cheddar cheese. How much calcium is in 3.25 servings of cheddar cheese?

Choose a Method **Find each product. Tell whether you use mental math, paper and pencil, or a calculator.**

37. 16×2.5 **38.** $60(0.5)$ **39.** 56.37×5.29

40. The average fuel rates for a hybrid car and an SUV are shown at the left. How much farther than the SUV can the hybrid car travel using 13 gallons of gas?

41. Astronomy Mercury is about 36 million miles from the sun. Jupiter is about 13.43 times that distance. About how far is Jupiter from the sun?

42. **Writing in Math** Explain how multiplying 0.3×0.4 is like multiplying 3×4. How are the two problems different?

43. Challenge Find the value that makes each statement true.
     a. $\blacksquare \div 0.2 = 0.7$ **b.** $\blacksquare \div 0.03 = 0.5$

Test Prep and Mixed Review   **Practice**

Multiple Choice

44. Abby's mother and father take Abby and three of her friends to a water park. Admission is $14 for adults and $11 for children. The steps for finding the total cost are below.
     Step K: Multiply $11 by 4.
     Step L: Add the products.
     Step M: Count two adults and four children.
     Step N: Multiply $14 by 2.

Which list shows the correct order of steps?
     Ⓐ L, M, K, N   Ⓒ K, N, L, M
     Ⓑ M, K, N, L   Ⓓ M, L, N, K

45. Which is a reasonable estimate of the sum $214 + 92 + 56$?
     Ⓕ 300   Ⓖ 350   Ⓗ 400   Ⓙ 450

46. Which statement about 2.315 is NOT true?
     Ⓐ $2.315 > 2.13$ Ⓒ $2.15 < 2.315$
     Ⓑ $2.31 < 2.315$ Ⓓ $2.315 > 2.51$

GO for Help

For Exercises	See Lesson
47–49	1-7

Find each sum or difference.

47. $7.32 + 4.29$ **48.** $11.07 - 1.2$ **49.** $6.5 - 0.32$

Multiplying and Dividing Decimals by 10, 100, and 1,000

There are shortcuts for multiplying and dividing decimals by 10, 100, and 1,000. You can use these shortcuts to multiply mentally.

ACTIVITY

1. Use a calculator to multiply.
   a. $2.6 \times 10 = \blacksquare$
   $2.6 \times 100 = \blacksquare$
   $2.6 \times 1{,}000 = \blacksquare$

   b. $0.45 \times 10 = \blacksquare$
   $0.45 \times 100 = \blacksquare$
   $0.45 \times 1{,}000 = \blacksquare$

2. **a. Patterns** What do you notice about the movement of the decimal point in your answer when you multiply by 10? By 100? By 1,000?
   b. Write a rule for multiplying a decimal by 10, 100, and 1,000.

3. Use a calculator to divide.
   a. $2.6 \div 10 = \blacksquare$
   $2.6 \div 100 = \blacksquare$
   $2.6 \div 1{,}000 = \blacksquare$

   b. $0.45 \div 10 = \blacksquare$
   $0.45 \div 100 = \blacksquare$
   $0.45 \div 1{,}000 = \blacksquare$

4. **a. Patterns** What do you notice about the movement of the decimal point when you divide by 10? By 100? By 1,000?
   b. Write a shortcut for dividing a decimal by 10, 100, and 1,000.

Exercises

Use mental math to find each answer.

1. 6.2×10
2. $122.9 \div 10$
3. $161.7 \div 100$
4. $1{,}000(4.3)$
5. $1.5 \div 100$
6. $1{,}000 \cdot 0.89$

7. Use a calculator to multiply.
   a. 527×0.1
   b. 527×0.01
   c. 527×0.001
   d. 527×0.0001
   e. Patterns What do you notice about the movement of the decimal point in your answers for parts (a)–(d)?

Checkpoint Quiz 2

Lessons 1-5 through 1-8

1. Write 12.035 in words.

2. Order the numbers 9, 8.7, 9.31, 8.0, and 8.05 from least to greatest.

Round each decimal to the nearest tenth.

3. 7.83   4. 7.98   5. 17.051

Find each sum, difference, or product.

6. $1.25 + 6.07$ 7. $9.06 - 0.8$ 8. 5.2×6.3 9. $1.7 - 0.28$

10. Jo made 7 pounds of cookies. She gave 3.25 pounds to her friends and 0.7 pounds to each of her three brothers. How many pounds did she have left?

MATH GAMES

Slide and Score

What You'll Need

- Six note cards with × 10, × 100, × 1,000, ÷ 10, ÷ 100, and ÷ 1,000 written on them
- Two chips to use as decimal points
- Two strips of paper with 4 1 2 3 5 and 5 3 1 4 2 written on them

How To Play

- Place the chips after the first digit in each number. The chips are used as decimal points. Line up the decimal points.
- A player draws a card and performs the operation on one of the numbers. Then the player lines up the decimal points again. The player receives points for any two numbers in a column. In the game below, the player will receive 3 points when the decimal is moved to the left.
- Replace the operation card and shuffle. A player's turn continues until the operation cannot be performed on either number. The winner is the first person to score 11 points.

÷100   ×10   ×100   ÷1,000   ×1,000

4 1 2.3 5

5 3.1 4 2

Dividing Decimals

Check Skills You'll Need

1. Vocabulary Review How is a *dividend* different from a *divisor*?

Simplify.

2. 935 ÷ 5

3. 296 ÷ 8

4. 636 ÷ 12

 for Help
Skills Handbook
p. 642

What You'll Learn

To divide decimals and to solve problems involving decimals

Why Learn This?

Sometimes you want to share costs with your friends. You can divide decimals to find the amount each person should pay.

Dividing decimals is similar to dividing whole numbers.

EXAMPLE **Dividing by a Whole Number**

1 Transportation and tickets for 12 friends to an amusement park cost $364.20. How much will each person pay?

You are looking for the size of equal groups, so divide.

Estimate $364.20 \div 12 \approx 360 \div 12$, or 30

Vocabulary Tip

You can indicate division three ways:

$15 \div 3$

$3\overline{)15}$

$\dfrac{15}{3}$ ← dividend
      ← divisor

$$
\begin{array}{r}
30.35 \\
12\overline{)364.20} \\
-36 \\
\overline{04} \\
-0 \\
\overline{42} \\
-36 \\
\overline{60} \\
-60 \\
\overline{0}
\end{array}
$$

← Divide as with whole numbers. Place the decimal point in the quotient above the decimal point in the dividend.

Each person will pay $30.35 for transportation and a ticket.

Check for Reasonableness 30.35 is close to 30.

Quick Check

1. a. Find $8\overline{)385.6}$.   **b.** Find $9.12 \div 6$.

One way to think about dividing decimals is to break the dividend into equal groups. The model below shows $0.8 \div 0.2$, or how many groups of 0.2 are in 0.8.

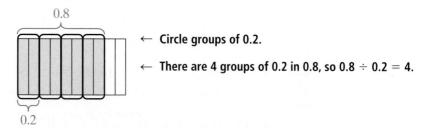

← Circle groups of 0.2.

← There are 4 groups of 0.2 in 0.8, so $0.8 \div 0.2 = 4$.

0.8

0.2

Study the pattern of quotients below.

	Dividend	÷	Divisor	=	Quotient
	0.8	÷	0.2	=	4
Multiply dividend and divisor by 10. →	8	÷	2	=	4
Multiply dividend and divisor by 100. →	80	÷	20	=	4

The pattern shows that when you multiply both the dividend and the divisor by the same number, the quotient remains the same.

KEY CONCEPTS **Dividing Decimals**

To divide a decimal by a decimal, multiply both the dividend and the divisor by 10, 100, or 1,000 so that the divisor is a whole number.

EXAMPLE **Dividing a Decimal by a Decimal**

2 **Recipes** You use 0.5 pounds of berries to make one smoothie. How many smoothies can you make with 2.25 pounds of berries?

Multiply 0.5 by 10 to make the divisor a whole number.

$0.5)\overline{2.25}$

Also multiply 2.25 by 10.

$$\begin{array}{r} 4.5 \\ 5)\overline{22.5} \\ -20 \\ \hline 25 \\ -25 \\ \hline 0 \end{array}$$

← Divide as with whole numbers. Place the decimal point in the quotient above the decimal point in the dividend.

You can make 4.5 smoothies.

✓ Quick Check

2. You have $2.75. You want to buy trading cards that cost $.25 each. How many can you buy?

1. **Vocabulary** When you divide both the dividend and the divisor by the same number, the (dividend, divisor, quotient) remains the same.

2. **Number Sense** Is the quotient of $3.05 \div 1.25$ *greater than*, *less than*, or *equal to* 3? Explain your reasoning.

3. Draw a model to find $0.6 \div 0.2$.

Complete each division.

4.
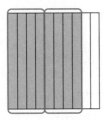

$0.8 \div 0.4 = \blacksquare$
$8 \div 4 = \blacksquare$

5.

$0.9 \div 0.3 = \blacksquare$
$9 \div 3 = \blacksquare$

6.
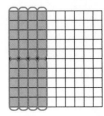

$0.40 \div 0.05 = \blacksquare$
$40 \div 5 = \blacksquare$

For more exercises, see Extra Skills and Word Problems.

GO for Help

For Exercises	See Example
7–14	1
15–21	2

Find each quotient.

7. $328.25 \div 13$

8. $7\overline{)255.5}$

9. $237.6 \div 33$

10. $32\overline{)258.24}$

11. $84\overline{)26.46}$

12. $144.54 \div 6$

13. $27\overline{)99.36}$

14. $38.27 \div 43$

15. $29.5 \div 0.4$

16. $8.9\overline{)6.497}$

17. $3.1\overline{)10.261}$

18. $16.8 \div 2.4$

19. $0.96\overline{)0.144}$

20. $10.54 \div 0.17$

21. $5.9\overline{)0.649}$

22. **Guided Problem Solving** Seventeen customers bought two movie tickets each. The total cost was $263.50. What was the price per ticket?
   • What was the total number of tickets purchased?
   • What operation should you use to find the price per ticket?

23. **School Supplies** A stack of paper measures 0.9 centimeter thick. Each piece of paper is 0.01 centimeter thick.
   a. How many pieces of paper are in the stack?
   b. Could each of 25 students get three pieces of paper?

24. **Bridges** The Great Seto Bridge in Japan is 9,368 meters long. A bicyclist riding across the bridge can travel 500 meters in 1 minute. A person walking can travel 100 meters in 1 minute. How many minutes shorter is the bicycle trip than the walk?

25. Five friends share three pizzas that cost $12.75 each. How much does each friend pay?

Find each quotient. Round to the nearest hundredth.

26. $64.97 \div 3.2$ 27. $10.126 \div 2.3$ 28. $3.3\overline{)26.81}$

29. $5.637 \div 0.17$ 30. $6.24\overline{)78.28}$ 31. $0.12\overline{)1.2542}$

GO Online
Homework Video Tutor
Visit: PHSchool.com
Web Code: aqe-0109

32. A utility company charges $.12 for each kilowatt-hour of electricity you use. Your electric bill was $125.10. How many kilowatt-hours did you use?

33. **Reasoning** Which quotient is greater, $127.34 \div 0.673$ or $127.34 \div 0.671$? Explain your reasoning.

34. **Challenge** You and a friend are paid $38.25 for doing yard work. You work 2.5 hours and your friend works 2 hours. How much should you get for your share of the work? Explain.

Test Prep and Mixed Review   Practice

Multiple Choice

35. Four friends line up from shortest to tallest. Mac is shorter than Nate and taller than Ben. Charlie is taller than Mac and not on either end of the line. Which friend is first in line?
    Ⓐ Ben   Ⓑ Charlie   Ⓒ Mac   Ⓓ Nate

36. Kelly bought a pair of jeans, a pair of sneakers, and four shirts. What missing piece of information is needed to find the total amount Kelly spent?
    Ⓕ the price of a shirt
    Ⓖ the amount of money Kelly has
    Ⓗ the original prices before the discount
    Ⓙ the number of shirts Kelly bought

Sale!
Jeans $24.99
Sneakers $34.99
Shirts 2 for the price of 1

GO for Help

For Exercises	See Lesson
37–38	1-6

Order each set of decimals from least to greatest.

37. 8.3, 8.03, 8.308, 8.035   38. 1.8, 1.18, 1.801, 1.081

Using Decimals

Archaeologists are detectives who solve mysteries. The items they unearth provide clues about the people who once lived in a region. For example, archaeologists can measure the length of bones to determine the approximate heights of people.

ACTIVITY

1. The table at the right shows the length of the humerus, or arm bone, for five skeletons from an archaeological dig. Estimate the height of Male 1 in inches. Use the steps below.

Skeleton	Length of Humerus (cm)
Male 1	35
Female 1	32.5
Male 2	31.5
Female 2	■
■	24.5

Male	Female
Step 1 Multiply the length of the humerus by 2.9.	**Step 1** Multiply the length of the humerus by 2.8.
Step 2 Add 70.6 to the result.	**Step 2** Add 74.8 to the result.
Step 3 Divide by 2.54 to find the height in inches.	**Step 3** Divide by 2.54 to find the height in inches.

2. Find the height in inches of Female 1 and Male 2.

3. Measure the length of your own humerus in centimeters. To do this, measure from your elbow to the edge of your shoulder. Use this value to estimate your height in inches. How accurate is this estimate?

4. Suppose that the height of Female 2 is 148 cm. Work backward to estimate the length of her humerus.

5. The person listed in the bottom row of the chart was 140 cm tall. Is it more likely that this person was a male or a female? Support your answer with data and calculations.

6. **Writing in Math** Write a short paragraph explaining how this technique for estimating a person's height might have been developed. How accurate is it?

Choosing the Right Operation

Rubber Band Ball John Bain made the largest rubber-band ball in the world. The ball was 5 feet tall. It took 550,000 rubber bands, and 4 years, 2 months to put together. About how many rubber bands did Mr. Bain add each month?

What You Might Think

What do I know?
What do I want to find out?

How can I show the main idea?

How do I solve the problem?

What is the answer?

What You Might Write

550,000 rubber bands were used. It took 4 years, 2 months, or 50 months, to build. I want to find the number of rubber bands he used each month.

Draw a diagram.

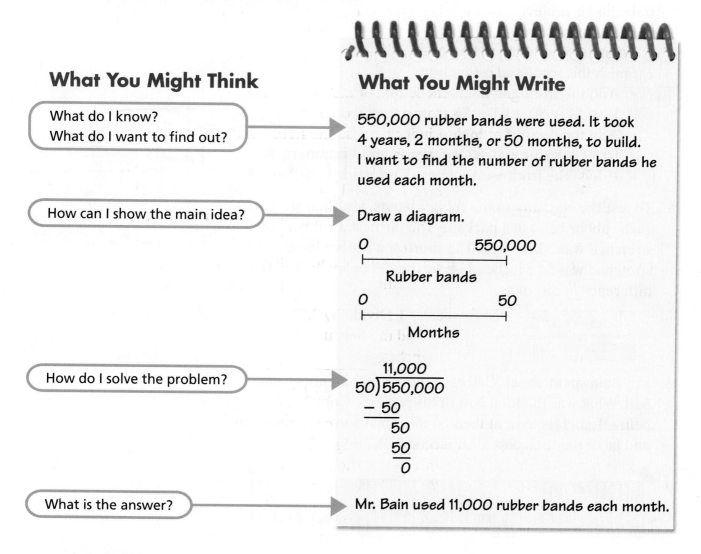

Mr. Bain used 11,000 rubber bands each month.

Think It Through

1. Why does the diagram show 0–550,000 rubber bands on a line the same length as the line for 0–50 months?

2. Explain why 4 years, 2 months is the same as $4 \times 12 + 2$ months.

3. **Estimation** Use estimation to show that the answer is reasonable.

Exercises

4. Suppose Mr. Bain started with 5 packages of rubber bands. The packages cost $1.39, $1.59, $0.89, $1.98, and $1.13. Use front-end estimation to determine about how much he spent to begin his project.

   a. What do you know?

   b. What are you trying to find out?

   c. Finish this front-end estimation.
   - Add the front-end numbers below.
     $1 + $1 + $0 + $1 + $1
   - Add the decimal numbers.
     $0.39 + $0.59 + $0.89 + $0.98 + $0.13 is about $■.
   - Adjust the front-end estimate. The estimate is then $■.

5. To test the elasticity of the rubber bands, Mr. Bain stretched each rubber band in a package. The farthest a rubber band stretched was 38.5 inches. The shortest a rubber band stretched was 34.8 inches. Use the model below to find the difference in distances.

38.5 inches	
34.8 inches	?

6. Mr. Bain spent about $240 each month on his rubber-band ball. What was the total cost of his project? Copy the drawing below. Label the cost at the first ■. Then solve the problem and label the total cost at the second ■.

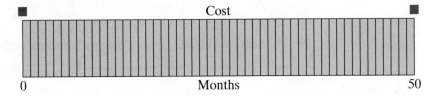

Cost

0   Months   50

7. You can make a chain 1 mile long using 63,360 paper clips. The world record is a chain 19.62 miles long. How many paper clips were used to make this chain?

8. A teacher made a paper-clip chain using 60,650 paper clips. It took the teacher about 26.75 hours to make the chain. About how many seconds did the teacher spend adding each paper clip?

Writing Gridded Responses

Some tests include gridded responses. When you find an answer, write the answer at the top of the grid. Then fill in the matching bubbles.

EXAMPLE **Using the Answer Grid**

A fitness trail is 3.4 miles long. You walk 2.7 miles of the trail. How many more miles must you walk to reach the end of the trail?

$3.4 \text{ miles} - 2.7 \text{ miles} = 0.7 \text{ mile}$

You can write the answer as 0.7 or .7. Here are the two ways to enter these answers. You do not include labels in the grid.

Start to grid your answer at the right side of the grid.
↓

Add the 0 to → the left of the decimal point.

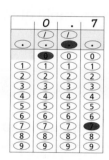

← Add the decimal point in the correct place. →

Exercises

Find each answer. If you have a grid, record your answer and fill in the bubbles.

1. A diver received scores of 6.5, 5.5, 6.0, 6.5, and 6.0 in a diving competition. What was his total score?

2. Compare each of the decimals. Which decimal is the greatest?
   0.23 0.256 0.236 0.26 0.24

3. You bought 2 books for $9 each. You also purchased 3 DVDs for $15 each. You paid with a $100 bill. What was your change in dollars?

4. Lisa bought 32.4 ounces of glue. She used 6.8 ounces to put together a model. How many ounces of glue did Lisa have left?

Chapter 1 Review

Vocabulary Review

 **Associative Property of Addition** (p. 12)
Associative Property of Multiplication (p. 13)
Commutative Property of Addition (p. 12)

Commutative Property of Multiplication (p. 13)
compatible numbers (p. 9)
expanded form (p. 23)
expression (p. 16)
front-end estimation (p. 32)

Identity Property of Addition (p. 12)
Identity Property of Multiplication (p. 13)
order of operations (p. 16)
standard form (p. 4)

Choose the correct vocabulary term to complete each sentence.

1. An example of the __?__ is $5 + 0 = 5$.

2. Numbers that are easy to compute mentally are called __?__.

3. The number 0.5830 is written in __?__.

4. $7 + 4 \times 2$ is a(n) __?__.

5. $5 + (6 + 8) = (5 + 6) + 8$ is an example of the __?__.

Go Online
PHSchool.com
For: Vocabulary Quiz
Web Code: aqj-0151

Skills and Concepts

Lessons 1-1, 1-2, 1-3

- To write and compare whole numbers
- To estimate with whole numbers by rounding and by using compatible numbers
- To understand and use the properties of numbers

You can round each number or use **compatible numbers** to estimate. You can use the **commutative, associative,** and **identity properties** to help you add and multiply mentally.

Write each number in words.

6. 5,000,025   7. 5,025

Write the numbers in order from least to greatest.

8. 1,010; 1,100; 1,001; 1,101   9. 2,332; 2,323; 2,322; 2,232

Estimate using rounding or compatible numbers.

10. $5,021 + 2,957$ 11. $52 + 29 + 97$ 12. $597 - 201$

13. $8,989 \div 3$ 14. 19×52 15. $6,012 \div 99$

Use mental math to find each sum or product.

16. $1 + 250 + 99$ 17. $2 \times 13 \times 5$ 18. $16 + 3 + 4 + 7$

Lesson 1-4

- To use the order of operations to simplify expressions and solve problems

An **expression** is a mathematical phrase that contains numbers and operation symbols. You can use the **order of operations** to find the value of an expression.

Find the value of each expression.

19. $30 - 5 + 4 \times 3$ **20.** $6 - (27 - 9) \div 3$ **21.** $5 \times 8 + 4 \div 2$

Lessons 1-5, 1-6

- To read, write, and round decimals
- To compare and order decimals using models and place value

You can write decimals in words, in **standard form,** and in **expanded form.** You can compare and order decimals using models, a number line, or place value.

Write each decimal in words.

22. 525.5   **23.** 0.5255   **24.** 5.025   **25.** 50.0025

Round each decimal to the underlined place.

26. 45.1̲6   **27.** 98.6̲45   **28.** 5.12̲5   **29.** 1.24̲6

Order each set of decimals from least to greatest.

30. 0.52, 0.4, 0.14, 0.06   **31.** 23, 23.2, 23.25, 23.03

Lesson 1-7

- To add and subtract decimals and to solve problems involving decimals

You can use estimation to tell whether your answer is reasonable. You can use **front-end estimation** to estimate a sum.

First estimate. Then find each sum or difference.

32. $337.4 + 20.08$ **33.** $1.741 - 0.81$ **34.** $1.6 + 1.8$

35. $9.6 - 7.9$ **36.** $4.12 - 0.253$ **37.** $2.01 + 5.39$

Lessons 1-8, 1-9

- To multiply and divide decimals and to solve problems involving decimals

When multiplying decimals, add the decimal places in the factors to place the decimal point in the product. When dividing decimals, multiply both the dividend and the divisor by the same number so that the divisor is a whole number.

Find each product or quotient.

38. 1.2×29.5 **39.** $12.12 \div 6$ **40.** $38.4 \div 0.08$ **41.** 0.54×17

42. $27.76 \div 4$ **43.** 3.21×9.8 **44.** 13×0.8 **45.** $8.5 \div 0.05$

Chapter 1 Test

Go Online
PHSchool.com
For: Online chapter test
Web Code: aqa-0152

Write each number in words.

1. 623.7

2. 2,086,374

3. 89.123

4. 35,743,620,000

5. 172,254

6. 3.024

Use <, =, or > to complete each statement.

7. 26,145 ▇ 25,641

8. 32.12 ▇ 32.42

9. 9.7 ▇ 9.70

10. 1,247 ▇ 1,241

Order each set of numbers from least to greatest.

11. 6,425; 6,542; 6,452; 7,642; 6,524

12. 0.27, 0.56, 0.212, 0.563, 0.276, 0.5

13. 81, 81.1, 80.08, 82, 81.5, 80.3

14. 1.63, 1, 1.064, 0.163, 1.036, 2.136, 2

15. **Estimation** Suppose your savings account has a balance of $238.52. You deposit $42.56. Then you withdraw $92.35. About how much is left in your savings account?

Use rounding, front-end estimation, or compatible numbers to estimate each answer.

16. $37 + 42 + 142$

17. 50.32×22.1

18. 4.63×50.491

19. $98 \div 24$

20. $1.01 + 2.89$

21. $62.85 - 24.12$

22. **DVDs** Five DVDs cost a total of $75. Explain whether the best estimate for the cost of one DVD is greater than or less than $14.

Use mental math to find each answer.

23. $829 + 71$

24. $24 + (72 + 64)$

25. $25 \times 6 \times 4$

26. $10 \times 7 \times 20$

27. You buy movie tickets for yourself and three friends. Each ticket costs $7. You pay with two $20 bills. How much change do you get back?

Find the value of each expression.

28. $16 \div (4 \times 4)$

29. $8 - 4 \div 2$

30. $5 + (32 - 16)$

31. $(9 - 1 \times 3) \div 2$

First estimate. Then find each sum or difference.

32. $3.89 + 15.3$

33. $4.6 - 2.07$

34. $41.2 - 19.8$

35. $53.7 + 28.6$

Find each product or quotient.

36. 9.063×24

37. $0.36(15)$

38. $21.6 \div 0.06$

39. $7 \div 0.14$

40. **Pet Food** Zelda spent $6.24 on pet food. The food costs $.24 per cup. How many cups of pet food did Zelda purchase?

41. **Money** There are 40 quarters in a roll of quarters. What is the value of 9 rolls of quarters?

Reading Comprehension

Read each passage below. Then answer the questions based on what you have read.

> **Rainfall** Hilo, Hawaii, usually receives 129.19 inches of rain each year. Compare that to Phoenix, Arizona, which receives 7.66 inches of rain a year. In Hilo, the wettest month is April, with 15.26 inches of rain, while the driest month is June, with 6.2 inches of rain. Phoenix's wettest month is December, with 1 inch, and its driest is May, with 0.12 inch.

1. In Hilo, how many more inches of rain typically fall in April than in June?
   - Ⓐ 0.88 inch
   - Ⓒ 9.06 inches
   - Ⓑ 15.26 inches
   - Ⓓ 21.46 inches

2. In July, Phoenix typically gets 0.83 inch of rain. About how many times as much rain falls in July as in May?
   - Ⓕ 6
   - Ⓖ 7
   - Ⓗ 8
   - Ⓙ 9

3. How many inches of rain does Hilo receive in a typical ten-year period?
   - Ⓐ 1,291.9 inches
   - Ⓒ 76.60 inches
   - Ⓑ 12.919 inches
   - Ⓓ 0.766 inches

4. Hilos yearly rainfall is about how many times the yearly rainfall is Phoenix?
   - Ⓕ 1,040 times
   - Ⓗ 138 times
   - Ⓖ 122 times
   - Ⓙ 16 times

> **Coins** Did you know that some coins contain more pure metal than others? American Gold Eagle coins are 0.9166 gold and Canadian Maple Leaf coins are 0.9999 gold. American Silver Eagle coins are 0.999 silver while American Platinum Eagle coins are 0.9995 platinum.

5. How might you write the purity of the American Silver Eagle coin in order to compare it with the other coins?
   - Ⓐ 0.99
   - Ⓒ 0.0999
   - Ⓑ 0.9990
   - Ⓓ 0.9999

6. What portion of the American Gold Eagle coin is NOT gold?
   - Ⓕ 0.0004
   - Ⓗ 0.0034
   - Ⓖ 0.0834
   - Ⓙ 0.0934

7. Which of the five coins mentioned contains the greatest portion of pure metal?
   - Ⓐ American Silver Eagle
   - Ⓑ American Gold Eagle
   - Ⓒ Canadian Maple Leaf
   - Ⓓ American Platinum Eagle

8. How much gold is in an American Gold Eagle coin that weighs 0.1 ounce?
   - Ⓕ 9.166 ounces
   - Ⓗ 0.9166 ounce
   - Ⓖ 0.91660 ounce
   - Ⓙ 0.09166 ounce

Applying Decimals

That's an Order Ancient Mesopotamians bought and traded grain and other items. They developed a writing system to keep track of their goods and money. Today, we use order forms and receipts to purchase items and record the money we spend.

Put It All Together

1. Find the five missing values in the sample order form. (*Hint:* Some missing values cannot be found without finding others first.)

2. **Open-Ended** Suppose you have a clothing budget of $500.
   a. **Research** Make a list of items you would like to purchase. Find their prices.
   b. Use an order form like the sample. Complete the Quantity, Description, and Unit Price columns for the items on your list. At least four of the values in the Quantity column should be greater than 1.
   c. Find the total for each row by multiplying the quantity by the unit price. Follow the directions on the order form to fill in the rest of the boxes. Make sure you stay within your budget!
   d. Copy your order form onto another sheet of paper. Leave some boxes blank as in the sample. Trade order forms with another student and find each other's missing values.

Order Form

Quantity	Description	Unit Price	Total
■	20-gallon aquarium	$119.99	$119.99
1	Air pump	$14.95	$14.95
2	Water filter	■	$64.98
3	Tropical fish food	$7.49	$22.47
■	Gravel, one bag	$1.99	■
3	Driftwood decoration	$13.25	$39.75
Subtotal (Add the totals from above.)			■
6% Shipping (Multiply subtotal by 0.06.)			$16.44
Total (Add subtotal and shipping.)			$290.52

Tally Sticks

People have used notched sticks for tallying totals for thousands of years. Larger notches denote greater amounts.

Calculations and More

Handheld calculators, which have taken the place of adding machines, perform many mathematical operations. This one can display graphs.

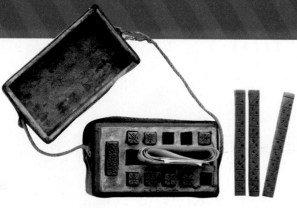

Napier's Rods

You can use Napier's rods to find products. The rods in the photo show multiples of 4, 7, and 9.

Go Online
PHSchool.com
For: Information about completing order forms
Web Code: aqe-0153

Cuneiform

Ancient Babylonians wrote their numbers in cuneiform, printed with sticks and wedges on clay tablets. The Babylonian number system is sexagesimal, which means it is based on counting 60's. This system remains in our measures of time and angles.

Counting Sheep

The cuneiform characters on this clay tablet are a tally of sheep and goats from an area called Tello, in ancient Mesopotamia.

What You've Learned

- In Chapter 1, you compared and ordered whole numbers and decimals.

- You used addition, subtraction, multiplication, and division to solve problems involving decimals.

- You used order of operations to simplify expressions.

 Check Your Readiness

GO for Help

For Exercises	See Lesson
1–2	1-6
3–9	1-7
10–12	1-9

Ordering Decimals.

Order each set of decimals from least to greatest.

1. 0.12, 0.13, 0.45, 0.35, 0.21

2. 45.1, 44.0, 46.01, 45.01

Adding Decimals

Find each sum.

3. 13.2 + 23.6 + 26.3   4. 152.3 + 143.6 + 128

5. 49.0 + 22.2 + 11.22 + 23.4   6. 6.09 + 1.5 + 4.68 + 13.6

Subtracting Decimals

Find each difference.

7. 109.55 − 89.34   8. 10.42 − 9.36   9. 75 − 73.2

Dividing Decimals

Find each quotient.

10. 142.03 ÷ 10   11. 361.6 ÷ 16   12. 100.75 ÷ 25

What You'll Learn Next

- In this chapter, you will find the mean, median, mode, and range of a set of data.

- You will select and use different types of data graphs, including line plots, line graphs, bar graphs, and stem-and-leaf plots.

- You will solve problems by collecting, organizing, displaying, and interpreting data.

 Problem Solving Application On pages 104 and 105, you will work an extended activity on mountain peaks.

Exploring the Mean

Three friends went apple picking. The friends want to make sure that each person has the same number of apples.

ACTIVITY

1. The diagram below shows the number of apples picked by each friend. Use objects to represent the apples. Make a pile of "apples" for each of the friends.

Janelle	Ciara	Macario
12 apples	6 apples	9 apples

2. Describe a method you can use to even out the number of apples so that each person has the same number. What is this number?

3. Graph the number of apples each friend picked on the number line. Then draw a small star on the number of apples each friend will get after sharing.

4. **Writing in Math** The value indicated by the star on your number line is called "the mean." Use what you have learned to write a definition for the word *mean*.

5. Make four piles with 13, 16, 18, and 19 "apples." Use the method you described in Step 2 to create four equal piles. What problem did you encounter? How can you solve this problem?

6. A dance committee is inflating balloons for a dance. The mean number of balloons inflated by each person is 9. Use objects to represent the number of balloons in the table at the right. How many balloons did Eric inflate?

Dance Committee

Name	Number of Balloons
Jamil	12
Ashley	10
Hoshi	4
Eric	■

Finding the Mean

Check Skills You'll Need

1. **Vocabulary Review**
When dividing, the result other than the remainder is the ___?___.

Find each quotient.

2. $330 \div 12$

3. $6\overline{)256.5}$

4. $237.4 \div 4$

GO for Help
Lesson 1-9

What You'll Learn

To find and analyze the mean of a data set using models and calculations

🔊 **New Vocabulary** mean, outlier

Why Learn This?

Meteorologists analyze data. They often use a measure, such as the mean, to help describe a set of data.

The **mean** of a set of data is the sum of the data divided by the number of data items. To find the mean of a set of data, you can adjust all of the values so the values are the same.

EXAMPLE **Using a Model to Find the Mean**

1. On four days it rained 2 inches, 4 inches, 5 inches, and 1 inch. Find the mean amount of rain.

You can draw a picture or use objects to model the situation.

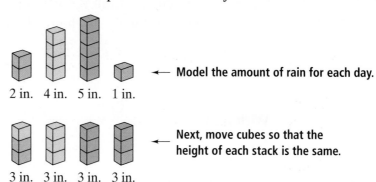

2 in. 4 in. 5 in. 1 in. ← Model the amount of rain for each day.

3 in. 3 in. 3 in. 3 in. ← Next, move cubes so that the height of each stack is the same.

The mean amount of rain is 3 inches.

Quick Check

1. Use a model to find the mean of 3, 6, 3, 4, 2, and 6.

The thorny lizard survives high temperatures by using its spikes to collect moisture at night.

EXAMPLE Calculating the Mean

2 You measure the temperature outside each day during the week. The temperatures are 95°, 96°, 103°, 99°, and 96°. Find the mean temperature.

$$95 + 96 + 103 + 99 + 96 = 489 \quad \leftarrow \text{Add the temperatures.}$$

$$\frac{489}{5} = 97.8 \quad \leftarrow \text{Divide by the number of readings.}$$

The mean temperature is 97.8°.

Check for Reasonableness The mean is between the lowest value, 95, and the greatest value, 103. So, the answer 97.8 is reasonable.

✓ Quick Check

2. You play a word game. Your scores are 12, 23, 13, 32, and 20. Find your mean score.

An **outlier** is a data item that is much greater or less than the other data items. If a data set has an outlier, then the mean may not describe the data very well.

EXAMPLE Analyzing the Mean

3 Your quiz scores in science are listed at the left. Find the mean test score with and without the outlier. What effect does the outlier have on the mean?

Quiz Scores		
81	77	92
89	81	87
75	42	81

Since 42 is much less than the other scores, the outlier is 42. Find the mean with and without the outlier.

With the outlier: $\dfrac{81 + 77 + 92 + 89 + 81 + 87 + 75 + 42 + 81}{9}$

$$\approx 78.333$$

Without the outlier: $\dfrac{81 + 77 + 92 + 89 + 81 + 87 + 75 + 81}{8}$

$$= 82.875$$

The outlier reduced the mean quiz score by about 5 points.

✓ Quick Check

3. You keep track of the number of hours you baby-sit for six days: 1.25, 1.50, 1.50, 1.75, 2.0, 5.5. What effect does the outlier have on the mean?

1. **Vocabulary** Explain how to find the mean of five test scores.

Use a model to find the mean of each data set.

2. 3, 2, 8, 4, 3

3. 5, 3, 7, 10, 6, 5

4. **Open-Ended** Explain why the mean might not be a good measure for a set of data when the set includes outliers. Write a set of data items that supports your explanation.

Homework Exercises

For more exercises, see Extra Skills and Word Problems.

GO for Help

For Exercises	See Example
5–13	1–2
14–16	3

Find the mean of each data set. You may find a model helpful.

5. 3, 4, 7, 2, 5, 9

6. 6, 4, 5, 9, 7, 6, 8, 3

7. 12, 9, 11, 8, 9, 12, 9

8. 14, 16, 28, 17, 20   ⁶

9. 121, 95, 115, 92, 113, 108, 91

10. 2.4, 1.8, 3.5, 2.3, 6.5   ¹¹
                                      ¹³
11. 500, 450, 475, 450, 500

12. 23, 24, 27, 25, 26, 22, 21   ¹⁵
                                         ¹⁶

13. You keep track of the time you spend doing homework each evening. You spend 58 minutes, 36 minutes, 44 minutes, and 37 minutes. Find the mean of these times.

For each set of data, identify any outliers. Then determine the effect that the outlier has on the mean.

14. 95, 90, 87, 85, 79, 82, 87, 40, 90, 80

15. 8, 7, 10, 12, 8, 11, 8, 6, 9, 50, 8, 10, 7, 7

16. 200; 225; 3,000; 500; 325; 311; 295; 485; 359; 325

GPS 17. **Guided Problem Solving** The prices for a gallon of milk at four stores are $1.99, $2.29, $2.19, and $1.88. Is the mean a good measure of the price of milk in the four stores? Explain.
  • **Understand the Problem** You have to determine whether any outliers affect the mean.
  • **Make a Plan** How will you find the mean?

18. **Data Collection** Measure the height, in inches, of five different cups in your home. Find the mean height.

Find the mean of each data set.

19. 10, 4, 11.7, 30, 7.9, 11, 8.2, 3, 8, 9.2, 14.2, 5.2

20. 2.4, 5.3, 3.5, 2.6, 2.3, 3.5, 2.8, 4.3, 4.5, 3.8

21. The table shows the monthly rainfall for one year in Hilo, Hawaii.
 a. Find the mean amount of rain to the nearest inch.
 b. **Writing in Math** Why are most of the data items less than the mean?

22. (**Algebra**) The mean of 22, 19, 25, and x is 23. Find x.

23. Shelby made a list of her test scores: 88, 100, 92, 80, 85, 94, and 90. What is the lowest score she can get on her next test to have a mean score of 90?

24. **Challenge** The mean of 22.3, 19.7, 25.4, and another number is 23.4. Find the missing number.

Rainfall in Hilo, Hawaii

Month	Rainfall (in.)
January	5
February	1
March	15
April	43
May	9
June	9
July	11
August	11
September	14
October	12
November	36
December	6

SOURCE: *The Weather Almanac*

Dense rain forests are found in Hawaii because of its wet, tropical climate.

Test Prep and Mixed Review

Practice

Multiple Choice

25. Which number is between the two points graphed on the number line?
 Ⓐ 1.44 Ⓑ 1.55 Ⓒ 1.63 Ⓓ 1.72

26. Kristi received scores of 5.2 and 2.3 on her two ice-skating routines. What is the difference between these scores?
 Ⓕ 2.1 Ⓖ 2.9 Ⓗ 3.1 Ⓙ 3.9

27. Duke has football practice for 2 hours after school every day. If he goes to practice 5 days, which method can be used to find the total number of hours Duke practices?
 Ⓐ Add 2 and 5. Ⓒ Multiply 5 by 2.
 Ⓑ Subtract 2 from 5. Ⓓ Divide 5 by 2.

GO **for Help**

For Exercises	See Lesson
28–30	1-8

Find each product.

28. 4.2 × 9.6   **29.** 3.07 × 6.3   **30.** 4.25 × 1.04

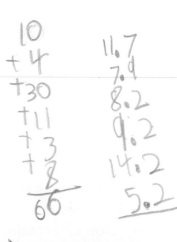

Vocabulary Builder

High-Use Academic Words

High-use academic words are words that you
see often in textbooks and on tests. These words
are not math vocabulary terms, but knowing them
will help you to succeed in mathematics.

Direction Words

Some words tell what to do in a problem. I need to understand what
these words are asking so that I give the correct answer.

Word	Meaning
Describe	To include enough detail that the topic or subject can be understood
Find	To realize, understand, or locate something by studying or observing
Analyze	To explain in depth how things are related to each other

Exercises

Use the activities listed at the right for Exercises 1–2.

1. Describe to your friend how you will spend your Saturday.

2. Find the total time it will take to complete the activities.

For Exercises 3–5, use the quiz scores 50, 86, 90, 94, and 95.

3. Describe how to calculate your mean score.

4. Find the outlier for the data.

5. Analyze how the outlier affects the mean.

6. **a. Word Knowledge** Think about the word *average*.
   Choose the letter for how well you know the word.
   A. I know its meaning.
   B. I've seen it, but I don't know its meaning.
   C. I don't know it.
   b. Research Look up and write the definition of *average*.
   c. Use the word in a sentence involving mathematics.

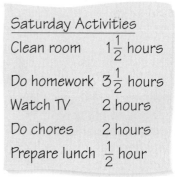

Saturday Activities
Clean room $1\frac{1}{2}$ hours
Do homework $3\frac{1}{2}$ hours
Watch TV 2 hours
Do chores 2 hours
Prepare lunch $\frac{1}{2}$ hour

Median and Mode

Check Skills You'll Need

1. **Vocabulary Review**
   To find the mean of 1, 2, 3, 4, and 5, you add the numbers and divide by __?__.

Find the mean of each set of data.

2. 4, 16, 20, 40

3. 12, 23, 19, 32, 26

4. 5, 15, 75, 105, 85

 **for Help**
Lesson 2-1

What You'll Learn

To find and analyze the median and mode of a data set

🔊 **New Vocabulary** median, mode

Why Learn This?

Scientists use the mean, median, and mode to describe sets of data, including fish populations.

The **median** is the middle number in a set of ordered data. The median gives a good description of numerical data with outliers.

4 7 **9** 13 25
       ↑
    median

For an even number of data items, you can find the median by adding the two middle numbers and dividing by 2.

EXAMPLE Finding the Median

Test Prep Tip

A griddable answer is not always a decimal.

1 **Gridded Response** A biologist studying the ecology of a river makes a weekly fish count. The results are 19, 18, 22, 23, 20, 24, 23, 20, 34, and 19. Find the median number of fish.

18, 19, 19, 20, **20, 22**, 23, 23, 24, 34 ← Order the data. Since there are 10 items, use the two middle values.

$$\frac{20 + 22}{2} = \frac{42}{2}, \text{ or } 21$$ ← Find the mean of 20 and 22.

The median number of fish is 21.

Quick Check

1. Weekly sales of comics at a store are 39, 19, 28, 9, 32, 35, and 17 comics. What is the median number of comics sold?

The **mode** is the data item(s) that appears most often. A data set may have more than one mode. If all data items occur the same number of times, there is no mode. The mode is useful when the data items are repeated or not numerical.

Video Tutor Help

Visit: PHSchool.com
Web Code: aqe-0775

EXAMPLE **Finding the Mode**

② The list shows the favorite lunches of 15 students. Find the mode.

Group the data.

pizza, pizza, pizza, pizza, pizza
hamburger, hamburger, hamburger
taco, taco, taco, taco
spaghetti, spaghetti, spaghetti

Pizza occurs the most. It is the mode.

_____
Favorite Lunch
_____

hamburger, pizza, taco,
pizza, spaghetti, taco,
spaghetti, hamburger,
hamburger, pizza, taco,
pizza, pizza, spaghetti,
taco

✓ Quick Check

2. How many students would have to switch from hamburger to taco as their favorite lunch for taco to be the only mode?

EXAMPLE **Analyzing Data**

Amount of Time Spent on Internet (minutes)			
50	276	57	50
62	53	72	71
63	60	22	

③ Find the mean, median, and mode for the number of minutes spent on the Internet. Does the mean, median, or mode best describe the typical amount of time spent on the Internet?

mean $\dfrac{50 + 276 + 57 + 50 + 62 + 53 + 72 + 71 + 63 + 60 + 22}{11} = \dfrac{836}{11}$

$= 76$

median 22 50 50 53 57 60 62 63 71 72 276: 60

mode 50

The mode and mean are close to only a few data points. The median is close to most of the data items. So the median best describes the typical amount of time spent on the Internet.

✓ Quick Check

3. The top five women's 1-meter diving scores are 288.75, 261.83, 254.85, 254.1, and 246.8. Does the mean, median, or mode best describe these data? Explain.

Check Your Understanding

1. **Vocabulary** The (mean, median, mode) of the following data is 4: 1, 2, 2, 4, 7, 9, 20.

2. **Open-Ended** Create a set of data with more than one mode.

Vocabulary Tip

The word *median* means "middle."

Find the median and mode(s) of each data set.

3. 5, 7, 8, 8, 8, 10, 12

4. 1, 1, 1, 2, 3, 4, 5, 5, 5

5. Add two data items to 40, 20, and 60 so that the median and mode are 60.

Homework Exercises

For more exercises, see Extra Skills and Word Problems.

GO for Help

For Exercises	See Example
6–12	1
13–16	2
17	3

Find the median of each data set.

6. 8, 42, 13, 7, 50, 91

7. 0, 1, 1, 1, 0, 1, 1, 0, 0, 0

8. 14.1, 20.7, 24.3, 16.0, 20.8

9. 500, 450, 475, 450, 500

10. 60.2, 63.5, 62, 62.2, 63.4, 61.1, 60.8

11. 1,205; 1,190; 1,225; 1,239; 1,187; 1,763

12. **Birds** Here are the number of birds spotted by a bird watcher: 2, 7, 3, 8, 10, and 2. What is the median number of birds?

Find the mode(s) of each data set.

13. 8, 7, 8, 9, 8, 7

14. sad, glad, glad, mad, sad

15. 15, 12, 17, 13, 20, 19

16. 23, 24, 27, 25, 26, 23, 21

17. **Fitness** For a week you keep track of the number of push-ups you do each morning: 9, 9, 4, 12, 11, 12, and 12. Does the mean, median, or mode best describe the set of data?

GPS 18. **Guided Problem Solving** Your homework grades are 92, 87, 74, 96, 83, 88, 91, 82, and 85. What score on your next homework will make the median and the mode equal?
- List the scores in order from least to greatest.
- You can use the strategy *Systematic Guess and Check* to help you find the solution.

42 48 51 52

Find the mean, median, and mode of each data set.

19. 13.5, 15, 13.5, 11, 13   **20.** 32, 28.3, 26.8, 31, 24.4

21. Number Sense The median of four numbers is 48. Three of the numbers are 42, 51, and 52. What is the other number?

22. Writing in Math Your scores on five math tests are 96, 88, 96, 85, and 30. Write a letter to your teacher stating which measure—mean, median, or mode—you think your teacher should use to determine your grade.

23. A company is asking students which types of shoe designs they prefer. Which is the best measure for describing the selections, the mean, the median, or the mode? Explain.

24. Books The page lengths of five books are 198, 240, 153, 410, and 374. What is the median?

Careers Shoe designers use survey and research data to decide what features to include in a shoe.

25. a. Mountains Find the mean and median heights of the peaks listed in the table at the right.
b. The height of Asia's highest peak is 8,850 meters. If you add it to the data, what is the change in the mean? In the median?

Highest Peaks

Continent	Altitude (meters)
Africa	5,895
Europe	5,642
North America	6,194
South America	6,960

SOURCE: *Time Almanac*

26. Challenge Use an example to explain why teachers do not use the median to calculate final grades.

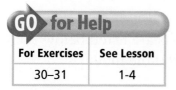
Test Prep and Mixed Review   **Practice**

Gridded Response

1 7 6 3
1 2 0 5
2 9 0 8

GO for Help

For Exercises	See Lesson
30–31	1-4

27. A shoe store recorded the sale of the following shoe sizes: 5, 7, 5, 11, 8, 11, 7, 6, 5, 8, 9, 10, 7, 6, and 7. What is the mode?

28. The height of a tree is 2.7 meters. The height of a second tree is 1.8 meters. What is the difference of the heights in meters?

29. A lilac bush is 1 foot tall when you buy it. The bush will grow about 1.5 feet each year. What will be the height of the bush in feet after 6 years?

Find the value of each expression.

30. $10 - 2 \times 4 - 1$ **31.** $200 \div (32 - 12) + 5$

Frequency Tables and Line Plots

Check Skills You'll Need

1. **Vocabulary Review** What is the *mode* of a set of data?

Find the mean, median, and mode of each data set.

2. 6, 4, 6, 7, 4, 3, 8, 4

3. 1.5, 0, 3, 0, 2, 8.5, 1

GO for Help
Lesson 2-2

What You'll Learn

To analyze a set of data by finding the range and by making frequency tables and line plots

◀》 **New Vocabulary** frequency table, line plot, range

Why Learn This?

Data, such as your classmates' favorite colors, are easier to read in a table or graph than in a list.

A **frequency table** is a table that lists each item in a data set with the number of times the item occurs.

Favorite Colors

Blue	Blue
Purple	Red
Red	Orange
Blue	Yellow
Blue	Green
Yellow	Blue
Green	Yellow
Purple	Blue

EXAMPLE Frequency Table

1 Your classmates' favorite colors are shown above. Organize the data in a frequency table. Find the mode.

Favorite Color

Color	Tally	Frequency
Blue	⦀⦀	6
Green	‖	2
Orange	∣	1
Purple	‖	2
Red	‖	2
Yellow	‖∣	3

Make a tally mark for each color chosen.

The number of tally marks in each row is the frequency.

Students selected blue most often. So the mode is blue.

Quick Check

1. The first initials of the names of 15 students are listed below. Organize the data in a frequency table. Find the mode.
   A J B K L C K D L S T D V P L

A **line plot** is a graph that shows the shape of a data set by stacking **X**'s above each data value on a number line.

EXAMPLE **Using a Line Plot**

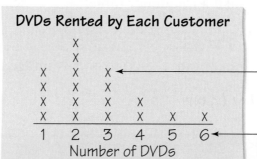

For: Line Plots Activity
Use: Interactive
   Textbook, 2-3

2 **Movies** The number of DVDs each customer rents when he or she visits a video store are 3, 5, 1, 2, 2, 1, 2, 3, 3, 4, 1, 2, 6, 2, 2, 4, 3, 1. Use a line plot to interpret the data.

DVDs Rented by Each Customer

```
            X
            X
X    X      X                              ← Each X represents
X    X      X                                one customer.
X    X      X    X
X    X      X    X    X    X                ← The scale of a graph includes
1    2      3    4    5    6                  all of the data values. The
        Number of DVDs                       scale is 1 to 6 in this line plot.
```

Customers usually rent between one and three DVDs. Most customers rent two DVDs.

Quick Check

2. Use a line plot to interpret the number of sales calls made each hour: 2, 3, 0, 7, 1, 1, 9, 8, 2, 8, 1, 2, 8, 7, 1, 8, 6, 1.

The **range** of a data set is the difference between the least and greatest values.

EXAMPLE **Finding the Range**

3 **Geography** In 1849 and 1850, six different surveyors made the following measurements of the height of Mount Everest.

28,990 ft; 28,992 ft; 28,999 ft; 29,002 ft; 29,005 ft; 29,026 ft

What is the range of the measurements?

$29,026 - 28,990 = 36$ ← Subtract the least from the greatest value.

The range of the measurements is 36 feet.

Quick Check

3. The numbers of pottery items made by students are 36, 21, 9, 34, 36, 10, 4, 35, 30, 7, 5, and 10. Find the range of the data.

1. **Vocabulary** How is a line plot similar to a frequency table?

The ages for required school attendance in ten states are 6, 7, 6, 5, 7, 6, 8, 6, 5, and 7. Use the data for Exercises 2–5.

2. Make a frequency table.   3. Make a line plot.

4. What is the range of the data? Is this a data point? Explain.

5. **Reasoning** Describe an advantage of using a line plot rather than a frequency table.

Homework Exercises

For more exercises, see Extra Skills and Word Problems.

Organize each set of data in a frequency table. Find the mode.

GO▶ for Help	
For Exercises	**See Example**
6–7	1
8–9	2
10–11	3

6. days in each month: 31, 28, 31, 30, 31, 30, 31, 31, 30, 31, 30, 31

7. vehicles in a parking lot:

pickup	compact	compact	mid-size
compact	SUV	mid-size	SUV
mid-size	compact	station wagon	pickup

Use a line plot to interpret each set of data.

8. lengths of baseball bats (inches):
   30 29 31 28 29 29 30 32 30 29 28 30 30

9. word lengths (letters): 7 2 6 1 7 6 9 1 8 4 2 3 10

Find the range for each set of data.

10. the ages of the first ten U.S. presidents when they took office:
    57, 61, 57, 57, 58, 57, 61, 54, 68, 51

11. heights of trees (meters): 2.3, 1.8, 3.4, 2.5, 2.9, 3.1, 3.2, 3.5, 2.8

GPS 12. **Guided Problem Solving** You spent $44 to purchase two of the least expensive tickets to the ballet. Each ticket you purchased was the same price. The range of the ticket prices is $55. How much is the most expensive ticket?
   • What is the cost of one of the least expensive tickets?
   • How can you use the range to find the cost of the most expensive ticket?

13. Speed Limits On a highway, the minimum speed allowed is 40 miles per hour. The maximum speed is 65 miles per hour. What is the range of speeds allowed on the highway?

14. Social Studies A town in Wales, United Kingdom, is named Llanfairpwllgwyngyllgogerychwyrndrobwllllantysiliogogogoch.
  a. Make a frequency table for the letters in the town's name.
  b. **Writing in Math** Use the mean, median, or mode to describe the data in your table. Explain your choice.

Nineteen water samples were taken from a river. The number of organisms counted in each sample is shown in the line plot.

15. What do the numbers represent?

16. Find the median and mode.

17. Why might you not want to use the mean to describe the data?

```
x
x
x   x
x   x   x
x   x   x
x   x   x   x
x   x   x   x   x
0   1   2   3   4
```

18. a. Make a frequency table and a line plot of the quiz scores.
  b. Use either the frequency table or line plot to identify any outliers. Which display did you use? Explain your choice.

Quiz Scores		
8	2	9
7	8	6
10	10	8
8	7	10

19. Challenge Make two sets of data with the same range but different means.

Test Prep and Mixed Review
Practice

Multiple Choice

20. Which statement is supported by the graph?
  Ⓐ More students received a D than a B.
  Ⓑ Six students received a C or better.
  Ⓒ Most students received an A or a D.
  Ⓓ Two more students received a C than the number who received a B.

**Semester
Science Grades**
```
              x
              x
x   x   x
x   x   x   x
x   x   x   x
A   B   C   D
Letter Grades
```

21. Find the median of the numbers.
12, 9, 6, 15, 10, 8, 14, 5, 0, 10, 4, 16, 12, 12, 8
  Ⓕ 8   Ⓖ 9   Ⓗ 10   Ⓙ 12

Use mental math to find each sum.

22. $17 + 23$ **23.** $46 + 0 + 14$ **24.** $5 + 32 + 15$

Bar Graphs and Line Graphs

✓ Check Skills You'll Need

1. **Vocabulary Review** What is the *range* of a set of data?

Make a line plot for each set of data.

2. 5, 6, 7, 8, 6, 5, 8, 7

3. 13, 17, 10, 21, 17

GO **for Help**
Lesson 2-3

What You'll Learn

To make and analyze bar graphs and line graphs

🔊 **New Vocabulary** bar graph, line graph

Why Learn This?

To make healthy eating decisions, you need to compare the amounts of nutrients in foods. Graphs help you "see" data by comparing size or showing change.

A **bar graph** uses vertical or horizontal bars to show comparisons.

Calcium Content

Food Item (1 cup)	Calcium (mg)
Milk	300
Yogurt	250
Cottage cheese	150
Ice cream	200
Broccoli	80

EXAMPLE Bar Graph

1 **Nutrition** Make a bar graph to display the data above. Compare the amount of calcium in milk to the amount in cottage cheese.

Draw and label the horizontal and vertical axes.

Choose an appropriate title.

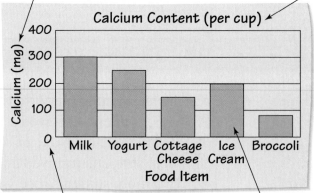

Choose a scale. The data go from 80 to 300 so use 0 to 400 as the scale. Mark it with intervals of 100.

Draw bars of equal widths. The heights will vary.

Vocabulary Tip

An *interval* is the amount of space between the values on the scale.

The amount of calcium in one cup of milk is twice the amount in one cup of cottage cheese.

✓ Quick Check

● 1. Find the amount of calcium in a cup of milk and a cup of broccoli.

A **line graph** uses a series of line segments to show changes in data. Usually, a line graph shows changes over time.

EXAMPLE Using a Line Graph

② **Temperature** Use the data at the left to make a line graph. Describe the change in temperature between 10 A.M. and 4 P.M.

Temperatures Throughout the Day	
Time	Temperature
8 A.M.	62°F
10 A.M.	70°F
NOON	78°F
2 P.M.	81°F
4 P.M.	76°F
6 P.M.	74°F

The range is 81 – 62, or about 20. Mark 60 to 85 in units of 5.

Choose an appropriate title.

Plot a point for each data item. Then connect the points with straight line segments.

Draw and label the axes.

The break symbol means that the values between 0 and 60 are not shown.

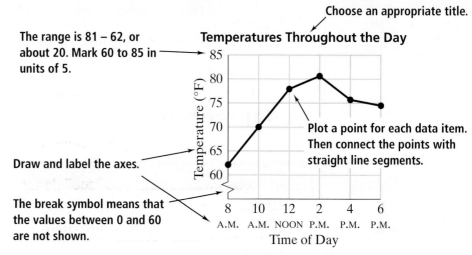

The temperature increased from 10 A.M. to 2 P.M. Then it began to decrease.

✓ Quick Check

2. Based on the line graph above, is the temperature likely to be greater than or less than 75°F at 8 P.M.? Explain.

EXAMPLE Selecting a Type of Graph

③ **Multiple Choice** Which type of data display is the most appropriate to show a comparison of the data in the table at the left?

Ⓐ organized list   Ⓒ line graph
Ⓑ bar graph   Ⓓ frequency table

World's Busiest Airports	
Airport	Passengers per Year (millions)
Atlanta	79
Chicago	70
London	63
Tokyo	63
Los Angeles	55

SOURCE: *Time Almanac*

Since you want to show comparison, use a bar graph. The correct answer is choice B.

✓ Quick Check

3. Which type of data display is the most appropriate to display the data at the right? Explain.

Ticket Sales				
Week	1	2	3	4
Tickets Sold	22	35	33	46

Check Your Understanding

1. **Vocabulary** A (line, bar) graph uses a series of line segments to show changes in data.

Length of Circus Tours

Circus	Number of Days
A	100
B	130
C	160
D	90

Use the table at the left for Exercises 2–4.

2. What type of display is the most appropriate for the data?

3. Which information would you choose for the vertical axis?

4. Make a graph of the data. Use the graph to compare the number of days Circus D toured to the number of days Circus C toured.

Homework Exercises

For more exercises, see Extra Skills and Word Problems.

GO for Help

For Exercises	See Example
5–6	1
7	2
8	3

Budgets Use the table at the right.

5. Make a bar graph to display the planned budgets.

6. Make a bar graph to display the actual budgets.

Monthly Budget

Cost Item	Planned	Actual
Dining Out	$40	$28
Clothes	$35	$42
Concerts	$18	$6
Movies	$22	$22

7. **Hot Lunches** Make a line graph of the data below.

Students Buying Hot Lunch

Day	Mon.	Tue.	Wed.	Thur.	Fri.
Number of Students	125	143	165	48	183

8. Which type of data display is the most appropriate to display the data below? Explain.

Allowance Each Week

Amount of money ($)	3	4	5	6	7
Number of students	10	21	34	12	6

9. **Guided Problem Solving** Make a graph to show how the number of customers changed over the week. Describe the change shown in the graph.
   - What type of graph will you use?
   - What values will you use for the horizontal and vertical axes?

Music World Customers

Day	Number
Monday	72
Tuesday	94
Wednesday	172
Thursday	106
Friday	181
Saturday	234

10. Writing in Math Explain how you can use range when planning to draw a line graph.

11. Prime Ministers Make a bar graph to show how many years each prime minister was in office.

Golda Meir,
Israel, 5 years

Indira Gandhi,
India, 18 years

Margaret Thatcher,
United Kingdom, 11 years

Gro Harlem Brundtland,
Norway, 10 years

12. Data Collection Make a line graph showing the amount of time you spend on homework each day for one week.

13. Challenge A histogram is a bar graph that shows the frequency of each data value. Histograms often combine data into equal-sized groups. Use the frequency table at the right to make a histogram.

Hours of Battery Life

Hours	Tally	Frequency
8–11	III	3
12–15	IIII	4
16–19	II	2
20–23	III	3

Test Prep and Mixed Review
Practice

Multiple Choice

14. Which statement is supported by the graph below?
- (A) Flu cases increased from September to December.
- (B) The lowest number of flu cases was in October.
- (C) There was a decrease in flu cases.
- (D) The highest number of flu cases was in November.

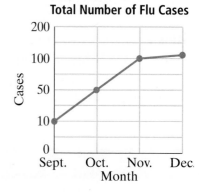

15. What is the median price?
$5.95, $2.50, $3.75, $4.95, $8.95, $5.25, $6.95, $4.50
- (F) $4.95
- (G) $5.10
- (H) $5.25
- (J) $5.95

Use <, =, or > to complete each statement.

16. 1.45 ■ 1.4   **17.** 0.75 ■ 0.752   **18.** 3.20 ■ 3.2

Making Bar Graphs

You can use a graphing calculator to make
a bar graph.

EXAMPLE

A number cube was rolled 15 times with the following results: 1, 2,
5, 1, 3, 6, 2, 4, 6, 1, 5, 2, 4, 2, 6. Make a bar graph using the data.

Step 1 Prepare your graphing calculator.

Press **LIST** and delete any data already in the list.
Press **2nd** [PLOT] 4: PlotsOff **ENTER** to turn off the
plots. Press **Y=** and clear any equations.

```
STAT PLOTS
1:Plot1...Off
   ▥ L1    1
2:Plot2...Off
   ⌐ L1   L2   ▫
3:Plot3...Off
   ⌐ L1   L2   ▫
4↓PlotsOff
```

Step 2 Enter the data.

Press **LIST**. Enter each number rolled in the L1
column. Press **ENTER** after typing each number.

```
L1      L2      L3      1
1
5
2
4
2
▬▬▬▬
L1(15) = 6
```

Step 3 Select the type of graph.

Press **2nd** [PLOT] 1 to select the first plot. Highlight
On and press **ENTER**. Next, use the arrow keys to select
bar graph for the type of graph, L1 for the Xlist, and
1 as the frequency.

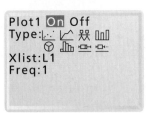

```
Plot1  On  Off
Type: ⌐ ⌐ 梁 ▥
      ◷ ▥ ▫ ▫
Xlist:L1
Freq:1
```

Step 4 Display the graph.

Press **ZOOM** 4: ZQuadrant1 to display the data.
This zoom feature selects a window size to view
the bar graph.

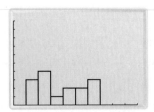

Exercises

1. Roll a number cube 15 times. Combine the results with the
   data from the Example. Make a new bar graph.

2. **Data Collection** Make a bar graph of your classmates'
   heights on the graphing calculator.

Double Bar and Line Graphs

You can plot two data sets on the same graph to compare them easily.

EXAMPLE

A bookstore tracks sales of cooking and travel books. Make a double bar graph and a double line graph of the data at the right.

Use a different color for each data set in the graphs.

Books Sold Each Month

Month	Jan.	Feb.	Mar.	Apr.
Cooking	86	98	112	110
Travel	100	106	88	102

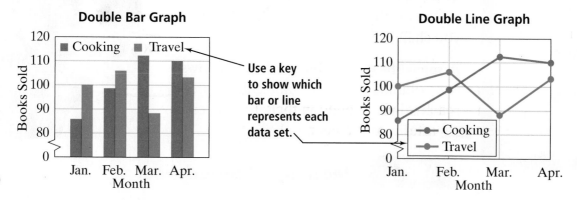

Use a key to show which bar or line represents each data set.

Exercises

Use the example above for Exercises 1 and 2.

1. Which graph shows most clearly how book sales changed from January to February?

2. Which graph shows most clearly the differences in sales between the two types of books?

Use the table at the right for Exercises 3 and 4.

3. Make a double bar graph. Show the differences between the numbers of endangered plants and animals.

4. Make a double line graph. Show how the numbers of endangered plants and animals have changed over time.

Endangered Species in the United States

Year	1985	1990	1995	2000	2005
Plants	93	179	432	592	599
Animals	207	263	324	379	389

Source: U.S. Fish and Wildlife Service.
Go to **PHSchool.com** for a data update.
Web Code: aqg-9041

Using Spreadsheets to Organize Data

Check Skills You'll Need

1. Vocabulary Review
The sum of two whole numbers is (never, usually) greater than either number.

Find each sum.

2. 88 + 71

3. 424 + 390

 for Help
Skills Handbook, p. 638

What You'll Learn

To make spreadsheets to display data and solve problems

◀)) **New Vocabulary** spreadsheet, cell

Why Learn This?

You can use formulas in a spreadsheet to automatically recalculate values when you change an entry.

A **spreadsheet** is a table made up of rows and columns used to organize data. A **cell** is a box in a spreadsheet where a specific row and column meet.

EXAMPLE **Reading a Spreadsheet**

1 **Music** The spreadsheet below shows the lengths of 15 CDs from five different categories. Identify the value in cell B5. Tell what this number represents.

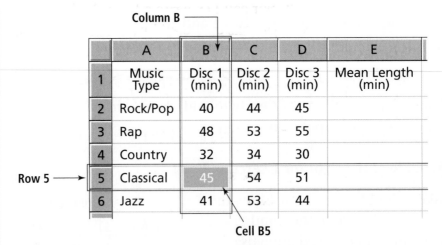

Column B

	A	B Disc 1 (min)	C Disc 2 (min)	D Disc 3 (min)	E Mean Length (min)
1	Music Type	Disc 1 (min)	Disc 2 (min)	Disc 3 (min)	Mean Length (min)
2	Rock/Pop	40	44	45	
3	Rap	48	53	55	
4	Country	32	34	30	
5	Classical	45	54	51	
6	Jazz	41	53	44	

Row 5

Cell B5

The value in B5 is 45. The first classical CD is 45 minutes long.

Quick Check

1. What is the value in cell D4? What does this number represent?

A computer automatically enters a value in a cell of a spreadsheet when you assign a formula to that cell. A formula is a statement of a mathematical relationship. An equal sign (=) tells the computer that an expression is a formula.

EXAMPLE Formulas in a Spreadsheet

2 The spreadsheet below gives the numbers of cans three classrooms collected during two weeks of a food drive. Write a formula for cell D2 that will find the total number of cans collected by Room 105.

Technology Tip

These operation symbols are used in spreadsheets:

+ addition
− subtraction
* multiplication
/ division

	A	B	C	D
1	Room Number	Week 1 (cans)	Week 2 (cans)	Total (cans)
2	105	389	416	■ ← D2
3	106	592	462	■
4	107	481	493	■
5				■

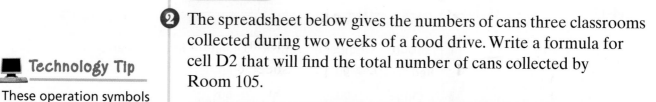

Total number of cans = 389 + 416

D2 = B2 + C2 ← Write an expression for cell D2.

Here is the formula for cell D2: = B2 + C2.

Quick Check

2. For cell D5, write a formula that will calculate the total number of cans collected by all three classrooms.

Check Your Understanding

1. **Vocabulary** How is a cell related to a spreadsheet?

Use the spreadsheet at the left for each matching question.

	A	B
1	Sandals	Pairs
2	Sporty	15
3	Casual	19
4	Total	■

2. What is the value in cell B3?

3. What is the value in cell B2?

4. What is a formula for cell B4 that adds the values in cells B2 and B3?

5. What is the value in cell B4?

A. = B3 + B4
B. 15
C. Sporty
D. 19
E. 34
F. = B2 + B3

Homework Exercises

For more exercises, see Extra Skills and Word Problems.

GO for Help table

For Exercises	See Example
6–13	1
14–16	2

Use the spreadsheet below for Exercises 6–15.

Four groups of students made videos. They received scores for originality, effort, and quality.

	A	B	C	D	E	F
1	Group	Originality	Effort	Quality	Total	Mean Score
2	Red	90	85	80	▪	▪
3	Orange	90	90	60	▪	▪
4	Yellow	95	100	75	▪	▪
5	Green	65	80	80	▪	▪

Identify the cell(s) for each category.

6. Effort   **7.** Mean Score   **8.** Green   **9.** Total

Find the value for the given cell.

10. C4   **11.** C5   **12.** B4   **13.** B2

Write a formula to find each quantity.

14. the total in cell E4   **15.** the mean score in cell F4

Wages Suppose your cousin works part time and earns $7 per hour. The spreadsheet shows a typical schedule for a week.

	A	B	C	D	E
1	Day	Time In (P.M.)	Time Out (P.M.)	Hours Worked	Amount Earned
2	9/15	3	8	▪	▪
3	9/17	4	8	▪	▪
4	9/19	3	6	▪	▪
5			Total:	▪	▪

16. Write a formula for cell D2. Then calculate the value in D2.

17. Guided Problem Solving Refer to the spreadsheet above. How much money did your cousin earn on 9/19?
- Use the formula for cell D2 to write a formula for the number of hours worked on 9/19.
- How can you use the value in D4 in the formula for E4?

Chapter 2 Data and Graphs

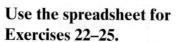

As a fundraiser, students sell nail polish for $3 per bottle. Find the value for each cell.

18. A3   **19.** B7

20. C1   **21.** C2

	A	B	C
1	Type	Number of Bottles Sold	Amount Collected (dollars)
2	Grape	8	▪
3	Glitter	10	▪
4	Pink	6	▪
5	Berry	12	▪
6	Electric	15	▪
7	Blue	5	▪
8	Grand Total		▪

Use the spreadsheet for Exercises 22–25.

22. Write a formula for cell C2.

23. a. Writing in Math Explain how the formula for C2 can be used to calculate the values in cells C3 through C7.
  b. Calculate the values in C3 through C7.

24. Write a formula for cell C8. Then calculate its value.

25. Challenge Write a formula that finds the mean amount collected for the six types of nail polish.

Test Prep and Mixed Review

Practice

Multiple Choice

26. The line plot shows the number of slices in loaves of bread. Which statement is NOT supported by the graph?
  Ⓐ 24 different loaves of bread were counted.
  Ⓑ The median value is 18.
  Ⓒ The range of slices is 5.
  Ⓓ The most frequent number of slices is 20.

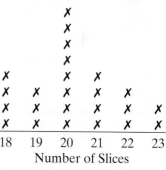

Slices in Loaves of Bread

27. A student lists her test scores for a quarter: 84, 80, 82, 85, 89, 90, and 92. What is the range of scores?
  Ⓕ 92   Ⓖ 12   Ⓗ 8   Ⓙ 7

28. Estimate each sum. Which is closest to 3,000?
  Ⓐ 612 + 898 + 1,690   Ⓒ 990 + 1,020 + 2,009
  Ⓑ 2,009 + 494 + 708   Ⓓ 1,498 + 898 + 612

GO for Help

For Exercises	See Lesson
29–30	2-2

Find the median of each data set.

29. 5, 4, 7, 8, 3, 4, 11, 3, 7, 8, 7   **30.** 2.8, 1.6, 0, 0.8, 1, 0

Technology

Spreadsheets and Graphs

You can use spreadsheet programs to make bar graphs, line graphs, and scatter plots. A **scatter plot** is a graph that relates two sets of data.

Enter and highlight the data you want to graph. Use the menu to choose the type of graph and the labels. Finally, insert the labels.

EXAMPLE

Sierra makes a table showing the amount of time she studies for each test and the grade she gets on the test. She enters her data in the spreadsheet below. Sierra then chooses a scatter plot because it shows the relationship between sets of data.

	A	B
1	Minutes Studied	Test Score
2	75	89
3	45	92
4	15	65
5	30	75
6	60	90

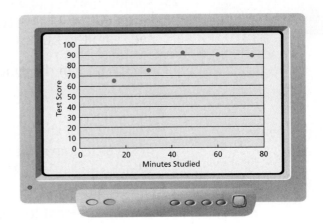

Exercises

Enter the data below in a spreadsheet. Use the program to make a graph of the data. Explain why you chose the type of graph you used.

1. **Allowance Spent at the Mall**

Time in Mall (hours)	2	4	3	1
Amount Spent ($)	$10	$24	$15	$8

2. **How Often People Need to Search for Keys**

Category	Never	Once a year	Once a month	Once a week	Once a day
Number of Responses	31	15	23	9	2

Use the line plot for Exercises 1–4.

1. Find the mean, the median, and the mode of the data.

2. Find the range of temperatures.

3. Are there any outliers? Explain.

4. Does the mean, median, or mode best describe these data? Explain.

High Temperatures

```
                    X
                    X    X
          X         X    X              X
  X   X   X    X    X    X         X              X
  17  18  19   20   21   22   23   24   25   26
            Temperature (°C)
```

5. **Nutrition** The grams of fat per serving for 24 breakfast cereals are 0, 1, 3, 1, 1, 2, 2, 0, 3, 1, 3, 2, 0, 1, 0, 2, 1, 1, 0, 0, 0, 2, 1, and 0. Make a frequency table for the data.

Use the spreadsheet for Exercises 6–8.

6. For cell B6 in the spreadsheet, write a formula to calculate the total collected from the fundraisers.

7. How much money was collected from the fundraisers?

8. Make a bar graph using the data.

9. Suppose your bank account balance is $37 in January, $40 in February, $55 in March, and $15 in April. Draw a line graph of the data.

	A	B
1	Fundraiser	Collected ($)
2	Book sale	200
3	Car wash	125
4	Food stand	325
5	Paper drive	150
6	TOTAL:	▪

MATH AT WORK

Park Ranger

Do you enjoy working outdoors? Are you interested in history? If so, maybe a career as a park ranger is for you. Park rangers use mathematics to predict the number of visitors, measure rainfall and tree growth, plan trails, solve problems involving acid rain or deforestation, and construct timelines.

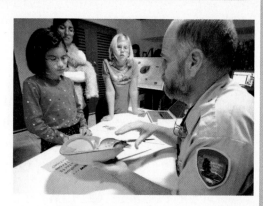

Go Online
PHSchool.com
For: Information on national parks
Web Code: aqb-2031

Stem-and-Leaf Plots

Check Skills You'll Need

1. **Vocabulary Review**
What is the *median* of a set of data?

Find the median of each data set.

2. 23, 32, 32, 15, 52

3. 15, 10, 32, 21, 10

4. 6.7, 4.6, 5.8, 3.8

 **for Help**
Lesson 2-2

What You'll Learn

To make and analyze stem-and-leaf plots

 **New Vocabulary** stem-and-leaf plot

Why Learn This?

You can use a stem-and-leaf plot to group and interpret data, including how long it takes to get ready for school.

A **stem-and-leaf plot** is a graph that uses the digits of each number to show the shape of the data. Each data value is broken into a "stem" and a "leaf."

stem → 5 | 8 ← leaf

EXAMPLE Interpreting a Stem-and-Leaf Plot

1 The times students take to get ready for school are shown below. How many students take less than 30 minutes? How many take more than 40 minutes?

Test Prep Tip

To read the data in a stem-and-leaf plot, combine the stem with each leaf in the same row.

Times to Get Ready for School (minutes)

2	3 3 5 7 8 8
3	3 4 5 7 7 7 9
4	0 0 2 3 3 5
5	8

Key: 2 | 3 means 23 minutes

6 students take less than 30 minutes. Their times are 23, 23, 25, 27, 28, and 28.

5 students take more than 40 minutes. Their times are 42, 43, 43, 45, and 58.

Six students take less than 30 minutes. Five students take more than 40 minutes.

Quick Check

1. What is the range of the data?

0–60 Miles per Hour Times (seconds)	
8.2	7.0
7.3	8.9
7.2	8.3
8.0	7.0
7.7	7.6
8.1	8.7
8.1	7.3
7.2	10.5
7.6	8.5
6.5	6.8

EXAMPLE **Making a Stem-and-Leaf Plot**

2 **Cars** The table at the left shows times that it takes compact cars to reach 60 miles per hour. Make a stem-and-leaf plot of the data.

Step 1 Write the stems in order. Use the whole-number part. Draw a vertical line to the right of the stems.

```
stems →   6|
          7|
          8|
          9|
         10|
```

Step 2 Write the leaves in order. There is no nonzero digit in the hundredths place. So use the values in the tenths place.

```
 6| 5 8              ←leaves
 7| 0 0 2 2 3 3 6 6 7
 8| 0 1 1 2 3 5 7 9
 9|
10| 5
```

Step 3 Choose a title and include a key. The key explains what your stems and leaves represent.

0–60 Miles per Hour Times (seconds)
```
 6| 5 8
 7| 0 0 2 2 3 3 6 6 7
 8| 0 1 1 2 3 5 7 9
 9|
10| 5
```
Key: 6 | 5 means 6.5   ←key

✓ Quick Check

2. **Elections** The data below show the numbers of students who voted for class president each year. Make a stem-and-leaf plot.
137, 125, 145, 123, 181, 132, 155, 141, 140, 133, 138, 127, 150, 126, 124, 130, 125, 138, 144, 121, 136
(*Hint:* Use the ones digit for the leaves.)

● More Than One Way

Your class collected data on how long it takes each student to get to school. The data are below. Use a data display to find the most frequent time.

times, in minutes: 8, 10, 6, 10, 22, 15, 9, 7, 10, 14, 9, 7, 10, 45, 18, 10, 6, 15, 13, 18, 13, 6, 3

Zach's Method

I can use a frequency table.

Time (min)	Tally	Frequency
3	I	1
6	III	3
7	II	2
8	I	1
9	II	2
10	ⅢⅡ	5

Time (min)	Tally	Frequency
13	II	2
14	I	1
15	II	2
18	II	2
22	I	1
45	I	1

The most frequent time is 10 minutes.

Lauren's Method

I can use a stem-and-leaf plot and choose the time with the most leaves.

Time Spent Traveling to School (minutes)

```
0 | 3 6 6 6 7 7 8 9 9
1 | 0 0 0 0 0 3 3 4 5 5 8 8
2 | 2
3 |
4 | 5
```

Key: 2 | 2 means 22 minutes

The most frequent time is 10 minutes.

Choose a Method

Students are asked how many minutes they think they need for tutoring after school: 30, 45, or 60. The results are shown below. Use a data display to show how long should be set aside for after-school tutoring. Explain why you chose the method you used.
60, 45, 60, 30, 30, 60, 60, 45, 60, 30, 30, 60, 60, 45, 30, 60, 45

Online active math

For: Stem-and-Leaf Plot Activity
Use: Interactive Textbook, 2-5

1. **Vocabulary** A graph that uses the digits of each number to show the shape of the data is a (line, stem-and-leaf) plot.

Use the stem-and-leaf plot at the right.

3	6 8
4	1 1 2 3 4
5	0
6	2
7	5 7 9

Key: 3 | 6 means 36 seconds

2. What do the stem 3 and leaf 8 represent?

3. How many of the times in the plot are greater than 50 seconds?

4. Copy the stem-and-leaf plot. Add the following data items: 38 seconds and 89 seconds.

5. **Writing in Math** What advantage does a stem-and-leaf plot have that a list of values does not have?

For more exercises, see Extra Skills and Word Problems.

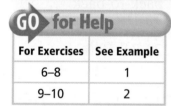

GO for Help

For Exercises	See Example
6–8	1
9–10	2

Use the stem-and-leaf plot at the right.

6. What does "0 | 8" represent?

7. How many entries have a value of 15?

8. How many customers waited less than 9 seconds?

Number of Seconds Customers on Hold

0	7 8 8 8 9 9
1	0 2 2 3 4 5 5 5 6 7 7

Key: 0 | 7 means 7 seconds

Make a stem-and-leaf plot for each set of data.

9. heights of tomato plants (inches): 27, 40, 31, 33, 35, 33, 26, 36, 41, 29, 30, 36

10. number of jelly beans in a scoop: 47, 28, 38, 47, 58, 34, 76, 35, 32, 45, 53, 43, 35, 27

GPS 11. **Guided Problem Solving** Some volcano eruptions last longer than others. The data below list the numbers of days different eruptions of the Mauna Loa volcano in Hawaii lasted. Make a stem-and-leaf plot.

23 24 46 15 39 12 48 16 61 25 16 20 21 15

• How many stems should your plot have?
• How many leaves should your plot have?

12. **Population** The table shows the rounded populations of nine states. Make a stem-and-leaf plot.

13. The ages of 18 people are shown below.

    21 12 15 13 35 24 16 23 9
    40 19 12 15 13 12 20 11 12

    a. Make a stem-and-leaf plot and a line plot.
    b. Which more clearly shows the number of people in their teens? Explain.

14. The heights of nine people are below. Use a stem-and-leaf plot to find the median, the mode, and any outliers.

    Heights in inches: 70, 59, 64, 66, 79, 67, 82, 68, 61

State	Population (millions)
Arizona	5.7
Colorado	4.6
Indiana	6.2
Kentucky	4.1
Maryland	5.6
Minnesota	5.0
Oregon	3.6
Tennessee	5.9
Wisconsin	5.5

SOURCE: U.S. Census Bureau.
Go to **PHSchool.com** for a data update. Web Code: aqg-9041

15. **Data Collection** Choose a paragraph from a book or magazine. Make a stem-and-leaf plot for the number of letters in each word. Use the plot to find the median word length.

Group A		Group B
9 5 3	2	8
1 0	3	4 7

Key:
means ← 3 | 2 | 8 → means
23   28

16. **Challenge** The back-to-back stem-and-leaf plot shown at the left displays two sets of data. Make a back-to-back stem-and-leaf plot for the data below.

    Group D: 24, 26, 33, 35, 39   Group F: 25, 29, 34, 36, 37

ⒶⒷⒸⒹ Test Prep and Mixed Review   **Practice**

Multiple Choice

17. Use the stem-and-leaf plot. How many data items are greater than 67?
    Ⓐ 7
    Ⓑ 6
    Ⓒ 5
    Ⓓ 3

4	0 9
5	2 4 4 5 9
6	3 7 7 7 8 8 9
7	2 4 6

Key: 4 | 0 means 40

18. The favorite activities of eight students are sports, reading, drawing, games, games, drawing, sports, and sports. Find the mode.
    Ⓕ reading   Ⓖ drawing   Ⓗ sports   Ⓙ no mode

19. Which decimal represents $\frac{6}{25}$?
    Ⓐ 0.24   Ⓑ 0.25   Ⓒ 0.30   Ⓓ 0.6

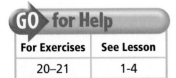

For Exercises	See Lesson
20–21	1-4

Find the value of each expression.

20. $13 + 5 \times 12 - 4$

21. $22 + 44 \div 22 - 11$

Solving Multiple-Step Problems

The table below shows some gasoline prices. At those prices, how much more would it cost to fill a 22-gallon gas tank in Hawaii than in Georgia?

Gas Prices (dollars per gallon)

Higher Prices		Lower Prices	
Hawaii	2.416	New Jersey	1.872
California	2.302	Texas	1.935
Oregon	2.130	Georgia	1.951

SOURCE: AAA Fuel Gauge Report

What You Might Think

What do I know?

What am I trying to find out?

What diagram can I draw to show the situation?

What hidden question needs to be answered?

How do I solve the problem?

What is the answer?

What You Might Write

Hawaii: $2.416 per gal Georgia: $1.951 per gal

I want to know how much more it costs to fill a 22-gallon tank in Hawaii than in Georgia.

Cost of gas in Hawaii	
Cost in Georgia	?

How much more does 1 gallon cost in Hawaii than in Georgia?

$2.416 − $1.951 = $0.465. This is the additional cost per gallon in Hawaii.
$0.465 per gal × 22 gal = $10.23

It costs $10.23 more to fill a 22-gallon tank in Hawaii than in Georgia.

Think It Through

1. How does the diagram show that subtraction is the operation needed to find how much more gas costs in Hawaii?

2. **Check for Reasonableness** How can you use rounding to decide whether the answer is reasonable? Check the answer.

3. **Reasoning** Is there another way to solve the problem? Explain. (*Hint:* Use the total cost to fill a 22-gallon tank.)

Exercises

4. How much less does it cost to fill an 18-gallon tank than a 23-gallon tank in Texas?
   a. What do you know?
   b. What hidden question needs to be answered?
   c. Solve the problem. Decide if the answer is reasonable. Tell how you decided.

5. Use the graph at the right. How much more did a gallon of gas cost in Week 11 than in Week 1?

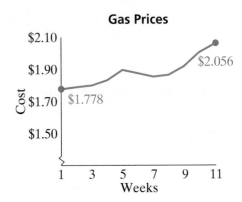

Gas Prices

6. A cab driver filled his car with 15.5 gallons of gasoline at $2.45 per gallon. He then bought snacks for $7.85. Use the diagram below to help you find the total cost. Is your answer reasonable? Explain.

Total cost	
Cost of gas	Cost of snacks

7. The tax on a gallon of gasoline in Texas is $.20. If there were no tax on gasoline, what would it cost to fill an 18.5 gallon tank in Texas? Use the diagram below to help answer the hidden question.

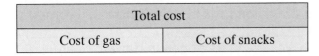

$1.935	
$0.20	Cost per gallon without tax

8. Find the mean, median, and mode of the data from the stem-and-leaf plot shown. What would you use for a newspaper headline about the typical gasoline price at these neighborhood stations? Explain your reasoning.

9. Airlines measure the amount of fuel in an airplane in pounds. One gallon of fuel weighs 6.1 pounds. One gallon of water weighs 8.3 pounds. How much less does the fuel in a 5-gallon can weigh than the water in a 5-gallon bucket?

Neighborhood Gas Prices

2.9	1 3 4 5 8
2.8	0 0 0 7 7 9 9
2.7	0 2 2 8 8
2.6	5 7 8
2.5	
2.4	
2.3	5

Key: 2.7 | 2 means $2.72

Misleading Graphs and Statistics

Check Skills You'll Need

1. **Vocabulary Review**
   What is the *mean* of a set of data?

   Find the mean for each set of data.

2. 21, 25, 52, 81.5, 98

3. 8.5, 9, 11, 19, 20

4. 111, 121, 131, 161

 **for Help**
Lesson 2-1

What You'll Learn

To identify misleading graphs and statistics

Why Learn This?

Companies often present data in ways that are meant to influence you. You will be able to make better decisions if you carefully analyze the data.

As you look at data displays, consider these questions: Is the information shown accurately? Is the presentation meant to influence you?

EXAMPLE **Misleading Line Graphs**

1. **Multiple Choice** Each month, residents of a town were asked, "Do you think the mayor is doing a good job?" The results are shown. Which statement tells why the graph may be misleading?

   Ⓐ The months on the horizontal axis are not consecutive.

   Ⓑ The title is misleading.

   Ⓒ The vertical scale uses unequal intervals.

   Ⓓ The graph does not start at 0.

   The graph uses unequal intervals on the vertical scale. The answer is choice C.

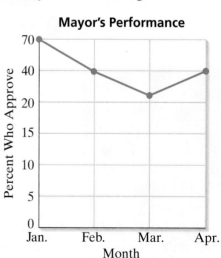

Mayor's Performance

Test Prep Tip

A graph can be misleading if the scales have uneven intervals or if the graph does not begin at 0.

✓ Quick Check

1. Redraw the graph so it is not misleading.

A graph can be misleading if the vertical scale does not start at 0.

EXAMPLE **Misleading Bar Graphs**

2 **Advertising** An auto dealer made the graph at the right.

a. What impression does the graph give?

It looks like there was a dramatic increase in sales.

b. Why is the graph misleading?

The vertical scale does not begin at 0. So you are looking at just the top of the graph.

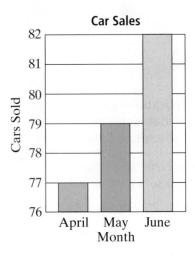

Car Sales

Cars Sold — April, May, June — Month

✅ Quick Check

2. Use the graph in Example 2.
   a. Compare the height of the bar for June to the height of the bar for May.
   b. How many more cars were sold in June than in May?

**GO for Help**

For help with finding the mean, the median, and the mode, go to Lessons 2-1 and 2-2.

Statistics can also be misleading. For example, the mean can be a distorted measure of a data set that contains outliers.

EXAMPLE **Identifying Misleading Statistics**

3 Five players on a professional basketball team have a mean salary of $2.2 million. Their five salaries are shown at the right. Explain why the mean may not be the best measure for describing the players' salaries.

Players' Salaries
$7,200,000
$1,200,000
$1,000,000
$800,000
$800,000

Only one person makes more than the mean of $2.2 million. The $7.2 million salary is an outlier that greatly increases the mean.

✅ Quick Check

3. In Example 3, which would better describe the basketball players' salaries, the median or the mode? Explain.

Use the graph for Exercises 1–4.

1. What impression does the graph give?

2. How does the height of the bar for Week 1 compare to the height of the bar for Week 4?

3. How many more sales were made in Week 1 than in Week 4?

4. Why is the graph misleading?

Homework Exercises

For more exercises, see **Extra Skills and Word Problems.**

GO for Help

For Exercise	See Example
5	1
6	2
7	3

Decide whether each graph is misleading. If a graph is misleading, what impression does the graph give? Explain why the graph is misleading. Then redraw the graph so it is not misleading.

5.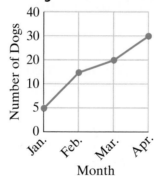

6.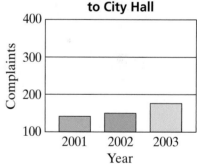

7. **Tests** A student scored 100%, 100%, 90%, 70%, and 60% on five quizzes. Which measure makes his grades look best—the mean, the median, or the mode?

8. **Guided Problem Solving** The prices of different digital cameras at a store are $138, $138, $138, $179, $189, $198, $219, $249, and $449. Would a salesperson use the mean, median, or mode to encourage you to purchase a digital camera? Explain.
   - Does the salesperson want the highest or lowest price to represent the data?
   - What are the mean, median, and mode of the prices?

9. **Election Results** Two graphs of the same election results are shown. Which graph might be preferred by Candidate A? Which might be preferred by Candidate B? Explain.

I.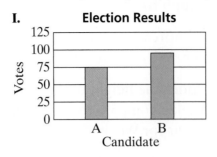

II.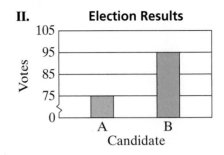

10. **Reasoning** How does the impression made by a line graph change when you make the horizontal scale shorter but keep the vertical scale the same?

Money Pledged to a Public Radio Station

Year	Amount Pledged
1	$34,096
2	$39,021
3	$41,132
4	$42,209
5	$44,172
6	$45,071
7	$45,759

Fundraising Use the table at the left for Exercises 11–13.

11. Draw a bar graph that suggests that the money pledged increased greatly from Year 1 to Year 7.

12. Draw a bar graph that suggests that the money pledged increased slowly from Year 1 to Year 7.

13. **Writing in Math** If you wanted to summarize the data using a low value, would you use the mean, the median, or the mode? Explain.

14. **Challenge** Which number could you remove from this list to make the mean and the median equal: 2, 7, 12, 14, 17?

Test Prep and Mixed Review **Practice**

Multiple Choice

15. Find the median of 4.5, 4, 4.5, 5.5, 6, and 6.5.
    Ⓐ 4　　Ⓑ 4.5　　Ⓒ 5　　Ⓓ 5.5

16. Which of the following statements is NOT supported by the graph?
    Ⓕ The initial height was 2 cm.
    Ⓖ The height was about 7 cm at 3 weeks.
    Ⓗ The height increased over time.
    Ⓙ The height was about 8 cm at 4 weeks.

Plant Growth

Make a stem-and-leaf plot of the data.

17. 33, 42, 16, 45, 14, 14, 28, 37, 16, 23, 33, 25, 16

Random Samples and Surveys

Surveys and polls collect data about a group of people called a *population*. Surveying a large population is difficult. So pollsters select a *sample*, or part of the population. In a *random sample*, each member of the population has the same chance of being selected.

EXAMPLE **Random Samples**

1. You want to know the favorite band of students at your school. Which strategy is most likely to result in a random sample?

   a. Ask the students in your class.
   b. Ask every tenth student who enters the school.
   c. Ask the players on the football team.
   d. Post a survey on the school bulletin board.

If you limit your survey to your class or to the football team, you are not giving every student in the school the same chance of being selected. A survey on the bulletin board will not get answers from students who do not read the bulletin board.

By asking every tenth student who enters the school, you are most likely getting a random sample, because each student has the same chance of being selected.

Exercises

1. You survey mall customers to find out their favorite store. Is each method likely to give a random sample? Explain.
   a. Survey shoppers in a clothing store.
   b. Walk around the mall and survey shoppers.
   c. Ask your friends where they shop.

2. **Data Collection** Write a survey question on a topic that interests you. Plan and carry out a survey that includes both a random sample and a non-random sample. Use a data display to compare your results.

Checkpoint Quiz 2

1. Make a stem-and-leaf plot for test scores: 92, 76, 85, 85, 68, 81, 84, 89, 84, 91, 97, 95, 86, and 64.

Use the stem-and-leaf plot at the right for Exercises 2–5.

2. What is the median life span?

3. How many of the animals have a life span greater than 15 years?

4. What is the range of the data?

5. Does the mean, the median, or the mode best describe the data? Explain.

6. A car dealer wants to advertise that its compact car is the roomiest, with 75.6 cubic feet inside. The cars of three competitors have 63.4 cubic feet, 70.1 cubic feet, and 68.7 cubic feet of space. Explain how to make a bar graph that shows a very large difference among the cars.

Life Spans of Different Animals

```
0 | 4 4 5 6 9
1 | 0 0 1 1 3 5 5 5 5 8
2 | 0 0 0 1 2 5
3 |
4 | 0
```

Key: 1 | 8 means 18 years

MATH GAMES

Bar Graph Race

What You'll Need

- three number cubes
- a graph for each player, labeled as shown

How To Play

- Each player takes a turn rolling the three number cubes. The player then chooses two of the numbers rolled and adds them.
- The player fills in one square on the graph in the column labeled with the sum.
- Once any player fills a column completely, no other players may play in that column on their own graphs.
- If a player cannot fill a square, then the player loses a turn.
- The first player to fill in three columns wins.

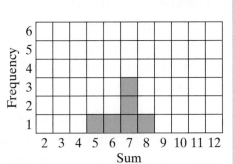

Answering the Question Asked

When answering a question, be sure to answer the question that is asked. Read the question carefully and identify the answer that you are asked to find. Some answer choices are answers to related questions, so you have to be careful.

EXAMPLE

1 In Mrs. Sanchez's class, students received the scores shown in the line plot. How many students took the test?

  Ⓐ 9   Ⓑ 19   Ⓒ 20   Ⓓ 28

The question asks for the number of students who took the test. The total number of scores is $4 + 4 + 4 + 1 + 6 + 9 = 28$. The correct answer is choice D.

The number of students who scored 20 points is 9. The mode is 20. The median is 19. But none of these is what is asked for.

Student Scores

```
                          X
                          X
                          X
                      X   X
                      X   X
  X   X   X           X   X
  X   X   X           X   X
  X   X   X           X   X
  X   X   X   X   X   X
 15  16  17  18  19  20
          Score
```

EXAMPLE

2 The stem-and-leaf plot shows the heights of 11 students in inches. What is the median height?

  Ⓕ 60 in.   Ⓖ 62 in.   Ⓗ 63 in.   Ⓙ 64 in.

The question asks for the median height. For eleven data items, the sixth is the median. The sixth height is 62 in. The correct answer is choice G.

The mode is 60 in. The mean is 63 in. Answer J is the average of 57 in. and 71 in., or 64 in. But none of these is what is asked for.

Heights of Students

5	7 8
6	0 0 1 2 3 4 7
7	0 1

Key: 5 | 8 means 58 inches

Exercises

1. In Example 2, how tall is the tallest student who is less than 70 in. tall?

  Ⓐ 60 in.   Ⓑ 67 in.   Ⓒ 70 in.   Ⓓ 71 in.

2. In Example 2, what is the range of data?

  Ⓕ 14 in.   Ⓖ 57 in.   Ⓗ 64 in.   Ⓙ 71 in.

Chapter 2 Review

Vocabulary Review

 bar graph (p. 74)
cell (p. 80)
frequency table (p. 70)
line graph (p. 75)
line plot (p. 71)

mean (p. 61)
median (p. 66)
mode (p. 67)
outlier (p. 62)

range (p. 71)
scatter plot (p. 84)
spreadsheet (p. 80)
stem-and-leaf plot (p. 86)

Choose the correct vocabulary term to complete each sentence.

1. A(n) __?__ lists each item in a data set with the number of times it occurs.

2. The __?__ of a data set is the sum of the values divided by the number of values.

3. A(n) __?__ of a data set is much greater or much less than the other data values.

A. mean

B. mode

C. frequency table

D. median

E. line graph

F. spreadsheet

G. outlier

Go Online
PHSchool.com
For: Vocabulary quiz
Web Code: aqj-0251

4. On the computer, you can use a(n) __?__ to organize data in a table.

5. A(n) __?__ typically shows changes over time.

Skills and Concepts

Lessons 2-1 and 2-2

• To find and analyze the mean of a data set using models and calculations

• To find and analyze the median and mode of a data set

The **mean** of a set of data is the sum of the values divided by the number of data items. The **median** is the middle value when data are arranged in numerical order. The **mode** is the value or item that appears most often.

Find the mean, median, and mode of each data set.

6. 34, 49, 63, 43, 50, 50, 26

7. 3, 7, 1, 9, 9, 5, 8

Lesson 2-3

• To analyze a set of data by finding the range and by making frequency tables and line plots

A **frequency table** lists each item in a data set with the number of times the item occurs. A **line plot** displays a data set by stacking **✗**'s above each data value on a number line.

8. Make a frequency table showing the number of times each vowel occurs in the paragraph above. Consider y a vowel.

9. Make a line plot showing the number of times the words *the, and, a,* and *of* appear in the paragraph above.

Lesson 2-4

- To make and analyze bar graphs and line graphs

A **bar graph** is used to compare amounts. A **line graph** shows how an amount changes over time.

Tickets Use the table at the right.

10. Make a line graph of the data.

11. Make a bar graph of the data.

12. Is a line graph or bar graph more appropriate for the ticket price data? Explain.

Ticket Prices

Year	Price
1985	$10
1990	$15
1995	$20
2000	$25
2005	$30

Lesson 2-5

- To use spreadsheets to display data and solve problems

You can use a **spreadsheet** to organize and analyze data. A **cell** is the spreadsheet box where a row and column meet. A formula is a statement of a mathematical relationship.

	A	B	C	D	E
1	Date	Kite Sales ($)	String Sales ($)	Book Sales ($)	Total Sales ($)
2	9/9	50	8	145	■
3	9/10	75	6	125	■

13. Which cells are for kite sales?

14. What is the value of B3?

15. Write the formula for cell E2.

Lessons 2-6 and 2-7

- To make and analyze stem-and-leaf plots
- To identify misleading graphs and statistics

A **stem-and-leaf plot** uses digits to show the shape of data.

16. Make a stem-and-leaf plot of the data: 507, 301, 479, 367, 543, 388, 512, 479, 483, 379, 548, 341, 399, 465.

Which measure best describes the data—mean, median, or mode?

17. 72, 67, 62, 77, 82

18. 1, 1.5, 4.5, 8, 4.5, 12

19. win, loss, tie, tie, tie, loss

20. 0, 3, 39, 2, 1, 7, 4, 9, 5

21. Every week you take a math quiz. The data in Exercise 18 show the scores of your first 5 quizzes. Explain how you would graph the data to show a very small difference in scores.

1. Find the mean, median, mode, and range of the data set: 31, 20, 31, 51, 27.

The numbers of children in 15 families are 1, 3, 2, 1, 3, 1, 2, 6, 2, 3, 3, 4, 3, 4, and 5.

2. Find the median, mode, and range.

3. Make a frequency table of the data.

4. Make a line plot of the data.

5. **Profits** A business has weekly profits of $5,000, $3,000, $2,000, $2,500, and $5,000. Why is using the mode to describe this data set misleading?

6. The spreadsheet below shows three quiz scores for two students. Write formulas for cells E2 and E3.

	A	B	C	D	E
1	Student	Q 1	Q 2	Q 3	Mean
2	Yori	81	95	88	▪
3	Sarah	78	81	87	▪

7. Make a stem-and-leaf plot for these state-fair pumpkin weights (pounds): 288, 207, 210, 212, 226, 233, 212, 218, 247, 262, 269, 203, 271.

Reading Twelve people estimated the time, in minutes, they spend reading each day. Their responses are below.
20, 5, 45, 90, 60, 45, 30, 10, 30, 45, 15, 25

8. Find the mean, median, mode, and range of the data.

9. Which would you use to describe the data—the mean, median, or mode?

10. **Writing in Math** What type of data display would you use for the data? Explain.

11. **Enrollment** Use the bar graph below. Which grade level has the fewest students enrolled?

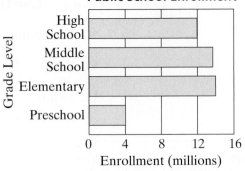

Public School Enrollment

SOURCE: U.S. Department of Education. Go to **PHSchool.com** for a data update. Web Code: aqg-9041

12. **Hot Lunches** Use the line graph below. What is the median number of students buying lunch?

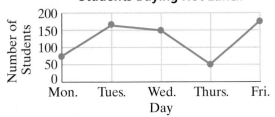

Students Buying Hot Lunch

Use the stem-and-leaf plot below.

5	0 2 6
6	1 3 6 7
7	4 8 9
8	0 1

Key: 5 | 0 means 5.0

13. How many stems are there?

14. How many leaves are there?

15. Find the range.

16. Find the median.

Reading Comprehension

Read each passage and answer the questions that follow.

> **Age of Leadership** In 1787 twelve of the original thirteen states sent delegates to Philadelphia to work on forming a government for our new country. In all, 55 delegates attended. You probably know some of their names: James Madison (36 years old), Alexander Hamilton (32), George Washington (55), and Benjamin Franklin (the oldest delegate, at 81).

1. What is the mean age of the delegates mentioned in the passage?
   - (A) 32
   - (B) 45
   - (C) 51
   - (D) 55

2. What is the median age of the delegates mentioned?
   - (F) 32
   - (G) 45.5
   - (H) 51
   - (J) 55

3. The mean age of all of the delegates was 42. What was the sum of the ages of all 55 delegates?
   - (A) 2,106 years
   - (B) 2,310 years
   - (C) 2,501 years
   - (D) 2,525 years

4. Franklin was in poor health and did not attend many of the meetings. Suppose a 60-year-old delegate replaced him. How would that affect the mean and the median ages of the four delegates mentioned in the passage?
   - (F) The mean would be lower.
   - (G) The median would be lower.
   - (H) The mean and median would both be lower.
   - (J) Neither the mean nor the median would change.

> **Math in Space** The first American astronaut to circle Earth was John Glenn. In 1962, Glenn made three orbits at an average speed of 17,544 miles per hour. He traveled a total distance of 75,679 miles. This was only a short trip into space. Soon astronauts would be looking beyond Earth orbit to the moon, about 240,000 miles away.

5. Based on the passage, about how far did Glenn travel in one orbit around Earth?
   - (A) 25 miles
   - (B) 17,544 miles
   - (C) 25,000 miles
   - (D) 52,632 miles

6. About how long did an average orbit take?
   - (F) 1.4 hours
   - (G) 4.3 hours
   - (H) 10 hours
   - (J) 13 hours

7. At Glenn's rate of travel, about how long would it take to reach the moon?
   - (A) 10 hours
   - (B) 14 hours
   - (C) 24 hours
   - (D) 38 hours

8. *Apollo 11* took about 3 days to go from Earth orbit to moon orbit. About how fast was *Apollo 11*'s average speed?
   - (F) 80,000 mi/h
   - (G) 17,544 mi/h
   - (H) 10,000 mi/h
   - (J) 3,333 mi/h

Applying Data Analysis

A Peak Experience Earth's highest natural features, its great mountains, dwarf even the tallest structures made by humans. The air at the top of Mt. Everest, in the Himalayan mountains, is three times thinner than the air at sea level. Because of the thin air, numbing cold, and unpredictable weather, it takes even the most experienced climbers many weeks to reach the top of Mt. Everest.

Mt. Aconcagua is the highest peak in South America at 6,960 meters.

Mt. Elbrus is Europe's highest peak at 5,642 meters.

Mt. Kilimanjaro, in Tanzania, rises to 5,895 meters.

Mt. Everest towers over volcanoes like Mt. Kilimanjaro, Fujiyama, and Mt. Vesuvius.

Fujiyama is Japan's highest peak at 3,776 meters.

Mt. Vesuvius, in Italy, is 1,277 meters high.

It's All Relative

Although Kilimanjaro is 2,955 meters shorter than Everest, it is still 40 times as tall as the Great Pyramid in Egypt.

Volcanic Storm

Mount St. Helens, a volcano in Washington state, erupted on May 18, 1980, throwing huge clouds of ash into the sky. Before the eruption, the summit was 2,950 meters high. Afterward, it was about 400 meters lower.

Mt. Cook is New Zealand's highest peak at 3,754 meters.

Mt. St. Helens: 2,550 meters

Put It All Together

Data File Use the information on these two pages and on page 650 to answer these questions.

1. **a.** Write the names of the mountain peaks in the table on page 650 in order from highest to lowest elevation.
   b. Graph the data (in meters) on a number line. Label each point with the name of the mountain.
   c. Insert data points and labels for New Zealand's highest mountain, Mt. Cook, and the Matterhorn, in the European Alps.
2. How tall is Hawaii's Mauna Kea?

Mt. Everest: 8,850 meters

Yaks can live at elevations as high as 6,000 meters.

Edmund Hillary and Sherpa Tenzing Norgay, the first people to climb Mt. Everest, pitched their base camp at 5,486 meters.

Mauna Kea   Mt. Everest

Mauna Kea is a volcano in Hawaii. Measured from its base on the ocean floor, Mauna Kea is 1,352 meters taller than Mt. Everest.

Mt. McKinley is the highest peak in North America at 6,194 meters.

Vinson Massif, Antarctica: 4,897 meters

The Matterhorn, in the European Alps, is 4,478 meters above sea level.

Mont Blanc, in the European Alps: 4,810 meters

3. What did the height of Mount St. Helens become after its eruption in 1980?

4. A mountain climber scaled both Mont Blanc and the Matterhorn. How many meters did she climb?

5. a. **Estimation** About how tall is the Great Pyramid of Egypt?
   b. About how many times taller than the Great Pyramid is Mt. Everest?

6. **Number Sense** Suppose a Sherpa has guided climbers 12 times from a base camp at 5,486 meters to the peak of Mt. Everest. How many kilometers of vertical elevation has he traveled as a guide?

Straight to the Top
Sherpas are people who live in the Himalayas. Many Sherpas act as guides on Mt. Everest.

Go Online
PHSchool.com
For: Information about mountains
Web Code: aqe-0253

CHAPTER 3

Patterns and Variables

What You've Learned

- In Chapter 1, you learned to add, subtract, multiply, and divide decimals.

- You used rounding and compatible numbers to estimate with decimals.

- You used the order of operations to simplify expressions.

 **Check Your Readiness**

GO for Help

For Exercises	See Lesson
1–4	1-4
5–10	1-7
11–13	1-8
14–16	1-9

Using the Order of Operations
Find the value of each expression.

1. $3 \times 8 + 5$

2. $36 + 6 \div 2$

3. $48 - 6 \times 5$

4. $(23 - 18) \times 6$

Adding and Subtracting Decimals
First estimate. Then find each sum or difference.

5. $36.05 + 6.1$

6. $36 - 26.5$

7. $0.05 + 5.05$

8. $5.2 - 3.04$

9. $5.12 - 2.85$

10. $9.8 + 4.56$

Multiplying Decimals
Find each product.

11. 3.79×5

12. 6.4×3.04

13. 43.7×7.1

Dividing Decimals
Find each quotient.

14. $13.2 \div 4$

15. $85 \div 0.5$

16. $1.917 \div 2.7$

What You'll Learn Next

- In this chapter, you will learn to use algebraic expressions to describe relationships and patterns.

- You will use mental math to estimate solutions to equations.

- You will use addition, subtraction, multiplication, and division to solve equations.

- You will write equations to solve problems.

◀)) Key Vocabulary

- algebraic expression (p. 113)
- arithmetic sequence (p. 123)
- conjecture (p. 108)
- Distributive Property (p. 144)
- equation (p. 124)
- evaluate (p. 114)
- inverse operations (p. 130)
- numerical expression (p. 113)
- open sentence (p. 125)
- sequence (p. 109)
- solution (p. 125)
- term (p. 108)
- variable (p. 113)

 Problem Solving Application On pages 154 and 155, you will work an extended activity on patterns.

3-1 Describing a Pattern

Check Skills You'll Need

1. **Vocabulary Review** To order numbers, you compare the place and ? of each digit.

Order each set of decimals from least to greatest.

2. 3.331, 3.1, 3.31

3. 0.105, 0.0105, 10.5

for Help
Lesson 1-6

What You'll Learn

To find and write rules for number patterns

🔊 **New Vocabulary** term, conjecture, sequence

Why Learn This?

You can see patterns in nature, art, and music. You can use math to describe the patterns.

The numbers 1, 4, 7, 10, . . . form a number pattern. Each number in the pattern is a **term.** The three dots after the number 10 tell you that the pattern continues.

When you predict terms in a number pattern, you are making a conjecture. A **conjecture** is a prediction about what may happen.

EXAMPLE Finding Number Patterns

1 **Decorating** Jacob is making a pattern of tiles. The first four designs are shown. How many tiles will be in the fifth and sixth designs?

   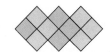

Count the tiles in each design. You can make a table to display the information. Each design has three more tiles than the one before it.

Design Number	1	2	3	4	5	6
Number of Tiles	1	4	7	10	13	16

← Add 3 to 10 to get the fifth term.
Add 3 to 13 to get the sixth term.

+3 +3

So the fifth and sixth designs have 13 and 16 tiles.

Quick Check

1. The eighth design will go all the way across Jacob's wall. How many tiles will be in the eighth design?

Sometimes you can use a rule to describe a pattern. A rule states the first term and an explanation of the operations you use to find the next term.

For: Exploring Patterns Activity
Use: Interactive Textbook, 3-1

EXAMPLE Using a Rule to Write a Pattern

② Write the first six terms in the number pattern described by this rule: *Start with 1 and multiply by 2 repeatedly.*

The first term is 1.

$\times 2 \quad \times 2 \quad \times 2 \quad \times 2 \quad \times 2$

1, 2, 4, 8, 16, 32 ← Multiply each term by 2 to find the next term.

✓ **Quick Check**

2. Write the first six terms in each number pattern.
   a. Start with 90 and subtract 15 repeatedly.
   b. Start with 1 and multiply by 3 repeatedly.

A **sequence** is a set of numbers that follow a pattern.

EXAMPLE Writing a Rule

③ **Multiple Choice** Each number in the sequence below has the same relationship to the number immediately before it.

14.7, 13.4, 12.1, 10.8, . . .

How can you find the next number in the sequence?
Ⓐ By adding 1.3 to the previous number
Ⓑ By subtracting 1.3 from the previous number
Ⓒ By multiplying the previous number by 1.3
Ⓓ By dividing the previous number by 1.3

$-1.3 \quad -1.3 \quad -1.3 \quad -1.3$

14.7, 13.4, 12.1, 10.8, 9.5 ← To get from one term to the next, subtract 1.3.

The rule is *start with 14.7 and subtract 1.3 repeatedly.* The correct answer is choice B.

Test Prep Tip ⒶⒷⒸⒹ

Always check your answer by testing the answer in the original problem.

✓ **Quick Check**

3. Write a rule for each pattern. Then write the next three terms.
   a. 1.5, 4.5, 13.5, 40.5, . . .
   b. 256, 128, 64, . . .

Check Your Understanding

1. **Vocabulary** A prediction about what may happen is a _?_.

2. Look at the coins. Describe a pattern that you see.

Write a rule for each number pattern.

3. 53, 49, 45, 41, . . . Start with ■ and subtract ■ repeatedly.

4. 2; 10; 50; 250; . . . Start with ■ and multiply by ■ repeatedly.

Homework Exercises

For more exercises, see Extra Skills and Word Problems.

GO for Help

For Exercises	See Example
5–9	1
10–11	2
12–15	3

Write the next two terms in each number pattern.

5. 2, 6, 10, 14, . . .

6. 99, 88, 77, 66, . . .

7. 1, 5, 25, 125, . . .

8. 1, 1.4, 1.8, 2.2, . . .

9. The years 2000, 2004, 2008, and 2012 are leap years. Find the next three leap years.

Write the first six terms in each number pattern.

10. Start with 7 and add 4 repeatedly.

11. Start with 512 and divide by 2 repeatedly.

Write a rule for each pattern. Then write the next three terms.

12. 100, 89, 78, 67, . . .

13. 0.12, 1.2, 12, 120, . . .

14. 600,000; 60,000; 6,000; . . .

15. $2.85, $5.70, $8.55, . . .

GPS 16. **Guided Problem Solving** You buy 75 pounds of food for your pet llama. You feed her 6.7 pounds of food each day. You will buy more food when you have less than 20 pounds left. After how many days will you buy more llama food?

- The rule is *start with* ■ *and subtract* ■ *repeatedly.*

Day	0	1	2	3	4
Amount of Food (lb)	75	68.3	■	■	■

−6.7 −6.7 −6.7 −6.7

17. Look for a pattern in the table. Find each missing term.

Number of Feet	1	2	3	4	5
Number of Inches	12	24	36	■	■

18. **Business** A dry cleaner charges $5.00 to clean one item. She offers to clean a second item for $4.50 and a third item for $4.00.
   a. If she continues to subtract $.50 for each additional item, how much will it cost to clean six items?
   b. If the pattern continues, which item will be cleaned for free?

19. **Astronomy** Edmond Halley (1656–1742) first saw the comet named for him in 1682. He correctly predicted that it would return about every 76 years. About how old will you be when the comet returns next?

20. **Open-Ended** Write a number pattern and its rule. The third term in your number pattern must equal 12.

21. **Geometry** Draw the next design for the pattern.

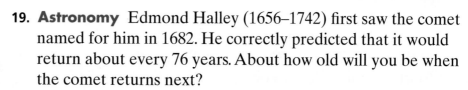

22. **Challenge** Write a rule for 156, 78, 76, 38, 36, 18, 16, . . . Then write the next three terms in the pattern.

Test Prep and Mixed Review   **Practice**

Multiple Choice

23. Each number in the sequence 2, 8, 14, 20, . . . has the same relationship to the number immediately before it. How can you find the next number in the sequence?
   Ⓐ Multiply the previous number by 4.
   Ⓑ Divide the previous number by 4.
   Ⓒ Add 6 to the previous number.
   Ⓓ Subtract 6 from the previous number.

24. A gasoline pump shows $2.949 as the price of one gallon of gasoline. About how much gasoline can you buy for $24?
   Ⓕ 8 gallons   Ⓖ 10 gallons   Ⓗ 14 gallons   Ⓙ 16 gallons

GO for Help

For Exercises	See Lesson
25–27	1-7

First estimate. Then find each sum or difference.

25. $17.2 - 4.5$ **26.** $2.005 + 2.307$ **27.** $8.01 + 1.7 + 1.09$

Patterns and Expressions

You can use a table to record data as you explore a pattern. A table can help you represent the pattern using symbols.

ACTIVITY

1. The first three designs in a pattern are shown at the right. Continue the pattern. Sketch the fourth and fifth designs on grid paper.

2. How many squares are in the fourth design? In the fifth design?

3. Copy and complete the table.

Design Number	1	2	3	4	5	6	7
Number of Squares	1	5	■	■	■	■	■

4. **Reasoning** Describe how you will find the number of squares in the tenth design of the pattern.

ACTIVITY

5. In each diagram, segments already join point *A* to the points on the circle. Copy each diagram. Join point *A* to the other points on the circle.

6. Copy and complete the table at the right.

Number of points on circle	4	5	6
Number of segments added to each diagram	■	■	■

7. Extend your table to include 7 and 8 points on a circle.

8. (**Algebra**) How many segments would you draw for *n* points on a circle?

3-2 Variables and Expressions

Check Skills You'll Need

1. **Vocabulary Review** What is a mathematical *expression*?

Find the value of each expression.

2. $40 - 16 \div 2$

3. $3 \times 5 + 12 \div 3$

4. $7 \times (95 - 32)$

 **for Help**
Lesson 1-4

What You'll Learn

To evaluate algebraic expressions

🔊 **New Vocabulary** numerical expression, variable, algebraic expression, evaluate

Why Learn This?

You do not know how many people will attend a school fair. You can use a variable to represent the number of people.

A **numerical expression** is a mathematical phrase with only numbers and operation symbols $(+, -, \times, \div)$. An example of a numerical expression is $8 + 5 - 2$.

In the expressions below, n, d, b, and x are variables. A **variable** is a symbol that can represent one or more numbers. A mathematical expression with one or more variables is an **algebraic expression.**

$$n + 2 \qquad 5d \qquad 7b - 2 \qquad 12x \div 3$$

You can use algebra tiles to model algebraic expressions.

☐ A yellow tile represents 1.

▌ A green tile represents a variable.

Test Prep Tip

The expression $5d$ means "5 times a number d." It can also be written as $5 \times d$ and $5 \cdot d$.

EXAMPLE Modeling With Algebra Tiles

❶ Model the expression $5x + 3$ with algebra tiles.

← 5 green tiles represent $5x$.
3 yellow tiles represent 3.

✓ Quick Check

1. Draw algebra tiles to model the expression $x + 2$.

The title screen of a video game usually asks, "How many players?" The number of players is a variable. The game software uses your entry to set up the game.

To **evaluate** an algebraic expression, you replace each variable with a number. Then you use the order of operations to simplify the expression.

EXAMPLE Evaluating an Algebraic Expression

② Evaluate $2x - 8$ for $x = 11$.

$$2x - 8 = 2(11) - 8 \quad \leftarrow \text{Replace } x \text{ with 11.}$$
$$= 22 - 8 \quad \leftarrow \text{Multiply 2 and 11.}$$
$$= 14 \quad \leftarrow \text{Subtract.}$$

✓ **Quick Check**

2. Evaluate each expression for $x = 7$.
   a. $3x + 15$ b. $5x \div 7$ c. $56 - 4x$

You can evaluate an expression using more than one value. Make a table to organize the different values.

EXAMPLE Application: Fundraising

③ You earn $3 for each person who plays the game at your booth at the school fair. The expression $3p$ represents the amount of money you earn, where p is the number of people who play your game. Copy and complete the table for the given number of people.

School Fair Booth Earnings

Number of People	Process	Amount Earned	
p	$3 \times p$	$3p$	← Substitute each number of people for p.
15	$3 \times$ ■	■	← $3 \times 15 = 45$
40	$3 \times$ ■	■	← $3 \times 40 = 120$
65	$3 \times$ ■	■	← $3 \times 65 = 195$

✓ **Quick Check**

3. How much will you earn from 85 people coming to your booth?

1. **Vocabulary** How are numerical and algebraic expressions different? Give examples.

2. **Number Sense** Will the expression $50 - x$ get *larger*, *smaller*, or *stay the same* as the value of x increases?

Evaluate each expression for $x = 8$.

3. $x + 12$ 4. $80 \div x$ 5. $2x$ 6. $x - 3$

Homework Exercises

For more exercises, see Extra Skills and Word Problems.

GO for Help

For Exercises	See Example
7–14	1
15–19	2
20–23	3

Draw algebra tiles to model each expression.

7. $3x + 5$ 8. $c + 3$ 9. 8 10. $z + 4$

11. $4 + 2x$ 12. $a + 6$ 13. $c + c + c$ 14. $3m + 2$

Evaluate each expression.

15. $24 \div d$ for $d = 3$ 16. $p + 8$ for $p = 6$ 17. $3r - 2$ for $r = 65$

18. $8b - 12$ for $b = 2.1$ 19. $18 - 3y$ for $y = 2.5$

20. **Biking** The rental fee for a bicycle is \$5, plus \$2 for each hour h the bike is rented. The expression for the total cost is $5 + 2h$. Copy and complete the table for the given number of hours.

Hour	Rental Fee
h	$5 + 2h$
1	▓
2	▓
3	▓

Copy and complete each table.

21.

x	x + 6
1	7
4	▓
7	▓

22.

x	7x
2	▓
4	▓
6	▓

23.

x	100 − x
20	▓
35	▓
50	▓

24. **Guided Problem Solving** The formula $P = 2\ell + 2w$ gives the distance around a rectangle with length ℓ and width w. Find P for a rectangle with length 7 cm and width 4 cm.
   • Replace each variable in the formula with the given values.

Evaluate each expression.

25. $11t - 6v$ for $t = 9$ and $v = 4$ **26.** $2ab$ for $a = 35$ and $b = 3$

27. The formula $N = 7 \times \ell \times h$ gives the number of bricks needed for a wall of length ℓ feet and height h feet. How many bricks are needed for a wall with length 22 feet and height 30 feet?

28. Dogs A dog walker charges $10 to walk a large dog and $6 to walk a small dog. She uses $10d + 6s$ to calculate her earnings, where d is the number of large dogs and s is the number of small dogs. How much does she earn for walking each group?
a. 4 large and 2 small dogs   **b.** 6 small dogs

29. Challenge Bob plays a game at the school fair. He starts with 0 points. He gets 25 throws. He wins 12 points for hitting the target and loses 8 points for each miss. Bob ends with a score of 0. How many hits and misses does Bob have?

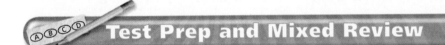

Test Prep and Mixed Review   **Practice**

Multiple Choice

30. Mr. Vasquez can seat 200 people in his restaurant. He has booths that seat 6 people and tables that seat 4 people. So far tonight, Mr. Vasquez has seated 8 full booths. Which method can he use to figure out how many more people he can seat?
Ⓐ Add the product of 6 and 8 to 4.
Ⓑ Subtract the product of 6 and 8 from 200.
Ⓒ Multiply 4 by the sum of 6 and 8.
Ⓓ Divide 200 by the sum of 6 and 4.

31. Each number in the sequence has the same relationship to the number immediately before it.

  1; 20; 400; 8,000; . . .

How can the next number in the sequence be found?
Ⓕ Add 20.   Ⓗ Multiply by 20.
Ⓖ Subtract 20.   Ⓙ Divide by 20.

32. Jenice rides her bike 3.4 miles to school. She takes a different route home. The route home is 3.7 miles. How many miles does Jenice ride each day?
Ⓐ 0.3 miles   Ⓑ 3.5 miles   Ⓒ 6.8 miles   Ⓓ 7.1 miles

GO for Help

For Exercises	See Lesson
33–35	1-8

Find each product.

33. 2.43×12 **34.** 4.05×1.5 **35.** 37.4×0.001

Modeling Expressions

You can draw a diagram to help understand
a word phrase.

Operation	Word Phrase	Diagram 1	Diagram 2
addition	a number m plus 3.2 the sum of a number m and 3.2 3.2 more than a number m	m 3.2	m 3.2
subtraction	a number p minus 6 the difference of a number p and 6 6 subtracted from a number p	p ? 6	p ? 6
multiplication	4 times a number k the product of 4 and a number k	k k k k	k k k k
division	the quotient of a number z and 5 a number z divided by 5	z ? ? ? ? ?	z ? ? ? ? ?

EXAMPLE

1 Draw a diagram for each word phrase.

   a. 2.5 more than x

   x 2.5 or x | 2.5

   b. the product of 3 and w

   w w w or w | w | w

Exercises

Copy and complete the table below. Each line is missing two parts.

Word Phrase	Diagram 1	Diagram 2
1. Height h divided by 6		
2.		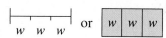
3.	r r r r r r r	
4. 6.3 smaller than t		

3-3 Writing Algebraic Expressions

Check Skills You'll Need

1. Vocabulary Review
What does it mean to *evaluate* an expression?

Evaluate each expression for $a = 7$.

2. $a + 3$

3. $7a - 19$

4. $6 \cdot (a + 1)$

5. $2 + (2a - 5)$

for Help
Lesson 3-2

What You'll Learn

To write algebraic expressions and use them to solve problems

Why Learn This?

Sometimes you need to find a quantity, cost, or amount. You can use an algebraic expression to model the cost of a night out with your family.

You can write a word phrase as an algebraic expression.

Operation	Word Phrase	Algebraic Expression
addition	a number m plus 45 the sum of a number m and 45 45 more than a number m	$m + 45$
subtraction	a number p minus 6 the difference of a number p and 6 6 subtracted from a number p	$p - 6$
multiplication	4 times a number k the product of 4 and a number k	$4k$
division	the quotient of a number z and 25 a number z divided by 25	$z \div 25, \frac{z}{25}$

Online
active math

Writing Algebraic Expressions

For: Algebraic Expressions Activity
Use: Interactive Textbook, 3-3

EXAMPLE From Words to Expressions

1 Write an expression for "the product of 7 and k."

$7 \cdot k$, or $7k$ ← *Product* means multiplication.

Quick Check

1. Write an expression for "2 more than x."

Drawing a diagram can help you write an expression for a real-world situation. Remember to state what the variable represents.

EXAMPLE **Application: Bowling**

2 You go bowling and bowl three games. Shoe rental for the day was $1.75. Write an algebraic expression for the total amount you pay.

Let g = the cost of the game. ← Choose a variable to represent the cost of one game.

Total Cost			
g	g	g	1.75

Each g represents the cost of one game.

The total cost is $3g + 1.75$.

Quick Check

2. Brandon is 28 years younger than his father. Write an expression using Brandon's age to describe his father's age.

You can see the relationship between numbers when they are organized in a table. You can use an algebraic expression to describe this relationship.

EXAMPLE **From a Pattern to an Expression**

Perimeter of Squares

Side Length	Perimeter
2 cm	8 cm
3 cm	12 cm
5 cm	20 cm

3 **Multiple Choice** The table at the left shows the length of the sides of three squares and their perimeters. Which expression can you use to find the perimeter of a square with a side s units long?

Ⓐ $s + 4$ Ⓑ $s - 4$ Ⓒ $4s$ Ⓓ $s \div 4$

Side Length	Process	Perimeter
2 cm	$4 \times 2 = 8$	8 cm
3 cm	$4 \times 3 = 12$	12 cm
5 cm	$4 \times 5 = 20$	20 cm
s cm	$4 \times s = 4s$	$4s$ cm

Look for a relationship between side length and perimeter. It might be "multiply by 4."

Check the rule for the other pairs of numbers.

The expression $4s$ describes the pattern. The correct answer is C.

Quick Check

3. Write an algebraic expression to describe the relationship in the table.

n	▨
2	6
5	9
7	11

More Than One Way

A long-distance call costs 10 cents, plus 4.5 cents for each minute. How much will an 8-minute call cost?

Jessica's Method

I can let m represent the number of minutes. To find the cost of the call, I can use the algebraic expression $10 + 4.5m$. Then I will evaluate the expression for $m = 8$.

$$10 + 4.5m = 10 + 4.5(8) \quad \leftarrow \text{Replace } m \text{ with 8.}$$
$$= 10 + 36 \quad \leftarrow \text{Multiply 4.5 and 8.}$$
$$= 46 \quad \leftarrow \text{Add 10 to 36.}$$

The telephone call will cost 46 cents.

Luis's Method

If one minute costs 4.5 cents, then a two-minute call will cost 9 cents. A four-minute call will cost 18 cents, and an eight-minute call will cost 36 cents. I need to add the 10 cents. So the total cost is 36 cents + 10 cents, or 46 cents.

Choose a Method
Another long-distance plan charges 5 cents per call, plus 4 cents for each minute. Find how much a 10-minute call costs with this plan. Explain why you chose the method you used.

Check Your Understanding

Total	
y	50

1. **Open-Ended** Write a problem that can be represented using the model at the left.

2. **Boating** Renting a paddle boat costs $8 per hour. Write an expression for the cost to rent a paddle boat for h hours.

Write an expression for each word phrase.

3. m increased by 4: ■ + ■

4. y divided by five: ■ ÷ ■

5. six times z: ■ × ■

6. 4 subtracted from m: ■ − ■

For more exercises, see Extra Skills and Word Problems.

GO for Help

For Exercises	See Example
7–16	1–2
17–22	3

Write an expression for each word phrase.

7. 34 less than k

8. 4 plus e

9. d more than 50

10. 23 times q

11. 7 decreased by b

12. b divided by 3

13. 13 minus d

14. a times 32

15. n less than 19

16. Jobs Three brothers earn money by doing yardwork. The brothers split the money equally. Write an expression that describes how much money each brother earns.

Write an expression to describe the relationship in each table.

17.

n	
10	7
12	9
15	12

18.

n	
1	7
2	14
3	21

19.

n	
3	5
4.5	6.5
7	9

20.

n	
42	7
54	9
72	12

21.

n	
1	11
2	22
3	33

22.

n	
30	23
45	38
52	45

23. Guided Problem Solving The largest pan of lasagna weighed 3,477 pounds. The length of the pan was ten times its width. The lasagna pan was 7 feet wide. Find the length.
- You can use the strategy *Draw a Picture* to help you solve the problem.

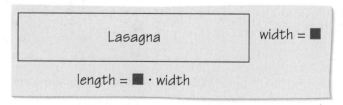

- The expression is ■. The length is ■.

GO Online
Homework Video Tutor
Visit: PHSchool.com
Web Code: aqe-0303

24. Zoos Admission to the zoo costs $3 per person. A family has a coupon for a discount of $5. There are p people in the family. Write an expression to represent how much the family pays.

Write an expression for each word phrase.

25. 5 less than the quotient of *m* and *n*

26. 12 greater than the product of 3 and *j*

27. Space Science In outer space, gravity has less effect on the human body. After a space flight, an astronaut's height can temporarily be 2 inches greater than her normal height *h*. Write an expression for an astronaut's height at the end of a flight.

28. Painting Customers in a paint store use the table at the right to decide how much paint they need.
   a. Write an expression for the number of gallons of paint needed for an area of *A* square feet.
   b. Paint costs $17.95 per gallon. Write an expression to find the cost of the paint needed for an area of *A* square feet.

Area sq. ft.	Gallons
400	1
800	2
2,000	5
3,200	8

29. Challenge A store that personalizes shirts charges $20 for a shirt plus $.75 for each letter. Write an algebraic expression for the cost of *t* shirts using *n* letters each.

Careers Astronaut researchers conduct scientific experiments in space.

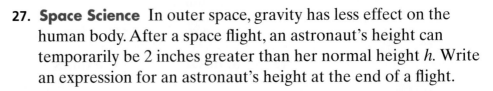
Test Prep and Mixed Review
Practice

Multiple Choice

30. Maria has a box of 20 cookies. She gives 2 cookies to each friend. Which expression shows the number of cookies Maria has left after giving cookies to *m* friends?
   Ⓐ $2m - 20$ Ⓑ $20 - 2m$ Ⓒ $20m - 2$ Ⓓ $20 + 2m$

31. The first four figures in a pattern are shown below.

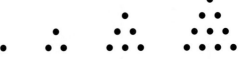

Which statement best describes the tenth figure in the pattern?
   Ⓕ The tenth figure has 10 dots in the bottom row.
   Ⓖ The tenth figure has 12 rows of dots.
   Ⓗ The tenth figure is 7 cm tall.
   Ⓙ The tenth figure has more than 100 dots.

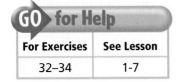

GO for Help

For Exercises	See Lesson
32–34	1-7

Find each sum.

32. $4.432 + 1.009$ **33.** $2.005 + 12.5$ **34.** $2.449 + 0.7$

Arithmetic Sequences

An **arithmetic sequence** is formed by adding a fixed number to or subtracting it from each previous term. You can use an algebraic expression to describe an arithmetic sequence.

EXAMPLE

Consider the sequence modeled in the table at the right. Write an expression to find the term in position n.

Look for a relationship between the position n and the term value.

Position, n	Term Value
1	3.5
2	4.5
3	5.5
4	6.5

Position, n	Process	Term Value
1	$1 + 2.5 = 3.5$	3.5
2	$2 + 2.5 = 4.5$	4.5

For the first two positions, you add 2.5 to the position n.

As the position increases by 1, the term value increases by 1. This can be written as n.

Use the rule to check the remaining values in the table.

Position, n	Process	Term Value
3	$3 + 2.5 = 5.5$	5.5
4	$4 + 2.5 = 6.5$	6.5

The rule applies to all of the number pairs in the table. Write the rule using an algebraic expression.

● The expression for the sequence in the table is $n + 2.5$.

Exercises

Write an algebraic expression for the sequence in each table.

1.

Position, n	Term Value
1	7
3	9
5	11
7	13

2.

Position, n	Term Value
10	6
11	7
12	8
13	9

3.

Position, n	Term Value
1	4
2	5
3	6
4	7

3-4 Using Number Sense to Solve One-Step Equations

✓ Check Skills You'll Need

1. **Vocabulary Review** How can you use front-end estimation to add $3.46 + $6.54?

First estimate. Then find each sum or difference.

2. 5.3 + 1.07

3. 6.1 − 2.4

4. 8 − 6.3

 **for Help**
Lesson 1-7

What You'll Learn

To use mental math to estimate and solve problems

🔊 **New Vocabulary** equation, open sentence, solution

Why Learn This?

Part of the fun of collecting is completing your collection. You can use an equation to find the number of items you still need.

An **equation** is a mathematical sentence that has an equal sign, =. An equation is like a balanced scale.

To be in balance, a scale must have weights with the same total on each side.

$$8 + 4 = 3 \times 4 \quad \leftarrow \begin{array}{l}\text{A true equation has equal values on} \\ \text{each side of the equal sign.}\end{array}$$

If each side of the equation does not have the same value, the equation is false. Use ≠ to indicate that an equation is false.

EXAMPLE **True Equations and False Equations**

1 Is the equation 6 + 13 = 18 true or false?

$$6 + 13 \overset{?}{=} 18 \quad \leftarrow \text{Write the equation.}$$
$$19 \qquad\qquad \leftarrow \text{Add } 6 + 13.$$
$$19 \neq 18 \quad \leftarrow \text{Compare.}$$

The equation is false.

Vocabulary Tip

Read "1 $\overset{?}{=}$ 2" as "Does 1 equal 2?" Read "1 ≠ 2" as "1 does not equal 2."

✓ Quick Check

1. Tell whether each equation is true or false.
   a. $7 \times 9 = 63$ **b.** $4 + 5 = 45$ **c.** $70 - 39 = 41$

An equation with one or more variables is an **open sentence.** A **solution** of an equation is the value of the variable that makes the equation true. For example, $x - 15 = 12$ is an open sentence. Since $27 - 15 = 12$, the value 27 is the solution to $x - 15 = 12$.

You can use mental math to find the solution of some equations.

EXAMPLE Using Mental Math

② **Baseball Cards** How many baseball cards do you need to add to the 14 cards you already own to have a total of 25 cards? Solve the equation $n + 14 = 25$, which models this situation.

What you think

I need to find a number that I can add to 14 and get 25. Since $11 + 14 = 25$, the solution is 11.

I need 11 more cards.

✓ **Quick Check**

2. **Mental Math** Solve each equation.
   a. $17 - x = 8$ **b.** $w \div 4 = 20$ **c.** $4.7 + c = 5.9$

EXAMPLE Guess, Check, and Revise

For help with problem solving strategies, go to the Problem Solving Handbook.

❸ Use the strategy *Guess, Check, and Revise* to solve $n - 43 = 19$.

Estimate Round the numbers to get a good starting point.

$$\begin{array}{ccc} n & - \ 43 & = \ 19 \\ \downarrow & \downarrow & \downarrow \\ n & - \ 40 & = \ 20 \end{array}$$

What you think

Using mental math, I know $60 - 40 = 20$, so n is close to 60.

I can try substituting 60 for n in the equation: $60 - 43 = 17$. The number 17 is too low. I will try $n = 65$: $65 - 43 = 22$. The number 22 is too high. I will try $n = 62$: $62 - 43 = 19$.

Since $62 - 43 = 19$ is true, the solution to $n - 43 = 19$ is 62.

✓ **Quick Check**

3. Use the strategy *Guess, Check, and Revise* to solve $k + 39 = 82$.

There are some open sentences that are true for every value you use for the variable. The algebraic equations that illustrate the number properties are true for all values of *a*, *b*, and *c*.

KEY CONCEPTS **Number Properties**

Identity Properties

The sum of 0 and any number is that number.

The product of 1 and any number is that number.

Arithmetic $0 + 9 = 9$ $\qquad$ $1 \times 9 = 9$
Algebra $\quad 0 + a = a$ $\qquad$ $1 \times a = a$

Commutative Properties Changing the order of addends or factors does not change the sum or the product.

Arithmetic $9 + 6 = 6 + 9$ $\qquad$ $9 \times 6 = 6 \times 9$
Algebra $\quad a + b = b + a$ $\qquad$ $a \times b = b \times a$

Associative Properties Changing the grouping of numbers does not change the sum or the product.

Arithmetic

$9 + (6 + 4) = (9 + 6) + 4$ $\qquad$ $9 \cdot (6 \times 4) = (9 \cdot 6) \times 4$

Algebra

$a + (b + c) = (a + b) + c$ $\qquad$ $a(bc) = (ab)c$

✓ Check Your Understanding

1. **Vocabulary** Why is an equation with one or more variables called an open sentence?

2. **Writing in Math** Explain how to use the strategy *Guess, Check, and Revise* to solve $y + 19 = 42$.

3. **Number Sense** Use the balance scale at the left. What value for *n* will make the equation $n + 3 = 18$ a true equation?

Find the missing number that makes the equation true.

4. ■ $+ 3 = 5$ 5. ■ $\times 4 = 12$

Tell whether each equation is true or false.

6. $5 + 14 = 14 + 5$ 7. $0 \times 9 = 9$ 8. $2 \times 5 = 5 + 2$

9. $0 + 3 = 3$ 10. $1 \cdot y = y$ 11. $x + 1 = x$

For more exercises, see Extra Skills and Word Problems.

GO for Help

For Exercises	See Example
12–14	1
15–20	2
21–26	3

Tell whether each equation is true or false.

12. $3 + 50 = 80$ **13.** $3 + 4 + 2 = 3 + 6$ **14.** $0 \times 5.7 = 5.7$

Solve each equation. Use either mental math or the strategy
Guess, Check, and Revise.

15. $x + 5 = 7$ **16.** $4x = 32$ **17.** $x + 2 = 6.3$

18. $g \div 4 = 2$ **19.** $p - 6 = 25$ **20.** $r + 14 = 23$

21. $6d = 612$ **22.** $k + 9 = 28$ **23.** $p \times 4 = 792$

24. $588 = 3n$ **25.** $b - 23 = 68$ **26.** $w + 13 = 71$

27. Guided Problem Solving Suppose you spent $74.95 for a shirt and a jacket. The shirt cost $20.25. Solve the equation $20.25 + j = 74.95$ to find how much you spent on the jacket.
- You can work a simpler problem to estimate an answer. Use number sense to solve $20 + j = 75$.

28. Pollution When burned, 18 gallons of gasoline produce about 360 pounds of carbon dioxide. Solve the equation $18n = 360$ to find how much carbon dioxide 1 gallon of gasoline produces.

GO Online

Homework Video Tutor
Visit: PHSchool.com
Web Code: aqe-0304

29. You have c pounds of cashews and 2.7 pounds of peanuts. You have 6 pounds of nuts altogether. Solve the equation $c + 2.7 = 6$ to find how many pounds of cashews you have.

30. Challenge Use estimation to check whether 59.4 is a reasonable solution to $x + 27.6 = 31.8$. Explain your answer.

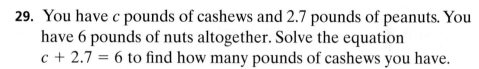

Test Prep and Mixed Review

Practice

Multiple Choice

31. Sue was 30 years old when her daughter Amy was born. If s represents Sue's age, which expression describes Amy's age?
   Ⓐ $s + 30$ Ⓑ $s - 30$ Ⓒ $30 - s$ Ⓓ $30s$

32. A bus has 25 passengers at the beginning of its route. At each stop, 5 people get off the bus and one person gets on. After how many stops will there be one passenger on the bus?
   Ⓕ 4   Ⓖ 5   Ⓗ 6   Ⓙ 10

GO for Help

For Exercise	See Lesson
33	3-1

33. Write the next three terms in the sequence 4, 12, 36, 108, . . .

Vocabulary Builder

High-Use Academic Words

High-use academic words are words that you will see often in textbooks and on tests. These words are not math vocabulary terms, but knowing them will help you to succeed in mathematics.

Direction Words

Some words tell what to do in a problem. I need to understand what these words are asking so that I give the correct answer.

Word	Meaning
Identify	To show that you recognize something
List	To present information in order or to give examples
Justify	To give reasons supporting a decision or conclusion

Exercises

1. Identify each animal as a pet or a wild animal.
   a. kitten   **b.** elephant   **c.** dog   **d.** crocodile

2. List five animals you could keep as a pet.

3. Justify your answer to Exercise 2.

4. Identify each expression as numerical or algebraic.
   a. $n \div 10$ **b.** $5 + (6 - 2) \div 3$ **c.** $5x - y$ **d.** $(1 + 3) \cdot (10 - 3)$

5. List 3 different examples of an algebraic expression.

6. Is $10x$ a numerical expression? Justify your answer.

7. **Word Knowledge** Think about the word *pattern*.
   a. Choose the letter for how well you know the word.
       A. I know its meaning.
       B. I've seen it, but I don't know its meaning.
       C. I don't know it.
   b. **Research** Look up and write a definition for *pattern*.
   c. Write a sentence involving mathematics and using the word *pattern*.

Write a rule for each pattern. Then write the next three terms.

1. 1, 6, 36, 216, . . .　　　**2.** 285, 270, 255, 240, . . .　　**3.** 50, 5, 0.5, 0.05, . . .

(Algebra) **Evaluate each expression for $x = 7$.**

4. $8x$　　　　　　　**5.** $3 \cdot (x - 4)$　　　　　**6.** $x \cdot (x + 3)$

Write an expression for each word phrase.

7. d less than 17　　　　**8.** a times e　　　　　**9.** 14 divided by q

---

3-5a 　Activity Lab

Hands On

Modeling Equations

To solve an equation using models, get
the variable by itself on one side.

EXAMPLE　Addition Equations

Solve $x + 7 = 15$.

$$x + 7 = 15$$

← Model the equation.

$$x + 7 - 7 = 15 - 7$$

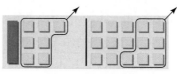

← Remove 7 tiles from each side.
This will keep the equation balanced.

$$x = 8$$

← Find the solution.

Exercises

Solve each equation by drawing models or using tiles.

1. $x + 2 = 7$　　　**2.** $5 + c = 35$　　　**3.** $7 + m = 21$　　　**4.** $8 = n + 5$

129

3-5 Solving Addition Equations

Check Skills You'll Need

1. **Vocabulary Review** How can you tell that an equation is an *open sentence*?

Use mental math to solve each equation.

2. $5 = 4 + t$

3. $x + 4 = 74$

4. $7 + x = 21$

 **for Help**
Lesson 3-4

What You'll Learn

To use subtraction to solve equations

🔊 **New Vocabulary** inverse operations, Subtraction Property of Equality

Why Learn This?

As living things grow, their height and weight change. You can use an equation to find the change.

In the equation $x + 4 = 38$, 4 is added to a variable. To solve the equation, you need to get the variable alone on one side of the equal sign.

To get the variable alone, you *undo* the operation. You undo adding 4 by subtracting 4. Operations that undo each other are **inverse operations.**

EXAMPLE Solving Equations by Subtracting

1. Solve $x + 4 = 38$.

Get x alone on one side of the equation.

$$x + 4 = 38$$
$$x + 4 - 4 = 38 - 4 \quad \leftarrow \text{Subtract 4 from each side to undo the addition and get } x \text{ by itself.}$$
$$x = 34 \quad \leftarrow \text{Simplify.}$$

Check $\quad x + 4 = 38 \quad \leftarrow$ Check your solution in the original equation.

$$34 + 4 \stackrel{?}{=} 38 \quad \leftarrow \text{Substitute 34 for } x.$$
$$38 = 38 ✔$$

GO for Help

For help with evaluating expressions, go to Lesson 3-2, Example 2.

✓ Quick Check

1. Solve $w + 4.3 = 9.1$. Check the solution.

When you solve problems using equations, drawing a diagram may help. The model indicates that the whole = part + part.

Whole	
Part	Part

EXAMPLE Application: Cats

2 When a kitten was brought home it weighed 15 ounces. After two years, the kitten had grown into a cat weighing 120 ounces. How many ounces did the cat gain?

Weight after 2 years	
Original weight	Ounces gained

Let g = the number of ounces gained.

120	
15	g

The equation $15 + g = 120$ models this situation.

$$15 + g = 120$$
$$15 + g - 15 = 120 - 15 \quad \leftarrow \text{Subtract 15 from each side to undo the addition.}$$
$$g = 105 \quad \leftarrow \text{Simplify.}$$

The cat gained 105 ounces.

✓ Quick Check

2. A cat has gained 1.8 pounds in a year. It now weighs 11.6 pounds. Write and solve an equation to find how much it weighed one year ago. Check the solution.

GO Online

Video Tutor Help
Visit: PHSchool.com
Web Code: aqe-0775

When you use inverse operations to solve equations, you are using a mathematical property. The property you use in this lesson is called the **Subtraction Property of Equality.**

KEY CONCEPTS Subtraction Property of Equality

If you subtract the same value from each side of an equation, the two sides remain equal.
Arithmetic $2 \cdot 3 = 6$, so $2 \cdot 3 - 4 = 6 - 4$.
Algebra If $a = b$, then $a - c = b - c$.

Check Your Understanding

1. **Vocabulary** What is the inverse operation of adding 6?

2. **Open-Ended** Write a real-world problem that can be represented using this model.

8	
n	3

Test Prep Tip

Drawing a diagram can help you model a real-world situation.

Solve each equation.

3. $d + 3 = 21$

21	
d	3

4. $k + 5.1 = 7.4$

7.4	
k	5.1

5. $x + 4.3 = 7$

7	
x	4.3

Homework Exercises

For more exercises, see Extra Skills and Word Problems.

GO for Help

For Exercises	See Example
6–17	1
18–19	2

Solve each equation. Check the solution. Remember, you can draw a diagram to help you solve an equation.

6. $x + 46 = 72$

7. $d + 5 = 53$

8. $y + 12 = 64$

9. $n + 17 = 56$

10. $m + 1.3 = 2.8$

11. $n + 4.5 = 10.8$

12. $14.7 = 5 + f$

13. $31 + y = 82$

14. $28 + g = 72$

15. $15 = k + 8.2$

16. $2.7 + g = 8.2$

17. $2.6 = 1.9 + g$

Write and solve an equation. Then check the solution.

18. You build 7 model airplanes during the summer. At the end of the summer, you have 25 model airplanes. How many model airplanes did you have before the summer?

19. **Music History** Wolfgang Amadeus Mozart wrote his first piano sonata in 1762, when he was 6 years old. In what year was Mozart born?

20. **Guided Problem Solving** Jeans that were on sale last week now cost $29.97. The savings were $4.99. Write and solve an equation to find the sale price of the jeans.
    • You can draw a diagram to help you write an equation.

Full price of jeans	
Sale price p	Savings $4.99

21. Music You add a 4-minute song to your digital music player. The player now has 2 hours of music. Use an equation to find how much music was on the player before you added the song.

22. In a number square, the sum of the numbers in each row, column, and main diagonal is the same.
   a. Find the sum for the number square at the right.
   b. Use the sum to write and solve equations to find the values of a, b, and c.

a	7	2
1	5	b
8	c	4

23. Biology A hippopotamus can hold its breath for about 15 minutes. It can hold its breath 5 minutes longer than a sea otter. Use an equation to find how long a sea otter can hold its breath.

Solve each equation. Then check the solution.

24. $y + 13.82 = 24$ **25.** $1.5 + x = 9.7$ **26.** $0.4 + g = 1.9$

27. $6.2 = j + 5.91$ **28.** $b + 0.87 = 1$ **29.** $11.4 = h + 5.9$

30. Challenge A large stepping stone weighs five times as much as a brick. Together, one brick and one stepping stone weigh 30 pounds. Find the weight of the stepping stone.

Test Prep and Mixed Review   **Practice**

Multiple Choice

31. The table shows the length and perimeter of different rectangles with a width of 3 cm. Which expression can be used to find the perimeter of a rectangle with a length of n units?

Side Length	Perimeter
5 cm	16 cm
10 cm	26 cm
15 cm	36 cm

   Ⓐ $n + 5$ Ⓑ $n + 10$ Ⓒ $n + 11$ Ⓓ $2n + 6$

32. Which of the following does NOT describe 1, 3, 5, 7, 9, . . .?
   Ⓕ List every other whole number, starting with 1.
   Ⓖ Start with 1 and add 2 repeatedly.
   Ⓗ The value of term n in $2n - 1$.
   Ⓙ Start with 1 and add 3 repeatedly.

(Algebra) Write the first five terms in each number pattern.

33. Start with 37 and add 3 repeatedly.

34. Start with 3.2 and multiply by 5 repeatedly.

GO for Help

For Exercises	See Lesson
33–34	3-1

3-6 Solving Subtraction Equations

Check Skills You'll Need

1. Vocabulary Review Explain why the number 4 is a *solution* to $x + 2 = 6$.

Use mental math to solve each equation.

2. $t - 4 = 10$

3. $x - 6 = 5$

4. $p - 7 = 3$

 **for Help**
Lesson 3-4

What You'll Learn

To use addition to solve equations

🔊 **New Vocabulary** Addition Property of Equality

Why Learn This?

Nutritional information on products can help you decide what you should eat. You can use an equation to find the nutritional contents of foods.

You learned to solve equations by subtracting the same amount from each side of an equation. You can also solve equations by using addition.

KEY CONCEPTS **Addition Property of Equality**

If you add the same value to each side of an equation, the two sides remain equal.

Arithmetic $2 \cdot 3 = 6$, so $2 \cdot 3 + 4 = 6 + 4$.
Algebra   If $a = b$, then $a + c = b + c$.

Some equations have a number subtracted on one side. To get the variable by itself, add the same number to each side of the equation.

EXAMPLE **Solving an Equation by Adding**

1 Solve $c - 12 = 43$.

c	
12	43

$$c - 12 + 12 = 43 + 12 \quad \leftarrow \text{Add 12 to each side to undo the subtraction.}$$

$$c = 55 \quad \leftarrow \text{Simplify.}$$

Quick Check

1. a. Solve $n - 53 = 28$.   **b.** Solve $x - 43 = 12$.

Another way to model a real-world situation is to state the problem as simply as you can. Then use your statement to write an equation.

EXAMPLE Application: Nutrition

Test Prep Tip Ⓐ Ⓑ Ⓒ Ⓓ
Verbs such as *is, are, has,* and *was* show you where to place the = sign.

② **Gridded Response** A serving of wheat flakes contains 3.7 mg of zinc. The amount of zinc in wheat flakes is 1.75 mg less than the amount in a breakfast bar. How much zinc is in a breakfast bar?

Words   amount in flakes is 1.75 less than amount in bar

Let b = the amount of zinc in a breakfast bar.

Equation   3.7   = b −   1.75

$$b - 1.75 = 3.7$$ ← Write the equation.

$$b - 1.75 + 1.75 = 3.7 + 1.75$$ ← Add 1.75 to each side to undo the subtraction.

$$b = 5.45$$ ← Simplify.

The breakfast bar contains 5.45 mg of zinc.

✓ Quick Check

2. **Temperature** The temperature dropped 9°F between 7 P.M. and midnight. It was 54°F at midnight. Use an equation to find the temperature at 7 P.M.

✓ Check Your Understanding

1. **Error Analysis** Your friend says the solution to $y - 4 = 24$ is 20. What did your friend do wrong?

2. Sheila is 2 years younger than Javon. Sheila is 10 years old. Write and solve an equation to find Javon's age.

   Words: Sheila is 2 years younger than Javon.

             Let j = Javon's age in years.

   Equation: ■ = j − ■

Match each equation with the correct solution.

3. $x - 3 = 7$

4. $x - 4 = 11$

5. $x - 5 = 6$

   A. 15
   B. 11
   C. 10

For more exercises, see Extra Skills and Word Problems.

GO for Help

For Exercises	See Example
6–17	1
18	2

Solve each equation. You may find a model helpful.

6. $x - 16 = 72$ **7.** $q - 2.4 = 1.8$ **8.** $n - 297 = 18$

9. $d - 68 = 40$ **10.** $y - 12 = 23$ **11.** $k - 56 = 107$

12. $5.8 = n - 0.35$ **13.** $0.6 = h - 2.9$ **14.** $q - 8.2 = 154$

15. $p - 1.23 = 8.77$ **16.** $n - 10.5 = 11.7$ **17.** $x - 5.7 = 5.7$

18. Geography The area of Cape Canaveral National Seashore in Florida is about 57,662 acres. That is about 72,772 acres less than the area of Padre Island National Seashore in Texas. Use an equation to find the area of Padre Island National Seashore.

19. Guided Problem Solving A healthy person has a normal temperature of about 98.6°F. Suppose a sick person needs to decrease his temperature by 3.7°F to return to normal. Use an equation to find the sick person's temperature.
- What equation will you use to model this problem?
- What operation will you use to solve the equation?

GO Online
Homework Video Tutor
Visit: PHSchool.com
Web Code: aqe-0306

20. You buy several posters. The total cost is $18.95. You have $7.05 left after you pay. Write and solve an equation to find how much money you had before this purchase.

21. Challenge Sue is 2 years older than Mary. Mary is 3 years younger than Bob. Sue is 11 years old. How old is Bob?

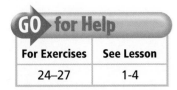
Test Prep and Mixed Review   Practice

Gridded Response

22. A store rents DVDs for $2 each, after you pay a membership fee of $10. Jeremy has spent a total of $26. How many DVDs has he rented?

23. The gas tank in the Rivera family car can hold a maximum of 18.2 gallons. After a trip, they filled the tank with 9.6 gallons of gas. How much gas was in the tank before it was filled?

GO for Help

For Exercises	See Lesson
24–27	1-4

Find the value of each expression.

24. $24 \div 4 - 2 \times 3$ **25.** $24 \div 3 - 2 \times 4$

26. $24 \div (3 - 2) \times 4$ **27.** $(24 \div 3 - 2) \times 4$

Checkpoint Quiz 2

Solve each equation.

1. $5 + x = 65$ **2.** $n - 3.2 = 15$ **3.** $z + 6 = 8.2$ **4.** $k - 4 = 3.6$

5. $14 = 3.2 + y$ **6.** $28 = 1.4 + a$ **7.** $23 = 16 + y$ **8.** $48 = 9.6 + a$

9. You pay for the refreshments at a movie theater with a $10 bill. The refreshments cost $5.73. Write an equation to find how much change you should receive. Solve the equation.

3-7a Activity Lab

Hands On

Modeling Division Equations

Models can help you understand the steps you need to follow to solve an equation.

EXAMPLE Solving Equations by Dividing

Solve $4x = 12$.

$4x = 12$  ← Model the equation.

$4x \div 4 = 12 \div 4$  ← Divide each side of the equation into 4 equal parts.

$x = 3$ 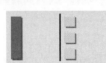 ← Find the solution.

Exercises

Solve each equation by drawing a model or using tiles.

1. $2x = 20$ **2.** $5c = 35$ **3.** $3g = 12$ **4.** $7m = 21$

5. Reasoning Explain how you could use a model to solve $6y = 1.8$.

3-7 Solving Multiplication and Division Equations

What You'll Learn

To use multiplication and division to solve equations

 New Vocabulary Division Property of Equality, Multiplication Property of Equality

Why Learn This?

Many products are sold in groups—cartons, cases, boxes, and bags. You can use an equation to find the cost of a single item.

You can use the **Division Property of Equality** to solve equations involving multiplication.

KEY CONCEPTS **Division Property of Equality**

If you divide each side of an equation by the same nonzero number, the two sides remain equal.

Arithmetic $4 \times 2 = 8$, so $4 \times 2 \div 2 = 8 \div 2$.
Algebra If $a = b$ and $c \neq 0$, then $a \div c = b \div c$.

You recall that $4n$ means 4 times n. To undo multiplication, you divide by the same number. So $4n \div 4 = n$.

🖩 Calculator Tip

Remember that you can never divide by zero. Your calculator will give you an error message if you try.

EXAMPLE **Solving an Equation by Dividing**

1 Solve $4n = 68$.

$$4n \div 4 = 68 \div 4 \quad \leftarrow \text{Divide each side by 4 to undo the multiplication and get } n \text{ alone.}$$
$$n = 17 \quad \leftarrow \text{Simplify.}$$

Check $\quad 4(17) \stackrel{?}{=} 68 \quad \leftarrow \text{Check your solution in the original equation. Replace } n \text{ with 17.}$

$$68 = 68 \; ✔$$

✓ Quick Check

1. Solve $0.8p = 32$. Then check the solution.

EXAMPLE Application: Photography

2 You buy a package containing six rolls of film for your camera. The total cost is $38.88. Use an equation to find the cost of one roll of film.

Use a diagram to model the situation.

Let c = the cost of one roll of film. The equation $6c$ = $38.88 models this situation.

$38.88					
c	c	c	c	c	c

Test Prep Tip

A model can help you understand what operation is needed for the equation.

$$6c = 38.88 \quad \leftarrow \text{Write the equation.}$$
$$6c \div 6 = 38.88 \div 6 \quad \leftarrow \begin{array}{l}\text{Divide each side by 6 to undo the}\\ \text{multiplication and get } c \text{ alone.}\end{array}$$
$$c = 6.48 \quad \leftarrow \text{Simplify.}$$

The cost of one roll of film is $6.48.

✓ Quick Check

2. A club sells greeting cards for a fundraiser. The profit for each card sold is $.35. The club's total profit is $302.75. Use an equation to find the total number of cards the club sells.

You can use the **Multiplication Property of Equality** to solve equations involving division.

KEY CONCEPTS Multiplication Property of Equality

If you multiply each side of an equation by the same number, the two sides remain equal.

Arithmetic $6 \div 2 = 3$, so $(6 \div 2) \times 2 = 3 \times 2$.

Algebra If $a = b$, then $a \cdot c = b \cdot c$.

EXAMPLE Solving an Equation by Multiplying

3 Solve $y \div 6.4 = 8$.

$$y \div 6.4 \times 6.4 = 8 \times 6.4 \quad \leftarrow \begin{array}{l}\text{Multiply by 6.4 to undo the}\\ \text{division and get } y \text{ alone.}\end{array}$$
$$y = 51.2 \quad \leftarrow \text{Simplify.}$$

✓ Quick Check

3. Solve $w \div 1.5 = 10$. Then check the solution.

Check Your Understanding

1. **Vocabulary** How are the Multiplication Property of Equality and the Division Property of Equality different?

Match each equation with the correct model below.

2. $4x = 20$ 3. $x \div 4 = 5$ 4. $5x = 20$ 5. $x \div 5 = 4$

A.
x				
4	4	4	4	4

B.
x			
5	5	5	5

C.
20			
x	x	x	x

D.
20				
x	x	x	x	x

Solve each equation.

6. $3x = 12.6$
   $3x \div \blacksquare = 12.6 \div \blacksquare$

7. $v \div 2 = 7$
   $v \div 2 \cdot \blacksquare = 7 \cdot \blacksquare$

Homework Exercises

For more exercises, see Extra Skills and Word Problems.

GO for Help

For Exercises	See Example
8–17	1–2
18–26	3

Solve each equation. Check the solution. You may find a model helpful.

8. $5a = 100$ 9. $8k = 76$ 10. $7n = 11.9$

11. $25h = 450$ 12. $0.4x = 1$ 13. $75 = 15c$

14. $16j = 80$ 15. $2.5g = 17.5$ 16. $10y = 5$

17. **Farming** An egg carton holds 12 eggs. One day a farmer gathers 8,616 eggs. Write and solve an equation to find how many cartons are needed for the eggs.

Solve each equation. Then check the solution.

18. $q \div 6 = 4$ 19. $a \div 7 = 63$ 20. $n \div 2.5 = 3$

21. $y \div 43 = 1,204$ 22. $10 = k \div 20$ 23. $12 = r \div 9$

24. $n \div 4 = 0.6$ 25. $t \div 0.3 = 1.4$ 26. $b \div 11 = 87$

GPS 27. **Guided Problem Solving** Each volleyball team in a league needs 6 players, 2 alternates, and a coach. How many teams can be formed with 288 people?
   • How many people are needed for each team?
   • Draw a diagram to model this situation.

28. Videos A video store charges the same price to rent each movie. The store collected a total of $80.73 for the rentals shown in the line plot. Use an equation to find the cost to rent one movie.

Number of Movie Rentals

```
                              x
                              x
x                    x        x
x                    x        x
x        x           x        x
x        x    x      x        x
x        x    x      x        x
x        x    x      x        x
M        T    W      T        F
```

29. Biology An elephant's height is about 5.5 times the length of her hind footprint. Use an equation to find the approximate height of an elephant whose hind footprint is 1.5 feet long.

Solve each equation. Check the solution.

30. $y \div 1.6 = 0.256$ **31.** $13 = 65x$ **32.** $30 = p \div 30$

33. $5.6k = 19.152$ **34.** $0.02g = 6$ **35.** $h \div 2.4 = 15$

36. Challenge One of the world's largest oil tankers, the *Jahre Viking*, is so long that if 3.5 identical tankers were placed end to end, they would measure about 1 mile long. Estimate the length, in feet, of the *Jahre Viking*. (*Hint*: 1 mile = 5,280 feet)

ABCD **Test Prep and Mixed Review**   **Practice**

Multiple Choice

37. Tickets to an event cost $25 each. Which equation can you use to find the number of tickets t that you can buy with $100?
  Ⓐ $4t = 100$ Ⓒ $4 + t = 100$
  Ⓑ $25t = 100$ Ⓓ $25 + t = 100$

38. Ashley bought a book for $15.99. She now has $32.12. How much money did Ashley have before she bought the book?
  Ⓕ $16.13   Ⓗ $47.11
  Ⓖ $17.13   Ⓙ $48.11

39. The table shows a sequence of terms. Which expression can be used to find the value of the term in position n?
  Ⓐ $n + 2$ Ⓒ $n + 3$
  Ⓑ $2n$ Ⓓ $3n$

Position, n	Value of Term
1	3
2	6
3	9
n	■

Use <, =, or > to complete each statement.

40. 6 ■ 1.6   **41.** 3.4 ■ 3.40   **42.** 8.05 ■ 5.08

Writing Equations to Solve Problems

Around the World On March 4, 2005, Steve Fossett set a record by completing a nonstop solo jet flight around the world. He landed with 1,515 pounds of fuel. A fuel leak caused a loss of 2,600 pounds of fuel. He started with 18,100 pounds of fuel. How much fuel did the jet use on the flight?

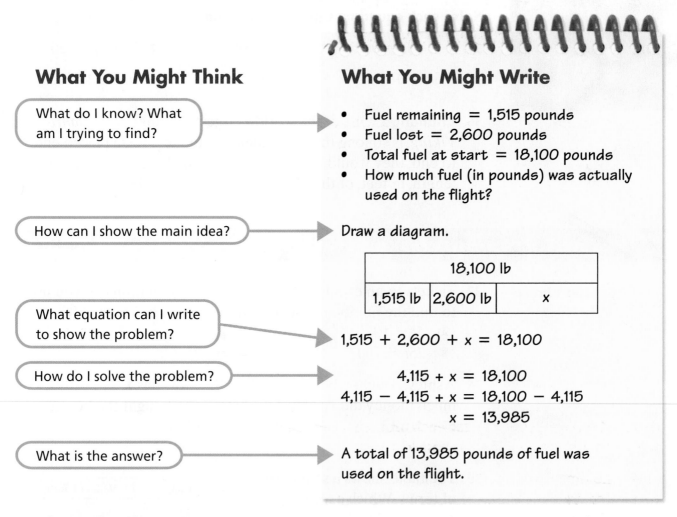

What You Might Think

What do I know? What am I trying to find?

How can I show the main idea?

What equation can I write to show the problem?

How do I solve the problem?

What is the answer?

What You Might Write

- Fuel remaining = 1,515 pounds
- Fuel lost = 2,600 pounds
- Total fuel at start = 18,100 pounds
- How much fuel (in pounds) was actually used on the flight?

Draw a diagram.

18,100 lb		
1,515 lb	2,600 lb	x

$1{,}515 + 2{,}600 + x = 18{,}100$

$$4{,}115 + x = 18{,}100$$
$$4{,}115 - 4{,}115 + x = 18{,}100 - 4{,}115$$
$$x = 13{,}985$$

A total of 13,985 pounds of fuel was used on the flight.

Think It Through

1. Is the answer above reasonable? Explain.

2. Refer to the diagram above. How do you know that the section for *x* must be the largest section?

3. **Reasoning** Suppose the plane had not lost 2,600 lbs of fuel. How much fuel would have been in the plane when it landed?

Exercises

4. The first flight around the world included stops. It was made by Lowell Smith and Alva Harvey in 1924. How many years passed between their flight and Fossett's flight?
   a. What do you know?
   b. What are you trying to find?
   c. Use the diagram below to write and solve an equation.

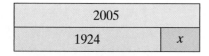

2005	
1924	x

   d. Decide if the answer is reasonable. Tell how you decided.

5. The first altitude record was set in a hot-air balloon. It rose to 82 feet. Fossett's plane flew at 45,000 feet. How many times higher was Fossett's altitude than that of the hot-air balloon? Use the diagram below to write and solve an equation. Round your answer to the nearest tenth.

45,000 ft			
82 ft	82 ft	82 ft	...

6. On October 3, 1967, William Knight flew an X-15 aircraft at 4,520 mph. This is 6.7 times the speed of sound. What is the speed of sound? Use the diagram at the right to help you write and solve an equation. Round your answer to the nearest tenth.

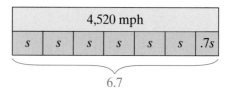

Write and solve an equation for each problem. You can draw a diagram to help you write an equation.

7. At one time the United States had the longest total length of railroad tracks in the world. The 149,129 miles of track could stretch around the world almost six times. What is the distance around the world?

8. In one year, London's Heathrow Airport had 44,262,000 passengers. In the same year, Germany's Frankfurt Airport had 27,546,000 passengers. How many more passengers were there in Heathrow Airport?

What You'll Learn

To use the Distributive Property to simplify expressions in problem solving situations

🔊 **New Vocabulary** Distributive Property

Why Learn This?

The amount you will earn at a job depends on the number of hours you work. The Distributive Property can help you use mental math to calculate your earnings quickly.

The **Distributive Property** shows how multiplication affects addition or subtraction.

The two rectangles below are drawn on graph paper. One rectangle has 3 × 5, or 15, squares. The other rectangle has 3 × 7, or 21, squares.

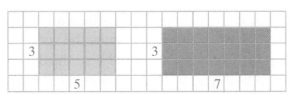

You can cut out and arrange the rectangles so that the sides with 3 units meet. This forms a rectangle with 3 × 12, or 36, squares.

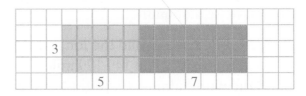

Notice that (3 × 5) + (3 × 7) = 3 × 12 = 3 × (5 + 7). This illustrates the Distributive Property.

$$3 \times (5 + 7) = (3 \times 5) + (3 \times 7)$$
$$= \quad 15 \quad + \quad 21$$
$$= \quad 36$$

Arithmetic	Algebra
$8 \times (4 + 6) = (8 \times 4) + (8 \times 6)$	$a(b + c) = ab + ac$
$7 \times (6 - 2) = (7 \times 6) - (7 \times 2)$	$a(b - c) = ab - ac$

You can use the Distributive Property to multiply mentally.

EXAMPLE Evaluating an Expression

1 Simplify 4×29.

What you think

I can think of 29 as $30 - 1$. Then I multiply both numbers by 4: $4 \times 30 = 120$ and $4 \times 1 = 4$. Now I subtract the two products: $120 - 4 = 116$.

Why it works

$$4 \times (30 - x)$$
$$4 \times 32 - 4x$$

$4 \times 29 = 4 \times (30 - 1)$	← Write 29 as $30 - 1$.
$= (4 \times 30) - (4 \times 1)$	← Use the Distributive Property.
$= 120 - 4 = 116$	← Simplify within parentheses and subtract.

Calculator Tip

Many calculators have a parenthesis key to help you solve problems.

Quick Check

1. Use the Distributive Property to simplify 5×68.

EXAMPLE Application: Wages

2 A summer job as an assistant camp counselor pays $6.50 per hour. How much does the counselor earn for working 8 hours?

$6.50 \times 8 = (6.00 + 0.50) \cdot 8$	← Write 6.50 as $6.00 + 0.50$.
$= (6.00 \times 8) + (0.50 \times 8)$	← Use the Distributive Property.
$= 48.00 + 4.00$	← Simplify within parentheses.
$= 52.00$	← Add.

The counselor earns $52 for working 8 hours.

Quick Check

2. A local bookstore charges $2.80 for each used book. What is the charge for 5 used books?

1. **Vocabulary** Which property of mathematics tells you that $(4 + 5) \times 7 = (4 \times 7) + (5 \times 7)$?
   Ⓐ associative   Ⓒ distributive
   Ⓑ commutative   Ⓓ identity

2. **Error Analysis** Who simplified $2 \times (3 + 5)$ correctly? Explain.

Thomas
$(2 \times 3) + (2 \times 5)$

Brian
$(2 + 3) \times (2 + 5)$

3. Which of these expressions is NOT equivalent to 19×12?
   Ⓕ $(19 \times 10) + (19 \times 2)$ Ⓗ $(10 \times 12) + (9 \times 12)$
   Ⓖ $(20 \times 12) - (1 \times 12)$ Ⓙ $(10 \times 10) + (9 \times 2)$

Use the Distributive Property to simplify each expression.

4. $6 \times 52 = 6 \times (50 + 2)$ 5. $4 \times 18 = 4 \times (20 - 2)$

For more exercises, see Extra Skills and Word Problems.

Use the Distributive Property to simplify each expression.

GO for Help

For Exercises	See Example
6–14	1
15	2

6. 8×28 7. 5×63 8. 4×34

9. 99×6 10. 7×83 11. 3×2.9

12. 9×48 13. 8.7×3 14. 52×6

15. Six students plan to go to a skating rink. The rink charges $4.50 per person. Find the total cost for the group.

16. **Guided Problem Solving** Mr. Garcia's company pays him 32.5 cents for each mile he drives. How much money does he receive for driving 40 miles?
    • How could you rewrite 32.5 as a sum?

17. **Fundraising** There are 50 people walking in a fundraising event. Each participant walks 5.3 miles. How many miles do the participants walk in all?

GO Online
Homework Video Tutor
Visit: PHSchool.com
Web Code: aqe-0308

18. **Writing in Math** Describe two ways to find the total area of the rectangle at the right.

[Rectangle diagram: 6.8 and 2 along the bottom, 2.5 on the right side]

Algebra Copy and complete each equation.

19. $4(7 - y) = (4 \cdot 7) - (4 \cdot \blacksquare)$ **20.** $9(a + b) = (\blacksquare \cdot a) + (9 \cdot \blacksquare)$

April 28   Arbor Day

21. Your class is selling calendars for $2.90 each. How much money does your class collect for selling 8 calendars?

22. **Gardening** Your school's ecology club plants 8 rows of trees in a vacant lot. Each row has 27 trees. Find the total number of trees that the ecology club plants.

23. **Reasoning** Which expression is NOT equivalent to the others?
- Ⓐ $(a \times c) + (b \times c)$
- Ⓒ $b \times (c + a)$
- Ⓑ $(b + a) \times c$
- Ⓓ $(a + b) \times c$

24. **Challenge** Add parentheses to $9 + 8 \times 7 - 6 \times 5 + 4 \times 3 + 2$ so that the value of the expression is 105.

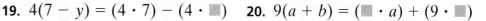

Test Prep and Mixed Review   **Practice**

Multiple Choice

25. Marissa earned $5 an hour baby-sitting. She worked for 4 hours and spent $8.75 of her earnings. Which equation could be used to determine how much money, m, Marissa had left?
- Ⓐ $m = 4 \times (\$5 - \$8.75)$
- Ⓒ $m = 4 \times \$5 + \$8.75$
- Ⓑ $m = 4 \times \$5 - \$8.75$
- Ⓓ $m = 4 \times (\$5 + \$8.75)$

26. Joey asked middle school students to name their favorite type of movie. Which graph correctly displays the data shown in the table?

Student Movie Preference

Movie	Drama	Comedy	Action
Students	140	260	200

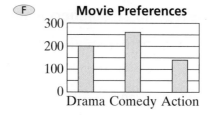

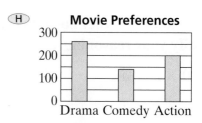

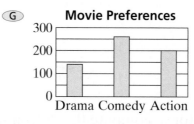

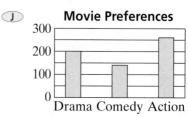

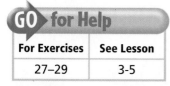

Tell whether each equation is true or false.

For Exercises	See Lesson
27–29	3-5

27. $5 \times 3 = 8$ **28.** $0 \times 9.8 = 9.8$ **29.** $1 \times 6.7 = 6.7$

Understanding Properties

Properties become more important as you "think algebraically." Understanding number properties and equality will help you solve algebraic equations.

EXAMPLE

Use a number property or number sense to determine whether the equation $8.8 + 12.5 + 1.2 = 1.2 + 8.8 + 12.5$ is true or false. Justify your reasoning.

$8.8 + 12.5 + 1.2 = 1.2 + 8.8 + 12.5$ ← The order of the numbers has changed. This is an example of the Commutative Property of Addition.

● The equation is true. It uses the Commutative Property of Addition.

Exercises

Determine whether each equation is true or false. Do not compute with paper and pencil. Use number properties and mental math to decide. Justify your reasoning.

1. $3.78 \times 14.95 \times 0 = 388.4 - 300 - 88.4$ **2.** $15.4 \times 10 = (15 \times 10) + (0.4 \times 10)$

3. $25.7 - (13 - 10) = (25.7 - 13) - 10$ **4.** $16 \times (3.8 \div 3.80) = 2 \times 8$

5. $60 \times 19.5 = 60 \times 2 - 60 \times 0.5$ **6.** $321 \times 3 = 300 \times 3 + 21 \times 3$

Determine whether each statement is true for all numbers a and b. Justify your reasoning.

7. $0 \times a = a$ **8.** $0 \div a = a$

9. $a - b + b = a$ **10.** $a \div 0 = 0$

11. $a \times b = b \times a$ **12.** $b + a - a = b$

13. $a \times b \div b = a$ (if $b \neq 0$)   **14.** $a \div b = b \div a$ (if $a, b \neq 0$)

15. $a \div b \times b = a$ (if $b \neq 0$)   **16.** $a \div a = b \div b$ (if $a, b \neq 0$)

17. Reasoning If you use a calculator to compute $0 \div 5$, you will get 0. If you calculate $5 \div 0$, you will get an error message. Use multiplication to explain why $5 \div 0$ is not defined.

Writing Short Responses

Short-response questions in this textbook are worth 2 points. To receive full credit, you must give the correct answer with units, if needed, and show your work or explain your reasoning.

$$\frac{a}{b} \times b \neq a$$

$$\frac{b}{a} \times b \neq a$$

$$\frac{a}{b} \neq \frac{b}{a}$$

$$b^2 = a^2$$

$$\frac{a \cdot b}{b} = a$$

EXAMPLE

Measurement Jenny stands on a scale. She weighs 104 pounds. Then she steps on the scale while holding her dog. Now the scale reads 121 pounds. Define a variable. Write and solve an equation to find the weight of the dog.

The problem asks you to define a variable, set up an equation, and solve the equation to find the weight of the dog. Below is a scoring guide that shows the number of points awarded for different answers.

Scoring

[2] The equation and solution are correct and all work is shown. The dog weighs 17 pounds.

[1] There is no equation, but there is a method to show that the dog weighs 17 pounds, OR an equation is written and solved. The response may contain minor errors.

[0] There is no response, no work shown, OR the response is completely incorrect.

Three responses are shown below, with the points each received.

2 points	1 point	0 points
Let d = weight of dog. $104 + d = 121$ $104 + d - 104 = 121 - 104$ $d = 17$ The dog weighs 17 pounds.	$121 - 104 = 17$ 17 pounds	27 pounds

Exercises

Use Example 1 to answer each question.

1. Why did each response receive the indicated number of points?

2. Write a 2-point response for solving the equation $121 - d = 104$.

Vocabulary Review

Fill in the blank.

1. Each number in a number pattern is called a(n) __?__.

2. A(n) __?__ contains one or more variables.

3. The value of the variable that makes an equation true is a(n) __?__.

4. A(n) __?__ is a symbol that stands for a number.

5. A(n) __?__ is a mathematical sentence with an equal sign.

Go **Online**
PHSchool.com
For: Vocabulary quiz
Web Code: aqj-0351

Skills and Concepts

Lesson 3-1
• To find and write rules for patterns

Each number in a number pattern is called a **term**. A **conjecture** predicts how a pattern may continue. You can describe a pattern with a rule.

Write a rule for each pattern. Then write the next three terms.

6. 2, 6, 18, 54, . . .   7. 7, 19, 31, 43, . . .   8. 7, 14, 28, 56, . . .

Lessons 3-2 and 3-3
• To evaluate algebraic expressions
• To write algebraic expressions and use them to solve problems

A **numerical expression** contains only numbers and operation symbols. An **algebraic expression** contains at least one **variable.**

Evaluate each expression.

9. $48 \div x$ for $x = 6$ 10. $c - 7$ for $c = 56$ 11. $14b$ for $b = 3$

Write an expression for each word phrase.

12. x divided by 12   13. 2 times b 14. h plus k

Lesson 3-4

- To use mental math to estimate and solve problems

An **equation** is a mathematical sentence that contains an equal sign. An **open sentence** is an equation that contains one or more variables. A value of the variable that makes an equation true is a **solution.**

Tell whether each equation is true or false.

15. $15 + 25 = 30$ **16.** $21 \div 3 = 7$ **17.** $6 \times 4 = 28$

Mental Math Solve each equation.

18. $x + 7 = 12$ **19.** $m + 13 = 21$ **20.** $4t = 32$

Lessons 3-5 and 3-6

- To use addition and subtraction to solve equations

You can use the **Addition Property of Equality** and the **Subtraction Property of Equality** to solve equations. Operations that undo each other are **inverse operations.**

Solve each equation.

21. $r - 1{,}078 = 4{,}562$ **22.** $m + 8 = 15$

23. $5.6 + x = 7$ **24.** $d - 2.16 = 3.9$

25. Paul is 2.7 pounds heavier than Elizabeth. Paul weighs 132.4 pounds. How much does Elizabeth weigh?

Lesson 3-7

- To use multiplication and division to solve equations

You can use the **Multiplication Property of Equality** and the **Division Property of Equality** to solve equations.

Solve each equation.

26. $78x = 4{,}368$ **27.** $t \div 4 = 32$ **28.** $1.2h = 3$

29. $7.2 = u \div 1.5$ **30.** $v \div 3.2 = 19$ **31.** $4.5 = 5n$

32. John has five times as much money as Stuart. John has $83.40. How much money does Stuart have?

Lesson 3-8

- To use the Distributive Property to simplify expressions in problem solving situations

You can use the **Distributive Property** to simplify an expression.

Use the Distributive Property to simplify each expression.

33. 7×28 **34.** 5×3.4 **35.** 11×57

Chapter 3 Test

Write the first six terms in each number pattern described.

1. Start with 10 and then multiply by 2 repeatedly.

2. Start with 50 and then subtract 4 repeatedly.

Write a rule for each number pattern. Then write the next three terms.

3. 6, 10, 14, 18, . . .   4. 64, 32, 16, 8, . . .

5. 78, 69, 60, 51, . . .   6. 4, 12, 36, 108, . . .

Evaluate each expression for $x = 12$.

7. $500 + (x - 8)$

8. $2x - 3$

9. $8 + x \div 2$

Write an algebraic expression for each model.

10.    11.

Use algebra tiles or a drawing to model each equation. Then solve.

12. $v + 3 = 8$ 13. $3g = 15$

Write an expression for each word phrase.

14. c more than 4   15. 8 less than $3d$

16. Gus is 8 years younger than his brother, Alex. Alex is x years old. Write an algebraic expression that describes how old Gus is.

17. **Writing in Math** Write a word problem that could be described by the expression $d + 4$.

Tell whether each equation is true or false.

18. $6 + 7 \times 3 = 39$

19. $1.5 \times (6 - 4) = 3$

$9 - 6 = 3$

Tell whether the given number is a solution to the equation.

20. $x + 1.5 = 32$; 17   21. $h - 8 = 2$; 28

Solve each equation.

22. $n - 4 = 8.4$

23. $25 + b = 138$

24. $k \div 12 = 3$

25. $11t = 99$

26. **Fundraising** A baseball team sold greeting cards to raise money for uniforms. The team received $.40 profit for each card sold. The total profit was $302. How many cards did the team sell?

27. **Patterns** Look at the pattern below. How many squares will be in the sixth figure?

Figure 1   Figure 2   Figure 3

Use the Distributive Property to simplify each expression.

28. 8×39 29. 4×71

30. 6×82 31. 3×98

Multiple Choice

Read each question. Then write the letter of the correct answer on your paper.

1. Which decimal is fifty-four hundredths?
Ⓐ 0.054 Ⓑ 0.54 Ⓒ 5.40 Ⓓ 54.00

2. Which inequality is NOT a true statement?
Ⓕ $0.04 > 0.01$ Ⓗ $0.48 < 0.4798$
Ⓖ $0.014 < 0.02$ Ⓙ $29.6 > 29.06$

3. Which sentence represents the Commutative Property of Multiplication?
Ⓐ $5 \times 2 = 10$
Ⓑ $5 \times (6 + 3) = 5 \times 9$
Ⓒ $5 \times 9 = 9 \times 5$
Ⓓ $(5 \times 6) \times 2 = 5 \times (6 \times 2)$

4. For 4 days, Akiko recorded the number of laps she jogged around a track. The numbers she recorded were 7, 11, 15, and 19. If she continues in the same pattern, how many laps will she jog on the sixth day?
Ⓕ 21 Ⓖ 23 Ⓗ 25 Ⓙ 27

5. Which word phrase does NOT describe the algebraic expression $b - 10$?
Ⓐ ten less than b Ⓒ b less than 10
Ⓑ b less ten Ⓓ b minus ten

6. Which expression has a value of 13?
Ⓕ $(3 + 2)^2$ Ⓗ $3^2 + 2^2$
Ⓖ $3 + (2)^2$ Ⓙ $3^3 + 2^2$

7. Which operation would you use to get the variable in $x - 15 = 40$ alone on one side of the equation?
Ⓐ Subtract 15 from each side.
Ⓑ Subtract x from each side.
Ⓒ Add 15 to each side.
Ⓓ Add 40 to each side.

8. What is the value of $2.5c + 2$ when $c = 6$?
Ⓕ 2.56 Ⓖ 17 Ⓗ 20 Ⓙ 256

9. Which expression is NOT equivalent to the others?
Ⓐ $13 \times (20 + 2)$
Ⓑ $13 \times 20 + 13 \times 2$
Ⓒ $(10 + 13) \times (10 + 12)$
Ⓓ $22 \times (10 + 3)$

10. Apples cost \$.38 each. You have \$4.00. What is the greatest number of apples you can buy?
Ⓕ 5 Ⓖ 9 Ⓗ 10 Ⓙ 11

Gridded Response

Record your answer in a grid.

11. What is the solution of $x \div 0.15 = 1.2$?

12. Cod sells for \$4.86 per pound. You buy two pieces, which cost a total of \$12.15. How many pounds of fish do you buy?

13. A sheet of metal has a thickness of 0.004 inches. In inches, how many inches thick is a stack of 100 sheets?

Short Response

14. a. Draw the fourth figure in the pattern.
b. How many white squares will the sixth figure have?

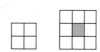

Figure 1 Figure 2 Figure 3

15. How many different sandwiches can you make from the choices of wheat bread, rye bread, or oatmeal bread with a filling of chicken, turkey, cheese, or peanut butter? Explain your method.

Applying Patterns

It's About Time Our day, month, and year are all based on the motion of Earth and the moon. One day is 24 hours long because that's how long it takes Earth to rotate once about its axis. The moon takes one month to orbit Earth, and Earth takes one year to orbit the sun. If we lived on another planet, each of these measures would be different, and we would have different measurements of time.

Earth's Moon

The moon contains almost the same elements, minerals, and rocks as Earth, but it has no water and no atmosphere. The moon orbits Earth in 29 days, 12 hours, 44 minutes, and 3 seconds, on average.

Pluto

In 1930, U.S. astronomer Clyde Tombaugh discovered Pluto, the ninth planet in the solar system. In 2006, the International Astronomical Union changed the status of Pluto to dwarf planet.

Pluto

Jupiter

Uranus

Sun

Venus

Mercury

Earth

Mars

Saturn

Measuring Time

The Jantar Mantar observatory, built between 1728 and 1734 in Jaipur, India, includes a giant sundial 27.5 meters high. You climb the steps to read the time, which is accurate to within a few seconds.

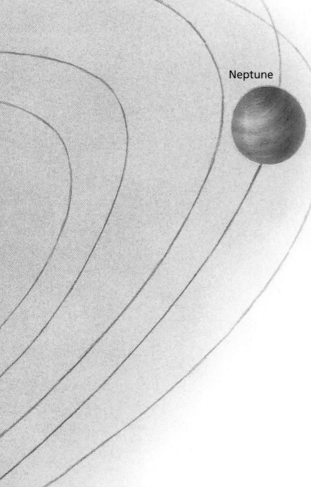

Neptune

The Solar System

All planets in our solar system orbit the sun in the same direction (counterclockwise when viewed from above), and most spin around their axes in the same direction, also.

Put It All Together

Planet	Length of Day (Earth hours)	Length of Year (Earth days)
☿ Mercury	1,407.51	87.97
♀ Venus	5,832.61	224.7
⊕ Earth	23.93	365.24
♂ Mars	24.62	686.98
♃ Jupiter	9.93	4,332.71
♄ Saturn	10.23	10,759.3
♅ Uranus	17.23	30,684
♆ Neptune	16.11	60,188.3
♇ Pluto*	153.29	90,777.3

SOURCE: *The Cambridge Planetary Handbook*
*In 2006, the International Astronomical Union changed the status of Pluto to dwarf planet.

1. a. How many Mercury years are equivalent to one Earth year? (Give your answer to the nearest whole number.)

   b. If you lived on Mercury, how old would you now be in Mercury years?

2. a. If you lived on Jupiter, how many birthdays would you be likely to celebrate in your lifetime? Explain.

   b. How many birthdays would you celebrate if you lived on Pluto? Explain.

3. Mars has two moons, Phobos and Deimos. Phobos orbits the planet every 7.5 hours, and Deimos every 30.25 hours.

   a. Writing in Math How might you define a "month" on Mars? Explain.

   b. Reasoning Do you think a Martian month would be a useful measure of time? Explain.

Go Online
PHSchool.com
For: Information about planets
Web Code: aqe-0353

Number Theory and Fractions

What You've Learned

- In Chapter 1, you compared and ordered whole numbers and decimals.

- You solved problems involving whole numbers and decimals.

- In Chapter 3, you wrote and simplified expressions using variables.

 **Check Your Readiness**

GO for Help

For Exercises	See Lesson
1–6	1-5
7–10	1-6
11–16	1-9

Reading and Writing Decimals
Write each decimal in words.

1. 0.4

2. 0.37

3. 1.8

4. 0.205

5. 20.88

6. 0.150

Comparing and Ordering Decimals
Order the decimals from least to greatest.

7. 4.2, 4.02, 4.21

8. 0.3, 0.33, 0.033

9. 6.032, 6.302, 6.203

10. 9.013, 9.103, 9.031

Dividing Decimals
Find each quotient.

11. $1.6 \div 2$

12. $3.85 \div 7$

13. $7.6 \div 0.4$

14. $290.4 \div 8$

15. $211.2 \div 1.6$

16. $583 \div 11$

What You'll Learn Next

- In this chapter, you will use divisibility rules, prime numbers, and factors to solve problems.

- You will write and simplify expressions using exponents.

- You will compare and order fractions and decimals.

- You will also convert between fractions and decimals.

 Problem Solving Application On pages 208 and 209, you will work an extended activity involving levers.

🔊 Key Vocabulary

- base (p. 162)
- common factor (p. 171)
- common multiple (p. 188)
- divisible (p. 158)
- equivalent fractions (p. 176)
- exponent (p. 162)
- factor (p. 166)
- improper fraction (p. 182)
- mixed number (p. 182)
- multiple (p. 188)
- prime factorization (p. 167)
- prime number (p. 166)
- proper fraction (p. 182)
- simplest form (p. 177)

Divisibility and Mental Math

What You'll Learn

To check for divisibility using mental math and to use divisibility to solve problems

🔊 **New Vocabulary** divisible, even number, odd number

Why Learn This?

When you plan an event, you can use divisibility rules to find how many tables you will need for your guests.

A whole number is **divisible** by a second whole number if the first number can be divided by the second number with a remainder of 0. You can use multiplication facts to test for divisibility.

GO for Help

For help with multiplying whole numbers, go to Skills Handbook, p. 640.

EXAMPLE **Using Mental Math for Divisibility**

1 **a.** Is 56 divisible by 7?

Think Since $56 = 8 \times 7$, 56 is divisible by 7.

b. Is 56 divisible by 4?

Think Since $56 = 8 \times 7$, and $4 \times 2 = 8$, 56 is divisible by 4.

✓ **Quick Check**

1. a. Is 64 divisible by 6?   **b.** Is 93 divisible by 3?

You can test for divisibility using the rules below.

KEY CONCEPTS **Divisibility of Whole Numbers**

A whole number is divisible by
- 2, if the number ends in 0, 2, 4, 6, or 8.
- 3, if the sum of the number's digits is divisible by 3.
- 5, if the number ends in 0 or 5.
- 9, if the sum of the number's digits is divisible by 9.
- 10, if the number ends in 0.

An **even number** is a whole number that ends with a 0, 2, 4, 6, or 8.
An **odd number** is a whole number that ends with a 1, 3, 5, 7, or 9.

EXAMPLE Divisibility by 2, 3, 5, and 10

② Test 715 for divisibility by 2, 3, 5, and 10.

2: 715 is not an even number. So 715 is not divisible by 2.

3: Find the sum of the digits in 715.

$7 + 1 + 5 = 13$ ← **Add the digits.**

The sum of the digits of 715 is 13, which is not divisible by 3. So 715 is not divisible by 3.

5: 715 ends in a 5. So 715 is divisible by 5.

10: 715 does not end in 0. So 715 is not divisible by 10.

So 715 is divisible by 5, but not by 2, 3, or 10.

✓ Quick Check

2. Test each number for divisibility by 2, 3, 5, and 10.
  a. 150 **b.** 1,021 **c.** 2,112

To test a number for divisibility by 9, you start by finding the sum of the number's digits—just as you did with divisibility by 3.

EXAMPLE Divisibility by 9

③ **Planning** There are 163 people signed up to play softball. Each team will have exactly 9 players. Will everyone who has signed up have a spot on one of the 9-person teams?

If 163 is divisible by 9, then everyone will have a spot on a team.

$1 + 6 + 3 = 10$ ← **Find the sum of the digits in 163.**
$10 \div 9$ has a remainder of 1.   ← **The sum is not divisible by 9.**

163 is not divisible by 9. Not everyone will have a spot on a team.

✓ Quick Check

3. Music A high school marching band has 126 members. Each row in the band formation on the field has 9 musicians. Will everyone in the band fit in a nine-person row?

1. **Vocabulary** How can you tell whether a number is odd or even?

2. **Number Sense** Since 54 is divisible by 6, 54 is also divisible by 2 and 3. Explain.

Match each number with its divisibility numbers.

3. 60

4. 48

5. 81

A. 3, 9
B. 2, 3
C. 2, 3, 5, 10

Homework Exercises

For more exercises, see Extra Skills and Word Problems.

For Exercises	See Examples
6–9	1
10–22	2
23–25	3

GO for Help

Is the first number divisible by the second? Use mental math.

6. 48 by 4   7. 46 by 4   8. 63 by 7   9. 122 by 6

Test each number for divisibility by 2, 3, 5, and 10.

10. 48,960   11. 2,385   12. 928

13. 672   14. 202,470   15. 53,559

16. 57   17. 92   18. 171

19. 962   20. 1,956   21. 11,160

22. A total of 114 people have signed up to play in a basketball tournament. There are 3 people on each team. Will everyone who has signed up have a spot on a 3-person team? Explain.

Test each number for divisibility by 9.

23. 1,187   24. 2,187   25. 17,595

26. **Guided Problem Solving** A theater group has 84 members. In how many different ways can the director split the group into teams of equal size?
   - Is there more than one way to divide the group?
   - How can you use divisibility rules to solve this problem?

What digit makes each number divisible by 9?

27. 9,0■5

28. ■7,302

29. 2■6,555

30. Time The number 60 is convenient for timekeeping because it can be easily divided by many numbers. Is 60 divisible by 2, 3, 4, 5, 6, 7, 8, 9, or 10?

31. Money Elissa and eight friends have lunch at a restaurant. The bill is $56.61. Can the friends split the bill into nine equal shares? Use the divisibility rule for 9 to explain your answer.

32. Patterns A number pattern begins 6, 12, 18, 24, . . .
   a. Write the next four numbers in the pattern.
   b. Which of the eight numbers are divisible by both 2 and 3?
   c. **Writing in Math** Write a rule for divisibility by 6.

33. You have $17 to spend on rides that cost $2 each. If you go on as many rides as you can afford, how much money will you have left?

34. Challenge Write all the three-digit numbers containing a 1, 2, and 3. Which of these numbers are divisible by 4? Explain.

Test Prep and Mixed Review
Practice

Multiple Choice

35. Rosa plants rows of flowers with exactly the same number in each row. Each row has more than one flower. She has 28 flowers. What is the largest number of rows she can make?
   Ⓐ 4   Ⓑ 7   Ⓒ 12   Ⓓ 14

36. Ben must buy all the equipment on the list. He estimates the total cost by rounding each price. Which is the closest to the amount Ben will spend?
   Ⓕ $77   Ⓗ $79
   Ⓖ $78   Ⓙ $80

Soccer Equipment	
Item	**Price($)**
Ball	14.98
Cleats	18.99
Shin guards	11.75
Team socks	6.25
Team jersey	28.50

37. A centimeter is one hundredth of a meter. Which measurement is equal to a centimeter?
   Ⓐ 0.1 m   Ⓑ 0.01 m   Ⓒ 0.001 m   Ⓓ 0.0001 m

GO for Help

For Exercises	See Lesson
38–41	3-2

Evaluate each expression.

38. $2(a - 1)$ for $a = 2$

39. $1 + 7a$ for $a = 5$

40. $6(b + 2)$ for $b = 3$

41. $3b - 2$ for $b = 3$

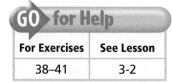

Exponents

Check Skills You'll Need

1. Vocabulary Review
A mathematical phrase containing numbers and symbols is an ? .

Find the value of each expression.

2. $3 \times 3 + 4 \times 4$

3. $1 \times 3 - 1 \times 3$

4. $1 + 1 \times 2 - 1$

for Help
Lesson 1-4

What You'll Learn

To use exponents and to simplify expressions with exponents

🔊 **New Vocabulary** exponent, base, power

Why Learn This?

Exponents are used to represent numbers. You need exponents to write large numbers like the number of stars in a galaxy.

You can write 625 as a product of factors.

$$625 = \underbrace{5 \times 5 \times 5 \times 5}_{\text{factors}}$$

The number 5 is used as a factor four times. An **exponent** tells you how many times a number, or **base,** is used as a factor.

$$5 \times 5 \times 5 \times 5 = 5^4 \quad \leftarrow \text{exponent}$$
$$\uparrow$$
$$\text{base}$$

Vocabulary Tip

You read 5^4 as "5 to the fourth power."

5^4 is a power. A **power** is a number that can be expressed using an exponent.

EXAMPLE   Using an Exponent

① Write $3 \times 3 \times 3 \times 3$ using an exponent. Name the base and the exponent.

$$3 \times 3 \times 3 \times 3 = 3^4 \quad \leftarrow 3^4 \text{ means that 3 is used as a factor 4 times.}$$

The base is 3, and the exponent is 4.

✓ Quick Check

1. Write each expression using an exponent. Name the base and the exponent.
    a. 3.94×3.94 **b.** $7 \times 7 \times 7 \times 7$ **c.** $x \cdot x \cdot x$

The area of the square is 3×3, or 3^2. You read 3^2 as "three squared."

The volume of the cube is $4 \times 4 \times 4$, or 4^3. You read 4^3 as "four cubed."

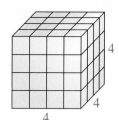

EXAMPLE Simplifying a Power

② **Science** You have 2^5 bones in your hand and arm. What is the value of 2^5?

$$2^5 = 2 \times 2 \times 2 \times 2 \times 2 = 32 \quad \leftarrow \text{The base 2 is used as a factor 5 times.}$$

The value of 2^5 is 32.

✓ **Quick Check**

2. **Astronomy** Phobos, the largest of Mars's moons, has a diameter of 3^3 kilometers. What is the value of 3^3?

The order of operations can be extended to include exponents.

KEY CONCEPTS Order of Operations

1. Do all operations within parentheses first.
2. Do all work with exponents.
3. Multiply and divide in order from left to right.
4. Add and subtract in order from left to right.

EXAMPLE Simplifying an Expression

Video Tutor Help
Visit: PHSchool.com
Web Code: aqe-0775

③ Simplify $3 \times (7^2 + 18 \div 2)$.

$$3 \times (49 + 18 \div 2) \quad \leftarrow \text{Simplify within parentheses. Simplify } 7^2.$$
$$3 \times (49 + 9) \quad \leftarrow \text{In parentheses, simplify } 18 \div 2.$$
$$3 \times (58) \quad \leftarrow \text{In parentheses, add } 49 + 9.$$
$$174 \quad \leftarrow \text{Multiply 3 and 58.}$$

✓ **Quick Check**

3. **a.** Simplify $2^3 - 6 \div 3$. **b.** Simplify $5 + (2 + 1)^2$.

1. **Vocabulary** How are exponents used to represent factors?

2. **Number Sense** Does 5^4 have the same value as 5×4? Explain.

Write each expression below using an exponent.

3. $3 \times 3 = 3^{\blacksquare}$ 4. $2 \times 2 \times 2 = \blacksquare^3$ 5. $9 \times 9 \times 9 = 9^{\blacksquare}$

Fill in each blank.

6. $4^2 = 4 \times 4 = \blacksquare$ 7. $2^3 = \blacksquare \times \blacksquare \times \blacksquare = 8$

Homework Exercises

For more exercises, see Extra Skills and Word Problems.

GO for Help

For Exercises	See Examples
8–16	1
17–20	2
21–26	3

Write each expression using an exponent. Name the base and the exponent.

8. $1 \times 1 \times 1 \times 1$ 9. 29 10. $3 \times 3 \times 3 \times 3$

11. $25 \times 25 \times 25$ 12. $2.5 \times 2.5 \times 2.5$ 13. $100 \times 100 \times 100$

14. $r \cdot r$ 15. $b \cdot b \cdot b \cdot b \cdot b$ 16. $25 \cdot n \cdot n \cdot n \cdot n$

17. A small plane needs 5^3 meters to take off or land. What is the value of 5^3?

Simplify each expression.

18. 5^2 19. 4^3 20. 2.5^2

21. $(2 + 3)^2$ 22. $(3^2 - 1)^2$ 23. $(9 - 7)^3 \times 6$

24. $(9 + 1)^2 - 1^3$ 25. $15^2 - (1 + 13^2)$ 26. $(10 - 8)^4 \times 3.5$

GPS 27. **Guided Problem Solving** A band of cumulus clouds is located at 10^4 feet. A commercial jet is traveling at 38,000 feet. What is the difference between the altitude of the clouds and the altitude of the jet?
   • How many feet is 10^4 feet?

28. **Geography** The population of Australia is more than 20,000,000 people. You can write 20,000,000 as $2 \times 10,000,000$. Write 10,000,000 using exponents.

Algebra **Evaluate each expression for $j = 2$ and $g = 4$.**

29. j^6

30. $(j + g)^3$

31. $(j + g)^2 + 4$

32. Patterns Copy the table.
a. Fill in the missing values.
b. **Writing in Math** Explain how the number of zeros in the standard form of a power of 10 relates to the exponent.
c. Extend the table to 10^8.
d. Write a rule for the number pattern.

Power	Standard Form
10^1	10
10^2	100
10^3	1,000
10^4	■
■	■

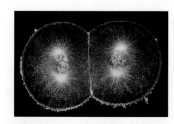

33. Biology A single-celled animal splits in two after one hour. Each new cell also splits in two after one hour. How many cells will there be after eight hours? Write your answer using an exponent.

34. Reasoning Does the expression $2^2 \cdot 3^2 - 2^3 - 1$ have the same value as $2^2 \cdot (3^2 - 2^3) - 1$? Explain.

35. Challenge In the equation $d = s^2$, d equals 32. Between what two whole numbers is the value of s?

Test Prep and Mixed Review

Practice

Multiple Choice

36. Yoel has 3 fewer coins than Selena. Selena has 15 coins. Which equation can be used to find k, the number of coins Yoel has?

  Ⓐ $k = 3 \cdot 5$ Ⓒ $k = 15 - 3$

  Ⓑ $k = 15 \div 3$ Ⓓ $k = 15 + 3$

37. Karen and her son share 30 grapes. Karen eats twice as many grapes as her son. How many grapes does Karen eat?

  Ⓕ 10   Ⓖ 15   Ⓗ 20   Ⓙ 30

38. The table shows the relationship between side length and volume of a cube. If the side length is n, what is the volume of the cube?

  Ⓐ $2n$ Ⓒ $3n$

  Ⓑ n^2 Ⓓ n^3

Side Length, n	Volume
1	1
2	8
3	27
n	■

39. The data below show lengths, in inches, of lake trout. Make a line plot using the data.

13 21 16 15 16 11 15 19 13 16 14 16 15 14 12

For Exercise	See Lesson
39	2-3

Prime Numbers and Prime Factorization

Check Skills You'll Need

1. **Vocabulary Review**
Is a number *divisible* by 5 always divisible by 10?

Test each number for divisibility by 2, 3, 5, 9, and 10.

2. 990   3. 901

4. 800   5. 2,080

 **for Help**
Lesson 4-1

What You'll Learn

To factor numbers and to find the prime factorization of numbers

🔊 **New Vocabulary** factor, composite number, prime number, prime factorization

Why Learn This?

Using factors, you can organize items or people in rows.

Divisibility rules can help you find factors. A **factor** is a whole number that divides a nonzero whole number with remainder 0.

EXAMPLE **Finding Factors**

1 An instructor plans a dance routine for 20 dancers in rows. Each row has the same number of dancers. What are the arrangements the instructor can use?

Look for pairs of factors for 20 to find the possible arrangements.

1×20 ← Write each pair of factors. Start with 1.

$2 \times 10, \; 4 \times 5$ ← 2 and 4 are factors. Skip 3, since 20 is not divisible by 3.

5×4 ← Stop when you repeat factors.

The arrangements are 1×20, 2×10, and 4×5.

✓ Quick Check

1. A gift box must hold the same number of pears in each row. You have 24 pears. What arrangements can you use?

A **composite number** is a whole number greater than 1 with more than two factors. A **prime number** is a whole number with exactly two factors, 1 and the number itself. The numbers 0 and 1 are neither prime nor composite.

EXAMPLE **Prime or Composite?**

2 Is the number prime or composite? Explain.

a. 51
Composite: 51 is divisible by 3. So 51 has more than two factors.

b. 53
Prime: 53 has only two factors, 1 and 53.

✓ **Quick Check**

2. Is the number prime or composite? Explain.
   a. 39   **b.** 47   **c.** 63

To write the **prime factorization** of a composite number, you write the number as a product of prime numbers. Each composite number has only one prime factorization.

When a factor repeats, use exponents to write your answer. You can use a division ladder or a factor tree to find the prime factorization of a number.

EXAMPLE **Prime Factorization**

3 Write the prime factorization of 84 using exponents.

For: Prime Factorization Activity
Use: Interactive Textbook, 4-3

Method 1 Use a division ladder.

2)84   ← **Divide 84 by the prime number 2. Work down.**
2)42   ← **The result is 42. Since 42 is even, divide by 2 again.**
3)21   ← **The result is 21. Divide by the prime number 3.**
　7   ← **The prime factorization is 2 × 2 × 3 × 7.**

Method 2 Use a factor tree.

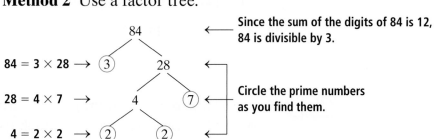

$84 = 3 \times 28 \rightarrow$ Since the sum of the digits of 84 is 12, 84 is divisible by 3.

$28 = 4 \times 7 \rightarrow$ Circle the prime numbers as you find them.

$4 = 2 \times 2 \rightarrow$

The prime factorization of 84 is $2 \times 2 \times 3 \times 7$, or $2^2 \times 3 \times 7$.

✓ **Quick Check**

3. Find the prime factorization of 27.

1. **Vocabulary** How is a prime number different from a composite number?

2. Find two prime numbers between 10 and 20, with a difference of 2.

3. Which number is not a composite number? Explain.

| 55 | 51 | 82 | 7 |

4. **Number Sense** Can two numbers have the same prime factorization? Explain.

Homework Exercises

For more exercises, see Extra Skills and Word Problems.

List the factors of each number.

GO for Help

For Exercises	See Examples
5–13	1
14–17	2
18–25	3

5. 28   6. 21   7. 17   8. 60

9. 48   10. 37   11. 144   12. 450

13. **Earth Science** For a science project, you want to display 36 rocks in rows, with the same number of rocks in each row. Find the arrangements that you can use.

Is each number *prime* or *composite*? Explain.

14. 19   15. 67   16. 57   17. 91

Find the prime factorization of each number.

18. 32   19. 42   20. 75   21. 400

22. 15   23. 45   24. 450   25. 10,000

26. **Guided Problem Solving** The yearbook editor must arrange 48 student photos on a page. Each row must have the same number of photos. What arrangements can she make?
   - **Make a Plan** What method can you use to find the factor pairs for 48?
   - **Check the Answer** How do you know that you have found all the factor pairs?

GO Online
Homework Video Tutor
Visit: PHSchool.com
Web Code: aqe-0403

Calculator **Find the number with the given prime factorization.**

27. $7 \times 11 \times 13$ **28.** $2^3 \times 5^2 \times 7 \times 11$

29. A clerk arranges 81 apples in a square crate. Each row has the same number of apples. How many rows does he make?

30. **Parades** A group has 36 ceremonial guards. When they march, they form rows of equal numbers of guards. What numbers of rows can they make? How many guards will be in each row?

31. (**Algebra**) Suppose p is a prime number greater than 2. Does $p + 1$ represent a prime or a composite number? Explain.

32. **Landscaping** A homeowner buys 116 square tiles to build a rectangular patio. The same number of tiles are in each row. What are the arrangements of tiles that he can make?

33. **Challenge** Find the pairs of prime numbers with a difference of two, between 1 and 100.

Test Prep and Mixed Review   **Practice**

Multiple Choice

34. What is the prime factorization of 48?
   Ⓐ $12 \cdot 4$ Ⓑ $6 \cdot 2^4$ Ⓒ $3 \cdot 2 \cdot 2^2$ Ⓓ $2^4 \cdot 3$

35. The graph below shows the results of a student survey. Which statement is supported by the graph?
   Ⓕ More students prefer pop or rock than jazz.
   Ⓖ More students prefer jazz than country.
   Ⓗ About half of the students prefer country and jazz.
   Ⓙ 100 students prefer pop or rock.

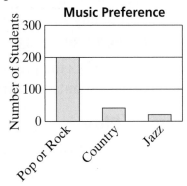

36. Which number is NOT a common factor of 12 and 30?
   Ⓐ 2   Ⓑ 3   Ⓒ 5   Ⓓ 6

GO for Help

For Exercises	See Lesson
37–38	1-4

Use <, =, or > to complete each statement.

37. $(8 + 10) \div 2 \blacksquare 14 \div (2 + 5)$

38. $3.5 + 2.5 \times 2 \blacksquare 24 \div 4 + 3$

✓ Checkpoint Quiz 1

Test each number for divisibility by 2, 3, 5, 9, and 10.

1. 375   **2.** 1,402   **3.** 240

Simplify each expression.

4. 4^3 **5.** $5 + (2^3 - 3)$ **6.** 5^5 **7.** $(6 + 2)^2$

Find the prime factorization of each number.

8. 42   **9.** 80   **10.** 1,000

11. A photographer is arranging 105 students in rows for a class picture. She wants the same number of students in each row. What are the different arrangements of students she can make?

MATH GAMES

Triple Prime Time

Getting Started

- Draw a 4-by-4 grid.
- Arrange the following numbers on your grid. Put each number in any square on the grid.

  12, 18, 20, 28, 30, 42, 45, 50, 63, 66, 70, 75, 105, 110, 154, 165
- The host writes the prime numbers **2, 3, 5, 7,** and **11** on slips of paper and puts the slips in a container.

How to Play

- The host draws a prime number, calls it out, and replaces it.
- Find a number on your grid that has the chosen prime number as a factor. Write the prime factor in that square. Each number on your grid has three prime factors.
- The host continues to draw slips and call numbers.
- When you record all three prime factors for a number, cross out the square. For example, you can cross out the square with 28 when you record 2, 2, and 7.
- The first player to cross out four squares in a row wins.

20	154	66	30
2, 2, 7 ~~28~~	18	5 50	165
63	110	12	2 42
70	75	45	105

Greatest Common Factor

Check Skills You'll Need

1. Vocabulary Review
Write a sentence about math using the words *factor* and *product.*

Find the prime factorization.

2. 45

3. 21

4. 99

GO for Help
Lesson 4-3

What You'll Learn

To find the GCF of two or more numbers

◄)) **New Vocabulary** common factor, greatest common factor (GCF)

Why Learn This?

A stamp club president distributes equally one set of 18 stamps and another set of 30 stamps to members present at a meeting. No stamps are left over. You can use factors to find the greatest possible number of club members at the meeting.

To find the greatest possible number of club members, you can find the factors that 18 and 30 share. A factor that two or more numbers share is a **common factor.**

The **greatest common factor (GCF)** of two or more numbers is the greatest factor shared by all the numbers. You can find the GCF of two numbers by listing their factors.

EXAMPLE **Using Lists of Factors**

1 Find the greatest common factor of 18 and 30.

List the factors of 18 and the factors of 30. Then circle the common factors.

Factors of 18: ①, ②, ③, ⑥, 9, 18   ← The common factors
Factors of 30: ①, ②, ③, 5, ⑥, 10, 15, 30   are 1, 2, 3, and 6.

The greatest common factor (GCF) is 6.

Quick Check

1. List the factors to find the GCF of each pair of numbers.
  a. 6, 21   **b.** 18, 49   **c.** 14, 28

You can also use a division ladder or factor trees to find the greatest common factor of two or more numbers.

EXAMPLE **Using a Division Ladder**

② **Gridded Response** Find the GCF of 42 and 56. Use a division ladder.

$2\overline{)42\quad56}$ ← Divide by 2, a common factor of 42 and 56.
$7\overline{)21\quad28}$ ← Divide by 7, a common factor of 21 and 28.
$\quad\ \ 3\quad\ \ 4$ ← 3 and 4 have no common factors.
Multiply the common factors: $2 \times 7 = 14$.

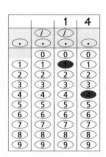

The GCF of 42 and 56 is 14.

✓ Quick Check

2. You want to cut two ribbons into equal lengths with nothing left over. The ribbons are 18 and 42 inches long. What is the longest possible length of ribbon you can cut?

EXAMPLE **Using Factor Trees**

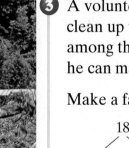

③ A volunteer divides 18 adults, 27 girls, and 36 boys into groups to clean up the park. He divides the adults, girls, and boys equally among the groups. What is the largest possible number of groups he can make?

Make a factor tree for each number.

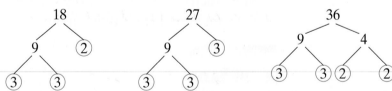

$18 = 3 \times 3 \times 2$
$27 = 3 \times 3 \times 3$ ← Write the prime factorization for each number.
$36 = 3 \times 3 \times 2 \times 2$

Identify common factors.

The GCF of 18, 27, and 36 is 9. The largest number of groups is 9.

✓ Quick Check

3. Use a factor tree to find the GCF.
   a. 48, 80, 128   b. 36, 60, 84

1. **Vocabulary** Explain why the GCF of two numbers is sometimes 1.

2. **Open-Ended** Write two numbers with a GCF of 4.

Match each pair of numbers to the GCF.

3. 18, 3

4. 8, 12

5. 22, 110

A. 22
B. 3
C. 4

Homework Exercises

For more exercises, see Extra Skills and Word Problems.

GO for Help

For Exercises	See Examples
6–11	1
12–17	2
18–23	3

List the factors to find the GCF of each set of numbers.

6. 14, 35

7. 24, 45

8. 26, 34

9. 30, 35

10. 48, 88

11. 36, 63

Use a division ladder to find the GCF of each set of numbers.

12. 10, 18

13. 24, 60

14. 11, 23

15. 27, 30

16. 12, 16, 28

17. 33, 55, 132

Use factor trees to find the GCF of each set of numbers.

18. 20, 60

19. 54, 84

20. 72, 120

21. 64, 125

22. 117, 130

23. 45, 150

24. **Guided Problem Solving** You want to make bouquets of balloons. You choose 18 yellow, 30 blue, and 42 red balloons. Each bouquet will have the same number of each color. What is the greatest possible number of bouquets you can make?
   • What method can you use to find the GCF?
   • What is the GCF? How many bouquets can you make?

25. Three groups of friends go to a movie. Each ticket costs the same amount. Each group spends a different total amount for tickets. The amounts are $27, $36, and $81. At most how much does each ticket cost?

Find the GCF of each set of numbers.

26. 300, 450   **27.** 280, 420   **28.** 200, 300, 400

29. Writing in Math Nine people plan to share equally 24 stamps from one set and 36 stamps from another set. Explain why 9 people cannot share the stamps equally.

30. Three friends pool their money to buy baseball cards. Brand A has 8 cards in each pack, Brand B has 12 cards, and Brand C has 15 cards. If they want to split each pack of cards equally, which two brands should they buy? Explain.

31. Summer Camp A camp director splits 14 counselors and 77 campers into activity groups. Each group should have the same number of counselors and the same number of campers. At most how many groups can she make? How many campers are in each group?

32. Reasoning Which number less than 50 has the most factors? Justify your answer.

33. Challenge There are four two-digit numbers that end with 6 and are less than 50. Find the GCF of the numbers.

Test Prep and Mixed Review   **Practice**

Gridded Response

34. You have 36 photos from a trip and 54 photos from a party. What is the GCF of 36 and 54?

35. The line plot shows the height, in inches, of students in a sixth-grade class. How many students are exactly 58 inches tall?

Sixth-Grade Students' Heights

```
                        ✗
                        ✗
            ✗           ✗    ✗
       ✗    ✗    ✗      ✗    ✗
  ✗    ✗    ✗    ✗      ✗    ✗    ✗
  ✗    ✗    ✗    ✗      ✗    ✗    ✗    ✗
  56   57   58   59     60   61   62   63
              Height (inches)
```

36. You buy 3 packs of notebook paper for $1.25 each and a binder for $1.50. Write an expression for the total cost of the items. Then find the total cost.

GO for Help

For Exercise	See Lesson
36	1-8

Modeling Fractions

A fraction describes a part of a set of items or a part of a whole item.

$\frac{3}{4}$ ← The numerator shows how many parts are being considered.
← The denominator shows the total number of parts.

EXAMPLE **Writing Fractions**

1 Write a fraction for each situation.

a. What fraction of the flowers are red?

There are 9 red flowers and 16 flowers altogether. So $\frac{9}{16}$ of the flowers are red.

b. What fraction of the pie is left?

The pie had 8 equal pieces. Five are left. So $\frac{5}{8}$ of the pie is left.

c. On the number line, what fraction describes the location of point A?

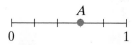

The segment from 0 to 1 is divided into 5 equal parts. Point A is three sections to the right of 0, so $\frac{3}{5}$ describes the location of point A.

Exercises

Name the fraction represented by each model.

1.

2.

3.

4.

Draw a fraction model for each situation.

5. $\frac{3}{4}$ as part of a set

6. $\frac{4}{7}$ as part of a rectangle

7. $\frac{5}{8}$ on a number line

8. Number Sense What number is represented when all parts of a fraction model are shaded? When no parts are shaded?

✓ Check Skills You'll Need

1. Vocabulary Review
How is a *common factor* different from the GCF?

Find the GCF of each set of numbers.

2. 20, 25

3. 12, 30

4. 5, 18

 **for Help**
Lesson 4-4

What You'll Learn

To find equivalent forms of fractions

🔊 **New Vocabulary** equivalent fractions, simplest form

Why Learn This?

Writing equivalent fractions often makes using fractions easier. Both models on the right show the same amount. You can describe the amount as $\frac{2}{3}$ or $\frac{4}{6}$.

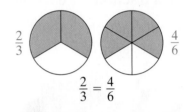

$$\frac{2}{3} = \frac{4}{6}$$

Equivalent fractions are fractions that name the same amount. The fractions $\frac{2}{3}$ and $\frac{4}{6}$ are equivalent fractions.

You form equivalent fractions by multiplying (or dividing) the numerator and denominator of a fraction by the same nonzero number.

EXAMPLE   Equivalent Fractions

1 Write two fractions equivalent to $\frac{6}{8}$.

$$\overset{\times 3}{\frac{6}{8} = \frac{18}{24}}$$ ← Multiply the numerator and denominator by 3.

$$\overset{\div 2}{\frac{6}{8} = \frac{3}{4}}$$ ← Divide the numerator and denominator by 2.

So $\frac{3}{4} = \frac{6}{8} = \frac{18}{24}$.

✓ Quick Check

1. Write two fractions equivalent to each fraction.

a. $\frac{4}{10}$

b. $\frac{5}{8}$

A fraction is in **simplest form** when the only common factor of the numerator and denominator is 1. One way to write a fraction in simplest form is to divide both the numerator and the denominator by their greatest common factor.

EXAMPLE Simplify a Fraction Using the GCF

2 Write $\frac{20}{28}$ in simplest form.

The GCF of 20 and 28 is 4.

$$\frac{20}{28} = \frac{20 \div 4}{28 \div 4} \quad \leftarrow \text{Divide the numerator and the denominator by the GCF.}$$

$$= \frac{5}{7} \quad \leftarrow \text{Simplify.}$$

The fraction $\frac{20}{28}$ written in simplest form is $\frac{5}{7}$.

✓ Quick Check

2. Write $\frac{24}{32}$ in simplest form.

EXAMPLE Using Prime Factorization

3 A pet store stocks 36 types of cat food, 42 types of dog food, 18 types of bird food, and 24 types of food for other pets. In simplest form, what fraction of the food is cat food?

Find the total number of food types.

$$36 + 42 + 18 + 24 = 120 \quad \leftarrow \text{Add the number of food types to find the denominator.}$$

$$\frac{36}{120} \quad \begin{array}{l} \leftarrow \text{number of cat food types} \\ \leftarrow \text{total number of food types} \end{array}$$

$$\frac{36}{120} = \frac{2 \cdot 2 \cdot 3 \cdot 3}{2 \cdot 2 \cdot 2 \cdot 3 \cdot 5} \quad \leftarrow \text{Write the prime factorizations of the numerator and the denominator.}$$

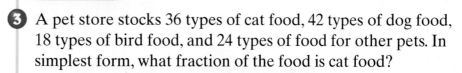

$$= \frac{\overset{1}{\cancel{2}} \cdot \overset{1}{\cancel{2}} \cdot \overset{1}{\cancel{3}} \cdot 3}{\underset{1}{\cancel{2}} \cdot \underset{1}{\cancel{2}} \cdot 2 \cdot \underset{1}{\cancel{3}} \cdot 5} \quad \leftarrow \text{Divide the common factors.}$$

$$= \frac{3}{10} \quad \leftarrow \text{Simplify.}$$

So $\frac{3}{10}$ of the food is cat food.

✓ Quick Check

3. In simplest form, what fraction of the food is dog food?

1. **Vocabulary** If the GCF of the numerator and the denominator is 1, then the fraction is in __?__.

2. Name each of the fractions modeled on the right. Are they equivalent?

Match each fraction with an equivalent fraction.

3. $\frac{9}{27}$ A. $\frac{1}{3}$

4. $\frac{5}{20}$ B. $\frac{2}{5}$

5. $\frac{6}{15}$ C. $\frac{1}{4}$

Homework Exercises

For more exercises, see Extra Skills and Word Problems.

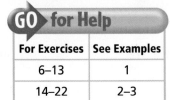

For Exercises	See Examples
6–13	1
14–22	2–3

Write two fractions equivalent to each fraction.

6. $\frac{2}{4}$ 7. $\frac{6}{7}$ 8. $\frac{12}{18}$ 9. $\frac{3}{16}$

10. $\frac{3}{10}$ 11. $\frac{3}{9}$ 12. $\frac{1}{20}$ 13. $\frac{15}{20}$

Write each fraction in simplest form.

14. $\frac{4}{6}$ 15. $\frac{10}{35}$ 16. $\frac{10}{20}$ 17. $\frac{40}{50}$

18. $\frac{15}{45}$ 19. $\frac{6}{8}$ 20. $\frac{12}{18}$ 21. $\frac{9}{21}$

22. **Sports** Over the last three seasons, a school football team has won 15 out of 25 games. In simplest form, what fraction of the games has the team won?

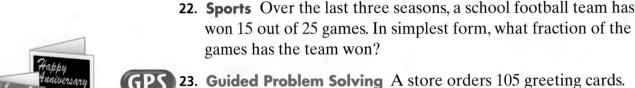

23. **Guided Problem Solving** A store orders 105 greeting cards. The order includes 50 birthday cards, 30 get-well cards, and some anniversary cards. In simplest form, what fraction of the cards are anniversary cards?
   • You can draw a picture to model the situation.

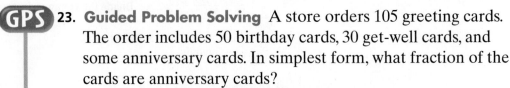

■ cards in all		
50 birthday	30 get-well	■ anniversary

State whether each fraction is in simplest form. If the fraction is not, write it in simplest form.

24. $\frac{3}{6}$ **25.** $\frac{1}{7}$ **26.** $\frac{15}{18}$ **27.** $\frac{17}{51}$

28. Traffic Planning Two traffic engineers are writing about the average driving time between two towns. One engineer writes the time as 45, but the other writes it as $\frac{3}{4}$. What could explain the difference?

29. On a chessboard, 32 of the squares are white. At the start of a game, each player places half of her 16 pieces on white squares. What fraction of the white squares have pieces on them?

30. Writing in Math How can you use the GCF of the numerator and the denominator to write a fraction in simplest form?

31. Challenge Evaluate $\frac{2a}{3a}$ for $a = 1, 2, 5,$ and 10.
   a. Write each result as a fraction.
   b. When a is a nonzero whole number, what do you think is the simplest form for $\frac{2a}{3a}$? Explain.

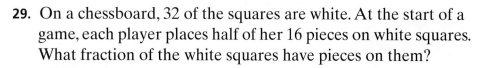

Test Prep and Mixed Review   Practice

Multiple Choice

32. What fraction of an hour is 40 minutes?

   (A) $\frac{3}{4}$ (B) $\frac{5}{6}$ (C) $\frac{2}{3}$ (D) $\frac{2}{5}$

33. On a field day, 84 girls and 78 boys will be split into teams. Each team will have the same number of girls and the same number of boys. At most how many teams are possible?

   (F) 2   (H) 13
   (G) 6   (J) 14

34. At a leadership conference, 96 students divide into discussion groups of equal sizes. Which method can you use to find the ways of forming the groups?

   (A) Find the factors of 96.
   (B) Find the multiples of 96.
   (C) Find the greatest common factor of 4 and 96.
   (D) Find the least common multiple of 96.

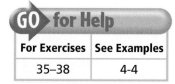

GO for Help

For Exercises	See Examples
35–38	4-4

Find the GCF of each pair of numbers.

35. 48, 56   **36.** 15, 21   **37.** 42, 72   **38.** 300, 450

Simplifying Fractions

You can use a fraction calculator to simplify a fraction. The calculator divides the numerator and denominator by a common factor and rewrites the fraction.

EXAMPLE

Use a fraction calculator to simplify $\frac{9}{27}$.

Keystroke	Display	
9 / 27	9/27	← Enter the fraction.
▶Simp	9/27 ▶ Simp	
ENTER =	9/27 ▶ Simp N/D → n/d 3/9	← The fraction is simplified once.
▶Simp	Ans ▶ Simp	
ENTER =	Ans ▶ Simp 1/3	← The fraction is in simplest form.

In simplest form, $\frac{9}{27} = \frac{1}{3}$.

Exercises

Use a fraction calculator to simplify each fraction.

1. $\frac{18}{51}$
2. $\frac{21}{49}$
3. $\frac{102}{387}$
4. $\frac{35}{56}$
5. $\frac{20}{65}$

6. $\frac{17}{68}$
7. $\frac{12}{15}$
8. $\frac{28}{32}$
9. $\frac{12}{30}$
10. $\frac{45}{75}$

11. $\frac{12}{96}$
12. $\frac{92}{132}$
13. $\frac{39}{117}$
14. $\frac{126}{324}$
15. $\frac{200}{385}$

16. **Writing in Math** How do you know from the calculator procedures shown in the example that the calculator does not use the greatest common factor (GCF) when simplifying?

Exploring Improper Fractions

You can use pattern blocks to name fractions that are equal to or greater than a whole.

EXAMPLES

1 The hexagon represents one whole. Use the pattern blocks to find what part of the whole two trapezoids represent.

Pattern Blocks

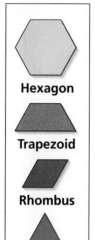

1    $\frac{1}{2}$ $\frac{2}{2}$

Each trapezoid is $\frac{1}{2}$ of the hexagon. So two trapezoids represent $\frac{2}{2}$ of the whole.

2 What part of the whole do three trapezoids represent?

Three trapezoids represent $\frac{3}{2}$ of the hexagon.

The trapezoids also represent one whole hexagon and half of a second hexagon.

Exercises

1. Use pattern blocks to complete the table at the right. A hexagon represents one whole.

2. **Reasoning** Can an improper fraction be written as a mixed number? Can a mixed number be written as an improper fraction? Explain.

3. Use pattern blocks to show that $\frac{4}{4}$ is equivalent to 1.

Fractional Parts	Fraction Name for One Part	Two Numbers for All Parts
4 blue rhombuses	$\frac{1}{3}$	$\frac{4}{3}$ and $1\frac{1}{3}$
8 green triangles		
7 green triangles		

What You'll Learn

To use mixed numbers and improper fractions

🔊 **New Vocabulary** proper fraction, improper fraction mixed number

Why Learn This?

You can use mixed numbers and improper fractions to describe distances. On the road sign at the right, the distance is written using the mixed number $2\frac{1}{2}$.

A **proper fraction** has a numerator that is less than its denominator. Example: $\frac{3}{8}$

An **improper fraction** has a numerator that is greater than or equal to its denominator. Example: $\frac{11}{8}$

A **mixed number** shows the sum of a whole number and a proper fraction, such as $2 + \frac{1}{2}$. Example: $2\frac{1}{2}$

NEXT 2½ MI

EXAMPLE Writing an Improper Fraction

1 Write $6\frac{2}{3}$ as an improper fraction.

Method 1

$$6\frac{2}{3} = 6 + \frac{2}{3}$$

$$= \frac{18}{3} + \frac{2}{3} \quad \leftarrow \text{Write 6 as } \frac{18}{3}.$$

$$= \frac{20}{3} \quad \leftarrow \text{Add.}$$

Method 2

$$6\frac{2}{3} = \frac{(3 \times 6) + 2}{3} \quad \leftarrow \text{Multiply the denominator times the whole number. Then add the numerator.}$$

$$= \frac{20}{3} \quad \leftarrow \text{The denominator stays the same.}$$

$6\frac{2}{3} = \frac{20}{3}$

You can also use a model to find the answer.

✓ Quick Check

1. Write $3\frac{4}{7}$ as an improper fraction.

EXAMPLE Application: Engines

2 A mechanic needs $3\frac{1}{4}$ gallons of oil for a diesel engine. How many quarts does the mechanic need? (*Hint:* 1 quart $= \frac{1}{4}$ gallon)

Since there are 4 quarts in a gallon, you find the number of quarts by finding the number of fourths in $3\frac{1}{4}$ gallons.

$$3\frac{1}{4} = \frac{13}{4} \quad \leftarrow \text{ Change } 3\frac{1}{4} \text{ to an improper fraction.}$$

There are 13 fourths in $3\frac{1}{4}$, so the mechanic needs 13 quarts of oil.

✓ Quick Check

2. To clean a fish tank you need $2\frac{1}{4}$ gallons of fresh water every two weeks. How many quarts do you need?

You can write an improper fraction greater than 1 as a mixed number. To do this, divide the numerator by the denominator.

EXAMPLE Writing a Fraction as a Mixed Number

3 Each orange slice is $\frac{1}{6}$ of an orange. How many oranges are represented by 9 slices?

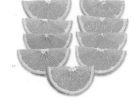

Write $\frac{9}{6}$ as a mixed number. Begin by dividing 9 by 6.

$$
\begin{array}{r}
1 \\
6)\overline{9} \\
-6 \\
\hline
3
\end{array}
$$
$\leftarrow$ The quotient represents one whole orange.

$\leftarrow$ The remainder represents three slices.

Write the remainder 3 as a fraction $\frac{3}{6}$.

$$\frac{9}{6} = 1\frac{3}{6}$$

$$= 1\frac{1}{2} \quad \leftarrow \text{ Simplify.}$$

Nine slices represent $1\frac{1}{2}$ oranges.

✓ Quick Check

3. Write each improper fraction as a mixed number in simplest form.

a. $\frac{40}{9}$ b. $\frac{32}{6}$ c. $\frac{23}{4}$

Check Your Understanding

Vocabulary Match each fraction to the fraction type.

1. $\frac{7}{8}$

2. $2\frac{4}{5}$

3. $\frac{7}{4}$

A. mixed number
B. improper fraction
C. proper fraction

Write a mixed number and an improper fraction for each model.

4.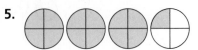

5.

Homework Exercises

For more exercises, see **Extra Skills and Word Problems.**

GO for **Help**

For Exercises	See Examples
6–14	1–2
15–22	3

Write each mixed number as an improper fraction. You may find a model helpful.

6. $1\frac{4}{5}$ **7.** $3\frac{1}{7}$ **8.** $5\frac{1}{4}$ **9.** $5\frac{1}{2}$

10. $1\frac{3}{11}$ **11.** $3\frac{3}{8}$ **12.** $2\frac{1}{16}$ **13.** $21\frac{1}{3}$

14. Cooking A recipe for cookies calls for $2\frac{2}{3}$ cups of flour. You have only a $\frac{1}{3}$-cup scoop for measuring. How many times must you fill the scoop to make the cookies?

Write each improper fraction as a mixed number in simplest form.

15. $\frac{17}{5}$ **16.** $\frac{10}{4}$ **17.** $\frac{27}{12}$ **18.** $\frac{9}{4}$

19. $\frac{21}{14}$ **20.** $\frac{18}{11}$ **21.** $\frac{21}{10}$ **22.** $\frac{16}{12}$

GPS **23. Guided Problem Solving** You estimate that 150 people will go to a picnic. Each person will drink about 2 cans of juice. Cans are sold in cases of 24. How many cases do you need?
- **Make a Plan** Find how many cans you need. Then find how many groups of 24 are in the total number of cans.
- **Check the Answer** Should your answer be a whole number?

Write each number as an improper fraction and as a mixed number.

24. 33 halves   **25.** 7 fifths   **26.** 106 fourths

27. 2 and 3 fifths   **28.** 8 and 7 ninths   **29.** 6 and 2 thirds

30. Catering A caterer plans to serve two slices of melon to each of 50 guests. She estimates getting 12 slices from each melon. Write the number of melons she will use as a mixed number. How many whole melons does she need?

31. A teacher needs at least 250 school T-shirts to raise money for the music program. The shirts come in boxes of 30. Each box costs $150. How much does the order cost?

32. Open-Ended Find a number between $\frac{6}{4}$ and $\frac{7}{4}$. Write your answer as an improper fraction and as a mixed number.

Find the length of each segment below. Use mixed numbers.

33.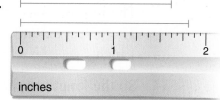

34.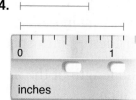

35. Challenge You cut $\frac{1}{2}$-inch squares of colored paper to make a mosaic. Each sheet of paper is $8\frac{1}{2}$ inches by 11 inches. How many squares can you make from each sheet?

Test Prep and Mixed Review

Practice

Multiple Choice

36. A music teacher ordered 6 pizzas. Each pizza had 8 slices. There were 20 slices left. How many pizzas were left?

     Ⓐ $2\frac{1}{4}$ Ⓑ $3\frac{1}{4}$ Ⓒ $2\frac{1}{2}$ Ⓓ $3\frac{1}{2}$

37. What is the prime factorization of 650?

     Ⓕ $2^2 \cdot 5 \cdot 13$ Ⓖ $2^2 \cdot 5^3$ Ⓗ $2 \cdot 5^2 \cdot 13$ Ⓙ $2^2 \cdot 5^2 \cdot 7$

38. Which number is NOT a factor of 60?

     Ⓐ 20   Ⓑ 15   Ⓒ 8   Ⓓ 5

State whether each equation is true or false.

39. $48 \div 6 = 8$ **40.** $12.6 \div 2 = 6.2$ **41.** $1.8 = 5.4 \div 3$

Fractions and Measurement

The marks on an inch ruler are based on fractions.

EXAMPLE **Fractions on a Ruler**

Biology Find the length for each insect shown below.

a.

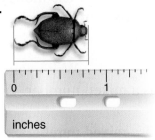

The ruler is marked every $\frac{1}{16}$ inch. The insect is the size of thirteen $\frac{1}{16}$-inch spaces.

So the length of the insect is $\frac{13}{16}$ inch.

b.

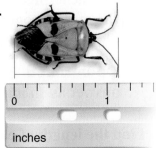

The ruler is marked every $\frac{1}{8}$ inch. The insect extends $\frac{1}{8}$ inch past 1 inch.

So the length of the insect is $1\frac{1}{8}$ inches.

Exercises

Find the length of each segment below.

1.

2.

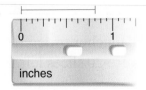

3.

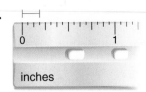

Use a ruler to measure the length of each segment or object below. Measure to the nearest sixteenth of an inch.

4. _____

5. _____

6. _____

7.

8.

9.

Making Word Lists

You can learn new vocabulary by making a word list using index cards.

- Write the term. Then write the definition.
- Include any math symbols related to the term.
- Give an example of the term.
- Give a nonexample showing how the term might *not* apply.

Greatest Common Factor (GCF)
Definition: The GCF of two or more numbers is the greatest factor shared by all the numbers.
Example: The GCF of 12 and 20 is 4.
Nonexample: 2 is a common factor of 12 and 20, but 2 is not the GCF.

For the vocabulary terms on page 157, make a word list with cards like the one shown above.

Checkpoint Quiz 2

Lessons 4-4 through 4-6

Find the GCF of each set of numbers.

1. 45, 80

2. 24, 72

3. 9, 18, 51

4. 18, 48

Write each mixed number as an improper fraction. Write each improper fraction as a mixed number in simplest form.

5. $3\frac{1}{5}$

6. $\frac{13}{8}$

7. $2\frac{2}{3}$

8. You are filling 8 bags with party favors, including small toys, balloons, and bags of peanuts. Each bag has the same number of toys, of balloons, and of bags of peanuts. You have 16 toys, 48 balloons, and 96 bags of peanuts. How many of each item will be in a bag?

Least Common Multiple

Check Skills You'll Need

1. **Vocabulary Review** How can you use a factor tree to find the *prime factorization* of a number?

Find the prime factorization of each number.

2. 80   3. 32

4. 208   5. 500

 **for Help**
Lesson 4-3

What You'll Learn

To find the LCM of two or more numbers

🔊 **New Vocabulary** multiple, common multiple, least common multiple (LCM)

Why Learn This?

You can use common multiples to make coordinating schedules easier.

Carmen gets her hair cut every four weeks. Maria gets her hair cut every six weeks. They both had their hair cut last week. How long will it be before they both get their hair cut again in the same week?

You can list multiples of 4 and 6 to answer this question. A **multiple** of a number is the product of that number and a nonzero whole number.

Multiples of 6
$6 \times 1 = 6$
$6 \times 2 = 12$
$6 \times 3 = 18$
$6 \times y = 6y$

A number that is a multiple of each of two or more numbers is a **common multiple.** The **least common multiple (LCM)** of two or more numbers is the least multiple that is common to all the numbers.

EXAMPLE   Find the LCM Using Lists of Multiples

1 Find the least common multiple of 4 and 6.

multiples of 4: 4, 8, ⑫, 16, 20, ㉔
multiples of 6: 6, ⑫, 18, ㉔

← List multiples of each number. 12 and 24 are common multiples.

The least common multiple is 12.

Quick Check

1. List multiples to find the LCM.
   a. 10, 12   b. 7, 10

Using Prime Factorizations

2 Scheduling A train for each of the train lines shown in the table on the left has just arrived. In how many minutes will a train for each line arrive at the same time again?

REGULAR SERVICE	
	EVERY
YELLOW LINE	8 min
GREEN LINE	10 min
PURPLE LINE	20 min

Write the prime factorizations for 8, 10, and 20. Then circle each different factor where it appears the greatest number of times.

$8 = \underline{2 \times 2 \times 2}$ ← **2 appears the most often here (three times).**
$10 = 2 \times \underline{5}$ ← **5 appears once.**
$20 = 2 \times 2 \times 5$ ← **Don't circle 5 again.**
$2 \times 2 \times 2 \times 5 = 40$ ← **Multiply the circled factors.**

The LCM is 40. The trains will arrive together in 40 minutes.

✓ Quick Check

2. Use prime factorization to find the LCM of 6, 8, and 12.

● More Than One Way

Find the LCM of 20, 30, and 45.

Michael's Method

I can use prime factorization to find the LCM.

$20 = \underline{2 \times 2} \times \underline{5}$ ← **2 appears twice. 5 appears once.**
$30 = 2 \times 3 \times 5$ ← **Don't circle 2 or 5 again.**
$45 = \underline{3 \times 3} \times 5$ ← **3 appears twice.**

$2 \times 2 \times 3 \times 3 \times 5 = 180$ ← **Multiply the circled factors.**

The LCM of 20, 30, and 45 is 180.

Amanda's Method

The greatest number is 45. I can list the multiples of 45 until I find one that is also a multiple of 20 and 30.

            90 is a multiple of 30, but not of 20.
45, 90, 135, 180 ← **180 is a multiple of both 20 and 30.**

So the LCM of 20, 30, and 45 is 180.

Choose a Method
Find the LCM of 6, 9, and 10. Explain why you chose your method.

1. **Vocabulary** Use the word *multiple* in a sentence about math.

List four multiples of each number.

2. 7   3. 8   4. 11

5. Find the LCM of 16 and 24 using prime factorizations.

Homework Exercises

For more exercises, see Extra Skills and Word Problems.

GO for Help

For Exercises	See Examples
6–17	1
18–27	2

List multiples to find the LCM of each set of numbers.

6. 4, 9   7. 5, 6   8. 12, 15

9. 10, 16   10. 14, 21   11. 20, 30

12. 25, 75   13. 8, 10   14. 3, 8, 12, 15

15. 4, 7, 12, 21   16. 25, 50, 125   17. 2, 3, 5, 7, 11

Use prime factorizations to find the LCM of each set of numbers.

18. 9, 21   19. 18, 24   20. 75, 100

21. 8, 14   22. 22, 55   23. 18, 108

24. 7, 12   25. 4, 7, 20   26. 30, 50, 200

27. **Shopping** You buy paper plates, napkins, and cups for a party. Plates come in packages of 15. Cups come in packages of 20, and napkins come in packages of 120. You want to have the same number of plates, cups, and napkins. How many packages of each item do you need to buy?

28. **Guided Problem Solving** Two ships sail between New York and London. One makes the round trip in 12 days. The other takes 16 days. They both leave London today. In how many days will both ships leave London together again?
    • How can you use multiples to solve this problem?
    • What are the multiples of 12 and 16?

29. **Business** During a promotion, a music store gives a free CD to every fifteenth customer and a free DVD to every fortieth customer. Which customer will be the first to get both gifts?

Find the LCM of each set of numbers or expressions.

30. 35, 45

31. 6, 8, 16

32. $2^2 \times 7$, 2×7^2

33. Number Sense A number N has both 8 and 10 as factors.
 a. Name three factors of the number N, other than 1.
 b. What is the smallest number N could be?

34. Fitness You lift weights every third day and swim every fourth day. If you do both activities today, in how many days will you do both activities again on the same day?

35. (**Algebra**) The LCM of 3 and 6 is 6. The LCM of 5 and 10 is 10. The LCM of x and $2x$ is ■ when x is a nonzero whole number.

36. Writing in Math What is the LCM for two numbers that have no common factors greater than 1? Explain your reasoning.

37. Challenge Find the LCM of $25xy$ and $200xy$.

Test Prep and Mixed Review   **Practice**

Multiple Choice

38. What is the least common multiple of 24 and 28?
 Ⓐ 4   Ⓑ 84   Ⓒ 168   Ⓓ 336

39. On January 1, Rosa waters all of her plants. She waters her cactus every 60 days, her fern every 4 days, and her violets every 3 days. How many times in a year will she water all her plants on the same day?
 Step K   Find the least common multiple.
 Step L   Divide 365 by the least common multiple.
 Step M   Find the prime factorizations for 3, 4, and 60.

 Which list shows the steps in the correct order?
 Ⓕ K, M, L   Ⓗ K, L, M
 Ⓖ M, K, L   Ⓙ M, L, K

40. Jon paid a membership fee of $30 to use a skate park. Each time he skated, he paid $2.50. Which equation can be used to find c, the cost of skating for s visits?
 Ⓐ $c = 2.5s + 30$ Ⓒ $c = 30s + 2.5$
 Ⓑ $c = 30(s + 2.5)$ Ⓓ $c = 2.5(s + 30)$

GO for Help

For Exercises	See Lesson
41–42	1-6

Order each set of decimals on a number line.

41. 0.51, 0.3, 0.49, 0.37, 0.6

42. 9.2, 9.28, 9.13, 9.25, 9.26

Comparing and Ordering Fractions

Check Skills You'll Need

1. **Vocabulary Review**
How is writing a fraction in *simplest form* related to finding *equivalent fractions?*

Write two fractions equivalent to each given fraction.

2. $\frac{7}{21}$ 3. $\frac{8}{40}$

4. $\frac{2}{3}$ 5. $\frac{25}{150}$

GO for Help
Lesson 4-5

What You'll Learn

To compare and order fractions

🔊 **New Vocabulary** least common denominator (LCD)

Why Learn This?

Carpenters, chefs, and musicians all use fractions when comparing measurements.

Models like those below can help you decide whether $\frac{2}{3}$ or $\frac{3}{5}$ is greater.

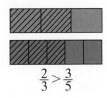

$$\frac{2}{3} > \frac{3}{5}$$

To compare fractions without using models, use the least common denominator. The **least common denominator (LCD)** of two or more fractions is the least common multiple (LCM) of their denominators.

EXAMPLE Comparing Fractions

1 Compare $\frac{5}{6}$ and $\frac{3}{4}$. Use <, =, or >.

First find the least common denominator. The least common multiple of 6 and 4 is 12, so 12 is the LCD.

$$\frac{5}{6} \overset{\times 2}{=} \frac{10}{12} \qquad \frac{3}{4} \overset{\times 3}{=} \frac{9}{12} \quad \leftarrow \text{Find equivalent fractions and compare.}$$

Then compare fractions. $\frac{10}{12} > \frac{9}{12}$, so $\frac{5}{6} > \frac{3}{4}$.

✓ Quick Check

1. Compare $\frac{6}{8}$ and $\frac{7}{9}$. Use <, =, or >.

EXAMPLE **Comparing Mixed Numbers**

Careers Tailors measure fabric to fit clothing.

2 **Tailoring** "Measure twice, cut once" is a useful motto for tailors to remember. A tailor needs fabric that is at least $6\frac{27}{32}$ inches wide. Is a $6\frac{3}{4}$-inch piece wide enough?

Since the whole numbers are the same, compare $\frac{27}{32}$ and $\frac{3}{4}$.

$$\frac{27}{32} = \frac{27}{32} \qquad \frac{3}{4} = \frac{24}{32} \qquad \leftarrow \text{Write equivalent fractions. Use the LCD, 32.}$$

$$\frac{27}{32} > \frac{24}{32} \qquad \leftarrow \text{Compare the fractions.}$$

So $6\frac{27}{32} > 6\frac{3}{4}$. The $6\frac{3}{4}$-inch piece is not wide enough.

✓ Quick Check

2. Is a $6\frac{7}{8}$-inch piece of fabric wide enough? Explain.

When you order fractions and mixed numbers, compare the two types of numbers separately. The fractions without a whole-number part will be less than the mixed numbers.

EXAMPLE **Ordering Fractions and Mixed Numbers**

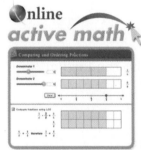

Online
active math

For: Ordering Fractions Activity
Use: Interactive Textbook, 4-8

3 Order from least to greatest: $1\frac{2}{3}$, $\frac{2}{5}$, $1\frac{7}{9}$, and $\frac{1}{4}$.

Step 1 Order the fractions. Find the LCM of 4 and 5. The LCD of the fractions is 20.

$$\frac{2}{5} = \frac{8}{20} \qquad \frac{1}{4} = \frac{5}{20} \qquad \leftarrow \text{Write equivalent fractions.}$$

$$\frac{5}{20} < \frac{8}{20} \qquad \leftarrow \text{Compare the fractions.}$$

So the order of the fractions is $\frac{1}{4} < \frac{2}{5}$.

Step 2 Order the mixed numbers. Since the whole-number parts are the same, compare $\frac{2}{3}$ and $\frac{7}{9}$.

$$\frac{2}{3} = \frac{6}{9}, \text{ so } \frac{6}{9} < \frac{7}{9}.$$

The order of the mixed numbers is $1\frac{2}{3} < 1\frac{7}{9}$.

Including the fractions first, the order is $\frac{1}{4} < \frac{2}{5} < 1\frac{2}{3} < 1\frac{7}{9}$.

✓ Quick Check

3. Order $2\frac{5}{6}$, $\frac{3}{8}$, $\frac{1}{3}$, $2\frac{4}{5}$, and $1\frac{2}{3}$ from least to greatest.

1. **Vocabulary** What is the LCD for fractions?

Find the least common denominator for each pair of fractions.

2. $\frac{1}{3}, \frac{1}{4}$

3. $\frac{7}{8}, \frac{1}{2}$

4. $\frac{4}{5}, \frac{1}{6}$

Mental Math Compare each pair of numbers. Use <, =, or >.

5. $\frac{1}{15}$ ■ $\frac{1}{20}$

6. $\frac{3}{4}$ ■ $\frac{3}{2}$

7. $\frac{2}{45}$ ■ $\frac{1}{30}$

Homework Exercises

For more exercises, see Extra Skills and Word Problems.

GO for Help

For Exercises	See Examples
8–16	1
17–23	2
24–29	3

Compare each pair of numbers. Use <, =, or >.

8. $\frac{3}{5}$ ■ $\frac{5}{8}$

9. $\frac{3}{4}$ ■ $\frac{3}{5}$

10. $\frac{1}{2}$ ■ $\frac{7}{16}$

11. $\frac{3}{5}$ ■ $\frac{12}{20}$

12. $\frac{5}{7}$ ■ $\frac{5}{6}$

13. $\frac{3}{11}$ ■ $\frac{1}{4}$

14. $\frac{2}{9}$ < $\frac{4}{15}$

15. $\frac{15}{16}$ ■ $\frac{7}{8}$

16. $\frac{9}{24}$ ■ $\frac{3}{8}$

17. $3\frac{1}{8}$ ■ $3\frac{1}{4}$

18. $7\frac{2}{3}$ ■ $7\frac{4}{6}$

19. $8\frac{7}{10}$ ■ $8\frac{3}{5}$

20. $2\frac{17}{18}$ ■ $2\frac{13}{16}$

21. $5\frac{4}{6}$ < $5\frac{5}{7}$

22. $3\frac{1}{4}$ ■ $3\frac{1}{5}$

23. Tim ran $1\frac{3}{4}$ miles. Naomi ran $1\frac{7}{10}$ miles. Who ran farther?

Order each set of numbers from least to greatest.

24. $\frac{2}{3}, \frac{5}{6}, \frac{3}{4}$

25. $3\frac{2}{3}, 3\frac{2}{5}, 3\frac{7}{15}$

26. $\frac{1}{8}, 2\frac{8}{9}, \frac{3}{10}, 2\frac{5}{6}$

27. $\frac{3}{12}, 2\frac{2}{3}, 3\frac{1}{4}, \frac{1}{2}$

28. $\frac{5}{8}, 1\frac{7}{12}, \frac{3}{4}, \frac{1}{2}, 2\frac{2}{3}$

29. $6\frac{5}{9}, 6\frac{2}{3}, 8\frac{1}{5}, 8\frac{2}{9}$

GPS 30. **Guided Problem Solving** Plywood comes in a variety of thicknesses for different uses. Put these thicknesses in order from least to greatest.

$\frac{3}{4}$ inch, $\frac{3}{8}$ inch, $\frac{1}{2}$ inch, $\frac{1}{4}$ inch, $\frac{5}{8}$ inch

- **Make a Plan** Find the least common denominator for the fractions. Then write equivalent fractions.
- **Carry Out the Plan** The least common denominator is ■. Compare the fractions.

GO **Online**
Homework Video Tutor
Visit: PHSchool.com
Web Code: aqe-0408

Number Sense Without using a common denominator, compare each pair of fractions using <, =, or >. Explain your reasoning.

31. $\frac{3}{7}$ ▇ $\frac{3}{8}$

32. $\frac{11}{16}$ ▇ $\frac{11}{12}$

33. $\frac{1}{8}$ ▇ $\frac{1}{18}$

34. Two sports drinks have the same price. The cherry flavored drink contains $12\frac{9}{20}$ ounces. The blueberry flavored drink contains $12\frac{7}{16}$ ounces. Which drink is the better buy?

35. Music Musical notes are based on fractions of a whole note.
 a. Order the fractions shown from greatest to least.
 b. Patterns Redraw the note symbols so they are in order. Do the symbols change in a pattern? Explain.

$\frac{1}{4}$ $\quad$ $\frac{1}{16}$ $\quad$ $\frac{1}{2}$ $\quad$ $\frac{1}{8}$
Fractions of a
Whole Note

36. Track Order the Olympic men's pole vault records below from greatest to least.
19 ft $1\frac{1}{2}$ in. $\quad$ 19 ft $2\frac{1}{4}$ in. $\quad$ 19 ft 2 in. $\quad$ 18 ft $8\frac{1}{4}$ in. $\quad$ 19 ft $4\frac{1}{4}$ in.

37. Writing in Math Explain how to compare two fractions that have the same numerators and different denominators.

38. Challenge Find a whole number x such that $\frac{2}{3} < \frac{x}{8} < 1$.

Test Prep and Mixed Review

Practice

Multiple Choice

39. Which measurement is between $\frac{3}{4}$ inch and $\frac{7}{8}$ inch on a ruler?

Ⓐ $\frac{5}{8}$ inch $\qquad$ Ⓑ $\frac{6}{8}$ inch $\qquad$ Ⓒ $\frac{12}{16}$ inch $\qquad$ Ⓓ $\frac{13}{16}$ inch

40. Brandon needs to buy equal numbers of hot dogs and buns. Hot dogs come in packages of 10. Hot dog buns come in packages of 8. What is the least number of buns he can buy?

Ⓕ 20 $\qquad$ Ⓖ 24 $\qquad$ Ⓗ 40 $\qquad$ Ⓙ 80

41. What is the prime factorization of 108?

Ⓐ $2^2 \cdot 3^3$ $\qquad$ Ⓑ $2^3 \cdot 2^2$ $\qquad$ Ⓒ $2^3 \cdot 3^3$ $\qquad$ Ⓓ $2^2 \cdot 3^2$

GO **for Help**

For Exercises	See Lesson
42–45	4-5

Write each fraction in simplest form.

42. $\frac{18}{42}$ $\qquad$ **43.** $\frac{16}{36}$ $\qquad$ **44.** $\frac{36}{132}$ $\qquad$ **45.** $\frac{36}{153}$

Practice Solving Problems

You can use number sense and equivalent fractions to order fractional amounts.

A set of wrenches falls out of its case. Arrange the wrenches by size from smallest to largest. The sizes, in inches, are $\frac{5}{16}$, $\frac{7}{8}$, $\frac{7}{32}$, $\frac{9}{16}$, $\frac{1}{2}$, $\frac{1}{8}$, and $\frac{21}{32}$.

What You Might Think

How can I use number sense to get started?

How can I order the fractions less than $\frac{1}{2}$? Greater than $\frac{1}{2}$?

What is the answer?

What You Might Write

Find the fractions that are less than $\frac{1}{2}$ and the fractions that are greater than $\frac{1}{2}$.

Less than $\frac{1}{2}$: $\frac{5}{16}$, $\frac{7}{32}$, $\frac{1}{8}$

Greater than $\frac{1}{2}$: $\frac{7}{8}$, $\frac{9}{16}$, $\frac{21}{32}$

Write the fractions with a common denominator (32).

Less than $\frac{1}{2}$: $\frac{10}{32}$, $\frac{7}{32}$, $\frac{4}{32}$

Greater than $\frac{1}{2}$: $\frac{28}{32}$, $\frac{18}{32}$, $\frac{21}{32}$

$\frac{1}{2} = \frac{16}{32}$

$\frac{4}{32}$, $\frac{7}{32}$, $\frac{10}{32}$, $\frac{16}{32}$, $\frac{18}{32}$, $\frac{21}{32}$, $\frac{28}{32}$ or

$\frac{1}{8}$, $\frac{7}{32}$, $\frac{5}{16}$, $\frac{1}{2}$, $\frac{9}{16}$, $\frac{21}{32}$, $\frac{7}{8}$

Think It Through

1. **Number Sense** How did you decide which fractions were greater than $\frac{1}{2}$ and which fractions were less than $\frac{1}{2}$?

2. **Reasoning** Without finding a common denominator, how can you use number sense to tell that $\frac{1}{8}$ is the least fraction and $\frac{7}{8}$ is the greatest fraction?

Exercises

3. Nail lengths, in inches, are given as mixed numbers. Arrange the nail lengths $2\frac{3}{4}$, $1\frac{3}{4}$, $1\frac{1}{2}$, $3\frac{1}{2}$, $3\frac{1}{4}$, 2, and $3\frac{3}{4}$ in order from least to greatest. (*Hint:* Start by grouping nails with the same whole-number part.)

4. **Patterns** Seven drill bits are arranged from smallest to largest in the table. They increase in size following a pattern. Find the diameters of the missing drill bits in simplest form.

Drill Bits

Bit Number	Diameter (inches)
1	$\frac{5}{16}$
2	$\frac{3}{8}$
3	■
4	$\frac{1}{2}$
5	■
6	$\frac{5}{8}$
7	$\frac{11}{16}$

5. U.S. presidential elections take place every 4 years. U.S. senators run for election every 6 years. A certain senator is elected in the same year as a presidential election. In how many years will the senator run for reelection in a presidential election year again?

6. The thickness and width of two pieces of lumber are given below. Write two true statements comparing the measurements of these pieces of lumber.

   Piece 1: $2\frac{1}{2}$ in. by $5\frac{1}{2}$ in.   Piece 2: $1\frac{1}{4}$ in. by $7\frac{1}{4}$ in.

7. You want to divide the field below into plots. The plots will be square and be the same size. Each plot will have whole-number side lengths. What is the largest plot size you can use to divide the entire field?

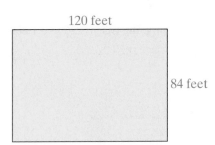

120 feet

84 feet

8. Your dog and cat each eat one can of food every day. Dog food comes in cases of 18 cans. Cat food comes in cases of 16 cans. What is the least number of cases of each type that you must buy so that you have the same number of cans of dog food and cat food?

Fractions and Decimals

Check Skills You'll Need

1. Vocabulary Review When you find 12 ÷ 3, you find how many groups of ■ are in ■.

Find each quotient.

2. 3 ÷ 2   **3.** 2 ÷ 3

4. 8 ÷ 5   **5.** 3 ÷ 10

 **for Help**
Lesson 1-9

What You'll Learn

To find equivalent forms of fractions and decimals and to order fractions and decimals

◀))) **New Vocabulary** terminating decimal, repeating decimal

Why Learn This?

You can write measurements in different ways—as decimals, as fractions, and as mixed numbers. To compare measurements, write them in the same way.

To write a decimal as a fraction, write the fraction as you would say the decimal. Then simplify.

Vocabulary Tip

Reading 0.225 as "two hundred twenty-five thousandths" can help you write 0.225 as a fraction.

EXAMPLE **Writing a Decimal as a Fraction**

1 Write 0.225 as a fraction in simplest form.

$0.225 = \frac{225}{1,000}$ ← Write "two hundred twenty-five thousandths" as a fraction.

$$\frac{225}{1,000} \overset{\div\,25}{\underset{\div\,25}{=}} \frac{9}{40}$$ ← Simplify. The GCF of 225 and 1,000 is 25.

So $0.225 = \frac{9}{40}$.

Quick Check

1. Write 5.08 as a mixed number.

A **terminating decimal** is a decimal that stops, or terminates. Examples are 0.5 and 1.25. A **repeating decimal** repeats the same digit or group of digits. A bar is drawn over the digits that repeat. You write $1.\overline{27}$ for 1.2727....

A fraction indicates division. To write a fraction as a decimal, divide the numerator by the denominator.

Writing a Fraction as a Decimal

② **Construction** A construction worker wants to drill a hole with a diameter that is no more than 0.6 in. Can she use a $\frac{5}{8}$-in. drill bit?

To write $\frac{5}{8}$ as a decimal, divide 5 by 8.

Method 1 Use pencil and paper.

$$\begin{array}{r} 0.625 \\ 8\overline{)5.000} \\ -48 \\ \hline 20 \\ -16 \\ \hline 40 \\ -40 \\ \hline 0 \end{array}$$ ← $\frac{5}{8}$ = 0.625

Method 2 Use a calculator.

5 ÷ 8 = 0.625

Since 0.625 > 0.6, the $\frac{5}{8}$-in. drill bit is too big.

✓ Quick Check

2. You answer 35 out of 40 test questions correctly. Your friend answers 0.8 of the questions correctly. Who scores higher?

EXAMPLE **Ordering Numbers**

Test Prep Tip

To order different types of numbers, you can rewrite the numbers either as all fractions or all decimals.

③ **Multiple Choice** Write 1.6, $1\frac{3}{15}$, 0.9, and $2\frac{2}{9}$ in order from least to greatest.

Ⓐ 0.9, 1.6, $1\frac{3}{15}$, $2\frac{2}{9}$

Ⓒ $2\frac{2}{9}$, 1.6, $1\frac{3}{15}$, 0.9

Ⓑ $2\frac{2}{9}$, $1\frac{3}{15}$, 1.6, 0.9

Ⓓ 0.9, $1\frac{3}{15}$, 1.6, $2\frac{2}{9}$

Write $1\frac{3}{15}$ as a decimal.

$1\frac{3}{15} = 1.2$ ← **Write as a decimal.**

$0.9 < 1.2 < 1.6$ ← **Compare the decimals.**

The order is 0.9, $1\frac{3}{15}$, 1.6, and $2\frac{2}{9}$. The correct answer is choice D.

✓ Quick Check

3. Write $2\frac{2}{3}$, $3\frac{1}{5}$, 1.8, and 2.7 in order from least to greatest.

 **for Help**

For help with dividing, go to Lesson 1-9, Example 1.

Write each decimal as a fraction in simplest form.

1. 0.3   **2.** 0.8   **3.** 0.75   **4.** 0.04

5. Explain why the mixed number $2\frac{3}{4}$ is the same as 2.75.

Match each fraction to a decimal.

6. $\frac{2}{5}$ **A.** 0.75

7. $\frac{3}{4}$ **B.** 0.40

                         C. 0.375

8. $\frac{3}{8}$

Write each set of numbers in order from least to greatest.

9. 1.6, $1\frac{3}{4}$, 2.3   **10.** $2\frac{1}{2}$, 3.7, 3.5   **11.** $3\frac{3}{8}$, $4\frac{3}{5}$, 3.1

Homework Exercises

For more exercises, see Extra Skills and Word Problems.

 **for Help**

For Exercises	See Examples
12–19	1
20–28	2–3

Write each decimal as a fraction or mixed number in simplest form.

12. 0.15   **13.** 0.17   **14.** 0.008   **15.** 5.5

16. 4.25   **17.** 3.149   **18.** 5.075   **19.** 8.32

Write each fraction or mixed number as a decimal.

20. $\frac{5}{6}$ **21.** $\frac{7}{15}$ **22.** $\frac{11}{8}$ **23.** $\frac{10}{9}$

24. $4\frac{7}{10}$ **25.** $1\frac{1}{10}$ **26.** $2\frac{7}{12}$ **27.** $5\frac{3}{20}$

28. Carpentry The sizes of four wrenches are 0.375, $1\frac{1}{8}$, 0.8125, and $1\frac{1}{16}$ inches. Order the wrench sizes from least to greatest.

GPS **29. Guided Problem Solving** A baseball player had 184 hits in 599 at-bats last season. Use a calculator to change the fraction $\frac{184}{599}$ to a decimal. Round to the nearest thousandth.
- What number do you enter first on your calculator?
- List the calculator keys in the order that you will use them.

Match each number with its location on the number line below.

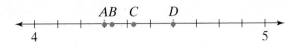

30. $4\frac{3}{5}$ **31.** 4.3 **32.** 4.43 **33.** $4\frac{1}{3}$

34. Shopping You order $1\frac{1}{4}$ pounds of cheese at a delicatessen. What decimal number appears on the digital scale?

35. Writing in Math Explain the steps you would use to write 0.125 as a fraction in simplest form.

36. Number Sense Change $\frac{2}{3}$, $\frac{3}{3}$, $\frac{4}{3}$, $\frac{5}{3}$, and $\frac{6}{3}$ to decimals. Describe when a denominator of 3 results in a repeating decimal.

37. Stocks Until 2001, stock prices were reported as mixed numbers. Find the dollar amounts represented by $6\frac{5}{8}$ and $8\frac{1}{2}$.

Write each number as a mixed number and as a decimal.

38. four and three fourths pounds

39. five and seven eighths inches

40. Challenge Use the same digit to make $\frac{\blacksquare 6}{125} = 0.\blacksquare 08$ true.

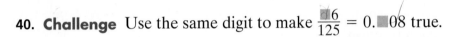

Test Prep and Mixed Review   **Practice**

Multiple Choice

41. Noah wants to write the fraction $\frac{5}{8}$ as a decimal. Which method should he use?
  Ⓐ Write the decimal 0.58.   Ⓒ Divide 5 by 8.
  Ⓑ Write the decimal 0.85.   Ⓓ Divide 8 by 5.

42. Five measuring cups stack inside one another. Which list shows the cup sizes from largest to smallest?
  Ⓕ $\frac{1}{8}$ c, $\frac{1}{4}$ c, $\frac{1}{3}$ c, $\frac{1}{2}$ c, 1 c   Ⓗ 1 c, $\frac{1}{2}$ c, $\frac{1}{4}$ c, $\frac{1}{3}$ c, $\frac{1}{8}$ c
  Ⓖ $\frac{1}{2}$ c, $\frac{1}{4}$ c, $\frac{1}{3}$ c, $\frac{1}{8}$ c, 1 c   Ⓙ 1 c, $\frac{1}{2}$ c, $\frac{1}{3}$ c, $\frac{1}{4}$ c, $\frac{1}{8}$ c

43. Which number is NOT a factor of 144?
  Ⓐ 12   Ⓑ 16   Ⓒ 22   Ⓓ 24

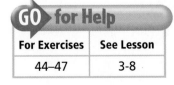

GO for Help

For Exercises	See Lesson
44–47	3-8

Use the Distributive Property to simplify each expression.

44. 3×42 **45.** 9×68 **46.** 7×2.9 **47.** 4×9.1

Conducting a Survey

The way you phrase a survey question can influence the way people answer it. A question that favors one answer over another is biased.

ACTIVITY

1. If your birthday is on an odd day, answer the question in Survey A. If your birthday is on an even day, write your answers to the question in Survey B.

2. Write the fraction of a day that you spend on each of the activities. There are 24 hours in a day.

3. Order your fractions from least to greatest. Write the name of each corresponding activity under each fraction.

4. Find the mean number of hours that students who answered the same survey question as you spend on each activity.

5. **Writing in Math** Compare your results to the results of the students who answered the other survey. Explain how the wording of the two survey questions could lead to differences in the way people responded.

6. Rewrite the question in your survey to remove any bias.

7. **Open-Ended** Choose a topic for a survey question. You might choose study habits, food preferences, favorite movies or books, family life, or computer use.
    a. Write one unbiased and one biased version of your survey question.
    b. **Data Collection** Survey 20 people. Ask 10 people your biased question. Then ask 10 people your unbiased question. Did the bias in your question influence your survey results? Explain.

Survey A
How many hours do you spend each week on these boring activities?
- playing an instrument
- playing video games
- watching television
- listening to music
- playing sports
- reading books

Survey B
How many hours do you spend each week on these fun activities?
- playing an instrument
- playing video games
- watching television
- listening to music
- playing sports
- reading books

Writing Extended Responses

An extended-response question in this book is worth a total of 4 points. To get full credit, you must show your work and explain your reasoning.

EXAMPLE

Mary plans to fence 80 square feet of her backyard for her dog. She wants the length and width to be whole numbers (in feet). What dimensions can she use? Tell how you know that you have found all possible pairs.

Here are four responses with the points each received.

4 points

1 ft by 80 ft, 2 ft by 40 ft, 4 ft by 20 ft, 5 ft by 16 ft, and 8 ft by 10 ft

These are all the pairs because there are no other whole numbers that divide 80 without a remainder.

The 4-point response shows all of the correct whole-number factors of 80 and the student's explanation of why the answer is complete.

3 points

8 and 10, 4 and 20, 5 and 14, 2 and 40, 1 and 80

There are no other whole numbers that divide 80 with no remainder, so this must be the answer.

The 3-point response has one error, and the student's explanation of the answer is complete.

2 points

8 ft by 10 ft, 1 ft by 80 ft, 2 ft by 40 ft, 5 ft by 16 ft, and 4 ft by 20 ft

The 2-point response gives all pairs of factors but does not have an explanation.

1 point

2 and 40, 1 and 80, 8 and 10

The 1-point response is missing some pairs and does not have an explanation.

Exercises

1. Read the 3-point response. What error did the student make?

2. Read the 1-point response. Which dimensions are missing?

Chapter 4 Review

Vocabulary Review

🔊 base (p. 162)
common factor (p. 171)
common multiple (p. 188)
composite number (p. 166)
divisible (p. 158)
equivalent fractions (p. 176)
even number (p. 159)
exponent (p. 162)

factor (p. 166)
greatest common factor (GCF) (p. 171)
improper fraction (p. 182)
least common denominator (LCD) (p. 192)
least common multiple (LCM) (p. 188)
mixed number (p. 182)

multiple (p. 188)
odd number (p. 159)
power (p. 162)
prime factorization (p. 167)
prime number (p. 166)
proper fraction (p. 182)
repeating decimal (p. 198)
simplest form (p. 177)
terminating decimal (p. 198)

Go Online
PHSchool.com

For: Vocabulary quiz
Web Code: aqj-0451

Choose the correct vocabulary term to complete each sentence.

1. Fractions that represent the same amount are ___?___ .

2. The number $5\frac{1}{8}$ is a(n) ___?___ .

3. The ___?___ of 42 is $2 \times 3 \times 7$.

Skills and Concepts

Lesson 4-1
• To check for divisibility using mental math and to use divisibility to solve problems

You can use divisibility rules to solve problems.

Test each number for divisibility by 2, 3, 5, 9, and 10.

4. 207   5. 585   6. 756   7. 3,330

Lessons 4-2 and 4-3
• To use exponents and to simplify expressions with exponents
• To factor numbers and to find the prime factorization of numbers

You can use an **exponent** to show how many times a number, or **base,** is used as a factor. A number expressed using an exponent is called a **power.**

Simplify each expression.

8. $3^2 + 2^3$ 9. $(15 - 1) - 3^2$

A **prime number** has exactly two factors, 1 and the number itself. A **composite number** has more than two factors. Writing a composite number as a product of prime numbers gives the **prime factorization** of the number.

Find the prime factorization of each number.

10. 28   11. 51   12. 100   13. 250

Lesson 4-4

- To find the GCF of two or more numbers

The **greatest common factor (GCF)** of two or more numbers is the greatest factor shared by all the numbers.

Find the GCF of each set of numbers.

14. $18, 28$ **15.** $12, 62$ **16.** $25, 35$ **17.** $16, 40$

Lessons 4-5 and 4-6

- To find equivalent forms of fractions
- To use mixed numbers and improper fractions

Equivalent fractions are fractions that name the same amount. A fraction is in **simplest form** when the only common factor of the numerator and the denominator is 1. A **mixed number** shows the sum of a whole number and a fraction. An **improper fraction** has a numerator that is greater than or equal to its denominator.

State whether each fraction is in simplest form. If the fraction is not, write the fraction in simplest form. Then write three other equivalent fractions for each fraction.

18. $\frac{5}{20}$ **19.** $\frac{4}{6}$ **20.** $\frac{1}{3}$ **21.** $\frac{2}{9}$

Rewrite each number as an improper fraction or a mixed number.

22. $4\frac{2}{3}$ **23.** $8\frac{1}{5}$ **24.** $\frac{13}{3}$ **25.** $\frac{58}{6}$

Lesson 4-7

- To find the LCM of two or more numbers

A number that is a multiple of each of two or more numbers is a **common multiple.** The **least common multiple (LCM)** of two or more numbers is the least multiple that is common to all the numbers.

Find the LCM of each set of numbers.

26. $12, 22$ **27.** $10, 20, 35$

Lessons 4-8, 4-9

- To compare and order fractions
- To find equivalent forms of fractions and decimals and to order fractions and decimals

To compare fractions with unlike denominators, find equivalent fractions that have a common denominator. To write a fraction as a decimal, divide the numerator by the denominator. Write a fraction for a decimal just as you would say the decimal.

Order the numbers from least to greatest.

28. $\frac{1}{2}, \frac{1}{4}, \frac{1}{6}$ **29.** $2\frac{4}{15}, 2\frac{1}{3}, 2\frac{2}{5}$ **30.** $\frac{17}{40}, \frac{7}{20}, \frac{5}{16}$

Write each number as a fraction or mixed number in simplest form or as a decimal.

31. $\frac{3}{16}$ **32.** $6\frac{5}{24}$ **33.** 0.06 **34.** 4.52

Go Online
PHSchool.com
For: Online chapter test
Web Code: aqa-0452

Test each number for divisibility by 2, 3, 5, 9, and 10.

1. 70   **2.** 405   **3.** 628   **4.** 837

State whether each number is prime or composite.

5. 19   **6.** 39   **7.** 51   **8.** 67

Find the prime factorization of each number.

9. 72   **10.** 80   **11.** 120

Find the GCF of each set of numbers.

12. 24, 36   **13.** 20, 25, 30   **14.** 7, 19

15. For a writing workshop, 15 coaches and 35 students will be split into groups, each with the same number of coaches and the same number of students. At most how many groups can there be?

16. Find the length of each segment.

a.
b.
c.

inches

Write each expression using an exponent. Name the base and the exponent.

17. $10 \times 10 \times 10 \times 10$

18. $p \cdot p \cdot p \cdot p \cdot p \cdot p$

Simplify each expression.

19. $4^3 - 1$ **20.** 2×3^2

21. $150 \div 5^2$ **22.** $36 - (8 - 6)^4$

23. Lawns Today, two neighbors water their lawns. One neighbor waters her lawn every four days. The other neighbor waters his lawn every three days. In how many days will they water their lawns on the same day again?

24. Write two fractions equivalent to each fraction.

a. $\frac{6}{18}$ **b.** $\frac{9}{24}$ **c.** $\frac{18}{20}$ **d.** $\frac{60}{100}$

25. Write $\frac{34}{51}$ in simplest form.

26. Writing in Math Explain how to use prime factorizations to find the LCM of two numbers. Include an example.

Find the LCM for each set of numbers.

27. 4, 8   **28.** 6, 11   **29.** 10, 12, 15

Compare each set of numbers using <, =, or >.

30. $1\frac{2}{5} \blacksquare 1\frac{1}{5}$ **31.** $\frac{15}{4} \blacksquare \frac{17}{5}$

32. $\frac{7}{14} \blacksquare \frac{1}{2}$ **33.** $2\frac{3}{5} \blacksquare 2\frac{7}{11}$

34. Order $1\frac{5}{6}$, $1\frac{7}{9}$, $\frac{35}{36}$, and $1\frac{3}{4}$ from least to greatest.

35. Fitness Lee jogged $\frac{1}{2}$ mile, Orlando jogged $\frac{2}{3}$ mile, and Holden jogged $\frac{3}{8}$ mile. Who jogged the longest distance?

Write each decimal as a fraction or mixed number in simplest form. Write each fraction as a decimal.

36. 0.04   **37.** $\frac{17}{40}$ **38.** 3.875

39. $\frac{8}{9}$ **40.** 2.14   **41.** $\frac{6}{11}$

Reading Comprehension

Read each passage and answer the questions that follow.

Sum Art Artists have often used mathematics in their work. The artist M.C. Escher used math ideas in many of his drawings. In the early sixteenth century, Albrecht Dürer included a 4 × 4 number square in one of his engravings, *Melancholia*. A number square has numbers arranged so that each row, column, and main diagonal has the same sum. Part of Dürer's number square is shown at the left.

16	3	2	a
5	b	11	c
d	6	7	e
f	15	14	1

1. What must be the sum of each row, column, and diagonal in Dürers number square?
   - Ⓐ 21
   - Ⓑ 23
   - Ⓒ 34
   - Ⓓ 38

2. What numbers do a and f represent?
   - Ⓕ 13 and 6
   - Ⓖ 14 and 4
   - Ⓗ 14 and 3
   - Ⓙ 13 and 4

3. What is the sum of $b + c$?
   - Ⓐ 15
   - Ⓑ 16
   - Ⓒ 17
   - Ⓓ 18

4. Two squares next to each other contain the year that Dürer made the engraving. In what year did Dürer engrave *Melancholia*?
   - Ⓕ 715
   - Ⓖ 911
   - Ⓗ 1112
   - Ⓙ 1514

Something to Prove One of the most famous unsolved math problems is Goldbach's Conjecture. In 1742, Christian Goldbach made the conjecture that every even number greater than 2 can be written as the sum of two prime numbers. For example, 6 = 3 + 3 and 10 = 3 + 7. Today, mathematicians are still trying to prove Goldbach's Conjecture.

5. To which of the following numbers does Goldbach's Conjecture apply?
   - Ⓐ 1
   - Ⓑ 2
   - Ⓒ 3
   - Ⓓ 4

6. Which of the following illustrates Goldbach's Conjecture for 100?
   - Ⓕ 100 = 35 + 65
   - Ⓖ 100 = 37 + 63
   - Ⓗ 100 = 39 + 61
   - Ⓙ 100 = 41 + 59

7. Which of the following does NOT illustrate Goldbach's Conjecture for 30?
   - Ⓐ 30 = 7 + 23
   - Ⓑ 30 = 21 + 9
   - Ⓒ 30 = 11 + 19
   - Ⓓ 30 = 17 + 13

8. Which of the following odd numbers would NOT be used to illustrate Goldbach's Conjecture?
   - Ⓕ 5
   - Ⓖ 7
   - Ⓗ 9
   - Ⓙ 11

Applying Fractions

Lifting With Levers The simplest machines have only a few moving parts and can be powered by hand. For example, you can use a lever like the one in the diagram below to help lift a heavy load. If you know the distances *a* and *b* in the diagram, and the weight of a load, you can find the force needed to lift the load.

Levers in Nature
The pincer of a fiddler crab is a Class 3 lever.

How to Measure Force
force $= \frac{a}{b} \times$ weight of load

Put It All Together

Data File Use the information on these two pages to answer these questions.

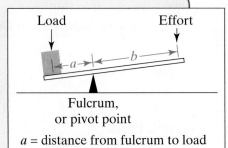

Load   Effort

Fulcrum, or pivot point

a = distance from fulcrum to load
b = distance from fulcrum to effort

1. a. Suppose *a* = 3 and *b* = 6. Find the fraction of the load the force will be.
   b. How much force would it take to lift 100 pounds?

Lever	Muscle Multiplier	Great Lifter	Load Lifter	Extra Muscle	Effort Less	Lever Greatness
a	6	4	5	10	8	5
b	10	6	8	15	14	9

2. The table shows the values of *a* and *b* in feet for six different levers.
   a. Use the force formula to write the fraction of the load required to work each lever. Write each fraction in simplest form.
   b. List the levers in order from least to most force required. Which levers need the same force?
   c. Convert each of the fractions to a decimal. Round to the nearest hundredth. Use the decimals to check the order of your list.

3. Open-Ended Make up your own set of levers.
   a. Choose *a* and *b* for six levers (make *a* less than *b*).
   b. Make a table to record the data about your levers. Name each lever.
   c. Exchange tables with a classmate. Write the fraction of the load required by each lever (in simplest form). Arrange the levers in order from least to most force required.

4. Reasoning For the levers on this page, *a* < *b*. What would happen if *a* > *b*? Can you think of a use for such a lever?

5. Writing in Math What class of lever is a wrench? Explain.

Levers in Playgrounds
A seesaw is a Class 1 lever. The fulcrum is between the load (one child) and the effort (the other child). The load and effort positions change as the seesaw rocks.

Levers at Work

A wheelbarrow is a Class 2 lever. The load (the hay) is between the fulcrum (the front wheel) and the effort (the girl in green).

Go Online
PHSchool.com
For: Information about levers
Web Code: aqe-0453

Three Classes of Levers

Class 1 Lever
Pliers

Fulcrum, between effort and load

Load

Effort

Class 2 Lever
Nutcracker

Load, between effort and fulcrum

Fulcrum

Effort

Class 3 Lever
Tongs

Effort, between load and fulcrum

Load

Fulcrum

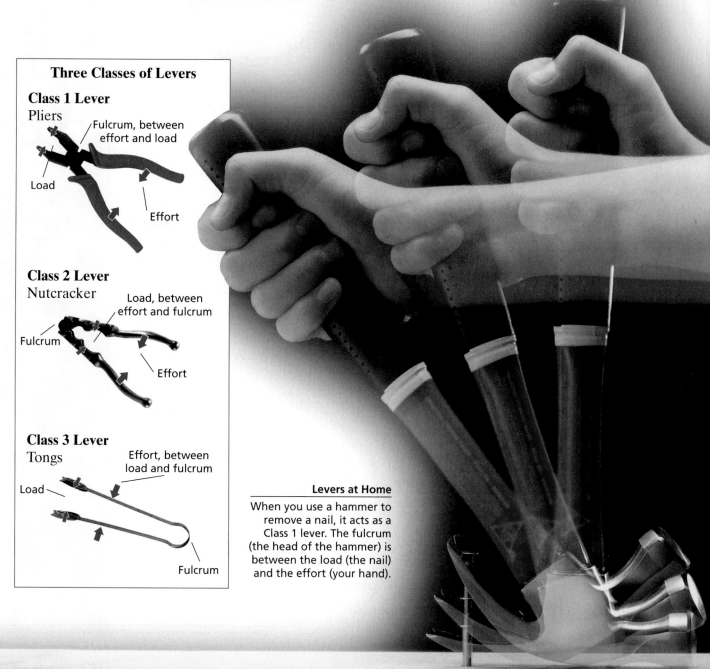

Levers at Home

When you use a hammer to remove a nail, it acts as a Class 1 lever. The fulcrum (the head of the hammer) is between the load (the nail) and the effort (your hand).

What You've Learned

- In Chapter 1, you used addition and subtraction to solve problems involving decimals.
- In Chapter 3, you solved equations using number sense, models, and the properties of equality.
- In Chapter 4, you compared and ordered fractions and mixed numbers.

Check Your Readiness

GO for Help	
For Exercises	See Lesson
1–4	1-5
5–10	4-5
11–13	4-7

Estimating With Decimals

Round each decimal to the nearest hundredth.

1. 2.58796

2. 1.98637

3. 6.219054

4. 7.654321

Finding Equivalent Fractions

Write each fraction in simplest form.

5. $\frac{5}{10}$

6. $\frac{6}{15}$

7. $\frac{12}{16}$

Writing Mixed Numbers and Improper Fractions

Write each improper fraction as a mixed number.

8. $\frac{87}{9}$

9. $\frac{21}{4}$

10. $\frac{15}{2}$

Finding the Least Common Multiple

Find the LCM of each pair of numbers.

11. 8, 18

12. 5, 16

13. 14, 30

What You'll Learn Next

- In this chapter, you will learn to model addition and subtraction problems involving fractions.

- You will use addition and subtraction to solve problems involving fractions.

- You will solve equations with fractions.

- You will use different units of time to solve problems involving elapsed time.

Problem Solving Application On pages 256 and 257, you will work an extended activity involving speeds.

🔊 Key Vocabulary

- benchmark (p. 212)
- elapsed time (p. 246)

Estimating Sums and Differences

1. Vocabulary Review What are *compatible numbers*?

Round each number to the nearest ten.

2. 64   **3.** 146

4. 895   **5.** 1,234

 **for Help**
Lesson 1-2

Vocabulary Tip

You can think of a *benchmark* as a reference point.

What You'll Learn

To estimate sums and differences with fractions and mixed numbers

🔊 **New Vocabulary** benchmark

Why Learn This?

You can use estimation to compare measurements, including heights, lengths, and weights.

A **benchmark** is a convenient number used to replace fractions that are less than 1. The benchmarks 0, $\frac{1}{2}$, and 1 are particularly useful when estimating sums and differences of fractions.

You can use benchmarks to estimate measurements. The following table will help you decide which benchmarks to use.

Description	Examples	Benchmark
Numerator is very small when compared to the denominator.	$\frac{1}{8}, \frac{3}{16}, \frac{2}{25}, \frac{9}{100}$	0
Numerator is about one half of denominator.	$\frac{3}{8}, \frac{9}{16}, \frac{11}{25}, \frac{52}{100}$	$\frac{1}{2}$
Numerator and denominator are close to each other.	$\frac{7}{8}, \frac{14}{16}, \frac{23}{25}, \frac{95}{100}$	1

EXAMPLE **Selecting a Fraction Benchmark**

1 Choose a benchmark for the measurement $\frac{7}{16}$ inch.

7 is about half of 16.

So choose the benchmark $\frac{1}{2}$ inch.

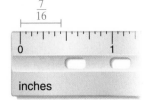

$\frac{7}{16}$

Quick Check

1. Choose a benchmark for the measurement $\frac{8}{9}$ inch.

You can use the benchmarks 0, $\frac{1}{2}$, and 1 to estimate sums and differences.

EXAMPLE **Estimating Sums and Differences**

2 Estimate $\frac{7}{12} + \frac{4}{5}$.

$$\frac{7}{12} + \frac{4}{5} \approx \frac{1}{2} + 1 \qquad \leftarrow \text{Replace each fraction with a benchmark.}$$

$$= 1\frac{1}{2} \qquad \leftarrow \text{Add.}$$

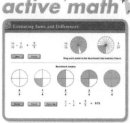

Online
active math

For: Estimating Sums and Differences Activity
Use: Interactive Textbook, 5-1

✓ Quick Check

2. a. Estimate $\frac{5}{6} + \frac{3}{7}$. **b.** Estimate $\frac{12}{13} - \frac{2}{25}$.

You can also round before estimating the sum or difference of two mixed numbers. The diagram below shows how to round $7\frac{9}{16}$ inches and $6\frac{1}{8}$ inches. If a mixed number has a fraction of $\frac{1}{2}$, round up.

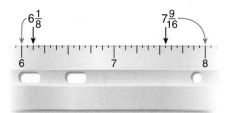

EXAMPLE **Estimating With Mixed Numbers**

3 **Measurement** Dave is $62\frac{3}{4}$ inches tall. Lina is $54\frac{1}{4}$ inches tall. Estimate the difference between their heights.

Estimate $62\frac{3}{4} - 54\frac{1}{4}$.

$62\frac{3}{4} \approx 63 \qquad \leftarrow \text{Since } \frac{3}{4} > \frac{1}{2}, \text{ round to 63.}$

$54\frac{1}{4} \approx 54 \qquad \leftarrow \text{Since } \frac{1}{4} < \frac{1}{2}, \text{ round to 54.}$

$63 - 54 = 9 \qquad \leftarrow \text{Estimate by finding the difference.}$

Dave is about 9 inches taller than Lina.

✓ Quick Check

3. It takes $3\frac{3}{4}$ hours to drive to the beach. It takes $8\frac{1}{2}$ hours to drive to the mountains. Estimate the difference in driving times.

1. **Vocabulary** How are finding a benchmark and rounding similar?

2. **Reasoning** Choose a benchmark for each fraction. Use $0, \frac{1}{2}$, or 1. Which of the fractions has a different benchmark from the others?

$$\frac{3}{8} \qquad \frac{7}{15} \qquad \frac{11}{57} \qquad \frac{45}{92}$$

Choose a benchmark for each fraction. Use $0, \frac{1}{2}$, or 1.

3. $\frac{1}{10}$ 4. $\frac{10}{20}$ 5. $\frac{48}{50}$ 6. $\frac{87}{200}$

For more exercises, see Extra Skills and Word Problems.

Choose a benchmark for each measurement. Use $0, \frac{1}{2}$, or 1.

For Exercises	See Example
7–12	1
13–18	2
19–25	3

7. $\frac{1}{8}$ inch   8. $\frac{4}{8}$ inch

9. $\frac{15}{16}$ inch   10. $\frac{3}{8}$ inch

11. $\frac{11}{16}$ inch   12. $\frac{3}{16}$ inch

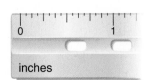

Estimate each sum or difference. Use the benchmarks $0, \frac{1}{2}$, and 1.

13. $\frac{5}{13} + \frac{4}{25}$ 14. $\frac{17}{19} - \frac{2}{13}$ 15. $\frac{70}{85} + \frac{32}{51}$

16. $\frac{11}{20} - \frac{2}{15}$ 17. $\frac{9}{16} - \frac{18}{37}$ 18. $\frac{5}{16} + \frac{7}{15}$

19. $4\frac{2}{9} + 6\frac{13}{27}$ 20. $9\frac{7}{15} - 3\frac{1}{2}$ 21. $22\frac{1}{9} - 16\frac{9}{11}$

22. $22\frac{8}{14} - 17\frac{3}{7}$ 23. $76\frac{6}{23} - 45\frac{1}{5}$ 24. $84\frac{3}{36} + 41\frac{7}{8}$

25. **Science** A kudzu plant is $1\frac{1}{12}$ feet tall. Over time, the plant grows to $4\frac{5}{6}$ feet. About how much does the plant grow?

26. **Guided Problem Solving** Your dog weighed $42\frac{3}{4}$ pounds. The dog gained $3\frac{1}{2}$ pounds. You put him on a diet and he lost $6\frac{1}{4}$ pounds. About how much does your dog weigh now?
    - You can use the strategy *Draw a Picture* to decide which operations are needed to solve the problem.
    - Use a benchmark for each mixed number.

27. Coins Use the table at the right to estimate the total width of the coins.

	U.S. Coins
Coin	**Diameter (inches)**
Dime	$\frac{11}{16}$
Penny	$\frac{3}{4}$
Nickel	$\frac{13}{16}$
Quarter	$\frac{15}{16}$

28. Number Sense You estimate $\frac{1}{8} + \frac{9}{16} + \frac{31}{32}$ using the benchmarks 0, $\frac{1}{2}$, and 1. Is your estimate less than or greater than the actual sum? Explain.

29. Writing in Math Why does it make sense to round a mixed number to the nearest whole number when estimating a sum or difference? Could you round to the nearest $\frac{1}{2}$ instead? Explain.

30. Estimation Use the table at the left.
a. About how much did each person grow during the summer?
b. Who grew the most?

Heights (inches)

Person	June	Sept.
Jocelyn	$61\frac{7}{8}$	$62\frac{1}{4}$
Carlos	$60\frac{3}{4}$	$61\frac{5}{8}$
Amanda	$59\frac{1}{8}$	$60\frac{5}{8}$

31. Challenge Use $<$, $=$, or $>$ to compare.

$$14\frac{9}{10} - \left(8\frac{1}{7} + 1\frac{8}{9}\right) \blacksquare 14\frac{9}{10} - 8\frac{1}{7} + 1\frac{8}{9}$$

Test Prep and Mixed Review   **Practice**

Multiple Choice

32. The length of a sticker is $\frac{3}{4}$ inch. The width is $\frac{7}{8}$ inch more than the length. What is a reasonable estimate for the width?
Ⓐ 1 inches   Ⓑ 2 inches   Ⓒ 3 inches   Ⓓ 4 inches

33. Which weight is nearest to the amount of cheese?

Ⓕ $\frac{1}{2}$ lb   Ⓗ $1\frac{1}{2}$ lb

Ⓖ 1 lb   Ⓙ 2 lb

IMPORTED SWISS CHEESE		
Weight	**Price per Unit**	**Total Cost**
1.47 lb	$5.29/lb	$7.78

34. Which statement about $\frac{3}{8}$ and 0.375 is true?

Ⓐ $\frac{3}{8} > 0.375$ Ⓒ $0.375 > \frac{3}{8}$

Ⓑ $\frac{3}{8} < 0.375$ Ⓓ $0.375 = \frac{3}{8}$

GO for Help

For Exercises	See Lesson
35–39	4-9

Write each fraction as a decimal.

35. $\frac{47}{1,000}$ **36.** $\frac{4}{5}$ **37.** $\frac{3}{500}$ **38.** $\frac{17}{20}$ **39.** $\frac{1}{8}$

Modeling Fraction Operations

You can use a paper model to help you add and
subtract fractions.

ACTIVITY

1. Draw and cut out a circle.
   Fold the circle in half. Then
   fold it in half three more
   times. When you unfold the
   circle, there are 16 sections.
   Each section represents $\frac{1}{16}$
   of the circle.

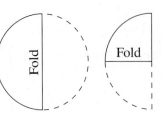

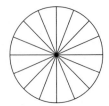

2. From the circle, cut a piece that contains 7 small sections. From
   the remaining part, cut another piece that contains 5 sections.
   Put the two pieces together. Use this model to find $\frac{7}{16} + \frac{5}{16}$.

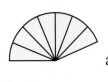 and is

3. Use new circles to model $\frac{11}{16}$ and $\frac{7}{16}$. Is the sum of $\frac{7}{16}$ and
   $\frac{11}{16}$ greater than 1? Find the sum of $\frac{7}{16}$ and $\frac{11}{16}$.

4. Place your model for $\frac{7}{16}$ on top of your model for $\frac{11}{16}$. How
   much of the $\frac{11}{16}$ model is not covered? Find $\frac{11}{16} - \frac{7}{16}$.

Exercises

Use models to add or subtract.

1. $\frac{1}{16} + \frac{9}{16}$ 2. $\frac{6}{8} - \frac{4}{8}$ 3. $\frac{3}{8} + \frac{7}{8}$ 4. $\frac{15}{16} - \frac{3}{16}$

5. a. **Patterns** Look at the numerators for the exercises that
      you modeled. What pattern do you see when you add
      or subtract fractions with the same denominator?
   b. Use the pattern to find $\frac{2}{5} + \frac{3}{5} + \frac{1}{5}$.

Fractions With Like Denominators

Check Skills You'll Need

1. **Vocabulary Review**
How can you tell when a fraction is in *simplest form*?

Write each fraction in simplest form.

2. $\frac{10}{40}$ 3. $\frac{8}{24}$

4. $\frac{20}{24}$ 5. $\frac{12}{28}$

 for Help
Lesson 4-5

What You'll Learn

To add and subtract fractions with like denominators

Why Learn This?

At a bake sale, $\frac{4}{12}$ of a cherry pie and $\frac{7}{12}$ of an apple pie are sold. You can find the total amount of pie sold by adding fractions.

To add fractions with like denominators, you add the numerators and do not change the denominators.

Vocabulary Tip

Like means "the same."

KEY CONCEPTS   **Adding With Like Denominators**

To add fractions with like denominators, add the numerators and keep the same denominator.

Arithmetic

$$\frac{2}{7} + \frac{3}{7} = \frac{2+3}{7} = \frac{5}{7}$$

Algebra

$$\frac{a}{c} + \frac{b}{c} = \frac{a+b}{c}$$

EXAMPLE   **Adding With Like Denominators**

1 Find $\frac{4}{12} + \frac{7}{12}$.

$$\frac{4}{12} + \frac{7}{12} = \frac{4+7}{12}$$ ← The fractions have like denominators. Add the numerators. The denominator stays the same.

$$= \frac{11}{12}$$ ← Simplify the numerator.

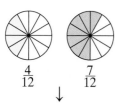

Quick Check

1. **a.** Add $\frac{1}{6} + \frac{1}{6}$.   **b.** Add $\frac{10}{21} + \frac{4}{21}$.

If the sum of fractions results in an improper fraction, rename the improper fraction as a mixed number.

EXAMPLE **Sums Greater Than 1**

For help with writing an improper fraction as a mixed number, go to Lesson 4-6, Example 3.

② Find $\frac{7}{9} + \frac{5}{9}$.

$$\frac{7}{9} + \frac{5}{9} = \frac{7+5}{9} \quad \leftarrow \text{Add the numerators. The denominator remains the same.}$$

$$= \frac{12}{9} \quad \leftarrow \text{Simplify the numerator.}$$

$$= 1\frac{3}{9} \quad \leftarrow \text{Write as a mixed number.}$$

$$= 1\frac{1}{3} \quad \leftarrow \text{Divide the numerator and denominator by the GCF, 3.}$$

✔ **Quick Check**

2. a. Find $\frac{5}{16} + \frac{13}{16}$. **b.** Find $\frac{11}{20} + \frac{17}{20}$.

To subtract fractions with like denominators, subtract the numerators and keep the same denominator. Write the answer in simplest form.

EXAMPLE **Subtracting With Like Denominators**

③ **Circus** A circus has ten seating sections. Eight sections are filled for the first show. Six sections are filled for the second show. How much more of the entire seating area is filled for the first show?

Eight sections out of ten means $\frac{8}{10}$. Six out of ten means $\frac{6}{10}$. The difference is $\frac{8}{10} - \frac{6}{10}$.

$$\frac{8}{10} - \frac{6}{10} = \frac{8-6}{10} \quad \leftarrow \begin{array}{l}\text{Subtract the numerators. The denominator} \\ \text{remains the same.}\end{array}$$

$$= \frac{2}{10} \quad \leftarrow \text{Simplify the numerator.}$$

$$= \frac{1}{5} \quad \leftarrow \text{Write the fraction in simplest form.}$$

In the circus, $\frac{1}{5}$ more of the seating area is full for the first show.

✔ **Quick Check**

3. A board is $\frac{11}{12}$ foot long. You need $\frac{7}{12}$ foot of the board for a brace. How much is left after you cut off the piece you need?

1. **Error Analysis** Which solution to $\frac{1}{5} + \frac{2}{5}$ is correct? Explain your reasoning.

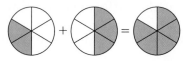

2. **Number Sense** Explain how you can tell when your answer is not in simplest form.

Write an addition or subtraction sentence for each model.

3.

4.

Homework Exercises

For more exercises, see Extra Skills and Word Problems.

GO for Help

For Exercises	See Example
5–8	1
9–12	2
13–22	3

Find each sum. You may find a model helpful.

5. $\frac{1}{4} + \frac{1}{4}$
6. $\frac{2}{5} + \frac{3}{5}$
7. $\frac{2}{9} + \frac{4}{9}$
8. $\frac{1}{6} + \frac{3}{6}$

9. $\frac{2}{3} + \frac{2}{3}$
10. $\frac{9}{10} + \frac{7}{10}$
11. $\frac{7}{12} + \frac{6}{12}$
12. $\frac{4}{5} + \frac{3}{5}$

Find each difference.

13. $\frac{17}{18} - \frac{5}{18}$
14. $\frac{15}{20} - \frac{3}{20}$
15. $\frac{4}{5} - \frac{3}{5}$

16. $\frac{6}{7} - \frac{3}{7}$
17. $\frac{5}{9} - \frac{2}{9}$
18. $\frac{9}{16} - \frac{3}{16}$

19. $\frac{8}{12} - \frac{5}{12}$
20. $\frac{17}{24} - \frac{7}{24}$
21. $\frac{3}{5} - \frac{1}{5}$

22. **Nature Trails** The blue trail at a national park is $\frac{7}{10}$ mile long. The orange trail is $\frac{6}{10}$ mile long. How much longer is the blue trail than the orange trail?

23. **Guided Problem Solving** You can run $\frac{5}{8}$ of a mile in ten minutes. Your friend can run $\frac{7}{8}$ of a mile in ten minutes. How much farther can your friend run in twenty minutes?
   - You can use the strategy *Work a Simpler Problem*. Find how much farther your friend runs in ten minutes.
   - How much farther can your friend run in twenty minutes?

GO Online
Homework Video Tutor
Visit: PHSchool.com
Web Code: aqe-0502

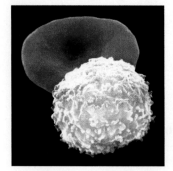

Find each sum.

24. $\frac{1}{20} + \frac{3}{20} + \frac{5}{20}$ **25.** $\frac{27}{100} + \frac{41}{100} + \frac{3}{100}$ **26.** $\frac{4}{15} + \frac{1}{15} + \frac{7}{15}$

27. A typical garden spider is $\frac{7}{8}$ inch long. A black widow spider is $\frac{3}{8}$ inch long. How much longer is the garden spider?

28. **Biology** Plasma makes up $\frac{11}{20}$ of your blood. Blood cells make up the other $\frac{9}{20}$. How much more of your blood is plasma than blood cells?

29. **Writing in Math** Explain how to find the sum of $\frac{5}{9}$ and $\frac{7}{9}$.

30. Suppose it rains $\frac{3}{8}$ inch on Friday and $\frac{7}{8}$ inch on Saturday.
   a. What is the total rainfall during the two days?
   b. What is the difference in rainfall for the two days?

31. **Challenge** Replace the ■ to make the equation true.
$\frac{7}{12} - \frac{■}{12} = \frac{1}{6}$

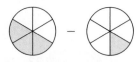
Test Prep and Mixed Review
Practice

Multiple Choice

32. Greg nails two boards together. Each board is $\frac{1}{4}$ inch thick. Greg needs to find the total combined thickness. Which process can he use to find the sum $\frac{1}{4} + \frac{1}{4}$?
   Ⓐ Add the denominators and add the numerators.
   Ⓑ Add the denominators and keep the same numerator.
   Ⓒ Keep the same denominator and the same numerator.
   Ⓓ Keep the same denominator and add the numerators.

33. Which measurement is closest to the length of the line?
   Ⓕ $1\frac{3}{4}$ in.   Ⓗ $1\frac{3}{16}$ in.
   Ⓖ $1\frac{7}{8}$ in.   Ⓙ $2\frac{1}{4}$ in.

34. Which expression represents the model?
   Ⓐ $\frac{1}{2} - \frac{1}{6}$ Ⓒ $\frac{3}{4} - \frac{1}{4}$
   Ⓑ $\frac{1}{3} - \frac{1}{6}$ Ⓓ $\frac{3}{5} - \frac{1}{5}$

GO for Help

For Exercises	See Lesson
35–38	4-5

Write two fractions equivalent to each fraction.

35. $\frac{3}{8}$ **36.** $\frac{1}{6}$ **37.** $\frac{2}{5}$ **38.** $\frac{7}{10}$

Modeling Unlike Denominators

In Lesson 5-2, you added and subtracted fractions with like denominators. To add or subtract fractions such as $\frac{5}{8}$ and $\frac{1}{4}$, first you must write the fractions with like denominators.

EXAMPLE

Use models to find each sum or difference.

a. $\frac{5}{8} + \frac{1}{4}$

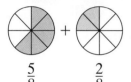

$\frac{5}{8}$ $\frac{1}{4}$

$\frac{5}{8} + \frac{2}{8}$ ← Change the model for $\frac{1}{4}$ so that it has the same number of sections as the model for $\frac{5}{8}$.

$\frac{7}{8}$ ← Add $\frac{2}{8}$ to the model for $\frac{5}{8}$.

b. $\frac{5}{6} - \frac{2}{3}$

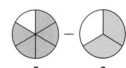

$\frac{5}{6}$ $\frac{2}{3}$

$\frac{5}{6} - \frac{4}{6}$ ← Change the model for $\frac{2}{3}$ so that it has the same number of sections as the model for $\frac{5}{6}$.

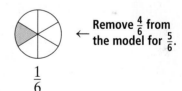 ← Remove $\frac{4}{6}$ from the model for $\frac{5}{6}$.

$\frac{1}{6}$

Exercises

Use models to find each sum or difference.

1.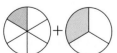

2.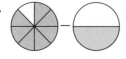

3.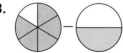

Use models to find each sum or difference.

4. $\frac{1}{8} + \frac{3}{4}$ **5.** $\frac{2}{3} - \frac{1}{6}$ **6.** $\frac{1}{2} + \frac{3}{8}$ **7.** $\frac{5}{6} - \frac{1}{3}$ **8.** $\frac{1}{2} + \frac{1}{3}$

9. **Writing in Math** Explain why you should use a common denominator to add or subtract fractions.

Fractions With Unlike Denominators

Check Skills You'll Need

1. **Vocabulary Review**
How do you use *factoring* when finding the *LCM*?

Find the LCM.

2. 6, 9   **3.** 5, 24

4. 30, 75   **5.** 4, 6, 15

GO for Help
Lesson 4-7

What You'll Learn

To add and subtract fractions with unlike denominators

Why Learn This?

Fractions, such as those used in survey data, sometimes have different denominators. You can use models to add fractions with unlike denominators. You can also write equivalent fractions with the same denominator.

GO Online

Video Tutor Help
Visit: PHSchool.com
Web Code: aqe-0775

EXAMPLE   **Adding With Unlike Denominators**

1 Find $\frac{1}{4} + \frac{1}{3}$.

Method 1 Model $\frac{1}{4} + \frac{1}{3}$.

← Use the fraction model for $\frac{1}{4}$.

← Use the fraction model for $\frac{1}{3}$.

← The LCD is 12. Find a twelfths fraction model with the same amount shaded.

$$\frac{1}{4} + \frac{1}{3} = \frac{7}{12}$$

Method 2 Use a common denominator.

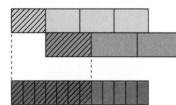

$$\frac{1}{4} \rightarrow \frac{1 \times 3}{4 \times 3} \rightarrow \frac{3}{12}$$

$$+\frac{1}{3} \rightarrow \frac{1 \times 4}{3 \times 4} \rightarrow +\frac{4}{12}$$

The LCD is 12. Write the fractions with the same denominator.

$$\frac{7}{12}$$ ← Add the numerators.

Quick Check

1. Find $\frac{3}{5} + \frac{1}{10}$. Use a model or a common denominator.

EXAMPLE **Application: Surveys**

2 Art students completed a survey about their favorite activity. Ceramics is the favorite of $\frac{2}{5}$ of the students. Drawing is the favorite of $\frac{3}{8}$ of the students. What fraction of the students chose either ceramics or drawing as their favorite activity?

Add $\frac{2}{5}$ and $\frac{3}{8}$ to find the total fraction of the students.

$$\frac{2}{5} \rightarrow \frac{2 \times 8}{5 \times 8} \rightarrow \frac{16}{40}$$

$$+\frac{3}{8} \rightarrow \frac{3 \times 5}{8 \times 5} \rightarrow +\frac{15}{40}$$

$$\frac{31}{40}$$

The LCD is 40. Write the fractions with the same denominator.

← Add the numerators.

The favorite activity of $\frac{31}{40}$ of the students is ceramics or drawing.

✓ Quick Check

2. You exercise for $\frac{1}{2}$ hour on Monday and $\frac{1}{3}$ hour on Tuesday. How long did you exercise on Monday and Tuesday?

You can also subtract fractions that have unlike denominators.

EXAMPLE **Subtracting Fractions**

3 **Multiple Choice** A property owner donates $\frac{1}{4}$ acre to a local park. After the donation, the size of the park is $\frac{5}{6}$ acre. Find the area of the park before the donation.

(A) $\frac{1}{3}$ acre (B) $\frac{2}{5}$ acre (C) $\frac{1}{2}$ acre (D) $\frac{7}{12}$ acre

Subtract $\frac{1}{4}$ from $\frac{5}{6}$ to find the original size of the park.

$$\frac{5}{6} \rightarrow \frac{5 \times 2}{6 \times 2} \rightarrow \frac{10}{12}$$

$$-\frac{1}{4} \rightarrow \frac{1 \times 3}{4 \times 3} \rightarrow -\frac{3}{12}$$

$$\frac{7}{12}$$

The LCD is 12. Write the fractions with the same denominator.

← Subtract the numerators.

The area of the park was $\frac{7}{12}$ acre. The correct answer is choice D.

Test Prep Tip Ⓐ Ⓑ Ⓒ Ⓓ

When you add or subtract fractions, find equivalent fractions with the same denominator.

✓ Quick Check

3. You have $\frac{2}{3}$ yard of felt. You use $\frac{1}{2}$ yard of the felt for a display. How much felt do you have left?

Check Your Understanding

Find each sum or difference.

1. $\frac{2}{5} + \frac{1}{2}$: Use a model.

2. $\frac{2}{3} - \frac{5}{12}$: Use a model.

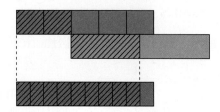 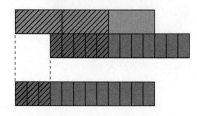

3. $\frac{1}{10} + \frac{2}{5}$: Use the LCD.

$$\frac{\frac{1}{10}}{+\frac{2}{5}} \quad \rightarrow \quad \frac{2 \times 2}{5 \times 2}$$

4. $\frac{7}{9} - \frac{1}{4}$: Use the LCD.

$$\frac{7}{9} \quad \rightarrow \quad \frac{7 \times 4}{9 \times 4}$$
$$-\frac{1}{4} \quad \rightarrow \quad \frac{1 \times 9}{4 \times 9}$$

Homework Exercises

For more exercises, see Extra Skills and Word Problems.

GO for Help

For Exercises	See Example
5–13	1–2
14–21	3

Find each sum. You may find a model helpful.

5. $\frac{1}{3} + \frac{1}{6}$

6. $\frac{1}{6} + \frac{1}{2}$

7. $\frac{8}{9} + \frac{5}{6}$

8. $\frac{5}{6} + \frac{1}{4}$

9. $\frac{1}{3} + \frac{2}{5}$

10. $\frac{3}{5} + \frac{3}{20}$

11. $\frac{3}{10} + \frac{1}{4}$

12. $\frac{3}{5} + \frac{1}{3}$

13. Pets You have two baby hamsters. One weighs $\frac{1}{4}$ pound and the other weighs $\frac{1}{5}$ pound. How much do they weigh together?

GO for Help

For help with writing equivalent fractions, go to lesson 4-5, Example 1.

Find each difference.

14. $\frac{13}{16} - \frac{1}{4}$

15. $\frac{17}{20} - \frac{2}{5}$

16. $\frac{9}{10} - \frac{3}{5}$

17. $\frac{3}{4} - \frac{1}{12}$

18. $\frac{5}{8} - \frac{1}{4}$

19. $\frac{4}{5} - \frac{2}{3}$

20. $\frac{7}{10} - \frac{1}{4}$

21. $\frac{5}{6} - \frac{1}{2}$

22. Guided Problem Solving A roller coaster can hold 48 people. There are 46 people on the ride. Younger adults fill $\frac{1}{3}$ of the seats. Senior citizens fill $\frac{1}{4}$ of the seats. What fraction of the roller coaster is filled by children?
- What is the least common denominator?
- What equivalent fractions should you use?

Use any method to add and subtract.

23. $\frac{5}{8} + \frac{9}{12} + \frac{1}{2}$ **24.** $\frac{11}{30} - \frac{1}{5} - \frac{1}{6}$ **25.** $\frac{2}{5} + \frac{1}{2} - \frac{1}{10}$

26. <u>**Writing in Math**</u> Find $\frac{5}{6} + \frac{7}{12}$ using a model or a common denominator. Explain why you chose the method you used.

27. **Weather** A meteorologist records the rainfall as $\frac{3}{10}$ inch from 9:00 to 10:00. You measure $\frac{7}{8}$ inch of rain from 10:00 to 11:00.
   a. **Estimation** Estimate the rainfall from 9:00 to 11:00.
   b. Find the total rainfall from 9:00 to 11:00.

28. You put $\frac{3}{4}$ cup of paint into a container. You use $\frac{1}{3}$ cup of the paint on a craft project. Later you add another $\frac{1}{2}$ cup of paint to the container. How much paint is in the container?

29. **Number Sense** You walk $\frac{1}{2}$ mile, $\frac{1}{3}$ mile, and then $\frac{1}{4}$ mile. Is the total distance *greater than, less than,* or *equal to* one mile?

30. **Challenge** Find $\frac{1}{2} + \frac{1}{4}$. Then find $\frac{1}{2} + \frac{1}{4} + \frac{1}{8}$. Now find $\frac{1}{2} + \frac{1}{4} + \frac{1}{8} + \frac{1}{16}$. If you continue this pattern, when will the sum be greater than 1? Explain.

Test Prep and Mixed Review   **Practice**

Multiple Choice

31. Sean needs $\frac{2}{3}$ cup of cheese for a casserole and $\frac{1}{4}$ cup of cheese for the topping. How many cups of cheese does Sean need?

    (A) $\frac{3}{12}$ cup   (B) $\frac{3}{7}$ cup   (C) $\frac{11}{12}$ cup   (D) 1 cup

32. Which sum represents the model shown?

    (F) $\frac{1}{6} + \frac{1}{3}$ (H) $\frac{1}{6} + \frac{2}{3}$

    (G) $\frac{1}{8} + \frac{1}{4}$ (J) $\frac{1}{8} + \frac{1}{3}$

33. Anna spends $\frac{1}{2}$ of her savings on a new bike and $\frac{1}{3}$ of her savings on gifts for her family. Which expression gives the fraction of Anna's savings that is left?

    (A) $\frac{1}{2} + \frac{1}{3}$ (C) $1 - \left(\frac{1}{2} + \frac{1}{3}\right)$

    (B) $1 + \frac{1}{2} - \frac{1}{3}$ (D) $1 - \left(\frac{1}{2} - \frac{1}{3}\right)$

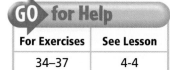
List the factors to find the GCF of each pair of numbers.

34. 16, 64   **35.** 33, 121   **36.** 40, 72   **37.** 60, 210

Estimate each sum or difference. Use the benchmarks 0, $\frac{1}{2}$, and 1.

1. $\frac{8}{9} + \frac{5}{16}$

2. $\frac{12}{13} - \frac{1}{9}$

3. $\frac{7}{12} + \frac{7}{8}$

4. $\frac{11}{12} - \frac{5}{6}$

Find each sum or difference. You may find a model helpful.

5. $\frac{3}{10} + \frac{9}{10}$

6. $\frac{5}{6} - \frac{1}{3}$

7. $\frac{7}{12} + \frac{2}{3}$

8. $\frac{9}{10} - \frac{1}{3}$

9. $\frac{1}{7} + \frac{5}{14}$

10. $\frac{17}{20} - \frac{3}{20}$

11. In a class, $\frac{1}{6}$ of the students have blue eyes, and $\frac{7}{9}$ of the students have brown eyes. Find how much more of the entire class has brown eyes than blue eyes.

12. You are still hungry after eating $\frac{2}{3}$ cup of wheat flakes, so you eat $\frac{1}{2}$ cup of corn flakes. How much cereal do you eat?

13. You mix $\frac{1}{4}$ gallon of yellow paint with $\frac{1}{8}$ gallon of red paint to make orange paint. How much orange paint do you have?

MATH AT WORK

Chef

Generally, there are two types of chefs—institutional chefs and restaurant chefs. No matter where a chef works, he or she will measure, mix, and cook meals according to recipes.

The art of cooking requires skill in many areas of mathematics. Knowing how to weigh and measure with both metric and customary measures is essential to following a recipe. A knowledge of estimation, ratios, and proportions will help a chef determine quantities and serving sizes.

Go Online
PHSchool.com **For:** Information on chefs
Web Code: aqb-2031

Using Mixed Numbers

You can use objects to help you understand addition of mixed numbers.

ACTIVITY

Cut string into lengths of $1\frac{3}{8}$ inches, $2\frac{1}{4}$ inches, $1\frac{7}{8}$ inches, $3\frac{1}{8}$ inches, and $3\frac{3}{4}$ inches.

1. Select the strings that measure $1\frac{3}{8}$ inches and $2\frac{1}{4}$ inches in length. Place the two pieces end to end. Estimate the total length of the two pieces.

2. Measure the total length of the two pieces of string.

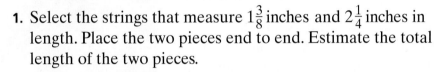

3. Check your measurement by writing an addition equation for the two pieces and finding the sum. Compare the sum to the measured length.
   a. How close was your estimate to the actual length?
   b. **Writing in Math** Explain why the measurement of the total length of the string should be the same as the sum of the two lengths.

4. Repeat Steps 1 through 3 for each pair of strings.

   a. $1\frac{7}{8}$ and $3\frac{3}{4}$
   b. $2\frac{1}{4}$ and $3\frac{3}{4}$

5. **Number Sense** Will the whole number in your answer always equal the sum of the whole numbers you are adding? Explain.

6. **Estimation** Which pairs of pieces of string have a total length between 6 inches and 7 inches? Which pairs have a difference in lengths less than 1 inch?

5-4   Adding Mixed Numbers

 **Check Skills You'll Need**

1. Vocabulary Review
Explain how you know that $\frac{36}{15}$ is an *improper fraction*.

Write each fraction as a mixed number in simplest form.

2. $\frac{8}{6}$ **3.** $\frac{15}{6}$

4. $\frac{7}{4}$ **5.** $\frac{25}{10}$

GO for Help
Lesson 4-6

What You'll Learn

To add mixed numbers with and without renaming

Why Learn This?

When you say, "I'll be there in an hour and a half," or, "I had band practice until quarter after five," you are using mixed numbers to talk about time.

You can find the sum of mixed numbers by adding the whole number and fraction parts separately. Then you combine the two parts to find the total.

EXAMPLE   Adding Mixed Numbers

1 You spent $8\frac{1}{4}$ hours on Saturday and $6\frac{1}{2}$ hours on Sunday working on a science project. How long did you work on the project?

Estimate $8\frac{1}{4} + 6\frac{1}{2} \approx 8 + 7 = 15$

$$
\begin{array}{ccc}
8\frac{1}{4} & \rightarrow & 8\frac{1}{4} \\
+6\frac{1}{2} & \rightarrow & +6\frac{2}{4} \\
\hline
& & 14\frac{3}{4}
\end{array}
$$

The LCD is 4. Write the fractions with the same denominator.

← Add the whole numbers. Then add the fractions.

You work a total of $14\frac{3}{4}$ hours on your science project.

Check for Reasonableness $14\frac{3}{4}$ is close to the estimate of 15. The answer is reasonable.

Quick Check

1. A giant tortoise traveled $2\frac{1}{3}$ yards and stopped. Then it traveled $3\frac{1}{2}$ yards. Find the total distance the giant tortoise traveled.

The sum of the fraction parts may be an improper fraction. If so, rename the sum as a mixed number.

Video Tutor Help

Visit: PHSchool.com
Web Code: aqe-0775

EXAMPLE **Renaming a Sum**

2 Find $15\frac{5}{6} + 3\frac{1}{2}$.

$$15\frac{5}{6} \quad \rightarrow \quad 15\frac{5}{6}$$

$$+3\frac{1}{2} \quad \rightarrow \quad +3\frac{3}{6} \qquad \leftarrow \text{The LCD is 6. Write } \frac{1}{2} \text{ as } \frac{3}{6}.$$

$$\overline{\qquad\qquad\qquad 18\frac{8}{6}} \qquad \leftarrow \begin{array}{l}\text{Add the whole numbers.}\\\text{Then add the fractions.}\end{array}$$

$$= 18 + 1\frac{2}{6} \qquad \leftarrow \text{Rename } \frac{8}{6} \text{ as } 1\frac{2}{6}.$$

$$= 19\frac{2}{6} \qquad \leftarrow \text{Add the whole numbers.}$$

$$= 19\frac{1}{3} \qquad \leftarrow \text{Simplify.}$$

Quick Check

2. a. Find $3\frac{5}{6} + 5\frac{11}{12}$.   **b.** Find $7\frac{3}{5} + 13\frac{2}{3}$.

EXAMPLE **Application: Music**

Test Prep Tip

Drawing a model can help you solve a problem.

Hours at Practice

Total	
$2\frac{1}{2}$	$1\frac{3}{4}$
Monday	Tuesday

3 **Multiple Choice** A band practiced for $2\frac{1}{2}$ hours on Monday and for $1\frac{3}{4}$ hours on Tuesday. How long did the band practice?

   Ⓐ $3\frac{1}{4}$ hours   Ⓑ $3\frac{2}{3}$ hours   Ⓒ $4\frac{1}{4}$ hours   Ⓓ $4\frac{2}{3}$ hours

Find $2\frac{1}{2} + 1\frac{3}{4}$.

$$2\frac{1}{2} \quad \rightarrow \quad 2\frac{2}{4} \qquad \leftarrow \text{The LCD is 4. Write } \frac{1}{2} \text{ as } \frac{2}{4}.$$

$$+1\frac{3}{4} \quad \rightarrow \quad +1\frac{3}{4}$$

$$\overline{\qquad\qquad\qquad 3\frac{5}{4}} \qquad \leftarrow \begin{array}{l}\text{Add the whole numbers.}\\\text{Then add the fractions.}\end{array}$$

$$= 3 + 1\frac{1}{4} \qquad \leftarrow \text{Rename } \frac{5}{4} \text{ as } 1\frac{1}{4}.$$

$$= 4\frac{1}{4} \qquad \leftarrow \text{Add the whole numbers.}$$

The band practiced for $4\frac{1}{4}$ hours. The correct answer is C.

Quick Check

3. Newspapers One advertisement in a newspaper is $1\frac{1}{4}$ inches long. Another advertisement is $2\frac{7}{8}$ inches long. How much space is needed for both advertisements?

1. **Open-Ended** Write an addition expression. Use two mixed numbers with a sum that is a whole number.

Mental Math Find each sum.

2. 1
   $+ 2\frac{1}{6}$

3. $2\frac{2}{3}$
   $+ 4$

4. $3\frac{5}{7}$
   $+ 1\frac{1}{7}$

5. $8\frac{1}{5}$
   $+ 3\frac{2}{5}$

Homework Exercises

For more exercises, see Extra Skills and Word Problems.

GO for Help

For Exercises	See Example
6–9	1
10–18	2–3

Find each sum. You can use a model to help you.

6. $3\frac{1}{9} + 2\frac{2}{3}$

7. $9\frac{1}{6} + 2\frac{1}{3}$

8. $2\frac{3}{5} + 7\frac{1}{3}$

9. $3\frac{1}{2} + 3\frac{1}{5}$

10. $11\frac{1}{3} + 6\frac{7}{9}$

11. $8\frac{5}{6} + 2\frac{1}{3}$

12. $5\frac{2}{3} + 4\frac{1}{2}$

13. $2\frac{5}{6} + 6\frac{2}{5}$

14. $2\frac{3}{4} + 1\frac{5}{8}$

15. $4\frac{5}{8} + 1\frac{3}{4}$

16. $3\frac{1}{3} + 2\frac{5}{6}$

17. $1\frac{1}{2} + 3\frac{5}{6}$

18. **Soccer** You play $12\frac{1}{6}$ minutes during the first half of a soccer game. Then you play $8\frac{3}{4}$ minutes during the second half. How many minutes do you play in total?

19. **Guided Problem Solving** You skate $1\frac{1}{4}$ miles from your house to the park. The park has a path that is $2\frac{3}{10}$ miles long. You skate once around the path and then skate home. What is the total distance you skate?

   • You can draw a picture to model the problem.

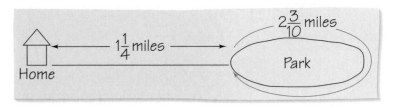

   • Which distance do you skate twice?

20. **Reasoning** One recipe uses $1\frac{3}{4}$ cups of milk. Another recipe uses $1\frac{1}{2}$ cups of milk. You have 3 cups of milk at home. Do you have enough milk to make both recipes? Explain.

GO Online

Homework Video Tutor

Visit: PHSchool.com
Web Code: aqe-0504

Estimation Compare using <, =, or >.

21. $5\frac{8}{9} + 7\frac{5}{6}$ ■ 13

22. $4\frac{5}{13} + 5\frac{4}{9}$ ■ $10\frac{12}{13}$

23. a. Tides At low tide, the depth of the water is $4\frac{11}{12}$ feet. At high tide, the water depth increases by $2\frac{3}{4}$ feet. How deep is the water at high tide?

b. The next day, the depth is $5\frac{1}{2}$ feet at low tide. The depth increases the same amount as the day before. What is the water depth at high tide?

24. Number Sense Is the sum of two mixed numbers *always*, *sometimes*, or *never* a mixed number? Give examples to support your answer.

25. Suppose you need the amounts of fabric shown in the table to make a flag. What is the total length of fabric you need?

26. Writing in Math How can you use mental math to find $5\frac{1}{3} + 3\frac{4}{5} + 3\frac{2}{3} + 6\frac{1}{5}$?

27. Challenge Find $7\frac{1}{3} + 7\frac{5}{6} - 7\frac{1}{9}$.

Careers Oceanographers study water, plants, and animals from the ocean.

Fabric Colors

Color	Length (yards)
Red	$3\frac{1}{4}$
White	$5\frac{1}{2}$
Blue	$4\frac{1}{4}$

Test Prep and Mixed Review **Practice**

Multiple Choice

28. Raul bikes $3\frac{1}{2}$ miles to a movie. Then he bikes $2\frac{3}{4}$ miles to the mall and 5 miles home. How many miles does he bike?

Ⓐ $10\frac{1}{4}$ mi   Ⓑ $10\frac{3}{4}$ mi   Ⓒ $11\frac{1}{4}$ mi   Ⓓ $11\frac{3}{4}$ mi

29. The tennis team sells pie at a fundraiser. Each pie is cut into 8 slices. The team sells 5 slices of apple pie, 8 slices of lemon pie, 2 slices of peach pie, and 3 slices of pumpkin pie. Which expression can you use to find the total number of pies sold?

Ⓕ $5 + 8 + 2 + 3$

Ⓖ $\frac{5}{8} + \frac{8}{8} + \frac{2}{8} + \frac{3}{8}$

Ⓗ $8(5 + 8 + 2 + 3)$

Ⓙ $\frac{5}{8} \times \frac{8}{8} \times \frac{2}{8} \times \frac{3}{8}$

30. Emily uses 30 feet of fencing to make a rectangular dog pen. Which dimensions are NOT possible for the pen?

Ⓐ 3 ft × 10 ft   Ⓑ 4 ft × 11 ft   Ⓒ 6 ft × 9 ft   Ⓓ 8 ft × 7 ft

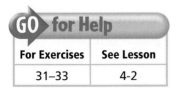

For Exercises | **See Lesson**
31–33 | 4-2

Simplify each expression.

31. $2^3 \times 3^2 + 5$ **32.** $5^3 \times 2^2 \div 10^2$ **33.** $6^2 \times 10^3$

Subtracting Mixed Numbers

Check Skills You'll Need

1. **Vocabulary Review** Explain how to find the *least common denominator* of $\frac{1}{4}$ and $\frac{1}{6}$.

Order each set of numbers from least to greatest.

2. $\frac{3}{5}, \frac{7}{10}, \frac{13}{20}$

3. $2\frac{1}{4}, 2\frac{3}{8}, 2\frac{5}{16}, 2\frac{7}{32}$

 **for Help**
Lesson 4-8

What You'll Learn

To subtract mixed numbers with and without renaming

Why Learn This?

Some scientists measure plant growth. They use mixed numbers when adding and subtracting the measurements.

When you subtract mixed numbers, you may need to write the fractions with a common denominator. Then you can subtract the whole number and the fraction parts separately.

EXAMPLE Subtracting Mixed Numbers

1 **Science** You grow plants for a science project. One plant is $11\frac{3}{4}$ inches tall. Another plant is $7\frac{5}{8}$ inches tall. Find the difference in the heights of the plants.

To find the difference in heights, find $11\frac{3}{4} - 7\frac{5}{8}$.

$$11\frac{3}{4} \quad \rightarrow \quad 11\frac{6}{8} \quad \leftarrow \text{The LCD is 8. Write } \frac{3}{4} \text{ as } \frac{6}{8}.$$

$$-7\frac{5}{8} \quad \rightarrow \quad -7\frac{5}{8}$$

$$\overline{\qquad\qquad\qquad\quad 4\frac{1}{8}} \quad \leftarrow \begin{array}{l}\text{Subtract the whole numbers.} \\ \text{Then subtract the fractions.}\end{array}$$

One plant is $4\frac{1}{8}$ inches taller than the other plant.

Calculator Tip

You can change mixed numbers to decimals on your calculator. You can rename $2\frac{5}{8}$ by entering 2 ➕ 5 ➗ 8 🟰.

Quick Check

1. Another plant is $14\frac{13}{16}$ inches tall. What is the difference between the heights of this plant and the $7\frac{5}{8}$-inch-tall plant?

GO for Help

For help writing mixed numbers as improper fractions, go to Lesson 4-6, Example 1.

Sometimes you need to rename whole numbers or fractions so you can subtract. Here is how to rename $3\frac{1}{4}$.

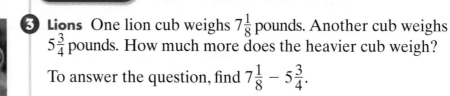

$$3\frac{1}{4} = 2 + 1\frac{1}{4}$$
$$= 2 + \frac{4}{4} + \frac{1}{4}$$
$$= 2\frac{5}{4}$$

$3\frac{1}{4}$ = $2\frac{5}{4}$

EXAMPLE **Renaming a Whole Number**

2 Find $7 - 2\frac{5}{8}$.

Write 7 as a mixed number. Use 8 for the denominator since you must subtract $\frac{5}{8}$.

$$
\begin{array}{ccc}
7 & \rightarrow & 6\frac{8}{8} \quad \leftarrow \text{Rename 7 as } 6 + 1 = 6 + \frac{8}{8}, \text{ or } 6\frac{8}{8}. \\
-2\frac{5}{8} & \rightarrow & -2\frac{5}{8} \\
\hline
& & 4\frac{3}{8} \quad \leftarrow \begin{array}{l}\text{Subtract the whole numbers.} \\ \text{Then subtract the fractions.}\end{array}
\end{array}
$$

✓ Quick Check

2. a. Find $5 - 3\frac{2}{3}$.　　　　　**b.** Find $10 - 4\frac{1}{4}$.

EXAMPLE **Renaming a Mixed Number**

3 **Lions** One lion cub weighs $7\frac{1}{8}$ pounds. Another cub weighs $5\frac{3}{4}$ pounds. How much more does the heavier cub weigh?

To answer the question, find $7\frac{1}{8} - 5\frac{3}{4}$.

$$
\begin{array}{ccc}
7\frac{1}{8} & \rightarrow & 6\frac{9}{8} \quad \leftarrow \text{Rename } 7\frac{1}{8} \text{ as } 6 + 1\frac{1}{8}, \text{ or } 6\frac{9}{8}. \\
-5\frac{3}{4} & \rightarrow & -5\frac{6}{8} \quad \leftarrow \text{The LCD is 8. Write } \frac{3}{4} \text{ as } \frac{6}{8}. \\
\hline
& & = 1\frac{3}{8} \quad \leftarrow \text{Subtract.}
\end{array}
$$

The heavier cub weighs $1\frac{3}{8}$ pounds more than the other cub.

✓ Quick Check

3. A picture frame is $1\frac{3}{4}$ feet wide and $3\frac{5}{6}$ feet long. How much longer is the picture frame than it is wide?

More Than One Way

Suppose you catch two fish. The first one is $9\frac{1}{8}$ inches long. The second one is $7\frac{1}{4}$ inches long. How much longer is the first fish?

Leon's Method

I need to subtract the lengths. Since $\frac{1}{8} < \frac{1}{4}$, I will rename $9\frac{1}{8}$.

$$
\begin{array}{r}
9\frac{1}{8} \\
-7\frac{1}{4} \\
\end{array}
\quad\rightarrow\quad
\begin{array}{r}
8\frac{9}{8} \\
-7\frac{2}{8} \\
\hline
= 1\frac{7}{8}
\end{array}
$$

← Rename $9\frac{1}{8}$ as $8 + 1\frac{1}{8}$, or $8\frac{9}{8}$.

← The LCD is 8. Write $\frac{1}{4}$ as $\frac{2}{8}$.

← Find the difference.

The first fish is $1\frac{7}{8}$ inches longer than the second fish.

Lauren's Method

I need to subtract the lengths. I will change both mixed numbers to improper fractions with the same denominator.

$9\frac{1}{8} - 7\frac{1}{4} = \frac{73}{8} - \frac{29}{4}$ ← Write as improper fractions.

$\phantom{9\frac{1}{8} - 7\frac{1}{4}} = \frac{73}{8} - \frac{58}{8}$ ← Rename as equivalent fractions with a like denominator.

$\phantom{9\frac{1}{8} - 7\frac{1}{4}} = \frac{15}{8}$, or $1\frac{7}{8}$ ← Subtract. Write the difference in simplest form.

The first fish is $1\frac{7}{8}$ inches longer than the second fish.

Choose a Method

Find $10\frac{1}{3} - 7\frac{8}{9}$. Describe your method and explain why it was appropriate.

Check Your Understanding

1. **Number Sense** Which mixed number is equal to $4\frac{5}{7}$?

   Ⓐ $3\frac{10}{7}$　　Ⓑ $3\frac{11}{7}$　　Ⓒ $3\frac{12}{7}$　　Ⓓ $3\frac{13}{7}$

Find each difference.

2. $12\frac{3}{4} - 10\frac{1}{4}$

3. $3\frac{4}{4} - 2\frac{3}{4}$

For more exercises, see Extra Skills and Word Problems.

GO for Help

For Exercises	See Example
4–13	1
14–16	2
17–21	3

Find each difference.

4. $9\frac{4}{7} - 2\frac{3}{14}$

5. $7\frac{3}{4} - 6\frac{2}{5}$

6. $2\frac{5}{8} - 1\frac{1}{4}$

7. $9\frac{4}{5} - 4\frac{4}{15}$

8. $21\frac{3}{8} - 11\frac{1}{4}$

9. $15\frac{11}{12} - 11\frac{1}{2}$

10. $12\frac{1}{4} - 4\frac{1}{8}$

11. $3\frac{2}{3} - 1\frac{1}{6}$

12. $19\frac{1}{3} - 7\frac{1}{5}$

13. You spend $2\frac{2}{3}$ hours reading and $1\frac{1}{2}$ hours watching a movie. How much more time do you spend reading than watching the movie?

Find each difference.

14.
$$\begin{array}{r} 8 \\ - 2\frac{3}{4} \\ \hline \end{array}$$

15.
$$\begin{array}{r} 23 \\ - 19\frac{5}{8} \\ \hline \end{array}$$

16.
$$\begin{array}{r} 32 \\ - 16\frac{1}{2} \\ \hline \end{array}$$

17. $10\frac{1}{10} - 3\frac{2}{5}$

18. $3\frac{3}{8} - 1\frac{3}{4}$

19. $4\frac{5}{12} - 1\frac{3}{4}$

20. $6\frac{1}{5} - 2\frac{2}{3}$

21. Biology In one hour, a bee can fly $5\frac{2}{3}$ miles. A moth can fly $11\frac{1}{6}$ miles in one hour. How much farther can the moth fly in one hour than the bee?

GPS **22. Guided Problem Solving** You have a board that is 12 feet long. You cut two pieces from the board that are both $3\frac{7}{12}$ feet long. How much of the board is left?
   • **Make a Plan** Subtract the first piece from 12 feet. Then subtract the second piece from the remaining length.
   • **Check the Answer** Draw a picture to determine whether your answer is reasonable.

12-foot board

$3\frac{7}{12}$ feet	$3\frac{7}{12}$ feet	answer

23. Weather On Monday, the snowfall in the mountains was $15\frac{3}{4}$ inches. On Tuesday, the snowfall was $18\frac{1}{2}$ inches. How much more snow fell on Tuesday?

24. <u>**Writing in Math**</u> You are finding $3\frac{1}{6} - 1\frac{5}{6}$. Explain why you would rewrite $3\frac{1}{6}$ as $2\frac{7}{6}$.

GO Online

Homework Video Tutor

Visit: PHSchool.com
Web Code: aqe-0505

25. Gardening Carlos plants a tree that is $3\frac{1}{2}$ feet tall. A year later the tree is $4\frac{5}{12}$ feet tall. How much has it grown?

26. Choose a Method Find $6\frac{2}{5} - 3\frac{1}{2}$. Did you subtract the mixed numbers or use improper fractions? Explain your choice.

Olympics Use the table for Exercises 27–29.

27. How much farther did Heike Drechsler jump in 1992 than in 2000?

28. Which two jumps were closest in length?

29. Find the difference between the longest and the shortest winning jumps.

Women's Olympic Long Jump Winners

Year	Winner, Country	Distance
1988	Jackie Joyner-Kersee, United States	24 ft $3\frac{1}{2}$ in.
1992	Heike Drechsler, Germany	23 ft $5\frac{1}{4}$ in.
1996	Chioma Ajunwa, Nigeria	23 ft $4\frac{1}{2}$ in.
2000	Heike Drechsler, Germany	22 ft $11\frac{1}{4}$ in.
2004	Tatyana Lebedeva, Russia	23 ft $2\frac{1}{2}$ in.

SOURCE: *ESPN Sports Almanac*

30. Challenge Solve the equation $x + 1\frac{2}{3} = 3\frac{1}{2}$.

Test Prep and Mixed Review

Practice

Multiple Choice

31. Lauren spent $1\frac{3}{4}$ hours doing math homework and $2\frac{1}{4}$ hours reading. How many more hours did Lauren spend reading?

ⓐ $\frac{1}{2}$ hour

ⓒ $1\frac{1}{2}$ hours

ⓑ $\frac{3}{4}$ hour

ⓓ $1\frac{3}{4}$ hours

32. James will use the following steps to find the sum $6\frac{5}{8} + 3\frac{7}{8}$.

Step K Write as a mixed number: $\frac{12}{8} = 1\frac{1}{2}$.

Step L Add fraction parts: $\frac{5}{8} + \frac{7}{8} = \frac{12}{8}$.

Step M Add whole number and fraction parts: $9 + 1\frac{1}{2} = 10\frac{1}{2}$.

Step N Add whole number parts: $6 + 3 = 9$.

Which list shows the steps in the correct order?
ⓕ M, N, L, K
ⓗ L, N, M, K
ⓖ L, K, M, N
ⓙ N, L, K, M

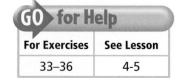

For Exercises	See Lesson
33–36	4-5

Write each fraction in simplest form.

33. $\frac{15}{25}$

34. $\frac{16}{56}$

35. $\frac{36}{54}$

36. $\frac{8}{4}$

Using a Fraction Calculator

You can use a fraction calculator to add and subtract fractions. Use the [/] key, which indicates division, for the fraction bar.

EXAMPLE

1 Find $\frac{5}{6} - \frac{3}{8}$.

Enter 5 [/] 6 [−] 3 [/] 8 [=] *11/24*.

$\frac{5}{6} - \frac{3}{8} = \frac{11}{24}$

You can also use a fraction calculator to add or subtract mixed numbers. Use the [UNIT] key to enter the whole number part. If you do not use the unit key, the calculator will interpret $1\frac{3}{4}$ as $\frac{13}{4}$.

EXAMPLE

2 Find $1\frac{3}{4} + 3\frac{1}{2}$.

Enter 1 [UNIT] 3 [/] 4 [+] 3 [UNIT] 1 [/] 2 [=] *21/4*.

To rename this number, press [2nd] [aᵇ/c] [=] *5 1/4*.

In simplest form, $1\frac{3}{4} + 3\frac{1}{2} = 5\frac{1}{4}$.

Exercises

Use a fraction calculator to find each sum or difference.

1. $\frac{3}{4} - \frac{2}{5}$ 2. $\frac{8}{9} + \frac{1}{12}$ 3. $\frac{11}{12} - \frac{3}{8}$ 4. $\frac{4}{5} + \frac{1}{20}$

5. $\frac{3}{10} - \frac{2}{9}$ 6. $\frac{22}{25} + \frac{9}{100}$ 7. $9\frac{3}{4} + 3\frac{3}{4}$ 8. $6\frac{9}{10} + 2\frac{1}{12}$

9. $18\frac{5}{12} - 9\frac{1}{2}$ 10. $1\frac{1}{10} + 8\frac{1}{12}$ 11. $13\frac{5}{12} - 5\frac{1}{3}$ 12. $14\frac{3}{10} - 3\frac{1}{2}$

13. **Writing in Math** How can you use a fraction calculator to simplify an improper fraction?

Find each sum or difference.

1. $2\frac{1}{2} + 3\frac{1}{8}$

2. $9\frac{1}{2} - 4\frac{3}{4}$

3. $6\frac{1}{3} + 8\frac{1}{2}$

4. $7\frac{5}{9} - 1\frac{2}{3}$

5. $3\frac{1}{3} + 2\frac{1}{2}$

6. $2\frac{1}{9} - 1\frac{2}{3}$

7. $4\frac{1}{2} + 5\frac{3}{8}$

8. $5\frac{2}{3} - 1\frac{1}{2}$

9. Music You spend $1\frac{1}{2}$ hours practicing piano and $2\frac{3}{4}$ hours working on homework. How many total hours have you spent doing both activities?

10. Travel A road sign says that the next exit is $2\frac{1}{4}$ miles ahead. You travel $1\frac{7}{10}$ miles according to your odometer. How much farther ahead is the next exit?

MATH GAMES

That's Some Sum!

What You'll Need

- Paper and pencil
- Two pencils or markers of different colors

How To Play

- Draw a square game board and divide it into 16 smaller squares. Write fractions in half of the squares and mixed numbers in the other half.
- Player 1 circles any two numbers and then finds their sum. The sum is added to that player's score.
- Player 2 circles two other numbers, finds the sum, and adds it to his or her score. Players take turns until all numbers have been chosen.
- Any answer may be challenged. If the answer is correct, the challenger loses a turn. If the challenger corrects the answer, that sum is added to the challenger's score. The other player's turn is over without any change to his or her score.
- The player with the greater total score wins.

Using Pictographs

A pictograph uses pictures or symbols to represent data. Each picture has the same value. The pictograph below shows that $4\frac{1}{2}$ thousand people have attended girls' basketball games.

Basketball Game Attendance

Boys' basketball

Girls' basketball

 = 1000 people in attendance

Exercises

1. What is the total number of pictures that represent data in the pictograph above? What is the total number of people who have attended girls' and boys' basketball games?

2. The pictograph at the right represents the hits that a player got in one season. How many hits did this player get?

3. For each pictograph below, describe a situation that the pictograph might represent. Then write and solve a mixed-number problem based on the pictograph.

   a.   **Pizzas Sold**

    = 10,000 pizzas

   b.   **Apartments for Rent**

   ☐☐☐☐ = 1,000 apartments

Number of Hits

Singles ◯◯◯◯◯◯◖

Doubles ◯◯◯◯

Triples ◯◯◖

Home runs ◯◯◯◗

◯◯ = 8 hits

4. **Reasoning** Suppose you are making a pictograph in which each picture represents 100 visits to a veterinarian. Why is it easier to use circular or square shapes than to use pictures of people or animals?

5. **Open-Ended** Draw a pictograph for the values $5\frac{3}{10}$ and $3\frac{7}{10}$. Write a problem that could be represented by your pictograph.

What You'll Learn

To solve equations with fractions

Why Learn This?

Weather reports include information such as temperature, humidity, and rainfall. You can use equations with fractions to find rainfall amounts.

Sometimes you can use mental math to solve equations that involve fractions or mixed numbers. Remember, you can also use a model to help you solve equations.

EXAMPLE **Using Mental Math in Equations**

1 Solve $3\frac{1}{8} + x = 15\frac{7}{8}$ using mental math.

	$15\frac{7}{8}$	
$3\frac{1}{8}$	x	

$3 + 12 = 15$ ← Use mental math to find the missing whole number.

$\frac{1}{8} + \frac{6}{8} = \frac{7}{8}$ ← Use mental math to find the missing fraction.

$x = 12\frac{6}{8}$ ← Combine the two parts.

Quick Check

1. Solve each equation using mental math.

a. $x - 1\frac{3}{8} = 1\frac{3}{8}$ **b.** $14\frac{1}{4} + x = 25\frac{1}{2}$ **c.** $5\frac{5}{6} - x = 2\frac{1}{6}$

You can use inverse operations to get the variable alone on one side of the equation.

EXAMPLE   Solving Equations With Fractions

2 Solve $x - \frac{1}{3} = \frac{5}{6}$.

$$x - \frac{1}{3} + \frac{1}{3} = \frac{5}{6} + \frac{1}{3} \qquad \leftarrow \text{Add } \tfrac{1}{3} \text{ to each side.}$$

$$x = \frac{5}{6} + \frac{2}{6} \qquad \leftarrow \text{The LCD is 6. Write } \tfrac{1}{3} \text{ as } \tfrac{2}{6}.$$

$$x = \frac{7}{6} \qquad \leftarrow \text{Add.}$$

$$x = 1\frac{1}{6} \qquad \leftarrow \text{Simplify.}$$

GO for Help

For help with adding fractions, go to Lesson 5-3, Example 1.

✓ Quick Check

2. a. Solve $n + \frac{1}{3} = \frac{11}{12}$. **b.** Solve $\frac{2}{5} + a = \frac{13}{20}$.

EXAMPLE   Application: Rainfall

3 During the first week of January, a rain gauge collected $\frac{1}{2}$ inch of rain. By the end of January, the total rainfall was $2\frac{3}{5}$ inches. How much rain fell after the first week of January?

Words	rainfall during first week of January	+	rainfall after first week of January	=	total rainfall in January

Let r = the rainfall after the first week of January.

Equation	$\frac{1}{2}$	+	r	=	$2\frac{3}{5}$

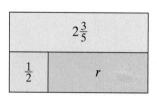

$$\frac{1}{2} + r = 2\frac{3}{5}$$

$$\frac{1}{2} + r - \frac{1}{2} = 2\frac{3}{5} - \frac{1}{2} \qquad \leftarrow \text{Subtract } \tfrac{1}{2} \text{ from each side.}$$

$$r = 2\frac{6}{10} - \frac{5}{10} \qquad \leftarrow \begin{array}{l}\text{The LCD is 10. Write each fraction} \\ \text{with a denominator of 10.}\end{array}$$

$$r = 2\frac{1}{10} \qquad \leftarrow \text{Subtract.}$$

After the first week of January, $2\frac{1}{10}$ inches of rain fell.

✓ Quick Check

3. You hammer a nail $2\frac{3}{8}$ inches long through a board. The nail pokes $\frac{5}{8}$ inch through the other side. How thick is the board?

Check Your Understanding

Match each equation with the correct solution.

1. $x - 3\frac{1}{5} = \frac{2}{5}$ **A.** $3\frac{1}{5}$

2. $x + 4\frac{3}{5} = 8$ **B.** $3\frac{2}{5}$

3. $x - 2\frac{1}{5} = 1\frac{3}{5}$ **C.** $3\frac{3}{5}$

               D. $3\frac{4}{5}$

4. $x + 4\frac{4}{5} = 8$

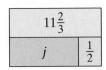

5. Your frog wins second place in a jumping contest. The winning jump of $11\frac{2}{3}$ feet is $\frac{1}{2}$ foot longer than your frog's jump. How far does your frog jump?

Homework Exercises

For more exercises, see Extra Skills and Word Problems.

Mental Math Solve each equation.

GO for Help

For Exercises	See Example
6–11	1
12–19	2
20–24	3

6. $x + 4\frac{2}{5} = 7\frac{4}{5}$ **7.** $a + 6\frac{1}{3} = 20\frac{2}{3}$ **8.** $c - \frac{3}{10} = 6\frac{9}{10}$

9. $7\frac{4}{5} = 2\frac{3}{5} + n$ **10.** $4\frac{3}{8} = k - 7\frac{1}{8}$ **11.** $12\frac{5}{6} = s + 2\frac{5}{6}$

Solve each equation. You may find a model helpful.

12. $x = \frac{2}{7} + \frac{5}{6}$ **13.** $\frac{2}{5} - \frac{1}{9} = x$ **14.** $x - \frac{5}{6} = \frac{7}{8}$

15. $\frac{5}{24} + g = \frac{1}{3}$ **16.** $\frac{4}{9} = y - \frac{2}{5}$ **17.** $t - \frac{7}{9} = \frac{1}{3}$

18. $\frac{11}{12} = n + \frac{2}{3}$ **19.** $\frac{5}{8} = a + \frac{1}{3}$ **20.** $3\frac{1}{5} = x - \frac{12}{25}$

21. $y - 2\frac{8}{9} = \frac{5}{6}$ **22.** $k - 4\frac{5}{6} = 2\frac{1}{4}$ **23.** $9\frac{7}{8} = b - \frac{3}{4}$

24. **Reading** A book has 8 chapters. You read $\frac{3}{8}$ of the book in a week. Use an equation to find how much you have left to read.

25. **Guided Problem Solving** You buy 12 pounds of beef for a class picnic. You use $5\frac{1}{2}$ pounds to make burgers and $4\frac{2}{3}$ pounds to make tacos. Use an equation to find how much beef remains.
- How much beef have you used in all?
- What equation represents this situation?

26. Patterns Solve each equation.

a. $\frac{1}{3} + x = \frac{1}{2}$ b. $\frac{1}{4} + x = \frac{1}{3}$ c. $\frac{1}{5} + x = \frac{1}{4}$

d. Predict the solution of $\frac{1}{9} + x = \frac{1}{8}$.

27. Landscaping The Service Club buys a 10-yard roll of edging to put around two trees in front of the school. The club uses $5\frac{2}{3}$ yards of edging for one tree and $3\frac{1}{2}$ yards for the other tree. How much edging is left?

28. The Golden Gate Bridge in California is about $\frac{4}{5}$ mile long. It is about $\frac{1}{2}$ mile longer than the Brooklyn Bridge in New York. About how long is the Brooklyn Bridge?

29. Writing in Math Refer to the table. Did the relay team beat their best total time of 6 minutes for this 1600-meter relay? Explain.

Relay Times (minutes)

Kim	$1\frac{1}{2}$
Alison	$1\frac{3}{8}$
Laura	$1\frac{3}{4}$
Jamie	$1\frac{1}{4}$

30. Your teacher asks your class to name one of the three primary colors. If $\frac{2}{5}$ of the class chooses yellow, and $\frac{1}{3}$ of the class chooses blue, what fraction of the class chooses red?

31. Number Sense Which variable, m or n, has the greater value?

$$m - \frac{3}{4} = \frac{37}{50} \qquad n - \frac{4}{5} = \frac{37}{50}$$

32. Challenge One girl can eat $\frac{1}{2}$ of an apple in $\frac{1}{3}$ of a minute. At this rate, how many apples can three girls eat in two minutes?

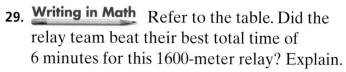
Test Prep and Mixed Review   **Practice**

Multiple Choice

33. Greg scores 98, 92, 76, 91, and 98 on 5 math quizzes. What is the median of Greg's quiz scores?

Ⓐ 76   Ⓑ 91   Ⓒ 92   Ⓓ 98

34. The table shows the amount Carla earns baby-sitting. Which expression can you use to find how much Carla earns for baby-sitting h hours?

Ⓕ $2h$ Ⓗ $h + 7$
Ⓖ $8h$ Ⓙ $h + 16$

Baby-sitting Money

Hours, h	Dollars
1	8
2	16
4	32
h	?

Order each set of numbers from least to greatest.

35. $\frac{1}{2}, \frac{2}{3}, \frac{4}{7}, \frac{3}{10}$ **36.** $\frac{3}{4}, \frac{4}{3}, \frac{1}{9}, \frac{11}{12}$ **37.** $\frac{2}{11}, \frac{0}{5}, \frac{5}{9}, \frac{8}{7}$

Practice Solving Problems

Carpentry You build a garden wall that is 36 inches tall. You place two $1\frac{1}{2}$-inch-by-$11\frac{1}{4}$-inch boards on top of each other. Each board is 5 feet long. How wide does the third board need to be to finish the wall?

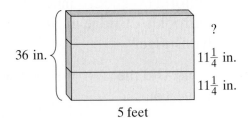

36 in. ? $11\frac{1}{4}$ in. $11\frac{1}{4}$ in. 5 feet

What You Might Think

> How can I use a diagram to show this situation?

> What equation can I write for this situation?

> What is the answer?

What You Might Write

36 in.		
$11\frac{1}{4}$ in.	$11\frac{1}{4}$ in.	w

Let w = width of unknown board.

$$11\frac{1}{4} + 11\frac{1}{4} + w = 36$$

$$22\frac{1}{2} + w = 36$$

$$22\frac{1}{2} + w - 22\frac{1}{2} = 36 - 22\frac{1}{2}$$

$$w = 13\frac{1}{2}$$

The third board needs to be $13\frac{1}{2}$ inches wide.

Think It Through

1. Can you solve the equation $11\frac{1}{4} + 11\frac{1}{4} + x = 36$ by subtracting $11\frac{1}{4}$ from each side? Explain.

2. **Check for Reasonableness** How can you use rounding to decide whether the answer is reasonable?

3. **Reasoning** Which strategies can you use to determine which information in the problem is unnecessary?

Exercises

4. Jack Earle starred in the 1924 movie *Jack & the Beanstalk.* He was 8 feet $6\frac{1}{2}$ inches tall. Trijntje Keever (1616–1633) was possibly the tallest woman ever at 8 feet $4\frac{1}{5}$ inches tall. How much shorter was Keever than Earle?

5. A textbook is $1\frac{15}{16}$ inches thick. The front and back covers are each $\frac{1}{8}$ inch thick. How thick is the book without its covers? Use the diagram below to write and solve an equation.

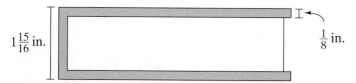

$1\frac{15}{16}$ in. $\frac{1}{8}$ in.

6. A standard business envelope is $4\frac{1}{8}$ inches high and 9 inches wide as shown at the right. An $8\frac{1}{2}$ inch-by-11 inch sheet of paper is folded and placed in the envelope. How much wider is the envelope than the paper?

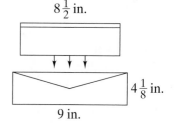

$8\frac{1}{2}$ in.

$4\frac{1}{8}$ in.

9 in.

7. An object needs to be shipped using one of the boxes in the table below. Either box is an appropriate length and width to fit the object. The object is $2\frac{3}{8}$ inches high. Which box would you use? How much extra space would there be?

Box Sizes (inches)

Length	Width	Height
$3\frac{3}{4}$	$3\frac{1}{2}$	$2\frac{9}{16}$
$3\frac{5}{8}$	$2\frac{11}{16}$	$2\frac{1}{4}$

8. What is the distance across the inside of the pipe shown at the right?

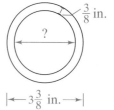

$\frac{3}{8}$ in.

?

$3\frac{3}{8}$ in.

9. An A-10 envelope is 6 inches wide and $9\frac{1}{2}$ inches long. The inside of the envelope is $5\frac{3}{4}$ inches wide and $9\frac{1}{8}$ inches long. What is the difference between an A-10 envelope's outside and inside dimensions?

10. <u>**Writing in Math**</u> Write a word problem that you can solve with the equation $1\frac{1}{2} + 1\frac{1}{2} + d = 10\frac{1}{2}$. Then solve your problem.

Measuring Elapsed Time

Check Skills You'll Need

1. **Vocabulary Review**
   Name four different *units of time.*

Write an equivalent time.

2. 8 hours 2 minutes

3. 5 days 3 hours

4. 3 weeks 5 days

for Help
Skills Handbook
p. 647

What You'll Learn

To add, subtract, and convert between units of time

🔊 **New Vocabulary** elapsed time

Why Learn This?

Trains, buses, and airplanes all follow schedules. You can calculate elapsed time to find how long something will last, such as a trip or your school day.

To add units of time, you may need to rewrite some units. You can rewrite 1 minute as 60 seconds, and 1 hour as 60 minutes. You can also rewrite days, weeks, months, and years.

EXAMPLE Adding Units of Time

1 An airplane taxis for 12 minutes before taking off. The flight time is 47 minutes. After landing, taxiing to the gate takes 11 minutes. What is the total gate-to-gate time for this flight?

$12 + 47 + 11 = 70$

70 minutes = 60 minutes + 10 minutes   ← 60 minutes equals one hour.

= 1 hour 10 minutes   ← Rewrite your answer using hours and minutes.

The total gate-to-gate time for the flight is 1 hour 10 minutes.

✓ Quick Check

1. You study math for 47 minutes and social studies for 39 minutes. What is the total time you spend studying?

The time between two events is called **elapsed time**. To estimate elapsed time, round each time. Then subtract.

EXAMPLE **Estimating Elapsed Time**

2 You begin practice at 1:55 P.M. and end at 5:17 P.M. Estimate the number of hours you practice.

To estimate the elapsed time, round 1:55 and 5:17. Then subtract.

5:17 ≈ 5:00	→	about 5 h after 12:00
1:55 ≈ 2:00	→	about 2 h after 12:00

Since 5:00 is 3 hours past 2:00, the elapsed time is about 3 hours.

✓ Quick Check

● **2.** Estimate the number of hours between 5:25 A.M. and 8:52 A.M.

To find elapsed time, subtract the hours and the minutes. When 12:00 falls between the two times, find the elapsed time between the beginning time and 12:00. Then add the ending time.

EXAMPLE **Calculating Elapsed Time**

3 **School** How long is a school day that begins at 8:15 A.M. and ends at 3:25 P.M.?

Since 12:00 noon falls between the two times, you first need to find the elapsed time from 8:15 A.M. to noon.

For: Elapsed Time Activity
Use: Interactive Textbook, 5-7

$$
\begin{array}{ll}
12:00 \;\rightarrow & 11\,\text{h}\;60\,\text{min} \quad \leftarrow \text{Rename 12:00 as 11 hours 60 minutes.} \\
\;\,8:15 \;\rightarrow & \underline{-\;8\,\text{h}\;15\,\text{min}} \quad \leftarrow \text{Subtract the beginning time.} \\
& \;\;\,3\,\text{h}\;45\,\text{min} \quad \leftarrow \text{Subtract.}
\end{array}
$$

Then you need to add the ending time to the elapsed time from 8:15 A.M. to noon.

$$
\begin{array}{ll}
& 3\,\text{h}\;45\,\text{min} \\
3:25 \;\rightarrow & \underline{+\;3\,\text{h}\;25\,\text{min}} \\
& 6\,\text{h}\;70\,\text{min}
\end{array}
$$

$6\,\text{h}\;70\,\text{min} = 7\,\text{h} + 10\,\text{min}$ ← Since 70 min is more than 1 h, rename.

The school day is 7 h 10 min long.

✓ Quick Check

● **3.** Find the elapsed time from 10:00 A.M. to 7:15 P.M.

You use elapsed time when reading schedules.

EXAMPLE **Reading and Using a Schedule**

4 **Bus Schedules** You arrive at the Willson Street bus stop 5 minutes after the 11:50 A.M. bus leaves.

Yellow Bus Line Buses Run Every 30 Minutes Monday–Friday	
Leave Willson St.	Arrive Kagy Blvd.
7:20 A.M.	7:45 A.M.
7:50 A.M.	8:15 A.M.
. . .	. . .
11:20 P.M.	11:45 P.M.

a. How long will you wait for the next bus?

The buses run every 30 min. You will wait 30 min − 5 min, or 25 min.

b. How long is the bus ride?

Use the first run, from 7:20 A.M. to 7:45 A.M. Since 45 − 20 = 25, the elapsed time is 25 min.

c. When will you arrive at Kagy Boulevard?

11:50 → 11 h 50 min

11 h 50 min + 30 min = 11 h 80 min ← Find when the next bus leaves.

= 12 h 20 min ← Since 80 min is more than 1 h, rename.

The next bus will leave at 12:20 P.M. The trip takes 25 min. Since 20 + 25 = 45, you will arrive at 12:45 P.M.

✓ Quick Check

4. It is a 50-minute walk from the bus stop on Kagy Boulevard to a gym. You arrive at the bus stop on Willson Street at 5:30 P.M. What time do you get to the gym?

✓ Check Your Understanding

1. **Vocabulary** The time between two events is called ___?___ .

2. **Reasoning** What is the least possible amount of time that has passed between the times shown on the clocks at the left?

3. Draw a clock showing the time 45 minutes after 7:10.

4. Which is equivalent to 205 minutes?
   Ⓐ 2 h 5 min Ⓑ 2 h 25 min Ⓒ 3 h 5 min Ⓓ 3 h 25 min

5. Find 45 min + 30 min + 10 min.

For more exercises, see Extra Skills and Word Problems.

GO for Help

For Exercises	See Example
6–9	1
10–13	2
14–17	3
18–20	4

Find the total time.

6. 43 min + 38 min

7. 52 min + 25 min

8. 58 min + 7 min + 56 min

9. 28 min + 49 min + 50 min

Estimation Estimate each elapsed time to the nearest hour.

10. from 1:38 A.M. to 4:50 A.M.

11. from 11:49 A.M. to 7:12 P.M.

12. from 2:25 P.M. to 3:35 P.M.

13. from 8:25 A.M. to 10:52 A.M.

Find the elapsed time for each interval.

14. from 5:25 P.M. to 11:11 P.M.

15. from 9:28 A.M. to 11:07 A.M.

16. from 11:25 A.M. to 2:45 P.M.

17. from 8:30 P.M. to 7:39 A.M.

Use the train schedule below for Exercises 18–20.

Train Schedule		
Station	Train A	Train B
Fairview	8:15 A.M.	8:42 A.M.
Huntville	8:26 A.M.	8:55 A.M.
Rush City	8:34 A.M.	9:04 A.M.
Grayland	8:45 A.M.	9:19 A.M.

18. Which train takes less time to go from Fairview to Grayland?

19. How long do you wait if you get to Rush City at 8:35 A.M.?

20. How long does Train B take to get to Grayland from Huntville?

GPS **21. Guided Problem Solving** You get home at 1:00 P.M. You make a list of things to do before a party that starts at 4:00 P.M. Make a schedule for your list.
- Which activities must you do in order?
- Can any activities be done at the same time?

> Decorate room (1 h)
> Mix cake (40 min)
> Bake cake (35 min)
> Cool cake (45 min)
> Frost cake (20 min)
> Shower and dress (25 min)

Time Zones The map below shows time zones in the United States. Find the time for each city when it is noon in Denver.

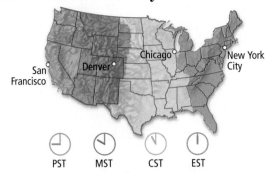

22. Chicago   **23.** New York City   **24.** San Francisco

25. ⟨Algebra⟩ Write an expression to find the time in New York when the time in San Francisco is x.

26. **Writing in Math** It is Monday in one part of the United States and Tuesday in another part. Explain how this is possible.

27. **Clowns** A clown wants to perform a 45-minute show at three birthday parties. The first party begins at 10:00 A.M. He needs to leave the third party by 2:15 P.M. He wants to allow one hour between each party. Make a schedule for the clown.

28. **Challenge** Find the elapsed time from Saturday at 7:15 A.M. to Sunday at 3:05 P.M.

⟨A⟩⟨B⟩⟨C⟩⟨D⟩ Test Prep and Mixed Review   **Practice**

Multiple Choice

29. Pablo makes a list of things to do before dinner. He leaves school at 3:15. If Pablo eats dinner at 6:00, how many minutes does he have to visit his neighbors?

Ride bike home	20 min
Feed the dog	10 min
Do homework	1 hour
Visit neighbors	40 min
Help prepare dinner	35 min

Ⓐ 40 min   Ⓑ 35 min   Ⓒ 30 min   Ⓓ 25 min

30. Miriam made 12.5 cups of soup for her family. After lunch 4.7 cups of soup were left. How many cups of soup did Miriam's family eat for lunch?

Ⓕ 17.2 cups   Ⓖ 16.2 cups   Ⓗ 8.8 cups   Ⓙ 7.8 cups

GO for Help

For Exercises	See Lesson
31–33	3-6

Solve each equation.

31. $23 = d - 16$ **32.** $15 = w + 9$ **33.** $9.1 - c = 5.3$

Reading for Understanding

Reading comprehension questions are based on a passage that gives facts. Read the directions and questions. Then read the passage. Look for information that helps you answer the questions.

Desert Area Deserts cover about $\frac{1}{5}$ of Earth's land surface. A desert is an area of land where less than 10 inches of precipitation (rain or the equivalent amount of snow) falls per year.

The Sahara is the world's largest desert, covering about $3\frac{1}{2}$ million square miles. The Sahara gets about 8 inches of rain each year.

Antarctica consists largely of desert. It is about 5 million square miles in area. The South Pole lies in the middle of the continent, and gets less than 1 inch of snow each year.

How much larger is Antarctica than the Sahara?

What is the question asking? What is the difference in area between Antarctica and the Sahara?

Identify the information you need. Antarctica is about 5 million square miles in area. The Sahara is about $3\frac{1}{2}$ million square miles in area.

Solve the problem. Find the difference in areas (million square miles).

Antarctica is about $1\frac{1}{2}$ million square miles larger than the Sahara.

$$\begin{array}{r} 5 \\ -\,3\frac{1}{2} \\ \hline \end{array} \quad \rightarrow \quad \begin{array}{r} 4\frac{2}{2} \\ -\,3\frac{1}{2} \\ \hline 1\frac{1}{2} \end{array}$$

Exercises

Use the passage above to answer Exercises 1 and 2.

1. In a year, how much more precipitation falls on the Sahara than on the South Pole?

2. Rain forests cover about $\frac{3}{50}$ of Earth's land surface. What fraction of Earth is covered by either desert or rain forest?

Chapter 5 Review

Go Online
PHSchool.com
For: Vocabulary quiz
Web Code: aqj-0551

Vocabulary Review

🔊 benchmark (p. 212)   elapsed time (p. 246)

Choose the vocabulary term that completes each sentence.

1. A(n) __?__ is a value that you use as an estimate for a fraction.

2. The time between two events is called __?__ .

Skills and Concepts

Lesson 5-1
• To estimate sums and differences with fractions and mixed numbers

A **benchmark** is a whole number or fraction that is easy to use when you estimate. You can use the benchmarks 0, $\frac{1}{2}$, or 1 to estimate sums and differences of fractions. To estimate sums and differences of mixed numbers, round to the nearest whole number.

Estimate each sum or difference. Use the benchmarks 0, $\frac{1}{2}$, and 1.

3. $\frac{8}{9} + \frac{3}{7}$ 4. $\frac{5}{8} - \frac{3}{12}$ 5. $\frac{4}{5} + \frac{1}{6}$ 6. $\frac{23}{35} - \frac{4}{7}$

Estimate each sum or difference.

7. $4\frac{1}{7} + 9\frac{7}{14}$ 8. $24\frac{11}{16} - 15\frac{1}{4}$

9. $8\frac{5}{6} + 6\frac{3}{8}$ 10. $45\frac{33}{35} - 40\frac{2}{7}$

11. You need $1\frac{1}{3}$ cups of lemon juice and $4\frac{3}{4}$ cups of water to make lemonade. Estimate the amount of lemonade you will make.

Lessons 5-2 and 5-3
• To add and subtract fractions with like denominators
• To add and subtract fractions with unlike denominators

To add or subtract fractions, write each fraction using a common denominator. Then add or subtract the numerators.

Find each sum or difference.

12. $\frac{2}{5} + \frac{5}{5}$ 13. $\frac{7}{8} - \frac{3}{8}$ 14. $\frac{3}{20} + \frac{9}{20}$ 15. $\frac{25}{36} - \frac{5}{36}$

16. $\frac{1}{8} + \frac{3}{4}$ 17. $\frac{4}{5} - \frac{3}{10}$ 18. $\frac{17}{24} - \frac{7}{12}$ 19. $\frac{11}{15} + \frac{1}{2}$

20. You rode your bicycle $\frac{2}{3}$ mile to school and $\frac{1}{5}$ mile to a friend's house. How far did you ride your bicycle?

Lesson 5-4

- To add mixed numbers with and without renaming

You can add mixed numbers by first adding the whole numbers and then adding the fraction parts.

Find each sum.

21. $3 + 4\frac{1}{8}$ **22.** $9\frac{8}{9} + 7\frac{4}{9}$ **23.** $35\frac{1}{5} + 28\frac{7}{10}$

24. Your sister is 10 years old and is $54\frac{1}{3}$ inches tall. Her doctor says she will grow about $2\frac{1}{2}$ inches during the next year and about $2\frac{3}{4}$ inches the year after that. About how tall will your sister be when she is 12 years old?

Lesson 5-5

- To subtract mixed numbers with and without renaming

You can subtract mixed numbers by first subtracting the whole numbers and then subtracting the fraction parts. Sometimes you need to rename whole numbers or fractions so you can subtract.

Find each difference.

25. $6 - 2\frac{2}{5}$ **26.** $10\frac{7}{8} - 4\frac{1}{2}$ **27.** $25\frac{1}{3} - 8\frac{5}{9}$

Lesson 5-6

- To solve equations with fractions

You can use mental math or the properties of inverse operations to solve equations involving fractions or mixed numbers.

Solve each equation.

28. $\frac{5}{7} = p + \frac{2}{7}$ **29.** $q + \frac{5}{8} = \frac{3}{4}$ **30.** $\frac{2}{3} = t - \frac{4}{9}$

31. $4\frac{2}{3} = x + 1\frac{1}{3}$ **32.** $k - 2\frac{1}{6} = 8\frac{8}{9}$ **33.** $13\frac{3}{5} + h = 20$

Lesson 5-7

- To add, subtract, and convert between units of time

The time between two events is called **elapsed time.** You may need to rewrite hours and minutes before you can add or subtract time.

Find the elapsed time for each interval.

34. from 8:15 A.M. to 11:56 A.M.

35. from 9:33 P.M. to 6:21 A.M.

36. You start doing things on your to-do list at 6:00 P.M. If you take a 25-minute break while doing homework, at what time will you complete your list?

Eat dinner	40 min
Homework	55 min
Walk dog	10 min

Chapter 5 Test

Go **O**nline
PHSchool.com **For:** Online chapter test
Web Code: aqa-0552

Estimate each sum or difference. Use the benchmarks 0, $\frac{1}{2}$, or 1.

1. $\frac{18}{35} + \frac{14}{16}$ **2.** $\frac{7}{50} + \frac{9}{16}$ **3.** $\frac{9}{10} + \frac{2}{26}$

4. How much did Sophia's hair grow during the month of May?

Sophia's Hair Length

May 1	$8\frac{1}{8}$ in.
May 31	$8\frac{5}{16}$ in.

Estimate each sum or difference.

5. $6\frac{5}{6} + 2\frac{1}{9}$ **6.** $11\frac{6}{7} - 3\frac{7}{9}$

7. $10\frac{5}{12} - 5\frac{1}{8}$

8. Lumber You need $\frac{3}{8}$ foot of lumber to fix a fence and $\frac{3}{4}$ foot of lumber to fix a shed. How much lumber do you need?

Find each sum or difference.

9. $\frac{4}{5} + \frac{2}{5}$ **10.** $\frac{11}{13} - \frac{7}{13}$

11. $\frac{4}{7} + \frac{6}{7}$ **12.** $1\frac{13}{15} - \frac{2}{3}$

13. $\frac{9}{20} + \frac{4}{5}$ **14.** $\frac{3}{4} - \frac{3}{8}$

15. $3\frac{3}{4} - 2\frac{8}{10}$ **16.** $8\frac{1}{5} + 4\frac{1}{6}$

Find each sum.

17. $\frac{1}{7} + \frac{2}{7} + \frac{5}{7}$ **18.** $\frac{4}{12} + \frac{2}{12} + \frac{5}{12}$

19. Dan ran $\frac{5}{6}$ mile. Sol ran $\frac{7}{8}$ mile.
 a. How much farther than Dan did Sol run?
 b. What was their combined distance?

20. <u>**Writing in Math**</u> Explain how you could mentally solve the equation $x - 7\frac{4}{5} = 3\frac{1}{10}$.

Solve each equation.

21. $\frac{6}{9} = \frac{1}{3} + g$

22. $y - \frac{4}{5} = \frac{11}{20}$

23. $4\frac{3}{4} + v = 17\frac{1}{8}$

24. $13\frac{2}{3} = k - 10\frac{7}{9}$

Use the table for Exercises 25–27.

Spruce Tree	Length of Cone (inches)
White	$1\frac{5}{8}$
Norway	$5\frac{1}{2}$
Black	$\frac{7}{8}$
Red	$1\frac{1}{4}$

25. Find the difference in length between the shortest and longest cones.

26. Which two cones differ in length by about $\frac{1}{2}$ inch?

27. What is the difference in length between the red spruce and white spruce tree cones?

How many minutes are in each amount of time?

28. 5 h 47 min   **29.** 23 h 8 min

30. Find the elapsed time between 6:33 A.M. and 7:20 P.M.

Multiple Choice
Read each question. Then write the letter of the correct answer on your paper.

1. On Venus the length of a day is 243.01 Earth days. On Mercury the length of a day is 58.65 Earth days. How much longer, in Earth days, is a Venus day than a Mercury day?
   - (A) 301.66
   - (B) 215.64
   - (C) 195.46
   - (D) 184.36

2. Suppose you buy a shirt for x dollars with a twenty-dollar bill. The cashier gives you $5.35 back. Which equation can you use to find the cost of the shirt?
   - (F) $5.35x = 20$
   - (G) $x + 5.35 = 20$
   - (H) $x \div 20 = 5.35$
   - (J) $5.35 - x = 20$

3. How much thicker is a quarter than a dime?

   - (A) $\frac{1}{20}$ mm
   - (B) $\frac{1}{4}$ mm
   - (C) $\frac{2}{5}$ mm
   - (D) $\frac{1}{2}$ mm

4. Which equation is NOT an example of the Distributive Property?
   - (F) $12(6.2) + 12(3.8) = 12(6.2 + 3.8)$
   - (G) $0.75(8.8) + 0.25(8.8) = 1(8.8)$
   - (H) $19.1(80) = 19.1(100) - 19.1(20)$
   - (J) $8.1 + 3.5 = 3.5 + 8.1$

5. Which set of numbers has a GCF of 3?
   - (A) 15, 30, 45
   - (B) 6, 30, 24
   - (C) 24, 36, 9
   - (D) 36, 27, 18

6. What is the best estimate for the sum of $12\frac{13}{16}$ and $23\frac{3}{8}$?
   - (F) 30
   - (G) 35
   - (H) 36
   - (J) 37

7. A store sells window glass that is $\frac{7}{32}$ inch, $\frac{3}{16}$ inch, $\frac{5}{16}$ inch, and $\frac{1}{8}$ inch thick. You need glass that is at least $\frac{1}{4}$ inch thick. Which thickness, in inches, should you buy?
   - (A) $\frac{1}{8}$
   - (B) $\frac{3}{16}$
   - (C) $\frac{5}{16}$
   - (D) $\frac{7}{32}$

8. What is the sum of $6\frac{3}{5}$ and $2\frac{4}{5}$?
   - (F) $8\frac{1}{5}$
   - (G) $8\frac{12}{25}$
   - (H) $9\frac{2}{5}$
   - (J) $9\frac{4}{5}$

Gridded Response
Record your answer in a grid.

9. Kerry boards the school bus at 7:48 A.M. and arrives at school at 8:13 A.M. How many minutes does he spend on the bus?

10. What is the solution of $x + \frac{3}{16} = \frac{3}{4}$? Write your answer in simplest form.

Short Response

11. What is the least common multiple of 36 and 45? Choose a method of either listing multiples or using prime factorizations. Show the steps you use to find this LCM.

12. From his home, a jogger runs 1 mile west, $3\frac{1}{2}$ miles north, 1 mile east, and $1\frac{1}{4}$ miles south. How far from home is he? Draw a diagram to help solve the problem. Then solve the problem.

Extended Response

13. At a book fair, a paperback sells for $.35 and a hardcover sells for $1.30. Your friend spends $6.00 on books. She buys three more paperbacks than hardcovers.
    - **a.** Write a list of possibilities for the number of books.
    - **b.** How many paperbacks does your friend buy?

Applying Mixed Numbers

Fast Fractions People love to race. Some races, like the Iditarod, the Tour de France, and the Paris–Dakar Rally, last days or even weeks. Other races can be over in a flash. The fastest runners can finish a 100-meter race in 10 or 11 seconds.

The Iditarod

The Iditarod is a dog sled race over at least 1,049 miles in Alaska. The fastest sled drivers, or mushers, finish in about 10 days.

Olympics

Track and field events are part of the summer Olympics.

Put It All Together

What You'll Need

- 3 number cubes

How to Play

- Work in a group. The goal of the game is to "run" each of four quarter-mile sections of a one-mile track.
- Roll three number cubes. Write a mixed number that includes a proper fraction. If all three numbers are the same, roll again.
- Take turns until each group member has times in minutes for each quarter-mile section of the track.
- If you roll the same three numbers more than once, you must make a different mixed number with them each time. If that is not possible, roll again.

1. Order your times from least to greatest.

2. a. Estimation Estimate the total time for each group member. Who do you think has the fastest time? Explain.

   b. Find your total time. Write your answer in simplest form.

   c. Compare your total to the totals for the others in your group. Who won the race?

3. Number Sense The record time for "running" this track is 4.95 minutes. Is it possible to beat this time? Explain.

4. Data File Pick one of the animals from page 650. How long would it take the animal to "run" the track? Who runs faster, you or the animal? Explain.

Go Online
PHSchool.com
For: Information about racing
Web Code: aqe-0553

Speed Skater
Catherine Raney of the 2002
U.S. Olympic team skated between
20 and 25 miles per hour during
the women's 5,000-meter final.

Tour de France
The Tour de
France bicycle
race lasts about three
weeks and covers about
2,000 miles.

CHAPTER 6

Multiplying and Dividing Fractions

What You've Learned

- In Chapter 1, you multiplied and divided decimals and solved problems using multiplication and division.
- In Chapter 4, you simplified and compared fractions. You also learned to express fractions as decimals.
- In Chapter 5, you added and subtracted fractions and mixed numbers.

Check Your Readiness

GO for Help	
For Exercises	**See Lesson**
1–6	3-7
7–12	4-4
13–18	4-5

Solving Equations

Solve each equation.

1. $3a = 12$

2. $5x = 25$

3. $p \div 3 = 4$

4. $14 = x \div 8$

5. $0.1n = 10$

6. $2 = g \div 0.3$

Finding the Greatest Common Factor

Find the GCF of each pair of numbers.

7. $12, 24$

8. $28, 35$

9. $27, 24$

10. $80, 100$

11. $36, 66$

12. $21, 42$

Writing Equivalent Fractions

Write each fraction in simplest form.

13. $\frac{15}{35}$

14. $\frac{24}{36}$

15. $\frac{16}{48}$

16. $\frac{24}{64}$

17. $\frac{18}{72}$

18. $\frac{21}{49}$

What You'll Learn Next

- In this chapter you will multiply and divide fractions and mixed numbers.

- You will use multiplication and division to solve problems involving fractions and mixed numbers.

- You will use fractions to change units of measure in the customary system.

 **Key Vocabulary**

- reciprocal (p. 272)

 Problem Solving Application On pages 302 and 303, you will work an extended activity involving carpentry.

Hands On

Modeling Fraction Multiplication

You can use a model to multiply fractions.

ACTIVITY

Use a model to find $\frac{1}{2} \times \frac{3}{4}$.

Step 1 Fold a piece of paper in half. Then fold it in half again.

Step 2 Your paper should be divided into four equal columns. Shade three of the four columns to represent $\frac{3}{4}$.

Step 3 Next, fold the paper in half. Unfold your paper. Shade one of the two rows to represent $\frac{1}{2}$.

1. **a.** How many small rectangles did you make?
   b. How many small rectangles did you shade twice?
   c. What fraction of the small rectangles did you shade twice?

2. How can you use your answer in Exercise 1 to find the product $\frac{1}{2} \times \frac{3}{4}$? What is $\frac{1}{2} \times \frac{3}{4}$?

Exercises

1. Find the product shown in the model.

Use a model to find each product.

2. $\frac{1}{2} \times \frac{2}{3}$

3. $\frac{1}{3} \times \frac{1}{4}$

4. $\frac{1}{3} \times \frac{1}{2}$

5. $\frac{1}{6} \times \frac{3}{4}$

6. Write a rule you can use to multiply two fractions without using a model.

Check Skills You'll Need

1. **Vocabulary Review** Give an example of *equivalent fractions.*

Write each fraction in simplest form.

2. $\frac{5}{10}$ 3. $\frac{9}{15}$

4. $\frac{28}{42}$ 5. $\frac{90}{100}$

 **for Help**
Lesson 4-5

What You'll Learn

To multiply fractions and to solve problems by multiplying fractions

Why Learn This?

Suppose you are building a model. You want to know the length of half of a $\frac{5}{6}$-inch piece of wood. You can multiply fractions to find part of a fractional quantity.

The model below shows $\frac{1}{2} \times \frac{5}{6}$.

$\frac{5}{6}$ of the columns are shaded with diagonal lines.

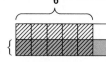

$\frac{1}{2}$ the columns are shaded blue.

5 out of 12 of the squares include both types of shading.

So $\frac{1}{2} \times \frac{5}{6} = \frac{5}{12}$. You can also find this product by multiplying the numerators and multiplying the denominators.

EXAMPLE Multiplying Two Fractions

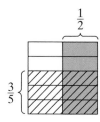

1 Find $\frac{3}{5}$ of $\frac{1}{2}$.

$$\frac{3}{5} \cdot \frac{1}{2} = \frac{3 \cdot 1}{5 \cdot 2}$$ ← Multiply the numerators.
   ← Multiply the denominators.

$$= \frac{3}{10}$$ ← Simplify.

Quick Check

1. **a.** Find $\frac{3}{5} \cdot \frac{1}{4}$.

   b. Find $\frac{2}{9} \times \frac{5}{7}$.

Arithmetic	Algebra
$\frac{3}{4} \times \frac{1}{2} = \frac{3 \times 1}{4 \times 2} = \frac{3}{8}$	$\frac{a}{b} \cdot \frac{c}{d} = \frac{ac}{bd}$, where b and d are not zero.

Vocabulary Tip

The word *of* usually suggests multiplication.

When the numerators and the denominators have a common factor, you can simplify before multiplying fractions.

$$\frac{3}{8} \cdot \frac{2}{5} = \frac{3 \cdot \overset{1}{2}}{\underset{4}{8} \cdot 5} \quad \leftarrow \text{Divide 8 and 2 by their GCF, 2.}$$

$$= \frac{3 \cdot 1}{4 \cdot 5} \quad \leftarrow \text{Multiply the numerators and the denominators.}$$

$$= \frac{3}{20} \quad \leftarrow \text{Simplify.}$$

To multiply a fraction by a whole number, write the whole number as an improper fraction with a denominator of 1.

EXAMPLE **Multiplying a Whole Number**

2 You are decorating a bulletin board using a piece of green ribbon that is $\frac{5}{6}$ yard long. You also need yellow ribbon that is nine times as long as the green ribbon. How much yellow ribbon do you need?

Draw a picture to help see how these lengths are related.

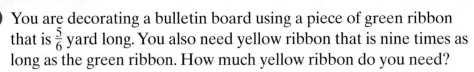

Find the length of the yellow ribbon by multiplying 9 and $\frac{5}{6}$.

$$9 \cdot \frac{5}{6} = \frac{9}{1} \cdot \frac{5}{6} \quad \leftarrow \text{Write 9 as } \frac{9}{1}.$$

$$= \frac{\overset{3}{9}}{1} \cdot \frac{5}{\underset{2}{6}} \quad \leftarrow \text{Divide 9 and 6 by their GCF, 3.}$$

$$= \frac{3 \cdot 5}{1 \cdot 2} \quad \leftarrow \text{Multiply the numerators and denominators.}$$

$$= \frac{15}{2}, \text{ or } 7\frac{1}{2} \quad \leftarrow \text{Simplify. Write as a mixed number.}$$

The yellow ribbon is $7\frac{1}{2}$ yards long.

✓ Quick Check

2. A baby alligator is $\frac{5}{6}$ foot long. An adult alligator is 12 times as long as the baby alligator. How long is the adult alligator?

1. **Number Sense** If you multiply 6 by $\frac{1}{2}$, is the answer greater than or less than the result of multiplying 6 by $\frac{1}{3}$? Explain.

Match each expression with its product.

2. $\frac{1}{4} \times \frac{1}{3}$ A. $\frac{3}{8}$

3. $\frac{2}{3} \cdot \frac{2}{5}$ B. $\frac{4}{15}$

4. $\frac{1}{2} \times \frac{3}{4}$ C. 6

5. $\frac{6}{7} \cdot 7$ D. $\frac{1}{12}$

Homework Exercises

For more exercises, see Extra Skills and Word Problems.

GO for Help

For Exercises	See Examples
6–13	1
14–21	2

Find each product. You may find a model helpful.

6. $\frac{1}{2} \times \frac{3}{8}$ 7. $\frac{5}{11} \times \frac{2}{7}$ 8. $\frac{3}{4} \times \frac{11}{12}$

9. $\frac{2}{9} \times \frac{4}{8}$ 10. $\frac{4}{9} \cdot \frac{3}{10}$ 11. $\frac{3}{5}$ of $\frac{2}{3}$

12. $\frac{4}{11} \cdot \frac{5}{8}$ 13. $\frac{9}{10}$ of $\frac{2}{5}$ 14. $\frac{3}{4} \cdot 20$

15. $\frac{3}{8} \times 5$ 16. $\frac{11}{14}$ of 28   17. $\frac{5}{12} \cdot 30$

18. $\frac{7}{9}$ of 21   19. $\frac{1}{6} \cdot 6$ 20. $\frac{3}{10} \times 45$

21. **Fitness** In gym class, you run $\frac{3}{4}$ mile. Your gym teacher runs 3 times that distance each day. How far does your teacher run?

22. **Guided Problem Solving** At the movies, you eat all but $\frac{1}{3}$ of a box of popcorn. Your friend eats $\frac{2}{3}$ of what is left. Who eats more popcorn, you or your friend?
    - **Understand the Problem** Draw a picture to help you understand the problem.
    - **Make a Plan** How can you find the answer using your picture?

GO Online
Homework Video Tutor
Visit: PHSchool.com
Web Code: aqe-0601

23. **Reasoning** Adding $\frac{3}{8}$ and $\frac{5}{8}$ is different from multiplying the two fractions. Explain why.

Algebra Evaluate each expression for $x = \frac{2}{3}$.

24. $15x$ **25.** $\frac{3}{2}x$ **26.** $\frac{9}{10}x$ **27.** $\frac{2}{3}x$

28. Budgets The graph at the right describes Paul's monthly spending. He makes $2,712 each month. How much does Paul spend each month on his rent and car combined?

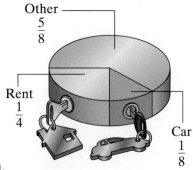

Other
$\frac{5}{8}$

Rent
$\frac{1}{4}$

Car
$\frac{1}{8}$

29. Writing in Math Is it necessary to have a common denominator when you multiply two fractions? Explain.

30. Monuments The width of the base of the Washington Monument is about $\frac{1}{10}$ of its height. The height of the monument is about 555 feet tall. Find the width of the base.

31. Challenge Find $8\frac{2}{3} \cdot 7\frac{1}{2}$.

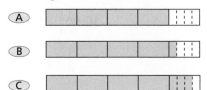

Test Prep and Mixed Review
Practice

Multiple Choice

32. Meg needs 5 yards of fencing to make a pen for her rabbit. She has $\frac{3}{4}$ yard of fencing. Each model below represents 5 yards of fencing. Which model can Meg use to find the amount of fencing she still needs?

Ⓐ
Ⓑ
Ⓒ
Ⓓ

33. What is the prime factorization of 420?
Ⓕ $2^2 \cdot 3 \cdot 3^5$ Ⓗ $2^2 \cdot 3 \cdot 5 \cdot 7$
Ⓖ $2 \cdot 3 \cdot 5 \cdot 7$ Ⓙ $2 \cdot 3 \cdot 5^2 \cdot 7$

34. Julio needs 2 hours to do his homework. He will take one 30-minute break. He wants to finish by 9:30 P.M. What is the latest time that Julio can begin his homework?
Ⓐ 6:00 P.M. Ⓑ 6:30 P.M. Ⓒ 7:00 P.M. Ⓓ 7:30 P.M.

GO for Help

For Exercises	See Lesson
35–38	5-3

Find each sum or difference.

35. $\frac{5}{6} + \frac{1}{3}$ **36.** $\frac{4}{5} - \frac{1}{2}$ **37.** $\frac{7}{9} - \frac{3}{5}$ **38.** $\frac{3}{10} + \frac{5}{8}$

Understanding Equality

A number sentence that uses the = symbol means that the value on the left side is the same as the value on the right side of the symbol. Balance scales may help you think about equality statements.

EXAMPLE   **Understanding Equality**

Is the equation $7 + 3.1 = 8 + 2.1$ true or false?

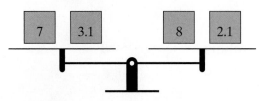

Compare the numbers on the left side to the numbers on the right.

Since 7 is one less than 8, and 3.1 is one more than 2.1, the weights on the left and right are equal. The scale is balanced.

● The equation is true.

Exercises

Find whether each statement is true. Explain your answer using logic and number sense. Do not compute.

1. $525 - 350 = 528 - 353$

2. $48.1 - 28.2 = 38.1 - 18.2$

3. $48.3 + 16 = 38.3 + 6$

4. $13 \times 40 = 130 \times 4$

5. $200 \times \frac{1}{2} = 400 \times \frac{1}{4}$

6. $20 \div 2.4 = 40 \div 4.8$

Use logic and number sense to find the value of the variable that makes the equation true.

7. $4 + 17.3 = 6 + x$

8. $73 - 21.5 = 83 - y$

9. $\frac{1}{3} \times 27 = z \times 9$

10. $32 \cdot 15 = x \cdot 30$

11. $75 \div 25 = y \div 50$

12. $100 \div 20 = 25 \div z$

Suppose the equation on the left is true. Use logic and number sense to find whether the equation on the right is true or false.

13. $37.4 + 68.8 = 106.2$ Does $(37.4 + 68.8) + 30 = 106.2 + 30$?

14. $224 \div 64 = 3.5$ Does $(224 \div 64) - 1.7 = 3.5 - 1.7$?

15. $4 \times 6.5 = 26$ Does $(4 \times 6.5) \div 2 = 26 \times 2$?

Multiplying Mixed Numbers

What You'll Learn

To estimate and find the products of mixed numbers

Why Learn This?

The dimensions of objects are not always expressed as whole numbers. You can multiply mixed numbers to find the area of objects.

To estimate the product of mixed numbers, round the mixed numbers to the nearest whole number. Then multiply. If the fraction in a mixed number is $\frac{1}{2}$ or greater, round up.

EXAMPLE   Estimating Products

For: Mixed Numbers Activity
Use: Interactive Textbook, 6-2

① One of the smallest newspapers ever printed had a page size of $1\frac{1}{4}$ inches wide by $2\frac{3}{4}$ inches long. Estimate the area of a page.

Step 1 Round the length and width to the nearest whole numbers.

Original size   Rounded size

$1\frac{1}{4}$ in.   1 in.

$2\frac{3}{4}$ in.   3 in.

Step 2 Multiply the whole numbers to estimate the area.

$$\text{area} = \text{length} \times \text{width}$$
$$\approx 3 \times 1$$
$$\approx 3$$

The area of a page was about 3 square inches.

✓ **Quick Check**

1. a. Estimate $5\frac{5}{6} \times 6\frac{4}{9}$.

    b. Estimate $7\frac{11}{16} \cdot 7\frac{1}{5}$.

To find the product of mixed numbers, write each mixed number as an improper fraction before multiplying.

EXAMPLE Multiplying Improper Fractions

2 Find the product $2\frac{2}{3} \times 3\frac{1}{4}$.

Estimate $2\frac{2}{3} \times 3\frac{1}{4} \approx 3 \times 3$, or 9

$2\frac{2}{3} \times 3\frac{1}{4} = \frac{8}{3} \times \frac{13}{4}$ ← Write the mixed numbers as improper fractions.

$\qquad = \frac{\overset{2}{\cancel{8}}}{3} \times \frac{13}{\underset{1}{\cancel{4}}}$ ← Divide 8 and 4 by their GCF, 4.

$\qquad = \frac{26}{3}$, or $8\frac{2}{3}$ ← Multiply the numerators and the denominators. Then write the product as a mixed number.

Check for Reasonableness $8\frac{2}{3}$ is near the estimate of 9, so the answer is reasonable.

Test Prep Tip

Estimate first. Then compare your computation to your estimate to decide if your answer is reasonable.

✓ Quick Check

2. a. Find $10\frac{1}{4} \times 2\frac{3}{4}$. **b.** Find $7\frac{1}{3} \times 3\frac{3}{4}$.

EXAMPLE Application: Skiing

3 A student skis $3\frac{1}{2}$ miles in an hour. An instructor can ski $1\frac{1}{3}$ times as far in an hour. How far does the instructor ski in an hour?

The diagram shows the distance that the student skis in one hour. The instructor skis $1\frac{1}{3}$ times as far as the student skis.

$\boxed{\begin{array}{c}\text{number of miles}\\\text{the instructor skis}\end{array}} = 1\frac{1}{3} \times \boxed{\begin{array}{c}\text{number of miles}\\\text{the student skis}\end{array}}$

$\qquad\qquad = 1\frac{1}{3} \times 3\frac{1}{2}$

$\qquad\qquad = \frac{4}{3} \times \frac{7}{2}$ ← Write the mixed numbers as improper fractions.

$\qquad\qquad = \frac{\overset{2}{\cancel{4}}}{3} \times \frac{7}{\underset{1}{\cancel{2}}}$ ← Divide 4 and 2 by their GCF, 2.

$\qquad\qquad = \frac{14}{3}$, or $4\frac{2}{3}$ ← Multiply the numerators and the denominators. Then write the product as a mixed number.

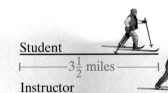

Student
├── $3\frac{1}{2}$ miles ──┤
Instructor

The instructor skis $4\frac{2}{3}$ miles in one hour.

✓ Quick Check

3. How many miles can the student ski in $\frac{3}{4}$ hour?

More Than One Way

Use the recipe at the right. How should you adjust the amount of tahini if you have $2\frac{2}{3}$ pounds of chickpeas?

HUMMUS

1 lb chickpeas
12 oz tahini
1 tbsp lemon juice
2 cloves garlic
Chop garlic and mix.
Add paprika, salt, cumin to taste.

Lauren's Method

Since I have $2\frac{2}{3}$ times as many pounds of chickpeas, I need $2\frac{2}{3}$ times as much tahini. I will multiply $2\frac{2}{3}$ times 12 ounces.

$2\frac{2}{3} \cdot 12 = \frac{8}{3} \cdot \frac{12}{1}$ ← Write the numbers as improper fractions.

$= \frac{8}{\underset{1}{3}} \cdot \frac{\overset{4}{12}}{1}$ ← Divide 3 and 12 by their GCF, 3.

$= \frac{32}{1}$, or 32 ← Multiply. Then simplify.

I need 32 ounces of tahini.

Luis's Method

I can think of $2\frac{2}{3}$ as more than doubling the original recipe amount of chickpeas.

I need to double the recipe amount by using two 12-ounce jars of tahini. Then I need $\frac{2}{3}$ of another 12-ounce jar of tahini.

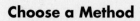

12 oz   12 oz $\frac{2}{3}$ full

$2\frac{2}{3} \times 12 = 2 \times 12 + \frac{2}{3} \times 12$

$= 24 + \frac{2}{1} \times 4$

$= 24 + 8$

$= 32$

I need 32 ounces of tahini.

Choose a Method

Find $7 \times 3\frac{2}{5}$. Describe your method and explain why you chose it.

1. **Number Sense** Which product is larger, 3×3 or $3 \times 3\frac{1}{2}$? Justify your answer.

Change each mixed number to an improper fraction.

2. $1\frac{2}{5}$ 3. $3\frac{1}{3}$ 4. $2\frac{2}{3}$

Find each product.

5. $\frac{2}{3} \cdot \frac{3}{4}$ 6. $2\frac{1}{2} \times 1\frac{2}{3}$ 7. $2\frac{1}{2} \cdot 1\frac{1}{4}$

Homework Exercises

For more exercises, see Extra Skills and Word Problems.

GO for Help

For Exercises	See Examples
8–14	1
15–21	2–3

Estimate each product.

8. $3\frac{1}{2} \cdot 1\frac{1}{4}$ 9. $14\frac{2}{3} \cdot 5\frac{1}{3}$ 10. $5\frac{1}{2} \cdot 10\frac{3}{10}$

11. $7\frac{3}{4} \times 9\frac{1}{2}$ 12. $15\frac{9}{10} \cdot 3\frac{1}{5}$ 13. $2\frac{3}{4} \times 6\frac{1}{8}$

14. Andrew earns $6.25 per hour. He works $4\frac{1}{2}$ hours per day, 5 days per week. Estimate how much money he earns per week.

Find each product.

15. $7\frac{1}{2} \cdot 8\frac{2}{3}$ 16. $5\frac{1}{3} \times 2\frac{1}{4}$ 17. $3\frac{1}{9} \cdot 3\frac{3}{8}$

18. $2\frac{4}{5} \times 12\frac{1}{2}$ 19. $1\frac{1}{3} \cdot 10\frac{1}{2}$ 20. $3\frac{1}{5} \cdot 1\frac{7}{8}$

21. **Sewing** A quilt pattern has squares with $7\frac{1}{2}$-inch sides. You want to make squares that are $\frac{2}{3}$ of the pattern's size. Find the new dimensions of a square.

22. **Guided Problem Solving** A carpenter needs six pieces of wood $3\frac{1}{2}$ feet long. The carpenter has two 10-foot boards. Does the carpenter have enough wood? Explain.
    • What is the total length of wood needed?
    • What is the total length of wood the carpenter has?

23. **Track and Field** A women's long-jump record is about $1\frac{1}{6}$ the distance of the 15–16-year-old girls' record of $20\frac{13}{24}$ feet. Find the distance of the women's record to the nearest foot.

GO Online
Homework Video Tutor
Visit: PHSchool.com
Web Code: aqe-0602

24. $9x$ **25.** $2\frac{5}{8} \cdot x$ **26.** $3x + 2$ **27.** $7\frac{1}{2}x + 5\frac{1}{4}x$

28. a. A mother is $1\frac{3}{8}$ times as tall as her daughter. The girl is $1\frac{1}{3}$ times as tall as her brother. The mother is how many times as tall as her son?

   b. If the son is 3 feet tall, how tall is his mother?

29. Design A painting is $1\frac{3}{4}$ feet by $1\frac{5}{8}$ feet. What size will a copy of the painting be if its length and width are $1\frac{1}{3}$ the size of the original?

30. You earn $7.25 per hour. You work $4\frac{1}{2}$ hours each day for 3 days each week. How much money do you earn in two weeks?

31. Writing in Math Describe some items with lengths and widths that are mixed numbers.

32. Challenge Find $\left(2\frac{1}{3}\right) \cdot \left(1\frac{1}{2}\right)^2$.

Test Prep and Mixed Review

Practice

Multiple Choice

33. Which measurement is closest to $\frac{1}{2}$ inch?

Ⓐ $\frac{1}{4}$ inch   Ⓑ $\frac{5}{16}$ inch   Ⓒ $\frac{5}{8}$ inch   Ⓓ $\frac{3}{4}$ inch

34. The length of a credit card is $3\frac{3}{8}$ inches. Its width is $2\frac{1}{8}$ inches. Which expression shows how much greater the length of the card is than the width?

Ⓕ $3\frac{3}{8} - 2\frac{1}{8}$ Ⓗ $3\frac{3}{8} + 2\frac{1}{8}$

Ⓖ $3\frac{1}{8} - 2\frac{3}{8}$ Ⓙ $3\frac{1}{8} + 2\frac{3}{8}$

35. Gerry wants to find a number between 90 and 100 that is divisible by 3 and 4. He chooses 92. Why is Gerry's answer incorrect?

Ⓐ 92 is a prime number.
Ⓑ 92 is not divisible by 3.
Ⓒ 92 is divisible by 3 and 4.
Ⓓ 92 is not divisible by 4.

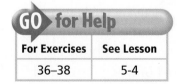

For Exercises	See Lesson
36–38	5-4

Find each sum.

36. $3\frac{2}{5} + 4\frac{1}{5}$ **37.** $2\frac{1}{6} + 1\frac{5}{6}$ **38.** $5\frac{3}{8} + 2\frac{1}{4}$

Fraction Division

Suppose you divide three large cheese quesadillas into eighths at a party. How many pieces do you have?

You can use a circle model to represent each quesadilla.

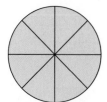 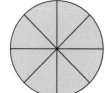 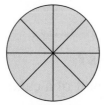

Each circle is divided into eighths. You have 24 pieces. So $3 \div \frac{1}{8} = 24$.

ACTIVITY

1. **a.** Draw three circles and cut them out. Divide each circle in half by cutting it. How many halves are there?
   b. What is $3 \div \frac{1}{2}$?

2. Divide four, five, and six circles into halves. Copy and complete the table.

Number of Circles	Fraction	Number of Pieces	Division Problem
3	$\frac{1}{2}$	■	$3 \div \frac{1}{2} = ■$
4	$\frac{1}{2}$	■	■
5	$\frac{1}{2}$	■	■
6	$\frac{1}{2}$	■	■

3. **a. Patterns** How does the number of pieces relate to the number of circles in the table?
   b. What happens when you divide a number by $\frac{1}{2}$?

4. **Number Sense** How are dividing by $\frac{1}{2}$ and multiplying by 2 related? Explain.

5. Use circle models to find each quotient.

   a. $4 \div \frac{1}{3}$ **b.** $5 \div \frac{1}{3}$ **c.** $4 \div \frac{1}{4}$

Check Skills You'll Need

1. **Vocabulary Review**
How do you find the *greatest common factor* of 4 and 15?

Find each product.

2. $8 \times \frac{3}{4}$ 3. $\frac{4}{5} \cdot \frac{1}{4}$

4. $\frac{1}{3}$ of $\frac{3}{7}$ 5. $\frac{10}{11} \cdot \frac{2}{5}$

for Help
Lesson 6-1

What You'll Learn

To divide fractions and to solve problems by dividing fractions

◀)) **New Vocabulary** reciprocal

Why Learn This?

Suppose you have half of a cake to share. You can find how many eighths you can cut from the cake by dividing by $\frac{1}{8}$.

The model below shows that there are four eighths in $\frac{1}{2}$. So $\frac{1}{2} \div \frac{1}{8} = 4$.

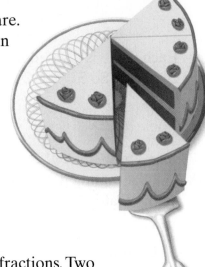

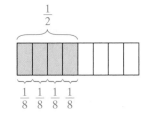

You can also use reciprocals to divide fractions. Two numbers are **reciprocals** if their product is 1. The numerators and denominators are switched in reciprocals such as $\frac{2}{3}$ and $\frac{3}{2}$.

Video Tutor Help

Visit: PHSchool.com
Web Code: aqe-0775

EXAMPLE   **Writing a Reciprocal**

1 Write the reciprocal of each number.

a. 9

Since $9 \times \frac{1}{9} = 1$, the reciprocal of 9 is $\frac{1}{9}$.

b. $\frac{7}{8}$

Since $\frac{7}{8} \times \frac{8}{7} = 1$, the reciprocal of $\frac{7}{8}$ is $\frac{8}{7}$.

Quick Check

1. a. Find the reciprocal of $\frac{3}{4}$.   **b.** Find the reciprocal of 7.

To divide by a fraction, multiply by the reciprocal of the fraction. You can remember this by thinking "invert and multiply."

KEY CONCEPTS **Dividing Fractions**

Arithmetic

$$\frac{3}{5} \div \frac{1}{3} = \frac{3}{5} \cdot \frac{3}{1}$$

Algebra

$$\frac{a}{b} \div \frac{c}{d} = \frac{a}{b} \cdot \frac{d}{c},$$

where b, c, and d are not 0.

EXAMPLES **Dividing With Fractions**

2️⃣ Find $\frac{5}{10} \div \frac{5}{6}$.

$$\frac{5}{10} \div \frac{5}{6} = \frac{5}{10} \times \frac{6}{5}$$ ← Multiply by $\frac{6}{5}$, the reciprocal of $\frac{5}{6}$.

$$= \frac{\overset{1}{\cancel{5}}}{\underset{5}{\cancel{10}}} \times \frac{\overset{3}{\cancel{6}}}{\underset{1}{\cancel{5}}}$$ ← Divide the numerator 5 and the denominator 5 by their GCF, 5. Divide 10 and 6 by their GCF, 2.

$$= \frac{1 \cdot 3}{5 \cdot 1}$$ ← Multiply.

$$= \frac{3}{5}$$ ← Simplify.

3️⃣ **Feeding Birds** You have 7 cups of birdseed. You use $\frac{2}{3}$ cup of seed each week. How long will your birdseed last?

You want to find how many $\frac{2}{3}$-cup portions are in 7 cups of seed, so divide 7 by $\frac{2}{3}$.

$$7 \div \frac{2}{3} = \frac{7}{1} \div \frac{2}{3}$$ ← Write 7 as $\frac{7}{1}$.

$$= \frac{7}{1} \times \frac{3}{2}$$ ← Multiply by $\frac{3}{2}$, the reciprocal of $\frac{2}{3}$.

$$= \frac{21}{2}$$ ← Multiply.

$$= 10\frac{1}{2}$$ ← Simplify.

The birdseed will last $10\frac{1}{2}$ weeks.

✓ **Quick Check**

2. a. Find $\frac{9}{16} \div \frac{3}{4}$.   **b.** Find $\frac{4}{5} \div \frac{1}{3}$.

3. Your art teacher cuts $\frac{5}{6}$ yard of fabric into five equal pieces. How long is each piece of fabric?

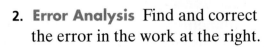

1. Vocabulary The product of reciprocals always equals __?__.

2. Error Analysis Find and correct the error in the work at the right.

$$\frac{11}{9} \div \frac{2}{3} = \frac{\cancel{9}^3}{11} \times \frac{2}{\cancel{3}_1}$$
$$= \frac{6}{11}$$

3. Open-Ended Write a fraction and its reciprocal.

Find each quotient.

4. $5 \div \frac{3}{8}$

5. $\frac{10}{16} \div \frac{5}{16}$

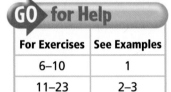

Homework Exercises

For more exercises, see Extra Skills and Word Problems.

For Exercises	See Examples
6–10	1
11–23	2–3

Write the reciprocal of each number.

6. $\frac{2}{5}$ **7.** $\frac{1}{7}$ **8.** 11   **9.** $\frac{5}{3}$ **10.** $\frac{4}{11}$

Find each quotient. You may find a model helpful.

11. $7 \div \frac{3}{5}$ **12.** $9 \div \frac{4}{9}$ **13.** $6 \div \frac{2}{5}$

14. $8 \div \frac{3}{7}$ **15.** $\frac{8}{9} \div \frac{1}{3}$ **16.** $\frac{1}{4} \div \frac{1}{4}$

17. $\frac{11}{2} \div \frac{3}{4}$ **18.** $\frac{1}{5} \div \frac{1}{4}$ **19.** $\frac{4}{9} \div \frac{2}{3}$

20. $\frac{9}{2} \div \frac{1}{2}$ **21.** $\frac{8}{9} \div \frac{4}{5}$ **22.** $\frac{3}{4} \div \frac{1}{8}$

23. A piece of iron $\frac{2}{3}$ yard long is cut into six equal pieces. How long is each piece in feet?

24. Guided Problem Solving A road crew has $\frac{3}{4}$ ton of stone to divide evenly among four sidewalks. How much stone does the crew use for each sidewalk?
- What amount are you dividing evenly?
- Into how many groups are you dividing the stone?

25. Measurement How many $\frac{1}{4}$ inches are in $\frac{1}{2}$ foot? Draw a diagram that models the problem.

26. Writing in Math Explain how dividing a number by 2 and dividing a number by $\frac{1}{2}$ are different. Include a diagram.

(Algebra) **Evaluate each expression for** $a = \frac{1}{2}$, $b = \frac{1}{4}$, **and** $c = \frac{3}{8}$.

27. $a \div b$ **28.** $b \div c$ **29.** $c \div b$

30. Baking A recipe for a loaf of banana bread requires $\frac{2}{3}$ cup of vegetable oil. You have 3 cups of oil. How many loaves of banana bread can you make with the oil?

Use the table for Exercises 31–32.

31. How many times as many people live in Argentina as in Peru?

32. The population of Brasilia, Brazil's capital, is about $\frac{1}{85}$ of the country's population. What fraction of the total population of South America lives in Brasilia?

33. Challenge Simplify $\left(\frac{2}{7}\right)^2 \div \left(\frac{1}{7}\right)^2$.

South American Population

Country	Portion of South America's Population
Brazil	$\frac{1}{2}$
Colombia	$\frac{1}{9}$
Argentina	$\frac{1}{10}$
Peru	$\frac{1}{13}$

Source: U.S. Census Bureau. Go to **PHSchool.com** for a data update.
Web Code: aqg-9041

Test Prep and Mixed Review   Practice

Multiple Choice

34. You want to buy enough fabric to make three stuffed bears. Each bear requires a certain amount of fabric. You want to know how much the fabric will cost for the three stuffed bears.

     Step P   Multiply the number of yards needed for each bear by 3.

     Step Q   Multiply the cost of the fabric by the total number of yards you need.

     Step R   Identify the cost of the fabric and the amount of fabric needed for each bear.

     Which list shows the steps in the correct order for finding how much the fabric for the stuffed bears will cost?

     (A) R, P, Q   (B) R, Q, P   (C) Q, P, R   (D) Q, R, P

35. You buy 2 shirts for $7.99 each and a pair of pants for $19.99. How much do you spend before tax?

     (F) $27.98   (G) $35.97   (H) $39.98   (J) $55.96

GO for Help

For Exercises	See Lesson
36–39	4-1

Test each number for divisibility by 2, 3, 5, 9, or 10.

36. 1,250   **37.** 372

38. 55,600   **39.** 445

What You'll Learn

To estimate and compute the quotient of mixed numbers

Why Learn This?

You may need to divide mixed numbers in measurements to make home repairs or change a recipe.

To estimate the quotient of two mixed numbers, round each number to the nearest whole number. Then divide.

EXAMPLE Estimating Quotients

1 **Carpentry** A homeowner wants to cover a wall $59\frac{1}{2}$ inches wide with wood panels. Each wood panel is $4\frac{3}{8}$ inches wide. Estimate the number of panels needed to cover the wall.

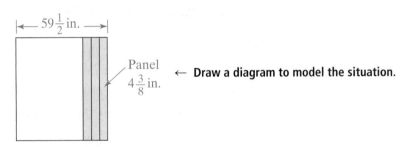

← Draw a diagram to model the situation.

$59\frac{1}{2} \div 4\frac{3}{8}$ ← Round each mixed number to the nearest whole number.
$\downarrow \qquad \downarrow$
$60 \div 4 = 15$ ← Divide.

About 15 panels are needed to cover the wall.

Quick Check

1. **a.** Estimate $7\frac{2}{5} \div 1\frac{3}{7}$. **b.** Estimate $14\frac{9}{16} \div 3\frac{8}{19}$.

To divide with mixed numbers, start by writing the numbers as improper fractions.

EXAMPLE **Application: Baking**

② **Multiple Choice** A baker has $2\frac{1}{4}$ cups of blueberries to make three batches of muffins. How many cups of blueberries should the baker put into each batch?

Ⓐ $\frac{4}{27}$ Ⓑ $\frac{3}{4}$ Ⓒ $\frac{4}{3}$ Ⓓ $6\frac{3}{4}$

Estimate Since $2\frac{1}{4} < 3$, the quotient is less than 1.

| blueberries ÷ batches | ← Divide the number of cups by the number of batches. |

$$2\frac{1}{4} \div 3 = \frac{9}{4} \div \frac{3}{1}$$ ← Write the numbers as improper fractions.

$$= \frac{9}{4} \times \frac{1}{3}$$ ← Multiply by $\frac{1}{3}$, the reciprocal of 3.

$$= \frac{\overset{3}{9}}{4} \times \frac{1}{\underset{1}{3}}$$ ← Divide 9 and 3 by their GCF, 3.

$$= \frac{3}{4}$$ ← Multiply.

The baker should put $\frac{3}{4}$ cup of blueberries into each batch. The correct answer is choice B.

✓ Quick Check

2. The baker has $3\frac{3}{4}$ cups of walnuts to make three batches of muffins. How many cups of walnuts should go into each batch?

EXAMPLE **Dividing Mixed Numbers**

③ Find $10\frac{1}{2} \div 1\frac{3}{4}$.

$$10\frac{1}{2} \div 1\frac{3}{4} = \frac{21}{2} \div \frac{7}{4}$$ ← Write the mixed numbers as improper fractions.

$$= \frac{21}{2} \times \frac{4}{7}$$ ← Multiply by $\frac{4}{7}$, the reciprocal of $\frac{7}{4}$.

$$= \frac{\overset{3}{21}}{\underset{1}{2}} \times \frac{\overset{2}{4}}{\underset{1}{7}}$$ ← Divide 21 and 7 by their GCF, 7. Divide 2 and 4 by their GCF, 2.

$$= \frac{6}{1}$$ ← Multiply.

$$= 6$$ ← Simplify.

✓ Quick Check

3. a. Find $7 \div 1\frac{1}{6}$.   **b.** Find $6\frac{5}{6} \div 3\frac{1}{3}$.

Video Tutor Help
Visit: PHSchool.com
Web Code: aqe-0775

1. **Estimation** Estimate $8\frac{3}{4} \div 3\frac{1}{3}$.

2. **Open-Ended** Write a word problem that you can solve using $2\frac{1}{2} \div 1\frac{1}{4}$. Explain what each number represents.

3. **Error Analysis** Who is correct, Jocelyn or Annie?

Jocelyn

$$4\frac{1}{2} \div 1\frac{1}{3} = \frac{8}{2} \div \frac{4}{3}$$
$$= \frac{\overset{1}{\cancel{2}}\overset{2}{\cancel{8}}}{\overset{}{\cancel{2}}\,1} \cdot \frac{3}{\cancel{4}}$$
$$= 3$$

Annie

$$4\frac{1}{2} \div 1\frac{1}{3} = \frac{9}{2} \div \frac{4}{3}$$
$$= \frac{9}{2} \cdot \frac{3}{4}$$
$$= \frac{27}{8}$$
$$= 3\frac{3}{8}$$

Homework Exercises

For more exercises, see Extra Skills and Word Problems.

Estimate each quotient.

GO for Help

For Exercises	See Examples
4–8	1
9–11	2
12–17	3

4. $50\frac{1}{4} \div 5\frac{3}{16}$

5. $48\frac{8}{10} \div 7\frac{3}{7}$

6. $99 \div 8\frac{2}{3}$

7. During a storm the level of a river rose $10\frac{1}{2}$ inches in $4\frac{1}{2}$ hours. Estimate how many inches per hour the level rose.

8. The average adult's height is about 8 times the length of the person's head. A man is $6\frac{1}{2}$ feet tall. About how long is his head?

Find each quotient.

9. $3\frac{1}{6} \div 2$

10. $2\frac{1}{2} \div 7$

11. $1 \div 4\frac{1}{2}$

12. $3\frac{1}{3} \div 1\frac{1}{2}$

13. $7\frac{1}{3} \div 1\frac{5}{6}$

14. $3\frac{1}{4} \div 1\frac{1}{2}$

15. $2\frac{1}{2} \div 1\frac{1}{8}$

16. $10\frac{1}{3} \div 3\frac{1}{3}$

17. $2\frac{1}{10} \div 4\frac{2}{3}$

Test Prep Tip ⒶⒷⒸⒹ

Drawing a model may help you solve a problem.

GPS 18. **Guided Problem Solving** Sunlight takes about $8\frac{1}{2}$ minutes to travel approximately 93 million miles from the sun to Earth. How many miles does light travel in one minute?

• What operation can you use to find the number of miles light travels in one minute?

• How can you use estimation to check your answer?

Find the number that completes each equation.

19. $2\frac{3}{5} \div 2\frac{1}{2} = \blacksquare$ **20.** $2\frac{3}{5} \div \blacksquare = 1$ **21.** $\blacksquare \div \frac{1}{2} = 1\frac{3}{4}$

22. Construction An attic ceiling 24 feet wide needs insulation. Each strip of insulation is $1\frac{1}{3}$ feet wide. Estimate the number of insulation strips that are needed.

23. Gardening A gardener is building a border for a flower garden with a row of red bricks. The row is $136\frac{1}{2}$ inches long. Each brick is $10\frac{1}{2}$ inches long and costs \$.35. How much will the border cost?

24. Writing in Math Explain how you can use mental math to find $12 \div \frac{1}{5}$.

25. Books A bookstore has a shelf that is $37\frac{1}{2}$ inches long. Each book is $1\frac{1}{4}$ inches thick. How many books can fit on the shelf?

26. Challenge Evaluate each expression for $x = 1\frac{1}{3}$.

a. $(x + x) \div \frac{1}{2}$ **b.** $(x + 1) \div 1\frac{1}{2}$

Test Prep and Mixed Review   **Practice**

Multiple Choice

27. You serve three different kinds of pizza for dinner. The shaded areas show the amount of pizza left over. How much pizza was eaten?

Ⓐ $1\frac{3}{4}$ Ⓑ 2 Ⓒ $2\frac{1}{12}$ Ⓓ $2\frac{1}{8}$

28. Mr. Perez is driving 380 miles home from vacation at an average speed of 60 miles per hour. Which method can Mr. Perez use to find how long it will take him to drive home?
Ⓕ Add 380 and 60.
Ⓖ Divide 380 by 60.
Ⓗ Multiply 380 by 60.
Ⓙ Subtract 60 from 380.

29. Find the greatest common factor of 12 and 20.
Ⓐ 2   Ⓑ 3   Ⓒ 4   Ⓓ 5

Find the prime factorization of each number.

30. 144   **31.** 98   **32.** 276   **33.** 5,000

Using a Calculator for Fractions

Many calculators do not have fraction keys. You can use a calculator without fraction keys to check your computations with fractions by changing the fractions to decimals. The example below is for a calculator that follows the order of operations.

Round repeating decimals to several decimal places. When you compute with rounded decimals, results may be slightly different.

EXAMPLES

1 Check $2\frac{3}{8} \times 4\frac{7}{10} = 11\frac{13}{80}$.

Change the fraction part to a decimal by dividing the numerator by the denominator. Then add the quotient to the whole number.

$$2\frac{3}{8} \qquad \times \qquad 4\frac{7}{10} \qquad \overset{?}{=} \qquad 11\frac{13}{80}$$

2 ➕ 3 ➗ 8 🟰 *2.375*   4 ➕ 7 ➗ 10 🟰 *4.7*   11 ➕ 13 ➗ 80 🟰 *11.1625*

2.375 ✖ *4.7* 🟰 *11.1625*   ← **Use a calculator to find 2.375 × 4.7.**

Since $2.375 \div 4.7 = 11.1625$, and $11\frac{13}{80} = 11.1625$, the answer checks.

2 Check $2\frac{2}{7} \div 1\frac{1}{3} = 1\frac{5}{7}$.

Find the decimal equivalent of each fraction. Use three decimal places.

$$2\frac{2}{7} \qquad \div \qquad 1\frac{1}{3} \qquad \overset{?}{=} \qquad 1\frac{5}{7}$$

2 ➕ 2 ➗ 7 🟰 *2.285...*   1 ➕ 1 ➗ 3 🟰 *1.333...*   1 ➕ 5 ➗ 7 🟰 *1.714...*

2.285 ➗ *1.333* 🟰 *1.714*   ← **Use a calculator to find 2.285 ÷ 1.333.**

Since 1.714 is equal to 1.714, the answer $1\frac{5}{7}$ checks.

Exercises

Write a decimal number equation to check each fraction equation. Round repeating decimals to three decimal places.

1. $3\frac{1}{5} \times 1\frac{3}{4} = 5\frac{3}{5}$ **2.** $9\frac{3}{10} - 3\frac{2}{5} = 5\frac{9}{10}$ **3.** $6\frac{1}{2} \div 1\frac{3}{5} = 4\frac{1}{16}$ **4.** $2\frac{5}{7} + 7\frac{1}{2} = 10\frac{3}{14}$

Find each product or quotient.

1. $\frac{5}{12}$ of 36

2. $5\frac{1}{4} \times 4\frac{1}{2}$

3. $24 \div \frac{3}{8}$

4. $1\frac{1}{9} \div 6\frac{2}{3}$

5. $\frac{2}{7} \cdot 5\frac{1}{3}$

6. $2\frac{2}{5} \div 4$

7. $8\frac{1}{6} \times 2$

8. $7\frac{4}{9} \div 3\frac{1}{3}$

9. $5\frac{2}{3} \div \frac{1}{6}$

10. $\frac{3}{5} \cdot 7\frac{1}{2}$

11. $3\frac{3}{10} \div 1\frac{1}{2}$

12. $5\frac{1}{6} \times 3$

13. How tall is a tree that is 9 times as tall as a $4\frac{1}{3}$-foot sapling?

14. How many $\frac{1}{2}$-inch-thick cookies can you slice from 1 foot of cookie dough? You may find a diagram helpful.

15. You must cover a wall $72\frac{3}{8}$ inches wide with wood panels. If each panel is $5\frac{5}{8}$ inches wide, about how many panels will you need?

MATH GAMES

Estimate That Product!

What You'll Need

- 20 cards or paper slips, each with a fraction or mixed number written on it
- fraction calculator (optional)

How To Play

- Three students are needed to play. One student acts as the judge. Two students are the players.
- The judge shuffles the cards and then turns over two cards.
- Players have 10 seconds to write an estimate for the product.
- The judge finds the product. The judge also computes the difference between each estimate and the actual product.
- The player with the estimate closer to the actual product earns one point. If there is a tie, each player gets one point.
- The first player to earn five points wins.

281

 6-5

Solving Fraction Equations by Multiplying

1. Vocabulary Review How is the *Division Property of Equality* used to solve $4y = 24$?

Find each product.

2. $\frac{1}{3} \cdot \frac{7}{10}$ **3.** $\frac{2}{3} \cdot \frac{9}{22}$

4. $\frac{3}{7} \cdot \frac{14}{15}$ **5.** $\frac{9}{10} \cdot \frac{2}{5}$

GO **for Help**
Lesson 3-7

What You'll Learn

To write fraction equations and solve them by multiplying

Why Learn This?

Projects, such as making flags from fabric, sometimes require you to solve an equation involving fractions.

The Multiplication Property of Equality states that if you multiply each side of an equation by the same number, the two sides remain equal.

★ ★ ★ ★
City of
Aurora
★ ★ ★ ★

EXAMPLE **Solving Equations by Multiplying**

1 **Multiple Choice** Solve $\frac{x}{8} = 20$.

Ⓐ $2\frac{1}{2}$ Ⓑ 12 Ⓒ 20 Ⓓ 160

Recall that the fraction $\frac{x}{8}$ can also be written as $x \div 8$.

$$\frac{x}{8} = 20$$

$8 \cdot \frac{x}{8} = 8 \cdot 20$ ← Multiply each side by 8 to undo the division and get *x* by itself.

$\frac{1}{8} \cdot \frac{x}{8}_{1} = 160$ ← Write 8 as $\frac{8}{1}$.

$\frac{x}{1} = 160$ ← Multiply the numerators and the denominators.

$x = 160$ ← Simplify.

The solution is 160. The correct answer is choice D.

✓ Quick Check

1. a. Solve $\frac{x}{2} = 15$. **b.** Solve $\frac{n}{6} = 12$.

To solve $\frac{2}{3}x = 8$, multiply each side of the equation by the reciprocal of $\frac{2}{3}$, or $\frac{3}{2}$.

EXAMPLE Using Reciprocals to Solve Equations

② Solve $\frac{2}{3}x = 8$. Check the solution.

$$\frac{2}{3}x = 8$$

$$\frac{3}{2} \cdot \left(\frac{2}{3}x\right) = \frac{3}{2} \cdot (8) \quad \leftarrow \text{Multiply each side by } \frac{3}{2}\text{, the reciprocal of } \frac{2}{3}.$$

$$1 \cdot x = 12 \quad \leftarrow \text{Multiply.}$$

$$x = 12 \quad \leftarrow \text{Simplify.}$$

Check $\frac{2}{3}x = 8 \quad \leftarrow \text{Start with the original equation.}$

$$\frac{2}{3} \cdot (12) \stackrel{?}{=} 8 \quad \leftarrow \text{Substitute 12 for } x \text{ in the original equation.}$$

$$8 = 8 \ ✔ \quad \leftarrow \text{The solution checks.}$$

GO for Help

For help multiplying fractions, go to Lesson 6-1, Example 1.

✓ Quick Check

2. Solve $\frac{7}{8}x = 42$. Check the solution.

EXAMPLE Writing and Solving Equations

③ A volunteer group has 6 yards of material to make flags for Community Day. Each flag uses $\frac{5}{8}$ yard of material. How many flags can the group make?

Words yards per flag $\times$ number of flags $=$ total yards

Let b = number of flags

Equation $\frac{5}{8}$ $\times$ b $=$ 6

GO for Help

For help writing an equation, go to Lesson 3-7, Example 3.

$$\frac{5}{8}b = 6 \quad \leftarrow \text{Write the equation.}$$

$$\frac{8}{5} \cdot \left(\frac{5}{8}b\right) = \frac{8}{5} \cdot \frac{6}{1} \quad \leftarrow \text{Multiply each side by } \frac{8}{5}\text{, the reciprocal of } \frac{5}{8}.$$
$$\qquad\qquad\qquad\qquad \text{Write 6 as } \frac{6}{1}.$$

$$1 \cdot b = \frac{48}{5} \quad \leftarrow \text{Multiply.}$$

$$b = 9\frac{3}{5} \quad \leftarrow \text{Simplify.}$$

The group can make 9 flags.

✓ Quick Check

3. How many flags can the group make with 13 yards of material?

1. **Writing in Math** Without solving the problem, how can you tell that the solution to $\frac{b}{4} = 2.5$ is greater than 8?

Name the reciprocal you use to solve each equation.

2. $\frac{m}{3} = 9$

3. $\frac{2}{5}x = 5$

4. $\frac{5}{9}z = 30$

Solve each equation. If possible, use mental math.

5. $\frac{v}{4} = 11$

6. $\frac{s}{5} = 35$

7. $\frac{4}{5}y = 8$

Homework Exercises

For more exercises, see Extra Skills and Word Problems.

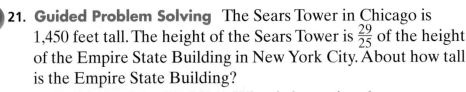

GO for Help	
For Exercises	**See Examples**
8–13	1
14–20	2–3

Solve each equation. Check the solution.

8. $\frac{x}{3} = 12$

9. $\frac{a}{7} = 8$

10. $\frac{j}{12} = 27$

11. $\frac{x}{15} = 3$

12. $\frac{t}{2} = 75$

13. $\frac{r}{12} = 1.5$

14. $\frac{1}{2}m = 6$

15. $\frac{2}{3}r = 10$

16. $\frac{3}{5}n = 9$

17. $\frac{7}{8}b = 14$

18. $\frac{3}{20}x = 5$

19. $\frac{3}{4}y = 21$

20. **Coin Collecting** The value of Gerald's coins is $\frac{7}{12}$ the value of his brother's coins. Gerald's coins are worth $14. What is the value of his brother's coins? Write and solve an equation.

GPS 21. **Guided Problem Solving** The Sears Tower in Chicago is 1,450 feet tall. The height of the Sears Tower is $\frac{29}{25}$ of the height of the Empire State Building in New York City. About how tall is the Empire State Building?
   - **Understand the Problem** What information do you have? What information do you want to find?
   - **Check the Answer** Estimate the height of the Empire State Building.

22. **Costumes** A costume uses $\frac{5}{6}$ yard of ribbon. You have 9 costumes to make. How many yards of ribbon do you need?

Homework Video Tutor

Visit: PHSchool.com
Web Code: aqe-0605

Solve each equation. Check the solution.

23. $2\frac{2}{5}p = 10$ **24.** $\frac{1}{6}m = \frac{3}{20}$ **25.** $\frac{2}{7}n = \frac{1}{14}$

Write and solve an equation.

26. Shopping The price of a shirt is $\frac{5}{6}$ of the price of a pair of pants. The shirt costs $12.50. How much do the pants cost?

27. A local bike race is broken into 12 stages. Each stage is $14\frac{1}{2}$ miles. What is the total distance of the bike race?

28. Travel Use the map. The distance from Cleveland to Pittsburgh is about $\frac{2}{5}$ of the distance from Cleveland to Chicago. About how far is Cleveland from Chicago?

29. Challenge Solve the equation $2\frac{5}{8}y = 10\frac{1}{2}$. Check the solution.

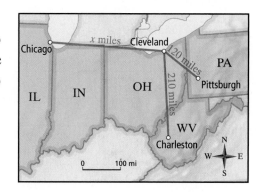

Test Prep and Mixed Review   **Practice**

Multiple Choice

30. Suchin has three pieces of string to tie up newspapers for recycling. The lengths are 10 feet, 36 feet, and 22 feet. Estimate the amount of string Suchin has.

Ⓐ 55 ft   Ⓑ 60 ft   Ⓒ 70 ft   Ⓓ 75 ft

31. Enrique mixes $\frac{1}{4}$ pound of peanuts with $\frac{1}{8}$ pound of cashews. Which strip is shaded to show the total number of pounds he has? Each strip represents one pound.

Ⓕ
Ⓖ
Ⓗ
Ⓙ

32. Bridget needs $1\frac{1}{4}$ yards of solid fabric and $4\frac{5}{8}$ yards of print fabric. About how much fabric does Bridget need in all?

Ⓐ 16 yd   Ⓑ 6 yd   Ⓒ 5 yd   Ⓓ 1 yd

GO for Help

For Exercises	See Lesson
33–35	5-5

Find each difference.

33. $15\frac{6}{9} - 13\frac{5}{12}$ **34.** $23\frac{2}{3} - 4\frac{1}{2}$ **35.** $26 - 4\frac{1}{9}$

Online lesson quiz, PHSchool.com, Web Code: aqa-0605   6-5 Solving Fraction Equations by Multiplying   **285**

Practice Solving Problems

Movies The table below shows the total earnings for five movies. How many times greater were the earnings for *Shrek 2* than for *Finding Nemo?*

Movie	Earnings ($100 millions)
Shrek 2	$4\frac{2}{5}$
Spider-Man	$4\frac{1}{25}$
Finding Nemo	$3\frac{2}{5}$
Pirates of the Caribbean	$3\frac{1}{20}$
Home Alone	$2\frac{9}{10}$

SOURCE: *U.S. Almanac*

What You Might Think

How can I use a diagram to show this situation?

I can use division to find how many times $3\frac{2}{5}$ fits into $4\frac{2}{5}$. What equation can I write and solve?

What is the answer?

What You Might Write

$$4\frac{2}{5}$$

$$3\frac{2}{5}$$

Let x = the number of times $3\frac{2}{5}$ fits into $4\frac{2}{5}$.

$$x = 4\frac{2}{5} \div 3\frac{2}{5}$$

$$x = \frac{22}{5} \div \frac{17}{5}, \text{ or } \frac{22}{5} \times \frac{5}{17}$$

$$x = \frac{22}{17}, \text{ or } 1\frac{5}{17}$$

The earnings for *Shrek 2* were $1\frac{5}{17}$ times greater than the earnings for *Finding Nemo*.

Think It Through

1. Why should you use division to solve the problem?

2. **Number Sense** Before solving the problem, should you expect your answer to be *greater than* or *less than* 1? Explain.

3. **Check for Reasonableness** How can you use estimation to decide whether the answer is reasonable?

Exercises

4. **a. Gas Prices** In the table below, how much greater is the average price of gasoline in the Netherlands than in the United States?

   b. How many times greater is the average price of gas in the Netherlands than in the United States?

Gas Prices

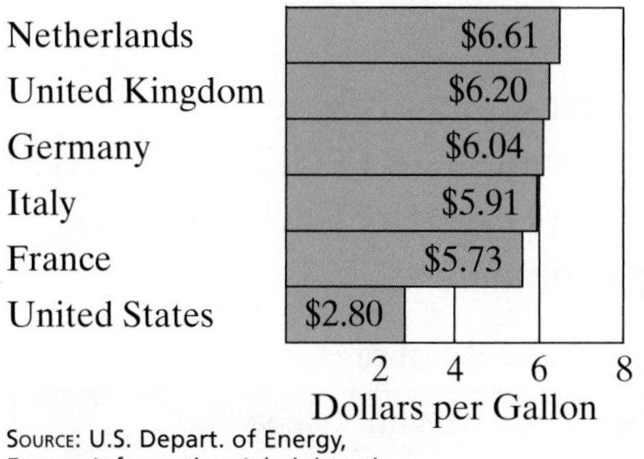

Netherlands	$6.61
United Kingdom	$6.20
Germany	$6.04
Italy	$5.91
France	$5.73
United States	$2.80

2 4 6 8
Dollars per Gallon

Source: U.S. Depart. of Energy,
Energy Information Administration

5. A lap around a motocross track is $\frac{3}{4}$ mile. How many laps do you need to complete to finish a 6-mile race?

6. How high is a stack of 12 pieces of lumber if each piece is $1\frac{1}{4}$ inches thick?

Use the chart below for Exercises 7 and 8.

Minimum Wage

State	Hourly Wage
Alaska	$7.15
New York	$6.75
Texas	$5.15
Kansas	$2.65

Source: U.S. Department of Labor,
Employment Standards Administration

7. How much less would you earn working at minimum wage in a 40-hour week in Texas than in New York?

8. **Estimation** Estimate the total amount you would earn in Alaska working 8 hours per day for 20 days.

The Customary System

Check Skills You'll Need

1. **Vocabulary Review**
Describe how to *compare* $\frac{3}{4}$ and $\frac{10}{12}$.

Compare each pair of numbers. Use <, =, or >.

2. $\frac{1}{2} \blacksquare \frac{1}{3}$

3. $\frac{5}{6} \blacksquare \frac{5}{7}$

4. $4 \blacksquare 3\frac{1}{4}$

 **for Help**
Lesson 4-8

What You'll Learn

To choose appropriate units and to estimate in the customary system

Why Learn This?

The customary system of measurement is based on units of measurement that have been used since 1824. The United States and a few other countries use this system. Each unit in the customary system has a separate name.

Customary Units of Measure

	Name	Symbol	Approximate Comparison
Length	inch	in.	Length of soda bottle cap
	foot	ft	Length of an adult male's foot
	yard	yd	Length across a door
	mile	mi	Length of 14 football fields
Weight	ounce	oz	Weight of a slice of bread
	pound	lb	Weight of a loaf of bread
	ton	t	Weight of two grand pianos
Capacity	fluid ounce	fl oz	Amount in a mouthful of mouthwash
	cup	c	Amount of milk in a single-serving carton
	pint	pt	Amount in a container of cream
	quart	qt	Amount in a bottle of fruit punch
	gallon	gal	Amount in a large can of paint

You can describe 128 fluid ounces of juice as 16 cups, 8 pints, 4 quarts, or 1 gallon. Using larger units of measure is helpful for larger quantities and estimates.

Quantity	Measurement	Less Helpful Measurement
Weight of a person	160 pounds	2,560 ounces
Distance from home to school	About 1 mile	About 63,360 inches
Amount of water in a swimming pool	About 17,000 gallons	About 272,000 cups

Use smaller units for smaller quantities and where you need to be exact.

288   Chapter 6   Multiplying and Dividing Fractions

EXAMPLE Choosing a Unit of Length

① Choose an appropriate customary unit of length to describe the height of a flagpole.

A mile is too large a unit. Use feet or yards.

✓ Quick Check

1. Choose an appropriate unit of length. Explain your choice.
   a. pencil   **b.** adult whale

EXAMPLE Choosing a Unit of Weight

② Which customary unit of weight describes a bag of ice?

The customary units that describe weight are ounces, pounds, and tons. The weight of a bag of ice is best described in pounds.

✓ Quick Check

2. Choose an appropriate unit of weight for a refrigerator.

You use a unit of capacity to describe amounts of liquid.

1 fluid   1 cup   1 pint   1 quart   1 gallon
ounce

EXAMPLE Choosing a Unit of Capacity

③ Choose an appropriate customary unit of capacity to describe the amount of liquid a water bottle can hold.

The capacity of a water bottle is not large, so it is best described in fluid ounces.

✓ Quick Check

3. Choose an appropriate unit of capacity. Explain your choice.
   a. a gasoline tanker truck   **b.** container of yogurt

Check Your Understanding

1. **Open-Ended** Give two examples of items in your daily life that you measure using gallons.

Vocabulary Tip

An *attribute* is a quality or characteristic.

Choose an appropriate customary unit of measure for each attribute of the milk carton.

2. height of the carton

3. amount of milk

4. weight of full carton

Homework Exercises

For more exercises, see Extra Skills and Word Problems.

GO for Help

For Exercises	See Examples
5–8	1
9–12	2
13–16	3

Choose an appropriate unit of length. Explain your choice.

5. backyard

6. distance to the moon

7. car's license plate

8. photograph

Choose an appropriate unit of weight. Explain your choice.

9. bag of oranges

10. package of chewing gum

11. bowling ball

12. pickup truck

Choose an appropriate unit of capacity. Explain your choice.

13. sample shampoo bottle

14. soup bowl

15. lawnmower gasoline tank

16. toothpaste tube

GPS 17. **Guided Problem Solving** In England, land used to be measured in furlongs. A furlong was the distance oxen could drag a plow before needing to rest. A standard furlong equals 660 feet. Which is longer, 2 furlongs or 440 yards? (*Hint:* There are 3 feet in 1 yard.)
   - How many feet are in 440 yards?
   - How many feet are in 2 furlongs?

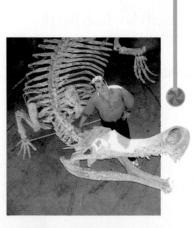

18. **Prehistoric Creatures** Scientists discovered the fossil of a huge African crocodile that was more than 40 feet long. About how many door widths are equal to the length of the crocodile?

Compare, using <, =, or >.

19. weight of a pen ▮ 6 oz

20. height of a tree ▮ 0.5 mi

21. ✏ **Writing in Math** Explain why inches are not an appropriate unit of length for the distance from your home to school.

22. **a.** Order the heights of the objects in the image below from shortest to tallest.
    b. Order the capacities from least to greatest.

Plastic flask   Glass graduated   Glass beaker
                  cylinder

23. **Challenge** Jewelers use troy ounces to weigh precious stones. A troy pound contains 12 troy ounces. Each troy ounce equals 480 grains. How many grains will two troy ounces of stones weigh?

Test Prep and Mixed Review   Practice

Multiple Choice

24. Which measure of capacity is appropriate to use in describing the amount of milk in a cereal bowl?

    Ⓐ ounce   Ⓑ cup   Ⓒ quart   Ⓓ gallon

25. Each student pays $12 to go on a field trip. You have collected $108. Which equation can you use to find the number of students *s* who have paid?

    Ⓕ $s = 108 \div 12$ Ⓗ $s = 108 + 12$
    Ⓖ $s = 108 \times 12$ Ⓙ $s = 108 - 12$

26. Boris walks $\frac{3}{8}$ of a mile to school. After school he walks $\frac{3}{4}$ mile. Which model can you use to find the total distance Boris walks?

    Ⓐ [▦] + [▦]   Ⓒ [▦] + [▦]

    Ⓑ [▦] + [▦]   Ⓓ [▦] + [▦]

GO for Help

For Exercises	See Lesson
27–28	5-7

Find the elapsed time for each pair of times.

27. 9:30 A.M. and 11:29 A.M.   28. 8:15 A.M. and 2:30 P.M.

Changing Units in the Customary System

Check Skills You'll Need

1. Vocabulary Review
What is the difference between a *mixed number* and an *improper fraction*?

Add or subtract.

2. $\frac{1}{2} + \frac{2}{3}$

3. $\frac{5}{6} - \frac{1}{4}$

4. $\frac{3}{4} - \frac{3}{5}$

5. $\frac{2}{3} + 1\frac{1}{9}$

for Help
Lesson 5-3

What You'll Learn

To convert between units in the customary system

Why Learn This?

Measures in the customary system are often written using more than one unit of measure. To solve problems with more than one unit, you may need to change units.

Length	Weight	Capacity
12 in. = 1 ft	16 oz = 1 lb	8 fl oz = 1 cup
36 in. = 1 yd	2,000 lb = 1 t	2 cups = 1 pt
3 ft = 1 yd		4 cups = 1 qt
5,280 ft = 1 mi		2 pt = 1 qt
		4 qt = 1 gal

To change from a larger unit to a smaller unit, you multiply.

EXAMPLE Larger Units to Smaller Units

1 Find the number of quarts in 5 gallons.

$5 \text{ gal} = (5 \times 4) \text{ qt}$ ← **Multiply to change to a smaller unit.**

$\qquad = 20 \text{ qt}$ ← **Multiply.**

There are 20 quarts in 5 gallons.

Vocabulary Tip

A *quart* is a quarter of a gallon.

Quick Check

1. Find the number of pounds in 2 tons.

To change from a smaller unit to a larger unit, you divide.

EXAMPLE Smaller Units to Larger Units

② You need 8 feet of fabric to make a costume. How many yards of fabric should you buy?

A foot is smaller than a yard, so divide.

$$8 \text{ ft} = \left(8 \div 3\right)\text{yd} \quad \leftarrow \begin{array}{l}\textbf{3 feet equals 1 yard,}\\ \textbf{so divide 8 by 3.}\end{array}$$

$$= 2\frac{2}{3}\text{ yd} \quad \leftarrow \textbf{Simplify.}$$

You should buy $2\frac{2}{3}$ yards of fabric.

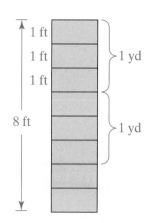

✓ **Quick Check**

2. You need 5 cups of milk to make hot chocolate. How many quarts of milk should you buy? $1\frac{1}{4}$ qt

Sometimes you need to rename units when you add or subtract.

EXAMPLE Renaming Units

③ **Multiple Choice** At age 12, Robert Wadlow was 6 ft 11 in. tall. At age 19, he was 8 ft 7 in. tall. How much did Robert grow from age 12 to age 19?

  Ⓐ 1 ft 1 in.　　Ⓑ 1 ft 8 in.　　Ⓒ 2 ft 3 in.　　Ⓓ 2 ft 8 in.

Think:　8 ft 7 in. = 7 ft + 1 ft + 7 in.　　← **Write 8 ft as 7 ft + 1 ft.**

　　　　　　= 7 ft + 12 in. + 7 in.　← **Rename 1 ft as 12 in.**

　　　　　　= 7 ft 19 in.　　　　　← **Combine 12 in. and 7 in.**

Subtract:　　8 ft　7 in.　　　7 ft　19 in.　← **Rename 8 ft 7 in. as 7 ft 19 in.**
　　　　　　− 6 ft 11 in.　　− 6 ft 11 in.
　　　　　　　　　　　　　　　1 ft　8 in.　← **Subtract.**

Robert grew 1 ft 8 in. The correct answer is choice B.

✓ **Quick Check**

3. A baby weighed 6 pounds 8 ounces at birth. She has since gained 1 pound 9 ounces. How much does she weigh now?

1. *Draw a picture* to show how many yards are in 12 feet.

State whether you multiply or divide to change units.

2. pounds to ounces   3. feet to yards   4. quarts to gallons

Is the statement true or false? If false, rewrite the statement to make it true.

5. 6 ft = 3 yd   6. 4 c = 32 fl oz   7. $2\frac{1}{2}$ t = 4,500 lb

Homework Exercises

For more exercises, see Extra Skills and Word Problems.

GO for Help

For Exercises	See Examples
8–12	1
13–20	2
21–24	3

Complete each statement. You may find a model helpful.

8. 6 lb = ▮ oz   9. 3 mi = ▮ ft   10. 68 qt = ▮ pt

11. 3 yd = ▮ ft   12. 6 qt = ▮ pt   13. 40 in. = ▮ ft

14. 5,500 lb = ▮ t   15. $27\frac{1}{4}$ c = ▮ pt   16. 2,640 ft = ▮ mi

17. 32 oz = ▮ lb   18. 9 fl oz = ▮ qt   19. 24 c = ▮ gal

20. You buy 12 ounces of cheese at the store. How many pounds of cheese do you buy?

Find the sum or difference.

21. 6 gal 3 qt
   + 4 gal 1 qt

22. 4 ft 8 in.
   − 1 ft 9 in.

23. 8 qt 1 cup
   − 6 qt 1 pt

24. A female African lion is 5 ft 8 in. long. A male African lion is 7 ft 3 in. long. What is the difference in their lengths?

25. **Guided Problem Solving** The 38,000-foot Mont Blanc Tunnel connects Italy and France through a mountain. The 31-mile Channel Tunnel connects France and England under the English Channel. Which tunnel is longer?
   • How many feet are in a mile?
   • Should you change feet to miles, or miles to feet?

26. **Wildlife** The whale shark, the largest fish in the world, can be 50 feet long. How long is the whale shark in inches?

Use <, =, or > to complete each statement.

27. 18 fl oz ■ 2 c   **28.** $3\frac{1}{2}$ lb ■ 56 oz   **29.** $1\frac{1}{2}$ t ■ 4,000 lb

30. <u>**Writing in Math**</u> Describe a situation in daily life in which you need to change from one unit of measure to another.

31. You have 12 gallons of punch. You estimate that each guest will drink 3 cups. Do you have enough punch for 60 guests? Justify your answer.

32. **Costume Design** A costume designer makes a figure skater's costume. The designer needs two 34-inch strips of fabric. How many yards of fabric does the designer need?

33. (**Algebra**) The equation $3x = y$ can be used to convert feet to yards, or yards to feet. Which unit of length is represented by each of the variables x and y? Explain.

34. Trucks must weigh 80,000 lb or less to use the highways. In tons, what is the maximum weight allowed for a truck?

35. **Challenge** Use the drawing to find the weight of each block. Explain your reasoning.

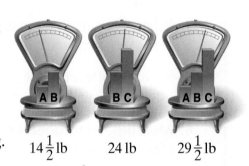

A B	B C	A B C
$14\frac{1}{2}$ lb	24 lb	$29\frac{1}{2}$ lb

Test Prep and Mixed Review

Practice

Multiple Choice

36. Mrs. Kim hired a baby sitter. She paid the babysitter $7 each hour for 3 hours. She spent a total of $55 for the evening. How much did Mrs. Kim spend while she was out?
   Ⓐ $21   Ⓑ $24   Ⓒ $34   Ⓓ $48

37. A football field is 100 yards long. How many lengths of a football field would equal a mile?
   Ⓕ 13.2   Ⓖ 17.6   Ⓗ 26.4   Ⓙ 52.8

38. What is the greatest common factor of 24, 32, and 56?
   Ⓐ 12   Ⓑ 8   Ⓒ 4   Ⓓ 2

Write each difference in simplest form.

For Exercises	See Lesson
39–41	5-5

39. $8\frac{4}{7} - 3\frac{5}{14}$ **40.** $4\frac{3}{8} - 1\frac{5}{16}$ **41.** $7\frac{2}{9} - 5\frac{5}{6}$

Measuring Objects

You can describe objects using different measures.

ACTIVITY

1. Examine your textbook. What are some attributes you can use to describe the size of your textbook?

2. Measure the length of your textbook to the nearest $\frac{1}{16}$ inch. Record your measurement. Next, measure the width of your textbook.

3. Compare your measurements to the measurements made by other students in the class.

4. What other attributes can you find to describe your textbook? What tools can you use to measure those attributes?

5. Select a different object in your class or at home. What attributes can you use to describe the object?

6. Measure the attributes of the object. Write them on a card. Hand the card to a classmate. Can your classmate tell what object your measurements describe?

✓ Checkpoint Quiz 2

Lessons 6-5 through 6-7

1. Solve $\frac{2}{3}x = 7$.

2. Solve $\frac{1}{3} = \frac{5}{6}h$.

3. Solve $\frac{1}{2}m = 23$.

4. Solve $\frac{b}{4} = \frac{2}{5}$.

Choose an appropriate unit for each measurement.

5. distance from school to a park

6. weight of your gym shoes

7. A 25-mile course has markers at the start, the end, and every $\frac{1}{2}$ mile. How many markers are there?

Eliminating Answers

In a multiple-choice problem, you can often eliminate some of the answer choices.

EXAMPLE

A plant that you bought two years ago is 3 feet 2 inches tall. It was 1 foot 11 inches tall when you bought it. How many inches has the plant grown since you bought it?

  Ⓐ 3 in.   Ⓑ 11 in.   Ⓒ 15 in.   Ⓓ 61 in.

- The plant is 3 feet 2 inches tall. So it could not have grown 61 inches. Eliminate choice D.

- 3 feet 2 inches is about 3 feet, and 1 foot 11 inches is about 2 feet. So the plant has grown about 1 foot or 12 inches. Eliminate choice A, which is much less than the estimate.

- 11 inches is less than 1 foot. So 11 inches + 1 foot 11 inches is less than 2 feet 11 inches. Eliminate choice B.

- The correct answer is choice C.

Exercises

Identify two choices that you can easily eliminate. Explain why. Then solve the problem.

1. A truck is carrying a load that weighs $15\frac{3}{5}$ tons. The total weight of the truck and the load is $36\frac{1}{2}$ tons. How many tons does the truck weigh?

  Ⓐ $14\frac{9}{10}$ Ⓑ $20\frac{9}{10}$ Ⓒ $21\frac{1}{10}$ Ⓓ $52\frac{1}{10}$

2. The height of a door is 86 inches. A person standing in the doorway is 53 inches tall. Find the approximate distance in feet between the person's head and the top of the door.

  Ⓕ 1 ft   Ⓖ 2 ft   Ⓗ 3 ft   Ⓙ 4 ft

3. You have 2 gallons of juice. How many cups of juice are equivalent to 2 gallons?

  Ⓐ 64 cups   Ⓑ 32 cups   Ⓒ 24 cups   Ⓓ 4 cups

Vocabulary Review

🔊 reciprocal (p. 272)

Skills and Concepts

Lessons 6-1 and 6-2
- To multiply fractions and to sove problems by multiplying fractions
- To estimate and find the products of mixed numbers

To multiply fractions, multiply the numerators and then multiply the denominators.

To multiply with mixed numbers, first write the mixed numbers as improper fractions. Then multiply the fractions.

Estimate each product.

1. $3\frac{1}{3} \times 4\frac{1}{8}$ 2. $5\frac{2}{3} \cdot 1\frac{5}{6}$ 3. $8\frac{3}{8} \times 9\frac{11}{15}$ 4. $7\frac{10}{23} \cdot 12\frac{3}{16}$

Find each product.

5. $\frac{1}{2} \cdot \frac{3}{5}$ 6. $\frac{12}{13} \times \frac{1}{18}$

7. $\frac{7}{9} \cdot \frac{18}{35}$ 8. $\frac{5}{8} \times 24$

9. $25 \cdot \frac{7}{10}$ 10. $5\frac{1}{6} \times \frac{3}{4}$

11. $3\frac{1}{3} \times 2\frac{2}{25}$ 12. $4\frac{5}{11} \cdot 4\frac{9}{14}$

13. **Dessert** A recipe for fruit salad calls for $\frac{2}{3}$ cup peaches. How many cups of peaches do you need to make $\frac{1}{2}$ of the original recipe?

Lesson 6-3
- To divide fractions and to solve problems by dividing fractions

Two numbers are **reciprocals** if their product is 1. The numbers $\frac{2}{3}$ and $\frac{3}{2}$ are reciprocals, as are $\frac{1}{5}$ and 5. To divide by a fraction, multiply by the reciprocal of the fraction.

Find each quotient.

14. $8 \div \frac{1}{2}$ 15. $4 \div \frac{12}{17}$ 16. $\frac{3}{11} \div \frac{3}{5}$ 17. $\frac{5}{6} \div \frac{15}{16}$

18. $\frac{4}{7} \div \frac{2}{5}$ 19. $\frac{18}{25} \div 9$ 20. $3\frac{3}{4} \div \frac{13}{15}$ 21. $4\frac{1}{7} \div \frac{1}{3}$

22. You can pick a bucket of tomatoes every $\frac{1}{6}$ hour. How many buckets can you pick in $3\frac{1}{3}$ hours?

Lesson 6-4

- To estimate and compute the quotient of mixed numbers

To divide mixed numbers, first write the numbers as improper fractions. Then multiply by the reciprocal of the divisor.

Estimate each quotient. Then find the quotient.

23. $2\frac{1}{5} \div 2\frac{1}{3}$ **24.** $8\frac{2}{3} \div 3\frac{2}{11}$ **25.** $12\frac{2}{7} \div 3\frac{5}{9}$ **26.** $13\frac{1}{2} \div 7\frac{5}{16}$

27. A hair stylist schedules appointments every $\frac{1}{3}$ hour. About how many appointments can a hair stylist schedule in $6\frac{1}{2}$ hours?

Lesson 6-5

- To write fraction equations and solve them by multiplying

To solve equations in which a variable is multiplied by a fraction, multiply both sides of the equation by the reciprocal of the fraction. If the variable is multiplied by a mixed number, write the mixed number as an improper fraction. Then solve.

Solve each equation.

28. $\frac{m}{6} = 16$ **29.** $\frac{2}{5}x = 10$ **30.** $\frac{3}{8}k = \frac{3}{4}$ **31.** $\frac{6}{7}y = \frac{9}{14}$

32. $\frac{5}{6}z = 3\frac{1}{3}$ **33.** $\frac{4}{5}w = 1\frac{3}{5}$ **34.** $\frac{2}{3}x = 4\frac{4}{5}$ **35.** $5a = 1\frac{3}{10}$

Lessons 6-6 and 6-7

- To choose appropriate units and to estimate in the customary system
- To convert between units in the customary system

When deciding what unit of measurement to use, first decide whether you are measuring length, weight, or capacity. The table below can help you change measurements.

Length	Weight	Capacity
12 inches = 1 foot	16 ounces = 1 pound	8 fluid ounces = 1 cup
3 feet = 1 yard	2,000 pounds = 1 ton	2 cups = 1 pint
5,280 feet = 1 mile		2 pints = 1 quart
		4 quarts = 1 gallon

Choose an appropriate customary unit for each measurement.

36. weight of a car   **37.** capacity of a can of soda

Complete each statement.

38. 880 in. = ■ ft   **39.** $2\frac{1}{2}$ gal = ■ c   **40.** 12,000 lb = ■ t

41. You are making bows from 50 yards of ribbon. How many feet of ribbon do you have?

Go Online
PHSchool.com
For: Online chapter test
Web Code: aqa-0652

Estimate each product.

1. $4\frac{2}{3} \times 1\frac{2}{7}$ 2. $5\frac{3}{4} \cdot 7\frac{4}{9}$

3. $2\frac{1}{2} \cdot \frac{11}{19}$ 4. $9\frac{1}{8} \times 2\frac{5}{6}$

Find each product.

5. $\frac{3}{8}$ of 32   6. $\frac{5}{6} \cdot \frac{12}{25}$

7. $\frac{7}{9} \cdot 5\frac{4}{7}$ 8. $3\frac{1}{3} \times 2\frac{3}{4}$

9. **Building Design** A log cabin has walls built with 12 logs lying horizontally on top of one another. If each log is $\frac{3}{4}$ foot thick, how high is each wall?

10. Jolene weighs 96 pounds. Jolene's father weighs $1\frac{7}{8}$ times as much as she does. How much does her father weigh?

Find each quotient.

11. $15 \div \frac{9}{11}$

12. $\frac{2}{5} \div \frac{8}{25}$

13. $\frac{5}{7} \div 25$

14. $6\frac{3}{4} \div 4\frac{1}{2}$

Estimate each quotient.

15. $10\frac{4}{17} \div 4\frac{5}{9}$

16. $30\frac{2}{7} \div 15\frac{1}{10}$

17. **Encyclopedias** Several volumes of an encyclopedia fill a shelf. Each volume is $1\frac{1}{4}$ inches wide, and the shelf is $27\frac{1}{2}$ inches long. How many volumes are in the encyclopedia?

Solve for x.

18. $\frac{1}{3}x = 5$ 19. $\frac{2}{3}x = \frac{7}{24}$

20. $\frac{1}{3}x = 3\frac{1}{7}$ 21. $\frac{x}{3} = 8$

22. How many miles equal 63,360 inches?

23. How many gallons equal $36\frac{1}{2}$ quarts?

24. Instead of walking from school to the grocery store, Scott walks 2 miles from school to the video store. His walk is $\frac{5}{6}$ of the distance to the grocery store. How far from school is the grocery store?

25. There are $1\frac{1}{3}$ times as many girls as there are boys at a party. If there are 18 boys, how many people are at the party?

Complete each statement.

26. $5\frac{3}{4}$ ft = ■ yd

27. 150 lb = ■ oz

Use <, =, or > to complete each statement.

28. 15 qt ■ $3\frac{1}{2}$ gal

29. 16 fl oz ■ 1 pt

30. **Writing in Math** Explain how you can use the Distributive Property to find $7\frac{2}{5} \times 5$.

31. Give an appropriate customary unit of measurement for each object.
    a. weight of an airplane
    b. length of a soccer field
    c. amount of water in a bathtub
    d. amount of mouthwash in one mouthful
    e. weight of a mouse
    f. length of a child's foot

Reading Comprehension

Read each passage and answer the questions that follow.

In the Dough Here is a recipe for making modeling dough.

1 cup flour	$1\frac{1}{2}$ teaspoons cream of tartar
$\frac{1}{2}$ cup salt	1 tablespoon vegetable oil
1 cup water	a few drops of food coloring

Heat the vegetable oil in a pan. Then add the other ingredients. Stir constantly. Let dough cool. Store in an airtight container.

1. How many cups of flour, salt, and water does the recipe call for?

   A $1\frac{1}{2}$ cups C $2\frac{1}{2}$ cups

   B 2 cups D $2\frac{3}{4}$ cups

2. Suppose you only have enough flour to make half a batch of dough. How much salt would you need?

   F $\frac{1}{4}$ cup H $\frac{3}{4}$ cup

   G $\frac{1}{2}$ cup J 1 cup

3. Suppose you only have 1 teaspoon of cream of tartar. By what fraction will you need to multiply the other ingredients in order to make dough with the same consistency?

   A $\frac{1}{3}$ B $\frac{1}{2}$ C $\frac{2}{3}$ D $\frac{3}{4}$

4. What fraction of a cup of cream of tartar does the recipe call for? (There are 48 teaspoons in 1 cup.)

   F $\frac{1}{32}$ G $\frac{1}{16}$ H $\frac{1}{3}$ J $\frac{1}{2}$

Video Value Carlos, Lisa, and Lenny found a box of used computer games at a yard sale. Carlos wanted four of the games, Lisa wanted two of them, and Lenny wanted the other six. The price for the box of computer games was $18. They planned to split the cost according to how many games each person wanted.

5. What fraction of the computer games did Lisa pick?

   A $\frac{1}{6}$ B $\frac{1}{4}$ C $\frac{1}{3}$ D $\frac{2}{3}$

6. How much should Lenny pay?

   F $4 G $6 H $9 J $12

7. How much should Lisa pay?

   A $3 B $4 C $6 D $8

8. What fraction of the computer games did Lenny and Carlos pick together?

   F $\frac{2}{3}$ G $\frac{3}{4}$ H $\frac{5}{6}$ J $\frac{7}{8}$

Problem Solving Application

Applying Mixed Numbers

Swimming to Win Suppose you want to build a set of shelves to hold the trophies and photographs for your school's swim team. Knowing how to work with fractions and mixed numbers can help you design and build shelves.

Put It All Together

1. Suppose you are building a trophy case $36\frac{3}{4}$ inches tall with three evenly spaced shelves, each $\frac{3}{4}$ inch thick. Let h represent the height of each shelf. Calculate h.

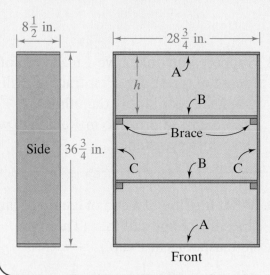

8½ in.

28¾ in.

A

h

B

Brace

Side 36¾ in.

C   B   C

A

Front

2. Calculate the length of each of the boards needed to build the trophy case, including the top and bottom (A), the shelves (B), and the sides (C). Sketch each piece with its dimensions labeled.

3. a. A lumberyard sells boards that are 8 feet long and boards that are 10 feet long. How many 8-foot boards would you need to buy? How many 10-foot boards would you need? Draw a diagram to support your answers.

b. The price of the lumber is $3.25 per foot. How much would the lumber for the project cost?

Off the Block

To power your dive off the starting block, grip the block with your hands and toes and put your weight on your back foot. Next, pull hard with your arms and push with your feet.

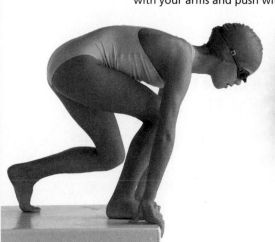

302

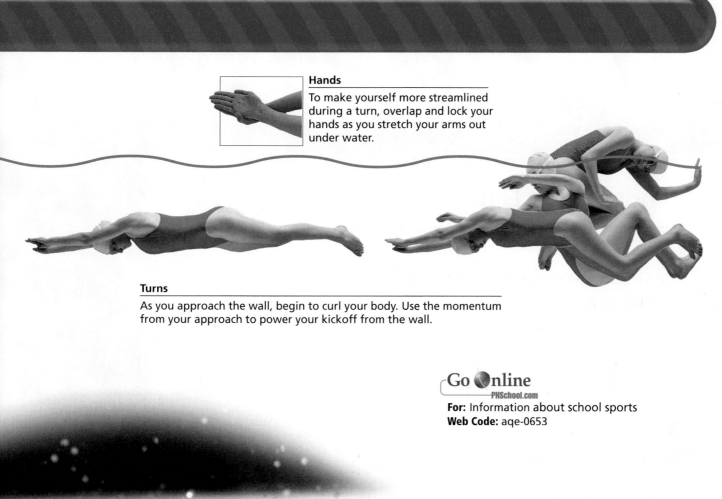

Hands

To make yourself more streamlined during a turn, overlap and lock your hands as you stretch your arms out under water.

Turns

As you approach the wall, begin to curl your body. Use the momentum from your approach to power your kickoff from the wall.

Go Online
PHSchool.com
For: Information about school sports
Web Code: aqe-0653

The Butterfly Stroke

The butterfly was invented in the early 1930s but was considered a form of the breaststroke until 1952. Originally the kick was similar to the breaststroke kick, but now swimmers use the more efficient "dolphin kick."

As your arms sweep backward, raise your head out of the water and take a breath.

Ratios, Proportions, and Percents

What You've Learned

- In Chapter 1, you used multiplication and division to solve problems involving decimals.
- In Chapter 5, you solved equations with fractions.
- In Chapter 6, you used multiplication and division to solve problems involving fractions and mixed numbers.

Check Your Readiness

GO for Help

For Exercises	See Lessons
1–4	3-7
5–8	4-5
9–12	4-8
13–16	6-3

Solving Equations

Solve for n.

1. $n \div 8 = 6$

2. $\dfrac{n}{7} = 6$

3. $3 \times n = 72$

4. $6n = 54$

Simplifying Fractions

Write each fraction in simplest form.

5. $\dfrac{10}{25}$

6. $\dfrac{20}{44}$

7. $\dfrac{34}{51}$

8. $\dfrac{27}{81}$

Comparing Fractions

Compare. Use <, =, or >.

9. $\dfrac{7}{9} \ \blacksquare \ \dfrac{3}{4}$

10. $\dfrac{2}{3} \ \blacksquare \ \dfrac{3}{5}$

11. $\dfrac{12}{15} \ \blacksquare \ \dfrac{12}{9}$

12. $\dfrac{24}{48} \ \blacksquare \ \dfrac{1}{2}$

Multiplying and Dividing Fractions

Find each product or quotient.

13. $\dfrac{4}{7} \times \dfrac{2}{3}$

14. $\dfrac{12}{14} \times \dfrac{7}{12}$

15. $\dfrac{7}{9} \div \dfrac{1}{5}$

16. $\dfrac{11}{12} \div \dfrac{2}{9}$

What You'll Learn Next

- In this chapter, you will use multiplication and division to solve problems involving ratios and rates.

- You will use ratios to describe proportional situations.

- You will use proportions to solve problems, including problems involving scale drawings.

- You will find and estimate percents and use percents to draw circle graphs.

🔊 Key Vocabulary

- circle graph (p. 341)
- cross products (p. 317)
- equivalent ratios (p. 307)
- percent (p. 331)
- proportion (p. 316)
- rate (p. 312)
- ratio (p. 306)
- scale (p. 326)
- unit cost (p. 313)
- unit rate (p. 312)

 Problem Solving Application On pages 358 and 359, you will work an extended activity involving scale.

7-1 Ratios

What You'll Learn

To write ratios to compare real-world quantities

◀)) **New Vocabulary** ratio, equivalent ratios

Why Learn This?

In recipes, the amounts of the ingredients are related to each other. You can use ratios to compare these amounts.

A **ratio** is a comparison of two numbers by division. The table below shows three ways to write the ratio of cups of party mix to cups of pretzels. All three ratios are read "six to two."

PARTY MIX
Makes 6 cups
4 cups cereal
2 cups pretzels
3 tbsp Worcestershire
        sauce

	Ways to Write a Ratio		
Statement	**In Words**	**With a Symbol**	**As a Fraction**
6 cups party mix to 2 cups pretzels	6 to 2	6 : 2	$\frac{6}{2}$

EXAMPLE **Three Ways to Write a Ratio**

1 **Recipes** Use the party mix recipe above. Write the ratio of cups of cereal to cups of pretzels in three ways.

The recipe calls for 4 cups of cereal and 2 cups of pretzels.

cereal to pretzels →   4 to 2   or   4 : 2   or $\frac{4}{2}$

✓ Quick Check

1. Use the recipe above. Write each ratio in three ways.
   a. pretzels to cereal
   b. pretzels to party mix

Two ratios that name the same number are **equivalent ratios.** You can find equivalent ratios by multiplying or dividing each term of a ratio by the same nonzero number.

EXAMPLE   **Writing Equivalent Ratios**

② Write two different ratios equivalent to 4 : 6.

Divide each → $\div 2$ $4:6$ $\div 2$ $\times 3$ $4:6$ $\times 3$ ← Multiply each
term by 2. $2:3$ $12:18$ term by 3.

Two ratios equivalent to 4 : 6 are 2 : 3 and 12 : 18.

✓ Quick Check

2. Write two different ratios equivalent to each ratio.

   a. $\dfrac{10}{35}$ **b.** 12 : 3   **c.** 8 to 22

Just as with fractions, you can write ratios in simplest form. To do this, you can divide the terms of the ratio by their greatest common factor (GCF).

EXAMPLE   **Writing a Ratio in Simplest Form**

③ Write the ratio of bats to balls in simplest form.

There are 8 bats and 12 balls, so the ratio of bats to balls is 8 to 12.

$$\dfrac{8}{12} \overset{\div 4}{\underset{\div 4}{=}} \dfrac{2}{3}$$ ← Write the ratio in simplest form.

In simplest form, the ratio of bats to balls is 2 to 3.

✓ Quick Check

3. You use 3 cups of popcorn kernels to make 24 quarts of popcorn. Write the ratio of the amount of kernels to the amount of popcorn in simplest form.

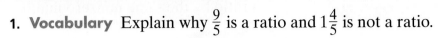

Check Your Understanding

1. **Vocabulary** Explain why $\frac{9}{5}$ is a ratio and $1\frac{4}{5}$ is not a ratio.

2. Which ratios below are NOT equivalent to 6 : 10?

    6 to 10 $\frac{8}{12}$ 12 : 20 $\frac{3}{5}$ 4 to 8

Use the picture at the left. Match each relationship on the left with the correct ratio on the right.

3. cups to bowls

4. coasters to blue cups

5. yellow cups to blue bowls

6. bowls to total number of items

A. 1 to 3
B. 2 to 1
C. 2 to 3
D. 6 to 5

Homework Exercises

For more exercises, see Extra Skills and Word Problems.

GO for Help

For Exercises	See Examples
7–9	1
10–13	2
14–21	3

Use the table for Exercises 7–9. Write each ratio in three ways.

School Play Ticket Sales

Students	35
Adults	24
Seniors	11

7. students to adults

8. adults to seniors

9. seniors to total number of people

Write two different ratios equivalent to each ratio.

10. 6 to 18   11. $\frac{4}{14}$ 12. 8 : 10   13. $\frac{30}{40}$

Write each ratio in simplest form.

14. $\frac{6}{15}$ 15. 40 : 30   16. 42 to 50   17. $\frac{14}{42}$

18. 9 to 81   19. 75 : 15   20. 8 : 36   21. $\frac{18}{12}$

22. **Guided Problem Solving** A jar contains 20 white marbles, 30 black marbles, and some red marbles. Half of the marbles are black. Find the ratio of white marbles to red marbles.
    • How many marbles are in the jar?
    • How can you find the number of red marbles?

Homework Video Tutor

Visit: PHSchool.com
Web Code: aqe-0701

Find the value that makes each pair of ratios equivalent.

23. 6 to 9, ■ to 3

24. 32 : 90, 16 : ■

25. ■ to 96, 4 to 6

26. $\dfrac{\blacksquare}{20}, \dfrac{50}{50}$

27. 50 : 150, 75 : ■

28. $\dfrac{72}{24}, \dfrac{\blacksquare}{6}$

29. A typical adult cat has 12 fewer teeth than a typical adult dog. An adult dog has 42 teeth. Write the ratio of an adult cat's teeth to an adult dog's teeth in simplest form.

30. **Writing in Math** Explain the steps you would use to rewrite 48 : 56 as 6 : 7.

31. **Science** You find that 14 students in your class of 20 students choose to make a volcano for a science project. You represent the ratio 14 to 20 using the fraction $\dfrac{7}{10}$. Does the ratio $\dfrac{7}{10}$ accurately describe the data? Explain.

32. **Open-Ended** Write a ratio of the number of vowels to the number of consonants in your first name.

33. **Challenge** Write $8x : 16x$ in simplest form.

Test Prep and Mixed Review

Practice

Multiple Choice

34. The table shows participation in three races. Which fraction represents the ratio of the number of 5-km runners to the number of 10-km runners?

Fun Run

Distance (km)	Number of Runners
10	96
5	128
1	52

Ⓐ $\dfrac{3}{4}$ Ⓒ $\dfrac{24}{13}$

Ⓑ $\dfrac{4}{3}$ Ⓓ $\dfrac{32}{13}$

35. The final score of a basketball game is 60 to 48. A prize is given to the person in the seat numbered with the least common multiple of 60 and 48. What is the prize-winning seat number?

Ⓕ 12   Ⓖ 120   Ⓗ 240   Ⓙ 480

36. Anders bought a can of juice labeled "12 fluid ounces." How many cups of juice are in the can?

Ⓐ $\dfrac{1}{2}$ cup   Ⓑ $\dfrac{3}{4}$ cup   Ⓒ $1\dfrac{1}{2}$ cups   Ⓓ $1\dfrac{3}{4}$ cups

GO for Help

For Exercises	See Lesson
37–40	6-1

Write each product in simplest form.

37. $\dfrac{2}{5} \times \dfrac{3}{7}$

38. $\dfrac{3}{4} \times \dfrac{5}{8}$

39. $\dfrac{1}{6}$ of $\dfrac{3}{5}$

40. $\dfrac{3}{16} \cdot \dfrac{16}{21}$

Modeling Ratios

You can use paper strips to model ratios. Cut four strips of paper with equal lengths. Fold and shade the paper strips to represent ratios.

EXAMPLE **Modeling Part to Part**

1 A punch recipe calls for 4 oranges and 2 lemons.

The ratio of oranges to lemons can be written as 4 : 2, 4 to 2, or $\frac{4}{2}$.

EXAMPLE **Modeling Part to Whole**

2 Five out of eight students walk to school.

The ratio of walkers to students can be written as 5 : 8, 5 to 8, or $\frac{5}{8}$.

Exercises

Use paper strips to model each ratio. Write each ratio in three different ways.

1. Three out of five kittens in a litter are male.

2. Seven out of ten high school seniors take a science course.

3. One out of four pairs of shoes sold in the summer are sandals.

4. Use the drawing of the blue jays and goldfinches at the right. Write three different ratios to describe the drawing.

5. **Writing in Math** You are given a part-to-part ratio, as in Example 1. Explain how to find the total number of parts.

6. **Reasoning** The ratio of girls to boys in a class is 6 to 8. Does this mean there are 14 students in the class? Explain.

Vocabulary Builder

High-Use Academic Words

High-use academic words are words that you will see often in textbooks and on tests. These words are not math vocabulary terms, but knowing them will help you to succeed in mathematics.

Direction Words

Some words tell what to do in a problem. I need to understand what these words are asking so that I give the correct answer.

Word	Meaning
Define	To give an accurate meaning with sufficient detail
Classify	To assign things to different groups based on their characteristics
Contrast	To show how two things are different; to include details or examples

Exercises

1. Define *salad*.

2. Classify each object as a fruit or a vegetable.
   a. apple **b.** carrot **c.** lettuce **d.** banana **e.** corn

3. Contrast a fruit salad and a vegetable salad.

4. Define *ratio*.

5. Classify each pair of ratios as equal or unequal.
   a. $\frac{1}{2}, \frac{3}{6}$ **b.** $\frac{2}{5}, \frac{4}{10}$ **c.** $\frac{5}{6}, \frac{1}{12}$ **d.** $\frac{1}{3}, \frac{3}{9}$

6. **Word Knowledge** Think about the word *comparison*.
   a. Choose the letter for how well you know the word.
      A. I know its meaning.
      B. I've seen it, but I don't know its meaning.
      C. I don't know it.
   b. **Research** Look up and write the definition of *comparison*.
   c. Use the word in a sentence involving mathematics.

7-2

Unit Rates

Check Skills You'll Need

1. Vocabulary Review Which operation is used in a ratio?

Write each ratio in simplest form.

2. $\frac{48}{12}$ **3.** $\frac{36}{9}$

4. $\frac{75}{15}$ **5.** $\frac{42}{7}$

GO for Help
Lesson 7-1

What You'll Learn

To find and use unit rates and unit costs

🔊 **New Vocabulary** rate, unit rate, unit price

Why Learn This?

Exercise is important for good health. You can use unit rates to find your heart rate.

A **rate** is a ratio involving two quantities in different units. The rate $\frac{150 \text{ heartbeats}}{2 \text{ minutes}}$ compares heartbeats to minutes. The rate for one unit of a given quantity is called the **unit rate.** Its denominator is 1.

$$\frac{150 \text{ heartbeats}}{2 \text{ minutes}} \overset{\div 2}{\underset{\div 2}{=}} \frac{75 \text{ heartbeats}}{1 \text{ minute}}$$

The unit rate is 75 heartbeats per minute.

EXAMPLE · **Finding a Unit Rate**

1 A box of wheat crackers contains 6 servings and has a total of 420 Calories. Find the number of Calories in 1 serving.

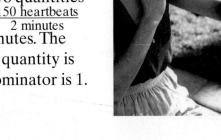

420 Calories → ← 6 servings

■ Calories → ← 1 serving

The model shows that

$$\frac{\text{total}}{\text{Calories}} \div \frac{\text{number of}}{\text{servings}} = \frac{\text{Calories}}{\text{per serving}}.$$

$$\begin{array}{c} \text{Calories} \rightarrow \\ \text{servings} \rightarrow \end{array} \frac{420}{6} \div \frac{6}{6} = \frac{70}{1} \quad \leftarrow \textbf{Divide by 6 to find the calories in one serving.}$$

The unit rate is $\frac{70 \text{ Calories}}{1 \text{ serving}}$, or 70 Calories per serving.

✓ **Quick Check**

1. Find the unit rate for $2.37 for 3 pounds of grapes.

A unit rate that gives the cost per unit is a **unit cost.** Unit costs help you compare prices.

EXAMPLE Comparing Unit Cost

② **Comparison Shopping** Two sizes of sports drink bottles are shown at the left. Which size is the better buy? Round each unit cost to the nearest cent.

Divide to find the unit cost for each size. First express each cost in cents.

$$\text{price} \rightarrow \frac{120 ¢}{24 \text{ oz}} \leftarrow \text{size} = 5¢ \text{ per fluid ounce}$$

$$\text{price} \rightarrow \frac{129 ¢}{32 \text{ oz}} \leftarrow \text{size} \approx 4¢ \text{ per fluid ounce}$$

The better buy costs less per fluid ounce. Since $.04 is less than $.05, the 32-ounce bottle is the better buy.

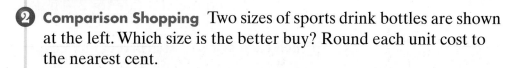

✓ **Quick Check**

2. You can buy 6 ounces of yogurt for $.68, or 32 ounces of yogurt for $2.89. Find each unit cost. Which is the better buy?

When you know a unit rate, you can use multiplication to solve a problem.

EXAMPLE Using a Unit Rate

Test Prep Tip

To write a whole number as a fraction, you can write the whole number in the numerator and 1 in the denominator.

③ **Multiple Choice** A car travels about 25 miles on 1 gallon of gas. About how far can the car travel on 8 gallons of gas?

  Ⓐ $3\frac{1}{3}$ miles   Ⓑ 8 miles   Ⓒ 33 miles   Ⓓ 200 miles

Write the unit rate as a ratio. Then find an equivalent ratio.

$$\frac{25 \text{ miles}}{1 \text{ gallon}} = \frac{200 \text{ miles}}{8 \text{ gallons}} \quad \leftarrow \textbf{Multiply each term by 8.}$$

The car can travel 200 miles on 8 gallons of gas. The correct answer is choice D.

✓ **Quick Check**

3. Write the unit rate as a ratio. Then find an equivalent ratio.
   a. You earn $5 in 1 hour. How much do you earn in 5 hours?
   b. You can type 25 words in 1 minute. How many words can you type in 10 minutes?

1. **Vocabulary** Which is a unit rate, $\frac{36 \text{ inches}}{3 \text{ feet}}$ or $\frac{12 \text{ inches}}{1 \text{ foot}}$? Explain.

2. **Health** Find the unit rate for 210 heartbeats in 3 minutes.

Match each price to the correct unit cost.

3. peaches: 6 for $3.84

4. bananas: 4 for $1.96

5. oranges: 3 for $2.16

6. pears: 5 for $2.90

   A. 49¢ each
   B. 58¢ each
   C. 64¢ each
   D. 72¢ each

Homework Exercises

For more exercises, see Extra Skills and Word Problems.

GO for Help

For Exercises	See Examples
7–10	1
11–13	2
14–16	3

Find the unit rate for each situation. You may find a model helpful.

7. 92 desks in 4 classrooms

8. $19.50 for 3 shirts

9. 45 miles in 5 hours

10. $29.85 for 3 presents

Comparison Shopping **Find each unit cost. Round to the nearest cent. Then determine the better buy.**

11. crackers: 16 ounces for $2.39; 20 ounces for $3.19

12. juice: 48 fluid ounces for $2.07; 32 fluid ounces for $1.64

13. apples: 3 pounds for $1.89; 1 pound for $.79

14. A book costs $6.75. Find the cost of 8 books.

15. There are 3 feet in 1 yard. Find the number of feet in a 15-yard run by a football player.

16. Five buses leave on a field trip. There are about 45 students per bus. About how many students are on the 5 buses?

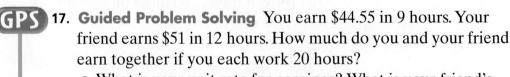

17. **Guided Problem Solving** You earn $44.55 in 9 hours. Your friend earns $51 in 12 hours. How much do you and your friend earn together if you each work 20 hours?
    - What is your unit rate for earnings? What is your friend's unit rate?
    - How can you use unit rates to find the total?

For Exercises 18–21, tell which unit rate is greater.

18. Dee reads 60 pages in 2 hours. Teri reads 99 pages in 3 hours.

19. Damian types 110 words in 5 minutes. Howard types 208 words in 8 minutes.

20. Jan bikes 18 miles in 2 hours. Nikki bikes 33 miles in 3 hours.

21. Tanya scores 81 points in 9 games. Tamaira scores 132 points in 12 games.

22. Jump Rope Crystal jumps 255 times in 3 minutes. The United States record for 11-year-olds is 882 jumps in 3 minutes.
   a. Find Crystal's unit rate for jumps per minute.
   b. Find the record-holder's unit rate for jumps per minute.
   c. How many more times per minute did the record-holder jump than Crystal?

23. Estimation A car travels 279.9 miles on 9.8 gallons of gasoline. Estimate the car's unit rate of miles per gallon. Explain how you found your estimate.

24. <u>Writing in Math</u> Explain why the speed limit on a highway is an example of a unit rate.

25. Challenge An airplane flies 2,750 miles in 5 hours. Find the unit rate in miles per second. Round your answer to the nearest hundredth.

Test Prep and Mixed Review **Practice**

Multiple Choice

26. There are 54 students and 18 computers in a classroom. Which ratio accurately compares the number of students to the number of computers?
   (A) 1 : 3   (B) 3 : 1   (C) 3 : 4   (D) 4 : 3

27. Each square below is divided into parts of equal size. In which square is the ratio of shaded to unshaded parts 2 : 1?

      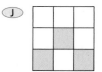

 for Help

For Exercises	See Lesson
28–30	6-4

Find each quotient.

28. $4\frac{2}{3} \div 1\frac{3}{4}$ **29.** $6\frac{1}{4} \div 2\frac{1}{2}$ **30.** $2\frac{2}{5} \div 7\frac{1}{5}$

Understanding Proportions

What You'll Learn

To understand proportions and to determine whether two ratios are proportional

◀)) **New Vocabulary** proportion, cross products

Why Learn This?

You need 4 scoops of mix and 10 cups of water to make lemonade. Will 12 scoops of mix and 30 cups of water make the same strength lemonade? You can use a proportion to find out.

A **proportion** is an equation stating that two ratios are equal.

One way to show that the ratios $\frac{4 \text{ scoops}}{10 \text{ cups}}$ and $\frac{12 \text{ scoops}}{30 \text{ cups}}$ form a proportion is to show that the ratios are equivalent.

EXAMPLE Identifying Proportions

① Do the ratios in each pair form a proportion?

a. $\frac{4}{10}, \frac{12}{30}$

$$\overset{\times 3}{\frac{4}{10} \overset{?}{=} \frac{12}{30}}_{\times 3}$$

$\frac{4}{10} = \frac{12}{30}$ ← Compare ratios →

$\frac{4}{10}$ and $\frac{12}{30}$ form a proportion.

b. $\frac{72}{81}, \frac{7}{9}$

$$\frac{72}{81} \overset{?}{=} \frac{7}{9} \quad \overset{72 \div 9 = 8,}{\underset{\text{not } 7}{\leftarrow}}$$
$$\div 9$$

$\frac{72}{81} \neq \frac{7}{9}$

$\frac{72}{81}$ and $\frac{7}{9}$ do *not* form a proportion.

✓ Quick Check

1. Do the ratios $\frac{8}{5}$ and $\frac{36}{20}$ form a proportion? Explain.

GO for Help

For help with the Multiplication Property of Equality, go to Lesson 3-7, Example 3.

There is a special relationship in equivalent ratios that form a proportion.

$$\frac{3}{4} = \frac{15}{20}$$ ← Start with a proportion.

$$3 \times 20 = 4 \times 15$$ ← Multiply the numerator of each ratio by the denominator of the other ratio.

$$60 = 60$$ ← The products are equal.

The products 20×3 and 4×15 are called cross products. You can find the **cross products** of two ratios by multiplying the numerator of each ratio by the denominator of the other ratio.

KEY CONCEPTS **Cross Products**

The cross products of a proportion are always equal.

Arithmetic: If $\frac{2}{4} = \frac{3}{6}$, then $2 \times 6 = 4 \times 3$.

Algebra: If $\frac{a}{b} = \frac{c}{d}$, and $b \neq 0$ and $d \neq 0$, then $ad = bc$.

You can use cross products to test whether two ratios are equivalent. If the cross products of two ratios are equal, they are equivalent. If the cross products of two ratios are not equal, they are not equivalent.

EXAMPLE **Using Cross Products**

② In one class, 4 of every 12 students have braces. In another class, 5 of every 15 students have braces. Are the ratios equivalent?

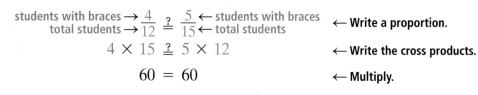

students with braces → $\frac{4}{12}$ $\overset{?}{=}$ $\frac{5}{15}$ ← students with braces
total students →   ← total students   ← Write a proportion.

$$4 \times 15 \overset{?}{=} 5 \times 12$$ ← Write the cross products.

$$60 = 60$$ ← Multiply.

The ratios $\frac{4}{12}$ and $\frac{5}{15}$ are equivalent.

✓ Quick Check

2. In a middle school, 1 out of every 12 students has a birthday in June. In a class of 26 students, there are 3 students with a birthday in June. Are these ratios equivalent? Explain.

1. **Vocabulary** Explain why $\frac{5}{6} = \frac{25}{30}$ is a proportion.

2. **Writing in Math** Explain how you can use fractions in simplest form to tell that $\frac{10}{40}$ and $\frac{25}{100}$ form a proportion.

3. Use the numbers below. Write four ratios that are equivalent to $\frac{12}{30}$.

> 2 4 5 6 10 15 24 60

4. Which ratios do NOT form a proportion?

    Ⓐ $\frac{4}{32}, \frac{1}{8}$ Ⓑ $\frac{9}{4}, \frac{3}{2}$ Ⓒ $\frac{16}{80}, \frac{1}{5}$ Ⓓ $\frac{21}{42}, \frac{9}{18}$

Homework Exercises

For more exercises, see Extra Skills and Word Problems.

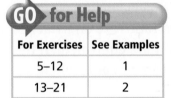

For Exercises	See Examples
5–12	1
13–21	2

Does each pair of ratios form a proportion?

5. $\frac{1}{2}, \frac{50}{100}$ 6. $\frac{10}{20}, \frac{30}{40}$ 7. $\frac{4}{12}, \frac{6}{8}$ 8. $\frac{42}{6}, \frac{504}{72}$

9. $\frac{9}{11}, \frac{63}{77}$ 10. $\frac{72}{27}, \frac{8}{3}$ 11. $\frac{16}{27}, \frac{4}{9}$ 12. $\frac{3}{2}, \frac{22}{16}$

13. $\frac{4}{12}, \frac{3}{9}$ 14. $\frac{32}{80}, \frac{4}{10}$ 15. $\frac{5}{7}, \frac{8}{10}$ 16. $\frac{6}{2}, \frac{8}{5}$

17. $\frac{93}{60}, \frac{62}{40}$ 18. $\frac{18}{9}, \frac{6}{3}$ 19. $\frac{10}{15}, \frac{3}{5}$ 20. $\frac{10}{16}, \frac{5}{8}$

21. **Cooking** A recipe calls for 2 cups of flour to make 3 dozen cookies. Is 3 cups of flour enough to make 60 cookies? Explain.

22. **Guided Problem Solving**
The table shows the results of a survey in different homerooms before a class election. In which homerooms did you receive the same ratio of votes to the total number of votes?

Student Election Survey

Homeroom	A	B	C
Votes for You	13	10	12
Total Votes	26	20	22

- Use a proportion to compare Homeroom A to Homeroom B.
- Compare Homeroom B to Homeroom C.

23. **Reasoning** Which value makes $\frac{4}{12} = \frac{\blacksquare}{18}$ a proportion?

    Ⓐ 2   Ⓑ 4   Ⓒ 6   Ⓓ 9

Does each pair of ratios form a proportion?

24. $\frac{3}{1.2}, \frac{0.5}{2}$

25. $\frac{20}{8}, \frac{3.5}{1.4}$

26. $\frac{8.4}{4.2}, \frac{20}{40}$

27. $\frac{6.1}{3.4}, \frac{7.4}{4.7}$

28. Choose a Method Would you use number sense, simplified fractions, or cross products to show that $\frac{141}{94}$ and $\frac{279}{186}$ form a proportion? Explain.

29. Architecture In one drawing, a line 4 centimeters long represents a wall 6 feet long. In another drawing, a line 6 centimeters long represents a wall 8 feet long. Do these ratios form a proportion?

30. In a ratio table, each ratio forms a proportion with every other ratio in the table. Copy and complete the ratio table below.

Hours	1	▦	4	6	▦	▦
Pay (Dollars)	5	10	▦	▦	35	50

31. (**Algebra**) Suppose you know that $\frac{a}{b}$ forms a proportion with $\frac{m}{n}$, and $\frac{a}{b}$ does not form a proportion with $\frac{x}{y}$. Does $\frac{m}{n}$ form a proportion with $\frac{x}{y}$? Explain.

32. Challenge You charge $7 to baby-sit for 2 hours. Last night you earned $17.50. How long did you baby-sit?

Ⓐ Ⓑ Ⓒ Ⓓ Test Prep and Mixed Review   **Practice**

Multiple Choice

33. A team's ratio of wins to losses is 3 to 4. Which of the following could be the team's record?
  Ⓐ 10 wins and 12 losses   Ⓒ 9 wins and 16 losses
  Ⓑ 12 wins and 16 losses   Ⓓ 40 wins and 30 losses

34. What is the prime factorization of 200?
  Ⓕ $2^3 \cdot 5^2$ Ⓖ $2^2 \cdot 5$ Ⓗ $2^3 \cdot 5$ Ⓙ $2^2 \cdot 5^2$

35. A class starts at 11:45 A.M. and lasts 85 minutes. At what time does the class end?
  Ⓐ 12:10 P.M.   Ⓒ 1:10 P.M.
  Ⓑ 12:40 P.M.   Ⓓ 1:40 P.M.

G⊙ for Help

For Exercises	See Lesson
36–39	5-5

Find each difference.

36. $7\frac{1}{2} - 6\frac{1}{4}$ **37.** $7\frac{2}{9} - 5\frac{1}{3}$ **38.** $4\frac{1}{4} - 1\frac{1}{2}$ **39.** $9\frac{1}{6} - 4\frac{2}{3}$

7-4 Solving Proportions

What You'll Learn

To solve proportions using number sense and cross products

Why Learn This?

You can use a proportion to find missing information or to make a prediction. For example, you can solve a proportion to predict the distance a car can travel.

You can sometimes use a unit rate to complete a proportion.

EXAMPLE Using a Unit Rate

1 **Cars** A hybrid car can travel 260 miles using 5 gallons of gas. How many miles can the car travel using 8 gallons of gas?

Write a proportion that compares miles driven to gallons of gas.

$$\text{miles} \rightarrow \frac{260}{5} = \frac{\blacksquare}{8} \leftarrow \text{miles} \\ \text{gallons} \rightarrow \qquad \leftarrow \text{gallons}$$

Find a unit rate for 260 miles and 5 gallons.

$$\frac{260}{5} \overset{\div 5}{\underset{\div 5}{=}} \frac{52}{1} \leftarrow \text{Divide each term by 5 to find the number of miles driven on one gallon of gas.}$$

So the unit rate is 52 miles per gallon.

$$52 \times 8 = 416 \leftarrow \text{Multiply the unit rate by the number of gallons.}$$

The car can travel 416 miles using 8 gallons of gas.

For: Proportions Activity
Use: Interactive Textbook, 7-4

Quick Check

1. Use a unit rate to solve $\frac{12}{4} = \frac{\blacksquare}{5}$.

You can solve some proportions using number sense.

EXAMPLE Solving a Proportion

2 Solve $\frac{x}{9} = \frac{4}{6}$.

$\frac{4}{6} = \frac{2}{3}$ ← Write the ratio as a fraction in simplest form.

$$\frac{x}{9} = \frac{2}{3}$$ ← Since 3 × 3 = 9, multiply 2 × 3 to find x.

$2 \times 3 = 6$, so $x = 6$.

✓ Quick Check

2. a. Solve $\frac{6}{8} = \frac{n}{20}$.

b. Solve $\frac{9}{12} = \frac{3}{x}$.

You can also use cross products to solve proportions.

EXAMPLE Using Cross Products

3 **Multiple Choice** A student buys 6 drawing pencils for $3.90. Which proportion can you use to find c, the cost of 10 pencils?

Ⓐ $\frac{6}{3.90} = \frac{c}{10}$

Ⓒ $\frac{6}{3.90} = \frac{10}{c}$

Ⓑ $\frac{c}{3.90} = \frac{6}{10}$

Ⓓ $\frac{10}{3.90} = \frac{10}{c}$

Write a proportion. Let c = the cost of 10 pencils.

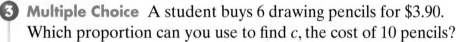

pencils → $\dfrac{6}{3.90}$ = $\dfrac{10}{c}$ ← pencils ← cost ($)   ← Write a proportion.

The correct answer is choice C. You can use cross products to solve the proportion.

$6 \cdot c = 3.90 \cdot 10$ ← Write the cross products.

$6c = 39$ ← Multiply.

$6c \div 6 = 39 \div 6$ ← Division Property of Equality

$c = 6.5$ ← Simplify.

The student pays $6.50 for 10 drawing pencils.

✓ Quick Check

3. If 5 notebooks cost $7.85, how much do 3 notebooks cost?

● More Than One Way

A package of 50 blank CDs costs $25. However, the store has run out of 50-packs. The manager agrees to sell you packages of 12 at the same unit price. How much should a 12-pack of CDs cost?

Jessica's Method

I'll set up a proportion and use equivalent fractions to solve it.

$$\frac{50 \text{ CDs}}{\$25} = \frac{12 \text{ CDs}}{x \text{ dollars}}$$

$$\frac{2}{1} = \frac{12}{x}$$

$$\frac{2}{1} \overset{\times 6}{\underset{\times 6}{=}} \frac{12}{x}$$

$$x = 6$$

A pack of 12 blank CDs should cost $6.

Michael's Method

I'll find the unit rate for the cost of one CD. Then I'll multiply.

$$\frac{\text{Cost}}{\text{Quantity}} \rightarrow \frac{25 \div 50}{50 \div 50} = \frac{0.5}{1}$$

Each CD costs $.50. Twelve CDs cost $12 \times \$.50 = \$6.00$.

A pack of 12 blank CDs should cost $6.

Choose a Method

An ad says "3 movies for $18." At that rate, what is the cost of 5 movies? Describe your method and explain why you chose it.

Check Your Understanding

1. **Writing in Math** Explain two ways that you can use to determine whether the ratios $\frac{45}{50}$ and $\frac{18}{20}$ form a proportion.

Solve each proportion. Each solution is either 1, 2, or 3.

2. $\frac{1}{5} = \frac{w}{10}$　　　3. $\frac{3}{d} = \frac{12}{4}$　　　4. $\frac{n}{3} = \frac{6}{6}$　　　5. $\frac{2}{1} = \frac{4}{z}$

For more exercises, see Extra Skills and Word Problems.

GO for Help

For Exercises	See Examples
6–12	1
13–22	2–3

Solve each proportion.

6. $\frac{35}{7} = \frac{105}{21}$

7. $\frac{12}{4} = \frac{\blacksquare}{28}$

8. $\frac{\blacksquare}{57} = \frac{38}{19}$

9. $\frac{190}{\blacksquare} = \frac{114}{3}$

10. $\frac{20}{\blacksquare} = \frac{55}{11}$

11. $\frac{32}{8} = \frac{40}{\blacksquare}$

12. **Groceries** The cost of 3 quarts of milk is $6.75. How much will 7 quarts of milk cost?

Solve each proportion.

13. $\frac{20}{6} = \frac{c}{12}$

14. $\frac{12}{n} = \frac{4}{21}$

15. $\frac{6}{22} = \frac{15}{a}$

16. $\frac{16}{27} = \frac{4}{m}$

17. $\frac{h}{2} = \frac{3}{16}$

18. $\frac{75}{12} = \frac{p}{8}$

19. $\frac{27}{84} = \frac{18}{t}$

20. $\frac{k}{17} = \frac{20}{68}$

21. $\frac{38}{x} = \frac{2}{6}$

22. **Cooking** A recipe for 10 oz of fondue requires 8 oz of cheese. How much cheese do you need for 36 oz of fondue?

GPS 23. **Guided Problem Solving** A photo 5 inches wide and 7 inches long is enlarged. The sides of the new photo are in proportion to the original. The new photo is 14 inches wide. Find the length of the new photo.
  - **Understand the Problem** You can draw a picture to see the problem.
  - **Make a Plan** You use a proportion. Write the widths in the numerator and the lengths in the denominator.

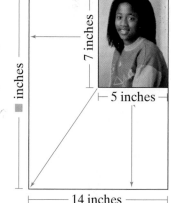

24. **Earth Science** A glacier moves about 12 inches every 36 hours. About how far does the glacier move in 1 week?

GO Online

Homework Video Tutor

Visit: PHSchool.com
Web Code: aqe-0704

25. **Printing** Your friend has a poster printed from a photograph that is 4 inches wide by 6 inches long. The poster is 22 inches wide and is proportional to the photograph. What is the length of the poster?

26. **(Algebra)** If the ratios $\frac{a}{b}$ and $\frac{x}{y}$ form a proportion, do the reciprocals $\frac{b}{a}$ and $\frac{y}{x}$ also form a proportion? Explain.

Solve each proportion.

27. $\dfrac{\$1.60}{3} = \dfrac{d}{12}$

28. $\dfrac{3.21}{k} = \dfrac{6}{8.2}$

29. $\dfrac{1.5}{3} = \dfrac{7.5}{h}$

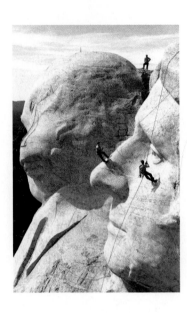

30. **Sculpture** The carvings at Mount Rushmore National Memorial in South Dakota are 60 feet from chin to forehead.
    a. The distance from chin to forehead is typically 9 inches long. The distance between the pupils of the eyes is 2.5 inches long. What is the approximate distance between the pupils in the carving of George Washington's head?
    b. **Reasoning** Did you need to convert feet to inches or inches to feet before you solved this proportion? Explain.

31. **Schools** There are 221 students and 13 teachers at a middle school. To keep the same student-to-teacher ratio, how many teachers are needed for 272 students?

32. **Choose a Method** A car can travel 54 miles on 3 gallons of gas. Find how far the car can travel on 8 gallons of gas. Explain why you chose the method you used.

33. **Challenge** Solve for x and y in the equation $\dfrac{x}{3} = \dfrac{8}{12} = \dfrac{14}{y}$.

Test Prep and Mixed Review

Practice

Multiple Choice

34. Veronica can walk 1 mile every 20 minutes. Which proportion can be used to find m, the number of miles she walks in 1 hour?

    Ⓐ $\dfrac{1}{20} = \dfrac{m}{60}$ Ⓑ $\dfrac{1}{20} = \dfrac{60}{m}$ Ⓒ $\dfrac{1}{20} = \dfrac{m}{1}$ Ⓓ $\dfrac{1}{20} = \dfrac{1}{m}$

35. Matt can type 216 words in 6 minutes. Lya can type 128 words in 4 minutes. Which statement is supported by the information?
    Ⓕ Matt can type faster than Lya.
    Ⓖ Lya can type faster than Matt.
    Ⓗ In 20 minutes, Matt can type 88 more words than Lya.
    Ⓙ Matt and Lya typing at the same time need 10 minutes to type 344 words.

36. Chris earns $25 for doing 3 hours of lawn work. About how much would Chris earn for doing 5 hours of lawn work?
    Ⓐ $40   Ⓑ $42   Ⓒ $45   Ⓓ $50

GO for Help

For Exercises	See Lesson
37–40	6-3

Find each quotient.

37. $4 \div \dfrac{4}{5}$

38. $\dfrac{4}{5} \div 4$

39. $\dfrac{4}{5} \div \dfrac{1}{5}$

40. $\dfrac{4}{5} \div 5$

Predicting Results

Last year your school used a spinner in a fundraising booth. Too many players won using the spinner. You make a new spinner to reduce the chance of winning. Your spinner has a ratio of "winning" area to "try again" area of 3 to 9.

ACTIVITY

1. Make a spinner. Divide your spinner into 12 equal sections. Shade 3 sections for the "winning" area. The ratio of "winning" area to "try again" area is 3 to 9.

2. Make another spinner with 4 equal sections. Shade 1 section for the "winning" section.

3. **Reasoning** If you spin your second spinner 60 times, how many times would you expect to win? Justify your prediction.

4. Spin each of your spinners 60 times. Record your results. Do your data agree with what you expected? Explain.

✓ Checkpoint Quiz 1   Lessons 7-1 through 7-4

1. Write 18 : 40 in words and as a fraction.

2. Cereal costs $.19 per ounce. How much does 15 oz of cereal cost?

3. Two movie tickets cost $15. What is the cost of five tickets?

Does each pair of ratios form a proportion?

4. $\dfrac{6}{45}, \dfrac{2}{18}$

5. $\dfrac{4}{7}, \dfrac{30}{42}$

6. $\dfrac{8}{12}, \dfrac{30}{45}$

Solve each proportion.

7. $\dfrac{21}{36} = \dfrac{7}{n}$

8. $\dfrac{54}{c} = \dfrac{9}{13}$

9. $\dfrac{x}{18} = \dfrac{\$6.30}{7}$

10. You buy six beverages for $2.97. Find the cost of 16 beverages.

Scale Drawings

What You'll Learn

To find the scale of a drawing and to use scales to find actual dimensions

◀◎ **New Vocabulary** scale

Why Learn This?

Mapmakers and architects make scale drawings. They apply ratios to make drawings that are smaller than the actual size of the objects they represent.

A **scale** is the ratio that compares a length in a drawing or model to the length in the original object. Usually you write a scale as a fraction in simplest form.

EXAMPLE Finding the Scale of a Drawing

1 In the drawing at the left, the height of the goat is 3 centimeters. Its actual height is 90 centimeters. What is the scale of the drawing?

Write a ratio to find the scale.

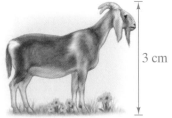
3 cm

$$\frac{\text{drawing height}}{\text{actual height}} \rightarrow \quad \frac{3 \text{ cm}}{90 \text{ cm}} = \frac{1 \text{ cm}}{30 \text{ cm}} \quad \leftarrow \text{Divide each measure by the GCF, 3.}$$

The scale of the drawing is 1 centimeter to 30 centimeters, or 1 : 30.

✓ Quick Check

1. The length of a drawing of an object is 6 inches. The length of the actual object is 84 inches. What is the scale of the drawing?

You can use a scale to calculate actual distances using a map.

EXAMPLE **Finding Distances on a Map**

2. Use the map and scale to find the actual distance from Winfield to Auburn.

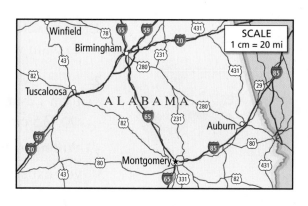

Step 1 Use a ruler to estimate the map distance from Winfield to Auburn. The distance is about 6 centimeters.

Vocabulary Tip

The scale on a map sometimes uses "=" to indicate the ratio: 1 cm = 20 mi.

Step 2 Write the scale as a ratio: $\dfrac{1 \text{ centimeter}}{20 \text{ miles}}$.

Step 3 Use a proportion. Let d = the actual distance.

$$\frac{1 \text{ cm}}{20 \text{ mi}} = \frac{6 \text{ cm}}{d \text{ mi}} \quad \begin{array}{l} \leftarrow \text{map distances} \\ \leftarrow \text{actual distances} \end{array}$$

$$\frac{1}{20} \overset{\times 6}{\underset{\times 6}{=}} \frac{6}{d}$$

Since $20 \times 6 = 120$, the distance is about 120 miles.

✓ Quick Check

2. Find the actual distance from Winfield to Montgomery.

EXAMPLE **Application: Architecture**

3. You use a scale of 1 inch : 10 feet to build a model of the White House. The White House is 58 feet tall. How tall is your model?

$$\frac{\text{model (in.)}}{\text{actual (ft.)}} \rightarrow \frac{1}{10} \quad \leftarrow \text{Write a ratio for the scale.}$$

$$\frac{1}{10} = \frac{h}{58} \quad \begin{array}{l} \leftarrow \text{Use } h \text{ to represent the model height.} \\ \leftarrow \text{actual height} \end{array}$$

$$58 = 10h \quad \leftarrow \text{Write the cross products. Then multiply.}$$

$$58 \div 10 = 10h \div 10 \quad \leftarrow \text{Divide each side by 10.}$$

$$5.8 = h \quad \leftarrow \text{Simplify.}$$

GO for Help

For help with cross products, go to Lesson 7-4, Example 3.

Your model is 5.8 inches tall.

✓ Quick Check

3. The White House is 170 feet long. How long is your model?

1. **Vocabulary** The scale on a map reads "1 in. : 50 miles." Explain what this means.

2. **Boats** Measure the length of the boat at the left. The scale is 1 cm : 3 m. What is a reasonable length for the actual boat?

  Ⓐ 2.5 cm   Ⓑ 2.5 m   Ⓒ 7.5 cm   Ⓓ 7.5 m

3. **Writing in Math** When you find actual distances on a map, do you expect to get exact or approximate answers? Explain.

Homework Exercises

For more exercises, see **Extra Skills and Word Problems.**

GO for Help

For Exercises	See Examples
4–6	1
7–10	2
11–15	3

Write each scale as a ratio.

4. a 10-inch-long drawing of a 40-inch-long table

5. a 15-foot-long model of a 300-foot-long fence

6. **Architecture** The height of a wall in a blueprint is 3 inches. The actual wall is 96 inches high. Find the scale of the blueprint.

Geography Use the map for Exercises 7–10. Find the actual distance between each pair of cities. Measure with a metric ruler. Round to the nearest mile.

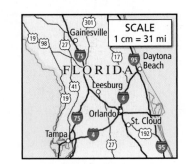

7. Gainesville and Leesburg

8. Gainesville and Orlando

9. Tampa and Daytona Beach

10. St. Cloud and Daytona Beach

Suppose you are making a model of each object. Use a scale of 1 inch : 9 inches to find the length or height of your model.

11. A chair is 36 inches tall.   12. A whale is 468 inches long.

13. A lizard is 12 inches long.   14. A stop sign is 117 inches tall.

GO Online

Homework Video Tutor

Visit: PHSchool.com
Web Code: aqe-0705

15. **Toy Design** From head to tail, the length of a *Tyrannosaurus rex* was about 40 feet. You want to design a model with a scale of 1 inch : 8 feet. How long will the model be?

16. Guided Problem Solving Suppose you are making a castle for your miniature figures. A 6-foot-tall knight is represented by a figure that is 30 mm tall. Actual castle walls are about 30 feet high. How high should you make the walls of the model?
- **Make a Plan** Use the scale as a ratio to write a proportion.
- **Carry Out the Plan** Solve the proportion $\frac{30 \text{ mm}}{6 \text{ feet}} = \frac{\blacksquare \text{ mm}}{30 \text{ feet}}$.

Map Scales Use a map scale of 1 centimeter : 100 kilometers. How many centimeters on the map represent each actual distance?

17. 125 kilometers

18. 80 kilometers

19. 170 kilometers

20. 2,500 kilometers

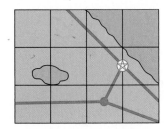

21. a. Number Sense Suppose you redraw the map at the left using a scale of 0.5 centimeter : 1 centimeter. Does your drawing enlarge or reduce the size of the map? Explain.
b. Redraw the map using the scale of 0.5 cm : 1 cm.

22. The table shows the measurements of a toy car and the actual car. Copy and complete the table.

Part	Toy Size	Actual Size
Car	3 in.	120 in.
Door handle	■	5 in.
Headlight	■	8 in.
Front bumper	0.18 ft	■
Rear window	■	4.5 ft

23. Challenge Make a scale drawing of a room in your home.

Test Prep and Mixed Review

Practice

Multiple Choice

24. On a map, 4 inches represents an actual distance of 200 miles. Which ratio best describes the scale of the map?
- Ⓐ 200 mi : 4 in.
- Ⓒ 4 in. : 200 mi
- Ⓑ 50 mi : 1 in.
- Ⓓ 1 in. : 50 mi

25. Jim cut 4 apple pies and 4 cherry pies into slices as shown at the right. He sold 23 slices of apple pie and 29 slices of cherry pie. Which expression shows the number of whole pies Jim sold?

- Ⓕ $\frac{23}{32} + \frac{29}{32}$
- Ⓖ $\frac{23}{12} + \frac{29}{12}$
- Ⓗ $\frac{23}{8} + \frac{29}{8}$
- Ⓙ $\frac{23}{4} + \frac{29}{4}$

GO for Help

For Exercises	See Lesson
26–29	6-1

Find each product.

26. $\frac{5}{16}$ of 32

27. $\frac{3}{4} \times 10$

28. $\frac{9}{10} \cdot 55$

29. $\frac{4}{5}$ of 100

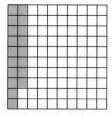

Modeling Percents

In Lesson 4-9, you learned to write a fraction with a denominator of 100 as a decimal. You can also write a fraction and a decimal as a percent.

In the grid model at the right, each small square represents $\frac{1}{100}$ of the whole. Forty-one of the 100 squares are shaded. This can be written as $\frac{41}{100}$, 0.41, or 41%.

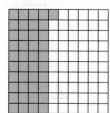

**Each column contains 10 squares.
Shade 4 columns and 1 additional square.**

ACTIVITY

1. On a piece of graph paper, draw a 10-by-10 grid model.

2. Suppose 50% of students in your school like broccoli. Use your grid model to represent 50%. How many squares will be shaded?

3. Write 50% as a fraction and as a decimal.

4. Make four grid models of the values in the table. Copy the table. Use your models to complete the table.

Fraction	$\frac{5}{100}$	■	■	■
Decimal	■	0.75	■	■
Percent	■	■	37%	100%

Exercises

Model each situation with a grid model.

1. A basketball player makes 82% of her free throws.

2. 67% of the seats in an auditorium are filled.

3. **Reasoning** Describe a grid model that represents 150%.

4. **a.** What percent of the grid at the right is shaded?
   b. What percent of the grid at the right is not shaded?
   c. **Writing in Math** Explain how you found your answer to part (b).

Percents, Fractions, and Decimals

What You'll Learn

To find equivalent forms of fractions, decimals, and percents

◀)) **New Vocabulary** percent

Why Learn This?

Newspapers use percents, fractions, and decimals to report data. To compare the data, you need to be able to convert from one form to another.

A **percent** is a ratio that compares a number to 100. The symbol for percent is %. You can write a percent as a fraction with a denominator of 100.

Math Test Scores Go Up by 12%

EXAMPLES **Representing Percents**

1 Write 36% as a fraction. Write your answer in simplest form.

$36\% = \frac{36}{100}$ ← Write the percent as a fraction with a denominator of 100.

$\quad\;\; = \frac{9}{25}$ ← Write the fraction in simplest form.

2 **Gridded Response** You read 36% of a book. Express this amount as a decimal.

$36\% = \frac{36}{100}$ ← Write the percent as a fraction with denominator 100.

$\quad\;\; = 0.36$ ← Write the fraction as a decimal.

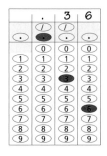

Quick Check

1. a. Write 55% as a fraction.   **b.** Write 4% as a fraction.

2. a. Write 25% as a decimal.   **b.** Write 2% as a decimal.

To write a decimal as a percent, you write a fraction first.

EXAMPLE **Writing a Decimal as a Percent**

3 Write 0.07 as a percent.

$$0.07 = \frac{7}{100} = 7\%$$ ← Write the decimal as a fraction with a denominator of 100.

✓ Quick Check

3. Write each decimal as a percent.
   a. 0.52   **b.** 0.05   **c.** 0.5

You can solve a proportion to convert a fraction to a percent.

EXAMPLE **Writing a Fraction as a Percent**

Careers Physicians measure heart rate and blood pressure.

4 **Doctors** According to a news article, 6 of every 25 doctors in the United States are women. As a fraction, 6 of every 25 is written $\frac{6}{25}$. Write $\frac{6}{25}$ as a percent.

$$\frac{6}{25} = \frac{p}{100}$$ ← Write a proportion. Percents have 100 in the denominator.

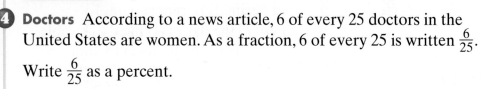

$$\frac{6}{25} = \frac{24}{100}$$ ← Find the fraction with a denominator of 100 equal to $\frac{6}{25}$.

$$\frac{6}{25} = \frac{24}{100} = 24\%$$ ← Write using a percent symbol.

In the United States, 24% of the doctors are women.

✓ Quick Check

4. The same article said that 1 of every 20 neurosurgeons in the United States is a woman. Write the fraction $\frac{1}{20}$ as a percent.

✓ Check Your Understanding

1. Vocabulary Explain why the ratio 4 : 10 is NOT a percent.

2. Which numbers at the left are equivalent to 20%?

$\frac{1}{5}$ 0.02 $\frac{20}{50}$ 0.20 $\frac{4}{12}$

0.2 $\frac{6}{24}$ 0.4 $\frac{20}{100}$ 0.05

3. Open-Ended Write a fraction and a decimal greater than 80%.

4. Mental Math Write 50% as a fraction in simplest form.

For more exercises, see Extra Skills and Word Problems.

GO for Help

For Exercises	See Example
5–14	1
15–25	2
26–30	3
31–36	4

Write each percent as a fraction in simplest form.

5. 70% **6.** 88% **7.** 5% **8.** 33% **9.** 14%

10. 15% **11.** 75% **12.** 18% **13.** 2% **14.** 42%

Write each percent as a decimal.

15. 15% **16.** 22% **17.** 82% **18.** 63% **19.** 10%

20. 40% **21.** 3% **22.** 7% **23.** 12% **24.** 100%

25. Quality Control A shipment of radios is packed incorrectly, and 6% arrive damaged. Write this amount as a decimal.

Write each decimal as a percent.

26. 0.17 **27.** 0.08 **28.** 0.98 **29.** 0.22 **30.** 0.44

Write each fraction as a percent.

31. $\frac{19}{20}$ **32.** $\frac{27}{50}$ **33.** $\frac{1}{4}$ **34.** $\frac{19}{25}$ **35.** $\frac{7}{25}$

36. School Play Three of every five students who tried out for a play made the cast. Write $\frac{3}{5}$ as a percent.

GPS 37. Guided Problem Solving About $\frac{7}{10}$ of Earth's surface is covered by water. What percent of Earth's surface is NOT covered by water?
  • You can draw a picture to model this problem.

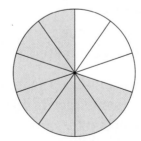

GO Online

Homework Video Tutor

Visit: PHSchool.com
Web Code: aqe-0706

Write the letter of the point on the number line that represents each number.

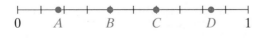

38. 0.4 **39.** 60% **40.** $\frac{5}{6}$ **41.** 18%

Order each set of numbers from least to greatest.

42. $46\%, \frac{1}{2}, 0.53, 5\%$ **43.** $\frac{1}{4}, 22\%, 0.24, \frac{1}{5}$

44. $63\%, \frac{3}{5}, 0.58, \frac{31}{50}$ **45.** $\frac{17}{20}, 95\%, 0.9, \frac{22}{25}$

46. Biology At least ninety-nine percent of all the kinds of plants and animals that have ever lived are now extinct. Write ninety-nine percent as a fraction and as a decimal.

47. Copy and complete the table below.

Fraction	$\frac{11}{50}$	$\frac{39}{50}$	$\frac{22}{25}$	■	■	$\frac{4}{5}$
Decimal	■	0.78	■	0.45	■	■
Percent	22%	■	■	■	42%	■

48. You answer 32 questions correctly on a 45-question test. You need a score of at least 70% to pass. Do you pass? Explain.

49. Fuel Gauge Use the fuel gauge below. What percent of the tank is full?

50. <u>Writing in Math</u> Explain how to write a decimal as a percent.

51. Challenge Find the percent of numbers from 1 to 100 that are prime numbers.

The paradise parrot once lived in Australia. It has been extinct since the early 1900s.

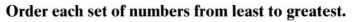

Test Prep and Mixed Review   **Practice**

Gridded Response

52. The formula $i = \frac{127}{50}c$ can be used to convert a measurement from centimeters to inches. Write a decimal equal to $\frac{127}{50}$.

53. Eric finishes a swimming race in 51.4 seconds. Bobby finishes the same race in 48.6 seconds. How much faster is Eric's time than Bobby's time, in seconds?

54. Billie Jean earns $12 for baby-sitting for 3 hours. How much will she earn in 4 hours, in dollars?

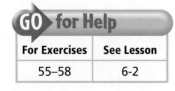

For Exercises	See Lesson
55–58	6-2

Estimate each product.

55. $2\frac{3}{4} \times 5\frac{1}{4}$ **56.** $6\frac{1}{8} \times 3\frac{3}{8}$ **57.** $4\frac{5}{8} \times 2\frac{2}{3}$ **58.** $3\frac{1}{2} \times 5\frac{1}{3}$

Write each percent as a decimal and as a fraction in simplest form.

1. 74%

2. 6%

3. 60%

Write each fraction as a percent.

4. $\dfrac{21}{25}$

5. $\dfrac{7}{10}$

6. $\dfrac{1}{20}$

Use the map below. Find the distance between each pair of cities.

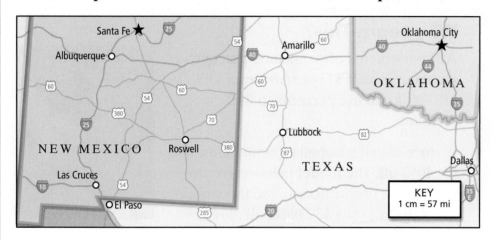

KEY
1 cm = 57 mi

7. Santa Fe and El Paso

8. Dallas and Albuquerque

9. Dallas and El Paso

10. Advertising A beverage cup is 6 inches tall. The beverage cup on a restaurant billboard is 18 feet tall. Write the scale of the billboard as a ratio in simplest form.

MATH AT WORK

Help-Desk Technician

Do you enjoy helping your family and friends with their computer-related questions? If so, a career as a help-desk technician might be for you. Help-desk technicians provide support to people who have hardware and software questions.

Help-desk technicians must be able to apply logical reasoning and problem-solving skills in order to assist their customers.

Go Online
PHSchool.com

For: Information on Help-Desk Technicians
Web Code: aqb-2031

Finding the Percent of a Number

Check Skills You'll Need

1. Vocabulary Review
How can you use *cross products* to solve a proportion?

Solve each proportion.

2. $\frac{m}{12} = \frac{6}{9}$

3. $\frac{6}{45} = \frac{2}{n}$

4. $\frac{54}{c} = \frac{9}{13}$

5. $\frac{92}{100} = \frac{q}{250}$

 **for Help**
Lesson 7-4

What You'll Learn

To use percents to find part of a whole

Why Learn This?

Advertisements often include percents such as "Save 25%" or "All items 40% off!" You can use percents to find discounts.

A store has all baseball equipment on sale for 40% off. The model below can help you write a proportion to find the amount you will save on a $32 baseball glove.

```
            part         whole
             ↓             ↓
   0         n            32
   [■■■■■■■■■■|■■■■■■■■■■■■■■]
  0%        40%         100%
```

$\frac{n}{32} = \frac{40}{100}$ ← The part *n* corresponds to 40% in the diagram.
  ← The full price $32 corresponds to 100%.

EXAMPLE **Using a Proportion**

1 Retail Sales Find 40% of $32.

amount saved → $\frac{n}{32} = \frac{40}{100}$ ← part
original price →   ← whole

$100 \times n = 40 \times 32$ ← **Write the cross products.**

$100n = 1{,}280$ ← **Multiply.**

$n = 12.8$ ← **Divide each side by 100.**

You will save $12.80 on the baseball glove.

✔ Quick Check

1. You buy a $40 shirt on sale for 20% off. Find 20% of $40.

You can find a percent of a number by using a decimal.

EXAMPLE **Using a Decimal**

② Find 22% of 288.

$$22\% = 0.22 \quad \leftarrow \text{Write 22\% as a decimal.}$$
$$0.22 \times 288 = 63.36 \quad \leftarrow \text{Multiply.}$$

So 22% of 288 is 63.36.

✓ Quick Check

2. **a.** Find 12% of 91.   **b.** Find 18% of 121.

The percents in the table below are found in real-world situations. You can change these to fractions or decimals to use mental math.

Test Prep Tip

Memorizing the values in the table at the right can help you find percents quickly on tests.

Equivalent Expressions for Mental Math

Percent	10%	20%	25%	50%	75%	80%
Fraction	$\frac{1}{10}$	$\frac{1}{5}$	$\frac{1}{4}$	$\frac{1}{2}$	$\frac{3}{4}$	$\frac{4}{5}$
Decimal	0.1	0.2	0.25	0.5	0.75	0.8

EXAMPLE **Using Mental Math**

③ Suppose 25% of 80 students in a survey vacationed in Florida. Find the number of students who vacationed in Florida.

What you think

$25\% = \frac{1}{4}; \frac{1}{4} \times 80 = 20.$

Twenty students vacationed in Florida.

Why it works

$$25\% = \frac{25}{100} = \frac{1}{4} \qquad \leftarrow \text{Write 25\% as a fraction in simplest form.}$$
$$\frac{1}{4} \times 80 = \frac{1}{4} \times \frac{80}{1} \qquad \leftarrow \text{Multiply } \frac{1}{4} \text{ by 80. Rewrite 80 as } \frac{80}{1}.$$
$$= \frac{80}{4} \qquad \leftarrow \text{Simplify.}$$
$$= 20 \qquad \leftarrow \text{Divide.}$$

✓ Quick Check

3. Use mental math to find 75% of 12.

Mental Math Find each answer.

1. 50% of 10   **2.** 25% of 40   **3.** 3% of 100

Use the table below for Exercises 4–5.

Frequency of Vowels in Written Passages

Letter	A	E	I	O	U
Frequency	8%	13%	6%	8%	3%

4. Find the number of E's expected in a passage of 100 letters.

5. Find the number of I's expected in a passage of 500 letters.

Homework Exercises

For more exercises, see **Extra Skills and Word Problems.**

GO for Help

For Exercises	See Examples
6–11	1
12–18	2
19–22	3

Find each answer. You may find a model useful.

6. 42% of 70   **7.** 8% of 210   **8.** 70% of 185

9. 11% of 600   **10.** 15% of 90   **11.** 65% of 240

12. 7% of 50   **13.** 18% of 170   **14.** 44% of 165

15. 43% of 61   **16.** 55% of 91   **17.** 30% of 490

18. Shopping You go to a sale where all items are 20% off. Your total clothes bill would have normally cost $80. Find the amount you save.

Find each answer using mental math.

19. 20% of 180   **20.** 80% of 40   **21.** 75% of 480

22. Dance Suppose 50% of 180 dancers said they prefer modern dance. How many dancers prefer modern dance?

GPS **23. Guided Problem Solving** You earn $240 for your first paycheck. You pay 22% of it in taxes. You decide to put 40% of the remaining money into savings. How much money will you have left to spend?
   • The amount you pay in taxes is ■. The money remaining after taxes is ■.
   • Write an expression to find the amount put into savings.

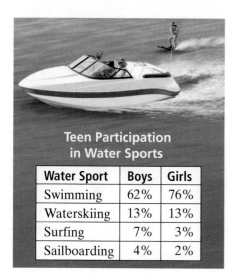

Teen Participation
in Water Sports

Water Sport	Boys	Girls
Swimming	62%	76%
Waterskiing	13%	13%
Surfing	7%	3%
Sailboarding	4%	2%

Recreation The results of a survey of 200 boys and 200 girls are shown at the left.

24. How many boys surf? **25.** How many girls surf?

26. How many boys swim? **27.** How many girls swim?

28. Travel Of 200 students surveyed, 30% said they have visited SeaWorld in Florida. Of those students, 60% saw Shamu. How many students saw Shamu?

29. Reasoning You want to buy a game that regularly costs $60. The store has a 40%-off sale. You also have a coupon for 10% off. Is taking 50% off the full price the same as taking 40% off the full price and then 10% off the sale price? Explain.

GO Online

Homework Video Tutor

Visit: PHSchool.com
Web Code: aqe-0707

Money You can find simple interest by multiplying the investment *P*, the yearly rate *r*, and the time *t*. Find the simple interest.

30. $P = \$500, r = 1\%, t = 2$ **31.** $P = \$1{,}000, r = 3\%, t = 4$

32. $P = \$895, r = 5\%, t = 2$ **33.** $P = \$4{,}500, r = 2\%, t = 3$

34. Vision In the United States, about 46% of the population wear glasses or contact lenses. A sample of 85 people is taken.
   a. About how many people would you expect to wear glasses or contact lenses?
   b. Writing in Math How did you find your answer to part (a)?

35. Challenge Store A offers a 60% discount. Store B has a sale for $\frac{2}{3}$ off. Which store gives the greater discount? Explain.

Test Prep and Mixed Review   **Practice**

Multiple Choice

36. The blood in a human body accounts for about 7% of total body weight. Which number is equal to 7%?
   Ⓐ 0.07   Ⓑ 0.7   Ⓒ $\frac{1}{7}$ Ⓓ $\frac{7}{10}$

37. How much of the model is shaded?
   Ⓕ 54%   Ⓗ 50%
   Ⓖ 52%   Ⓙ 48%

GO for Help

For Exercises	See Lesson
38–41	7-1

Write each ratio in simplest form.

38. $\frac{10}{45}$ **39.** 36 : 90   **40.** 18 to 21   **41.** $\frac{100}{150}$

Exploring Circle Graphs

You can make a circle graph to display data. You can use a paper strip to help you draw a circle graph.

 ACTIVITY

You ask 50 students to name their favorite sport. The results are shown in the table. Make a circle graph to display the data.

Favorite Sports

Football	27
Basketball	10
Baseball	5
Other	8

1. Cut a strip of paper slightly more than 50 cm long with a tab at the end as shown. Each centimeter represents 1 student.

54%	20%	10%	16%	Tab

2. Draw a line 27 cm from the left end of the strip. This section represents the students who prefer football.

3. Draw lines to make sections representing the other sports.

4. Form a ring with the strip. Line up the beginning of the strip with the 50-student line and tape the ends together.

5. Use a compass to draw a circle around your ring. Use your ring to mark sections around the edge of the circle.

6. Connect the marks to the center of the circle. Label each section with the name of the sport it represents.

7. Determine the percent of the students who prefer each sport. Label each section of the circle with the correct percent.

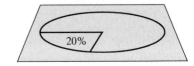

Exercises

Make a circle graph for each table of data.

1. **Favorite Colors**

Red	Blue	Green	Yellow
8	6	9	2

2. **Hours of Sleep Each Night**

Less Than 8	8–10	More Than 10
4	9	7

3. **Homework on Saturdays**

Usually	Sometimes	Never
12	31	7

What You'll Learn

To read and make circle graphs to represent real-world data

🔊 **New Vocabulary** circle graph

Why Learn This?

A circle graph is a useful way to represent data. You can use a circle graph to visually compare parts to a whole.

A **circle graph** is a graph of data in which the entire circle represents the whole. Each sector in the circle represents part of the whole.

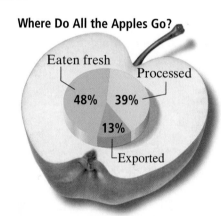

Where Do All the Apples Go?

Eaten fresh Processed
48%   39%
13%
Exported

EXAMPLES   Reading a Circle Graph

1 Use the circle graph above. How are 13% of apples used?

The circle graph is divided into three sections. The purple section is labeled 13%. 13% of apples are exported.

2 Use the circle graph above. Describe how many apples are eaten fresh.

A little less than half of the circle is labeled "Eaten fresh." 48% is close to 50%, or $\frac{1}{2}$.

Almost half of apples are eaten fresh.

Vocabulary Tip

A circle graph is often called a pie chart. Each wedge of a circle graph is a "piece of the pie."

✓ Quick Check

1. Using the circle graph above, how are 39% of the apples used?

2. Using the circle graph above, are more apples exported or processed? Justify your answer.

EXAMPLE **Sketching a Circle Graph**

③ **Sports** In one season, the Seattle Mariners baseball team stole a total of 174 bases. Sketch a circle graph of the data.

First use a calculator to change the data to percents of the total. Round to the nearest percent.

$$\frac{56}{174} \approx 32\% \qquad \frac{39}{174} \approx 22\%$$

$$\frac{34}{174} \approx 20\% \qquad \frac{45}{174} \approx 26\%$$

Stolen Bases by Seattle Mariners

Player	Total
Ichiro Suzuki	56
Mark McLemore	39
Mike Cameron	34
Other players combined	45
Total number of stolen bases	174

Use number sense to divide the circle.

$32\% \approx \frac{1}{3}$ 22% is slightly less than $\frac{1}{4}$ of the circle.

$26\% \approx \frac{1}{4}$ 20% is the percent left.

Stolen Bases by Seattle Mariners

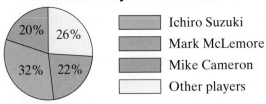

Label the divided circle with each percent. Use a different color for each player. Make a key, and add a title.

✓ Quick Check

3. Of 50 students surveyed, 13 bought a hot lunch, 9 packed a lunch, 6 bought a salad, and 22 bought a sandwich. Sketch a circle graph of the data.

✓ Check Your Understanding

1. **Vocabulary** A circle graph is a graph of data in which the entire circle represents the ___?___.

2. **Music** Use the circle graph at the right. Which instrument do more musicians play than any other?

3. **Reasoning** Explain why you cannot use $\frac{1}{2}$, $\frac{1}{3}$, and $\frac{1}{4}$ to sketch a complete circle graph.

Instruments Played by Amateurs

Drums 7%
Flute 11%
Piano 58%
Guitar 24%

For more exercises, see Extra Skills and Word Problems.

GO for Help

For Exercises	See Examples
4–7	1–2
8–11	3

Use the circle graph for Exercises 4–7.

Favorite Sport

□ Tennis
□ Basketball
□ Soccer
□ Baseball
□ Volleyball

4. Which sport is the least popular?

5. Which is more popular, basketball or volleyball?

6. List the sports from least to most popular.

7. Which sport is about twice as popular as basketball?

Sketch a circle graph for the given percents.

8. 10%, 40%, 50%

9. 5%, 14%, 33%, 48%

10. 12%, 26%, 62%

11. 12%, 34%, 21%, 33%

12. Guided Problem Solving The table below shows that taxes are a large part of the price of gas. Use two circle graphs to compare the tax a person in each country pays as a percentage of the price of gas.

Taxes on One Gallon of Gasoline

Country	Price (including tax)	Tax
United States	$2.39	$.39
United Kingdom	$6.09	$4.27

- What is the percentage of tax on one gallon of gas in each country?
- Sketch a circle graph for each country. Compare the tax to the price of gasoline in each country.

Sketch a circle graph for each set of fractions.

13. $\frac{1}{2}, \frac{1}{3}, \frac{1}{6}$

14. $\frac{3}{4}, \frac{1}{10}, \frac{1}{10}, \frac{1}{20}$

15. $\frac{3}{8}, \frac{1}{8}, \frac{4}{10}, \frac{1}{10}$

GO Online

Homework Video Tutor

Visit: PHSchool.com
Web Code: aqe-0708

16. Science The human body is made up of 21 chemical elements. Use the table at the right to make a circle graph.

17. Data Collection List the things you do on a Saturday. Estimate the hours you spend on each activity. Write each time as a percent of a 24-hour day. Make a circle graph.

Human Body Composition

Element	Percent
Oxygen	65
Carbon	18
Hydrogen	10
Nitrogen	3
Other	4

18. Surveys 100 students were asked how they spend their free time. Of those surveyed, 53% said they like to go to the mall, 80% said they like to watch TV, 72% said they like to spend time outside, and 34% said they like to search the Internet.

a. Writing in Math Explain why you cannot use a circle graph to display the data.

b. What kind of graph could you use to compare the data?

Coins Donated

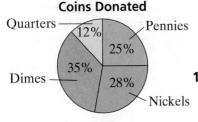

19. Challenge A class collected 700 coins for charity. Use the circle graph at the left to find how much money was donated.

Test Prep and Mixed Review

Practice

Multiple Choice

20. Of the 100 people Alex surveyed, 18 said spring was their favorite season, 55 said summer, 16 said fall, and 11 said winter. Which circle graph displays the data?

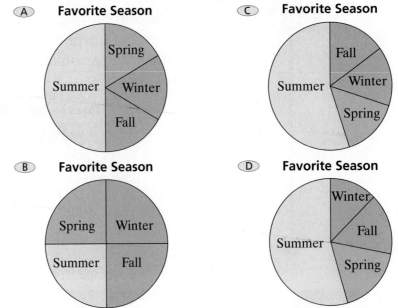

21. Camille earns $14 baby-sitting. She now has $81. Which equation can Camille use to find d, the amount of money she had before baby-sitting?

F $\quad d = 81 \div 14$

H $\quad d = 81 - 14$

G $\quad 14 = 81 \times d$

J $\quad 14 = 81 + d$

GO for Help

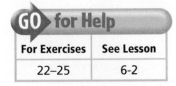

For Exercises	See Lesson
22–25	6-2

Algebra Evaluate each expression for $x = 3\frac{3}{4}$.

22. $8x$ **23.** $\frac{2}{5}x$ **24.** $\frac{4}{3}x$ **25.** $x \cdot 2\frac{1}{2}$

Reporting Survey Results

Sometimes you can combine categories in a survey and choose a data display to support one side of an issue.

ACTIVITY

1. Clear your calculator for this activity. Press [LIST] and clear any data already in the list. Press [2nd] [PLOT] 4: PlotsOff to turn off the plots. Press [Y=] and clear any equations.

2. Press [LIST]. Enter "Yes," "Undec," and "No" in the L1 column. Use "Undec" for "Undecided". To type letters, press [2nd] [TEXT] and use the arrow keys. Use quotation marks to begin and end each word. After each word, select Done and press [ENTER]. Press [ENTER] again to add the word to the list.

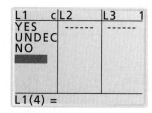

3. Using the table, sort the data into three categories: "Yes," "Undecided," and "No". Enter the totals in the L2 column.

Should the School Change Its Mascot?

Category	Yes	Undecided	No
Number of students	86	28	86
Percent			

4. To make a circle graph, press [2nd] [PLOT] 1: Plot1. Use the arrow keys and the [ENTER] key to select On and Circle Graph. CategList: shows L1, and Data List: shows L2. Then select Percent on the bottom line, and press [ENTER].

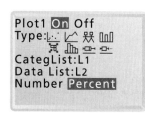

5. Press [GRAPH]. Use [TRACE] and the arrow buttons to display the key on the graph for each category.

6. Combine the "Undecided" and the "No" categories into a new category called "Not Yes." Make a circle graph using the resorted data. Enter the categories "Yes" and "Not Yes."

7. **Writing in Math** Use your graph to explain why the school should not change the mascot.

8. **Reasoning** Use the data above to make a circle graph using two categories different from the categories in Step 6. Show that most people would like to change the mascot.

Practice Solving Problems

Top Jobs A survey identified the four jobs most commonly held by high school sophomores. There were 425 students surveyed. How many students worked as a cashier or a grocery clerk?

Sophomore Job Survey

Job	Percent
Food Service	21
Child Care	13
Cashier or Grocery Clerk	6
Salesperson	4

What You Might Think

How can I use a diagram to show this situation?

I can use the diagram to write and solve a proportion.

What You Might Write

Let n = the number of students who worked as a cashier or a grocery clerk.

$$\frac{n}{425} = \frac{6}{100}$$

$$n \times 100 = 6 \times 425$$

$$100n = 2{,}550$$

$$\frac{100n}{100} = \frac{2{,}550}{100}$$

$$n = 25.5$$

What is the answer? Is it reasonable?

About 26 sophomores worked as a cashier or a grocery clerk.

10% of 425 is about 42, so 5% is about 21, which is close to 25.5.

Think It Through

1. Give two other proportions you can write for this situation.

2. **Reasoning** Why is the answer 26, not 25.5?

3. **Check for Reasonableness** Explain how the estimate was found.

Exercises

4. Use the survey data on the previous page to find how many more students were food service workers than cashiers or grocery clerks. (*Hint*: Find how many students worked in food service.)

5. Thirty-seven percent of the students in the survey on the previous page worked 10 hours or less each week. How many of the students worked more than 10 hours each week? Use the diagram below.

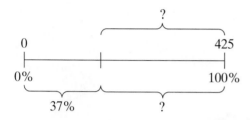

6. Carrie rode her bike a longer distance in less time today than she did yesterday. On which day did she ride faster? Explain.

7. Suppose an elevator in the Empire State Building takes 80 seconds to travel 950 feet. How far does the elevator travel in 1 minute?

8. The distance around the Talladega Motor Speedway track is 2.66 miles. In the drawing below, the backstretch is 1.6 inches. What is the actual length of the backstretch in feet?

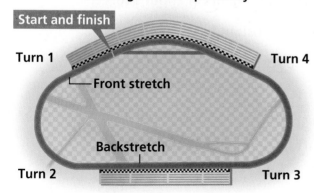

Talladega Motor Speedway

Scale: 1 in. = 2,500 ft

Estimating With Percents

What You'll Learn

To use mental math and estimation with percents

Why Learn This?

When shopping, you need to know whether you have enough money to buy an item. You can use mental math to estimate prices.

EXAMPLE Estimating Cost

1 **Sales Tax** Suppose you buy the scarf above. The sales tax rate is 5%. Estimate the total cost of the scarf to the nearest dollar.

Method 1 Estimate the cost and multiply.

Round the cost of the scarf to $15.

$$5\% \text{ of } 15 = 0.05 \times 15 \quad \leftarrow \text{Write 5\% as 0.05.}$$
$$= 0.75 \quad \leftarrow \text{Multiply to find the tax.}$$
$$15 + 0.75 = 15.75 \quad \leftarrow \text{Find the sum of the price and the tax.}$$

The cost of the scarf including tax is about $16.

Method 2 Estimate the cost and use number sense.

Round the cost of the scarf to $15. 10% of $15 is $1.50.

Since 5% is half of 10%, 5% of $15 is half of $1.50, or $.75. So the tax is about $.75. The total cost is about $15 + $.75 = $15.75.

The cost of the scarf including tax is about $16.

✓ Quick Check

1. Use a 6% tax rate to estimate the total cost for the hat shown with the scarf above.

EXAMPLE **Estimating a Tip**

2 **Dining Out** Estimate a 15% tip for a bill of $26.22.

What you think

The bill is about $26. 15% = 10% + 5%.
Since 10% of $26 is $2.60, 5% is half of $2.60, or $1.30.
A 15% tip of $26.22 is about $2.60 + $1.30 = $3.90, or about $4.

Why it works

$$15\% \times \$26 = (10\% + 5\%) \times \$26 \quad \leftarrow \text{Replace 15\% with 10\% + 5\%.}$$
$$= 10\% \times \$26 + 5\% \times \$26 \quad \leftarrow \text{Distributive Property}$$
$$= \$2.60 + (5\% \times \$26) \quad \leftarrow \text{Find 10\%} \times \$26.$$
$$= \$2.60 + \left(\frac{1}{2} \times 10\% \times \$26\right) \quad \leftarrow \text{Replace 5\% with } \frac{1}{2} \times \text{10\%.}$$
$$= \$2.60 + \$1.30 \quad \leftarrow \text{Simplify inside the parentheses.}$$
$$= \$3.90, \text{ or about } \$4.00 \quad \leftarrow \text{Add.}$$

✓ Quick Check

2. Estimate a 15% tip for a bill of $41.63.

EXAMPLE **Estimating a Sale Price**

3 **Sales** The regular price for a pair of hiking boots is $57.95. The store is having a 30%-off sale. Estimate the sale price.

Method 1

The regular price is about $60. If the sale price is 30% off, you pay 100% − 30%, or 70% of the regular price.
70% of $60 is $42. The sale price is about $42.

Method 2

The sale price is 30% off the regular cost.

$$30\% \times \$60 = 0.3 \times \$60 \quad \leftarrow \text{Write 30\% as 0.3.}$$
$$= \$18 \quad \leftarrow \text{Simplify.}$$

Subtract the amount saved from the regular price.
$60 − $18 = $42. The sale price is about $42.

✓ Quick Check

3. Estimate the sale price of a $40.19 baseball glove at 40% off.

1. **Mental Math** There is a 10% tax on a game priced at $49.99. About how much is the total cost of the game?

2. **Reasoning** When estimating tax, is it better to round a price like $34.48 up to $35 or down to $34? Explain your choice.

Write a numerical expression you can use to estimate the amount of tax or discount.

3. cost: $19.99; sales tax: 9%

4. cost: $499.95; discount: 30%

5. cost: $39.80; sales tax: 5%

6. cost: $109.80; discount: 25%

Homework Exercises

For more exercises, see **Extra Skills and Word Problems.**

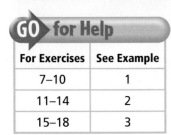

For Exercises	See Example
7–10	1
11–14	2
15–18	3

Use a sales tax rate of 7%. Estimate the total cost for each item.

7. a game that costs $27.60

8. a bicycle that costs $129

9. a book that costs $14.59

10. a DVD that costs $19.95

Estimate a 15% tip for each amount.

11. $41.90   12. $8.60   13. $79.10   14. $40.60

Estimate the sale price of each item.

15. 40% off a $42 necklace

16. 50% off a $789 sofa

17. 70% off a $16.99 shirt

18. 90% off a $68 jacket

19. **Guided Problem Solving** The regular price of a bicycle helmet is $28. You get a discount of 25%. Then you must pay a 6% sales tax. Find the total cost for the bicycle helmet.
    • What is the sale price of the helmet?
    • How much tax will you pay on the sale price?

GO Online
Homework Video Tutor
Visit: PHSchool.com
Web Code: aqe-0709

20. **Jobs** You get the following tips. Estimate the value of each tip.
    a. 20% of $14.20   **b.** 10% of $24.75   **c.** 15% of $19.70
    d. Which tip has the greatest value?

21. **Writing in Math** Suppose 5% tax on a restaurant bill is $4.36. Explain how you can use this amount to find a 20% tip and a 15% tip.

Estimate each amount. State whether your answer is an overestimate or an underestimate of the exact answer.

22. 90% of 49   **23.** 12% of 302   **24.** 1.2% of 490

25. The snowboard at the left is on sale for $12.74. The snowboard is on sale for 60% off. Find the regular price of the snowboard.

Sale Price
$12.74

Sales Tax Use the sales tax rate table. Estimate the sales tax and the total cost of each item below for each state in the table.

26. erasers: $.79   **27.** art book: $64.45

28. journal: $5.29

State Sales Tax

State	Tax
Florida	6%
Georgia	4%
Massachusetts	5%
Tennessee	7%

SOURCE: *The World Almanac*

29. Challenge By age two, a child's height is usually about 50% of his or her full adult height. Estimate the adult height of a two-year-old whose height is 2 feet 9 inches.

Test Prep and Mixed Review   **Practice**

Multiple Choice

30. Samantha and her friends buy 11 shirts, each priced at $24. About how much do the shirts cost all together?

   (A) $200   (B) $250   (C) $300   (D) $350

31. The chart shows the ratio of men to women in the United States population for three age groups. Which statement is best supported by the data?

Age (years)	Ratio (men : women)
55–64	92 : 100
65–74	84 : 100
75 and older	46 : 100

   (F) The ratio of men to women increases as age increases.

   (G) The ratio of men to women decreases as age increases.

   (H) The ratio of men to women decreases as age decreases.

   (J) There is no relationship between the ratio and age.

32. You read 80% of a book. What fractional part of the book do you have left to read?

   (A) $\frac{1}{5}$ (B) $\frac{1}{4}$ (C) $\frac{3}{4}$ (D) $\frac{4}{5}$

GO for Help

For Exercises	See Lesson
33–36	5-7

How many minutes are in each amount of time?

33. 1 h 15 min   **34.** 2 h 10 min   **35.** 5 h 45 min   **36.** 6 h 20 min

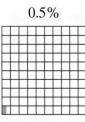
Percents Under 1% or Over 100%

Percents can be less than 1% or greater than 100%.

0.5%

Less than 1%

100%   +   5%   =   105%

Greater than 100%

EXAMPLES

1 Write 0.4% as a decimal.

$0.4\% = \dfrac{0.4}{100}$ ← Write the percent as a fraction.

$= 0.004$ ← Write the fraction as a decimal.

As a decimal, 0.4% is 0.004. As a fraction, 0.4% is $\dfrac{4}{1,000}$.

2 **Nutrition** A vitamin supplement provides 150% of the Recommended Daily Allowance (RDA) of vitamin C. The RDA is 60 milligrams. How many milligrams of vitamin C are in the vitamin supplement?

150% of 60 = 1.50 × 60   ← Write the percent as a decimal.

$= 90$ ← Multiply.

The vitamin supplement contains 90 milligrams of vitamin C.

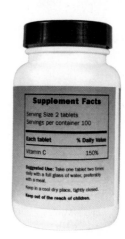

Exercises

Write each percent as a decimal.

1. 0.2%   **2.** 0.75%   **3.** 110%   **4.** 250%

Find each answer.

5. 400% of 5   **6.** 150% of 18   **7.** 0.5% of 300   **8.** 0.25% of 12

Working Backward

The problem-solving strategy *Work Backward* is useful when taking multiple-choice tests. Work backward by testing each choice in the original problem. You will eliminate incorrect answers. Eventually you will find the correct answer.

EXAMPLE

A fruit stand is selling 8 bananas for $1.00. At this rate, how much will 20 bananas cost?

(A) $1.50   (B) $2.00   (C) $2.50   (D) $3.00

Use mental math to test the choices that are easy to use.

$2.00 is twice $1.00. Twice 8 is only 16, so choice B is not the answer.

$3.00 is three times $1.00. Three times 8 is 24, so choice D is not the correct answer.

Since 20 is between 16 and 24, the cost must be between $2.00 and $3.00. The correct answer is choice C.

Exercises

1. Omar made an overseas phone call. The rate was $2.40 for the first minute and $.55 for each additional minute. His bill was $6.80. How can Omar find the total amount charged for additional minutes?
   (A) Subtract 2.40 from 6.80.
   (B) Add 0.55 and 6.80.
   (C) Subtract 0.55 from 6.80.
   (D) Add 2.40 and 6.80.

2. At a copy center, 100 copies cost $4.00. At this rate, how much will 450 copies cost?
   (F) $16.00   (G) $18.00   (H) $20.00   (J) $22.00

3. What method should NOT be used to find 88% of 40?
   (A) 0.88×40
   (B) $\frac{88}{100} \times 40$
   (C) $\frac{n}{40} = \frac{88}{100}$
   (D) $\frac{40}{n} = \frac{88}{100}$

Chapter 7 Review

Vocabulary Review

🔊 **circle graph** (p. 341)
cross products (p. 317)
equivalent ratios (p. 307)
percent (p. 331)

proportion (p. 316)
rate (p. 312)
ratio (p. 306)

scale (p. 326)
unit cost (p. 313)
unit rate (p. 312)

Go **Online**
PHSchool.com

For: Vocabulary quiz
Web Code: aqj-0751

Choose the vocabulary term from the column on the right that best completes the sentence.

1. Two equivalent ratios can be written as a __?__ .
2. You can use a __?__ to compare a part to a part.
3. An example of a __?__ is 25 miles per hour.
4. You can use a __?__ to compare a number to 100.

A. percent
B. proportion
C. rate
D. ratio

Skills and Concepts

Lesson 7-1
• To write ratios to compare real-world quantities

A **ratio** compares two quantities by division. To write a ratio in simplest form, divide both numbers by their GCF. **Equivalent ratios** name the same number.

A jar contains 8 tacks, 15 bolts, and 23 nails. Write each ratio in three ways.

5. bolts to nails 6. bolts to tacks 7. nails to tacks 8. bolts to total

Write each ratio in simplest form.

9. 8 to 32 10. $\frac{18}{30}$ 11. 24 ft : 8 yd 12. $\frac{45 \text{ boys}}{54 \text{ girls}}$

Lesson 7-2
• To find and use unit rates and unit costs

A **rate** is a ratio that compares quantities measured in different units. To find a **unit rate,** divide the numerator by the denominator. A **unit price** gives the cost per unit.

13. You run 1 mile in 8 minutes. How long do you take to run 5 miles?

14. You earn $400 in 32 hours. How much do you earn in 1 hour?

15. **Bread** One loaf of bread costs $3.09 for 32 ounces, and another costs $1.40 for 24 ounces. Which is the better buy?

354 Chapter 7 Chapter Review

Lessons 7-3 and 7-4
- To understand proportions and to determine whether two ratios are proportional
- To solve proportions using number sense and cross products

A **proportion** is an equation stating that two ratios are equal.

Does each pair of ratios form a proportion?

16. $\frac{2}{5}, \frac{1}{3}$ **17.** $\frac{6}{16}, \frac{21}{56}$ **18.** $\frac{15}{9}, \frac{5}{3}$ **19.** $\frac{3}{8}, \frac{9}{16}$

20. There are 944 marbles in a bag. If 3 out of 8 marbles are yellow, how many marbles are yellow?

Lesson 7-5
- To find the scale of a drawing and to use scales to find actual dimensions

A **scale** is a ratio that compares a length on a drawing or a model to an actual length.

Ships The *S.S. United States,* a passenger ship, is 990 feet long. Find the length of a model with each given scale.

21. 1 foot : 10 feet   **22.** 3 inches : 20 feet

23. 2 inches : 15 feet

Lessons 7-6 and 7-7
- To find equivalent forms of fractions, decimals, and percents
- To use percents to find part of a whole

A **percent** is a ratio that compares a number to 100.

Write each percent as a fraction in simplest form and as a decimal.

24. 30%   **25.** 25%   **26.** 56%   **27.** 12%

28. There are 200 students in your class, and 30% of them joined the school band. How many students in your class joined the band?

29. Three out of 5 children enjoy swimming. What percent like to swim?

Lesson 7-8
- To read and make circle graphs to represent real-world data

30. Books Use the data in the table below to make a circle graph.

Favorite Types of Books

Mysteries	Biographies	Fiction	Humor
22%	13%	55%	10%

Lesson 7-9
- To use mental math and estimation with percents

You can use mental math to estimate percents.

Estimate each amount.

31. 20% of 48   **32.** 6% of $19.99   **33.** 15% of $38.56

Chapter 7 Test

You have 3 nickels, 11 dimes, and 5 quarters in your pocket. Write each ratio in three ways.

1. nickels to quarters
2. dimes to nickels
3. dimes to all coins
4. quarters to dimes

5. Use the figure below. Find the ratio of the shaded region to the unshaded region in simplest form.

Write three ratios equivalent to each ratio.

6. 3 to 2
7. $\frac{3}{18}$
8. 6 : 8

9. A car can travel 28 miles per gallon of gas. How far can the car travel on 8 gallons of gas?

10. A 6-ounce bottle of juice costs $.96. An 8-ounce bottle costs $1.12. Which is the better buy?

Does each pair of ratios form a proportion?

11. $\frac{5}{3}, \frac{15}{9}$
12. $\frac{3}{4}, \frac{4}{5}$
13. $\frac{8}{12}, \frac{12}{8}$

Solve each proportion.

14. $\frac{4}{5} = \frac{x}{25}$
15. $\frac{6}{4} = \frac{9}{m}$
16. $\frac{a}{25} = \frac{3}{10}$

17. A grocery store sells 6 pounds of apples for $4. How much will 8 pounds of apples cost? Round your answer to the nearest cent.

18. **Writing in Math** The ratio of girls to boys in a science class is 5 to 6. Can there be 15 boys in the class? Explain why or why not.

Use a map scale of 1 inch : 30 miles to find each actual distance.

19. 3 inches
20. 6 inches
21. 0.5 inches

22. A scale model of a tiger measures 1.5 feet long. The tiger's actual length is 9 feet. What is the scale of the model?

Write each percent as a decimal and as a fraction.

23. 25%
24. 6%
25. 98%

Write each decimal or fraction as a percent. If necessary, round to the nearest percent.

26. 0.48
27. 0.02
28. $\frac{1}{10}$
29. $\frac{3}{15}$
30. $\frac{5}{6}$
31. $0.\overline{9}$

Find each percent.

32. 5% of 200
33. 80% of 8
34. 2% of 50

35. Suppose 86% of 50 people at a law firm like their jobs. How many people like their jobs?

36. Use the circle graph.
    a. How do *most* students get to school?
    b. What method do students use *least*?

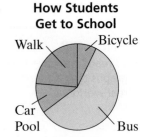

How Students Get to School

Estimate a 15% tip for each bill amount.

37. $32.04
38. $48.76
39. $12.83

40. Suppose you buy a DVD for $12.98. The sales tax is 7%. Estimate the total cost.

Multiple Choice
Choose the correct letter.

1. Find the product of $\frac{2}{9}$ and $\frac{5}{7}$.

   Ⓐ $\frac{10}{63}$ Ⓒ $\frac{14}{45}$

   Ⓑ $\frac{5}{31}$ Ⓓ $3\frac{3}{14}$

2. Which could you use to describe how to find $1\frac{3}{4}$ divided by $\frac{1}{2}$?

   Ⓕ Multiply $\frac{1}{2}$ and $\frac{7}{4}$.

   Ⓖ Multiply $\frac{1}{2}$ and $\frac{4}{7}$.

   Ⓗ Multiply $\frac{4}{7}$ and 2.

   Ⓙ Multiply $\frac{7}{4}$ and 2.

3. You bought a 12-bag variety pack of dried fruit. Each bag of dried fruit contains c ounces. How many ounces of dried fruit did you buy?

   Ⓐ $c \div 12$ Ⓒ $c + 12$
   Ⓑ $12 \div c$ Ⓓ $12c$

4. Which statement is false?

   Ⓕ $\frac{8}{10} = \frac{32}{40}$ Ⓗ $\frac{24}{42} = \frac{28}{49}$

   Ⓖ $\frac{1}{3} = \frac{12}{36}$ Ⓙ $\frac{13}{14} = \frac{169}{196}$

5. Which decimal represents the portion of the model that is NOT shaded?

   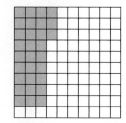

   Ⓐ 0.3   Ⓑ 0.33   Ⓒ 0.67   Ⓓ 0.7

6. Which of the following numbers is divisible by 2, 3, 5, 9 and 10?

   Ⓕ 1,350   Ⓗ 945
   Ⓖ 1,010   Ⓙ 120

7. Choose an appropriate unit for measuring the length of a driveway.

   Ⓐ inches Ⓑ feet   Ⓒ miles Ⓓ tons

8. Solve $x - \frac{1}{10} = \frac{1}{2}$.

   Ⓕ $\frac{1}{10}$ Ⓖ $\frac{1}{6}$ Ⓗ $\frac{2}{5}$ Ⓙ $\frac{3}{5}$

9. At a car dealer, $\frac{2}{5}$ of the vehicles sold during the year were minivans. What percent of the vehicles sold were minivans?

   Ⓐ 2.5%   Ⓑ 20%   Ⓒ 25%   Ⓓ 40%

Gridded Response

10. A bank teller spends about 8 minutes helping each customer. How long does the teller spend with 7 customers?

11. Solve $\frac{k}{9} = \frac{2}{5}$ for k. Write your answer as an improper fraction.

12. Find the product of $7\frac{5}{6}$ and $2\frac{1}{2}$. Write your answer as a decimal rounded to the nearest hundredth.

Short Response

13. Summer vacation is 68 days long and $\frac{3}{4}$ of the vacation has gone by. How many days are left? Explain.

Extended Response

14. Your dinner bill comes to $19.68. Estimate your total cost for dinner with a 5% tax and a 20% tip on the original bill. Justify your reasoning.

15. A customer service agent gets a phone call about every 12 minutes in a 7-hour work day. How many calls does she get in a 5-day work week? Explain how you found your answer.

Problem Solving Application

Applying Proportions

Prehistoric Giants Dinosaurs first appeared on Earth about 230 million years ago and died out about 65 million years ago. Today, scientists study dinosaur remains to learn more about them. For example, scientists can calculate the size of a dinosaur by measuring bones they have found. Then they use proportions to estimate the dimensions of other bones.

Fossilized Bones

Skeletons of animals that die in soft earth or mud can become fossils. Over time, the skeleton sinks and mud covers it. The mud turns to stone, preserving the skeleton.

Put It All Together

Data File Use the information on these two pages and on page 651 to answer these questions.

Materials centimeter ruler, poster board

1. Copy the table.
   a. Measure the dinosaur in the center of the page. Complete the first column of the table.
   b. Measure the height of one of the eight schoolgirls. Then measure your own height (in centimeters). Use the measurements to estimate the scale of the dinosaur.
   c. Use your scale to estimate the actual dimensions of the dinosaur. Complete the second column of the table.

2. a. **Open-Ended** Choose a large object such as your family's car, your bicycle, your bed, or a desk in your classroom. Measure at least four different parts of the object in centimeters.
   b. Choose a scale that will allow a drawing of both the dinosaur and your object to fit on (and cover as much as possible of) the poster board. Write the scale in a corner of the poster board.
   c. Calculate the poster dimensions for the dinosaur and the object. Complete the third column of your table.
   d. Use the dimensions from part (c) to draw the dinosaur and the object on the poster board.

3. **Research** Choose an animal from the table on page 651. Find out what the animal looks like. Calculate its size using the scale for your poster. If possible, add a drawing of it to your poster.

Dinosaur Measurements (centimeters)

Body Part	Math Book Length	Actual Length	Poster Length
Height	■	■	■
Tail	■	■	■
Thigh	■	■	■
Foot	■	■	■
Neck	■	■	■

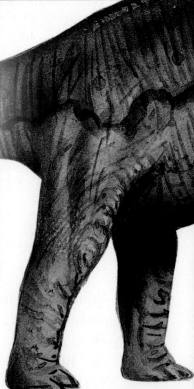

Sue and Sue

In 1990, fossil hunter Sue Hendrickson discovered Sue, a *Tyrannosaurus rex* fossil that is nearly 90% complete. Here she poses with a reconstructed back foot.

How Tall Is That?

A *Brachiosaurus* was about the height of eight middle school students.

Compsognathus

Compsognathus was one of the smallest dinosaurs, about the size of a turkey.

Digging Up Dinosaurs

A paleontologist carefully chisels fossils from rock.

Go Online
PHSchool.com

For: Information about dinosaurs
Web Code: aqe-0753

What You've Learned

- In Chapter 3, you solved one-step equations by using number sense and inverse operations.

- In Chapter 7, you used ratios to describe proportional situations.

- You used proportions to solve problems.

 Check Your Readiness

GO for Help

For Exercises	See Lesson
1–4	3-4
5–7	3-5
8–10	3-6
11–16	7-3

Using Number Sense to Solve Equations
Use mental math to solve each equation.

1. $a + 9 = 18$

2. $y \div 3 = 3$

3. $11k = 44$

4. $c - 5 = 5$

Solving Equations
Solve each equation. Then check the solution.

5. $0.23 + x = 1.5$

6. $p + 120.5 = 180$

7. $62.9 + b = 90$

8. $d - 13 = 4.5$

9. $g - 22 = 11.3$

10. $c - 0.45 = 11.62$

Recognizing Proportions
Do the ratios in each pair form a proportion?

11. $\frac{3}{4}, \frac{18}{24}$

12. $\frac{11}{12}, \frac{121}{144}$

13. $\frac{16}{20}, \frac{64}{100}$

14. $\frac{12}{15}, \frac{24}{30}$

15. $\frac{5}{8}, \frac{15}{20}$

16. $\frac{4}{9}, \frac{16}{36}$

What You'll Learn Next

- In this chapter, you will identify points, lines, and planes.
- You will measure angles and classify them as acute, obtuse, or right.
- You will identify and classify geometric figures.
- You will use proportions to test congruency and similarity in geometric figures.

 Problem Solving Application On pages 412 and 413, you will work an extended activity on building a house.

◀)) Key Vocabulary

- angle (p. 367)
- line (p. 362)
- line symmetry (p. 398)
- parallel lines (p. 363)
- point (p. 362)
- polygon (p. 386)
- quadrilateral (p. 387)
- ray (p. 362)
- reflection (p. 403)
- rotation (p. 403)
- segment (p. 362)
- similar figures (p. 393)
- translation (p. 402)

Points, Lines, Segments, and Rays

What You'll Learn

To identify and work with points, lines, segments, and rays

🔊 **New Vocabulary** point, line, segment, ray, plane, intersecting lines, parallel lines, skew lines

Why Learn This?

The stars in constellations are like points that can be connected to form an image. To find the constellation Orion, the Hunter, look for the three stars in a row that form the belt.

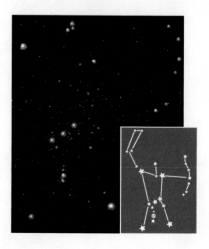

A **point** is a location in space. It has no size. You name a point with a capital letter.

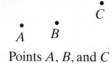
Points *A*, *B*, and *C*

A **line** is a series of points that extends in two opposite directions without end. It has no thickness. To name a line, use any two points. Read $\overleftrightarrow{DE}$ as "line *DE*."

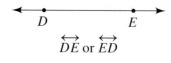
$\overleftrightarrow{DE}$ or $\overleftrightarrow{ED}$

A **segment** consists of two endpoints and all the points of the line between the endpoints. You name a segment by its endpoints. Read $\overline{DE}$ as "segment *DE*."

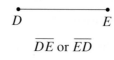
$\overline{DE}$ or $\overline{ED}$

Vocabulary Tip

A ray of sunlight begins at the sun and travels in one direction.

A **ray** consists of one endpoint and all the points of the line on one side of the endpoint. To name a ray, use its endpoint first and then any other point on the ray. Read $\overrightarrow{DE}$ as "ray *DE*."

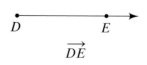
$\overrightarrow{DE}$

Naming Lines, Segments, and Rays

1 Name a line, a segment, and a ray.

line: $\overleftrightarrow{XW}$ or $\overleftrightarrow{WX}$

segment: $\overline{WX}$ or $\overline{XW}$

ray: $\overrightarrow{WX}$ or $\overrightarrow{XW}$

✓ **Quick Check**

1. Use the figure at the right.
   a. Give two names for the line.
   b. Name three segments.

A **plane** is a flat surface with no thickness that extends in all directions on the surface. Plane *ABCD* is shown at the left.

Two lines that lie in the same plane are either intersecting or parallel. **Intersecting lines** are lines that have exactly one point in common. **Parallel lines** are lines that have no points in common. Parallel segments lie in parallel lines.

Skew lines are lines that are not parallel and do not intersect. Skew lines lie in different planes.

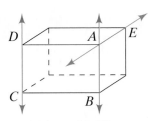

Plane *ABCD*

$\overleftrightarrow{AB}$ is parallel to $\overleftrightarrow{DC}$.

$\overleftrightarrow{AD}$ intersects $\overleftrightarrow{AB}$.

$\overleftrightarrow{AE}$ and $\overleftrightarrow{DC}$ are skew.

EXAMPLE **Application: Maps**

2 Are the lines indicated on the map below parallel or intersecting?

a. $\overleftrightarrow{AB}$ and $\overleftrightarrow{CD}$

$\overleftrightarrow{AB}$ and $\overleftrightarrow{CD}$ intersect at point *C*.

b. $\overleftrightarrow{AB}$ and $\overleftrightarrow{TW}$

$\overleftrightarrow{AB}$ and $\overleftrightarrow{TW}$ are parallel.

For: Lines and Rays Activity
Use: Interactive Textbook, 8-1

✓ **Quick Check**

2. a. Name two streets on the map that are parallel.
   b. Name two streets on the map that intersect.

1. **Vocabulary** Which figure can be represented by a log?
   Ⓐ point   Ⓑ line   Ⓒ segment   Ⓓ ray

Match each figure with its name.

2. E •———————————• F   **A.** $\overleftrightarrow{EF}$

3. ←——•——————•——→ E   F   **B.** $\overline{EF}$

4. ←——•——————•—— E   F   **C.** $\overrightarrow{EF}$

5. •——————•——→ E   F   **D.** $\overrightarrow{FE}$

Homework Exercises

For more exercises, see Extra Skills and Word Problems.

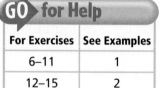

Name each line, segment, or ray.

For Exercises	See Examples
6–11	1
12–15	2

6. •———————• F   G

7. ←——•——————•——→ J   K

8. •————————• H   J

9. •——————•——→ Q   P

10. ←——•——•—→ X   Y

11. •———————• D   W

Use the diagram at the right. Name each of the following figures.

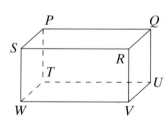

12. a line parallel to $\overleftrightarrow{PQ}$

13. two skew lines

14. a line parallel to $\overleftrightarrow{SW}$ and $\overleftrightarrow{RV}$

15. two intersecting lines

16. **Guided Problem Solving** Use the picture of the cereal box. Describe how $\overleftrightarrow{AB}$ is related to $\overleftrightarrow{DC}$, $\overleftrightarrow{GH}$, and $\overleftrightarrow{BC}$.

- **Understand the Problem** Are any of the lines parallel, skew, or intersecting?
- **Carry Out the Plan** $\overleftrightarrow{AB}$ is parallel to ■. $\overleftrightarrow{AB}$ is skew to ■. $\overleftrightarrow{AB}$ intersects ■.

Use *sometimes*, *always*, or *never* to complete each sentence.

17. A ray __?__ has one endpoint.

18. Skew lines __?__ intersect.

19. <u>Writing in Math</u> Explain why $\overleftrightarrow{AB}$ represents a line and $\overline{AB}$ represents a line segment.

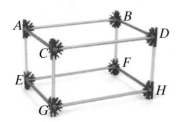

Use the diagram at the left. Name each of the following.

20. the segments intersecting $\overline{GH}$

21. a line parallel to $\overleftrightarrow{AB}$

22. the intersection of $\overleftrightarrow{EF}$ and $\overleftrightarrow{AE}$

23. a segment skew to $\overline{AC}$

24. a. Given two points on a line, A and B, describe the points that $\overrightarrow{AB}$ and $\overrightarrow{BA}$ have in common.
   b. Reasoning If $\overrightarrow{AB}$ contains C, but $\overrightarrow{CA}$ does not contain B, then where on the line must point C be located?

25. Challenge On a road map, where would you find an example to illustrate a pair of skew lines? Explain.

Test Prep and Mixed Review   **Practice**

Multiple Choice

26. Sung-Pil made two batches of cookies. He needed $2\frac{3}{4}$ cups of flour for each batch. How much flour did Sung-Pil use?
   Ⓐ $4\frac{1}{2}$ c   Ⓑ $4\frac{3}{4}$ c   Ⓒ $5\frac{1}{2}$ c   Ⓓ $5\frac{3}{4}$ c

27. Mrs. Ortiz is making two dozen gift baskets. She wants eight ounces of cheese in each basket. How many pounds of cheese does she need?
   Ⓕ 10 lb   Ⓖ 11 lb   Ⓗ 12 lb   Ⓙ 16 lb

28. A chorus has 125 members. There are 40 sopranos. What percent of the singers in the chorus are sopranos?
   Ⓐ 22%   Ⓑ 30%   Ⓒ 32%   Ⓓ 35%

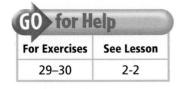

For Exercises	See Lesson
29–30	2-2

Find the median of each data set.

29. 5, 6, 8, 9, 10, 4, 7

30. 600, 550, 475, 520, 500

Using Angle Benchmarks

You can think of an angle as a wedge or section of a circle. You can use wedges of different sizes to describe the size of angles.

ACTIVITY

1. Trace each of the wedges below. Then cut out each wedge.

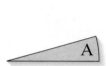 A 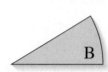 B 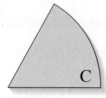 C

2. Use wedges A, B, and C as benchmarks to describe angles.

a.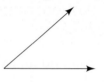

The size of this angle is between the size of wedges B and C.

b.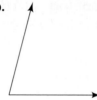

This angle is the same size as wedge C and wedge A combined.

Exercises

1. Compare each angle to wedges A, B, and C.

a.

b.

c.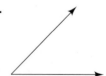

2. The measure of wedge A is 15°. Wedge B measures 30°, and wedge C measures 60°. Use the measures of angles A, B, and C to estimate the measures of the angles in Exercise 1.

3. Reasoning Use one corner of a rectangle to serve as a benchmark angle for 90°. Estimate the size of the angle.

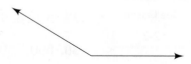

8-2 Angles

Check Skills You'll Need

1. Vocabulary Review How is a *ray* different from a *line*?

Use the diagram.

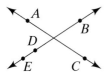

2. Name a line, a segment, and a ray.

3. Name $\overleftrightarrow{DE}$ in two other ways.

GO for Help
Lesson 8-1

What You'll Learn

To measure and classify angles

🔊 **New Vocabulary** angle, vertex, degrees, acute angle, right angle, obtuse angle, straight angle, perpendicular lines

Why Learn This?

You can describe a hockey stick using geometry vocabulary. An **angle** is a figure formed by two rays with a common endpoint. The angle at the right can be called ∠Y, ∠XYZ, or ∠ZYX. The **vertex** is the point of intersection of two sides of an angle or figure.

You measure angles in units called **degrees**. Use the symbol (°) for degrees. Use a *protractor* to measure angles.

sides   vertex

EXAMPLE **Application: Ice Hockey**

1 Measure the angle between the hockey stick and the ground.

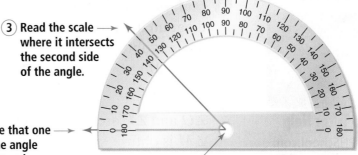

③ Read the scale where it intersects the second side of the angle.

② Make sure that one side of the angle passes through zero on the scale. Start measuring from zero.

① Place the point of the protractor on the vertex of the angle.

The angle measure is 45°.

✓ Quick Check

1. Use a protractor to measure the angle at the left.

You can classify angles by their measures.

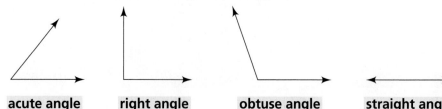

acute angle
Measures less than 90°.

right angle
Measures 90°.

obtuse angle
Measures between 90° and 180°.

straight angle
Measures 180°.

Test Prep Tip

The right angle symbol, ⌐, indicates that the angle measures 90°.

Lines that intersect to form right angles are called **perpendicular lines.** The symbol ⌐ in the diagram shows that ∠AED is a right angle and that $\overleftrightarrow{AB}$ is perpendicular to $\overleftrightarrow{CD}$.

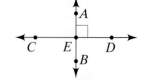

EXAMPLE **Classifying Angles**

2 Classify each angle as *acute, right, obtuse,* or *straight.*

a.

acute

b.

obtuse

c.

right

Quick Check

2. Estimate the measure of the angle. Classify the angle as *acute, right, obtuse,* or *straight.*

GO **Online**

Video Tutor Help
Visit: PHSchool.com
Web Code: aqe-0775

EXAMPLE **Application: Construction**

3 **Multiple Choice** The deck shown in the diagram has different types of angles. Which angle is obtuse?

Ⓐ ∠M Ⓒ ∠O
Ⓑ ∠N Ⓓ ∠P

∠O and ∠P are right angles. ∠N is less than 90°. ∠M is obtuse, since it is between 90° and 180°.

The correct answer is choice A.

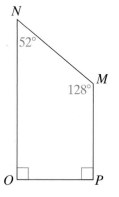

Quick Check

3. Classify the angles in Example 3 as *acute, right, obtuse,* or *straight.*
   a. ∠N   b. ∠O   c. ∠P

More Than One Way

Use a protractor to measure the angle.

Elena's Method

I place the center point of the protractor on the vertex of the angle. Then I turn the protractor so that 0° lines up with the inner scale for one side of the angle. The second side crosses the inner scale at 50°.

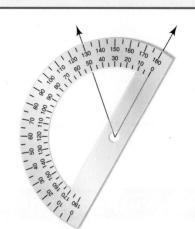

The angle measures 50°.

Zack's Method

I place the center point of the protractor on the vertex of the angle. I read the outer scale where each side intersects the protractor. Then I find the difference between the two scale readings.

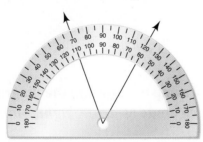

Since 120 − 70 = 50, the angle measures 50°.

Choose a Method
Measure the angle. Describe the method you chose.

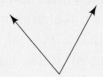

1. **Vocabulary** How are a right angle and an obtuse angle different?

2. **Reasoning** Does increasing the lengths of the sides of an angle change the measurement of the angle? Explain.

Without using your protractor, sketch angles with the following measures. Then use your protractor to see how close you are.

3. 30°

4. 60°

5. 120°

Homework Exercises

For more exercises, see Extra Skills and Word Problems.

GO for Help

For Exercises	See Examples
6–8	1
9–11	2
12–15	3

Measurement Use a protractor to measure each angle.

6.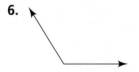

7.

8.

Classify each angle as *acute, right, obtuse,* **or** *straight.*

9.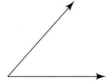

10.

11.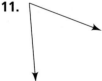

You build a ramp as shown in the diagram. Classify each angle as *acute, right, obtuse,* **or** *straight.*

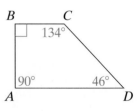

12. ∠A

13. ∠C

14. ∠B

15. ∠D

 16. Guided Problem Solving You are facing north. You turn 270° counterclockwise. Which direction are you now facing?
- **Make a Plan** Make a sketch showing the four basic compass directions. Recall that 270 = 90 × 3. Then act out the problem by turning 90° to the left three times.
- **Carry Out the Plan** Which direction will you face after each counterclockwise turn?

Use a protractor to draw angles with the following measures.

17. $30°$ **18.** $135°$ **19.** $90°$ **20.** $75°$

**Use the figure for Exercises 21–24.
Estimate the measure of each angle.
Then measure each angle.**

21. $\angle AGB$ **22.** $\angle BGD$

23. $\angle BGF$ **24.** $\angle EGB$

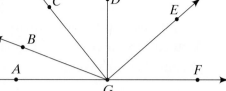

25. Photography A 35-mm camera lens has a 45° field of view. What kind of angle is this?

26. Open-Ended Give three examples of perpendicular lines in your classroom.

27. Writing in Math Explain how to fold a piece of paper so that the fold lines form four right angles.

28. A surveyor draws two boundary lines. One line points east. Another line points northeast. Sketch the 45° angle.

29. Challenge Find the measure of the angle formed by the hour hand and the minute hand of a clock at 12:30 A.M.

Careers Photographers use different lenses to achieve various effects.

Test Prep and Mixed Review   **Practice**

Multiple Choice

30. Which angle is obtuse?

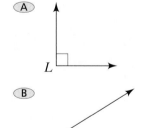

31. A bus has 25 riders at the start of its route. At each stop, 5 riders get off the bus and 1 rider gets on. How many stops will the bus make before only one rider is left on the bus?

Ⓕ 4   Ⓗ 6
Ⓖ 5   Ⓙ 10

32. Choose an appropriate unit of length to measure a soccer field. Explain your choice.

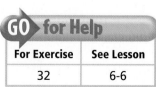

For Exercise	See Lesson
32	6-6

Basic Constructions

A *perpendicular bisector* is a line that is perpendicular to a segment and passes through that segment's *midpoint*. You can use a compass and straightedge to construct a perpendicular bisector.

EXAMPLE

1 Use a compass and a straightedge to construct the perpendicular bisector of $\overline{AB}$.

Step 1 Open the compass to more than half the length of $\overline{AB}$. Put the tip of the compass point at A. Draw a part of a circle, or *arc*, that intersects $\overline{AB}$.

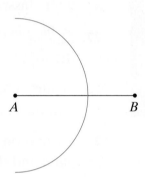

Step 2 Keep the compass open to the same width. Put the tip of the compass at B. Draw another arc that intersects $\overline{AB}$. Label the points of intersection of the two arcs C and D.

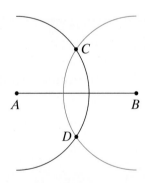

Step 3 Draw $\overleftrightarrow{CD}$. Label the intersection of $\overleftrightarrow{CD}$ and $\overline{AB}$ point M.

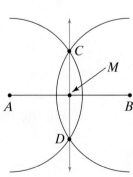

$\overleftrightarrow{CD}$ intersects $\overline{AB}$ at its midpoint M.

$\overleftrightarrow{CD}$ is the perpendicular bisector of $\overline{AB}$.

An *angle bisector* is a ray that divides an angle into two angles with equal measures.

EXAMPLE

2 Use a compass and a straightedge to construct the angle bisector of $\angle E$.

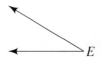

Step 1 Put the tip of the compass at E. Draw an arc that intersects both sides of $\angle E$. Label the points of intersection F and G.

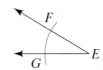

Step 2 Place the tip of the compass at F. Draw a large arc.

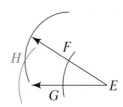

Step 3 Keep the compass open to the same width and place the tip at G. Draw another large arc. Label the point of intersection of the two large arcs H.

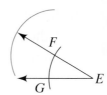

Step 4 Draw $\overrightarrow{EH}$.

$\overrightarrow{EH}$ divides $\angle FEG$ into two angles with equal measures, $\angle FEH$ and $\angle HEG$.

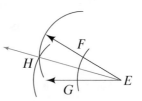

$\overrightarrow{EH}$ is the angle bisector of $\angle FEG$.

Exercises

1. Draw $\overline{JK}$ two inches long. Then construct its perpendicular bisector.

2. Draw an obtuse angle and construct its bisector.

3. **Writing in Math** Explain how you can use perpendicular bisectors and angle bisectors to construct a 45° angle.

8-3 Special Pairs of Angles

Check Skills You'll Need

1. **Vocabulary Review** Give an example of an object with an *acute angle* in your classroom.

Use a protractor to draw each angle.

2. 30°   3. 60°

4. 45°   5. 120°

GO for Help
Lesson 8-2

What You'll Learn

To use the relationship between special pairs of angles

◀)) **New Vocabulary** complementary angles, supplementary angles, vertical angles, congruent angles

Why Learn This?

Landscapers use special angle pairs to cut stones and bricks for tiles and pathways.

If the sum of the measures of two angles is 90°, the angles are **complementary angles.** If the sum of the measures of two angles is 180°, the angles are **supplementary angles.**

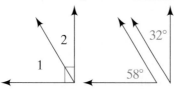   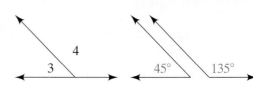

Complementary angles   Supplementary angles

Two angles, the sum of   Two angles, the sum of
whose measures is 90°   whose measures is 180°

EXAMPLE Finding the Complement of an Angle

1 (**Algebra**) Find the value of x at the right.

Let x = the measure of the angle's complement.

$$x + 60° = 90°$$ ← The angles are complementary.

$$x + 60° - 60° = 90° - 60°$$ ← Subtract 60° from each side.

$$x = 30°$$ ← Simplify.

Vocabulary Tip

The *complement* of an angle is the angle complementary to it.

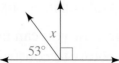

Quick Check

1. Find the value of x.

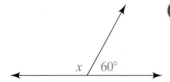

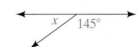 **EXAMPLE** **Using Supplementary Angles**

2 (**Algebra**) Find the value of x at the left.

$$x + 60° = 180° \quad \leftarrow \text{The angles are supplementary.}$$
$$x + 60° - 60° = 180° - 60° \quad \leftarrow \text{Subtract 60° from each side.}$$
$$x = 120° \quad \leftarrow \text{Simplify.}$$

The value of x is 120°.

Quick Check

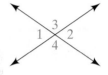

● **2.** Find the value of x.

Two intersecting lines form **vertical angles**. Angles 1 and 2 are vertical angles. Angles 3 and 4 are also vertical angles. Vertical angles have equal measures. Angles with equal measures are **congruent angles.**

EXAMPLE **Vertical Angles**

3 Two boards intersect at the corner of the barn door shown below. The measure of ∠2 is 38°. Find the measures of ∠1 and ∠4.

$$m\angle1 + 38° = 180° \quad \leftarrow \angle\text{1 and } \angle\text{2 are supplementary.}$$
$$m\angle1 + 38° - 38° = 180° - 38° \quad \leftarrow \text{Subtract 38° from each side.}$$
$$m\angle1 = 142° \quad \leftarrow \text{Simplify.}$$

$$m\angle4 = 38° \quad \leftarrow \angle\text{2 and } \angle\text{4 are vertical angles.}$$

The measure of ∠1 is 142°. The measure of ∠4 is 38°.

You read $m\angle1$ as "the measure of angle one."

Quick Check

3. The measure of ∠5 in the photo above is 142°. Find the measures of ∠6 and ∠7.

Check Your Understanding

1. **Vocabulary** Two angles are complementary. Explain why they are not supplementary angles.

2. **Writing in Math** Describe how to draw a pair of supplementary angles without using a protractor.

Match each pair of angle measurements with the correct term.

3. 47° and 47°

4. 9° and 81°

5. 89° and 91°

A. complementary angles
B. supplementary angles
C. congruent angles

Homework Exercises

For more exercises, see Extra Skills and Word Problems.

GO for Help

For Exercises	See Examples
6–10	1
11–17	2
18	3

Find the complement of each angle measure.

6. 12°   7. 45°   8. 33°   9. 68°   10. 4°

Find the supplement of each angle measure.

11. 90°   12. 176°   13. 110°   14. 144°

Find the value of *x* in each figure.

15.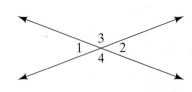

16.

17.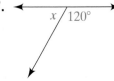

18. The measure of ∠1 at the left is 40°. What are the measures of ∠2, ∠3, and ∠4? Explain your reasoning.

19. **Guided Problem Solving** An angle formed at the intersection at the right has a measure of 46°. Find the measures of ∠1, ∠2, ∠3, and ∠4.
   - Which angles are vertical angles?
   - How can you use what you know about special angle pairs to find the measure of each angle?

Complete each sentence with *sometimes*, *always*, or *never*.

20. Two acute angles are ? complementary.

21. Two obtuse angles are ? supplementary.

(**Algebra**) **Find the value of *x* in each figure.**

22.

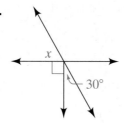

23.

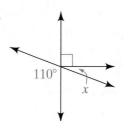

24. Architecture Before renovations, the Leaning Tower of Pisa stood at an angle of about 5° from vertical. What was the measure of the acute angle that the tower made with the ground? What was the measure of the obtuse angle?

25. Reasoning An angle measures 115°. Explain why you cannot find both a complement and a supplement of the angle.

26. Challenge The circle is cut into unequal sections. One section forms an angle whose measure is 65°. Find the measures of the angles formed by the other two sections.

Test Prep and Mixed Review

Practice

Multiple Choice

27. Find the measure of ∠*QTR* to the nearest degree.
  Ⓐ 180°
  Ⓑ 110°
  Ⓒ 70°
  Ⓓ 40°

28. Alejandra types about 65 words per minute. Which proportion can she use to find the number of words that she can type in 30 minutes?

  Ⓕ $\frac{65}{1} = \frac{w}{30}$ Ⓖ $\frac{1}{65} = \frac{w}{30}$ Ⓗ $\frac{65}{60} = \frac{w}{30}$ Ⓙ $\frac{60}{65} = \frac{w}{30}$

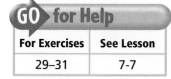

For Exercises	See Lesson
29–31	7-7

Find each answer.

29. 5% of 100

30. 30% of 50

31. 75% of 42

Exploring Parallel Lines

A line that intersects two or more lines is a **transversal.**
When a transversal crosses two parallel lines, the eight
angles formed are related.

ACTIVITY

1. On a piece of notebook paper, draw two lines using the lines
   of the paper. What kind of lines did you draw?

2. Draw a slanted line, or transversal, through the lines. Label
   the angles formed as shown in the diagram below.

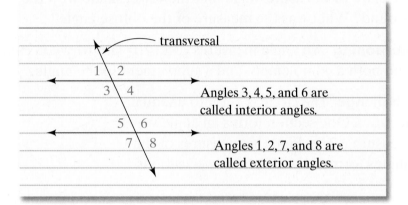

transversal

Angles 3, 4, 5, and 6 are
called interior angles.

Angles 1, 2, 7, and 8 are
called exterior angles.

3. Use your protractor to measure each of the eight
   angles. Record your measurements.

4. Find two pairs of interior angles that have the same
   measure. Next, find two pairs of exterior angles
   that have the same measure.

5. Find two interior angles that have the same
   measure as ∠8. Then find two pairs of interior
   angles that are supplementary.

6. Obtain a picture that shows parallel lines intersected by
   a transversal. Following the guitar example at the right,
   highlight the lines. Then label angles that have the
   same measure with the same number.

7. **Reasoning** Draw two parallel lines. Draw two parallel
   transversals that form 40° angles with your parallel
   lines. Label all of the congruent angles in your drawing.

Use the diagram to name the figures.

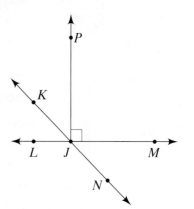

1. two lines

2. two rays

3. a right angle

4. an acute angle

5. an obtuse angle

6. a straight angle

7. a pair of vertical angles

8. an angle congruent to ∠MJN

9. a pair of complementary angles

10. a pair of supplementary angles

8-4a Activity Lab

Technology

Investigating Angles in a Triangle

Geometry software is a fun way to investigate relationships among angles of a triangle.

ACTIVITY

1. Draw a triangle. Label the vertices *A*, *B*, and *C*.

2. Measure the three interior angles.

3. Make a table to show the angles, their measures, and the sum of the measures.

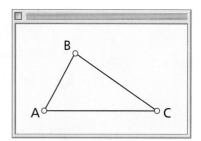

4. Change the shape of the triangle by dragging *A*, *B*, or *C*. Make a new column in your table to find the sum of the angle measures.

5. Make a conjecture about the sum of the measures of the angles of a triangle. Compare your results with those of other students.

6. **Reasoning** Can a triangle have two obtuse angles? Justify your answer.

8-4   Classifying Triangles

✓ Check Skills You'll Need

1. **Vocabulary Review** Can an *obtuse angle* have a *complementary angle*? Explain.

Classify each angle as *acute, right, obtuse,* or *straight.*

2. 45°   3. 105°

4. 90°   5. 180°

 **for Help**
Lesson 8-2

What You'll Learn

To classify triangles by their angles and their sides

🔊 **New Vocabulary**   triangle, acute triangle, obtuse triangle, right triangle, congruent segments, equilateral triangle, isosceles triangle, scalene triangle

Why Learn This?

Different types of shapes are frequently used in construction. For example, engineers use triangles to make bridges strong.

A **triangle** is a closed figure made of three line segments that meet only at their endpoints. The sum of the angle measures is 180°. You can classify triangles by their angle measures.

Classifying by Angles

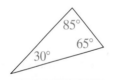
acute triangle
Three acute angles

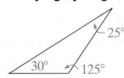
obtuse triangle
One obtuse angle

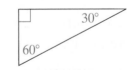
right triangle
One right angle

EXAMPLE   Classifying Triangles by Angles

1 Classify each triangle by its angles.

a.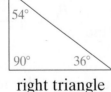
right triangle

b.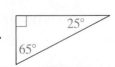
obtuse triangle

c.
50°
70° 60°
acute triangle

✓ Quick Check

1. Classify the triangle by its angles.

380   **Chapter 8** Tools of Geometry

Finding an Angle's Measure

2 **Gridded Response** Find the value of *x* in degrees.

Solve an equation to find the value of *x*.

$$x + 20° + 90° = 180° \quad \leftarrow \text{The sum of the angle measures is 180°.}$$

$$x + 110° = 180° \quad \leftarrow \text{Add 20° and 90°.}$$

$$x + 110° - 110° = 180° - 110° \quad \leftarrow \text{Subtract 110° from each side.}$$

$$x = 70° \quad \leftarrow \text{Simplify.}$$

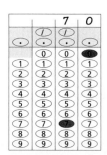

Quick Check

2. The angles of a triangle measure 58°, 72°, and *x*. Find *x*.

Segments that are the same length are **congruent segments.** You can classify triangles by the number of congruent segments or sides.

Classifying by Sides

 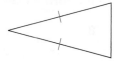 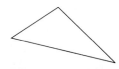

equilateral triangle
Three congruent sides

isosceles triangle
At least two
congruent sides

scalene triangle
No congruent sides

Video Tutor Help
Visit: PHSchool.com
Web Code: aqe-0775

EXAMPLE **Classifying Triangles by Sides**

3 Classify each triangle by its sides.

a.
isosceles triangle

b.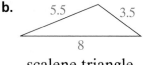
scalene triangle

c.
equilateral triangle

Quick Check

3. Classify the triangle at the right by its sides.
Explain your reasoning.

Vocabulary Classify each triangle by its angles and sides.

1.

2.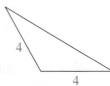

3.

4. The sides of a triangle measure 5 in., 12 in., and 13 in. The triangle has a 90° angle. Classify the triangle.

Homework Exercises

For more exercises, see Extra Skills and Word Problems.

GO for Help

For Exercises	See Examples
5–7	1
8–10	2
11–16	3

Classify each triangle by its angles.

5.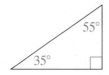

6.

7.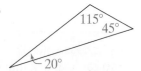

(**Algebra**) **Find the value of *x*, the measure of the third angle.**

8.

9.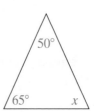

10.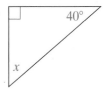

Classify each triangle by its sides.

11.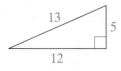

12.

13.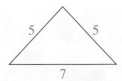

14. sides: 3, 3, 5

15. sides: 6, 9, 4

16. sides: 11, 11, 11

GPS 17. **Guided Problem Solving** The triominoes shown are pieces from a game. Classify the shape of a triomino by its sides and angles.
- What is the measure of the largest angle?
- How many sides are congruent?

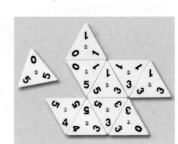

Classify each triangle by its angles.

18. $15°, 60°, x$ **19.** $14°, x, 76°$ **20.** $x, 60°, 61°$

Use the diagram below of the drafting triangles.

21. Classify each triangle by its angles.

22. Classify each triangle by its sides.

23. <u>Writing in Math</u> Explain why you only need to know the measure of two angles of a triangle in order to classify it by its angles.

24. A designer for a boat company describes the sail shown in the photo at the left. Describe the triangle, classifying it by its angles and sides.

25. (Algebra) The angles in an equilateral triangle are congruent. Write an equation for the sum of angles in an equilateral triangle.

26. Sketch an obtuse scalene triangle.

27. **Challenge** An isosceles triangle has two congruent angles. Write an expression to represent the measure of the third angle of the triangle.

Test Prep and Mixed Review   **Practice**

Gridded Response

28. A triangle has angles that measure $37°$ and $52°$. What is the measure of the triangle's third angle in degrees?

29. What is the value of the fifth term in the number sequence?
10, 20, 40, 80

30. There are 24 nonswimmers and 20 swimmers in a swimming program. What is the ratio of nonswimmers to swimmers? Write your answer as a decimal.

GO **for Help**

For Exercises	See Lesson
31–32	7-8

Use the graph at the right. A market researcher asked 200 people to choose their favorite dessert.

31. How many people prefer pie?

32. How many more people prefer ice cream than prefer cake?

Vocabulary Builder

High-Use Academic Words

High-use academic words are words that you will see often in textbooks and on tests. These words are not math vocabulary terms, but knowing them will help you to succeed in mathematics.

Direction Words

Some words tell what to do in a problem. I need to understand what these words are asking so that I give the correct answer.

Word	Meaning
Measure	To use a tool to find the size, length, quantity, or rate of something
State	To express something with words
Draw	To make an accurate picture that represents something

Exercises

1. Measure the length of your classroom by using your textbook. How many textbooks long is your classroom?

2. State the features of your classroom.

3. Draw a picture of your classroom.

4. Measure the perimeter of the rectangle.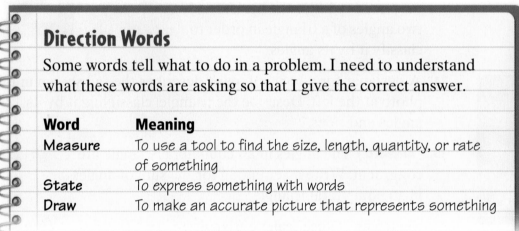

5. State the features of the rectangle.

6. Draw the rectangle on your paper.

7. **Word Knowledge** Think about the word *trace*.
   a. Choose the letter for how well you know the word.
      A. I know its meaning.
      B. I've seen it, but I don't know its meaning.
      C. I don't know it.
   b. **Research** Look up and write the definition of *trace*.
   c. Use the word in a sentence involving mathematics.

Angles in a Quadrilateral

This activity explores the four corners of a four-sided figure.

ACTIVITY

1. Trace the four-sided figure at the right.

2. Tear off the four corners of the figure. Place them together around a common point as shown below.

3. What is the sum of angles 1, 2, 3, and 4?

4. Draw another four-sided figure. Repeat Steps 2 and 3. Do you get the same result?

5. Draw another four-sided figure. Label it *PQRS*. Draw a segment that connects two opposite vertices.

6. **Reasoning** How many triangles did you form? What is the relationship between the sum of the angles of figure *PQRS* and the sum of the angles of the triangles? Explain.

7. Make a conjecture about the sum of the angles of a four-sided figure.

Exercises

1. A ferry leaves port *W*. As shown in the diagram at the right, it stops at points *X, Y,* and *Z*. What is the measure of ∠*W*?

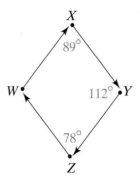

Find the value of *x*.

2.

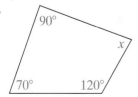

3.

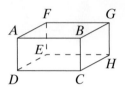

What You'll Learn

To identify regular polygons and to classify quadrilaterals

◀)) **New Vocabulary** polygon, regular polygon, irregular polygon, quadrilateral, parallelogram, rectangle, rhombus, square, trapezoid

Why Learn This?

Signs have shapes to help you recognize them from a distance.

A **polygon** is a closed figure that has three or more line segments that do not cross.

| polygon | polygon | not a polygon | not a polygon |

To name a polygon, just count the number of sides. Then refer to the table below.

EXAMPLE   **Identifying Polygons**

1 Identify each polygon according to the number of sides it has.

Polygon	Number of Sides
Triangle	3
Quadrilateral	4
Pentagon	5
Hexagon	6
Octagon	8
Decagon	10

a.

pentagon

b.

octagon

c.

quadrilateral

✓ Quick Check

1. Identify each polygon according to the number of sides it has.

   a.

   b.

   c.

A **regular polygon** is a polygon with all sides congruent and all angles congruent. An **irregular polygon** is a polygon with sides that are not all congruent or angles that are not all congruent.

EXAMPLE **Identifying Regular Polygons**

② Determine whether each polygon is regular or irregular.

a.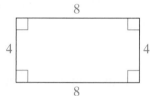

regular hexagon

b.

irregular quadrilateral

☑ Quick Check

2. Determine whether each polygon is regular or irregular.

a.

b.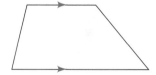

Online active math

For: Quadrilaterals Activity
Use: Interactive Textbook, 8-5

A polygon with four sides is called a **quadrilateral.** Some quadrilaterals have special names.

Test Prep Tip
Arrows on a drawing indicate that sides are parallel.

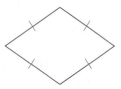

Parallelogram
Has two pairs of parallel sides

Trapezoid
Has exactly one pair of parallel sides

Rectangle
Parallelogram with four right angles

Rhombus
Parallelogram with four congruent sides

Square
Parallelogram with four right angles and four congruent sides

EXAMPLE Classifying Quadrilaterals

③ A baseball diamond is a quadrilateral. Write all of its names. Which is the best name? Explain.

Parallelogram: Both pairs of opposite sides are parallel.

Rectangle: The four angles are right angles.

Rhombus: The four sides are congruent.

Square: This is the best description of a baseball diamond. A square has four right angles and four congruent sides.

✓ Quick Check

3. Write all of the names for the quadrilateral. Which is the best name? Explain.

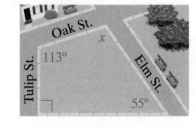

GO for Help

For help with quadrilateral angle measures, go to Activity Lab 8-5a.

The sum of the angle measures of a quadrilateral is 360°.

EXAMPLE Finding an Angle Measure

④ **Multiple Choice** A family buys the lot of land shown. What is the measure of angle x, where Oak Street and Elm Street intersect?

Ⓐ 35°   Ⓒ 78°
Ⓑ 67°   Ⓓ 102°

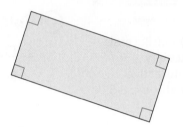

The four property lines form a quadrilateral. Write an equation.

$x + 55° + 90° + 113° = 360°$ ← The sum of the angle measures is 360°.

$x + 258° = 360°$ ← Add.

$x + 258° - 258° = 360° - 258°$ ← Subtract 258° from each side.

$x = 102°$ ← Simplify.

The correct answer is choice D.

✓ Quick Check

4. You landscape a yard using the design at the right. Find the measure of ∠a.

1. **Vocabulary** How can you tell whether a rectangle is a square?

2. What is the name of a five-sided polygon?

3. **Writing in Math** Describe how a figure that is *not* a polygon is different from one that is a polygon.

Homework Exercises

For more exercises, see Extra Skills and Word Problems.

GO for Help

For Exercises	See Examples
4–6	1
7–9	2
10–12	3
13–15	4

Identify each polygon according to the number of sides it has.

4.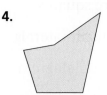

5.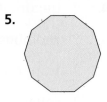

6.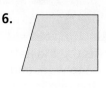

Determine whether each polygon is regular or irregular.

7.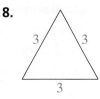

8.

9.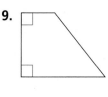

Write all of the names for each quadrilateral.

10.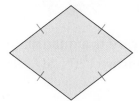

11.

12.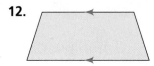

Find the value of each variable.

13.

14.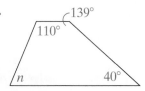

15.

16. **Guided Problem Solving** You need to draw a quadrilateral with two pairs of parallel sides. All of the sides are congruent. There are no right angles. Draw and label the quadrilateral.

   • Use 4 pencils of equal length as a model.

Use graph paper to draw an example of each quadrilateral.

17. trapezoid

18. rectangle

19. rhombus

20. parallelogram

21. quadrilateral with only one right angle

22. Science What shape is the Raft of Treetops platform at the left? Draw the polygon. Add two lines to divide it into a quadrilateral and two triangles.

23. Draw a parallelogram that has a 30° angle.

Complete each sentence with *All, Some,* or *No.*

24. ___?___ quadrilaterals are squares.

25. ___?___ rhombuses are quadrilaterals.

26. ___?___ trapezoids are parallelograms.

27. ___?___ squares are rectangles.

28. Challenge A diagonal of a polygon is a segment that connects two vertices that are not next to each other. Draw the diagonals for a quadrilateral, a pentagon, and a hexagon. Predict the number of diagonals in an octagon.

Scientists use the Raft of Treetops to work and sleep atop rain forests.

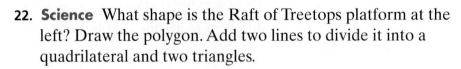

Test Prep and Mixed Review **Practice**

Multiple Choice

29. Jordan's backyard is a quadrilateral. The angles measure 120°, 90°, 95°, and *b*. What is *b*?
  Ⓐ 35° Ⓒ 55°
  Ⓑ 45° Ⓓ 135°

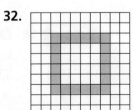

30. Which number is NOT a multiple of 15?
  Ⓕ 5 Ⓖ 15 Ⓗ 75 Ⓙ 90

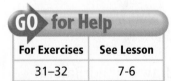

For Exercises	See Lesson
31–32	7-6

What percent of each grid is shaded?

31.

32.

Classify each triangle by its angles.

1. 20°, 60°, 100°

2. 40°, 50°, 90°

3. 60°, 60°, 60°

Classify each triangle by its sides.

4. 8, 9, and 8 units

5. 3, 4, and 5 units

6. 10, 10, and 10 units

7. The perimeter of an equilateral triangle is 12 m. Find the length of a side.

Identify each polygon according to the number of sides it has.

8.

9.

10.

Write the names for each quadrilateral. Then give the best name.

11.

12.

13.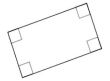

MATH AT WORK

Cartoonist

A career as a cartoonist could be just right for you if you enjoy reading and can draw well. Some cartoonists produce comic strips meant for amusement. Others illustrate articles, books, or advertisements.

Cartoonists use lines, angles, measures, and perspective to draw cartoons.

Go Online
PHSchool.com **For:** Information on cartoonists,
Web Code: aqb-2031

Congruent and Similar Figures

Check Skills You'll Need

1. Vocabulary Review
How can you tell that two angles are *congruent*?

Classify each triangle by its sides.

2.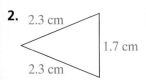
2.3 cm
1.7 cm
2.3 cm

3.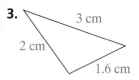
3 cm
2 cm
1.6 cm

GO for Help
Lesson 8-3

What You'll Learn

To identify congruent and similar figures

🔊 **New Vocabulary** congruent figures, similar figures

Why Learn This?

Designers use congruent figures in art and architecture. You can fit some congruent figures together without gaps or spaces.

Congruent figures are figures that have exactly the same size and shape. Congruent figures have congruent *corresponding sides* and congruent *corresponding angles*. The matching sides and angles are corresponding parts.

Suppose you rotate the blue trapezoid. It will fit exactly over the green trapezoid.

EXAMPLE   Identifying Congruent Figures

GO for Help

Figures are congruent even if you must flip or turn a figure to fit over another figure.

① Tell whether each triangle is congruent to triangle *PQR*.

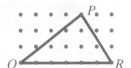
P
Q   R

a.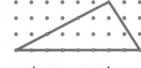
congruent

b.
not congruent

✓ Quick Check

1. Tell whether each trapezoid is congruent to the first trapezoid.

a.

b.

Similar figures have the same shape, but not necessarily the same size. Corresponding angles of similar figures are congruent. Lengths of corresponding sides of similar figures are proportional.

EXAMPLE Identifying Similar Figures

2 Show that the triangles are similar.

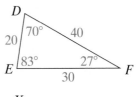

The measures of $\angle D$ and $\angle X$ are 70°.
The measures of $\angle E$ and $\angle Y$ are 83°.
The measures of $\angle F$ and $\angle Z$ are 27°.

$\frac{20}{30} = \frac{2}{3}$, $\frac{40}{60} = \frac{2}{3}$, and $\frac{30}{45} = \frac{2}{3}$

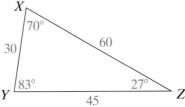

The measures of corresponding angles are equal. The lengths of corresponding sides form equal ratios. The triangles are similar.

GO for Help

For help with checking proportions, go to Lesson 7-3, Example 1.

Quick Check

2. Is the triangle at the right similar to triangle DEF in Example 2? Explain your reasoning.

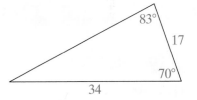

If the angles of two triangles are congruent, then the triangles are similar. The sides must also be congruent for the triangles to be congruent.

EXAMPLE Application: Architecture

3 Triangles ABC and CDE are similar. The measure of $\angle A$ is 70°. The measure of $\angle B$ is 55°. What is the measure of $\angle E$? Explain.

The measure of $\angle ACB$ is 55°, since the sum of the angles in a triangle equals 180°. $\angle ACB$ and $\angle E$ are corresponding angles. So the measure of $\angle E$ is 55°.

Online active math

For: Congruence Activity
Use: Interactive Textbook, 8-6

Quick Check

3. The measure of $\overline{AB}$ is 4 units, the measure of $\overline{BC}$ is 5 units, and the measure of $\overline{CD}$ is 12 units. Find the measure of $\overline{DE}$.

1. **Vocabulary** Congruent and similar figures have __?__ angles.

2. **Reasoning** Are all right triangles similar? Explain your answer using words and a sketch.

Match the congruent triangles.

3. 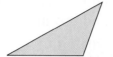   4.   5.

A.    B.   C.

For more exercises, see Extra Skills and Word Problems.

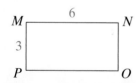

For Exercises	See Examples
6–7	1
8–11	2
12–14	3

Tell whether each figure is congruent to trapezoid *ABDC*.

6.   7.

Which rectangles are similar to rectangle *MNOP* at the left?

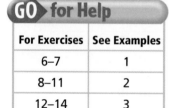

8. 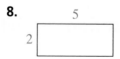   9. 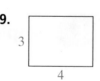   10.   11.

Each figure is similar to triangle *PQR*. Find *x* in each figure.

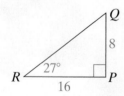

12.   13. 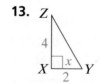   14.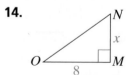

 15. **Guided Problem Solving** You need to replace a broken window. Should the new window glass be congruent to the original window glass? Explain.
- How are congruent and similar rectangles different?
- Can two rectangles be both similar and congruent?

16. List the pairs of figures that are similar. If necessary, use a protractor to measure the angles.

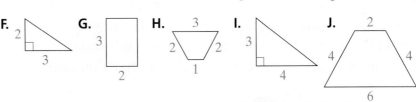

17. Triangles *MNO* and *PQR* at the left are similar.

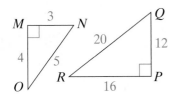

  a. List the pairs of congruent angles.

  b. Write the proportions for the corresponding sides.

18. **Writing in Math** Are congruent figures always similar? Explain.

(**Algebra**) **Each pair of figures is congruent. Find *x*.**

19.   **20.**

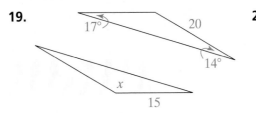
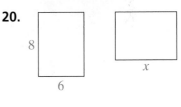

21. **Challenge** How many congruent triangles are in the figure at the left? How many similar triangles?

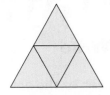

Test Prep and Mixed Review **Practice**

Multiple Choice

22. The angle at each vertex of a regular pentagon is 108°. What type of angle is at each vertex of a regular pentagon?

  Ⓐ Acute   Ⓒ Right
  Ⓑ Obtuse   Ⓓ Straight

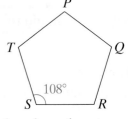

23. Eighteen classes are on a field trip. Each class has about 25 students. About how many students are on the trip?
  Ⓕ 43   Ⓖ 45   Ⓗ 430   Ⓙ 450

GO for Help

For Exercise	See Lesson
24	2-4

24. Make a line graph from the data in the table below.

Net Profit per Week

Week	1	2	3	4	5
Store A	$1,500	$800	$700	$950	$1,000

GPS Guided Problem Solving

Practice Solving Problems

In the Ball Park   The distance from home plate to the center of the pitcher's mound in the scale drawing is about 0.3 inch. About how far is the actual distance from home plate to the center of the pitcher's mound?

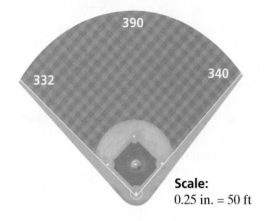

Scale:
0.25 in. = 50 ft

What You Might Think

(What do I know?)

(What am I trying to find?)

(How can I write and solve a proportion to find the answer?)

(What is the answer?)

What You Might Write

- A scale drawing is similar to the actual object, so the distances are proportional.

- scale: 0.25 in. = 50 ft

- scale distance is about 0.3 in.

the actual distance from home plate to the center of the pitcher's mound

Let d = the actual distance from home plate to the center of the pitcher's mound.

$$\frac{0.25}{50} = \frac{0.3}{d}$$

$$0.25d = 15$$

$$d = 60$$

The actual distance from home plate to the center of the pitcher's mound is 60 feet.

Think It Through

1. Why is a proportion used to find the answer?

2. **Check for Reasonableness** How do you know the answer is reasonable? (*Hint:* Notice that 0.25 inch is close to 0.3 inch.)

Exercises

3. The actual distance from home plate to the center-field wall in another ballpark is 400 feet. How long should you draw that distance in a drawing with a scale of 0.25 inch = 50 feet?
   a. How can you use the scale 0.25 inch = 50 feet to write a proportion?
   b. **Check for Reasonableness** How can you decide if the answer is reasonable?

4. The dimensions of your science book are $8\frac{3}{4}$ inches by 11 inches. Is the photo of the book at the right similar to the shape of your science book? Explain.

5. Draw a right triangle similar to the one below. Make the lengths of the sides in your drawing $a = 4$ inches and $b = 3$ inches. What are the lengths of all of the sides for both triangles?

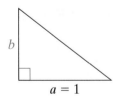

6. Draw a figure similar to the one below but larger. Tell how you know the figures are similar.

7. A box in a drawing is 2 in. wide, $5\frac{1}{2}$ in. long, and $3\frac{1}{4}$ in. high. The scale is $\frac{3}{4}$ in. = 2 ft. What are the dimensions of the actual box?

What You'll Learn

To find lines of symmetry

🔊 **New Vocabulary** line symmetry, line of symmetry

Why Learn This?

You often see symmetry in nature, as in the butterfly at the right. You can also find symmetrical designs in fabrics, flags, architecture, and art.

A figure has **line symmetry** if a line can divide the figure so that each half is a mirror image of the other. This dividing line is called a **line of symmetry.** If you fold a drawing on its line of symmetry, the two sides match.

EXAMPLE   Testing for Line Symmetry

1. For each figure, is the dashed line a line of symmetry? Explain.

a.

No, if you fold the figure along the line, the two parts do not match.

b.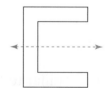

Yes, if you fold the figure along the line, the two parts match.

✓ Quick Check

1. Is the red dashed line in the figure a line of symmetry? Explain.

Some figures have more than one line of symmetry.

EXAMPLE **Application: Nature**

2 How many lines of symmetry does each figure have? Draw them.

a.

The leaf has one line of symmetry.

b.

The snowflake has 6 lines of symmetry.

✓ Quick Check

2. How many lines of symmetry does each figure have? Trace the figure and draw the lines of symmetry.

a.

b.

✓ Check Your Understanding

1. **Vocabulary** Is the dashed line in the square at the right a line of symmetry?

2. **Reasoning** How many lines of symmetry does a square have? Draw a diagram to support your answer.

3. **Open-Ended** The word CODE has a horizontal line of symmetry. Find another word that has a horizontal line of symmetry.

← ‑ ‑ **CODE** ‑ ‑ →

For more exercises, see Extra Skills and Word Problems.

GO for Help

For Exercises	See Examples
4–6	1
7–9	2

Is the dashed line in each figure a line of symmetry? Explain.

4.

5.

6.

How many lines of symmetry does each figure have? Trace the figure and draw the lines of symmetry.

7. 8.  9.

10. **Guided Problem Solving** An artist designs the logo in the sketch at the right. How many lines of symmetry does the logo have?
   - **Make a Plan** Look for vertical, horizontal, and other lines of symmetry.
   - **Check the Answer** Trace the logo and fold it along its lines of symmetry.

Tell whether each design has line symmetry.

11.

12.

13.

Nature Tell how many lines of symmetry each object has.

14.

15.

16. **Reasoning** How many lines of symmetry does a circle have? Explain your reasoning.

17. <u>**Writing in Math**</u>  Sketch a scalene, an equilateral, and an isosceles triangle. Use dashed lines to show the lines of symmetry. Describe the lines of symmetry.

18. **Flags** How many lines of symmetry does each flag have?

19. **Challenge** Research a Native American design with lines of symmetry. Trace the design. Draw all the lines of symmetry.

Test Prep and Mixed Review

Practice

Multiple Choice

20. Which set of angle measures can you use to draw a triangle?
    Ⓐ 82°, 55°, 47°
    Ⓒ 25°, 30°, 35°
    Ⓑ 90°, 30°, 60°
    Ⓓ 50°, 20°, 30°

21. In a survey, 35% of teenagers said they would keep their computer if they could keep only one electronic device. Another 30% chose a television, 20% chose a telephone, and 15% chose a radio. Which graph accurately displays the results of the survey?

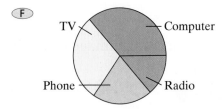 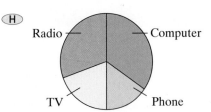

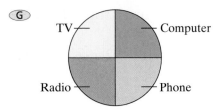 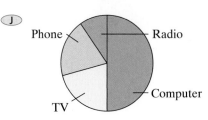

Use the diagram to name the figures.

22. three points not on the same line

23. three rays

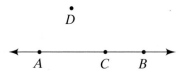

Transformations

✓ Check Skills You'll Need

1. **Vocabulary Review** How can you fold paper to determine if a figure has *line symmetry?*

Trace each figure and draw the lines of symmetry.

2.

3.

for Help
Lesson 8-7

What You'll Learn

To identify and draw translations, reflections, and rotations

🔊 **New Vocabulary** transformation, image, translation, reflection, line of reflection, rotation, center of rotation

Why Learn This?

Quilters make interesting patterns by transforming shapes to different positions.

A **transformation** of a figure is a change in its position, shape, or size. The new figure is the **image** of the original. Three types of transformations change only the position of the figure. They are translations, reflections, and rotations.

A **translation,** or slide, is a transformation that moves every point of a figure the same distance and in the same direction.

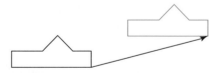

The blue figure is the image of the black figure after a translation.

EXAMPLE **Identifying Translations**

1. Is the second figure a translation of the first figure?

a.

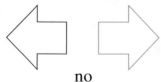

no

b.

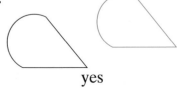

yes

✓ Quick Check

1. Is the second figure a translation of the first figure?

A **reflection,** or flip, is a transformation that flips a figure over a line called the **line of reflection.**

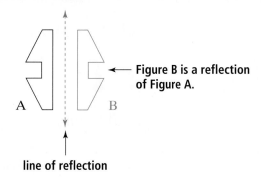

Figure B is a reflection of Figure A.

line of reflection

EXAMPLE **Drawing Reflections**

② Draw the reflection of Figure A over the red line of reflection.

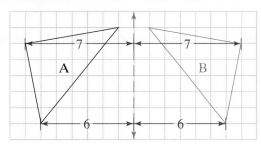

Use the grid to locate the vertices equidistant from the line of reflection.

Then connect the vertices.

✓ Quick Check

2. Copy the figure on graph paper. Draw its reflection over the given line.

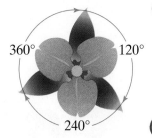

Vocabulary Tip

The hands on a clock rotate. The direction they rotate is called *clockwise*.

A **rotation,** or turn, is a transformation that turns a figure about a point. This point stays fixed and is called the **center of rotation.** You can describe a rotation using degrees.

EXAMPLE **Application: Nature**

③ Through how many degrees can you rotate the flower at the left so that the image and the original flower match?

The image matches the original flower after rotations of 120°, 240°, and 360°.

✓ Quick Check

3. Tell whether each figure below is a rotation of the first shape.

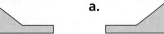

a.   b.   c.

Vocabulary Match each type of transformation to its name.

1.

2.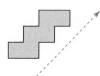

3.

A. reflection

B. translation

C. rotation

4. What clockwise rotation of a figure will produce the same image as a counterclockwise rotation of 180°?

Homework Exercises

For more exercises, see Extra Skills and Word Problems.

GO for Help

For Exercises	See Examples
5–7	1
8–10	2
11–14	3

Is the second figure a translation of the first figure?

5.

6.

7.

Copy each diagram. Draw its reflection over the given line.

8.

9.

10.

Tell whether each shape is a rotation of the shape at the left.

11.   12. 13.   14.

GPS 15. **Guided Problem Solving** How many degrees can you rotate the figure so that the image matches the original? List all possibilities less than 360°.
- **Understand the Problem** Turn the figure so that it looks exactly the same.
- **Check the Answer** Trace and color the figure. Rotate to check the answer.

Make three copies of the figure below for Exercises 16–18.

16. Draw a 90° clockwise rotation of the figure.

17. Draw a translation of the figure.

18. Draw a line of reflection below the figure. Then draw the reflection of the figure over the line.

19. Describe a translation of the figure in the fabric.

20. Describe the transformation the blades of a windmill make.

21. Reasoning What transformations can you use to change the image of the letter C so that it faces left?

22. <u>Writing in Math</u> Describe how translations and reflections are alike and how they are different. Include examples.

23. Open-Ended Design a pattern that consists of translations, reflections, and rotations of one basic figure. Explain in words how to find each transformation in your design.

24. Challenge State the least number of degrees you must rotate an equilateral triangle for the image to fit exactly over the original triangle.

Test Prep and Mixed Review

Practice

Multiple Choice

25. The ratio of adults to children at a skating rink is about 1 to 3. If a manager counts 42 children at the rink, about how many adults would the manager expect to be at the rink?

   Ⓐ 13   Ⓑ 14   Ⓒ 15   Ⓓ 16

26. The stem-and-leaf plot shows the length, in minutes, of 20 movies. What is the mode of the data?

   Ⓕ 86   Ⓗ 88

   Ⓖ 87   Ⓙ 90

Length of Movies	
6	0 5
7	4 5 9
8	1 2 4 5 6 8 8
9	0 0 0 2 5
10	6
11	5
12	2

Key: 7 | 8 means 78 minutes

Solve each equation.

27. $x + 5\frac{2}{9} = 14\frac{1}{3}$ **28.** $27\frac{1}{2} = x + 5\frac{3}{4}$

29. $25 - 17\frac{2}{3} = x$ **30.** $x + 6\frac{2}{3} = 18$

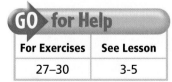

GO for Help

For Exercises	See Lesson
27–30	3-5

Tessellations

A **tessellation** is a pattern of repeated, congruent shapes. It covers a surface without gaps or overlaps. You can use a trapezoid to make a tessellation.

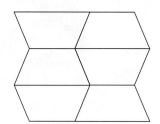

ACTIVITY

1. Draw a $1\frac{1}{2}$-inch square and cut it out. Inside the square, draw a trapezoid and a triangle with one side of each shape on a side of the square.

2. Cut out the figures and move each to the opposite side of the square. Tape them in place.

3. Trace the figure repeatedly to make a tessellation. Compare your tessellation to the figure below.

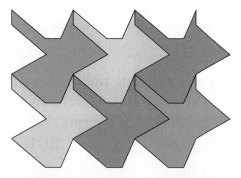

4. Repeat the activity using two other shapes inside a square.

Exercises

Does each figure tessellate? Use a drawing to support your answer.

1.

2.
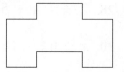

3.

4.

Drawing a Picture

Often, you can find a solution to a problem more easily if you draw a picture to show the information in the problem.

EXAMPLE

Rectangle A and rectangle B share an edge of 16 inches. The shorter side of rectangle A is 8 inches. If rectangle A is similar to rectangle B, which proportion can you use to find s, the longer side of rectangle B?

Ⓐ $\dfrac{8}{16} = \dfrac{s}{16}$ 　　　Ⓑ $\dfrac{8}{16} = \dfrac{16}{s}$ 　　　Ⓒ $\dfrac{8}{16} = \dfrac{s}{8}$ 　　　Ⓓ $\dfrac{8}{16} = \dfrac{8}{s}$

Step 1 Draw a picture of the two rectangles to visualize the information.

Step 2 Use the side lengths to set up a proportion.

shorter side of A → 　$\dfrac{8}{16} = \dfrac{16}{s}$　 ← shorter side of B
longer side of A → 　　　　　 ← longer side of B

● The correct answer is choice B.

Exercises

1. Triangle ABC is similar to triangle XYZ. Angle B and angle Y are right angles. If $\overline{AB}$ is 4 inches, $\overline{AC}$ is 8 inches, and $\overline{XZ}$ is 16 inches, which proportion can you use to find s, the length of $\overline{XY}$?

   Ⓐ $\dfrac{4}{16} = \dfrac{s}{8}$ 　　　　　　　　Ⓒ $\dfrac{4}{8} = \dfrac{s}{16}$

   Ⓑ $\dfrac{4}{16} = \dfrac{8}{s}$ 　　　　　　　　Ⓓ $\dfrac{4}{8} = \dfrac{16}{s}$

2. $\overleftrightarrow{MN}$ and $\overleftrightarrow{RS}$ intersect at point W. If $m\angle MWR = 130°$ and $m\angle MRW = 20°$, what is the measure of $\angle WMR$?

   Ⓕ $20°$ 　　　　　　　　　　Ⓗ $50°$

   Ⓖ $30°$ 　　　　　　　　　　Ⓙ $70°$

Vocabulary Review

🔊 acute angle (p. 368)
acute triangle (p. 380)
angle (p. 367)
center of rotation (p. 403)
complementary angles
    (p. 374)
congruent angles (p. 375)
congruent figures (p. 392)
congruent segments (p. 381)
degrees (p. 367)
equilateral triangle (p. 381)
image (p. 402)
intersecting lines (p. 363)
irregular polygon (p. 387)
isosceles triangle (p. 381)
line (p. 362)
line of reflection (p. 403)

line of symmetry (p. 398)
line symmetry (p. 398)
obtuse angle (p. 368)
obtuse triangle (p. 380)
parallel lines (p. 363)
parallelogram (p. 387)
perpendicular lines (p. 368)
plane (p. 363)
point (p. 362)
polygon (p. 386)
quadrilateral (p. 387)
ray (p. 362)
rectangle (p. 387)
reflection (p. 403)
regular polygon (p. 387)
rhombus (p. 387)
right angle (p. 368)

right triangle (p. 380)
rotation (p. 403)
scalene triangle (p. 381)
segment (p. 362)
similar figures (p. 393)
skew lines (p. 363)
square (p. 387)
straight angle (p. 368)
supplementary angles
    (p. 374)
transformation (p. 402)
translation (p. 402)
transversal (p. 378)
trapezoid (p. 387)
triangle (p. 380)
vertex (p. 367)
vertical angles (p. 375)

Choose the correct term to complete each sentence.

1. The measure of an (acute, obtuse) angle is between 90° and 180°.

2. An (isosceles, equilateral) triangle has three congruent sides.

3. Lines that intersect to form right angles are (skew, perpendicular).

4. A (rectangle, rhombus) always has four right angles.

5. A (ray, line) extends in two opposite directions without end.

Go Online
PHSchool.com
For: Vocabulary quiz
Web Code: aqj-0851

Skills and Concepts

Lesson 8-1

• To identify and work with points, lines, segments, and rays

A **point** has no size, only location. A **line** continues without end in opposite directions. A **segment** is part of a line and has two endpoints. A **ray** is part of a line and has one endpoint.

Parallel lines are lines in the same plane that do not intersect. **Skew lines** lie in different planes.

6. Name two parallel lines.

7. Name two rays with endpoint *B*.

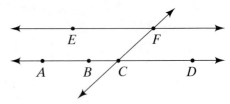

Lessons 8-2 and 8-3

- To measure and classify angles
- To use relationships between special pairs of angles

Angles are classified as **acute, right, obtuse,** or **straight.** Two intersecting lines form two pairs of **vertical angles.** The sum of the measures of two **complementary angles** is 90°. The sum of the measures of two **supplementary angles** is 180°.

Name each of the following.

8. a pair of vertical angles

9. an obtuse angle

10. two congruent angles

11. an acute angle

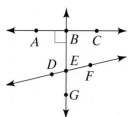

Lessons 8-4 and 8-5

- To classify triangles by their angles and their sides
- To identify regular polygons and to classify quadrilaterals

You can classify a triangle as **acute, obtuse,** or **right.** You can also classify a triangle as **scalene, isosceles,** or **equilateral.**

Polygons with four sides are called **quadrilaterals.** Three special types of **parallelograms** are the **rhombus,** the **rectangle,** and the **square.**

Give the best name for each polygon.

12.    13.   14.

Lessons 8-6, 8-7, and 8-8

- To identify congruent and similar figures
- To find lines of symmetry
- To identify and draw translations, reflections, and rotations

Congruent figures have the same size and shape. **Similar** figures have the same shape, but not necessarily the same size. **Translations, reflections,** and **rotations** are transformations that change the position of a figure.

Do the triangles appear to be congruent or similar?

15. 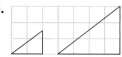   16.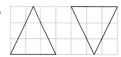

17. Draw a translation and a reflection of the figure shown.

Go **O**nline
PHSchool.com **For:** Online chapter test
Web Code: aqa-0852

1. Draw three points that do not lie on the same line. Label them *X, Y,* and *Z.* Draw $\overleftrightarrow{XY}$ and $\overrightarrow{YZ}$.

Measure each angle. Then classify it as *acute, right, obtuse,* or *straight.*

2.

3.

4.

5.

Find the complement and the supplement of each angle measure.

6. 72°

7. 42°

Classify each triangle as *acute, right,* or *obtuse.*

8.
27°
41°
112°

9.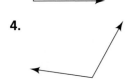
55°
35°

Classify each triangle as *scalene, isosceles,* or *equilateral.*

10.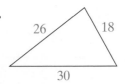
15 15
15

11.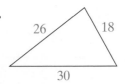
26 18
30

12. Draw a quadrilateral with the given number of lines of symmetry.
    a. 0   b. 1   c. 2   d. 4

Write the best name for each figure.

13.

14.

15.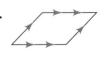

16.

17. **Writing in Math** Describe how congruent figures and similar figures are alike and how they are different.

How many lines of symmetry does each quadrilateral have?

18.

19.

Use the shape below for Exercises 20–22.

20. Draw a translation of the shape.

21. Draw a reflection of the shape. Show the line of reflection.

22. Draw a 180° clockwise rotation of the shape. Show the point you chose as the center of rotation.

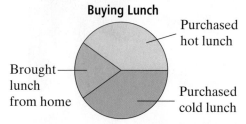
Multiple Choice
Choose the best answer.

1. What information does the circle graph below NOT tell you about Jen?

Buying Lunch

Purchased hot lunch

Brought lunch from home

Purchased cold lunch

- Ⓐ Jen purchased lunch more often than she brought it from home.
- Ⓑ Jen purchased hot lunches about as often as cold lunches.
- Ⓒ Jen brought lunch from home more often than she purchased cold lunch.
- Ⓓ Jen purchased hot lunch more often than she brought lunch from home.

2. A hot air balloon is 2,250 feet in the air. It is scheduled to land at 3:30 P.M. It descends 90 feet every minute. When should the balloonist start descending?
- Ⓕ 3:55 P.M.
- Ⓗ 2:55 P.M.
- Ⓖ 3:05 P.M.
- Ⓙ 2:45 P.M.

3. In order to conclude that *MNOP* is a rhombus, what do you need to know?
- Ⓐ $\overline{MO}$ has length 8.
- Ⓑ $\overline{MO}$ is perpendicular to $\overline{NP}$.
- Ⓒ $\overline{NP}$ and $\overline{MO}$ are congruent.
- Ⓓ $\overline{MP}$ and $\overline{PO}$ both have length 8.

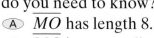

4. Which set of decimals is ordered from least to greatest?
- Ⓕ 0.2, 0.02, 0.22
- Ⓖ 0.15, 0.51, 1.05
- Ⓗ 0.24, 0.3, 0.05
- Ⓙ 0.49, 0.4, 0.05

5. The Amazon River in South America carries one sixth of Earth's water that flows into oceans. About what percent is this?
- Ⓐ 17%
- Ⓑ 12.5%
- Ⓒ 10%
- Ⓓ 6%

6. Which is ordered from least to greatest?
- Ⓕ $\frac{3}{7}, \frac{5}{7}, \frac{7}{11}$
- Ⓗ $\frac{1}{3}, \frac{2}{3}, \frac{4}{5}$
- Ⓖ $\frac{1}{4}, \frac{1}{2}, \frac{2}{5}$
- Ⓙ $\frac{1}{8}, \frac{2}{5}, \frac{3}{10}$

Gridded Response

7. $31.2 \times \blacksquare = 0.0312$. What is $\blacksquare$?

8. What is the value of $3 + 4 \times 2^3$?

9. What is the degree measurement of a supplement of a 32° angle?

10. The greatest angle in a right triangle measures __?__ degrees.

Short Response

11. Which of the mean, median, mode, or range is the greatest for these data? Explain.
81, 70, 95, 73, 74, 91, 86, 74

12. a. Bagels cost $6 per dozen. Find the cost of 5 bagels. Use a proportion.
b. Find the unit cost for a bagel.

Extended Response

13. Can you conclude that the two triangles below are NOT similar? Explain.

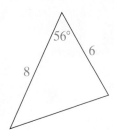

Applying Geometry

Building Outside the Box Before your home was built, it was probably drawn as a two-dimensional plan, or blueprint. A blueprint lets an architect experiment on paper with different ideas. The architect can discuss these ideas with the owner before construction begins. A blueprint also gives clear directions to a contractor on what to build. Most houses and apartments are rectangles with rectangular rooms, but they can be any shape.

Using a Blueprint

Builders read blueprints and translate the two-dimensional notes into three-dimensional buildings. A builder refers to a blueprint many times a day during the building process.

Reading a Blueprint

A blueprint shows the layout of individual floors of your home in $\frac{1}{4}$ inch–to–1 foot scale. It includes the dimensions of each room and closet and provides a key so you know what various symbols mean.

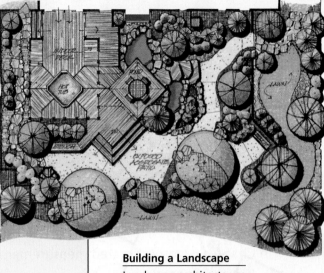

Put It All Together

Materials ruler

1. The blueprint shows a home where no room is rectangular.
   a. What shape is the home?
   b. Identify the shape of each room.

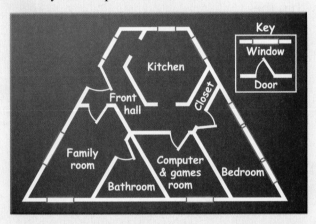

2. **Open-Ended** Suppose you are designing your own home. Make a list of the rooms you would like to include. Feel free to include rooms for hobbies or other special interests.

3. Make a rough sketch of the home, showing the shape and location of each room.
   - Use at least five different shapes from this chapter.
   - Include at least two rooms that are congruent to each other. Make one a translation or rotation of the other.
   - Remember to include hallways and doorways so that people can get into the rooms!

4. Use a ruler to make a final drawing of your design. Show windows and doors using the key in the blueprint. Label the rooms. Add furniture to your drawing if you wish.

5. **Writing in Math** Why do you think homes usually have rectangular rooms?

Go Online
PHSchool.com
For: Information about architecture
Web Code: aqe-0853

CHAPTER 9

Geometry and Measurement

What You've Learned

- In Chapter 6, you estimated measurements in the customary system.
- You also converted units of measure within the customary system.
- In Chapter 8, you identified and classified angles and two-dimensional figures.

Check Your Readiness

GO for Help

For Exercises	See Lessons
1–2	6-6
3–8	6-7
9–11	8-4, 8-5

Choosing Units of Measurement

Choose an appropriate unit for each measurement.

1. weight of a newborn baby

2. distance to the sun

Changing Units

Complete each statement.

3. ■ oz = 9 lb   4. 46 in. = ■ ft   5. $7\frac{1}{4}$ c = ■ pt

Use <, =, or > to complete each statement.

6. 14 ft ■ 4 yd   7. $2\frac{1}{2}$ gal ■ 11 qt   8. 5 c ■ 37 fl oz

Classifying Polygons

Classify each figure. Classify the triangle by its sides.

9.

10.

11.

414   Chapter 9

What You'll Learn Next

- In this chapter, you will use the metric system of measurement and convert units of measure within the metric system.

- You will use formulas to find the circumference and area of a circle.

- You will find the perimeters and areas of parallelograms and triangles.

- You will identify three-dimensional figures and find their surface areas and volumes.

 Problem Solving Application On pages 472 and 473, you will work an extended activity on measurement.

🔊 Key Vocabulary

- area (p. 426)
- chord (p. 438)
- circle (p. 438)
- circumference (p. 439)
- diameter (p. 438)
- metric system (p. 416)
- perimeter (p. 426)
- prism (p. 449)
- radius (p. 438)
- surface area (p. 454)
- volume (p. 458)

Metric Units of Length, Mass, and Capacity

Check Skills You'll Need

1. **Vocabulary Review** Name a *customary unit of measure* for length, weight, and capacity.

Name an appropriate unit for each measurement.

2. the length of a gymnasium

3. the capacity of a juice box

GO for Help
Lesson 6-6

What You'll Learn

To use metric units of measure and to choose appropriate units of length, mass, and capacity

◀ᵼ))) **New Vocabulary** metric system, meter (m), mass, gram (g), capacity, liter (L)

Why Learn This?

The **metric system** of measurement is a decimal system. Computing with decimals is easier than other systems. The metric system uses prefixes to indicate the size of metric units. The table at the right shows the most common prefixes.

The standard unit of length in the metric system is the **meter (m)**. A meter is a little longer than a yard.

Metric Prefixes

Prefix	Meaning
kilo-	1,000
centi-	$\frac{1}{100}$ or 0.01
milli-	$\frac{1}{1,000}$ or 0.001

Metric Units of Length

Unit	Relationship to a Meter	Example
kilometer (km)	1 km = 1,000 meters	2.5 times around an indoor track
meter (m)	1 meter	height of a doorknob from the floor
centimeter (cm)	1 cm = 0.01 meter	thickness of a CD case
millimeter (mm)	1 mm = 0.001 meter	thickness of a CD

EXAMPLE Choosing a Unit of Length

❶ Choose an appropriate metric unit of length for a pencil.

A pencil is much shorter than a meter but much longer than a millimeter. The most appropriate unit of measure is centimeters.

✓ Quick Check

● **1.** Choose an appropriate metric unit of length for a city block.

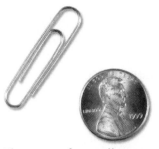

The mass of a small paper clip is 1 gram. The mass of a penny is about 2.5 grams.

Solids are sometimes measured in units of mass. **Mass** is a measure of the amount of matter in an object. The standard unit of mass is the **gram (g).**

Unit of Mass	Relationship to a Gram	Example
kilogram (kg)	1 kg = 1,000 grams	mass of 4 videocassettes
gram (g)	1 gram	mass of a small paper clip
milligram (mg)	1 mg = 0.001 gram	mass of an eyelash

EXAMPLE **Choosing a Unit of Mass**

2 Choose an appropriate metric unit of mass for your math book.

The mass of a math book is much greater than the mass of a paper clip. The appropriate unit of measure is kilograms.

☑️ **Quick Check**

2. Choose an appropriate metric unit of mass.
    a. a car   **b.** a desk   **c.** a robin's feather

Containers are measured in units of capacity. **Capacity** is a measure of the amount of space an object contains. The standard unit of capacity is the **liter (L).** A liter is a little more than a quart.

Unit of Capacity	Relationship to a Liter	Example
kiloliter (kL)	1 kL = 1,000 liters	2 or 3 bathtubs
liter (L)	1 liter	juice bottle
milliliter (mL)	1 mL = 0.001 liter	eye dropper

EXAMPLE **Choosing a Unit of Capacity**

3 Choose an appropriate metric unit of capacity for a bottle cap.

A bottle cap holds about 10 to 20 drops of water. The appropriate unit of measure is milliliters.

☑️ **Quick Check**

3. Choose an appropriate metric unit of capacity.
    a. a car's fuel tank   **b.** a pond   **c.** a test tube

1. **Vocabulary** Tell whether each measurement is a unit of length, mass, or capacity.
   a. 13 mg　　　　b. 13 m　　　　c. 13 kL

Open-Ended For each unit, name two items that you would measure using the unit.

2. milligram　　　3. centimeter　　　4. kilogram

Is each statement true or false? If it is false, explain why.

5. 1,000 mg = 1 g　　　　6. 100 kg = 100,000 g

7. 10 L = 1,000 mL　　　　8. 1 mm = 10 cm

Homework Exercises

For more exercises, see Extra Skills and Word Problems.

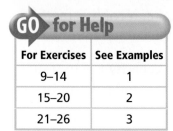

For Exercises	See Examples
9–14	1
15–20	2
21–26	3

Choose an appropriate metric unit of length.

9. width of a highway　　　10. length of an eyelash

11. height of your desk　　　12. width of your finger

13. width of your classroom door

14. distance across the state of Ohio

Choose an appropriate metric unit of mass.

15. a pencil　　　16. a pin　　　17. a chair

18. a pea　　　19. a potato　　　20. a shirt button

Choose an appropriate metric unit of capacity.

21. a watering can　　22. a juice box　　23. a large lake

24. a bucket of paint　25. an oil truck　　26. a glass of milk

27. **Guided Problem Solving** You have two 650-milliliter bottles of sunscreen lotion. Is a 1-liter container large enough to hold all of the lotion from the two bottles?
    - What is the total volume of lotion you have?
    - Is the total volume of lotion *greater than* or *less than* 1 liter?

Complete each statement.

28. 1 g = ■ kg   **29.** 1 mL = ■ L   **30.** ■ cm = 1 m

31. Estimation The width of a door is about 1 meter. How can you estimate the length of a wall that contains the door?

Is each measurement reasonable? Explain.

32. A giraffe is 550 centimeters tall.

33. A ladybug has a mass of 4 kilograms.

34. A sidewalk is 30 kilometers wide.

35. You place eight 12-centimeter pencils end to end. Is the total length *greater than* or *less than* 1 meter? Justify your answer.

36. Groceries You buy a bag of oranges. Should the price be calculated using length, mass, or capacity? Explain.

37. Writing in Math Explain the difference between mass and capacity. Give an example of each using one container.

38. Challenge The deciliter (dL) is sometimes used in medical laboratory testing. The prefix *deci-* means one tenth, or 0.1. Complete each statement.
   a. 15 L = ■ dL   **b.** 273 dL = ■ L

Test Prep and Mixed Review   **Practice**

Multiple Choice

39. Which measurement is NOT reasonable?
   Ⓐ A teenager's height is 180 centimeters.
   Ⓑ A container holds 2 liters of juice.
   Ⓒ A pebble has a mass of 3 grams.
   Ⓓ A truck has a mass of 80 kilograms.

40. A trapezoid is shown. Find the measure of ∠T.
   Ⓕ 60°
   Ⓖ 70°
   Ⓗ 130°
   Ⓙ 150°

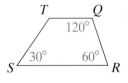

Find the complement and the supplement of each angle.

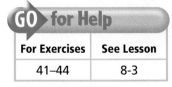
41. 44°   **42.** 16°   **43.** 81°   **44.** 62.5°

Metric Units

These activities provide practice working with metric units of volume and length.

ACTIVITY

1. What is the measure of the volume of liquid in the container at the right?

   The liquid reaches a height of 28 units. The units on this container are milliliters. So the amount in the container is 28 milliliters, or 28 mL.

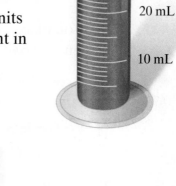

2. What is the measure of the segment below in millimeters and in centimeters?

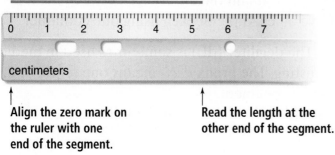

Align the zero mark on the ruler with one end of the segment.

Read the length at the other end of the segment.

The length is 53 millimeters, or 5.3 centimeters.

Exercises

1. What is the measure of the volume of liquid in the container at the right?

Measure each segment in millimeters and in centimeters.

2. ───────────

3. ────

4. ─────────────

5. **Writing in Math** The width of a leaf measures between 4 and 5 centimeters. Explain how you can write your answer in centimeters and in millimeters.

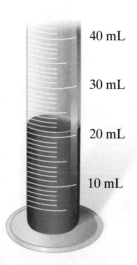

What You'll Learn

To convert between metric measurements

Why Learn This?

Most countries around the world use the metric system to describe distance, volume, and mass.

You can rewrite one metric unit as another metric unit by multiplying or dividing by a power of 10.

Next 96 km

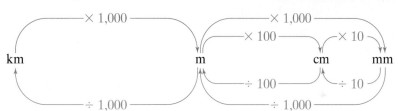

You can think of converting larger units to smaller units as creating many small units from a larger unit. To do this, you multiply.

EXAMPLE Converting to Smaller Units

① A door is 3.2 meters tall. What is 3.2 meters in centimeters?

The meter is a larger unit than the centimeter. To convert meters to centimeters, multiply by 100.

$$3.2 \times 100 = 320.$$ ← **To multiply by 100, move the decimal point 2 places to the right.**

3.2 m = 320 cm

✓ Quick Check

1. Convert each measurement
   a. 15 cm to millimeters
   b. 837 km to meters

You can think of converting smaller units to larger units as combining many smaller units. To do this, you divide. You will end up with fewer larger units than smaller units.

EXAMPLE Converting to Larger Units

2 **Multiple Choice** The distance from the equator to the North Pole on the Earth's surface is approximately 10,000,000 m. What is the approximate distance in kilometers?

   Ⓐ 1,000 km   Ⓒ 100,000 km

   Ⓑ 10,000 km   Ⓓ 100,000,000 km

The meter is a smaller unit than the kilometer. So to convert meters to kilometers, divide by 1,000.

   $10,000,000 \div 1,000 = 10,000.000$ ← **To divide by 1,000, move the decimal point 3 places to the left.**

The equator is about 10,000 km from the North Pole. The correct answer is choice B.

✓ Quick Check

2. A sprinter runs 60,000 m each week. How many kilometers does the sprinter run each week?

You can also convert grams or liters to related units.

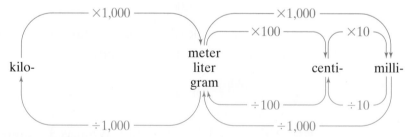

Test Prep Tip

The prefix *kilo-* means "thousand". Knowing what each metric prefix means can help you convert units.

EXAMPLE Converting Units of Mass or Capacity

3 Complete the statement 325 cL = ▮ L.

To convert centiliters to liters, divide by 100.

   $325 \div 100 = 3.25 \rightarrow 3.25$ liters ← **To divide by 100, move the decimal point 2 places to the left.**

✓ Quick Check

3. Complete each statement.

   a. 15 mg = ▮ g   **b.** 386 L = ▮ kL   **c.** 8.2 cg = ▮ g

1. **Number Sense** Which measurement is greater, 500 millimeters or 5 meters? Explain.

State whether you multiply or divide to change units.

2. meters to kilometers

3. liters to kiloliters

4. centigrams to milligrams

5. centimeters to meters

Homework Exercises

For more exercises, see Extra Skills and Word Problems.

GO for Help

For Exercises	See Examples
6–9	1
10–14	2
15–23	3

Convert each measurement.

6. 1.3 km to meters

7. 6,000 m to centimeters

8. 59 cm to millimeters

9. 200 km to centimeters

10. 206 cm to meters

11. 142 cm to kilometers

12. 7.5 mm to centimeters

13. 6,900 m to kilometers

14. **Animals** One of the world's longest dogs measured 240 cm. How many meters long was this dog?

Complete each statement.

15. 3,070 mm = ▅ m

16. 586 cg = ▅ g

17. 0.61 km = ▅ m

18. 0.04 m = ▅ cm

19. 4,500 g = ▅ mg

20. 6.4 kL = ▅ L

21. 150 cL = ▅ L

22. 120 mg = ▅ g

23. 3,000 L = ▅ mL

GPS 24. **Guided Problem Solving** A carpenter is installing a pocket door in a wall. The opening for the door needs to be 2.5 cm greater than two times the width of the door. How many centimeters wide should you make the opening for a door that is 0.8 m wide?
   • How many centimeters wide is the door?
   • How wide is the opening for the door?

25. **Science** Light travels at approximately 299,792,458 meters per second. Approximately how many kilometers does light travel in one second?

GO Online
Homework Video Tutor
Visit: PHSchool.com
Web Code: aqe-0902

Convert each measurement to meters, liters, or grams.

26. 8 kL   **27.** 7,000 mg   **28.** 0.24 km   **29.** 34,000 cm

30. 0.07 cL   **31.** 52 kg   **32.** 8.6 mm   **33.** 41.5 cg

34. (**Algebra**) Write an expression that can be used to find the number of milligrams in n grams.

Number of Grams	1	3	5	6	n
Number of Milligrams	1,000	3,000	5,000	6,000	■

35. Waves The world's largest wave was about 0.524 km tall. The height of the wave shown at the left is about 5 m. How many meters greater was the height of the largest wave than the height of this wave?

36. A bottle contains 1 liter of juice. Which measurement at the right is closest to 1 liter?

Test #	Measurement
1	1,002.3 mL
2	100.1 cL
3	0.000997 kL

37. Writing in Math When you convert metric measurements, how do you decide whether to multiply or divide?

38. Challenge A cup of whole milk contains 8.5 grams of fat. Two cups of skim milk contain 800 milligrams of fat. Find the difference in fat content per cup of milk.

Test Prep and Mixed Review   Practice

Multiple Choice

39. The diameter of Pluto is about 3,000,000 m. What is the approximate diameter of Pluto in kilometers?
  Ⓐ 300 km   Ⓒ 30,000 km
  Ⓑ 3,000 km   Ⓓ 3,000,000 km

40. Which unit should Lisa use to measure the length of a baseball bat?
  Ⓕ millimeter   Ⓗ liter
  Ⓖ centimeter   Ⓙ kilometer

GO for Help

For Exercises	See Lesson
41–43	8-3

Classify each triangle by its angles and its sides.

41.   **42.**   **43.**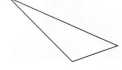

Vocabulary Builder

Using Concept Maps

One way to show connections among ideas is to draw a diagram called a concept map. The lines in a concept map connect related ideas.

EXAMPLE

Make a concept map with the terms related to transformations from Chapter 8.

- center of rotation
- reflection
- rotation
- translation
- transformation
- line of reflection

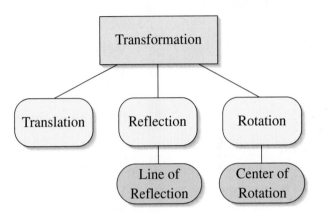

Exercises

1. Use the list below to make a concept map for the metric system.

metric system	millimeter	mass	kiloliter
length	gram	milliliter	centimeter
meter	kilometer	liter	milligram
kilogram	capacity		

2. Compete the concept map below as you study the next few lessons. Fill in the ovals using the appropriate terms listed below. Include area formulas on your concept map.

area
parallelogram
square
height
width
triangle
rectangle
base
length
side

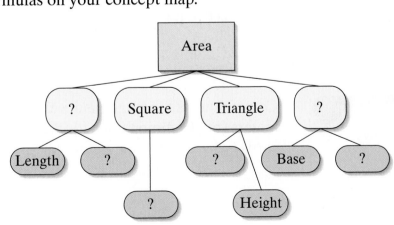

Perimeters and Areas of Rectangles

Check Skills You'll Need

1. **Vocabulary Review** Name the *base* and the *exponent* in 3^2.

Simplify each expression.

2. 4^2

3. 6^2

4. 5.4^2

5. 1.6^2

for Help
Lesson 4-2

What You'll Learn

To solve problems involving perimeters and areas of rectangles

 **New Vocabulary** perimeter, area

Why Learn This?

The length of a fence around a figure is a different measure from the area enclosed by the fence. You need to know how to find both measurements.

The **perimeter** of a figure is the distance around the figure. You can find the perimeter P of a rectangle by adding the lengths and widths of the rectangle.

$$P = \ell + w + \ell + w$$

So the perimeter is twice ℓ plus twice w, or twice the sum of ℓ and w.

$$P = 2\ell + 2w \qquad \text{or} \qquad P = 2(\ell + w)$$

The **area** of a figure is the number of square units the figure contains. You can find the area A of a rectangle by multiplying the length ℓ times the width w.

KEY CONCEPTS   Perimeter and Area of a Rectangle

$$P = 2(\ell + w)$$

$$A = \ell \times w$$

Vocabulary Tip

Read the symbol ft² as "square feet."

Common units for length and width are feet (ft), yards (yd), and meters (m). Common units for area are square feet (ft^2), square yards (yd^2), and square meters (m^2).

EXAMPLE Finding Perimeter and Area

① A landscaper plants grass and installs a fence around a rectangular backyard. Find the perimeter and area of the backyard.

70 ft

House | Backyard | 25 ft ← The length is 70 ft.
The width is 25 ft.

Test Prep Tip

Some formulas are provided for you to use during the test.

$P = 2(\ell + w)$ ← Use the formula for perimeter.

$= 2(70 + 25)$ ← Substitute 70 for ℓ and 25 for w.

$= 2 \times 95$ ← Add.

$= 190$ ← Multiply.

$A = \ell \times w$ ← Use the formula for area.

$= 70 \times 25$ ← Substitute 70 for ℓ and 25 for w.

$= 1{,}750$ ← Multiply.

The perimeter is 190 feet. The area is 1,750 square feet.

✓ Quick Check

1. Find the perimeter and area of a rectangle with a length of 8 ft and a width of 5 ft.

EXAMPLE Finding the Area of a Square

Area of Squares

Side Length (in.)	Area (in.^{2})
2	4
4	16
6	36
8	64
s	■

② **Multiple Choice** The table at the left shows the area of a square with different side lengths. Which expression can be used to find the area of a square with a side s units in length?

Ⓐ $2s$ Ⓑ $4s$ Ⓒ s^2 Ⓓ s^4

Look for a relationship between the side length and the area.

$2 \times 2 = 2^2$

$4 \times 4 = 4^2$ ← Square each side length to find the area.

$s \times s = s^2$

The expression s^2 can be used to find the area of a square with a side that is s units in length. The correct answer is choice C.

✓ Quick Check

2. Find the area of a square given side $s = 7$ in.

● More Than One Way

Leon and Lauren will run laps around the school playground. The playground is 310 feet long and 215 feet wide. How many laps will they run if they run about 1 mile?

Leon's Method

I can draw a model of the playground and label each side. Then I'll add the four sides to find the length of one lap.

$310 + 215 + 310 + 215 = 1{,}050$

Each lap is 1,050 feet. Since 1 mile equals 5,280 feet, I will divide.

$5{,}280 \div 1{,}050 \approx 5$

I will run 5 laps around the playground to run about 1 mile.

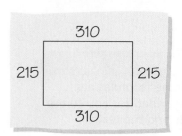

Lauren's Method

I can use the formula for perimeter. I'll substitute 310 feet for the length and 215 feet for the width.

$$
\begin{aligned}
P &= 2(\ell + w) \\
&= 2(310 + 215) \\
&= 2 \times 525 \\
&= 1{,}050
\end{aligned}
$$

The perimeter of the playground is 1,050 feet. There are 5,280 feet in a mile, so I'll divide.

$5{,}280 \div 1{,}050 \approx 5$

I will run 5 laps around the playground to run about 1 mile.

Choose a Method

Baseball diamonds are in the shape of a square. Major league diamonds are 90 feet on each side. Little League diamonds are 60 feet on each side. What is the difference between the perimeters of the diamonds in the two leagues? Describe your method.

1. **Vocabulary** Explain the difference between the perimeter and area of a figure.

Find the perimeter and area of each rectangle.

2.
4 in.

4 in.

3.
4 ft

9 ft

4.
16 m

8 m

Homework Exercises

For more exercises, see **Extra Skills and Word Problems.**

GO for Help

For Exercises	See Examples
5–13	1
14–16	2

Find the perimeter and area of each rectangle.

5. $\ell = 12$ in., $w = 7$ in.

6. $\ell = 8$ ft, $w = 5$ ft

7. $\ell = 13$ in., $w = 9$ in.

8. $\ell = 2$ m, $w = 7$ m

9. $\ell = 44$ m, $w = 30$ m

10. $\ell = 87$ ft, $w = 56$ ft

11. $\ell = 12$ in., $w = 15$ in.

12. $\ell = 42$ in., $w = 26$ in.

13. You want to frame a picture and hang it on your wall. The picture is 18 inches wide and 30 inches tall. Find the perimeter and area of the picture.

Find the area of each square.

14. $s = 8$ ft

15. $s = 5$ m

16. $s = 1.4$ in.

GPS 17. **Guided Problem Solving** A family is planting grass and a garden in the backyard. The rectangular backyard measures 131 ft by 52 ft. The garden measures 13 ft by 9 ft. What is the area of the backyard that will be grass?
- You can draw a picture to help visualize the situation.
- Subtract the area of the garden from the area of the backyard to find the area that will be grass.

18. **Stamps** The world's smallest stamp, shown at the left, measures 0.31 inch by 0.37 inch. Find the area of the stamp.

19. **Reasoning** How many square feet are in a square yard? Draw a picture and explain your answer.

Use a ruler to measure the length and width of each rectangle to the nearest millimeter. Then find the perimeter and area.

20.

21.

22.

Careers Interior decorators coordinate colors of paint in schools and offices.

23. **Decorating** You are going to paint a wall in your room. The wall is 12 feet long and 8 feet high. A window in the wall is 3 feet wide and 4 feet high. Find the area that you paint.

24. **Number Sense** A rectangle has a length of 4.5 inches and a width of 3 inches. How would the area change if you doubled both dimensions? Explain your reasoning.

25. **a.** Draw and label all the rectangles with a perimeter of 24 units. Use only whole units.
    b. Find the area of each rectangle. Record your data in a table as shown below.

Length	Width	Perimeter	Area
11 units	1 unit	24 units	11 square units

c. What is true about the rectangle with the greatest area?

26. **Writing in Math** You know the area of a rectangle. Can you find its perimeter? Use examples to explain why or why not.

27. **Challenge** How many square inches are in a square yard? Justify your answer.

Test Prep and Mixed Review

Practice

Multiple Choice

28. A rectangle has length ℓ and width w. Which equation can you NOT use to find the perimeter P of the rectangle?
    Ⓐ $P = \ell \cdot w$ Ⓒ $P = 2(\ell + w)$
    Ⓑ $P = 2\ell + 2w$ Ⓓ $P = \ell + \ell + w + w$

29. Which container could hold 80,000 milliliters?
    Ⓕ 0.5-kiloliter drum   Ⓗ 500-milliliter beaker
    Ⓖ 28-liter fuel tank   Ⓙ 2-liter bottle

GO for Help

For Exercise	See Lesson
30	7-5

30. The scale on a map is 1 cm : 10 km. How many centimeters on the map represent an actual distance of 25 kilometers?

Comparing Areas

In this activity, you will investigate how to find the areas of parallelograms and triangles.

ACTIVITY

1. On graph paper, draw a parallelogram that does not have a right angle. Cut out your parallelogram.

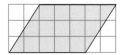

2. Draw a segment from one vertex that is perpendicular to the opposite base. Cut along that segment.

3. Arrange both pieces of the parallelogram to form a rectangle.

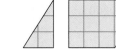

4. **Number Sense** Find the area of your rectangle. Is this area the same as the area of your parallelogram? Explain.

5. Repeat Steps 1–4 using a different parallelogram that does not have a right angle.

6. Write a formula that you can use to find the area of a parallelogram in the diagram on the right. Explain why the formula works. Then find the area of the parallelogram.

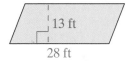

13 ft

28 ft

ACTIVITY

7. Draw two identical triangles on graph paper. Cut out both triangles.

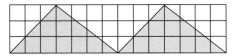

8. Arrange and tape both triangles to form a parallelogram. Then repeat Steps 2–4.

9. Repeat Steps 7 and 8 using a different triangle.

10. **Writing in Math** Write a formula that you can use to find the area of the triangle on the right. Explain why the formula works. Then find the area of the triangle.

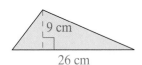

9 cm

26 cm

Check Skills You'll Need

1. **Vocabulary Review**
   The *area* of a rectangle is measured using __?__ units.

Find the perimeter and area of each rectangle.

2. $\ell = 6$ in.; $w = 4$ in.

3. $\ell = 12$ m; $w = 5$ m

GO for Help
Lesson 9-3

What You'll Learn

To solve problems involving areas of parallelograms, triangles, and complex figures

 **New Vocabulary** base of a parallelogram, height of a parallelogram, base of a triangle, height of a triangle

Why Learn This?

Conservation groups purchase land to protect wildlife. The value of the land depends in part on its area.

The area of a parallelogram is the product of the base and the height. Any side can be considered the **base of a parallelogram**. The **height of a parallelogram** is the perpendicular distance between opposite bases.

KEY CONCEPTS **Area of a Parallelogram**

$$A = b \times h$$

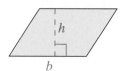

EXAMPLE **Finding the Area of a Parallelogram**

1 Find the area of the parallelogram.

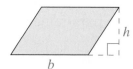

$A = b \times h$ ← Use the formula for the area of a parallelogram.

$\quad = 5 \times 3$ ← Substitute 5 for b and 3 for h.

$\quad = 15$ ← Simplify.

The area of the parallelogram is 15 m^2.

Quick Check

1. Find the area of a parallelogram with $b = 14$ m and $h = 5$ m.

Any side of a triangle can be the **base of a triangle.** The **height of a triangle** is the length of the perpendicular segment from a vertex to the base opposite that vertex.

The diagram at the right shows that the area of a triangle is half of the area of a parallelogram with the same base length and height, or $A = \frac{1}{2}b \times h$.

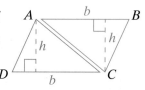

EXAMPLE   Finding the Area of a Triangle

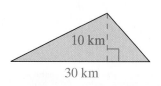

② **Conservation** A conservation group plans to buy a triangular plot of land shown at the left. What is the area of the plot?

$A = \frac{1}{2}b \times h$ ← Use the formula for the area of a triangle.

$= \frac{1}{2} \times 30 \times 10$ ← Substitute 30 for *b* and 10 for *h*.

$= 150$ ← Simplify.

The area of the plot is 150 km².

✓ Quick Check

2. A triangle has a base of 30 m and a height of 17.3 m. Find the triangle's area.

Sometimes you can split a complex figure into smaller polygons.

EXAMPLE   Finding the Area of a Complex Figure

③ Find the area of the figure.

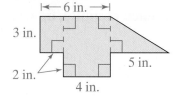

Split the polygon into two ← rectangles and a triangle, as shown by the dashed lines.

Area of smaller rectangle: $3 \times 2 = 6$, or 6 in.²

Area of larger rectangle: $5 \times 4 = 20$, or 20 in.²

Area of triangle: $\frac{1}{2}(5 \times 3) = \frac{1}{2} \times 15$, or 7.5 in.²

Find the area of each polygon.

The total area is $6 + 20 + 7.5$, or 33.5 in.².

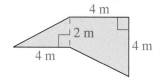

✓ Quick Check

3. Find the area of the figure at the left.

1. **Vocabulary** Explain why the height of a triangle depends on which side you select for the base.

2. If you double the length of the base of a triangle, how does the area of the triangle change?

3. **Reasoning** Draw a triangle and a rectangle that have the same base and the same height. How are the areas of the two figures related?

Homework Exercises

For more exercises, see Extra Skills and Word Problems.

GO for Help

For Exercises	See Examples
4–6	1
7–10	2
11–12	3

Find the area of each parallelogram or triangle.

4.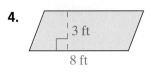
3 ft
8 ft

5.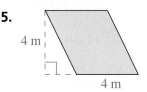
4 m
4 m

6.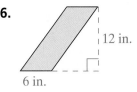
12 in.
6 in.

7.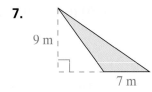
9 m
7 m

8.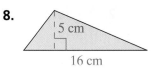
5 cm
16 cm

9.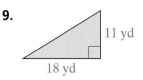
11 yd
18 yd

10. **Art** You sprinkle glitter on a triangular area of a card. The triangle has a base of 5 cm and a height of 10 cm. What is the area of the triangle?

Find the area of each complex figure.

11.
5 ft
1 ft
1 ft
2 ft
2 ft

12.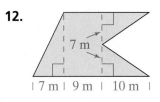
7 m
7 m 9 m 10 m

GPS 13. **Guided Problem Solving** Find the area of the trapezoid at the right.
   • How can you split the trapezoid into two triangles?
   • Find the area of the two triangles.

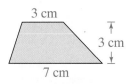
3 cm
3 cm
7 cm

Find the area of each figure.

14.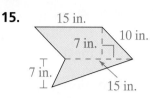
4.2 in. | 5 in.
6 in.

15.
15 in.
7 in. | 10 in.
7 in.
15 in.

16.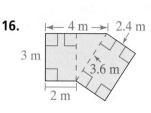
4 m | 2.4 m
3 m
3.6 m
2 m

Parking spaces are sometimes shaped like parallelograms.

17. Parking Each space at the left has a width of 10.5 feet and a length of 21 feet. Find the area of a parking space.

18. Number Sense Two parallelograms have the same base length. The height of the first is half the height of the second. What is the ratio of the area of the smaller parallelogram to the area of the larger one?

19. (**Algebra**) A parallelogram has an area of 66 in.² and a base length of 5 inches. What is the height of the parallelogram?

20. Writing in Math Suppose you know the perimeter and the height of an equilateral triangle. Explain how you would find the area of the triangle.

21. Challenge A parallelogram has an area of 4 ft² and a base length of 8 in. What is the height of the parallelogram?

Test Prep and Mixed Review **Practice**

Multiple Choice

22. Hue cut out the triangle at the right for a craft project. What is the area of the triangle?
(A) 12 ft² (C) 54 ft²
(B) 24 ft² (D) 10 ft²

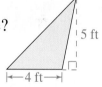
5 ft
4 ft

23. Isaac makes 3 out of 5 free throws. If he attempts 100 free throws, how many would you expect him to make?
(F) 15 (G) 30 (H) 60 (J) 75

24. Lorenzo started doing homework at 4:15 P.M. He finished at 6:00 P.M. How long did Lorenzo spend doing homework?
(A) 1 hour 15 minutes
(B) 1 hour 45 minutes
(C) 2 hours 15 minutes
(D) 2 hours 45 minutes

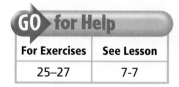

For Exercises	See Lesson
25–27	7-7

Find each answer.

25. 50% of 492 **26.** 35% of 84 **27.** 15% of 120

1. Choose an appropriate metric unit of length for a baseball bat.

2. Choose an appropriate metric unit of mass for a backpack.

Convert each measurement to meters, liters, or grams.

3. 62 milliliters

4. 4.3 kilograms

5. 178 centimeters

6. 0.31 centigrams

7. 0.5 kiloliters

8. 83 milligrams

Find the perimeter and area of a figure with the given dimensions.

9. square: $s = 8.5$ cm

10. rectangle: $\ell = 9$ mi, $w = 4$ mi

Find the area of each figure.

11.
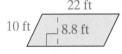
22 ft
10 ft 8.8 ft

12.
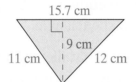
15.7 cm
9 cm
11 cm   12 cm

13.
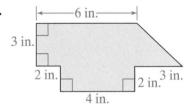
6 in.
3 in.
2 in.
2 in. 3 in.
4 in.

 **MATH AT WORK**

Event Planner

Event planners organize and arrange all the details for parties, business meetings, and other group activities. Their responsibilities include finding the meeting place, choosing the menu, and arranging the decorations for an event.

Geometry is useful to event planners as they determine dimensions for room sizes, arrange rectangular or circular tables, and plan serving areas.

Go Online
PHSchool.com
For: Information on event planners
Web Code: aqb-2031

Exploring Circles

Recall that the perimeter of a figure is the distance around the figure. In this activity, you will explore the distance around a circle.

ACTIVITY

Materials: several circular objects, metric tape measure

1. Find several objects with circular bases, such as a can or a wastebasket.

2. Copy the table shown below.

Object	Distance around the circle	Distance across the circle	Distance around the circle / Distance across the circle

3. Measure the longest distance across each circle to the nearest tenth of a centimeter. Record the results in your table.

4. Measure the distance around each circle by wrapping the tape measure around the outside of each circle. Measure to the nearest tenth of a centimeter. Record the results in your table.

5. **Calculator** Find the ratio $\frac{\text{distance around the circle}}{\text{distance across the circle}}$ for each circle, to the nearest tenth. Record the results in your table.

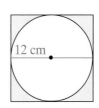

6. **Patterns** What do you notice about the relationship between the distance around a circle and the distance across the circle?

7. **(Algebra)** Suppose the distance across a circle is x. Write an expression to approximate the distance around the circle.

8. a. Estimate the distance around the circle in the diagram.
   b. Find the perimeter of the square.
   c. What is the difference between your estimate of the distance around the circle and the perimeter of the square?

12 cm

9-5 Circles and Circumference

✓ Check Skills You'll Need

1. Vocabulary Review
When you multiply two or more numbers, you are finding a _?_.

Estimate each product.

2. 2×3.14

3. 3.14×8

4. $2 \times 3.14 \times 35$

5. $2 \times 3.14 \times 10$

 **for Help**
Lesson 1-8

What You'll Learn

To identify the parts of a circle and to find the radius, diameter, and circumference

🔊 **New Vocabulary** circle, radius, chord, diameter, circumference

Why Learn This?

To build a circular structure, such as a Ferris wheel, engineers must understand the relationships between the parts of a circle.

A **circle** is the set of points in a plane that are the same distance from a given point called the center.

A **radius** is a segment that connects the center to the circle.

A **chord** is a segment that has both endpoints on the circle.

A **diameter** is a chord that passes through the center of a circle.

Center

EXAMPLE Identifying Parts of a Circle

Vocabulary Tip

Radii (RAY dee eye) is the plural of radius.

1 **a.** List the radii shown in circle P.
The radii are $\overline{PA}$, $\overline{PB}$, $\overline{PC}$, and $\overline{PD}$.

b. List the chords shown in circle P.
The chords are $\overline{AB}$, $\overline{BC}$, $\overline{CD}$, $\overline{DA}$, $\overline{AC}$, and $\overline{BD}$.

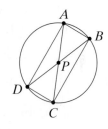

✓ Quick Check

● **1.** List the diameters shown in circle P.

In Example 1, the diameter $\overline{AC}$ consists of two radii $\overline{PA}$ and $\overline{PC}$. The length of a diameter of a circle is twice the length of a radius.

Finding the Radius and Diameter

2 **Amusement Parks** The diameter of a Ferris wheel is 250 feet. What is its radius?

$$r = \frac{1}{2} \times 250 \quad \leftarrow \text{The radius is half the diameter, or } r = \frac{1}{2}d.$$

$$= 125 \qquad \leftarrow \text{Simplify.}$$

The radius of the Ferris wheel is 125 feet.

✓ Quick Check

2. Find the radius when $d = 8$ cm.

For help with the ratio of circumference to diameter, see Activity Lab 9-5a.

The distance around a circle is its **circumference.** The ratio of the circumference C of a circle to its diameter d is the same for *every* circle. The symbol π (read "pi") represents this ratio. So $\pi = \frac{C}{d}$.

You can rewrite the relationship $\pi = \frac{C}{d}$ as $C = \pi \times d$, or πd.

KEY CONCEPTS **Circumference of a Circle**

$C = \pi d$

$C = 2\pi r$

EXAMPLE **Finding Circumference**

3 **Multiple Choice** A regulation archery target is a circle with a 24-inch radius. Which equation can be used to find the circumference of the archery target?

Ⓐ $C = 2 \cdot 12$ Ⓒ $C = \pi \cdot 24$

Ⓑ $C = \pi \cdot 12$ Ⓓ $C = 2\pi \cdot 24$

$$C = 2\pi r \qquad\quad \leftarrow \text{Use the formula for the circumference of a circle.}$$

$$= 2 \times \pi \times 24 \quad \leftarrow \text{Substitute 24 for } r.$$

$$= 48\pi \qquad\qquad \leftarrow \text{Multiply.}$$

The correct answer is choice D.

✓ Quick Check

3. A circle has a radius of 11 m. What expression describes the circumference of the circle in meters?

Pi is a nonrepeating, nonterminating decimal. Two approximations for π are 3.14 and $\frac{22}{7}$. Use $\frac{22}{7}$ when measurements are a multiple of 7 or involve fractions. You can also use the π key on a calculator.

EXAMPLE **Calculating Circumference of a Circle**

4 Find the circumference of a circle with a 48-inch diameter. Round to the nearest inch.

Test Prep Tip

Be careful to use the correct formula to find circumference.

$C = \pi d$ ← Use the formula for the circumference of a circle.

$\approx 3.14 \times 48$ ← Substitute 48 for d and 3.14 for π.

$= 150.72$ ← Multiply.

The circumference is 151 inches.

✓ Quick Check

4. Find the circumference of a circle with a diameter of 5.8 centimeters. Round to the nearest centimeter.

Check Your Understanding

1. **Vocabulary** Is it possible for a chord of a circle not to be a diameter of the circle? Explain.

2. **Reasoning** Draw a circle with a radius greater than 2 in. and a circumference less than 15 in.

Homework Exercises

For more exercises, see Extra Skills and Word Problems.

GO for Help

For Exercises	See Examples
3–6	1
7–10	2
11–17	3–4

Identify each of the following for circle Q.

3. three radii   4. one diameter

5. two chords   6. center

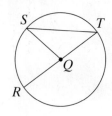

Find the unknown length for each circle.

7. $r = 35$ mi, $d = $ ■   8. $d = 6.8$ yd, $r = $ ■

9. $r = 18$ ft, $d = $ ■   10. $d = 0.25$ km, $r = $ ■

11. A circular water tank has a radius of 4 m. What expression describes the circumference of the tank in meters?

Find the circumference of each circle.

12.
9 cm

13.
5 in.

14.
23 ft

15. $d = 28$ mi   **16.** $r = 7$ ft   **17.** $d = 10$ m

18. Guided Problem Solving You need to cut a circular piece of wood with a circumference of 20.5 cm. What radius should you use to draw the circle?
- Which formula should you use to find the radius, $C = \pi d$ or $C = 2\pi r$?
- How can you use the formula to find the radius?

Estimate the radius of a circle with the given circumference.

19. 192 ft   **20.** 1,273 m   **21.** 3.75 in.   **22.** 12.4 mi

23. A dog trainer uses hoops with diameters of 24 and 30 inches. What is the difference between the circumferences? Use 3 for π.

24. Writing in Math A pebble is stuck in a bicycle's tire. As the tire turns, the pebble leaves a mark every 69 inches. Explain how you would find the circumference of the tire.

25. Challenge The diameter of a bicycle wheel is 2 feet. How far will the bicycle travel when the wheel makes one full turn?

Test Prep and Mixed Review   **Practice**

Multiple Choice

26. Which statement about the parts of a circle is NOT true?
Ⓐ The radius is half as long as the diameter.
Ⓑ The diameter is four times as long as the radius.
Ⓒ The circumference is about 6 times the radius.
Ⓓ The circumference is about 3 times the diameter.

27. Which type of angle measures 180°?
Ⓕ Acute   Ⓗ Right
Ⓖ Obtuse   Ⓙ Straight

GO for Help

For Exercises	See Lesson
28–29	2-2

Find the median of each data set.

28. 50, 20, 42, 45, 48, 50   **29.** 8.0, 7.5, 6.6, 7.8, 7.5

GPS Guided Problem Solving

Practice Solving Problems

Suppose you used 1 gallon of paint to paint a wall that is 20 ft long and 12 ft high. Each dimension of another wall is twice the dimension of the wall you painted. Will 2 gallons be enough paint for the larger wall? Explain.

What You Might Think

What do I know? What do I want to find?

What is the area of the painted wall?

What is the area of the wall with dimensions twice as great?

How many square feet will 2 gallons of paint cover?

Is the area of the unpainted wall twice the area of the painted wall?

What You Might Write

- I used 1 gallon to paint a wall 20 ft by 12 ft.

- I need to find out whether 2 gallons will be enough paint for a wall that is twice the length and width of the wall I painted.

$A = 20$ ft $\times 12$ ft or 240 ft^2. So 1 gallon of paint covered 240 ft^2.

The unpainted wall is 40 ft by 24 ft. The area of the unpainted wall is 40 ft $\times$ 24 ft, or 960 ft^2.

One gallon covered 240 ft^2, so 2 gallons will cover 2×240 ft^2, or 480 ft^2.

The area of the unpainted wall is more than twice as much as the area of the painted wall. So 2 gallons is not enough paint.

Think It Through

1. Suppose you want to paint 720 ft^2. How many gallons of paint do you need?

2. Find the number of square feet painted per gallon. Write your answer as a unit rate.

3. **Check for Reasonableness** How many gallons of paint are needed to paint the unpainted wall? How did you decide?

Exercises

4. You have 34 feet of fence to enclose a rectangular garden. You want the length of each side to be a whole number. What dimensions of the garden enclose the greatest area?
 a. What do you know?
 b. What do you want to find?
 c. Find the enclosed area.

$$A = b \times h$$
$$= \blacksquare \times \blacksquare$$
$$= \blacksquare \text{ ft}^2$$

5. What will it cost to tile the floor shown below with 1-foot square tiles costing $3.75 each? Assume that you can buy the exact number of tiles you need.

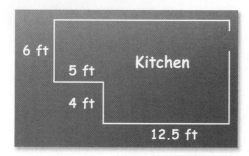

6. A rectangular figure is 9 times the area of the figure shown below. Draw the larger figure showing its dimensions. Explain how you decided on the dimensions.

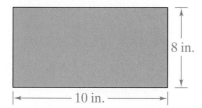

7. In one season, the total payroll for the Cleveland Browns was $87.7 million. The total payroll for the San Francisco 49ers was $63.0 million. About how many times greater was the payroll for the Browns?

What You'll Learn

To find the area of a circle

Why Learn This?

To plant crops on a farm using a center-pivot irrigation system, farmers must calculate the area of a circle.

Suppose you cut a circle into equal-sized wedges. You can rearrange the wedges into a figure that resembles a parallelogram.

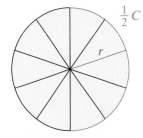

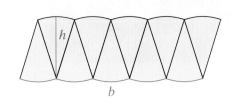

The base of the parallelogram is one half of the circumference of the circle, or πr. The height of the parallelogram is the same length as the circle's radius.

$A = b \times h$ ← Use the formula for the area of a parallelogram.

$= \pi r \times r$ ← Substitute πr for b and r for h.

$= \pi r^2$ ← Simplify.

The calculations suggest a formula for the area of a circle.

GO for Help

For help finding the area of a parallelogram, go to Lesson 9-4, Example 1.

KEY CONCEPTS **Area of a Circle**

$A = \pi r^2$

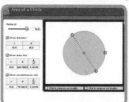
EXAMPLE Finding the Area of a Circle

① Find the area of the circle at the right.

5 ft

Estimate $A \approx 3 \times 5^2$, or 75

$$A = \pi r^2 \quad \leftarrow \text{Use the formula for the area of a circle.}$$

$$\approx 3.14 \times 5^2 \quad \leftarrow \text{Substitute 5 for } r \text{ and 3.14 for } \pi.$$

$$= 78.5 \quad \leftarrow \text{Multiply.}$$

The area is about 78.5 square feet.

Check for Reasonableness The estimate, 75 square feet, is close to 78.5 square feet. So the answer is reasonable.

✓ Quick Check

1. Find the area of each circle. Use 3.14 for π.

a.

12 km

b.

3 in.

c.
8 yd

When the radius or diameter of a circle is a multiple of 7 or a fraction, you may find it easier to use $\frac{22}{7}$ for π.

EXAMPLE Application: Mirrors

Circular mirrors are used in telescopes.

② Find the area of the circular mirror at the left with a diameter of 14 inches. Use $\frac{22}{7}$ for π.

The radius is one half of the diameter, or 7 inches.

$$A = \pi r^2 \quad \leftarrow \text{Use the formula for the area of a circle.}$$

$$\approx \frac{22}{7} \times 7^2 \quad \leftarrow \text{Use } \frac{22}{7} \text{ for } \pi \text{ and 7 for } r.$$

$$= \frac{22}{\overset{}{\underset{1}{7}}} \times \overset{7}{49} \quad \leftarrow \text{Divide 7 and 49 by their GCF, 7.}$$

$$= 154 \quad \leftarrow \text{Multiply.}$$

The area of the mirror is about 154 square inches.

✓ Quick Check

2. Find the area of a large pizza with a 14-inch diameter. Use $\frac{22}{7}$ for π.

1. Find the area of a pie with a radius of 14 cm. Use $\frac{22}{7}$ for π.

2. **Patterns** Find the area of each circle. Use 3.14 for π.
   a. $r = 2$ in.   **b.** $r = 4$ in.   **c.** $r = 8$ in.
   d. What happens to the area of a circle when you double the radius?

Mental Math **Estimate the area of each circle. Use 3 for π.**

3. $r = 2$ in.   4. $d = 6$ mm   5. $r = 20$ cm   6. $d = 16$ ft

Homework Exercises

For more exercises, see Extra Skills and Word Problems.

 for Help

For Exercises	See Examples
7–12	1
13–16	2

Find the area of each circle. Use 3.14 for π.

7.
8 mm

8.
26 km

9.
37 ft

10. $d = 32$ in.   11. $r = 11$ yd   12. $d = 12$ cm

Find the area of each circle. Use $\frac{22}{7}$ for π.

13.
$2\frac{1}{3}$ mm

14.
$4\frac{1}{2}$ in.

15.
21 mi

16. **Camping** Campers arrange stones in a circle around their campfire site. The circle has a diameter of 14 feet. Find the area of the site.

17. **Guided Problem Solving** The Aztecs used their knowledge of astronomy and mathematics to make a calendar. They carved the calendar, called the Sun Stone, on a circular stone 3.6 meters in diameter. Find the area of the Sun Stone. Use 3.14 for π.
   • What is the radius of the stone?
   • What unit of measure will your answer include?

Find the area of each circle. Use 3.14 for π. Round your answer to the nearest tenth.

18. $r = 1.1$ mi   **19.** $d = 2.4$ cm   **20.** $r = 0.5$ m   **21.** $d = 13.7$ ft

22. <u>Writing in Math</u> Does a circular pan with a diameter of 20 in. have a greater area than a square pan 18 inches long? Explain.

Vocabulary Tip

The prefix *semi-* means "half." A semicircle is one half of a circle.

23. Games The hopscotch figure at the right is composed of squares and a semicircle. Suppose the side lengths of each square are 2 feet. Find the area of the hopscotch figure.

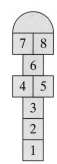

24. You can pick up the signal of one radio station within 45 miles of the station. Find the approximate area of the broadcast region.

Find the area of each yellow region. Use 3.14 for π.

25.

12 cm

26.
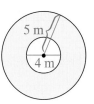
5 m
4 m

27.
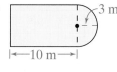
3 m
10 m

28. Find the area of a circle with a circumference of 31.4 units.

29. Challenge The diameter of a circle is tripled. How does this affect the area of the circle?

Test Prep and Mixed Review
Practice

Multiple Choice

30. Which expression can Jack use to find the area of a circle with diameter d and radius r?
(A) πr^2 (B) $2\pi r$ (C) πd^2 (D) πd

31. The circumference of a circle is about 18.84 meters. Estimate the approximate length of the radius of the circle.
(F) 3 m   (G) 6 m   (H) 9 m   (J) 12 m

Trace each figure and draw the lines of symmetry.

32.

33.

34.
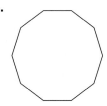

Three-Dimensional Views

You can draw three-dimensional objects so that they appear to have length, width, and height. You can also draw different views of the blocks.

ACTIVITY

FRONT   RIGHT

1. Stack 6 blocks as shown at the right.

2. Make three different drawings. Draw a view from the:
   a. top   **b.** front   **c.** right side

Top View

Front View

Right Side View

Exercises

Use blocks or centimeter cubes to build the figures below. Then draw the top, front, and right side views of each figure.

1.

FRONT   RIGHT

2.

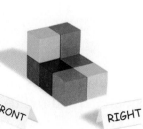

FRONT   RIGHT

3.

FRONT   RIGHT

Reasoning Use the drawings below. Make a figure of blocks for each set of views.

4.

Top View

Front View

Right Side View

5.

Top View

Front View

Right Side View

Check Skills You'll Need

1. Vocabulary Review
Describe a *rectangle* that is not a *square*.

Identify each polygon by the numbers of sides.

2.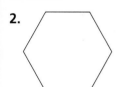

3.

GO for Help
Lesson 8-5

What You'll Learn

To identify three-dimensional figures

🔊 **New Vocabulary** three-dimensional figure, faces, edge, vertex, prism, cube, pyramid, cylinder, cone, sphere

Why Learn This?

Architects use shapes to design buildings. To identify these figures, you need to understand how they differ.

A **three-dimensional figure** is a figure that does not lie in a plane. It has three dimensions: length, width, and height.

The flat surfaces of a three-dimensional figure are called **faces**.

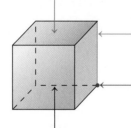

An **edge** is a segment where two faces meet.

A **vertex** is a point where two or more edges meet.

When you draw three-dimensional figures, use dashed lines to indicate "hidden" edges.

A **prism** is a three-dimensional figure with two parallel and congruent faces that are polygons. These faces are called bases. The prism above is a **cube**. All of its faces are congruent.

Vocabulary Tip

Three-dimensional is often abbreviated as 3-D.

Base Shape	Name of Prism
Triangle	Triangular Prism
Rectangle	Rectangular Prism
Pentagon	Pentagonal Prism
Hexagon	Hexagonal Prism
Heptagon	Heptagonal Prism
Octagon	Octagonal Prism

You name a prism by the shape of its bases.

Test Prep Tip

When naming a 3-D figure, identify the shape of its base. Then determine whether the faces meet at one vertex.

EXAMPLE **Naming Prisms**

1 Name the prism shown.

Each base is a hexagon. So the figure is a hexagonal prism.

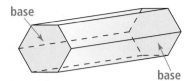
base

base

✓ Quick Check

1. Name each prism.

a.

b.

c.

A **pyramid** is a three-dimensional figure with one polygon for a base. All of the other faces are triangles. The faces all meet at one vertex. You name a pyramid by its base.

Some three-dimensional figures do not have polygons for bases.

rectangular pyramid

A **cylinder** has two congruent parallel bases that are circles.

A **cone** has one circular base and one vertex.

A **sphere** has no base.

EXAMPLE **Identifying Three-Dimensional Figures**

2 **Museum** The American Museum of Natural History in New York City is shown at the right. Name a three-dimensional figure in the photo.

The sphere in the photo is a three-dimensional figure without a base.

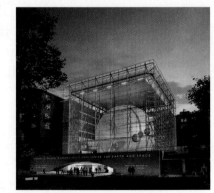

✓ Quick Check

2. Name another three-dimensional figure in the photo.

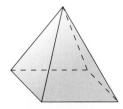

1. **Vocabulary** How are a prism and a pyramid alike? How are they different?

2. **Writing in Math** Describe the shape of the square pyramid at the left.

Label each figure as a *cylinder, cone,* or *sphere*.

3.

4.

5.

Homework Exercises

For more exercises, see Extra Skills and Word Problems.

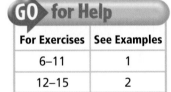

For Exercises	See Examples
6–11	1
12–15	2

Name each prism.

6.

7.

8.

9.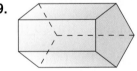

10.

11.

Structures Name a three-dimensional figure in each photo.

12.

13.

14.

15.

16. Guided Problem Solving Name the figure at the right. Find the number of faces, vertices, and edges in the figure.
- What is the shape of the base in the figure?
- How many faces does the figure have?

17. Name the figure. Then find the number of faces, vertices, and edges in the figure.

18. Reasoning In a prism, what shape are the faces that are not the base?

Art You can use translations to draw three-dimensional figures.

Step 1 Draw a figure on graph paper.	**Step 2** Translate the figure.	**Step 3** Connect each vertex with its image.	**Step 4** Use dashes for hidden lines.

19. Start with a triangle. Draw a three-dimensional figure.

20. Start with a pentagon. Draw a three-dimensional figure.

21. Challenge Describe the translation used in Steps 1–4. Redraw the rectangle. Use a different translation to draw the figure.

Test Prep and Mixed Review   Practice

Multiple Choice

22. A meteorologist listed the high temperatures for one week as 74°F, 70°F, 72°F, 75°F, 79°F, 80°F, and 82°F. What was the range of high temperatures?
- Ⓐ 82°F
- Ⓑ 70°F
- Ⓒ 12°F
- Ⓓ 8°F

23. Brittany drank one gallon of water in one weekend. Which measurement could NOT be expressed as one gallon?
- Ⓕ 4 quarts
- Ⓖ 8 pints
- Ⓗ 16 cups
- Ⓙ 32 ounces

24. A shirt that originally costs $20 is marked 30% off. Find the sale price.

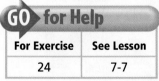

For Exercise	See Lesson
24	7-7

Surface Areas of Prisms

Check Skills You'll Need

1. **Vocabulary Review** Describe the *area* of a piece of paper.

Find the area of each rectangle.

2. $\ell = 7$ m, $w = 3$ m

3. $\ell = 10$ m, $w = 6$ m

GO for Help
Lesson 9-3

What You'll Learn

To use nets and to find the surface areas of rectangular prisms

◀)) **New Vocabulary** net, surface area

Why Learn This?

Package designers make creative labels. The surface area of an object is the space designers have to work with.

A **net** is a pattern you can fold to form a three-dimensional figure.

	Front	
	Top	
Side	Back	Side
	Bottom	

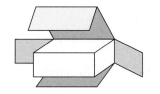 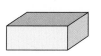

EXAMPLE Drawing a Net

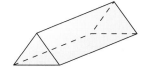

1 Draw a net for the triangular prism at the left.

Step 1 Draw one base. ⟶ Back

Step 2 Draw one face that connects the two bases.

| Left side | Bottom | Right side |

Step 4 Draw the remaining faces.

Step 3 Draw the other base. ⟶ Front

Quick Check

1. Draw a net for a cube.

The surface area of a three-dimensional figure is the sum of the areas of its surfaces.

h = 10 cm

w = 3 cm

ℓ = 6 cm

EXAMPLE Finding the Surface Area of a Prism

2 **Package Design** Find the surface area of the juice box at the left.

Step 1 Draw and label a net for the prism.

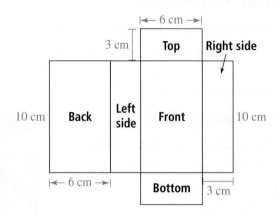

Step 2 Find and add the areas of all the rectangles.

    Top   Back   Left   Front   Right   Bottom

$3 \times 6 + 10 \times 6 + 10 \times 3 + 10 \times 6 + 10 \times 3 + 3 \times 6$

$= \quad 18 \quad + \quad 60 \quad + \quad 30 \quad + \quad 60 \quad + \quad 30 \quad + \quad 18$

$= 216$

The surface area of the juice box is 216 square centimeters.

✓ Quick Check

2. Find the surface area of the prism.

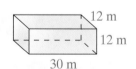

12 m

12 m

30 m

✓ Check Your Understanding

1. **Vocabulary** Describe how a net can help you find the surface area of an object.

Find the surface area. A small cube measures 1 cm on a side.

2.

3.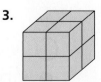

For more exercises, see Extra Skills and Word Problems.

GO for Help

For Exercises	See Examples
4–6	1
7–13	2

Draw a net for each three-dimensional figure.

4.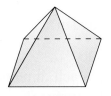

5.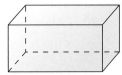

6.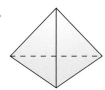

Find the surface area of each prism.

7.
3 cm · 3 cm · 5 cm

8.
8 m · 17 m · 15 m · 10 m

9.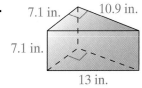
6 ft · 6 ft · 6 ft

10.
9 m · 8 m · 12 m

11.
20 in. · 15 in. · 7 in.

12.
7.1 in. · 10.9 in. · 7.1 in. · 13 in.

13. The platform of the Taj Mahal in India is a rectangular prism. It is 95 m long, 95 m wide, and 7 m high. Find the surface area of the platform.

14. **Guided Problem Solving**
Find the surface area of the spaghetti box.
Spaghetti · 7 cm · 27 cm · 3 cm
- **Understand the Problem**
  Draw a net of the figure, and label all sides.
- **Make a Plan** Find the area of each surface of the box. Then add the areas to find the total surface area.

15. **Writing in Math** Suppose each dimension of a rectangular prism is doubled. How is the surface area affected?

16. Which of the following cannot be the dimensions of the piece of wrapping paper used to wrap the box?
4 in. · 9 in. · 15 in.
- Ⓐ 20 in. by 28 in.
- Ⓒ 40 in. by 10 in.
- Ⓑ 36 in. by 18 in.
- Ⓓ 24 in. by 24 in.

17. **Reasoning** The surface area of a cube is 54 square inches. What is the length of each edge?

GO Online
Homework Video Tutor
Visit: PHSchool.com
Web Code: aqe-0908

Find the surface area of each rectangular prism.

18. $\ell = 3$ m, $w = 2.2$ m, $h = 11$ m

19. $\ell = 6.3$ in., $w = 5$ in., $h = 8$ in.

20. (Algebra) What is the surface area of a cube whose edges are s units long?

21. Challenge Suppose each dimension of a cube is increased. What happens to the surface area when each dimension is doubled? Tripled? Quadrupled?

Test Prep and Mixed Review

Practice

Multiple Choice

22. Oscar pays $6 to enter the county fair. Then his mother gives him $10. He buys 20 ride tickets for $12 and a cold drink for $3. Oscar has $4 left. Which expression can Oscar use to find the amount of money he had before entering the fair?

    Ⓐ $4 - 3 - 12 + 10 - 6$ Ⓒ $6 + 10 - 12 - 3 + 4$

    Ⓑ $4 + 3 + 12 - 10 + 6$ Ⓓ $6 - 10 + 12 + 3 - 4$

23. Find the area of the circle at the right.

    Ⓕ 5π ft^2

    Ⓖ 10π ft^2

    Ⓗ 25π ft^2

    Ⓙ 100π ft^2

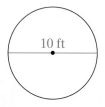

24. Which of the following is the measure of an obtuse angle?

    Ⓐ $5°$ Ⓑ $90°$ Ⓒ $135°$ Ⓓ $180°$

25. The circle graph shows the percents of chorus members who sing soprano, alto, tenor, and bass. Which statement is NOT supported by the circle graph?

    Ⓕ The chorus has the same number of sopranos and altos.

    Ⓖ The chorus has 100 members.

    Ⓗ One fourth of the members sing bass.

    Ⓙ The fewest members sing tenor.

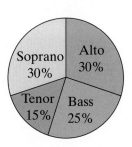

GO for Help

For Exercises	See Lesson
26–29	9-1

Choose an appropriate metric unit of measure.

26. capacity of a pond

27. capacity of a thimble

28. mass of a pencil

29. mass of a brick

Exploring Volume

You can use centimeter cubes to find how much space is inside a rectangular prism.

1. Use centimeter cubes to build each rectangular prism. Use your models to find the missing values in the table.

Rectangular Prism	Length	Width	Height	Total Number of Cubes
height width length	2	4	3	▪
height width length	▪	▪	▪	▪
height width length	▪	▪	▪	▪

2. Use 60 cubes to build a rectangular prism with a width of 3 cubes and a height of 4 cubes.

3. Find the length of your rectangular prism.

4. **Algebra** Use the words *base* and *height* to write a formula to calculate the volume of a rectangular prism.

5. **Reasoning** Use your formula to find the volume of a rectangular prism that is 10 cm long, 5 cm wide, and 4 cm high.

6. Use centimeter cubes to find eleven rectangular prisms that have a volume of 24 cubic centimeters. Record in a table the width, length, and height of each prism.

7. **Writing in Math** Add a column to your table and record the surface areas. Explain why rectangular prisms with the same volume can have different surface areas.

Volumes of Rectangular Prisms

What You'll Learn

To find the volume of rectangular prisms

🔊 **New Vocabulary** volume, cubic unit

Why Learn This?

The volume of a fish tank tells you how much water the tank can hold. You can use volume to find the amount of space that is inside an object.

A **cubic unit** is the amount of space in a cube that measures 1 unit long by 1 unit wide by 1 unit high. The **volume** of a three-dimensional figure is the number of cubic units needed to fill the space inside the figure.

EXAMPLE Counting Cubes to Find Volume

1 Find the volume of the rectangular prism.

Each layer of the prism is 5 cubes by 3 cubes. This equals 5×3, or 15 cubes. The prism is 4 layers high. So the prism has a total of 4×15, or 60 cubes.

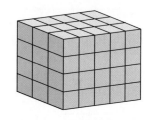

The volume of the prism is 60 cubic units.

✓ Quick Check

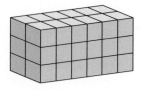

1. Find the volume of the rectangular prism at the left.

KEY CONCEPTS Volume of a Prism

volume = area of base × height
$$V = B \times h$$

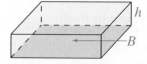

For a rectangular prism, the area of a base is $\ell \times w$, since the base is a rectangle. So the volume formula is $V = \ell \times w \times h$. Common cubic units used in measuring volume are cubic centimeters (cm^3), cubic inches, ($in.^3$), and cubic feet (ft^3).

EXAMPLE **Finding the Volume of a Prism**

10 in.

12 in.

20 in.

2 Fish Tanks Find the volume of the fish tank shown at the left.

$V = \ell \times w \times h$ ← Use the formula for the volume of a rectangular prism.

$\quad = 20 \times 10 \times 12$ ← Substitute 20 for ℓ, 10 for w, and 12 for h.

$\quad = 2,400$ ← Multiply.

The volume is 2,400 cubic inches, or 2,400 $in.^3$.

✓ Quick Check

2. Find the volume of a rectangular prism with a length of 8 meters, a width of 7 meters, and a height of 10 meters.

✓ Check Your Understanding

1. **Vocabulary** How are volume and area different?

2. **Number Sense** How does the volume of a cube change if its dimensions are doubled?

Find the volume of each rectangular prism.

3. $\ell = 6$ m, $w = 4$ m, $h = 11$ m   4. $\ell = 3$ ft, $w = 2$ ft, $h = 9$ ft

Homework Exercises

For more exercises, see **Extra Skills and Word Problems.**

Find the volume of each rectangular prism.

GO for Help

For Exercises	See Examples
5–7	1
8–10	2

5.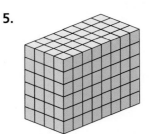

6.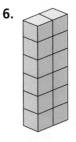

7.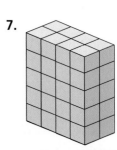

Find the volume of each rectangular prism.

8.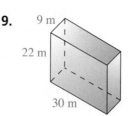
6 ft
5 ft
7 ft

9.
9 m
22 m
30 m

10.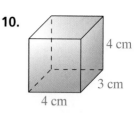
4 cm
3 cm
4 cm
4 cm

11. Guided Problem Solving The shape of a monument is a hexagonal prism. The area of the base is 5.4 square feet and the height is 13 feet. Find the volume.
 • Which formula should you use, $V = B \times h$ or $V = \ell \times w \times h$?

12. Writing in Math Two rectangular prisms have the same base area. The height of the second prism is twice the height of the first prism. How do their volumes compare? Explain.

13. Reasoning One ton of coal fills a bin that is 5 ft by 4 ft by 2 ft. Find the dimensions of a bin that holds 2 tons of coal.

14. A truck trailer has a length of 20 feet, a width of 8 feet, and a height of 7 feet. A second trailer has a base area of 108 square feet and a height of 8 feet. Which trailer has a greater volume? How much greater is it?

15. Challenge A swimming pool is 24 meters long and 16 meters wide. The average depth of the water is 2.5 meters. How many 2-liter bottles of water do you need to fill the pool? (*Hint*: $1 \text{ m}^3 = 1,000 \text{ L}$)

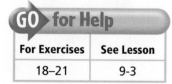
Test Prep and Mixed Review **Practice**

Multiple Choice

16. A rectangular prism measures 2 meters long, 50 centimeters wide, and 1 meter high. Find the volume of the prism.
 Ⓐ 1 cubic meter
 Ⓒ 100 cubic centimeters
 Ⓑ 100 cubic meters
 Ⓓ 10,000 cubic centimeters

17. What missing piece of information is needed to find the area of the parallelogram?
 Ⓕ Side length
 Ⓗ Height
 Ⓖ Base length
 Ⓙ Perimeter

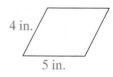
4 in.
5 in.

GO for Help

For Exercises	See Lesson
18–21	9-3

Find the area of each square with the given perimeter.

18. 12 m **19.** 24 ft **20.** 34 cm **21.** 25 in.

1. The circumference of a circular cover is 66 ft. What is the area of the cover?

Name each figure.

2.

3.

4.

5.

Use the rectangular prism at the right for Exercises 6 and 7.

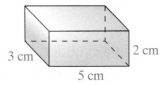
3 cm   2 cm   5 cm

6. Find the surface area.

7. Find the volume.

9-10a   Activity Lab

Hands On

Exploring Cylinders

A solid with a circular base is called a *cylinder*. You can find the surface area and volume of a cylinder.

ACTIVITY

1. On a sheet of paper, draw two circles, each with a diameter of 3.5 inches. Cut out each circle.

2. Find the area of each circle. Label each circle with its area. Label a second sheet of $8\frac{1}{2}'' \times 11''$ paper with its area.

3. Tape the $8\frac{1}{2}$-inch edges of the second sheet of paper to form a tube. Tape a circle to each open end to form a cylinder.

4. **Writing in Math** Explain how you can use the areas of the circles and rectangle to find the surface area of the cylinder.

5. Find the surface area of the cylinder.

$r = 1.75$ in.
$h = 8.5$ in.

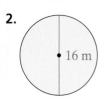

What You'll Learn

To find the surface area and volume of cylinders

Why Learn This?

Food cans are usually in the shape of a cylinder. Knowing how to find the volume of a cylinder can help you find the amount of food in one can.

If you carefully peel the label from a can as shown, you will see that the label is a rectangle.

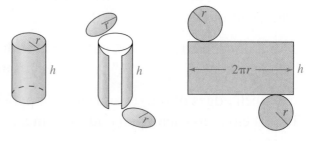

Fresh Golden

SWEET CORN

The height of the rectangle is the height of the can.

The base length of the rectangle is the circumference of the can.

Suppose you draw a net of the cylinder that is the actual vegetable can. You will see that the can is made up of a rectangle and two circles.

You can find the surface area of a cylinder by finding the area of its net.

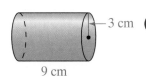

3 cm

9 cm

1 Find the surface area of the cylinder at the left. Use 3.14 for π.

Step 1 Draw and label a net for the cylinder.

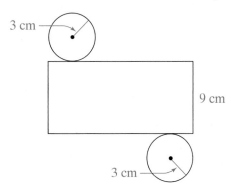

3 cm

9 cm

3 cm

Step 2 Find the area of one circle.

$$A = \pi r^2 \qquad \leftarrow \text{Use the formula.}$$

$$\approx 3.14 \times 3^2 \quad \leftarrow \text{Substitute 3 for } r \text{ and 3.14 for } \pi.$$

$$= 28.26 \qquad \leftarrow \text{Multiply.}$$

$$\approx 28.3 \qquad \leftarrow \text{Round to the nearest tenth.}$$

Step 3 Find the area of the rectangle.

$$A = \ell \times w \qquad \leftarrow \text{Use the formula.}$$

$$= \pi d \times h \qquad \leftarrow \begin{array}{l}\text{The length of the rectangle is the circumference} \\ \text{of the circle. The width of the rectangle} \\ \text{is the height of the cylinder.}\end{array}$$

$$\approx 3.14(6) \times 9 \quad \leftarrow \text{Substitute 6 for } d, \text{ 9 for } h, \text{ and 3.14 for } \pi.$$

$$= 169.56 \qquad \leftarrow \text{Multiply.}$$

$$\approx 169.6 \qquad \leftarrow \text{Round to the nearest tenth.}$$

Step 4 Add the areas of the two circles and the rectangle.

$$28.3 + 28.3 + 169.6 = 226.2$$

The surface area of the cylinder is about 226.2 square centimeters.

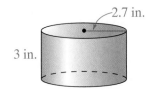

2.7 in.

3 in.

✓ Quick Check

1. Find the surface area of the cylinder at the left. Use 3.14 for π. Round to the nearest tenth.

The formula $V = B \times h$ applies to cylinders as well as prisms. For cylinders, use $A = \pi r^2$ to find the area of the base. Then multiply the area of the base by the height to find the volume of the cylinder.

EXAMPLE **Finding the Volume of a Cylinder**

2 **Food** Find the volume of the can of cheese at the left. Round to the nearest tenth. Use 3.14 for π.

Step 1 Find the area of the base.

$$B = \pi \times r^2 \qquad \leftarrow \text{Use } A = \pi r^2 \text{ to find the area of the base.}$$
$$\approx 3.14 \times 1.4^2 \qquad \leftarrow \text{Substitute 1.4 for } r \text{ and 3.14 for } \pi.$$
$$= 6.1544 \qquad \leftarrow \text{Multiply.}$$

Step 2 Find the volume.

$$V = B \times h$$
$$\approx 6.1544 \times 6 \qquad \leftarrow \text{Substitute 6.1544 for } B \text{ and 6 for } h.$$
$$= 36.9264 \qquad \leftarrow \text{Multiply.}$$

The volume is about 36.9 cubic inches, or 36.9 in.^{3}.

✓ Quick Check

2. Find the volume of a cylinder with a radius of 4 inches and a height of 9 inches. Round to the nearest cubic inch.

✓ Check Your Understanding

1. **Reasoning** Explain how the expression $2\pi r^2 + C \times h$ can be used to find the surface area of a cylinder.

2. **Writing in Math** Explain how doubling the height of a cylinder affects the volume of the cylinder.

Use the net of each cylinder to find each surface area. Use 3.14 for π.

3.
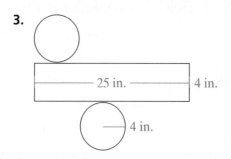
25 in.   4 in.

4 in.

4.
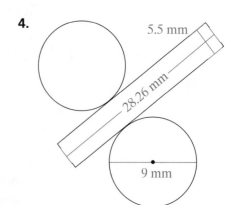
5.5 mm

28.26 mm

9 mm

For more exercises, see Extra Skills and Word Problems.

GO for Help

For Exercises	See Examples
5–7	1
8–13	2

Find the surface area of each cylinder. Use 3.14 for π. Round to the nearest tenth.

5.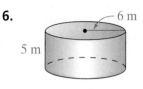
4 cm   10 cm

6.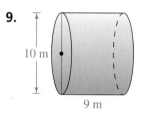
6 m
5 m

7.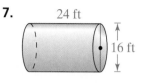
24 ft
16 ft

Find the volume of each cylinder. Use 3.14 for π. Round to the nearest tenth.

8.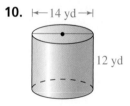
5 in.
3 in.

9.
10 m
9 m

10.
14 yd
12 yd

11.
19 ft
3 ft

12.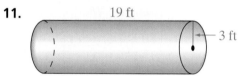
22 m
7 m

13. A drinking straw has the shape of a cylinder. Find the volume of a straw with a radius of 3 mm and a height of 200 mm.

14. **Guided Problem Solving** A tennis ball container is a cylinder with a height of 8.3 inches and a diameter of $2\frac{7}{8}$ inches. The container is open at the top. Find the surface area and volume of the tennis ball container. Use 3.14 for π.
   • What is the radius of the container?
   • Use the radius to find the area of the base.
   • Draw a net to help you find the surface area.

15. Find the surface area and volume of the battery below.

3.2 cm
5.5 cm

GO Online
Homework Video Tutor
Visit: PHSchool.com
Web Code: aqe-0910

16. **Packaging** A cardboard mailing tube is 3 inches in diameter and 20 inches long. The tube is open at both ends. Find the surface area and volume of the mailing tube.

Find the volume of each cylinder with the given dimensions. Round your answer to the nearest hundredth.

17. $r = 8.1$ cm, $h = 4$ cm

18. $r = 2.4$ in., $h = 5.4$ in.

19. $r = 9$ m, $h = 23.5$ m

20. $r = 8.2$ ft, $h = 3.2$ ft

21. (Algebra) The Great Pyramid of Khufu has a length of 230 meters, a width of 230 meters, and a height of 146 meters. Use the formula $V = \frac{1}{3} \times \ell \times w \times h$ to find the volume.

22. Challenge Find the height of a cylinder with a volume of 85 cubic feet and a radius of 2.6 feet.

ⒶⒷⒸⒹ **Test Prep and Mixed Review** **Practice**

Multiple Choice

23. The table shows edge lengths and volumes of rectangular prisms with a width of 2 inches and a height of 3 inches.

Volumes of Prisms

Length	Width	Height	Volume
1 in.	2 in.	3 in.	6 in.^{3}
2 in.	2 in.	3 in.	12 in.^{3}
3 in.	2 in.	3 in.	18 in.^{3}
n in.	2 in.	3 in.	■

Which expression can be used to find the volume, in cubic units, of a prism with a width of 2 in., a height of 3 in., and a length of n in.?

Ⓐ $n + 5$ 　　Ⓑ $n + 6$ 　　Ⓒ $5n$ 　　Ⓓ $6n$

24. Which process can Wyatt use to find the circumference of a circle?

Ⓕ Multiply the diameter by 2.
Ⓖ Multiply the radius by 2.
Ⓗ Multiply the diameter by 2π.
Ⓙ Multiply the radius by 2π.

25. Which unit should Timmy use to measure the length of a folder?

Ⓐ Inch 　　Ⓑ Foot 　　Ⓒ Yard 　　Ⓓ Mile

GO▸for Help

For Exercise	See Lesson
26	9-5

26. A dog is tied to a post with a 10-foot rope. The dog can run in a circle without wrapping the rope around the post. What is the circumference of the circle the dog makes? Round your answer to the nearest tenth.

Measuring to Solve

Some test questions ask you to measure with a protractor or ruler to solve a problem.

EXAMPLE

Emilio's yard is shaped like the quadrilateral below.

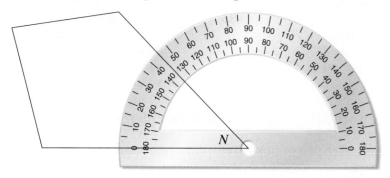

Find the measure of $\angle N$ to the nearest degree.

Ⓐ 45°   Ⓑ 55°   Ⓒ 135°   Ⓓ 145°

$\angle N$ is an acute angle, so its measure must be less than 90°. Since the side of the angle is between the 40° and 50° marks on the protractor, $\angle N$ has a measure of about 45°.

The angle measure is 45°. The correct answer is choice A.

Exercises

1. A hexagon is shown. Use a protractor to find the measure of $\angle R$ to the nearest degree.

   Ⓐ 25°
   Ⓑ 35°
   Ⓒ 155°
   Ⓓ 162°

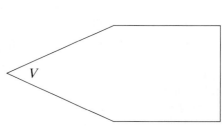

2. A pentagon is shown. Use a protractor to find the measure of $\angle V$ to the nearest degree.

   Ⓕ 48°   Ⓗ 125°
   Ⓖ 62°   Ⓙ 135°

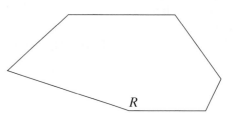

Vocabulary Review

area (p. 426)
base of a parallelogram
(p. 432)
base of a triangle (p. 433)
capacity (p. 417)
chord (p. 438)
circle (p. 438)
circumference (p. 439)
cone (p. 450)
cube (p. 449)
cubic unit (p. 458)

cylinder (p. 450)
diameter (p. 438)
edge (p. 449)
faces (p. 449)
gram (g) (p. 417)
height of a parallelogram
(p. 432)
height of a triangle (p. 433)
liter (L) (p. 417)
mass (p. 417)
meter (m) (p. 416)

metric system (p. 416)
net (p. 453)
perimeter (p. 426)
prism (p. 449)
pyramid (p. 450)
radius (p. 438)
sphere (p. 450)
surface area (p. 454)
three-dimensional figure
(p. 449)
vertex (p. 449)
volume (p. 458)

Go Online
PHSchool.com

For: Vocabulary Quiz
Web Code: aqj-0951

Choose the vocabulary term that best completes each sentence.

1. A rectangular prism has three pairs of congruent and parallel ___?___ .

2. A ___?___ is a three-dimensional figure with one base.

3. A ___?___ is a segment that connects a circle to its center.

Skills and Concepts

Lessons 9-1 and 9-2
• To use metric units of measure and to choose appropriate units of length, mass, and capacity
• To convert between metric measurements

The standard units of measurement in the **metric system** are the **meter (m),** the **gram (g),** and the **liter (L).** You can convert one metric unit to another by multiplying or dividing by a power of 10.

Complete each statement.

4. 0.3 kg = ■ g   5. 150 cm = ■ m   6. 5,700 mL = ■ L

Lessons 9-3 and 9-4
• To solve problems involving perimeters and areas of rectangles
• To solve problems involving areas of parallelograms, triangles, and complex figures

The **area** of a figure is the number of square units inside the figure. The formula for the area of a parallelogram is $A = b \times h$. The formula for the area of a triangle is $A = \frac{1}{2}b \times h$.

Find the perimeter and the area of each figure.

7.
6 ft
7 ft
8 ft

8.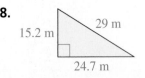
15.2 m
29 m
24.7 m

9.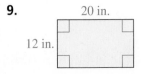
20 in.
12 in.

Lessons 9-5 and 9-6

- To identify the parts of a circle and to find the radius, diameter, and circumference
- To find the area of a circle

A **circle** has three kinds of segments: a **radius, chord,** and **diameter.** The distance around a circle is the **circumference.** The symbol π represents the ratio $\frac{\text{circumference}}{\text{diameter}}$.

Circumference: $C = \pi d$, or $C = 2\pi r$ Area: $A = \pi r^2$

Use circle O for Exercises 10–14. Use 3.14 for π.

10. Name three chords.

11. Name a diameter.

12. Name the radii.

13. Find the circumference.

14. Find the area of the circle. Round to the nearest square inch.

Lesson 9-7

- To identify three-dimensional figures

A **prism** is a **three-dimensional figure** with two parallel and congruent **faces** that are polygons. A **pyramid** has triangular faces and one base that is a polygon. You name a prism or a pyramid by the shape of its bases or base.

Name each figure.

15.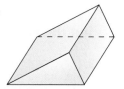

16.

17.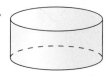

Lessons 9-8, 9-9, and 9-10

- To use nets and to find the surface areas of rectangular prisms
- To find the volume of rectangular prisms
- To find the surface area and volume of cylinders

The **surface area** of a three-dimensional figure is the sum of the areas of all its faces.

The **volume** of a three-dimensional figure is the number of cubic units needed to fill the space inside the figure. The formula for the volume of a prism or a cylinder is $V = B \times h$, where B is the area of the base.

Find the surface area and volume of each figure. Use 3.14 for π.

18.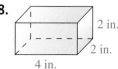

19.

20.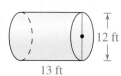

Choose an appropriate metric unit for each measurement.

1. length of a car

2. capacity of a cup

3. length of a skateboard

4. mass of a boat

5. capacity of a bucket

Convert each measurement.

6. 672 millimeters to centimeters

7. 25,040 milliliters to liters

8. 35.1 kilograms to grams

9. 125 liters to kiloliters

10. 42.9 meters to centimeters

Find the area of each figure.

11.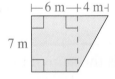
9 mm
21 mm

12.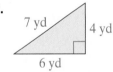
7 yd
4 yd
6 yd

13.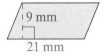
6 m   4 m
7 m

14.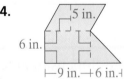
5 in.
6 in.
9 in.   6 in.

15. A garden is in the shape of a right triangle. The base of the triangle measures 8 feet. The height measures 4 feet. What is the area of the garden?

16. **Writing in Math** Which is larger, a pie plate with a radius of 5 inches, or a pie plate with a diameter of 9 inches? Explain.

Find the circumference and area of each circle. Round to the nearest tenth.

17.
15 ft

18.
18 km

19. **Food** A rectangular cracker has a length of 5 centimeters and an area of 20 square centimeters. Find the perimeter of the cracker.

20. **Manufacturing** A factory fills cans with tomato juice. Each can has a radius of 2 inches and a height of 8 inches. Find the volume of a can.

Find the surface area of each figure.

21.
12 m
14 m

22.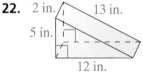
2 in.   13 in.
5 in.
12 in.

Find the volume of each figure.

23.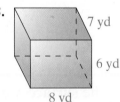
7 yd
6 yd
8 yd

24.
22 cm
17 cm

25. The volume of a rectangular prism is 504 square centimeters. The area of the base is 72 square centimeters. Find the height of the prism.

26. A company makes compost bins in the shape of a cylinder. The height and diameter of each bin is 36 inches. What is the volume of each bin?

Reading Comprehension

Read each passage and answer the questions that follow.

Clock Face The Clock Tower of the Palace of Westminster in London—what people often call "Big Ben"—is about 316 feet tall. The tower has four sides, each with a large clock. Each clock face is a circle about 22 feet in diameter. The minute hands are about 12 feet long, measuring from the center of the clock face to the tip of the hand. The Clock Tower can be seen from many parts of the city.

1. Which expression represents the circumference of the circle that the tip of one of the minute hands traces out in an hour?
   Ⓐ 6π Ⓑ 10π Ⓒ 12π Ⓓ 24π

2. If the minute hand were twice as long, how much farther would it travel every hour?
   Ⓕ half as far
   Ⓖ the same distance
   Ⓗ twice as far
   Ⓙ four times as far

3. Which expression represents the area of one of the clock faces?
   Ⓐ $10 \cdot 10 \cdot \pi$ Ⓒ $20 \cdot 20 \cdot \pi$
   Ⓑ $11 \cdot 11 \cdot \pi$ Ⓓ $22 \cdot 22 \cdot \pi$

4. If the radius of the clock face were twice as long, how many times greater would the area of the face be?
   Ⓕ the same
   Ⓖ two times
   Ⓗ four times
   Ⓙ eight times

Mountain Math It takes about $1\frac{1}{2}$ hours to get from Al's house to Mount Monadnock. First you go west 40 miles on a state highway. Then you turn right and go north another 30 miles, and you're there. On a clear day you can see the tallest buildings in Al's hometown from the top of the mountain.

5. Which choice does NOT correctly identify a point in this diagram?
   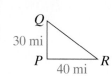
   Ⓐ Q is Al's house.
   Ⓑ R is Al's house.
   Ⓒ P is at the right turn.
   Ⓓ Q is the mountain.

6. How long will it take Al to drive to Mount Monadnock if he averages a rate of 56 miles per hour for the whole trip?
   Ⓕ 1 h
   Ⓖ 1.25 h
   Ⓗ 1.5 h
   Ⓙ 1.8 h

7. How many miles is the trip from Al's house to Mount Monadnock?
   Ⓐ 30 miles
   Ⓑ 40 miles
   Ⓒ 50 miles
   Ⓓ 70 miles

8. The odometer on Al's car shows how many miles the car travels. If the odometer shows 12,350 miles as Al leaves home, what will it show after a round trip to the mountain?
   Ⓕ 12,000 miles
   Ⓖ 12,490 miles
   Ⓗ 12,520 miles
   Ⓙ 12,900 miles

Applying Measurement

The Shape of Buildings to Come When architects design office or apartment buildings, they know that people will want as many windows as possible. The footprint, or area that a building covers, has to do with the arrangement of the windows. For example, a large square building may have inside rooms with no windows. Architects can change the shape of the footprint to make more outside walls.

Let the Sun in

This modern glass building connects two Victorian-era office buildings.

Straw bale   Frame

Straw-Bale Construction

College students in Wisconsin designed and built this straw-bale house. Wheat, oats, barley, rice, rye, and flax are all desirable straws for bale walls.

Biosphere 2

Originally constructed as a miniature Earth, Biosphere 2 is now a research facility. It covers 3.15 acres and includes five different environments: a coastal desert, a marsh, a grassy plain, a rain forest, and an ocean.

Rain forest

Grassy plain

Ocean

Kitchen

Put It All Together

Materials graph paper

1. Draw three rectangular footprints that you can make using 16 squares. Find each area and perimeter.

Footprint using 4 blocks

2. **Open-Ended** Draw several non-rectangular footprints that use 16 squares. Be creative! Find each perimeter.

3. **a.** Use 16 squares. Draw a square footprint with an open area in the center.

   b. Find the outside perimeter. Find the inside perimeter. Then find the total perimeter.

   c. Reasoning Why might an architect use a design like this for a building? Explain.

4. Consider all the footprints you have drawn. What arrangement of 16 squares gives the greatest total perimeter? The least total perimeter?

5. Buildings A, B, and C at the right are rectangular.

   a. Copy and complete the table. Calculate the volume and total exposed area of each building. (Include the top and four faces, but not the base.) How does the shape affect the surface area?

   b. Which shape gives the most space for windows? Which gives the least? Explain.

Building Entry

These binoculars are four stories tall and made from steel tubing and concrete. Each barrel is a conference room with a circular skylight at the top.

Building Data

Building	ℓ	w	h	Volume	Exposed Surface Area
A	3	2	4	■	■
B	6	2	2	■	■
C	1	3	8	■	■

A h ℓ w

B h ℓ w

C h ℓ w

Marsh

Library

Living quarters

Tree research buildings

Air supply

Control room

Go Online
PHSchool.com
For: Information about architecture
Web Code: aqe-0953

CHAPTER 10

Exploring Probability

What You've Learned

- In Chapters 5 and 6, you learned to write equivalent fractions and to add, subtract, and multiply fractions.

- In Chapter 7, you used ratios to describe proportional relationships, and you solved problems.

- You also converted between decimals, fractions, and percents.

 **Check Your Readiness**

GO for Help

For Exercises	See Lesson
1–4	1-7
5–8	5-2
9–12	6-1
13–16	7-6

Subtracting Decimals

Find each difference.

1. $1 - 0.32$ **2.** $1 - 0.08$

3. $1 - 0.6$ **4.** $1 - 0.234$

Adding Fractions With Like Denominators

Find each sum.

5. $\frac{2}{5} + \frac{1}{5}$ **6.** $\frac{3}{6} + \frac{1}{6}$ **7.** $\frac{2}{8} + \frac{5}{8}$ **8.** $\frac{3}{10} + \frac{3}{10}$

Multiplying Fractions

Find each product.

9. $\frac{1}{2} \times \frac{5}{6}$ **10.** $\frac{3}{4} \times \frac{8}{9}$ **11.** $\frac{7}{10} \times \frac{5}{14}$ **12.** $\frac{2}{3} \times \frac{8}{9}$

Writing Equivalent Numerical Expressions

Write each fraction as a decimal and then as a percent.

13. $\frac{2}{8}$ **14.** $\frac{3}{9}$ **15.** $\frac{4}{5}$ **16.** $\frac{7}{10}$

What You'll Learn Next

- In this chapter, you will construct sample spaces using lists and tree diagrams.

- You will find the probabilities of a simple event and of its complement.

- You will also find experimental probabilities.

- You will use probabilities and proportions to make predictions about populations.

 Problem Solving Application On pages 512 and 513, you will work an extended activity on games.

🔊 Key Vocabulary

- complement of an event (p. 483)
- compound event (p. 501)
- counting principle (p. 477)
- dependent event (p. 504)
- equally likely outcomes (p. 482)
- event (p. 476)
- experimental probability (p. 488)
- independent events (p. 500)
- outcome (p. 476)
- permutation (p. 481)
- population (p. 495)
- probability of an event (p. 482)
- sample (p. 495)
- sample space (p. 476)
- simulation (p. 498)
- tree diagram (p. 477)

Check Skills You'll Need

1. **Vocabulary Review**
   When you multiply, you can group numbers together using the ___?___ *Property*.

Find each product.

2. $5 \times 5 \times 2$

3. $25 \times 2 \times 40$

4. $3 \times 4 \times 1000$

for Help
Lesson 1-8

What You'll Learn

To construct sample spaces for events and to use the counting principle

🔊 **New Vocabulary** outcome, event, sample space, tree diagram, counting principle

Why Learn This?

A coin toss is used in sporting events to decide which team starts with the ball. If you toss a coin once, there are two possible outcomes—heads or tails. An **outcome** is the result of an action.

An **event** is an outcome or group of outcomes. The set of all possible outcomes is the **sample space.**

EXAMPLE Finding a Sample Space

1 Use the menu. Construct the sample space for selecting a main dish and a side dish. How many possible outcomes are there?

List all of the possible outcomes.

Lunch Menu

| Main Dish | Grilled Chicken |
| | Baked Chicken |

Side Dish	Salad
	Vegetable
	Rice

Grilled chicken	Salad	Baked chicken	Salad
Grilled chicken	Vegetable	Baked chicken	Vegetable
Grilled chicken	Rice	Baked chicken	Rice

The number of possible outcomes is six.

Test Prep Tip

"What is the size of the sample space?" can also be worded, "How many ways are there?", or "How many possible outcomes are there?"

Quick Check

1. A bicycle comes in three models and three colors. Construct the sample space to find how many bicycle choices you have. How many possible outcomes are there?

A **tree diagram** is an organized list of all possible outcomes.

EXAMPLE Using a Tree Diagram

② You roll a standard number cube and then toss a coin. List the possible outcomes. How many are there?

Draw the tree diagram at the left to list the possible outcomes.

The diagram shows 12 possible outcomes.

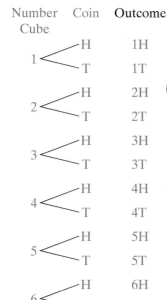

Number Cube	Coin	Outcome
1	H	1H
	T	1T
2	H	2H
	T	2T
3	H	3H
	T	3T
4	H	4H
	T	4T
5	H	5H
	T	5T
6	H	6H
	T	6T

✓ **Quick Check**

2. You can choose blue or khaki pants and a red, yellow, or green shirt. Construct the sample space using a tree diagram. How many outfits are possible?

The **counting principle** is a way to find the number of possible outcomes.

KEY CONCEPTS Counting Principle

There are *m* ways of making one choice and *n* ways of making a second choice. There are $m \times n$ ways to make the first choice followed by the second choice.

EXAMPLE Using the Counting Principle

③ **Multiple Choice** You choose one item from each category in the menu. How many different desserts can you order?

Ⓐ 20   Ⓒ 30
Ⓑ 25   Ⓓ 35

Ice Cream Menu

Flavors	Toppings
Vanilla	Nuts
Chocolate	Sprinkles
Strawberry	Cherries
Banana	**Cones**
Peach	Waffle
	Sugar

Flavors		Toppings		Cones		Desserts
↓		↓		↓		↓
5	×	3	×	2	=	30

You can order 30 different desserts. The correct answer is choice C.

✓ **Quick Check**

3. In the menu above, cherry ripple ice cream as a flavor and fudge as a topping are added. Find the new number of different desserts.

● More Than One Way

Each lunch for a school field trip has a turkey, roast beef, or bologna sandwich, an orange or apple for a fruit, and a cookie or muffin for dessert. Amanda and Zack would like to know the number of possible lunch choices.

Amanda's Method

I am going to draw a tree diagram to show all possible choices.

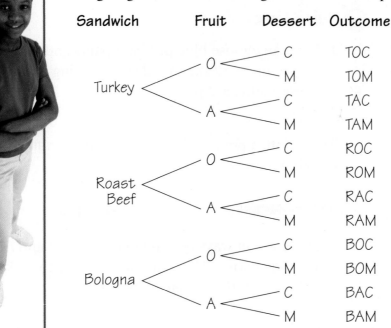

Sandwich	Fruit	Dessert	Outcome

The tree diagram shows 12 choices. There are 12 lunch choices.

Zack's Method

I will use the counting principle to find the number of possible choices.

Sandwich		Fruit		Dessert		Lunches
3	×	2	×	2	=	12

There are 12 lunch choices.

Choose a Method

A fourth sandwich type, peanut butter, is added to the menu above. How many lunch choices are offered now? Describe your method. Explain why you chose it.

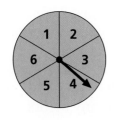

1. **Vocabulary** The list of all possible outcomes is called the __?__ .

2. You spin the spinner at the left. Then you toss a coin. Use a tree diagram to find the number of possible outcomes.

3. **Writing in Math** You like 5 paint colors and 6 wallpaper patterns. Describe how you would find the different ways to decorate using one paint color and one wallpaper pattern.

Homework Exercises

For more exercises, see Extra Skills and Word Problems.

GO for Help

For Exercises	See Examples
4–5	1
6–8	2
9–10	3

Construct a sample space. How many possible outcomes are there?

4. A music store sells electric guitars in 3 colors and 2 sizes. How many different guitars can you buy?

5. You can choose from a model car, plane, or boat. Each model comes in 3 colors. How many choices do you have?

Construct a sample space using a tree diagram. How many possible outcomes are there?

6. You spin the spinner at the right twice.

7. You toss a coin twice.

8. You toss a coin. Then you roll a number cube.

Use the counting principle. Find the number of possible outcomes.

9. You toss a coin three times.

10. A theater shows 8 movies at 3 prices five times each day. How many types of tickets does the theater sell?

11. **Guided Problem Solving** You buy 2 hats, 5 shirts, and 3 pairs of pants at a store. Your friend buys 4 hats, 4 shirts, and 2 pairs of pants. Who can make the greatest number of possible outfits using one hat, one shirt, and one pair of pants? Justify your answer.
    - Which method could you use to find the number of possible outcomes?
    - How many possible outfits can your friend make?

Careers Librarians assist people in finding information.

12. **Games** To play a game, you spin a spinner and draw a card. The spinner tells you to move 1, 2, 3, or 4 spaces. The cards read Free Turn, Lose a Turn, or No Change. It is your turn.
   a. Construct a sample space for the possible outcomes.
   b. To win the game, you need to move at least 2 spaces or draw a Free Turn card. How many of the possible outcomes will allow you to win on your next turn?

13. **Reasoning** A city has 30 libraries. Each library will receive a banner. There are 5 banner styles. How many colors will you need so that each library receives a different banner?

14. **Choose a Method** The table below shows features for a computer. You choose one keyboard, one monitor, and one printer. How many different choices can you make? Describe your method, and explain why you chose it.

Keyboard	Monitor	Printer
Standard	Color 15-in.	Inkjet
Extended	Color 17-in.	Color inkjet
Adjustable	Color 19-in.	Laser

15. **Challenge** Find the total number of four-digit numbers you can write using only digits that are even numbers.

Test Prep and Mixed Review **Practice**

Multiple Choice

16. Talia and Anthony run for class president. Josh, Matt, and Susan run for vice-president. What are the possible outcomes of the election?

   Ⓐ

Anthony	Susan
Anthony	Josh
Anthony	Matt

   Ⓒ

Talia	Susan
Talia	Josh
Talia	Matt

   Ⓑ

Anthony	Susan
Anthony	Josh
Anthony	Matt
Talia	Susan
Talia	Josh
Talia	Matt

   Ⓓ

Anthony	Susan
Anthony	Susan
Anthony	Josh
Talia	Josh
Talia	Matt
Talia	Matt

17. What is an appropriate unit of weight to describe a car?

Permutations

An arrangement of objects in a particular order is called a **permutation.** For the letters A and M, the permutations AM and MA are different, because the orders of the letters are different.

EXAMPLES

1 Find the permutations of the letters in FLY.

Make an organized list. Use each letter exactly once.

FLY   LFY   YFL

FYL   LYF   YLF

2 Find the two-digit permutations you can make with the digits 1, 3, 7, and 9. How many are there?

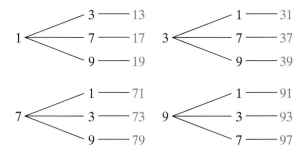

There are 12 permutations.

Exercises

1. Make an organized list to find the permutations of the letters in WORD.

Draw a tree diagram to find the permutations of each set.

2. two-digit permutations of the numbers 1, 2, 3, and 4

3. three-letter permutations of the letters in BOLT

4. In your garden you want to plant a row of carrots, a row of peppers, a row of tomatoes, and a row of peas. Find all of the possible arrangements of the rows.

Probability

Check Skills You'll Need

1. **Vocabulary Review**
   What does the word *percent* mean?

Write each number as a percent.

2. 0.32   3. $\frac{9}{25}$

4. $\frac{2}{5}$ 5. 0.02

for Help
Lesson 7-6

What You'll Learn

To find the probabilities of an event and of its complement

🔊 **New Vocabulary** equally likely outcomes, probability of an event, complement of an event

Why Learn This?

You can use probability to predict your chances of winning a game.

Suppose you spin the spinner below. The spinner is equally likely to land on each of the ten sections.

3 out of 10 possible outcomes are blue.

Outcomes that have the same chance of occurring are called **equally likely outcomes.** If you toss a coin once, there are two equally likely outcomes—heads or tails.

The **probability of an event** is a number that describes how likely it is that the event will occur.

On the spinner above, the probability of the event "blue" is 3 out of 10, or $\frac{3}{10}$. The probability of the event "not blue" is 7 out of 10, or $\frac{7}{10}$.

KEY CONCEPTS **Probability of an Event**

For equally likely outcomes:

the probability of an event $= \dfrac{\text{number of favorable outcomes}}{\text{total number of outcomes}}$

You can write $P(\text{blue})$ for the phrase "the probability of blue." For the spinner above, $P(\text{blue}) = \frac{3}{10}$.

Video Tutor Help

Visit: PHSchool.com
Web Code: aqe-0775

EXAMPLE Probability of an Event

1 You roll a number cube once. Find P(an even number).

There are 3 outcomes for the event "even" out of 6 equally likely outcomes.

$$P(\text{even}) = \frac{3}{6} \leftarrow \text{number of outcomes with even numbers}$$
$$\phantom{P(\text{even})} \leftarrow \text{total number of outcomes}$$
$$= \frac{1}{2} \quad \leftarrow \text{Simplify.}$$

The probability of rolling an even number is $\frac{1}{2}$.

Quick Check

1. You roll a number cube once. Find P(4 or 6).

The collection of outcomes *not* contained in the event is the **complement of an event.** The sum of the probabilities of an event and its complement is 1.

EXAMPLE Complement of an Event

2 Of 20 students in a class, 18 are 12 years old. A teacher selects a student at random. What is P(12 years old)? What is P(not 12 years old)?

$$P(12) = \frac{18}{20} \leftarrow \text{number of 12-year-old students}$$
$$ \leftarrow \text{total number of students}$$
$$= \frac{9}{10} \quad \leftarrow \text{Simplify.}$$

The event "not 12 years old" is the complement of the event "12 years old." The sum of the probabilities of an event and its complement is 1, so P(not 12 years old) = $1 - P$(12 years old).

$$P(\text{not 12 years old}) = 1 - P(\text{12 years old})$$
$$= 1 - \frac{9}{10} \qquad \leftarrow \text{Substitute } \frac{9}{10} \text{ for } P(12).$$
$$= \frac{1}{10} \qquad \leftarrow \text{Simplify.}$$

P(12 years old) is $\frac{9}{10}$. P(not 12 years old) is $\frac{1}{10}$.

Quick Check

2. You roll a number cube once. Find P(not 6).

Vocabulary Tip

Random means "equally likely."

Probabilities range from 0 to 1. An impossible event will never occur. Its probability is 0. If an event will definitely happen, then the event is certain. Its probability is 1.

You can write probabilities as fractions, decimals, or percents.

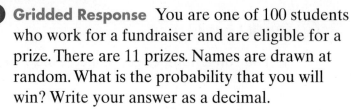

Impossible event		Event equally likely or unlikely		Certain event
↓ 0%	25%	50%	75%	100% ↓
0	$\frac{1}{4}$ or 0.25	$\frac{1}{2}$ or 0.5	$\frac{3}{4}$ or 0.75	1

EXAMPLE **Application: Fundraising**

3 **Gridded Response** You are one of 100 students who work for a fundraiser and are eligible for a prize. There are 11 prizes. Names are drawn at random. What is the probability that you will win? Write your answer as a decimal.

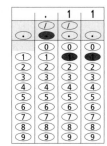

$$P(\text{win a prize}) = \frac{11}{100} \begin{array}{l} \leftarrow \text{number of prizes} \\ \leftarrow \text{total number of students} \end{array}$$

$$= 0.11$$

✓ Quick Check

3. In a bag of mixed nuts, 6 out of 10 nuts are pecans. What is the probability that a randomly selected nut is a pecan? Write your answer as a decimal.

✓ Check Your Understanding

1. Vocabulary What is the relationship between the probability of an event and the probability of its complement?

2. Reasoning You roll a number cube once. Is $P(3)$ different from $P(4)$? Explain.

3. Open-Ended Give an example of an impossible event. Then give an example of a certain event.

You spin the spinner once. Match each probability to a fraction.

4. $P(3)$

5. $P(4 \text{ or } 5)$

6. $P(\text{not } 6)$

A. $\frac{1}{6}$

B. $\frac{1}{3}$

C. $\frac{5}{6}$

For more exercises, see Extra Skills and Word Problems.

GO for Help

For Exercises	See Examples
7–10	1
11–12	2
13–16	3

A bag contains 4 red marbles, 3 yellow marbles, 2 black marbles, and 1 green marble. You select a marble at random. Find each probability.

7. $P(\text{red})$

8. $P(\text{yellow})$

9. $P(\text{black})$

10. $P(\text{green})$

11. Of 12 fish in a tank, 8 have spots. You catch a fish at random. What is $P(\text{spots})$? What is $P(\text{no spots})$?

12. A clown has 21 balloons to sell. Seven of the balloons in the bunch are yellow. You take the string of a balloon at random. What is $P(\text{yellow})$? What is $P(\text{not yellow})$?

Test Prep Tip

Sometimes it is easier to find the probability of an event by finding the probability of its complement.

Find the probability of each event. Write the probability as a decimal.

13. A spinner has equal sections of red, blue, pink, green, and yellow. You spin the spinner once and land on yellow.

14. You roll a number cube. You roll a number greater than 3.

15. You write the letters A, B, C, D, E, and F on pieces of paper. You select a piece of paper at random and pick a vowel.

16. Your name is selected at random from a list of 6 names.

17. Guided Problem Solving A package of 25 party favors contains 8 glitter balls. A package of 20 party favors contains 6 glitter balls. You randomly select a party favor from each package. In which package are you more likely to get a glitter ball as a party favor?
- Find the probability of choosing a glitter ball from each package.
- Use decimals or fractions to compare the probabilities.

18. Baseball A baseball team has the starting and relief pitchers shown in the table. The manager selects a pitcher at random. Find the probability that the pitcher is left-handed.

Pitchers on Baseball Team

Pitchers	Number
Left-handed starters	1
Right-handed starters	4
Left-handed relievers	2
Right-handed relievers	1

Find each probability for one roll of a number cube.

19. $P(\text{multiple of 3})$

20. $P(\text{not a multiple of 4})$

21. $P(\text{not a factor of 8})$

22. $P(\text{prime})$

Estimation You spin the spinner once. Estimate each probability. Give your answer as a decimal.

23. The spinner does *not* land on pink.

24. The spinner does *not* land on green.

25. The spinner does *not* land on yellow.

26. **Writing in Math** In a game, is the probability of "not winning" always the same as "losing"? Explain.

Vocabulary Tip

Icosahedron comes from two Greek words. *Icosa*– means "twenty" and *–hedron* means "surface."

27. **Geometry** You roll the icosahedron shown. It has 20 congruent faces and equal numbers of red, blue, yellow, and green faces. What is the probability that the top face will *not* be green?

28. **Challenge** A bag contains only red, green, and blue marbles. $P(\text{green}) = \frac{1}{3}$, and $P(\text{red}) = \frac{1}{2}$. There are 6 green marbles. How many blue marbles are there in the bag?

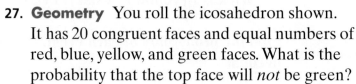

Test Prep and Mixed Review | **Practice**

Gridded Response

29. A spinner has equal-sized sections numbered 1 through 20. You spin the spinner once. What is the probability, written as a decimal, that you spin a multiple of 5?

30. The measurements of a wall and its window are shown in the diagram. How much wallpaper, in square feet, is needed to cover the wall?

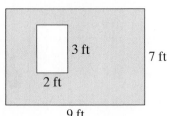

3 ft
2 ft
7 ft
9 ft

31. The ratio of adults to children in a preschool classroom is 1 to 8. If there are 2 adults in the class, how many children are there?

GO for Help

For Exercises	See Lesson
32–35	4-6

Write each improper fraction as a mixed number.

32. $\frac{49}{5}$

33. $\frac{17}{3}$

34. $\frac{49}{6}$

35. $\frac{51}{4}$

1. You have three shirts and two pairs of jeans. Construct a sample space of the possible outfits you can wear.

2. You roll a number cube and toss a coin. Draw a tree diagram to find the number of possible outcomes.

3. A store sells 8 flavors of frozen yogurt and 6 kinds of toppings. How many desserts can you order with 1 flavor of frozen yogurt and 1 topping?

A number cube is rolled. Find each probability.

4. $P(\text{less than 3})$

5. $P(8)$

6. $P(5 \text{ or } 6)$

Three coins are tossed. Find each probability.

7. $P(\text{exactly 1 tail})$

8. $P(\text{exactly 2 heads})$

9. $P(3 \text{ tails})$

10. $P(\text{all the same})$

11. $P(1 \text{ or more tails})$

12. $P(3 \text{ heads})$

13. Alicia gets her hair braided at a salon. She has a choice of 4 styles of braid, 5 ribbon colors, and 3 barrettes. Alicia may choose one style of braid, one ribbon color, and one barrette. How many different hairdos can she get?

MATH AT WORK

Board Game Designer

Board Game Designer is a career that could be just right for you if you love games. Game design requires an eye for color and a creative mind.

Game designers also use mathematical skills. In games with spinners or number cubes, designers use probability. To evaluate marketing information about a game, they use data analysis.

 **Go Online**
PHSchool.com

For: Information on board game designers
Web Code: aqb-2031

What You'll Learn

To find experimental probability

🔊 **New Vocabulary** experimental probability

Why Learn This?

The probabilities of some events are very difficult to calculate. Instead of using a formula, you can conduct an experiment.

To find the experimental probability of winning a tennis tournament, you can collect data for several tennis matches. Each match is a trial. Then you can write the **experimental probability** as a ratio of the number of times an event occurs to the total number of trials.

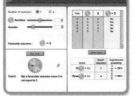
KEY CONCEPTS   Experimental Probability

$$P(\text{event}) = \frac{\text{number of times an event occurs}}{\text{total number of trials}}$$

EXAMPLE   Experimental Probability

1 In 20 tennis matches against Jennie, Ai-Ling wins 9 times. What is the experimental probability that Ai-Ling wins a match?

$P(\text{Ai-Ling wins}) = \dfrac{9}{20}$ ← number of matches Ai-Ling wins
      ← total number of matches

The experimental probability that Ai-Ling wins a match is $\frac{9}{20}$.

✓ Quick Check

● **1.** What is the experimental probability that Jennie wins a match?

A fair coin or number cube generates equally likely outcomes. If coins, cubes, or spinners are damaged or irregularly made, they may *not* be fair.

EXAMPLE Analyzing Experimental Probability

GO Online

Video Tutor Help

Visit: PHSchool.com
Web Code: aqe-0775

Fair Games You and your friend want to play a game, but your only number cube is chipped. To make a fair game, you roll the number cube 60 times. The results are shown in the table below.

Outcome	1	2	3	4	5	6
Number of Times Rolled	16	17	12	8	4	3

Which of the following games seems fair? Explain.

a. You win if the number rolled is 6. Your friend wins if the number rolled is 2.

$$P(6) = \frac{3}{60} \quad \leftarrow \text{There are 3 rolls of 6 in 60 trials.}$$

$$P(2) = \frac{17}{60} \quad \leftarrow \text{There are 17 rolls of 2 in 60 trials.}$$

You would expect $P(2)$ and $P(6)$ to be about the same with a fair number cube. Since this number cube strongly favors 2, the game seems to be unfair.

b. If the number rolled is even, you win. If it is odd, your friend wins.

$$17 + 8 + 3 = 28 \quad \leftarrow \text{Add to find the number of even rolls.}$$

$$16 + 12 + 4 = 32 \quad \leftarrow \text{Add to find the number of odd rolls.}$$

$$P(\text{even}) = \frac{28}{60} \quad \leftarrow \text{There are 28 even rolls in 60 trials.}$$

$$P(\text{odd}) = \frac{32}{60} \quad \leftarrow \text{There are 32 odd rolls in 60 trials.}$$

You would expect $P(\text{even})$ and $P(\text{odd})$ to be about the same with a fair number cube. The probabilities are about the same, so the game seems to be fair.

✓ Quick Check

2. Use the data in Example 2. Suppose you win with a 1, 3, or 6, and your friend wins with a 2, 4, or 5. Does this game seem fair? Explain.

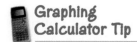
1. **Vocabulary** Why is experimental probability called "experimental"?

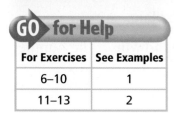
Graphing Calculator Tip

You can use a graphing calculator to simulate flips of a coin by randomly generating the numbers 1 and 2.

2. You toss a coin 20 times and record 8 tails. Find the experimental probability of the outcome tails.

A cooler contains 20 grape drinks, 13 cherry drinks, 8 lime drinks, and 9 lemon drinks. You select a drink at random.

3. Find $P(\text{grape})$. 4. Find $P(not \text{ lemon})$. 5. Find $P(\text{lime})$.

Homework Exercises

For more exercises, see Extra Skills and Word Problems.

GO for Help

For Exercises	See Examples
6–10	1
11–13	2

The table shows the results of students playing a video game. Find the experimental probability of each person winning.

Game Results

Player	Blake	Troy	Carla	Kate	Sara	Luis
Number of Wins	11	47	63	17	0	14
Number of Times Game is Played	25	80	294	17	15	30

6. Carla   7. Luis   8. Kate   9. Sara   10. Troy

The table below shows the results of tossing a chipped number cube 80 times. Tell whether each game seems fair. Explain.

Outcome	1	2	3	4	5	6
Number of Times Rolled	9	12	19	14	25	1

11. If even, then Player A wins. Otherwise, Player B wins.

12. If 1, 2, or 3, then Player A wins. Otherwise, Player B wins.

13. If 5 or 6, then Player A wins. Otherwise, Player B wins.

 14. **Guided Problem Solving** In your first 16 times at bat in softball, you get 6 hits. Find the experimental probability of getting a hit. Predict the number of hits you will get in 40 at-bats, if you keep hitting at the same rate.
   • Find the experimental probability for the first 16 at-bats.
   • Multiply the probability by the total number of trials.

15. Basketball A player makes 4 of 12 free throws. Find the experimental probability of the player missing a free throw.

16. <u>Writing in Math</u> You and your friend want to play a game that uses a spinner with five sections. Explain how you can use experimental probability to determine if the spinner is fair.

Data Collection Roll a pair of number cubes 50 times. Record your results. Find each experimental probability.

17. $P(1$ and $1)$ **18.** $P(\text{doubles})$ **19.** $P(\text{even and even})$

20. $P(\text{odd and odd})$ **21.** $P(2$ and $3)$ **22.** $P(4$ and $5)$

23. Snowboarding You and a friend go snowboarding. You make it down the mountain before your friend 13 times out of 20. What is the experimental probability that you make it down the mountain first? That your friend makes it down first?

24. a. You roll a number cube 12 times and roll a 3 once. Find the experimental probability of rolling a 3.
   b. Reasoning You calculate the probability of rolling 3 on a number cube as $\frac{1}{6}$. Explain why your calculation is different from the experimental probability you found in part (a).

25. Challenge A dartboard has an area of 40 square inches. In the center is a triangle. In 50 random throws, you hit the triangle 30 times. Estimate the area of the triangle.

Test Prep and Mixed Review **Practice**

Multiple Choice

26. A student rolls a number cube 40 times. The number 3 appears 8 times. What is the experimental probability of rolling a 3?

Ⓐ 8% Ⓑ 12.5% Ⓒ 0.20 Ⓓ $\frac{1}{4}$

27. The Yangs plan to remodel their kitchen. The kitchen is 12 feet wide. The scale of the floor plan for the kitchen is 1 inch to 8 feet. What is the width of the kitchen on the plan?

Ⓕ 1 in. Ⓖ $1\frac{1}{4}$ in. Ⓗ $1\frac{3}{8}$ in. Ⓙ $1\frac{1}{2}$ in.

GO for Help

For Exercises	See Lesson
28–30	8-6

Tell whether the figures are congruent or similar.

28. 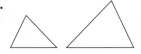 **29.** **30.**

Experimental and Theoretical Probabilities

When you calculated probability in Lesson 10-2, you found *theoretical* probability. Theoretical probability tells you what will *most likely* happen, but the actual outcome of an experiment is not always the most likely outcome.

ACTIVITY

You can calculate the theoretical probability that both children in a family with two children are girls. You can compare this prediction with the results of both an experiment and a survey.

1. List the possible outcomes for a family with exactly two children. Assume that the chance of having a boy child is equal to the chance of a girl child. Find the theoretical probability that both children are girls. Enter the probability in the first column of the table below.

	Theoretical Probability	Experimental Probability	
		Experiment	Survey
Fraction			
Percent			

2. Toss two coins together 20 times. Record your results using a table as shown below.

Coin Toss

Coin 1	Coin 2

Let heads represent a girl.   Let tails represent a boy.

3. Find the experimental probability of having two girls. Enter the probability in the second column of the table in Step 1.

4. Survey *all* of your classmates to determine how many families have exactly two children. Of those families, how many have two girls? Enter the data in the table.

5. Calculate and compare the percents in the bottom row of the table. Explain why the values may not be exactly the same.

Vocabulary Builder

High-Use Academic Words

High-use academic words are words that you will see often in textbooks and on tests. These words are not math vocabulary terms, but knowing them will help you to succeed in mathematics.

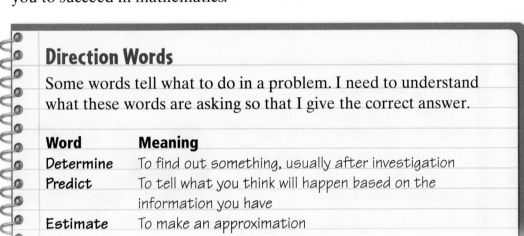

Direction Words

Some words tell what to do in a problem. I need to understand what these words are asking so that I give the correct answer.

Word	Meaning
Determine	To find out something, usually after investigation
Predict	To tell what you think will happen based on the information you have
Estimate	To make an approximation

Exercises

1. Determine what you will wear to school tomorrow.

2. Predict what you will wear to school in May.

3. Estimate the number of pairs of shoes you have in your closet.

Use the table at the right for Exercises 4–6.

4. Determine the probability of eating breakfast.

5. Of 75 students, predict how many students eat breakfast.

6. Of 81 students, estimate how many students eat breakfast.

Breakfast Survey

Do You Eat Breakfast?	Percent
Yes	75
No	25

7. **Word Knowledge** Think about the word *random*.
   a. Choose the letter for how well you know the word.
      A. I know its meaning.
      B. I've seen it, but I don't know its meaning.
      C. I don't know it.
   b. **Research** Look up and write the definition of *random*.
   c. Use the word in a sentence involving mathematics.

Making Predictions From Data

What You'll Learn

To make predictions using probabilities and samples

🔊 **New Vocabulary** population, sample

Why Learn This?

Probabilities can help you make a prediction about the outcome of an event, such as predicting the gender of each child in a family.

To predict the number of times an event will occur, multiply the probability of the event by the total number of trials.

$$P(\text{event}) \times \frac{\text{total number}}{\text{of trials}} = \frac{\text{number of predicted}}{\text{successes}}$$

A prediction cannot guarantee what will actually occur.

EXAMPLE Making a Prediction

1. For a family with two children, suppose there is a 25% chance that both children are boys. Out of 72 families with two children, how many are likely to have two boys?

$$P(\text{two boys}) \times \frac{\text{number of}}{\text{families}} = \frac{\text{number of families}}{\text{with 2 boys}}$$

$$\frac{1}{4} \qquad \times \qquad 72 \qquad = \qquad 18$$

← Write 25% as $\frac{1}{4}$. To find $\frac{1}{4}$ of a number, divide the number by 4.

About 18 of the families are likely to have two boys.

✓ Quick Check

1. At an arcade, Juanita plays a game 20 times. She has a 30% probability of winning. How many times can she expect to win?

A **population** is a group about which you want information. A **sample** is a part of the population. You use a sample and proportions to make predictions about the population.

EXAMPLE Application: Quality Control

2 A company makes 15,000 toy robots. The company inspects 200 robots at random. The sample has 5 faulty robots. Predict how many of the 15,000 robots are likely to be faulty.

Words $\dfrac{\text{number faulty in sample}}{\text{total number in sample}} = \dfrac{\text{number faulty in population}}{\text{total number in population}}$

Let n = the number of faulty robots in 15,000 robots.

Proportion $\dfrac{5}{200} = \dfrac{n}{15,000}$

$200n = 5 \cdot 15,000$ ← Write the cross products.

$200n = 75,000$ ← Simplify.

$\dfrac{200n}{200} = \dfrac{75,000}{200}$ ← Divide each side by 200.

$n = 375$ ← Simplify.

It is likely that about 375 toy robots are faulty.

✓ **Quick Check**

2. Suppose 1,000 toy robots are selected at random from 20,000 robots, and 54 robots are found faulty. Predict how many of the 20,000 robots are likely to be faulty.

✓ Check Your Understanding

1. **Vocabulary** How is a sample related to a population?

2. **Writing in Math** What is the advantage of taking a random sample instead of surveying an entire population?

3. A manufacturer finds that 50% of the light bulbs in a sample are defective. How many bulbs might be defective in 80 bulbs?
   Ⓐ 30　　　Ⓑ 40　　　Ⓒ 50　　　Ⓓ 60

4. You survey at random 40 people who saw a movie. Thirty-eight of them say that the movie was excellent. There were 600 people in the theater. How many of the 600 people are likely to think that the movie was excellent?

For more exercises, see Extra Skills and Word Problems.

GO for Help

For Exercises	See Examples
5–10	1
11–15	2

The probability of winning a game is 40%. How many times should you expect to win if you play each number of times?

5. 5 times   **6.** 10 times   **7.** 15 times

8. 30 times   **9.** 85 times   **10.** 120 times

11. Art A mayor wants opinions from students about murals displayed in City Hall. He selects a random sample of 120 students from 18,000 students in the city. Twenty-two of the students surveyed like Mural A. Predict how many of the 18,000 students will like Mural A.

A company makes shirts, pants, belts, and socks. It makes 24,000 of each item. For each sample, predict the number of items likely to be defective.

12. 6 defects in 500 shirts   **13.** 3 defects in 160 pairs of socks

14. 2 defects in 250 belts   **15.** 3 defects in 10 pairs of pants

16. Guided Problem Solving Park rangers are planning programs at a national park. They conduct a survey of 200 families at the park. The results are in the table below.

Reason for Visit	Number of Families
Camping	84
Hiking	72
Fishing	44

The total number of families visiting the park each summer is 15,600. Predict the number of families that will come to the park for each activity in the table.
- **Make a Plan** Write and solve a proportion for each activity.
- **Check the Answer** Since the results for all 200 families are in the table, the sum of your answers should be 15,600.

GO Online

Homework Video Tutor

Visit: PHSchool.com
Web Code: aqe-1004

17. Number Sense Suppose you take a sample of 15 pieces of colored fruit snacks and a sample of 60 pieces of colored fruit snacks from one day's production. Which sample is more likely to give you a prediction closer to the actual number of each color? Explain.

18. **Tour** A teacher asks 70 random students, "Did you see the electricity exhibit?" Fourteen answer yes. If 1,000 students went on the trip, how many likely saw the exhibit?

19. A sample of 100 gadgets is selected from one day's production of 5,000 gadgets. In the sample, 7 are defective. Predict the number of gadgets in the day's production that are *not* defective.

A computer dart game displays random points to represent darts being thrown. The areas of each section are shown.

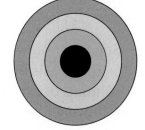

- black: 1 in.^{2}
- blue: 3 in.^{2}
- yellow: 6 in.^{2}
- orange: 10 in.^{2}

20. What is the probability that a point is in the yellow section?

21. What is the probability that a point is in the orange or yellow section?

22. What is the probability that a point is *not* in the black section?

23. **Challenge** A jar holds 80 marbles that are red, green, or blue. The probability of picking a red marble at random is $\frac{1}{5}$. Find the number of red marbles you would need to add to the jar to change the probability to $\frac{1}{2}$.

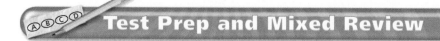

Ⓐ Ⓑ Ⓒ Ⓓ **Test Prep and Mixed Review** **Practice**

Multiple Choice

24. The ratio of adults to children in a musical is 1 to 3. Which of the following could be the numbers of adults and children in the musical?
   - Ⓐ 25 adults, 75 children
   - Ⓒ 20 adults, 80 children
   - Ⓑ 75 adults, 25 children
   - Ⓓ 80 adults, 20 children

25. You want to paint the walls of your room. A gallon of paint covers 400 square feet. Which method should you use to find how many gallons of paint you need?
   - Ⓕ Find the area of the walls and divide by 400.
   - Ⓖ Find the perimeter of the walls and divide by 400.
   - Ⓗ Find the area of the walls and multiply by 400.
   - Ⓙ Find the perimeter of the walls and multiply by 400.

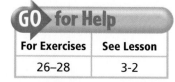

For Exercises	See Lesson
26–28	3-2

Evaluate each expression for $a = 3$, $b = 1.5$, and $c = 2$.

26. $3(a - 2)$

27. $7a \div c$

28. $1 + 4b$

Simulations

Sometimes it is difficult to collect data. Instead, you may be able to use a simulation. A **simulation** of a real-world situation is a model used to find probabilities. You can use computer spreadsheets to do simulations.

Suppose you want to simulate 25 spins of a spinner with 5 equal parts numbered 1 to 5. You can make rows and columns of random integers from 1 to 5 by entering the following formula in each cell.

=RANDBETWEEN (1, 5)

lowest number to choose from   **highest number to choose from**

You can use formulas to count results automatically. To count all the 3's in the 25 squares shown, you enter

=COUNTIF (A1:E5, 3)

upper left cell location / **number to count**

lower right cell location

According to the simulation, the experimental probability of spinning a 3 is $\frac{4}{25}$.

Random Numbers

	A	B	C	D	E	F
1	3	4	2	1	4	
2	2	4	4	2	4	
3	5	3	5	4	5	
4	4	3	1	4	2	
5	3	1	5	1	5	
6						
7						
8	Number of 3's:					
9	4					

ACTIVITY

1. **Basketball** Michelle plays basketball. She misses one free throw out of every three attempts.
   a. To simulate the probability of a successful free throw, let 1 = miss, 2 = make, and 3 = make. Write a spreadsheet formula to generate random numbers for this simulation.
   b. Use a spreadsheet to count the 1's in the first 6 rows.
   c. Out of 30 numbers, how many 1's would you expect?
   d. Generate 30 random numbers from 1 to 3. Find the experimental probability that Michelle misses a free throw.

2. a. **Writing in Math** Suppose you guess random answers to three true-or-false questions. Describe a simulation to find the probability that you answer each question correctly.
   b. Conduct the simulation in part (a). What is the probability that you answer each question correctly?

Tristan rolls a number cube 20 times. He rolls 4 twos, 3 fours, and 5 sixes. Find the experimental probability of each event.

1. rolling a 2

2. rolling a 4

3. rolling an even number

4. rolling an odd number

5. A pencil is dropped 20 times. It points left 8 times. Find the experimental probability that the pencil points left.

6. In a town survey, 40 out of 50 men say they eat lunch. The town has 35,000 men. Predict the number of men who eat lunch.

7. In a pet store's survey, 45 of 60 customers own a cat. How many of 420 customers are likely to own a cat?

8. A company has 20,000 hats. In a random sample of 80 hats, 3 are defective. Overall, how many are likely to be defective?

MATH GAMES

Probability Race

What You'll Need
- a number cube
- a strip of paper with 12 spaces, as shown at the right
- two different coins or chips for markers

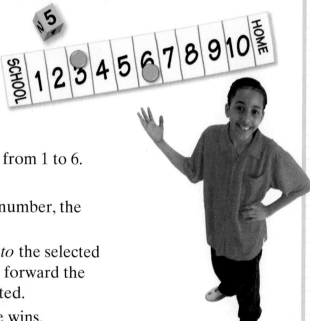

How To Play
- A player starts a turn by selecting a number from 1 to 6.
- The player rolls the number cube.
- If the number rolled is *less than* the selected number, the player does not move his or her marker.
- If the number rolled is *greater than or equal to* the selected number, the player moves his or her marker forward the number of spaces equal to the number selected.
- Players take turns. The first to land on home wins.

Independent Events

What You'll Learn

To find probabilities of independent events

🔊 **New Vocabulary** independent events, compound event

Why Learn This?

In many games, you can plan a winning strategy by finding the probability of two or more events happening.

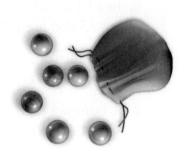

Suppose you draw a marble from the bag.

$$P(\text{blue}) = \frac{4}{6}, \text{ or } \frac{2}{3} \qquad P(\text{red}) = \frac{2}{6}, \text{ or } \frac{1}{3}$$

If you return or replace the marble, mix the marbles, and draw again, the probabilities do not change. If the occurrence of one event does not affect the probability of another event, then the two events are **independent events.**

EXAMPLE **Identifying Independent Events**

1 Decide whether the given events are independent. Explain.

a. You toss a coin twice. The first toss is heads. Then you make a second toss.

Independent: The first toss has no effect on the second toss.

b. You select a colored pen from a box of assorted colored pens. Your brother selects one after you.

Not independent: After you select one pen, there will be one pen fewer in the box. The first selection affects the second selection.

✓ Quick Check

1. You select a card from a deck of cards. Without replacing it, you select another card. Are the events independent? Explain.

A **compound event** consists of two or more separate events. When events are independent, you can find probability with a formula.

> **KEY CONCEPTS** **Probability of Independent Events**
>
> If A and B are independent events, then
>
> $$P(A, \text{then } B) = P(A) \times P(B).$$

For: Independent Events Activity
Use: Interactive Textbook, 10-5

EXAMPLE **Probability of Independent Events**

2. You have a bag containing three red cubes and two yellow cubes. You draw a cube from the bag and replace it. Then you draw a second cube. Find the probability that both cubes are red.

The events are independent. $P(\text{red})$ is $\frac{3}{5}$.

$$P(\text{red, then red}) = \frac{3}{5} \times \frac{3}{5} \qquad \leftarrow \text{Use the formula.}$$

$$= \frac{9}{25} \qquad \leftarrow \text{Multiply.}$$

The probability that both cubes are red is $\frac{9}{25}$.

✓ Quick Check

2. For the situation in Example 2, find $P(\text{yellow, then yellow})$.

You can multiply to find the probability of more than two events.

EXAMPLE **Application: Quiz Show**

3. Three questions are asked during a quiz show. Each question has choices A, B, C, and D. You guess each answer at random. What is the probability that you answer all questions correctly?

For each question, the probability of guessing the answer is $\frac{1}{4}$.

$$P(\text{three correct answers}) = \frac{1}{4} \times \frac{1}{4} \times \frac{1}{4}$$

$$= \frac{1}{64}$$

The probability that you answer all three questions correctly is $\frac{1}{64}$.

✓ Quick Check

3. You guess at random the answers of four true-or-false questions. What is the probability that all four answers are correct?

1. **Vocabulary** Rolling a number cube and picking a number card (are, are not) independent events.

2. **Mental Math** Find the probability of rolling the number 5 on a number cube and then tossing heads on a coin.

3. <u>**Writing in Math**</u> Give examples of two events that are independent and two events that are not independent.

Homework Exercises

For more exercises, see Extra Skills and Word Problems.

GO for Help

For Exercises	See Examples
4–6	1
7–12	2
13–16	3

Decide whether the events are independent. Explain your answer.

4. You have nickels and dimes in your pocket. You take out a dime at random and spend it. Then you take out a second coin at random.

5. You roll five number cubes and the numbers rolled are 1, 2, 3, 4, and 5.

6. A teacher selects one student and then another student.

A bag contains 3 red, 5 blue, and 2 green marbles. Marbles are drawn twice with replacement. Find each probability.

7. both red   8. both green   9. both blue

10. red, then blue   11. blue, then red   12. red, then green

A number cube is rolled three times. What is the probability of each sequence of rolls?

13. even, even, odd   14. 3, 4, 5   15. each less than 5

16. An envelope contains two $1 bills and four $5 bills. You select three bills at random with replacement. What is the probability of choosing only $5 bills?

17. **Guided Problem Solving** A new restaurant offers a choice of 4 main dishes and 3 desserts. You randomly choose a main dish and a dessert. What is the probability of choosing both the main dish and the dessert that are the chef's favorites?
   - Are the two events independent?
   - What two probabilities can you use to find the answer?

One letter is drawn from the set below and then replaced. Find each probability.

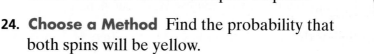

18. $P(\text{H, then U})$ **19.** $P(\text{Y, then S})$ **20.** $P(\text{A, then vowel})$

21. Biology Assume that parents are equally likely to have a boy or a girl. Find $P(\text{girl, then boy})$.

22. Bells Each day three church bells are rung in a random order. What is the probability that the smallest bell rings first three days in a row?

Suppose you spin the spinner twice.

23. Is the outcome of the second spin independent of the outcome of the first spin? Explain.

24. Choose a Method Find the probability that both spins will be yellow.

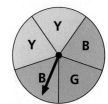

25. Challenge A bag of five apples contains three ripe apples and two rotten apples. If a ripe apple is selected first, what is the probability that a second apple selected is rotten?

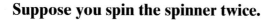
Test Prep and Mixed Review
Practice

Multiple Choice

26. Jerry's class has 24 students. His teacher puts each student's name in a hat. One name is drawn at random from the hat. What is the probability that Jerry's name will NOT be drawn?

Ⓐ $\frac{1}{24}$ Ⓑ $\frac{1}{23}$ Ⓒ $\frac{23}{24}$ Ⓓ $\frac{24}{23}$

27. Find the measure of the angle to the nearest degree.

Ⓕ $65°$ Ⓗ $115°$
Ⓖ $75°$ Ⓙ $125°$

for Help

For Exercises	See Lesson
28–29	9-9

Find the volume of each rectangular prism.

28.

4 cm
3 cm
4 cm

29.

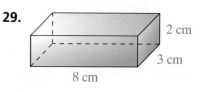

2 cm
3 cm
8 cm

Dependent Events

When the occurrence of one event affects the probability of the occurrence of another event, the two events are **dependent events.**

The formula for the probability of dependent events states that if event B depends on event A, then $P(A,$ then $B) = P(A) \times P(B$ after $A)$.

EXAMPLE

The cards at the right are placed in a bag and shaken. You choose two cards at random. Find the probability that you draw M out first and, without replacing it, draw A next.

The probability of drawing M first is $\frac{1}{4}$. Then, since M is not in the bag, A is one of 3 letters in the bag. So the probability of drawing A next is $\frac{1}{3}$.

$P(M,$ then $A) = P(M) \times P(A$ after $M)$ ← Use the formula for dependent events.

$\qquad = \frac{1}{4} \times \frac{1}{3}$ ← Substitute and multiply.

$\qquad = \frac{1}{12}$

Exercises

Twenty cards are numbered 1–20. You draw a card. Without replacing it, you draw a second card. Find each probability.

1. $P(1,$ then 20)

2. $P(3,$ then even)

3. $P($even, then 7)

A bag contains 3 blue marbles, 4 red marbles, and 2 white marbles. You draw a marble. Without replacing it, you draw a second marble. Find each probability.

4. $P($red, then blue)

5. $P($red, then white)

6. $P($both blue)

7. $P($both white)

8. <u>**Writing in Math**</u> You draw marbles at random without replacing them. Are these independent or dependent events? Explain.

Practice Solving Problems

You can use what you know about counting outcomes to solve problems.

A Close Vote Andres, Bonita, Chen, Debi, and Erin have the same number of votes in an election for three student council members. So a random selection is made. Letters A–E are put on cards to represent the first letter in each of their names. Three cards are then selected at random to choose the three council members. What is the probability that Erin (E) is selected?

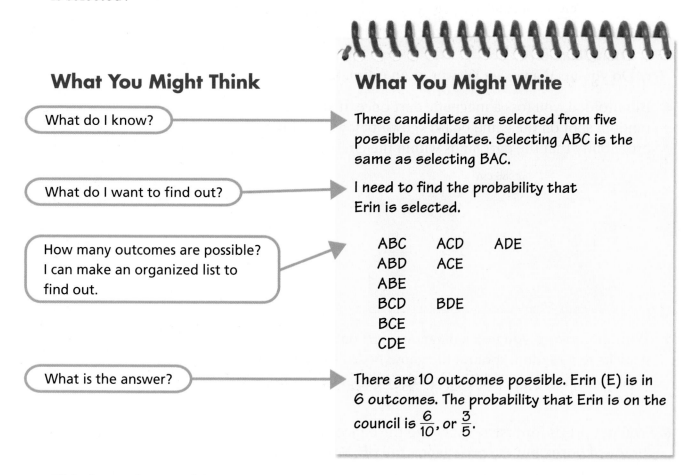

What You Might Think

What do I know?

What do I want to find out?

How many outcomes are possible? I can make an organized list to find out.

What is the answer?

What You Might Write

Three candidates are selected from five possible candidates. Selecting ABC is the same as selecting BAC.

I need to find the probability that Erin is selected.

ABC	ACD	ADE
ABD	ACE	
ABE		
BCD	BDE	
BCE		
CDE		

There are 10 outcomes possible. Erin (E) is in 6 outcomes. The probability that Erin is on the council is $\frac{6}{10}$, or $\frac{3}{5}$.

Think It Through

1. What does this statement mean: *Selecting ABC is the same as selecting BAC?*

2. **Check for Reasonableness** Does the probability of each of the other candidates being elected also equal $\frac{3}{5}$? Explain.

Exercises

3. The results from a survey of 1,012 adults are shown below. About how many of the people in the 2005 survey said they always wear a seat belt?

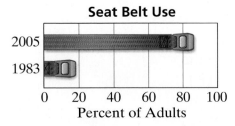

Seat Belt Use

a. What are you trying to find?
b. What data do you need?
c. Do you need an exact answer or an estimate? Explain.

4. Blindfolded, you toss a magnetic dart once. It sticks to a random spot on the game board shown below. What is the probability that the dart lands within the circle?

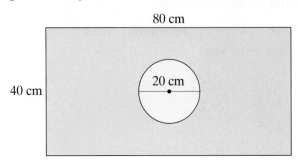

80 cm
40 cm
20 cm

5. Without looking, you toss a magnetic dart once, and it sticks to a random spot on the game board shown at the right. What is the probability that the dart lands inside the triangle?

6. You put prizes for first, second, and third place in separate wrapped boxes, but the prize labels fall off. You put a label on one of the boxes at random. What is the probability that the label is correct?

7. Suppose you have 6 blue socks, 8 red socks, and 4 black socks in the same drawer. Without looking, you pick one sock out of the drawer. Without returning it, you pick another. What is the probability that both socks are blue?

Interpreting Data

You may need to compare data displayed in a graph. You can use number sense to help you compare.

EXAMPLE

Several students were asked to name their favorite pizza topping. Their responses are displayed in the bar graph.

Which statement is best supported by the information in the graph?

Favorite Pizza Topping

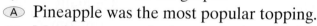

ⓐ Pineapple was the most popular topping.
ⓑ Mushroom was the least popular topping.
ⓒ Pepperoni was more popular than sausage.
ⓓ Sausage was the most popular topping.

- More people chose mushroom than pineapple, so you can eliminate choices A and B.
- Since only 5 people chose sausage, the answer is not D.
- Six people chose pepperoni. Only 5 people chose sausage. The correct answer is choice C.

Exercises

Games Played at Arcade

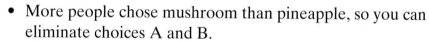

1. Which statement is best supported by the graph?
   ⓐ More people played 11 games than 15 games.
   ⓑ The same number of people played 11 games as played 14 games.
   ⓒ More than 50% of the people played 12 games.
   ⓓ Fewer than 5 people played 13 games.

2. What is the mode of the data represented in the graph above?
   ⓕ 4   ⓖ 12   ⓗ 13   ⓙ 26

Vocabulary Review

🔊 **complement of an event**
  (p. 483)
  compound events (p. 501)
  counting principle (p. 477)
  dependent event (p. 504)
  equally likely outcomes
  (p. 482)

event (p. 476)
experimental probability
  (p. 488)
independent events (p. 500)
outcome (p. 476)
permutation (p. 481)
population (p. 495)

probability of an event
  (p. 482)
sample (p. 495)
sample space (p. 476)
simulation (p. 498)
tree diagram (p. 477)

Choose the vocabulary term from the column at the right that best completes each sentence.

1. When tossing a coin, one possible __?__ is "coin shows heads."

2. __?__ have the same chance of occurring.

3. The __?__ can be used to find the number of outcomes in a compound event.

4. To make predictions about a population, you can use a(n) __?__ that represents that population.

A. counting principle
B. equally likely outcomes
C. event
D. sample

Go Online
PHSchool.com

For: Vocabulary quiz
Web Code: aqj-1051

Skills and Concepts

Lesson 10-1

• To construct sample spaces for events and to use the counting principle

You can make an organized list, draw a tree diagram, or use the **counting principle** to find the number of arrangements of objects.

The set of all possible outcomes is the **sample space.**

5. **Flags** Suppose you want to make a flag with four stripes colored red, blue, green, and white. Use the counting principle to find the number of ways you can order the colors.

Lesson 10-2

• To find the probabilities of an event and of its complement

An **event** is an outcome or group of outcomes. The **probability of an event** is the ratio

$$P(\text{event}) = \frac{\text{number of favorable outcomes}}{\text{total number of outcomes}}.$$

A number cube is rolled once. Find each probability.

6. $P(5)$ 7. $P(\text{even})$ 8. $P(4 \text{ or } 6)$

Lesson 10-3

• To find experimental probability

You can find probabilities by collecting data. For a series of trials, the **experimental probability** of an event is the ratio

$$P(\text{event}) = \frac{\text{number of times event occurs}}{\text{total number of trials}}.$$

9. Noel and Kayla play a game 30 times. Noel wins 20 times. What is the experimental probability that Kayla wins? That Noel wins?

You spin a spinner 60 times. It stops on blue 15 times, green 25 times, and red 20 times. Find each experimental probability.

10. $P(\text{blue})$ 11. $P(\text{red})$ 12. $P(\text{not green})$

Lesson 10-4

• To make predictions from probabilties and samples

You can predict the number of times an event will occur by multiplying the probability of the event by the total number of trials. If you want to make predictions about a **population,** you can use a **sample** to gather the information you need. You can model many situations with a **simulation.**

13. **Computers** Out of 300 computers, 22 are defective. How many defective computers would you expect in a group of 30,000?

14. The probability of rain in San Francisco on a given day is $\frac{1}{6}$. The probability of rain in Miami is $\frac{5}{6}$. Use two number cubes to find the simulated probability of rain in both cities.

Lesson 10-5

• To find probabilities of independent events

A **compound event** consists of two or more separate events. If A and B are independent events, you can find the probability of the compound event "A, then B" with the formula $P(A, \text{then } B) = P(A) \times P(B)$.

Decide whether the events are independent. Explain your answers.

15. A roll of a number cube is 3. The fourth roll of the number cube is 6.

16. You draw a pink cube from a bag containing pink and yellow cubes. Without replacing the pink cube, you draw a yellow cube.

A bag contains two red, four blue, and three green marbles. You draw marbles twice with replacement. Find each probability.

17. both green   18. green, then red   19. red, then blue

For Exercises 1 and 2, use the diagram below. Suppose you spin the spinner three times.

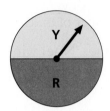

1. Make a tree diagram to show the sample space. How many possible outcomes are there?

2. Find P(yellow, then red, then yellow).

3. Suppose you read in the newspaper that the probability of rain is 10%. Write the probability as a fraction and as a decimal.

4. The figure at the right has faces numbered from 1 through 12. All outcomes are equally likely. Find each probability for one roll.
   a. P(even number)
   b. P(prime)
   c. P(7 or 8)
   d. P(13)

5. Pam and Tony play a game 18 times. Tony wins 8 times and Pam wins 10 times.
   a. Find the experimental probability that Pam wins.
   b. Find the experimental probability that Tony wins.
   c. **Writing in Math** If Pam and Tony play the game 18 more times, must the experimental probabilities remain the same? Explain.

6. A ranch has 132 cows. You pick 32 of them at random and find that 18 of those cows have spots. Predict the number of cows on the ranch that have spots.

7. A bag contains only blue and green chips. The probability of drawing a blue chip is $\frac{5}{12}$. Find P(green).

A bag contains 4 red, 4 blue, and 3 green cubes. Cubes are drawn twice with replacement. Find each probability.

8. P(blue, then green)

9. P(both red)

10. P(both green)

11. P(red, then blue)

12. Determine whether the events are independent. Explain your answers.
    a. You roll two number cubes. One shows a 3. The other shows a 1.
    b. You draw a red marble from a bag containing red and yellow marbles. You do not put the marble back. You draw another red marble.

13. Suppose you roll a number cube twice. What is the probability of getting a 2 on the first roll and a 5 on the second roll?

The letters of the word *PROBABILITY* are written on 11 cards. You draw a card at random, replace it, and draw a second card. Find each probability.

14. P(B, then R)

15. P(I, then vowel)

Reading Comprehension

Read each passage and answer the questions that follow.

> **E-commerce** In the future, purchasing items online is likely to become more popular than shopping at a store. During a recent year, the most popular items bought online were computer hardware goods. Online sales for the year were as follows: 24% for computer hardware, 13% for clothing and footwear, 4% for music and videos, and 3% for toys and games.

1. Suppose a website that sells all types of goods receives 200 orders. How many sales would you expect to be for computer hardware goods?
   - Ⓐ 4
   - Ⓑ 13
   - Ⓒ 24
   - Ⓓ 48

2. What is the probability, given as a fraction, that any online sale during the year will be for clothing and footwear?
   - Ⓕ $\frac{1}{24}$
   - Ⓖ $\frac{1}{13}$
   - Ⓗ $\frac{13}{100}$
   - Ⓙ $\frac{6}{25}$

3. What is the percentage of sales that will NOT be any of the items listed in the article?
   - Ⓐ 56%
   - Ⓑ 44%
   - Ⓒ 37%
   - Ⓓ 7%

4. Suppose an employee of an e-commerce company selects 20 orders at random. Of these, 4 are for clothing and footwear. In this sample, what is the experimental probability of a clothing or footwear order?
   - Ⓕ 2.6%
   - Ⓖ $\frac{13}{100}$
   - Ⓗ $\frac{1}{5}$
   - Ⓙ $\frac{4}{5}$

> **Sports Trends** Are "ball" sports becoming less popular? From 1993 to 2000, the number of youths who play baseball went down from 23% to 12%. In that same period, the number of youths who play basketball decreased from 58% to 46%. From 1993 to 2000, in-line skating participation increased from 17% to 30% and snowboarding participation rose by about 8%.

5. In 2000, what was the probability of a youth participating in in-line skating?
   - Ⓐ 0.58
   - Ⓑ 0.46
   - Ⓒ 0.30
   - Ⓓ 0.17

6. About which sport are you NOT given enough information to find the probability of a youth playing the sport in 1993?
   - Ⓕ baseball
   - Ⓖ basketball
   - Ⓗ in-line skating
   - Ⓙ snowboarding

7. In 1993, suppose 300 youths were asked what sports they played. How many youths were likely to say basketball?
   - Ⓐ 174
   - Ⓑ 138
   - Ⓒ 58
   - Ⓓ 46

8. Which sport discussed in the article had the greatest decrease in percentage of participation?
   - Ⓕ baseball
   - Ⓖ basketball
   - Ⓗ in-line skating
   - Ⓙ snowboarding

Applying Probability

Fair Chance? Toss a ring onto a post, hit a target with a baseball, or pop a balloon with a dart. The real pleasure comes from playing the game, but how likely are you to win? Sometimes you can figure it out by using geometry and probability together.

Horseshoes

The game of horseshoes uses special shoes with a maximum weight of 2 pounds 10 ounces. A shoe must fall within 6 inches of the stake to score.

Heads or Tails?

A coin toss has two possible outcomes: heads or tails.

Milk-bottle array

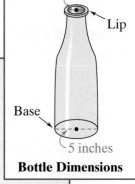

2 inches

Lip

Base

5 inches

Bottle Dimensions

Put It All Together

At the school fair, the student council set up 100 old milk bottles in rows. The challenge is to throw a coin into one of the bottles. The game seems easy because there are so many bottles.

1. The square at the right shows part of the bottle array from above. Copy the diagram. Label as many dimensions as you can.

2. Since a coin can land anywhere within one of these square regions, the diagram shows the possible outcomes of each throw. What is the area of the square?

3. A favorable outcome is when a coin lands inside a bottle.

   a. On your copy of the square, shade the regions in which the coin must land for a favorable outcome.

   b. **Reasoning** If you made several copies of the square and put the shaded regions together, what shapes would be shaded?

   c. Find the area of the shaded parts of your square.

4. a. Calculate the probability of winning the game. Write your answer as a percent.

   b. How many times would you expect to win if you played 100 times?

   c. **Number Sense** It costs $1 for one toss. The student council pays $1.75 for each prize. If 50 people play, how much money can the student council expect to raise with this game? Show your work.

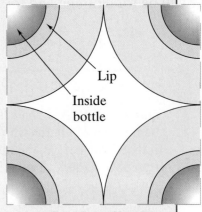

Lip

Inside bottle

Top view of bottles

Carnival Games
Some schools use carnival games as fundraisers.

Go Online
PHSchool.com
For: Information about games
Web code: aqe-1053

CHAPTER 11

Integers

What You've Learned

- In earlier chapters, you learned to add, subtract, multiply, and divide decimals and fractions.

- You wrote and solved equations.

- You graphed numbers on a number line and used graphs to analyze data.

 Check Your Readiness

GO for Help

For Exercises	See Lessons
1–2	3-5
3–4	3-6
5–10	3-7
11–16	4-8

(Algebra) Solving Equations

Solve each equation.

1. $a + 13 = 92$

2. $b + 12 = 43$

3. $c - 31 = 8$

4. $d - 23 = 8$

(Algebra) Solving Multiplication and Division Equations

Solve each equation.

5. $7g = 4.2$

6. $h \div 6 = 11$

7. $8j = 328$

8. $k \div 9 = 8$

9. $16m = 240$

10. $n \div 14 = 18$

Comparing and Ordering Fractions

Compare each pair of numbers. Use <, =, or >.

11. $\frac{1}{3} \blacksquare \frac{2}{5}$

12. $\frac{3}{4} \blacksquare \frac{2}{3}$

13. $\frac{2}{16} \blacksquare \frac{1}{8}$

Order each set of numbers from least to greatest.

14. $\frac{1}{8}, \frac{1}{3}, \frac{1}{12}$

15. $\frac{4}{9}, \frac{5}{6}, \frac{7}{12}$

16. $\frac{1}{4}, \frac{6}{7}, \frac{1}{2}$

What You'll Learn Next

- In this chapter, you will use integers, opposites, and absolute values to represent real-world situations.

- You will locate and graph points in the coordinate plane using ordered pairs of integers.

- You will add, subtract, multiply, and divide integers.

- You will solve equations using integers.

🔊 Key Vocabulary

- absolute value (p. 517)
- coordinate plane (p. 548)
- function (p. 558)
- integers (p. 516)
- opposites (p. 516)
- ordered pair (p. 548)
- origin (p. 548)
- quadrants (p. 548)

 Problem Solving Application On pages 568 and 569, you will work an extended activity on elevation.

Exploring Integers

What You'll Learn

To use integers, opposites, and absolute values to represent real-world situations

◀)) **New Vocabulary** opposites, integers, absolute value

Why Learn This?

You can use integers to represent real-world situations. In the tug-of-war below, the team on the right has gained 2 feet. The position of the flag is positive 2, or +2. You write +2 as 2.

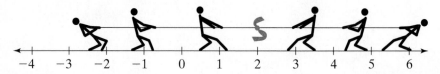

Suppose the team on the right had lost 2 feet instead. The position of the flag would have been negative 2, or −2.

$$-5 \quad -4 \quad -3 \quad -2 \quad -1 \quad 0 \quad 1 \quad 2 \quad 3 \quad 4 \quad 5$$

Opposites are two numbers that are the same distance from 0 on a number line but in opposite directions. **Integers** are the set of positive whole numbers, their opposites, and zero. The opposite of 0 is 0.

EXAMPLE   Representing Situations with Integers

1 Multiple Choice Dry ice is solid carbon dioxide, which freezes at about 109 degrees below zero Fahrenheit. Which integer represents the freezing point of dry ice?

   Ⓐ −109   Ⓑ −19   Ⓒ +19   Ⓓ +109

The freezing point is 109 degrees below zero. Use a negative sign for an integer less than zero: −109. The answer is choice A.

✓ Quick Check

1. The lowest elevation in New Orleans, Louisiana, is 8 feet below sea level. Use an integer to represent this elevation.

The "smoke" that makes a performance exciting is actually from dry ice.

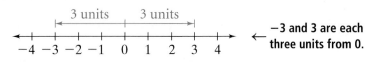

EXAMPLE Identifying Opposites

Calculator Tip

You can use the (-) key or the +/- key on your calculator to express an opposite.

2 Write the opposite of 3.

3 units | 3 units

```
←——+——+——+——+——+——+——+——+——+——→
  −4  −3  −2  −1   0   1   2   3   4
```

← −3 and 3 are each three units from 0.

The opposite of 3 is −3.

✓ Quick Check

● **2.** Write the opposite of −5.

The **absolute value** of a number is its distance from 0 on a number line. The symbol for the absolute value of a number n is $|n|$. Opposite numbers have the same absolute value.

EXAMPLE Finding Absolute Value

Test Prep Tip

Drawing a number line can help you answer questions involving integers.

3 Find $|-4|$ and $|2|$.

4 units | 2 units

```
←——•——+——+——+——•——+——•——+——+——→
  −4  −3  −2  −1   0   1   2   3   4
```

Since −4 is four units from 0, $|-4| = 4$. Since 2 is two units from 0, $|2| = 2$.

✓ Quick Check

● **3. a.** Find $|-1|$. **b.** Find $|7|$.

✓ Check Your Understanding

1. **Vocabulary** Give examples of numbers that are integers and numbers that are *not* integers.

2. **Open-Ended** Describe two different real-life situations that can be represented by the integer −9.

Match each integer with a point on the number line.

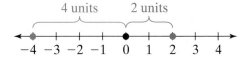

```
     M      N              P           Q
←——•——+——•——+——+——+——+——•——+——+——•——+——→
  −6  −5  −4  −3  −2  −1   0   1   2   3   4   5   6
```

3. −6   4. 5   5. 1   6. −4

Homework Exercises

For more exercises, see Extra Skills and Word Problems.

GO for Help

For Exercises	See Examples
7–12	1
13–20	2
21–28	3

Use an integer to represent each situation.

7. earned $100

8. 800 ft gain in elevation

9. 12° below 0°C

10. 4° above 0°F

11. a debt of $25

12. lost 5 pounds

Write the opposite of each integer.

13. −10   **14.** −21   **15.** 14   **16.** 0

17. 13   **18.** −8   **19.** 150   **20.** −1

Find each absolute value.

21. $|38|$ **22.** $|2|$ **23.** $|-9|$ **24.** $|-97|$

25. $|-4|$ **26.** $|17|$ **27.** $|-65|$ **28.** $|0|$

GPS **29. Guided Problem Solving** The reading on a thermometer outside is 55°F when you leave for school at 8:00 A.M. At 3:00 P.M., the reading is 72°F. What integer can you use to represent the change in temperature?

- You can use a number line to help visualize the problem.

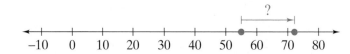

30. Starting at the fourth floor, an elevator goes down 3 floors and then up 8 floors. At which floor does the elevator stop?

31. Divers Dean dives 17 feet below the surface of Canyon Lake. Janet dives 25 feet below the lake's surface. Use absolute values to find who dives farther below the surface.

32. Writing in Math Can the absolute value of a number be negative? Explain your reasoning.

Write an integer for each point on the number line.

33. *A*   **34.** *B*   **35.** *C*   **36.** *D*

Write two numbers that have the given absolute value.

37. 3   **38.** 22   **39.** 101   **40.** 2,004

41. (**Algebra**) The absolute value of a certain integer n equals the opposite of n. If n does not equal 0, is n positive or negative?

42. History A timeline is a number line that shows dates.

Draw a timeline from 2000 B.C. to A.D. 2000 using intervals of 500 years. Then graph the following events on the timeline.

A.D. 1971   The first microcomputer is introduced.
776 B.C.   The first Olympic Games are held.
1600 B.C.   Stonehenge is completed.
A.D. 1492   Columbus lands in the New World.
1190 B.C.   The city of Troy falls to Greek warriors.

43. Challenge Explain how to locate 225 on the number line.

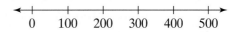

Microchips used in computers are made of silicon, a chemical element found in ordinary beach sand.

Test Prep and Mixed Review   **Practice**

Multiple Choice

44. Tara was 50 feet below the surface of the ocean. She then swam up 20 feet. Which integer represents her starting depth?
  Ⓐ −50   Ⓑ −20   Ⓒ 20   Ⓓ 50

45. Kaida has 4 red marbles, 3 blue marbles, and 5 green marbles in a bag. If she randomly draws one marble from the bag, what is the probability that she does NOT draw a red marble?
  Ⓕ $\frac{1}{8}$ Ⓖ $\frac{1}{3}$ Ⓗ $\frac{1}{2}$ Ⓙ $\frac{2}{3}$

GO for Help

For Exercises	See Lesson
46–48	9-4

Use the data in the graph for Exercises 46–48.

46. Which waterfall has the greatest height?

47. Which waterfall has the least height?

48. Which waterfalls are between 2,000 feet and 2,500 feet?

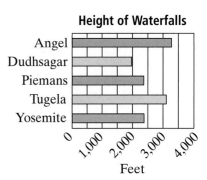

Height of Waterfalls

Comparing and Ordering Integers

Check Skills You'll Need

1. **Vocabulary Review** The symbol $<$ means ? , and the symbol $>$ means ? .

Compare each pair of numbers. Use $<$, $=$, or $>$.

2. $\frac{2}{3}$ ■ $\frac{7}{10}$

3. $\frac{2}{3}$ ■ $\frac{8}{12}$

4. $\frac{3}{5}$ ■ $\frac{5}{11}$

 **for Help**
Lesson 4-8

What You'll Learn

To compare and order integers

Why Learn This?

Negative points and scores are possible in some games. You need to compare and order integers to find who is winning.

You can use a number line to compare integers. As you move to the right on a number line, the numbers become greater.

$$\begin{array}{ccccccccc} -4 & -3 & -2 & -1 & 0 & 1 & 2 & 3 & 4 \end{array}$$

… negative integers   positive integers …

0 is neither positive nor negative.
The opposite of 0 is 0.

EXAMPLE   Comparing Integers

1 Compare -6 and -4.

$$\begin{array}{cccccc} -8 & -6 & -4 & -2 & 0 & 2 \end{array}$$

← Graph -4 and -6 on the same number line.

Since -6 is to the left of -4 on the number line, $-6 < -4$, or $-4 > -6$.

Quick Check

1. Compare, using $<$ or $>$.
   a. 5 ■ -3 b. -12 ■ 9

You can also use a number line to order integers.

EXAMPLE **Ordering Integers**

Tigers	−200
Bulldogs	+300
Lions	−400
Spartans	+100

② **Games** Order the scores on the scoreboard from least to greatest.

Use one hundred as the number line interval.

$$-400 \quad -300 \quad -200 \quad -100 \quad 0 \quad 100 \quad 200 \quad 300 \quad 400$$

$-400, -200, 100, 300$ ← **Order the scores from least to greatest.**

In order, the scores are $-400, -200, 100,$ and 300.

For: Comparing Integers Activity
Use: Interactive Textbook, 11-2

✓ Quick Check

2. Order these scores from least to greatest: $-25, 100, -50, 75$.

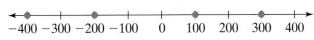
Check Your Understanding

1. Which statement is NOT true?
   Ⓐ $-9 < -7$ Ⓑ $-3 < 5$ Ⓒ $-5 > -3$ Ⓓ $-2 < 6$

2. Order $-2, 4, 0,$ and -6 from least to greatest.

3. **Writing in Math** Suppose a is negative and b is positive. Use a number line to explain how you know that $a < b$.

Homework Exercises

For more exercises, see **Extra Skills and Word Problems.**

GO for Help

For Exercises	See Examples
4–15	1
16–20	2

Compare, using < or >.

4. $-7 \blacksquare -8$ **5.** $-3 \blacksquare 3$ **6.** $0 \blacksquare -9$ **7.** $-7 \blacksquare 0$

8. $-5 \blacksquare 0$ **9.** $6 \blacksquare -18$ **10.** $-12 \blacksquare -2$ **11.** $0 \blacksquare -3$

12. $2 \blacksquare -12$ **13.** $-9 \blacksquare -17$ **14.** $-1 \blacksquare 10$ **15.** $-23 \blacksquare -4$

Order each set of integers from least to greatest.

16. $-9, -12, -4, -15$ **17.** $-2, 5, 0, -5, 2$

18. $40, -30, 30, -50, -60$ **19.** $-28, -16, -33, -13$

20. Golf In golf, a negative score is called "under par." List the golf scores $-1, +2, -3,$ and $+4$ from least to greatest.

21. Guided Problem Solving Here are the coldest and hottest temperatures on record for four Alaskan cities:
$-34°F, 85°F, -62°F, 96°F, -22°F, 90°F, -54°F, 86°F$.

Write the temperatures in order from coldest to hottest.
- Separate the list into negative and positive integers.
- Order each group of integers separately.

22. Number Sense What is the greatest negative integer?

23. How many integers are *greater than* -5 and *less than* 5?

24. Weather Order the temperatures below from least to greatest.
- Normal body temperature is about $37°C$.
- An average winter day on the polar ice cap is $-25°C$.
- The warmest day on record in Canada was $45°C$.
- The coldest day on record in Texas was $-31°C$.

25. (Algebra) Compare, using $<$ or $>$.
a. If $x > y$, then the opposite of x ■ the opposite of y.
b. If $x < y$, then the opposite of x ■ the opposite of y.

26. Challenge Write the numbers in order from least to greatest:
$-2, -1.3, \frac{1}{4}, 0, -4, -\frac{1}{2}, -2\frac{3}{4}, 3, -3.5, 2\frac{1}{2}$.

Test Prep and Mixed Review

Practice

Multiple Choice

27. The temperature on the moon varies from $-387°F$ to $253°F$. Which integer represents the highest moon temperature?
- Ⓐ -387
- Ⓑ -253
- Ⓒ 253
- Ⓓ 387

28. Two students measured the length of the shelves in a school library. The results are shown in the table. Which expression can be used to find the length, in yards, of shelf E?
- Ⓕ $3n$
- Ⓗ $n - 3$
- Ⓖ $\frac{3}{n}$
- Ⓙ $\frac{n}{3}$

Library Shelves

Shelf	Length (feet)	Length (yards)
A	3	1
B	6	2
C	12	4
D	15	5
E	n	■

For Exercises	See Lesson
29–31	9-4

Find the area of each parallelogram.

29.
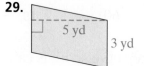
5 yd
3 yd

30.
6 km 9 km

31.
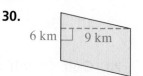
6.5 m
4 m

Modeling Addition of Integers

ACTIVITY

1. Find 5 + 2.

Show 5 "+" chips. Then add 2 "+" chips.   There are 7 "+" chips. So 5 + 2 = 7.

   →

2. Find −5 + (−2).

Show 5 "−" chips.   There are 7 "−" chips.
Then add 2 "−" chips.   So −5 + (−2) = −7.

   →

To add integers with different signs, use zero pairs. These chips
⊕ ⊖ are a *zero pair* because ⊕ + ⊖ = 0. Removing a zero pair
does not change the sum.

3. Find 5 + (−2).

Show 5 "+" chips.   Pair the "+" and "−" chips.   There are 3 "+" chips left.
Then add 2 "−" chips.   Remove the pairs.   So 5 + (−2) = 3.

   →   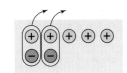   →

Exercises

Use chips or mental math to add the following integers.

1. 13 + (−8)   **2.** −4 + 3   **3.** −7 + (−2)   **4.** 8 + (−11)

5. Write a rule for adding each of the following: (a) two positive
integers, (b) two negative integers, and (c) two integers with
different signs.

11-3 Adding Integers

Check Skills You'll Need

1. Vocabulary Review Find two integers with an *absolute value* of 6.

Find each absolute value.

2. $|15|$ **3.** $|-12|$

4. $|-8|$ **5.** $|8|$

for Help
Lesson 11-1

What You'll Learn

To add integers and to solve problems by adding integers

Why Learn This?

Sometimes you add positive and negative integers, such as yards gained and yards lost in a football game.

You can use a number line to model the addition of integers. You start at 0, facing the positive direction. You move forward for a positive integer and backward for a negative integer. Here is how to model $3 + 2$.

Start at 0. Face the positive direction. Move forward 3 units for 3.

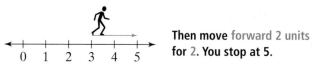

Then move forward 2 units for 2. You stop at 5.

EXAMPLE Using a Number Line to Add Integers

1 Use a number line to find $-3 + (-2)$.

Start at 0, and face the positive direction. Move backward 3 units for -3.

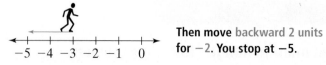

Then move backward 2 units for -2. You stop at -5.

So $-3 + (-2) = -5$.

Quick Check

1. Use a number line to find $-1 + (-3)$.

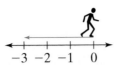 **Application: Sports**

2 A football team loses 3 yards on one play. On the next play, the team gains 2 yards. Find −3 + 2.

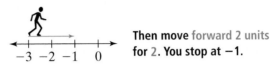

Start at 0, and face the positive direction.
Move backward 3 units for −3.

Then move forward 2 units
for 2. You stop at −1.

The result is a loss of 1 yard.

✓ Quick Check

2. Find −4 + 1.

KEY CONCEPTS **Adding Integers**

Same Signs The sum of two positive integers is positive. The sum of two negative integers is negative.

Examples: $2 + 6 = 8$ $-2 + (-6) = -8$

Different Signs Find the absolute value of each integer. Then subtract the lesser absolute value from the greater. The sum has the sign of the integer with the greater absolute value.

Examples: $3 + (-7) = -4$ $-3 + 7 = 4$

EXAMPLES **Adding Integers**

3 Find −3 + (−7).

$-3 + (-7) = -10$ ← The sum of two negative numbers is negative.

4 Find 8 + (−5).

$|8| = 8$ and $|-5| = 5$ ← Find the absolute value of each integer.
$8 - 5 = 3$ ← Subtract the absolute values.
$8 + (-5) = 3$ ← Since 8 has the greater absolute value, the sum is positive.

GO ▶ for Help

For help with absolute values, go to Lesson 11-1, Example 3.

✓ Quick Check

3. Find −9 + (−12).   **4.** Find −11 + 4.

Check Your Understanding

Complete each statement with *always, sometimes,* or *never.*

1. The sum of two negative integers is __?__ negative.

2. The sum of two positive integers is __?__ negative.

3. The sum of a positive integer and a negative integer is __?__ negative.

4. **Number Sense** Explain how you can tell whether the sum of two numbers is positive or negative before you add.

Homework Exercises

For more exercises, see Extra Skills and Word Problems.

GO for Help

For Exercises	See Examples
5–11	1–2
12–23	3–4

Use a number line to find each sum.

5. $-5 + (-3)$

6. $2 + 4$

7. $-2 + (-2)$

8. $6 + (-7)$

9. $-1 + 4$

10. $-6 + 6$

11. **Money** Suppose you borrow $8 from a friend. You pay him back $6. How much do you still owe?

Find each sum.

12. $-2 + (-7)$

13. $-6 + 3$

14. $9 + (-9)$

15. $-31 + (-16)$

16. $-12 + (-9)$

17. $13 + 29$

18. $91 + 28$

19. $-47 + (-41)$

20. $-51 + (-9)$

21. $23 + (-15)$

22. $-8 + 72$

23. $18 + (-39)$

24. **Guided Problem Solving** A jellyfish was 64 feet below sea level. It rose 19 feet. What integer describes the new position of the jellyfish?
    • What integer represents 64 feet below sea level?
    • What operation represents a rise of 19 feet?

25. **Temperature** At 7:30 A.M. on January 22, 1943, the temperature was −4°F in Spearfish, South Dakota. At 7:32 A.M. the temperature had risen 49 degrees. What was the temperature at 7:32 A.M.?

Find each sum.

26. $8 + (-1) + (-6) + 5$ **27.** $-2 + 6 + (-3) + (-4)$

28. <u>**Writing in Math**</u> Why do you use subtraction when you add a positive integer and a negative integer?

29. Open-Ended Use a positive integer and a negative integer to write a word problem about each bank account.
  a. The sum of the integers is negative.
  b. The sum of the integers is positive.
  c. The sum of the integers is zero.

30. Skyscrapers The mail center of a building is on the fifteenth floor. A clerk delivers mail by going up 5 floors, down 3 floors, and then down another 4 floors. Where is the clerk in relation to the mail center?

31. Submarines A submarine is 86 feet below sea level. The submarine then rises 16 feet and dives 58 feet. What integer describes the position of the submarine?

32. Challenge Copy the square shown. Write the integers $-4, -3, -2, -1, 0, 1, 2, 3,$ and 4 in the boxes so that the vertical, horizontal, and diagonal sums are 0.

 Test Prep and Mixed Review   **Practice**

Multiple Choice

33. Rita ate less than half of her sandwich for lunch. Which fraction is NOT less than $\frac{1}{2}$?

  Ⓐ $\frac{1}{4}$ Ⓑ $\frac{2}{5}$ Ⓒ $\frac{4}{7}$ Ⓓ $\frac{5}{11}$

34. A 5-kilometer run is about 3.1 miles long. How many meters long is a 5-kilometer run?

  Ⓕ 0.005 m   Ⓖ 0.05 m   Ⓗ 500 m   Ⓙ 5,000 m

35. You need to add three simplified fractions. The denominators are 9, 12, and 18. What is the least common denominator?

  Ⓐ 18   Ⓑ 36   Ⓒ 72   Ⓓ 108

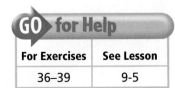

For Exercises	See Lesson
36–39	9-5

Name each of the following for circle _J_.

36. radii   **37.** diameters

38. chords   **39.** the center

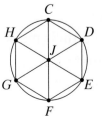

Find each absolute value.

1. $|-13|$

2. $|64|$

Find each sum.

3. $-8 + 5$

4. $-10 + (-2)$

5. You write a check for $32. What integer represents the change in your checking account balance?

6. Order 16, −17, 18, −15, and −14 from least to greatest.

7. In the morning, the temperature was −7°F. The temperature rose 19 degrees by noon. What was the temperature at noon?

MATH GAMES

A Race to the End

What You'll Need

- game board
- two different-colored number cubes
- two different-colored place markers

How To Play

- Each player places a marker on 0.
- Use one cube to represent positive integers and the other cube to represent negative integers.
- One player rolls the two number cubes.
- The player adds the integers represented by the cubes and then moves his or her marker the number of spaces in the direction indicated by the sum.
- Players take turns rolling both number cubes and moving their markers.
- The first player who reaches or goes past either end of the board wins.

Modeling Subtraction of Integers

ACTIVITY

1. Find $-5 - (-2)$.

Show 5 "−" chips.		Take away 2 "−" chips.		There are 3 "−" chips left. So $-5 - (-2) = -3$.
	→		→	

Remember that and ⊖ are a zero pair. Sometimes you need to insert zero pairs in order to subtract.

ACTIVITY

2. Find $5 - (-2)$.

Show 5 "+" chips.		Insert two zero pairs. Then take away 2 "−" chips.		There are 7 "+" chips left. So $5 - (-2) = 7$.
	→	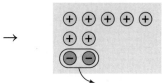	→	

3. Find $-5 - 2$.

Show 5 "−" chips.		Insert two zero pairs. Then take away 2 "+" chips.		There are 7 "−" chips left. So $-5 - 2 = -7$.
	→	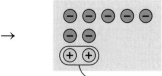	→	

Exercises

Use chips or mental math to help you subtract the following integers.

1. $5 - 8$ **2.** $-3 - 7$ **3.** $5 - (-9)$ **4.** $-8 - (-13)$

Subtracting Integers

What You'll Learn

To subtract integers and to solve problems by subtracting integers

Why Learn This?

You can subtract integers to find changes in the depth of vehicles or creatures underwater.

You can use a model to subtract integers. On a number line, the subtraction operation tells you to turn around and face the opposite direction.

EXAMPLE **Using a Number Line to Subtract**

Vocabulary Tip

The expression 3 − (−2) is read "3 minus negative 2."

1 Use a number line to find 3 − (−2).

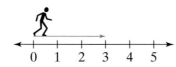

Start at 0. Face the positive direction. Move forward 3 units for 3.

The subtraction sign tells you to turn around.

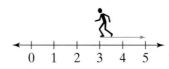

Then move backward 2 units for −2. You stop at 5.

So 3 − (−2) = 5.

✓ Quick Check

1. a. Find 5 − (−1).   **b.** Find −3 − 3.

Subtracting an integer is the same as adding its opposite.
$$3 - 2 = 1 \text{ and } 3 + (-2) = 1$$

KEY CONCEPTS **Subtracting Integers**

You subtract an integer by adding its opposite.

Examples:

$$10 - 6 = 10 + (-6) \qquad 10 - (-6) = 10 + 6$$
$$-10 - 6 = -10 + (-6) \qquad -10 - (-6) = -10 + 6$$

EXAMPLE **Subtracting Integers**

② **a.** Find $-8 - (-3)$.

$$-8 - (-3) = -8 + 3 \qquad \leftarrow \text{To subtract } -3, \text{ add its opposite, 3.}$$
$$= -5 \qquad \leftarrow \text{Simplify.}$$

b. Find $-2 - 7$.

$$-2 - 7 = -2 + (-7) \qquad \leftarrow \text{To subtract 7, add its opposite, } -7.$$
$$= -9 \qquad \leftarrow \text{Simplify.}$$

GO for Help

For help adding integers, go to Lesson 11-3, Example 3.

✓ Quick Check

2. Find $-6 - (-2)$.

EXAMPLE **Application: Submarines**

③ The submarine *Alvin* was 1,500 feet below sea level ($-1,500$). Then it moved to 1,872 feet below sea level ($-1,872$). How far did *Alvin* move?

Find $-1,872 - (-1,500)$.

$$-1,872 - (-1,500) = -1,872 + 1,500 \qquad \leftarrow \begin{array}{l} \text{To subtract } -1,500, \\ \text{add its opposite.} \end{array}$$
$$= -372 \qquad \leftarrow \text{Simplify.}$$

Alvin moved down 372 feet.

GO Online

Video Tutor Help

Visit: PHSchool.com
Web Code: aqe-0775

✓ Quick Check

3. Suppose *Alvin* moved from 1,872 feet below sea level to a position 1,250 feet below sea level. How far did *Alvin* move? Did it finish closer to sea level or farther from sea level?

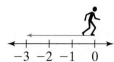
1. Write an expression you can model using the steps below.

2. **Writing in Math** Explain why $2 - 7$ is not the same as $7 - 2$.

Rewrite each difference as a sum.

3. $-10 - 3$ 4. $2 - (-8)$ 5. $-1 - (-3)$

Homework Exercises

For more exercises, see Extra Skills and Word Problems.

 for Help

For Exercises	See Examples
6–11	1
12–21	2–3

Use a number line to find each difference.

6. $7 - 4$ 7. $4 - (-5)$ 8. $3 - 8$

9. $-1 - 6$ 10. $-2 - (-3)$ 11. $-4 - (-1)$

Find each difference.

12. $-1 - (-1)$ 13. $2 - 7$ 14. $-4 - 3$

15. $-9 - 7$ 16. $81 - 106$ 17. $12 - (-17)$

18. $43 - (-21)$ 19. $-24 - (-12)$ 20. $-25 - (-57)$

21. **Biology** A fish was at 1,965 feet below sea level. It then swam down to 2,327 feet below sea level. How far did the fish swim?

GPS 22. **Guided Problem Solving** Temperatures on the surface of Mercury vary from $-279°F$ to $801°F$. What is the range of temperatures on the surface of Mercury?
- **Make a Plan** To find the range, you subtract the lowest temperature from the highest temperature.
- **Check the Answer** Round -292 to -300 to check your answer.

 **nline**
Homework Video Tutor
Visit: PHSchool.com
Web Code: aqe-1104

23. **Hiking** You are at the highest point of Lost Mine Trail. Your elevation is 6,850 feet. You hike down the trail to an elevation of 5,600 feet. What is your change in elevation?

Find each difference.

24. $17 - 18 - (-81)$ **25.** $-18 - 13 - 12$

26. $23 - (-18) - (-54)$ **27.** $16 - 28 - (-38)$

28. Time Zones Standard time is computed in relation to Greenwich Mean Time (GMT). The table shows the number of hours from GMT for each city. It is 1:30 P.M. GMT. Find the time for each city.

Cairo, Egypt	+2
Honolulu, Hawaii	−10
Los Angeles, Calif.	−8
Paris, France	+1
Sydney, Australia	+10
Tokyo, Japan	+9
Washington, D.C.	−5

29. (**Algebra**) Explain why $a - b$ is not always the same as $b - a$.

30. Challenge Copy and complete the pyramid so that each number represents the sum of the two numbers directly beneath it.

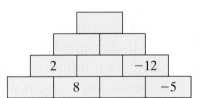

The two sides of this house are in different time zones.

 Test Prep and Mixed Review   **Practice**

Multiple Choice

31. The low temperature on Monday was 6 degrees below zero. The high temperature was 10 degrees above zero. Which integer represents the low temperature?

  (A) −16   (B) −6   (C) 6   (D) 16

32. Mr. Young has 20 students in his art class. He buys paint in packages of 12 jars. He wants to give the same number of jars of paint to each student. Arrange the steps below to find the least amount of paint Mr. Young needs to buy.

  Step K. Find the least common multiple of 12 and 20.
  Step L. List the multiples of 12 and the multiples of 20.
  Step M. Divide the least common multiple by 12.

  (F) K, M, L   (G) K, L, M   (H) L, K, M   (J) L, M, K

GO for Help

For Exercises	See Lesson
33–36	8-1

Use the figure to name the following.

33. three rays   **34.** three segments

35. three points   **36.** three lines

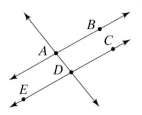

What You'll Learn

To multiply integers and to solve problems by multiplying integers

Why Learn This?

Computers multiply time by a negative rate to tell skydivers when to open their parachutes.

Recall that multiplication is an easy way to do repeated addition. You can use a number line to multiply integers. Always start at 0.

3×2 means three groups of 2 each: $3 \times 2 = 6$.

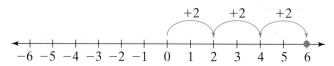

$3 \times (-2)$ means three groups of −2 each: $3 \times (-2) = -6$.

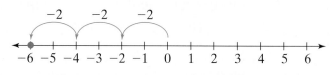

The integers 3 and −3 are opposites. You can think of -3×2 as the opposite of three groups of 2 each. So $-3 \times 2 = -6$.

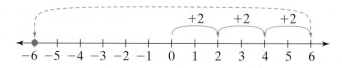

You can think of $-3 \times (-2)$ as the opposite of three groups of −2 each. Since $3 \times (-2) = -6$, $-3 \times (-2) = 6$.

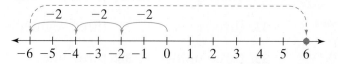

EXAMPLE **Using a Model to Multiply Integers**

1 Use a number line to find $4 \times (-3)$.

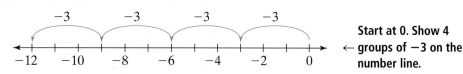

Start at 0. Show 4
← groups of -3 on the
number line.

The sum of 4 groups of -3 is -12. So $4 \times (-3) = -12$.

✓ Quick Check

1. a. Find $3 \times (-4)$.　　　　　**b.** Find $-3 \times (-4)$.

You can use the following rules to multiply integers.

KEY CONCEPTS **Multiplying Integers**

The product of two integers with the *same* signs is positive.
The product of two integers with *different* signs is negative.

Examples:　　　$4 \times 5 = 20$　　　$4 \times (-5) = -20$
　　　　　　　　　$-4 \times (-5) = 20$　　　$-4 \times 5 = -20$

EXAMPLES **Multiplying Integers**

GO ●nline

Video Tutor Help
Visit: PHSchool.com
Web Code: aqe-0775

2 Find $-5 \times (-6)$.

$-5 \times (-6) = 30$　← same signs, positive product

3 A skydiver falls 56 meters each second. The skydiver waits 8 seconds before opening her parachute. Use an integer to express the change in the skydiver's elevation.

$(-56) \times 8 = -448$　← Use a negative number to represent falling.

The integer -448 expresses the change in the skydiver's elevation.

✓ Quick Check

2. a. Find $-9 \times (-3)$.　　　　　**b.** Find $5 \times (-3)$.

3. The temperature drops 5°F each hour for four hours. Use an integer to express the total drop in temperature.

Check Your Understanding

1. <u>Writing in Math</u> Explain how to find $5 \times (-2)$.

2. Copy and complete the table with *positive* or *negative*.

Multiplication of Integers

positive	×	positive	=	?
negative	×	negative	=	?
positive	×	negative	=	?
negative	×	positive	=	?

State whether each product is positive or negative.

3. -8×4

4. $-3 \times (-5)$

5. $7 \times (-6)$

Homework Exercises

For more exercises, see Extra Skills and Word Problems.

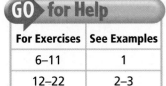

For Exercises	See Examples
6–11	1
12–22	2–3

Use a number line to find each product.

6. 6×3

7. $-4 \times (-2)$

8. $5 \times (-2)$

9. $8 \times (-1)$

10. -2×7

11. $-1 \times (-3)$

Find each product.

12. -7×5

13. $11 \times (-2)$

14. 7×12

15. $-6 \times (-9)$

16. $(-4) \times 9$

17. $15 \times (-3)$

18. $-25 \times (-5)$

19. -16×4

20. $-1 \times (-124)$

21. **Money** You withdraw $10 from a bank account once a week for four weeks. What integer expresses the change in value?

22. The temperature fell three degrees per hour for four hours. What was the total change in the temperature?

23. **Guided Problem Solving** A game show awards 25 points for correct answers and deducts 15 points for incorrect answers. Use the table to determine which player wins.
    - Find the score for each player.
    - Compare the scores. You may find a number line helpful.

Game Show Results

Player	Correct Answers	Incorrect Answers
A	9	21
B	5	8

Find each product.

24. $-3 \times (-4) \times (-5)$ **25.** $12 \times (-12) \times (-1)$

26. $-6 \times 2 \times (-2) \times 8$ **27.** $7 \times 3 \times (-3) \times 2$

28. Number Sense When does the product of two integers equal zero? When does the sum of two integers equal zero?

29. Ballooning Hot air balloons generally descend at a rate of 200 to 400 feet per minute. A balloon descends 235 feet per minute for 4 minutes. Write an integer to express the balloon's total movement.

30. a. Is the product of 3 negative integers positive or negative?
   b. Is the product of 4 negative integers positive or negative?
   c. What happens when you multiply five negative integers?
   d. Patterns Will the product of 101 negative integers be positive or negative? Explain.

31. Challenge Find $1 - 2 + 3 - 4 + 5 - 6$. Then change one of the operation symbols in the expression to multiplication so that the new value is eight times the original value.

Test Prep and Mixed Review

Practice

Multiple Choice

32. Rhonda runs in a marathon. Which statement is NOT supported by the graph?
   Ⓐ Rhonda ran the first 20 miles in 3 hours.
   Ⓑ Rhonda ran the last 6 miles in less than 1 hour.
   Ⓒ Rhonda ran the first half of the race in less than 2 hours.
   Ⓓ Rhonda ran the second half of the race in less than 2 hours.

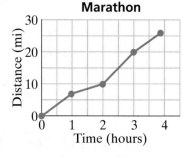

Marathon

33. Reed randomly chooses two marbles from a bag of yellow marbles and red marbles. Which list shows all of the possible combinations of marbles Reed could choose?
   Ⓕ 2 red; 2 yellow   Ⓗ 2 red; 2 yellow; 1 of each
   Ⓖ 1 red and 1 yellow   Ⓙ 1 red; 1 yellow; 2 of each

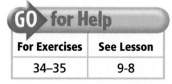

For Exercises	See Lesson
34–35	9-8

Find the surface area of each rectangular prism.

34. $\ell = 5$ m, $w = 3$ m, $h = 4$ m   **35.** $\ell = 9$ m, $w = 6$ m, $h = 7$ m

Practice Solving Problems

Interpreting Time You start a video tape at the beginning to record a show. The time readings on the recorder when you stop recording and when you finish rewinding are shown below. How long is the recording?

Time Stopped	18:54
Time Started	−4:15

What You Might Think

> What do I know? What do I want to find?

> What diagram can I draw to show the situation?

> What equation can I write using the diagram?

> What is the answer?

What You Might Write

- The timer shows 18:54 when I stop recording.

- After rewinding, the timer shows −4:15.

- I want to know how long the recording is.

```
|←————————— x —————————→|
┌────────────┬──────────────────────┐
│            │                      │
└────────────┴──────────────────────┘
 ↑          ↑                      ↑
−4:15      0:00                  18:54
```

Let t = the total length of the recording.

$$t = 18{:}54 - (-4{:}15)$$
$$= 18{:}54 + 4{:}15$$
$$= 22{:}69, \text{ or } 23{:}09$$

The recording is 23 minutes and 9 seconds.

Think It Through

1. Why did you use subtraction in the equation?

2. How was 22:69 changed to 23:09?

3. **Number Sense** Can you use the equation $-4{:}15 - 18{:}54 = t$ to show this situation? Explain.

Exercises

4. Use the graph below. Find the increase in pay a person would expect from earning an advanced degree after a bachelor's degree. Is that amount greater than the increase expected by someone earning a bachelor's degree after a high school diploma?

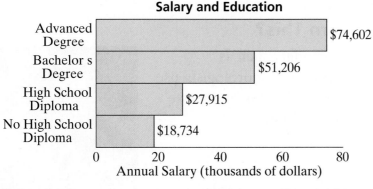

Salary and Education

a. Use the differences in the amounts earned to decide.

b. What is your conclusion? Explain.

The expected score in golf is called the "par" score. Golfers who play well score below par (−). Use the table below for Exercises 5–7.

Golf Earnings

Player	Score	Relative to Par	Earnings
Phil Mickelson	208	−8	$900,000
Bo Van Pelt	226	+10	$9,500

5. Draw a picture and write an equation to show by how many points Phil Mickelson outscored Bo Van Pelt in this tournament.

6. What was par for the tournament?

7. How much did Phil Mickelson earn per stroke under par?

8. **Reasoning** Time is sometimes given in terms of a 24-hour day. The time 0:00 represents midnight. The time 16:30 represents 16 hours and 30 minutes after midnight, or 4:30 P.M. Find both a positive and a negative number to represent 10:36 P.M.

What You'll Learn

To divide integers and to solve problems by dividing integers

Why Learn This?

Many professionals, such as stockbrokers and meteorologists, use rates of change. You can find a rate of change by dividing integers.

The rules for finding the sign of a quotient when dividing integers are similar to the rules for multiplying integers.

KEY CONCEPTS   **Dividing Integers**

The quotient of two integers with the same sign is positive.
The quotient of two integers with different signs is negative.

Examples: $20 \div 4 = 5$ $20 \div (-4) = -5$
$-20 \div (-4) = 5$ $-20 \div 4 = -5$

EXAMPLE   **Dividing Integers**

1 **a.** Find $-15 \div (-3)$.

$-15 \div (-3) = 5$ ← same signs, positive quotient

b. Find $-24 \div 8$.

$-24 \div 8 = -3$ ← different signs, negative quotient

✓ Quick Check

1. Find each quotient.
a. $-24 \div 6$ **b.** $-36 \div (-2)$ **c.** $48 \div (-12)$

Careers Meteorologists analyze and predict changes in the weather.

2 **Multiple Choice** The temperature changed from $0°C$ to $-56°C$ in four hours. Find the average rate of change in degrees per hour.

Ⓐ -52 Ⓑ -14 Ⓒ 14 Ⓓ 52

$-56 \div 4 = -14$ ← different signs, negative quotient

The average rate of change is $-14°C$ per hour.

The correct answer is choice B.

Quick Check

2. The value of one share of stock decreased $20 over the last five days. Find the average rate of change in dollars per day.

Check Your Understanding

1. **Error Analysis** Who found the correct quotient? Explain.

Zarita	Zurina
$-6 \div (-2) = 3$	$-6 \div (-2) = -3$

2. **Writing in Math** Explain how you know without computing that the quotient $-400 \div 25$ is less than 0.

3. Over three hours, the temperature decreased $6°$. Find the average rate of change in degrees per hour.

Tell whether each quotient is *positive* or *negative*.

4. $-24 \div (-3)$ 5. $30 \div (-10)$ 6. $-81 \div 9$

Homework Exercises

For more exercises, see **Extra Skills and Word Problems.**

GO for Help

For Exercises	See Examples
7–14	1
15–17	2

Find each quotient.

7. $-64 \div (-8)$ 8. $-25 \div (-5)$

9. $-12 \div (-2)$ 10. $-15 \div 3$

11. $72 \div (-1)$ 12. $-28 \div 4$

13. $100 \div (-20)$ 14. $-84 \div 7$

Find the average rate of change for each situation.

15. You climb 72 stairs in 4 minutes.

16. The price of shoes decreases $21 over 7 days.

17. A rock sinks 160 feet in 20 seconds.

 18. **Guided Problem Solving** Copy and complete the pyramid so that each number represents the product of the two numbers directly beneath it.

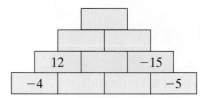

- You can *work a simpler problem* to complete the pyramid.
- Find the missing numbers below.

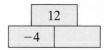 

19. The value of a share of stock decreased $30 over the last 5 days. Find the average rate of change in dollars per day.

20. **Reasoning** Is the mean of 5 negative numbers positive or negative? Explain your reasoning.

21. **Science** You fill a 500-mL bowl with fresh water and a 600-mL bowl with salt water. All of the fresh water evaporates in 4 days. All of the salt water evaporates in 5 days. Does fresh water evaporate faster than salt water? Explain.

22. **Challenge** Is the division of integers commutative? Give examples to support your answer.

Test Prep and Mixed Review   Practice

Multiple Choice   23. Stacia's hair grows at an average rate of 6 inches each year. How many months will it take for her hair to grow 18 inches?

Ⓐ 3   Ⓑ 24   Ⓒ 30   Ⓓ 36

24. What is the measure of $\angle W$?

Ⓕ 30°   Ⓗ 120°

Ⓖ 60°   Ⓙ 150°

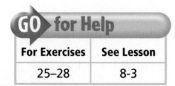
GO for Help

For Exercises	See Lesson
25–28	8-3

Find the complement and the supplement of each angle.

25. 50°   26. 19°   27. 67°   28. 81°

11-7 Solving Equations With Integers

What You'll Learn

To solve equations containing integers

Why Learn This?

Equations can help you find an unknown amount of money.

You can solve equations that contain integers the same way you solve other equations. Use the properties of equality and inverse operations to get the variable alone on one side of the equation.

EXAMPLE **Solving Equations with Integers**

1 Solve each equation. Check the solution.

a. $t + 9 = 5$

$t + 9 - 9 = 5 - 9$ ← Subtract 9 from each side to undo the addition.

$t = 5 + (-9)$ ← To subtract 9, add its opposite, -9.

$t = -4$ ← Simplify.

Check $-4 + 9 = 5$ ✔   ← Check by replacing t with -4.

b. $m \div 5 = -7$

$m \div 5 \times 5 = -7 \times 5$ ← Multiply each side by 5 to undo the division.

$m = -35$ ← Simplify.

Check $-35 \div 5 = -7$ ✔   ← Check by replacing m with -35.

✓ Quick Check

1. Solve each equation. Check the solution.
  a. $c - 15 = -5$ **b.** $k \div (-7) = -$ **c.** $-6z = 36$

EXAMPLE   Application: Budget

② **Gridded Response** You earn $200 during the summer and deposit it into a new savings account. You withdraw $25 on the first day of each month, starting in September. For how many months can you withdraw $25?

Words   [monthly withdrawal] times [number of months] equals [total of all withdrawals]

⬇ Let m = the number of months.

Equation -25 × m = -200

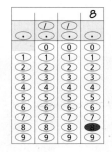

$$-25m = -200 \qquad \leftarrow \text{Write the equation.}$$
$$-25m \div (-25) = -200 \div (-25) \qquad \leftarrow \text{Divide each side by } -25.$$
$$m = 8 \qquad \leftarrow \text{Simplify.}$$

You can withdraw $25 per month for 8 months.

✓ Quick Check

2. Budget Use Example 2. If you make 10 monthly withdrawals instead of 8, how much can you withdraw each month?

✓ Check Your Understanding

1. **Open-Ended** Write a word problem that can be solved by using the equation $x - 10 = -50$.

2. **Reasoning** Is the first step in solving $8x = -56$ the *same as* or *different from* the first step in solving $-8x = 56$? Explain.

3. Suppose a scuba diver is 100 feet below sea level. The diver rises to the surface at a rate of 25 feet per minute. How long will it take the diver to reach the surface?

Mental Math **Match each equation with the correct solution.**

4. $-3x = -6$
5. $x - 6 = -7$
6. $-5x = -5$
7. $x \div 2 = 0$
8. $x + 3 = 1$

A. -2
B. -1
C. 0
D. 1
E. 2

For more exercises, see Extra Skills and Word Problems.

GO for Help

For Exercises	See Examples
9–20	1
21	2

Solve each equation. Check the solution.

9. $t + 12 = 9$ **10.** $v - 6 = -4$ **11.** $-3 + c = -8$

12. $w - 18 = -13$ **13.** $x - (-6) = 18$ **14.** $x + 20 = -20$

15. $-6y = 42$ **16.** $-4y = -64$ **17.** $7h = -84$

18. $c \div (-8) = 3$ **19.** $z \div (-7) = -1$ **20.** $p \div 2 = -2$

21. A metro train ride costs \$4. After the ride, your card has a balance of −\$3. Find your balance before the train ride.

22. Guided Problem Solving After the first round in a game show, a contestant had 250 points. At the end of the second round, the contestant had −300 points. How did the score change during the second round?
• First define the variable. Then write an equation.

23. Four friends divided a restaurant bill evenly. Each owed \$20. What was the total amount of the bill?

24. <u>Writing in Math</u> Explain why $t + 4 = -6$ and $t + 6 = -4$ have the same solution.

GO Online
Homework Video Tutor
Visit: PHSchool.com
Web Code: aqe-1107

25. Temperature At midnight the temperature was 0°F. It then began to decrease about 4 degrees per hour. After about how many hours did the temperature reach −20°F?

26. Challenge Solve the equation $2x - 10 = -8$ by using two inverse operations. Check the solution.

Test Prep and Mixed Review   **Practice**

Gridded Response

27. The Perez family drives 473.7 miles to a vacation spot. They drive the same route to get home. Find the total distance the family drives, in miles.

28. A diner offers 3 appetizers, 4 main courses, and 2 desserts. Latoya wants to order one appetizer, one main course, and one dessert. How many choices does she have?

GO for Help

For Exercises	See Lesson
29–30	3-6

Solve each equation.

29. $d - 25 = 39$ **30.** $n - 13 = 74$

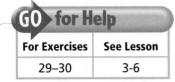

Thinking About Solutions

Thinking about numbers is a good first step when solving an equation. This will alert you to mistakes you might make when solving the equation.

EXAMPLE

Decide which statements are true for $x - 19\frac{1}{2} = 30$.

a. $x \approx 20$ **b.** x is negative.   **c.** $x > 30$

- "$x \approx 20$" is false. The left side of the equation would be close to 0.

- "x is negative" is false. The left side of the equation would be negative.

- "$x > 30$" is true. The left side must be large enough that when $19\frac{1}{2}$ is subtracted 30 remains.

● Statements (a) and (b) are false. Statement (c) is true.

Exercises

Use number sense to decide which statements are true for the given equation. More than one choice may be true. Explain your answer.

1. $x + 7 = -13$
   a. $x > 0$ **b.** x is an integer.   **c.** $x < -13$

2. $11x = 100$
   a. x is a whole number.   **b.** x is negative.   **c.** $x < 10$

3. $3x = -16$
   a. $x < 0$ **b.** $x \approx -50$ **c.** $x \approx 5$

4. $x + 8 = 3$
   a. $x > 0$ **b.** x is an integer.   **c.** $x < 0$

5. $100 - x = 49\frac{1}{2}$
   a. $x \approx 90$ **b.** $x > 0$ **c.** $x \approx 50$

6. Write two true statements about x for the equation $2x = -81$. Then write two false statements about the same equation.

Graphing Points

You can use a graphing calculator to explore how to graph points. An ordered pair is a pair of numbers that describe the location of a point on your screen.

First, prepare your calculator for this activity. Press 2nd [PLOT] 4: PlotsOff to turn off the plots. Press Y= and clear any equations. Press ZOOM 4: ZQuadrant1 to set the window.

ACTIVITY

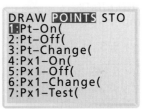

1. First press CLEAR.

2. Press DRAW to select the **Draw** menu. Press ▶ to highlight **Points.** Select 1: Pt-On. Then press ENTER.

3. To graph the point (6, 4), press 6 , 4) ENTER.

4. The ordered pair (6, 4) tells you the location of the point. How far to the right of the vertical line is the point (6, 4)? How far above the horizontal line is the point?

5. Repeat steps 1–3 to graph (4, 5). Describe the location of the point on the screen.

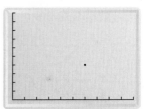

Exercises

Use a graphing calculator to graph each point.

6. (1, 6)   7. (9, 7)   8. (2, 3)   9. (6, 1)

10. **Reasoning** Without using a graphing calculator, describe the location of the point (4, 8). Draw a diagram to check your answer.

11. Graph (0, 4) on a calculator. Why does the point not appear on the screen?

12. **Writing in Math** Your classmate needs to graph (3, 14). Write directions for your classmate explaining how to graph the point on the calculator.

11-8

Graphing in the Coordinate Plane

✓ Check Skills You'll Need

1. Vocabulary Review
Opposites are the same distance from __?__ on a number line.

Graph each integer on a number line.

2. −2   **3.** 3

4. 0   **5.** −6

GO for Help
Lesson 11-1

What You'll Learn

To name and graph points on a coordinate plane

🔊 **New Vocabulary** coordinate plane, quadrants, origin, ordered pair

Why Learn This?

You can use coordinates to find and describe locations on a map.

The **coordinate plane** is a surface formed by the intersection of two number lines. The plane is divided into four regions, called **quadrants**. The **origin** is the point where the two number lines intersect.

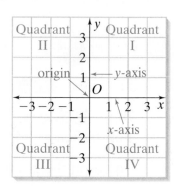

An **ordered pair** is a pair of numbers that describes the location of a point in a coordinate plane. The ordered pair (0, 0) describes the origin.

The *x*-coordinate tells ———┐   ┌——— The *y*-coordinate tells
how far to move right or   *x*   *y*   how far to move up or
left along the *x*-axis.   down along the *y*-axis.

EXAMPLE   Naming Coordinates

Vocabulary Tip

The plural of *axis* is *axes*.

① Find the coordinates of point *C*.

Point *C* is 1 unit to the right of the *y*-axis. So the *x*-coordinate is 1.

Point *C* is 3 units above the *x*-axis. So the *y*-coordinate is 3.

The coordinates of point *B* are (1, 3).

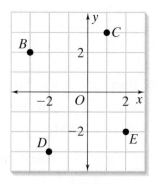

✓ Quick Check

1. Find the coordinates of each point in the coordinate plane.
     a. *B*   **b.** *D*   **c.** *E*

Online active math

For: Coordinate Plane Activity
Use: Interactive Textbook, 11-8

You can graph points if you know their coordinates. You move right from the *origin* to graph a positive *x*-coordinate and left from the *origin* to graph a negative *x*-coordinate. You move up from the *x*-axis to graph a positive *y*-coordinate and down from the *x*-axis to graph a negative *y*-coordinate.

EXAMPLE **Graphing Ordered Pairs**

② Graph point $P(3, 2)$ on a coordinate plane.

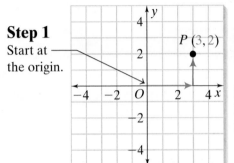

Step 1
Start at the origin.

Step 3
Move 2 units up.

Step 2
Move 3 units to the right.

✓ Quick Check

2. Graph each point on the same coordinate plane.
   a. $A(1, 3)$ **b.** $B(-3, 2)$ **c.** $C(-4, -4)$

EXAMPLE **Using Map Coordinates**

③ A student drew a map of certain locations in relation to home.

a. Identify the coordinates of the library.

The library is located at $(-2, 1)$.

b. You leave the library and ride your scooter 2 blocks north and then 4 blocks east. At which building do you arrive?

You are at the grocery store.

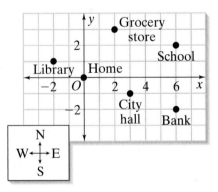

✓ Quick Check

3. **a.** Suppose you leave the library and walk 5 blocks east and then 2 blocks south. At which building do you arrive?
   b. What are the coordinates of the building?

11-8 Graphing in the Coordinate Plane **549**

1. **Vocabulary** Why is order important in an ordered pair?

2. **Open-Ended** Name four points on a coordinate plane that form a square when connected by straight lines.

3. Which point is NOT in the same quadrant as the other three?
   Ⓐ $(8, -4)$ Ⓑ $(-5, 6)$ Ⓒ $(1, -7)$ Ⓓ $(2, -2)$

Homework Exercises

For more exercises, see Extra Skills and Word Problems.

GO for Help

For Exercises	See Examples
4–11	1
12–17	2
18–20	3

Find the coordinates of each point at the right.

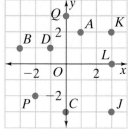

4. B 5. D 6. K 7. Q

Name the point with the given coordinates in the coordinate plane at the right.

8. $(1, 2)$ 9. $(-2, -2)$

10. $(3, -3)$ 11. $(0, -3)$

Graph each point on the same coordinate plane.

12. $A(1, 5)$ 13. $B(-5, -3)$ 14. $C(2, -4)$

15. $D(-2, 3)$ 16. $E(1, -4)$ 17. $F(-5, 5)$

Use the map below for Exercises 18–20.

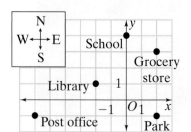

18. You travel 2 units north of the library and 4 units east. Where do you arrive?

19. Find the coordinates of the park.

20. Find the coordinates of the school.

 21. **Guided Problem Solving** A police car begins at $(-2, 8)$. It travels 6 blocks east and 10 blocks south to the courthouse. In which quadrant is the courthouse?
    • Which direction on the coordinate plane is east?
    • Which direction on the coordinate plane is south?

22. **Writing in Math** What do all points located on the y-axis have in common? Explain.

Name the quadrant or axis in which each point lies.

23. $(-2, -2)$ **24.** $(6, 4)$ **25.** $(0, 4)$ **26.** $(-1, 9)$

27. $(-3, 0)$ **28.** $(5, -8)$ **29.** $(8, 0)$ **30.** $(0, -10)$

31. Geometry A symmetrical four-pointed star has eight corner points. Seven of the points are $(-1, 1)$, $(0, 3)$, $(1, 1)$, $(3, 0)$, $(1, -1)$, $(0, -3)$, and $(-1, -1)$. What are the coordinates of the missing point?

32. Quilt Making Quilt designers often use coordinate grids to design patterns. Find the coordinates of the pattern shown at the right.

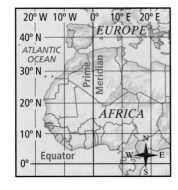

33. Geography Maps of Earth use a coordinate system to describe locations. The horizontal axis is the equator, and the vertical axis is the prime meridian.
  a. On what continent is 20° N latitude, 20° E longitude?
  b. On what continent is 48° N latitude, 5° E longitude?

34. (Algebra) On which axis does the point $(n, 0)$ lie?

35. Challenge A parallelogram has vertices at $(3, 2)$, $(2, 5)$, and $(6, 5)$. Find three possible points for the fourth vertex.

Test Prep and Mixed Review   Practice

Multiple Choice

36. Which ordered pair represents a point located inside both the circle and the rectangle at the right?
  Ⓐ $(1, 2)$ Ⓒ $(3, 2)$
  Ⓑ $(2, 4)$ Ⓓ $(5, 2)$

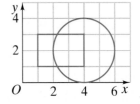

37. Belle cut a rectangle from paper for a geometry project.

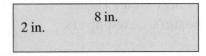

What is the perimeter of the rectangle in inches?
  Ⓕ 6   Ⓖ 10   Ⓗ 16   Ⓙ 20

GO for Help

For Exercise	See Lesson
38	9-6

38. Find the circumference and the area of a circle with a radius of 6 millimeters. Round your answer to the nearest millimeter.

Find each answer.

1. $-4 - (-2)$

2. $-10 - 2$

3. $12 \times (-3)$

4. -8×2

5. $14 \div (-2)$

6. $-21 \div (-3)$

Solve each equation.

7. $x + 5 = -8$

8. $r - 10 = -2$

9. $3d = -12$

10. The temperature decreased 15°F to −2°F. Write and solve an equation to find the starting temperature.

11. A police car begins at $(-2, 8)$. It travels 12 blocks south and 4 blocks east to the courthouse. What are the coordinates of the courthouse?

Name the coordinates of each point.

12. A

13. B

14. C

15. D

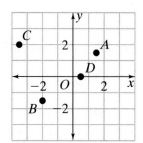

Reflections in the Coordinate Plane

In Chapter 8, you studied reflections. When you use the
x- or y-axis as the line of reflection, there is a relationship
between the coordinates of the reflected points.

EXAMPLES

1   List the ordered pairs of the vertices of the
    parallelograms that are in Quadrants I and II.
    Find a pattern.

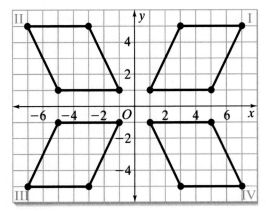

Quadrant I	
x	**y**
1	1
3	5
7	5
5	1

Quadrant II	
x	**y**
−1	1
−3	5
−7	5
−5	1

All corresponding x-coordinates are opposites and
all corresponding y-coordinates are the same.

2   List the ordered pairs of the vertices of the parallelograms that
    are in Quadrants I and IV. Find a pattern.

Quadrant I	
x	**y**
1	1
3	5
7	5
5	1

Quadrant IV	
x	**y**
1	−1
3	−5
7	−5
5	−1

All corresponding x-coordinates are the same and
all corresponding y-coordinates are opposites.

Exercises

**Plot the given points and connect them in order. Reflect the figure
over the y-axis. Then reflect the original figure over the x-axis.**

1. (2, 2), (4, 6), (6, 2), (2, 2)

2. (−1, −1), (−1, −6), (−7, −6), (−1, −1)

3. (1, −1), (4, −1), (4, −3), (3, −4), (2, −4), (1, −3), (1, −1)

11-9 Applications of Integers

Check Skills You'll Need

1. **Vocabulary Review** Explain how you use *absolute value* when you add integers.

Find each sum.

2. 12 + 26

3. (−9) + 18

4. 41 + (−54)

5. −19 + (−10)

 **for Help**
Lesson 11-3

What You'll Learn

To apply integers to profit and loss situations

Why Learn This?

Businesses, such as flower shops, keep track of the money they receive and spend. Money received is called income. Money spent is called expenses.

To find a balance, add the income (positive numbers) and the expenses (negative numbers). A positive balance means that there is a *profit*. A negative balance means that there is a *loss*.

EXAMPLE Finding Profit or Loss

① **Small Business** Find Flower Mania's profit or loss for February.

Income and Expenses for Flower Mania		
Month	Income	Expenses
Jan.	$11,917	−$14,803
Feb.	$12,739	−$9,482
Mar.	$11,775	−$10,954
Apr.	$13,620	−$15,149

$12,739 + (−$9,482) = $3,257 ← **Add income and expenses for February.**

Flower Mania had a profit of $3,257 for February.

Quick Check

1. Find the profit or loss for Flower Mania for January and for March.

You can use line graphs to look at trends of monthly balances.

EXAMPLE Drawing and Interpreting Graphs

2 Business Draw a line graph of the monthly profits and losses for Beth's Pottery Shop. During which month was the profit greatest?

Profit/Loss for Beth's Pottery Shop					
Month	Profit/Loss	Month	Profit/Loss	Month	Profit/Loss
Jan.	−$1,917	May	−$150	Sept.	−$417
Feb.	−$682	June	$250	Oct.	−$824
Mar.	$303	July	$933	Nov.	$1,566
Apr.	$781	Aug.	$1,110	Dec.	$1,945

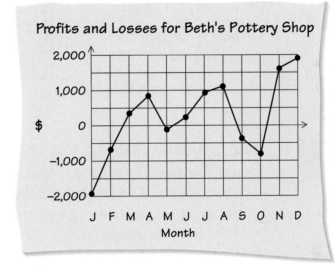

The balances vary from −$1,917 to $1,945. So make a scale from −$2,000 to $2,000. Use intervals of $500.

Beth's Pottery Shop made its greatest profit in December.

Quick Check

2. In which months did Beth's shop show a profit?

Check Your Understanding

1. **Vocabulary** State whether you would use a positive number or a negative number to represent each of the following.
   a. loss   b. income   c. expense   d. profit

2. **Number Sense** If expenses and income for a business are equal in July, how much money does the business make in July?

For more exercises, see Extra Skills and Word Problems.

GO for Help

For Exercises	See Examples
3–7	1
8–10	2

Use the data for Rad's Books. Find the profit or loss.

3. Week 1
4. Week 2
5. Week 3
6. Week 4

Income and Expenses for Rad's Books

Week	Income	Expenses
Week 1	$4,257	−$6,513
Week 2	$3,840	−$2,856
Week 3	$4,109	−$3,915
Week 4	$3,725	−$4,921

Use the table showing income and expenses for several days.

7. Find the profit or loss for each day.

8. Draw a line graph to show the profits and losses.

9. On which day was the profit greatest?

10. On which day was the loss greatest?

Day	Income	Expenses
Mon.	$94	−$85
Tues.	$78	−$60
Wed.	$13	−$22
Thurs.	$90	−$73
Fri.	$37	−$49
Sat.	$15	−$16

GPS 11. **Guided Problem Solving** You sell bottled water at sports games. You pay $20 per game to rent a cooler. You pay $1 each for bottles of water and sell them for $2 each. How many bottles must you sell during a game to make a profit of $100?
   • What are your expenses?
   • How much profit do you earn from each bottle of water?

12. You receive a total of $125 for your birthday. You spend $20 on a sweater, $15 on a CD, $8 on a book, $12 on a pair of sunglasses, and $35 on a bicycle helmet. How much money do you have left?

13. **Writing in Math** Explain how you can determine whether a company has made a profit.

14. **Accounting** Find the balance after each transaction in the checking account. What was the amount of the least balance?

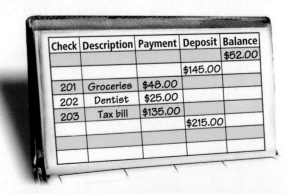

Check	Description	Payment	Deposit	Balance
				$52.00
			$145.00	
201	Groceries	$48.00		
202	Dentist	$25.00		
203	Tax bill	$135.00		
			$215.00	

Use the graph for Exercises 15–18.

15. How many CDs were sold in the fifth week?

16. How many more CDs were sold in the sixth week than were sold in the second week?

17. In which two weeks were the same number of CDs sold?

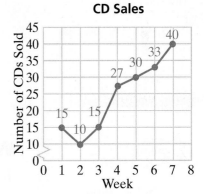

18. Which week showed a decrease in the number of CDs sold?

Population Use the table below for Exercises 19–22.

City	Population (thousands)					
	1950	1960	1970	1980	1990	2000
Miami, Fla.	249	292	335	347	359	362
Rochester, N.Y.	322	319	296	242	232	220

19. Display the data in a double line graph.

20. Use the graph you created in Exercise 19. Which city shows a positive trend in population? A negative trend in population?

21. In 1950, which city had a larger population?

22. **Challenge** Use your graph to predict the population of each city in 2020.

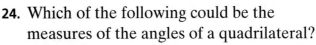
Test Prep and Mixed Review   **Practice**

Multiple Choice

23. Which point on the graph corresponds to the coordinate pair $\left(2\frac{1}{2}, 3\right)$?

    Ⓐ A   Ⓒ C
    Ⓑ B   Ⓓ D

24. Which of the following could be the measures of the angles of a quadrilateral?
    Ⓕ 40°, 65°, 55°, 20°   Ⓗ 80°, 120°, 90°, 90°
    Ⓖ 85°, 75°, 30°, 70°   Ⓙ 115°, 75°, 45°, 125°

GO for Help

For Exercises	See Lesson
25–29	8-2

Classify each angle as *acute, obtuse, right,* or *straight*.

25. 123°   26. 54°   27. 90°   28. 173°   29. 180°

11-10 Graphing Functions

Check Skills You'll Need

1. **Vocabulary Review** Explain how an *expression* and an *equation* are different.

Evaluate each expression for $x = 3$.

2. $8 + x$ **3.** $18 \div x$

4. $4x$ **5.** $21 - x$

 **for Help**
Lesson 3-2

What You'll Learn

To make a function table and to graph a function

◀ঠ) **New Vocabulary** function

Why Learn This?

Pretend you have a machine. You can put any number, or input, into the machine. The machine performs an operation on the number and provides a result, or output. A **function** is a rule that assigns exactly one output value to each input value.

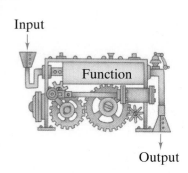

Input

Function

Output

Suppose you tell the machine to multiply by 4. A function table, such as the one at the right, shows the input and output values.

Input	Output
3	12
−7	−28

EXAMPLE Completing a Function Table

① Complete the function table if the rule is Output = Input · (−2).

Input	Output
−1	2
1	−2
3	−6

← Multiply −1 by −2. Place 2 in the Output column.

← Multiply 1 by −2. Place −2 in the Output column.

← Multiply 3 by −2. Place −6 in the Output column.

✓ Quick Check

1. Complete the function table for each rule.

a. Output = Input ÷ 4

Input	Output
16	■
−24	■
36	■

b. Output = Input − 8

Input	Output
−6	■
−1	■
4	■

You can write the function rule in Example 1 using variables.

Output = Input · (−2)

$y = x \cdot (-2)$ or $y = -2x$

You can graph a function on the coordinate plane. Use the horizontal axis for input (x) and the vertical axis for output (y).

EXAMPLE **Graphing a Function**

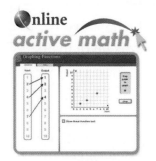

For: Graphing Functions Activity
Use: Interactive Textbook, 11-10

2 Make a table and graph some points of the function $y = x + 3$.

Input (x)	Output (y)
−2	1
−1	2
0	3
1	4
2	5

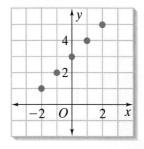

✓ Quick Check

2. Make a table and graph some points of the function $y = x - 3$.

In Example 2, the points lie on a line. This type of function is a linear function. You can join the points with a line.

Vocabulary Tip

The graph of a *linear* function is a *line*.

EXAMPLE **Application: Salaries**

3 Workers at a grocery store make $7 an hour. The function $m = 7h$ shows how the money m they earn relates to the number of hours h they work. Make a table and graph the function.

Hours Worked	Money Earned (dollars)
1	7
2	14
3	21
4	28

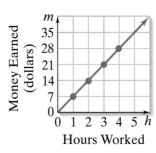

✓ Quick Check

3. A car is driven at a steady rate of 45 miles per hour. The function $d = 45t$ shows how time t relates to distance d. Make a table and graph the function.

More Than One Way

A pizza delivery person receives $5 each day he reports to work and $2 for each pizza he delivers. You can express this situation as the function $y = 5 + 2x$, where y = earnings and x = number of pizzas he delivers. How much will the delivery person earn in one day if he delivers 25 pizzas?

Jessica's Method

I can evaluate the equation to find the amount the delivery person earns. To do so, I replace x with the 25 pizzas he delivers.

$y = 5 + 2x$ ← Write the equation.

$y = 5 + 2(25)$ ← Substitute 25 for x.

$y = 55$

The delivery person will earn $55 for delivering 25 pizzas.

Leon's Method

If I make a table and a graph, I can tell how much the delivery person earns for delivering different numbers of pizzas.

x	y
0	5
5	15
10	25
15	35

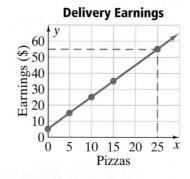

Delivery Earnings

All the points lie on a line, so I can use the graph to find the amount earned for 25 pizzas delivered. When $x = 25$, the y-value is 55. So the delivery person earned $55.

Choose a Method

Tracy is a member of a discount CD club. She pays an annual fee of $30 and $4 for each CD. The function $y = 30 + 4x$ models this situation. If Tracy buys 15 CDs during the year, what will be her total cost? Describe your method and explain why you chose it.

Use the function $y = 3x$.

1. **Vocabulary** Which variable represents the input?

2. Explain how to find the value of y when $x = 4$.

3. Describe the function: For each value of x, __?__ by 3 to find the value of y.

4. Make a table of values and graph the function.

Homework Exercises

For more exercises, see Extra Skills and Word Problems.

Complete the function table using the rule.

GO for Help

For Exercises	See Examples
5–6	1
7–12	2
13	3

5. Output = Input + 4

Input	Output
−5	▦
8	▦
31	▦

6. Output = Input − 4

Input	Output
−2	▦
5	▦
14	▦

Make a table and graph some points for each function.
Use −2, −1, 0, 1, and 2 for x.

7. $y = x + 2$

8. $y = x - 2$

9. $y = 2x$

10. $y = \dfrac{x}{2}$

11. $y = \dfrac{x}{2} + 1$

12. $y = -\dfrac{x}{2}$

13. **Library** Suppose a library charges a fine of $0.25 for each day a book is overdue. The function $f = 0.25d$ shows how the number of days d relates to the fine f. Make a table and graph the function.

14. **Guided Problem Solving** You buy shirts for $9 each. You have a coupon for $2 off your total purchase. Find the final price of seven shirts.
    • What function models this situation?
    • What number will you substitute for t, the price of a shirt?

GO Online
Homework Video Tutor
Visit: PHSchool.com
Web Code: aqe-1110

15. **Choose a Method** A store sells kicking tees by mail for $3 each. The shipping charge is $5. Find the total prices for 2, 3, 4, or 5 tees. Describe your method and explain why you chose it.

Complete each function table. Then write a rule for the function.

16.

Input	Output
3	5
4	6
5	7
6	■
7	■

17.

Input	Output
10	2
15	3
20	4
25	■
30	■

18. Business You start a cookie business. You know that the oven and materials will cost $600. You decide to charge $.75 for each cookie. The function $p = 0.75c - 600$ relates profit p to the number of cookies c that you sell.

    a. What will be your profit or loss if you sell 400 cookies? If you sell 500 cookies?

    b. How many cookies must you sell to break even?

Writing in Math Classify each function as *linear* or *not linear*. Explain your answer.

19. $y = x$

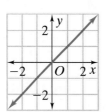

20. $y = x^2$

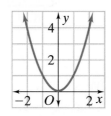

21. $y = \dfrac{1}{x}$

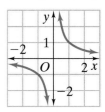

22. Challenge Graph $y = -2x$ and $y = -x^2$. What points do the graphs have in common? How are the graphs different?

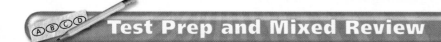
Test Prep and Mixed Review   **Practice**

Multiple Choice

23. Which ordered pair shows the coordinates of point P?

    Ⓐ $\left(1\frac{1}{2}, 2\right)$ Ⓒ $\left(2, 1\frac{1}{2}\right)$

    Ⓑ $\left(1, 2\frac{1}{2}\right)$ Ⓓ $\left(2\frac{1}{2}, 1\right)$

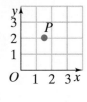

24. Tim drives his car 240 miles in 4 hours. If he travels at this rate, how far will Tim drive in the next 7 hours?

    Ⓕ 1,680 miles   Ⓖ 600 miles   Ⓗ 420 miles   Ⓙ 60 miles

25. You will drive for 5 hours and make three $\frac{1}{2}$-hour stops. You want to arrive at 3:30 P.M. What time should you leave?

GO for Help

For Exercise	See Lesson
25	5-7

Using a Variable

Use a variable to represent the unknown quantity. You can choose a letter that reminds you of what the variable represents. Then write an equation.

EXAMPLE

Admission to a county fair is $4.50 per person. The Rodriguez family pays $22.50 for admission to the fair. Which equation can you use to find p, the number of people in the Rodriguez family?

 Ⓐ $p = 22.50 + 4.50$ Ⓒ $p = 22.50 \times 4.50$
 Ⓑ $p = 22.50 - 4.50$ Ⓓ $p = 22.50 \div 4.50$

Words	number of people	equals	total cost	divided by	cost of one person

Let p = the number of people.

Equation	p	$=$	22.50	$\div$	4.50

$p = 22.50 \div 4.50$ ← **Write the equation.**

● The correct answer is choice D.

Exercises

1. Stephanie scored 17 points in the first half of a game. In all, she scored 25 points. Which equation can you use to find p, the number of points Stephanie scored in the second half?

 Ⓐ $p = 25 + 17$ Ⓒ $p = 25 \times 17$
 Ⓑ $p = 25 - 17$ Ⓓ $p = 25 \div 17$

2. You want to make 18 double-decker sandwiches. You need 3 slices of bread for each sandwich. Which equation can you use to find s, the number of slices of bread that you need?

 Ⓕ $s = 18 + 3$ Ⓗ $s = 18 \times 3$
 Ⓖ $s = 18 - 3$ Ⓙ $s = 18 \div 3$

3. Russell volunteers 36 hours at a hospital. He volunteers over a period of 15 weekends. Which equation can you use to find h, the average number of hours he works each weekend?

 Ⓐ $h = 36 + 15$ Ⓒ $h = 36 \times 15$
 Ⓑ $h = 36 - 15$ Ⓓ $h = 36 \div 15$

Chapter 11 Review

Vocabulary Review

🔊 absolute value (p. 517)
coordinate plane (p. 548)
function (p. 558)

integers (p. 516)
opposites (p. 516)
ordered pair (p. 548)

origin (p. 548)
quadrants (p. 548)

Go Online
PHSchool.com

For: Vocabulary quiz
Web Code: aqj-1151

Choose the vocabulary term that correctly completes each sentence.

1. A(n) __?__ assigns one output value to each input value.

2. The numbers −4, −2, −1, 0, and 3 are __?__.

3. __?__ are the regions of the coordinate plane.

4. −3 and 3 are __?__.

Skills and Concepts

Lessons 11-1, 11-2
- To use integers, opposites, and absolute values to represent real-world situations
- To compare and order integers

Integers are the set of positive whole numbers, their opposites, and 0. The **absolute value** of a number is its distance from 0 on a number line.

5. Write an integer to represent 14 degrees below zero.

Compare, using < or >.

6. $|-5|$ ■ $|4|$
7. -8 ■ 12
8. 4 ■ $|-9|$
9. -12 ■ -14

Order from least to greatest.

10. $-1, 1, 2, -2$
11. $0, -4, 5, -6$
12. $-3, 5, -7, 9$

Lessons 11-3, 11-4
- To add integers and to solve problems by adding integers
- To subtract integers and to solve problems by subtracting integers

The sum of two positive integers is positive. The sum of two negative integers is negative. The sum of integers with different signs has the sign of the number with the greater absolute value.

You subtract an integer by adding its opposite.

Find each sum or difference.

13. $3 + 8$
14. $5 + (-9)$
15. $-4 + 2$
16. $-7 + (-6)$

17. $11 - 3$
18. $2 - (-6)$
19. $-7 - 4$
20. $-10 - (-2)$

Lessons 11-5, 11-6
- To multiply integers and to solve problems by multiplying integers
- To divide integers and to solve problems by dividing integers

The product or quotient of two integers with the same sign is positive. The product or quotient of two integers with different signs is negative.

Find each product or quotient.

21. 4×9 22. $7 \times (-3)$ 23. -5×2 24. $-6 \times (-8)$

25. $16 \div 4$ 26. $25 \div (-5)$ 27. $-49 \div (-7)$ 28. $-32 \div 8$

Lesson 11-7
- To solve equations containing integers

You use properties of equality and inverse operations to solve equations.

Solve each equation.

29. $x + 3 = -12$ 30. $x - 3 = -12$

31. $-3x = 12$ 32. $\frac{x}{3} = -12$

Lesson 11-8
- To name and graph points on a coordinate plane

A **coordinate plane** is formed by the intersection of an x-axis and a y-axis at the **origin.** An **ordered pair** identifies the location of a point.

Graph each point on the same coordinate plane.

33. $A(0, 6)$ 34. $B(5, -4)$ 35. $C(-6, 1)$ 36. $D(-2, -3)$

Lesson 11-9
- To apply integers to profit and loss situations

The sum of a business's income and expenses is called a balance. A positive balance is a profit. A negative balance is a loss.

Use the table at the right.

37. Find the total balance for the four months.

38. Did Pie in the Sky Balloons have a profit or a loss during that time?

Pie in the Sky Balloons	
Month	Profit/Loss
January	–$985
February	$10,241
March	–$209
April	$17,239

Lesson 11-10
- To make a function table and to graph a function

A **function** assigns exactly one output value to each input value.

Make a table and graph each function. Use x-values -2, -1, 0, 1, and 2.

39. $y = x + 3$ 40. $y = 2x - 3$ 41. $y = \frac{x}{4}$

Go Online PHSchool.com **For:** Online chapter test **Web Code:** aqa-1152

1. What integer represents 7°F below 0°F?

2. Name the opposite of each integer.
   a. 89   **b.** −100

Compare, using <, =, or >.

3. 18 ▇ −24

4. −15 ▇ −9

5. 27 ▇ −27

6. Order the integers from least to greatest.
   3, −1, −13, 5, 0

7. **Writing in Math** Define *absolute value* and illustrate with a number line.

Find each answer.

8. $9 + (-4)$ 9. $-13 + 6$

10. $-7 + (-5)$ 11. $-2 - 8$

12. $-3 - (-3)$ 13. $3 - 9$

14. $5 \times (-4)$ 15. $-3 \times (-6)$

16. -2×7 17. $9 \div (-3)$

18. $-5 \div (-5)$ 19. $-12 \div 4$

20. Solve $d + 6 = -3$.

21. **Temperature** The temperature is 18°F at 1:00 A.M. The temperature falls 22 degrees by 6:00 A.M. Find the temperature at 6:00 A.M.

22. On a math quiz worth 50 points, a student misses 2 points on the first section, 3 points on the second, 2 points on the third, and 1 point on the last. Find the student's score.

Use the coordinate plane below for Exercises 23 and 24.

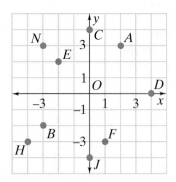

23. Name the point with the given coordinates.
   a. $(0, 4)$ **b.** $(-3, 3)$ **c.** $(-4, -3)$

24. Write the coordinates of each point.
   a. A **b.** B **c.** F **d.** J

25. Graph each point on a coordinate plane.
   a. $(-2, -3)$ **b.** $(4, -5)$ **c.** $(2, 6)$

26. **a.** Use the data below to find Royale Bakery's profit or loss for each month.
   b. Graph the profit and loss data.

Income and Expenses for Royale Bakery		
Month	Income	Expenses
Jan.	$1,314	−$828
Feb.	$2,120	−$120
Mar.	$1,019	−$1,285
Apr.	$1,438	−$765

27. Draw a graph for the linear function $y = x - 3$.

28. **Estimation** A climber starts at 50 feet above sea level at 7:00 A.M. At 11:00 A.M., she is 210 feet above sea level. If she maintains a steady rate, estimate her height above sea level at 12:30 P.M.

Multiple Choice
Choose the correct letter.

1. Evaluate the expression $b - a - 8$ when $a = 7$ and $b = 24$.
   Ⓐ -25 Ⓑ -9 Ⓒ 9 Ⓓ 11

2. Which amount is the same as $1\frac{1}{2}$ pints?
   Ⓕ 25 fluid ounces Ⓗ $\frac{3}{5}$ quart
   Ⓖ 3 cups Ⓙ $\frac{1}{8}$ gallon

3. Suppose you purchase 9 peaches, 6 oranges, 12 pears, and 8 plums. What is the ratio of plums to pears?
   Ⓐ $\frac{2}{3}$ Ⓒ $12 : 8$
   Ⓑ 9 to 12 Ⓓ $4 : 2$

4. Find the median of the following set of data: 9, 19, 9, 17, 13, 14, 11, 9, 13.
   Ⓕ 9 Ⓖ 10 Ⓗ $12\frac{2}{3}$ Ⓙ 13

5. Suppose you have a fresh lemonade stand. You spend $7 on the lemons, sugar, and cups. During the day, you sell 12 cups of lemonade for $.50 each. What is your profit or loss?
   Ⓐ $-$1$ Ⓑ $-$.50$ Ⓒ $$0$ Ⓓ $$1$

6. Which of the following is the area of a circle with a diameter of 9 inches? Round to the nearest square unit.
   Ⓕ 28 in.^{2} Ⓗ 64 in.^{2}
   Ⓖ 57 in.^{2} Ⓙ 254 in.^{2}

7. Simplify: $-8 + 9 \div 3$.
   Ⓐ $-\frac{1}{3}$ Ⓑ $\frac{1}{3}$ Ⓒ 5 Ⓓ -5

8. Which statement is false?
   Ⓕ A square is always a rectangle.
   Ⓖ Some rectangles are rhombuses.
   Ⓗ All quadrilaterals are parallelograms.
   Ⓙ A square is always a rhombus.

9. Which equation is NOT correct?
   Ⓐ $\frac{3}{4} + 2\frac{1}{2} = 3\frac{1}{4}$ Ⓒ $1\frac{7}{8} + 1\frac{5}{6} = 3\frac{17}{24}$
   Ⓑ $3\frac{4}{5} - \frac{6}{8} = 3\frac{1}{20}$ Ⓓ $5\frac{2}{5} - 2\frac{1}{3} = 3\frac{1}{10}$

10. Find the volume of a rectangular prism with the dimensions $\ell = 10$ m, $w = 7$ m, and $h = 8$ m.
    Ⓕ $V = 25$ m^3 Ⓗ $V = 56$ m^3
    Ⓖ $V = 70$ m^3 Ⓙ $V = 560$ m^3

11. The angles of 4 triangles have the following measures. Which of the triangles is obtuse?
    Ⓐ $86°, 53°, 41°$ Ⓒ $89°, 45.5°, 45.5°$
    Ⓑ $123°, 32°, 25°$ Ⓓ $74°, 71°, 35°$

Gridded Response

12. How many kilometers are in 120 meters?

13. Jack saves $32.75 from his newspaper delivery job. On Saturday, he spends $23.52 of his savings on a CD. How much does he have left?

Short Response

14. On a scale drawing, the scale shown is 1 in. to 10 ft. The length of a room is 2.5 in. on the drawing. Make a sketch and find the actual length of the room.

15. Write an integer to represent three degrees Fahrenheit below zero. Then graph the integer on a number line.

Extended Response

16. a. A parallelogram has a base of 9 in. and a height of 7 in. Find its area.
    b. The base and the height of the parallelogram are doubled. Is the area doubled? Explain.

Applying Integers

Peaks and Valleys Elevations in the United States vary from tens of thousands of feet above sea level to several hundred feet below sea level. Aerial photography and relief maps show these differences clearly.

Seattle, Washington

Mt. Whitney, California
Elevation: 14,495 feet
Highest point in the contiguous United States

Put It All Together

Data File Use the information on these two pages and on page 651 to answer these questions.

1. Which featured location has the highest elevation? The lowest elevation?

2. a. How much higher is the elevation of Vostok Station, Antarctica, than the elevation of Death Valley, California?

b. How much higher is the elevation of New Orleans, Louisiana, than the elevation of Death Valley, California?

3. Which location has an elevation 5,512 feet lower than Colorado Springs, Colorado? Show your work.
  A. Colossal Cave, Arizona   **B.** Detroit, Michigan
  C. Houston, Texas   **D.** New Orleans, Louisiana

4. Which location has an elevation 16 feet higher than New Orleans, Louisiana? Show your work.
  A. Atlantic Ocean   **B.** Death Valley, California
  C. Key West, Florida   **D.** Long Island, New York

5. Reasoning Which of these places do you think has the highest elevation: Boston, Massachusetts; Denver, Colorado; or Memphis, Tennessee? Explain.

Las Vegas, Nevada

Death Valley, California
Elevation: −282 feet
Average temperature: high 90.5°F, low 62.2°F
Lowest point in the contiguous United States.

Pacific Ocean
Elevation: Sea level (0 feet)

Go Online
PHSchool.com
For: Information about geography
Web Code: aqe-1153

Detroit, Michigan
Elevation: 633 feet
Average temperature:
high 58.4°F, low 41°F

Boston,
Massachusetts

Minneapolis,
Minnesota

Long Island, New York
Elevation: 16 feet
Average temperature:
high 61.2°F, low 43.5°F

Denver, Colorado

Chicago,
Illinois

Washington, D.C.

Colorado Springs,
Colorado
Elevation: 6,145 feet
Average temperature:
high 61.8°F, low 33.7°F

Oklahoma City,
Oklahoma

Memphis,
Tennessee

New Orleans, Louisiana
Elevation: −8 feet
Average temperature:
high 78°F, low 59.6°F

Atlantic Ocean
Elevation: Sea level (0 feet)

Houston, Texas
Elevation: 96 feet
Average temperature:
high 79.4°F, low 58.2°F

Key West, Florida
Elevation: 8 feet
Average temperature:
high 82.9°F, low 73.2°F

CHAPTER 12
Equations and Inequalities

What You've Learned

- In earlier chapters, you solved one-step equations and used equations to solve problems.
- In Chapter 8, you learned to identify right triangles.
- In Chapter 11, you learned to add, subtract, multiply, and divide integers.

 **Check Your Readiness**

Algebra **Solving Equations**

Solve each equation.

1. $c + 9 = 34$

2. $a + 5 = -8$

3. $y - 15 = 28$

4. $b - 21 = -11$

5. $9x = 117$

6. $5r = 35$

7. $14z = 266$

8. $m \div 4 = 16$

9. $s \div 9 = 7$

10. $y \div 25 = 5$

GO for Help

For Exercises	See Lessons
1–2	3-5
3–4	3-6
5–10	3-7
11–13	4-2
14–16	11-2

Writing Exponents

Write each expression using an exponent. Name the base and the exponent.

11. $4 \times 4 \times 4$

12. 2×2

13. $1 \times 1 \times 1 \times 1$

Comparing Integers

Compare using < or >.

14. $4 \ \blacksquare \ 8$

15. $-2 \ \blacksquare \ -1$

16. $-100 \ \blacksquare \ -101$

What You'll Learn Next

- In this chapter, you will solve two-step equations.

- You will solve and graph inequalities.

- You will find square roots and identify rational numbers.

- You will use the Pythagorean Theorem to solve problems involving right triangles.

🔊 **Key Vocabulary**

- graph of an inequality (p. 579)
- hypotenuse (p. 591)
- inequality (p. 578)
- legs (p. 591)
- perfect square (p. 588)
- Pythagorean Theorem (p. 591)
- rational number (p. 588)
- solution of an inequality (p. 579)
- square root (p. 587)
- two-step equation (p. 572)

 Problem Solving Application On pages 604 and 605, you will work an extended activity on electricity costs.

12-1 Solving Two-Step Equations

✓ Check Skills You'll Need

1. Vocabulary Review
Which symbol is always used in an *equation*?

Solve each equation.

2. $\frac{c}{4} = 5$ **3.** $\frac{n}{4} = 12$

4. $\frac{1}{7}x = 3$ **5.** $\frac{1}{8}y = 24$

 **for Help**
Lesson 3-7

What You'll Learn

To solve two-step equations and to use two-step equations to solve problems

🔊 **New Vocabulary** two-step equation

Why Learn This?

Suppose your dog has a litter of 3 puppies. You weigh the puppies in a basket. The empty basket weighs 2 pounds. The basket and puppies weigh a total of 14 pounds.

To find the average weight of a puppy, you can solve the equation $3x + 2 = 14$. Algebra tiles can help you understand the solution.

$3x + 2 = 14$ ← Model the equation.

$3x + 2 - 2 = 14 - 2$ ← Remove 2 tiles from each side.

$3x = 12$ ← Simplify.

$\frac{3x}{3} = \frac{12}{3}$ ← Divide each side into three equal groups.

$x = 4$ ← Simplify.

A **two-step equation,** such as $3x + 2 = 14$, is an equation that contains two operations. To solve a two-step equation, you use inverse operations and the properties of equality to get the variable alone. For many equations, you first undo the addition or subtraction. Then you undo the multiplication or division.

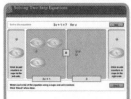
EXAMPLE Solving a Two-Step Equation

1 **Multiple Choice** Solve $2y + 3 = 11$.

(A) 4   (B) 7   (C) 16   (D) 28

$$2y + 3 = 11$$

$$2y + 3 - 3 = 11 - 3 \quad \leftarrow \text{Subtract 3 from each side to undo the addition.}$$

$$2y = 8 \quad \leftarrow \text{Simplify.}$$

$$\frac{2y}{2} = \frac{8}{2} \quad \leftarrow \text{Divide each side by 2 to undo the multiplication.}$$

$$y = 4 \quad \leftarrow \text{Simplify.}$$

The correct answer is choice A.

✓ Quick Check

1. Solve each equation. Check the solution.
   a. $5x + 3 = 18$ **b.** $3x - 4 = 23$

EXAMPLE Application: Party Planning

2 Three neighbors host a party. Each neighbor buys a watermelon for $8. They split the cost of paper goods, p, equally. If each neighbor spends $20, what is the total cost of the paper goods? Solve the equation $\frac{p}{3} + 8 = 20$.

$$\frac{p}{3} + 8 = 20$$

$$\frac{p}{3} + 8 - 8 = 20 - 8 \quad \leftarrow \text{Subtract 8 from each side to undo the addition.}$$

$$\frac{p}{3} = 12 \quad \leftarrow \text{Simplify.}$$

$$3 \cdot \frac{p}{3} = 12 \cdot 3 \quad \leftarrow \text{Multiply each side by 3 to undo the division.}$$

$$p = 36 \quad \leftarrow \text{Simplify.}$$

The total cost of the paper goods is $36.

✓ Quick Check

2. You and a friend split the cost of a moped rental. Your friend pays the bill. You owe your friend only $12, because your friend owed you $9 from yesterday. How much was the total bill? Let m represent the cost of the moped rental. Solve the equation $\frac{m}{2} - 9 = 12$.

More Than One Way

Solve $2b - 18 = 34$.

Michael's Method

First I add. Then I divide.

$$2b - 18 = 34$$
$$2b - 18 + 18 = 34 + 18 \quad \leftarrow \text{Add 18 to each side.}$$
$$2b = 52 \quad \leftarrow \text{Simplify.}$$
$$\frac{2b}{2} = \frac{52}{2} \quad \leftarrow \text{Divide each side by 2.}$$
$$b = 26 \quad \leftarrow \text{Simplify.}$$

Lauren's Method

Since each number in the equation is an even number, I begin by dividing each side of the equation by 2.

$$2b - 18 = 34$$
$$(2b - 18) \div 2 = 34 \div 2 \quad \leftarrow \text{Divide each side by 2.}$$
$$b - 9 = 17 \quad \leftarrow \text{Divide } 2b, 18, \text{ and 34 by 2.}$$
$$b - 9 + 9 = 17 + 9 \quad \leftarrow \text{Add 9 to each side.}$$
$$b = 26 \quad \leftarrow \text{Simplify.}$$

Choose a Method

Solve $5p + 75 = 245$. Describe your method and explain why you chose it.

Check Your Understanding

Vocabulary Identify each equation as one-step or two-step.

1. $6n + 3 = 21$ **2.** $b - 4 = 12$ **3.** $4j + 4 = 12$

4. Mental Math What is the solution of $3a - 1 = 11$?

5. Copy the equation. Then complete the solution.
$$2b + 4 = 12$$
$$2b + 4 - \blacksquare = 12 - \blacksquare$$

For more exercises, see Extra Skills and Word Problems.

GO for Help

For Exercises	See Examples
6–14	1
15–16	2

Solve each equation. Check your solution.

6. $2y + 5 = 9$

7. $2p + 13 = 3$

8. $5x + 7 = 22$

9. $\frac{a}{2} + 4 = 8$

10. $\frac{x}{3} + 2 = 5$

11. $\frac{n}{6} - 1 = 3$

12. $2y - 3 = -11$

13. $-6 = 4b - 10$

14. $1 + \frac{g}{2} = -5$

15. You need to buy a pair of pants and three shirts. You have $90 to spend on clothes. You do not pay sales tax. The pants you choose cost $24. How much can you spend on each shirt? Let s represent the cost of a shirt. Solve $3s + 24 = 90$.

16. You order a backpack for $34 and pens for $2 each. You spend $46, excluding the shipping cost and tax. How many pens do you order? Let p represent the number of pens. Solve $2p + 34 = 46$.

17. Guided Problem Solving Mr. Lewis donates $200 to his favorite charities. He begins by giving $35 to an animal shelter. He also makes $15 donations to several other charities. How many other charities does he support? Let c represent the number of other charities. Solve $35 + 15c = 200$.
  • Which operation do you undo first?
  • Which operation do you undo second?

18. You save $26 each week to buy a digital camera that costs $260. You have already saved $182. In how many weeks will you save $260? Let w represent the number of weeks. Solve $26w + 182 = 260$.

Mental Math Solve each equation.

19. $2y + 1 = 11$

20. $5c + 15 = 30$

21. $4d - 12 = 8$

22. $3n - 1 = 17$

23. $\frac{w}{2} - 6 = 4$

24. $\frac{a}{5} + 7 = 12$

25. Error Analysis What error is made in the solution of the equation $4 + \frac{m}{5} = 19$ at the right?

$$4 + \frac{m}{5} = 19$$
$$\frac{m}{5} = 15$$
$$m = 3 \; \times$$

26. Writing in Math How is solving $16e - 32 = 176$ different from solving $16e = 176$?

GO Online
Homework Video Tutor
Visit: PHSchool.com
Web Code: aqe-1201

Careers A sales representative for a clothing company sells the latest fashions to retail stores.

Choose the correct equation. Then solve the equation.

27. **Sales** A sales representative earns a weekly base salary of $250 and a commission of 8% on her weekly sales. (A commission is money earned that equals a percent of the sales.) At the end of one week, she earned $410. How much did she sell that week? Let s represent the total sales.
   Ⓐ $0.08s + 250 = 410$ Ⓑ $250 + 410 = 0.08s$

28. **Exercise** You pay $75 to join a health club and then pay a monthly fee. The total cost for the first year is $495. What is the monthly fee? Let m represent the monthly fee.
   Ⓐ $12m + 75 = 495$ Ⓑ $75 + 495 = 12m$

For each table, write a rule that uses two operations. Then complete the table. (*Hint:* Multiply or divide first.)

29.

Input	Output
2	7
4	11
7	17
8	▪
15	▪

30.

Input	Output
6	−6
9	−5
15	−3
30	▪
63	▪

31. **Challenge** Solve $\frac{a}{2} + \frac{2}{3} = 5\frac{1}{3}$.

Test Prep and Mixed Review
Practice

Multiple Choice

32. A triangle has angles that measure 90° and 32°. What is the measure of the third angle?
   Ⓐ 58°   Ⓑ 68°   Ⓒ 78°   Ⓓ 88°

33. Cameron's father tiles a floor with square tiles. Each box of tile holds 50 tiles. The floor measures 13 feet by 15 feet. What additional piece of information does Cameron's father need to find the number of boxes of tile he must buy?
   Ⓕ area of a tile   Ⓗ perimeter of the room
   Ⓖ area of the floor   Ⓙ height of the tile box

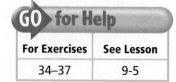

For Exercises	See Lesson
34–37	9-5

Find the radius or diameter of each circle.

34. $r = 12$ inches, $d = $ ▪   35. $d = \frac{1}{2}$ in., $r = $ ▪

36. $d = 0.36$ meter, $r = $ ▪   37. $r = 4.7$ cm, $d = $ ▪

Using Equation Language

Equations describe real-world situations. Solve the puzzles below using equation language.

ACTIVITY

A class makes puzzles with quarters that honor the 50 U.S. states. For each puzzle, find the number of quarters from each of three states.

1. Martin's Puzzle

Clue 1   10 quarters from Mississippi, Maryland, or Florida

Clue 2   4 fewer Mississippi quarters than Maryland quarters

Clue 3   3 times as many Maryland quarters as Florida quarters

2. Sara's Puzzle

Clue 1   6 Indiana quarters

Clue 2   2 more Kentucky quarters than Tennessee quarters

Clue 3   12 quarters from Indiana, Kentucky, or Tennessee

3. Joaquin's Puzzle

Clue 1 $\frac{1}{2}$ are Ohio quarters

Clue 2   18 quarters from Ohio, Texas, or Tennessee

Clue 3   Twice as many Tennessee quarters as Texas quarters

4. Donelle's Puzzle

Clue 1   15 quarters from Maine, Louisiana, or Idaho

Clue 2   1 fewer Maine quarter than Louisiana quarters

Clue 3   1 more Maine quarter than Idaho quarters

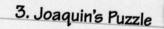

5. Make a puzzle by choosing quarters from three states. Then write clues. Include the total number of quarters as a clue.

6. Exchange puzzles with another student. Solve the puzzle.

7. **Writing in Math** 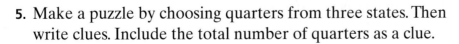 How did you solve Joaquin's puzzle? Explain.

12-2 Inequalities

✓ Check Skills You'll Need

1. **Vocabulary Review** How can you use a number line to *compare* integers?

Compare using < or >.

2. 4 ■ −9

3. −2 ■ −3

4. −94 ■ −93

5. 1,001 ■ 1,010

 **for Help**
Lesson 11-2

What You'll Learn

To express and identify solutions of inequalities

🔊 **New Vocabulary** inequality, graph of an inequality, solution of an inequality

Why Learn This?

Inequalities can tell you time limits, the height limits for amusement-park rides, and many other things.

An **inequality** is a mathematical sentence that contains <, >, ≤, ≥, or ≠. Real-world situations can sometimes be represented by inequalities.

DONT CROSS THIS FIELD UNLESS YOU CAN DO IT IN 9.9 SECONDS. THE BULL CAN DO IT IN 10

Inequality Symbols		
< less than	>	greater than
≤ less than or equal to	≥	greater than or equal to
	≠ not equal to	

EXAMPLE Writing an Inequality

① **Time** The sign above warns you to cross the field in less than 10 seconds. Write an inequality that represents the time limit.

Words   your time is less than bull's time

Let *t* = your time.

Inequality   *t*   <   10

The inequality is *t* < 10.

✓ Quick Check

1. Skydivers jump from an altitude of 14,500 feet or less. Write an inequality to express the altitude from which skydivers jump.

The **graph of an inequality** shows all solutions of the inequality. A **solution of an inequality** is any number that makes the inequality true. An open circle on a graph shows that the number is *not* a solution. A closed circle shows that the number *is* a solution.

> **EXAMPLE** Graphing Inequalities

2 Write the inequality. Then graph the inequality.

a. You ride your scooter more than 2 miles.

Let k = your distance.

$$k > 2$$

b. The temperature is 3 degrees or less.

Let t = temperature.

$$t \leq 3$$

✓ Quick Check

2. You spend at least 2 hours studying. Write the inequality for the situation. Then graph the inequality.

You can use an inequality to show which numbers meet a limit.

> **EXAMPLE** Identifying Solutions of an Inequality

3 **Roller Coasters** You must be at least 48 inches tall to ride a certain roller coaster. Which of the children in the table can ride the roller coaster?

Name	Height
Sally	$48\frac{1}{2}$ in.
Dean	48 in.
Kelsey	$46\frac{3}{4}$ in.

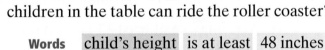

Words   child's height is at least 48 inches

     Let h = the child's height.

Inequality h $\geq$ 48

Decide whether the inequality is true or false for each person.

Sally $48\frac{1}{2} \geq 48$ Dean $48 \geq 48$ Kelsey $46\frac{3}{4} \geq 48$

     true   true   false

Sally and Dean may ride the roller coaster.

✓ Quick Check

3. Ian is 3 ft 11 in. tall. Is Ian tall enough to ride the roller coaster?

1. **Vocabulary** A graph of an inequality shows all the _?_ of the inequality.

2. **Reasoning** Are the solutions of $x < 3$ and $x \leq 3$ the same? Explain.

3. Write an inequality for the graph.

<−4 −3 −2 −1 0 1 2

Homework Exercises

For more exercises, see Extra Skills and Word Problems.

Write an inequality for each situation.

For Exercises	See Examples
4–6	1
7–9	2
10–11	3

GO for Help

4. No more than 45 students work in the car-wash fundraiser.

5. There are more than 15 ladybugs on the windowsill.

6. A sign reads, "Maximum height of vehicles is 12 feet."

Write an inequality for each situation. Then graph the inequality.

7. Four people or fewer are allowed on the ride at once.

8. Kristen has less than three days to write her paper.

9. You must deposit at least $20 to open a bank account.

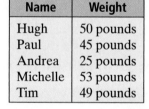

Name	Weight
Hugh	50 pounds
Paul	45 pounds
Andrea	25 pounds
Michelle	53 pounds
Tim	49 pounds

10. Use the table at the left. A child must weigh less than 50 pounds to ride on the playground animals. Who may ride the animals?

11. You must be at least 13 years old to buy a certain DVD. From the following list of students, who may buy the DVD? Carl (12 years, 9 months), Cara (15 years, 4 days), Molly (13 years), Peter (8 years, 11 months)

GPS 12. **Guided Problem Solving** Which appliances in the table below use an average of more than 50 kilowatt-hours of energy per month? Write an inequality and graph the solution.

Average Monthly Energy Use

Appliance	VCR	Dryer	Washer	Dishwasher
Energy (kilowatt-hours)	4	100	10	50

- Which symbol can you use to represent "more than"?
- On your graph, should you use an open or closed circle?

Tell whether each inequality is true or false.

13. $-2 \le 2$ **14.** $|-5| < 5$ **15.** $-4^2 < (-4)^2$

16. Football You must weigh 120 pounds or less to play in a junior football league. Use the table at the right. Who qualifies to play?

Name	Weight
Aaron	118 lb
Steve	109 lb
Mark	131 lb
James	120 lb

17. Writing in Math Describe how to graph $x < -20$.

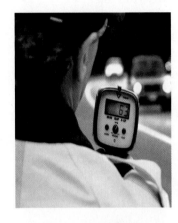

18. Driving The minimum speed limit on an interstate is 45 miles per hour. The maximum speed limit is 65 miles per hour.
  a. Write an inequality that describes the speed of a car going slower than the minimum limit.
  b. Write an inequality that describes the speed of a car going faster than the maximum limit.

19. Number Sense Graph the inequality $x \ne 4$.

20. Challenge Solve and graph $|x| < 2$.

Test Prep and Mixed Review   **Practice**

Multiple Choice

21. Chris wrote the coordinates of 5 vertices of the hexagon at the right.

$(3, 7), (1, 4), (7, 6), (1, 3), (4, 1)$

Which ordered pair represents the vertex that is NOT listed?
  Ⓐ $(7, 2)$ Ⓒ $(2, 5)$
  Ⓑ $(7, 4)$ Ⓓ $(2, 7)$

22. Abby plans to practice piano 30 minutes per day, 5 days per week, over the next 10 weeks. How can she find the total number of minutes she will practice?
  Ⓕ Multiply 30 and 5.   Ⓗ Multiply 30, 5, and 10.
  Ⓖ Multiply 5 and 10.   Ⓙ Multiply 0.5, 5, and 10.

23. What kind of angle is $\angle Z$?
  Ⓐ Acute   Ⓒ Obtuse
  Ⓑ Right   Ⓓ Straight

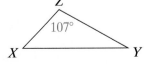

24. Tom won 84 games and lost 24 games. Find the experimental probability of Tom winning a game.

12-3

Solving One-Step Inequalities

What You'll Learn

To solve one-step inequalities by adding or subtracting

Why Learn This?

You can solve inequalities when you need to find an unknown amount. For example, you can determine how close you are to meeting a goal in sports or in business.

To solve an inequality, use inverse operations to get the variable alone.

EXAMPLES Solving Inequalities

1 Solve $s - 7 < 3$.

$$s - 7 < 3$$
$$s - 7 + 7 < 3 + 7 \quad \leftarrow \text{Add 7 to each side to undo the subtraction.}$$
$$s < 10 \quad \leftarrow \text{Simplify.}$$

2 Solve $n + 12 \geq 18$.

$$n + 12 \geq 18$$
$$n + 12 - 12 \geq 18 - 12 \quad \leftarrow \text{Subtract 12 from each side to undo the addition.}$$
$$n \geq 6 \quad \leftarrow \text{Simplify.}$$

Quick Check

1. Solve $u - 6 \leq 3$.

2. Solve $z + 15 > 24$.

You can also solve inequalities in real-world situations.

EXAMPLE **Application: Running**

3 A marathon runner plans to run at least 55 miles this week. He has already run 42 miles. Write and solve an inequality to find how many more miles he plans to run this week.

Words   miles run + miles left is at least 55 miles

   Let m = number of miles left.

Inequality   42   + m ≥   55

$$42 + m \geq 55$$
$$42 + m - 42 \geq 55 - 42 \quad \leftarrow \text{Subtract 42 from each side.}$$
$$m \geq 13 \quad \leftarrow \text{Simplify.}$$

The marathon runner plans to run at least 13 more miles this week.

✓ Quick Check

3. A restaurant can serve a maximum of 115 people. There are now 97 people dining in the restaurant. Write and solve an inequality to find how many more people can be served.

✓ Check Your Understanding

Name the operation used to solve each inequality.

1. $c - 4 \geq 8$ **2.** $n + 2 < 13$ **3.** $t + 11 \leq 11$

4. Reasoning What number is a solution of $y + 2 \geq 10$ but is not a solution of $y + 2 > 10$?

5. Mental Math Solve $c - 2 \leq 8$.

Homework Exercises

For more exercises, see Extra Skills and Word Problems.

Solve each inequality.

For Exercises	See Examples
6–11	1
12–18	2–3

GO for Help

6. $x - 2 \geq 5$ **7.** $z - 5 < 0$ **8.** $k - 21 > 1$

9. $j - 2 > -9$ **10.** $n - 96 < -58$ **11.** $s - 4 \leq 8$

12. $r + 5 \geq 7$ **13.** $y + 12 \leq 11$ **14.** $w + 2 > -7$

15. $14 + d \leq 24$ **16.** $13 + f > 7$ **17.** $5 + g \leq 62$

18. You have $15 to spend on souvenirs. You buy a visor for $7.99. Write and solve an inequality to find how much more money you can spend.

19. Guided Problem Solving Your bank requires a minimum of $250 in an account to avoid fees. You have $143 in your account. Write and solve an inequality to find how much money you must deposit to avoid fees.
  • **Make a Plan** Decide which operation to use in the inequality. Undo the operation in the inequality.
  • **Check the Answer** Draw a graph of the inequality.

20. Writing in Math Explain how you know that $3n > 3n$ has no solutions.

GO Online
Homework Video Tutor
Visit: PHSchool.com
Web Code: aqe-1203

21. To avoid a storm, a pilot of a vintage biplane flies up 2,500 feet but stays below 32,000 feet. Write an inequality to find the maximum original altitude of the plane.

22. Budgeting You want to spend less than $30 on two T-shirts and a pair of shorts. The pair of shorts costs $13. Each of the T-shirts costs the same amount. Write and solve an inequality to find how much money you can spend on each T-shirt.

23. Challenge Which integers are solutions to both $x + 7 \leq 9$ and $x + 7 > 4$?

 **Test Prep and Mixed Review** **Practice**

Multiple Choice

24. The elevation of Death Valley in California is 282 feet below sea level. Mount McKinley in Alaska is 20,320 feet above sea level. What integer represents the elevation of Death Valley?
  Ⓐ −20,320   Ⓑ −282   Ⓒ 282   Ⓓ 20,320

25. Which line segment is twice as long as the radius?
  Ⓕ $\overline{DE}$ Ⓗ $\overline{FG}$
  Ⓖ $\overline{DF}$ Ⓙ $\overline{EG}$

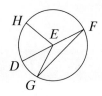

GO for Help

For Exercises	See Lesson
26–28	9-7

Name each figure.

26.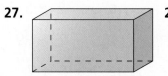

27.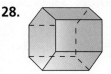

28.

12-3b Activity Lab

Applying Inequalities

You can use floating bar graphs to represent inequalities. On the graph below, each bar represents a range of costs for an item that you might want to buy.

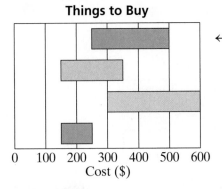

Things to Buy

Cost ($)

The cost of a bicycle goes from ← $250 to $500. Represent the cost using $x \geq 250$ and $x \leq 500$.

- bicycle
- digital music player
- computer
- digital camera

ACTIVITY

1. You have saved $120 for a computer. Use the floating bar graph above. Write and solve two inequalities to find the minimum and maximum amount of money you still need to save for the computer.

2. You begin saving $25 per week for a digital camera. Write and solve two inequalities to find the minimum and maximum number of weeks it will take to save the money you need.

✓ Checkpoint Quiz 1

Lessons 12-1 through 12-3

Solve each equation.

1. $4t + 5 = 37$ 2. $\frac{r}{2} - 8 = -4$ 3. $5m - 8 = 57$

Solve each inequality. Graph the solution on a number line.

4. $p + 8 < 3$ 5. $n - 5 \geq -17$ 6. $d + 2 \leq 6$

Exploring Squares

You will need a geoboard and rubber bands. Look at the geoboard at the right. Each side of the square is 1 unit long. The area is 1 square unit.

ACTIVITY

1. **a.** Use your geoboard to make squares with areas of 4, 9, and 16 square units.
   b. Copy the table at the right. Enter the length of a side for each square you made in part (a).

Area of Square (units²)	Length of Side (units)
1	
4	
9	
16	

2. **a.** Look at your table. What pattern(s) do you notice?
   b. Continue the table for squares with areas of 25, 36, and 49 square units.

3. Use your geoboard to make the figure shown at the right. The figure is a square with an area of 2 square units.
   a. Use your table to estimate the length of a side of this square.
   b. Recall that the formula for the area of a square is $A = s^2$. Use a calculator and the *Systematic Guess and Check* strategy. To the nearest hundredth, find the length of a side of a square with an area of 2 square units.

4. **a.** Use your calculator and the *Systematic Guess and Check* strategy. To the nearest hundredth, find the length of a side of a square with an area of 8 square units.
   b. How does the side length you found in Step 3b compare with your answer to Step 4a?

5. Use your geoboard to make a square with an area of 8 square units.

6. **Challenge** Use your geoboard to make a square with an area of 5 square units.

Exploring Square Roots and Rational Numbers

Check Skills You'll Need

1. **Vocabulary Review**
   What operation can you use to find 4 *squared*?

Write each expression using an exponent.

2. $4 \times 4 \times 4 \times 4 \times 4$

3. $999 \times 999 \times 999$

4. 3.6×3.6

for Help
Lesson 4-2

What You'll Learn

To find square roots and to identify rational numbers

◀)) **New Vocabulary** square root, perfect square, rational number

Why Learn This?

Suppose you know the area of a square object or space, such as a garden. You can use square roots to find the length of the garden without measuring.

In the diagram, the area of a square with side length 3 is 3^2, or 9. The inverse of squaring is finding the square root. The square root of 9 is 3. In symbols, $\sqrt{9} = 3$.

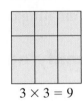

$3 \times 3 = 9$

A **square root** of a given number is a number that, when multiplied by itself, equals the given number.

For: Square Root Activity
Use: Interactive Textbook, 12-4

EXAMPLE **Finding Square Roots**

1. **a.** Find $\sqrt{64}$.

   $8 \times 8 = 64$, so $\sqrt{64} = 8$.

   b. Find $\sqrt{49}$.

   $7 \times 7 = 49$, so $\sqrt{49} = 7$.

Quick Check

1. Find $\sqrt{100}$.

A **perfect square** is the square of a whole number. The number 64 is a perfect square because $64 = 8^2$. You can use a calculator to approximate the square root of a number that is not a perfect square.

EXAMPLE Using a Calculator

2 **Gridded Response** You need 50 square feet of land to plant a square garden. How long will the side be? Find $\sqrt{50}$ to the nearest tenth.

$\sqrt{50} \approx 7.071067812$ ← Press **2nd** x^2 **50** $=$.

≈ 7.1 ← Round to the nearest tenth.

The side is about 7.1 feet.

Quick Check

2. Find $\sqrt{10}$ to the nearest tenth.

A **rational number** is any number that can be written as a quotient of two integers in which the denominator is not zero. You can write any integer as a quotient with a denominator of 1, so all integers are rational numbers. Examples of rational numbers are $2 \left(\text{or } \frac{2}{1} \right)$, $\frac{4}{5}$, $0.38 \left(\text{or } \frac{38}{100} \right)$, and $-8 \left(\text{or } \frac{-8}{1} \right)$.

The square root of a whole number is a rational number only when the whole number is a perfect square. Rational numbers in decimal form are either terminating or repeating.

EXAMPLE Identifying Rational Numbers

Vocabulary Tip

A repeating decimal, such as $2.\overline{3}$, can be written with a bar over the repeating digits. A decimal that does not repeat *cannot* be written with a bar.

3 Tell whether each number is rational.

a. 6.7

Rational: 6.7 is a terminating decimal.

b. $\frac{1}{5}$

Rational: $\frac{1}{5}$ is a quotient of integers.

c. $\sqrt{26}$

Not rational: 26 is not a perfect square.

d. 3.22272228 . . .

Not rational: the decimal does not repeat or terminate.

Quick Check

3. Is 12.112111211112 . . . a rational number? Explain.

1. **Vocabulary** Is $\sqrt{4}$ a rational number? Explain.

2. Which number is NOT a perfect square?

   Ⓐ 9

   Ⓑ 16

   Ⓒ 32

   Ⓓ 36

3. Find $\sqrt{7}$ to the nearest tenth. Use a calculator.

4. **Estimate** Is $\sqrt{5}$ closer to 2 or 3? Draw a number line. Then justify your reasoning.

Homework Exercises

For more exercises, see **Extra Skills and Word Problems.**

GO for Help

For Exercises	See Examples
5–12	1
13–17	2
18–29	3

Find each square root without using a calculator.

5. $\sqrt{1}$
6. $\sqrt{25}$
7. $\sqrt{81}$
8. $\sqrt{9}$

9. $\sqrt{16}$
10. $\sqrt{36}$
11. $\sqrt{100}$
12. $\sqrt{144}$

🖩 **Calculator** **Find each square root to the nearest tenth.**

13. $\sqrt{21}$
14. $\sqrt{33}$
15. $\sqrt{51}$
16. $\sqrt{75}$

17. The area of a square quilt is 40 ft². How long is each side?

Tell whether each number is rational.

18. $6.\overline{8}$
19. $\frac{9}{11}$
20. $\sqrt{1}$

21. $-2\frac{1}{2}$
22. $\frac{7}{9}$
23. $\sqrt{18}$

24. 6.2319743
25. $3\frac{1}{3}$
26. $\sqrt{49}$

27. 15
28. $0.101001\ldots$
29. $\sqrt{32}$

 30. **Guided Problem Solving** A square patio has an area of 169 square feet. What is the perimeter of the patio?
   - **Make a Plan** Draw a picture. Find the side length of the square using square roots. Then find the perimeter.
   - **Check the Answer** How can you check to make sure you are using the correct side lenghts for the patio?

Estimation Estimate to the nearest whole number.

31. $\sqrt{6}$　　　**32.** $\sqrt{7}$　　　**33.** $\sqrt{11}$　　　**34.** $\sqrt{26}$

35. Reasoning Is $\sqrt{2}$ greater than 1? Is $\sqrt{2}$ greater than 2? Explain.

36. Calculator Use a calculator and evaluate $\sqrt{27}$, $\sqrt{9} \times \sqrt{3}$, and $3 \times \sqrt{3}$. What do you notice about the answers?

37. Egyptian Pyramids The area of the square base of the Great Pyramid at Giza is 52,900 square meters. What is the length of each side of the base of the pyramid?

38. Simplify each expression.

　a. $\left(\sqrt{2}\right)^2$　　　**b.** $\left(\sqrt{3}\right)^2$　　　**c.** $\left(\sqrt{16}\right)^2$

　d. Patterns What happens when you square the square root of a number?

39. Writing in Math Find two consecutive whole numbers between which $\sqrt{29}$ is located. Explain your choice.

40. Challenge Find two perfect squares whose sum is 100.

Test Prep and Mixed Review　　　**Practice**

Multiple Choice

41. Which point on the graph shows the location of the ordered pair $\left(2, \frac{2}{3}\right)$?

　Ⓐ Q　　　Ⓒ S
　Ⓑ R　　　Ⓓ T

42. Casey withdraws $12 from his bank account. Then he deposits $27. What integer represents the withdrawal?

　Ⓕ 12　　　Ⓗ −27
　Ⓖ 27　　　Ⓙ −12

43. Ana serves 72 customers every 4 hours at a snack bar. Which is the ratio of hours to customers served?

　Ⓐ 1 : 18　　　Ⓑ 18 : 1　　　Ⓒ 72 : 4　　　Ⓓ 36 : 2

GO for Help

For Exercises	See Lesson
44–47	9-6

Find the area of each circle to the nearest tenth. Use 3.14 for π.

44. $r = 2$ in.　　**45.** $d = 4$ ft　　**46.** $r = 6$ m　　**47.** $d = 15$ km

12-5

Introducing the Pythagorean Theorem

Check Skills You'll Need

1. Vocabulary Review
List 3 numbers that are examples of *perfect squares*.

Find each square root.

2. $\sqrt{9}$ **3.** $\sqrt{64}$

4. $\sqrt{25}$ **5.** $\sqrt{36}$

6. $\sqrt{121}$ **7.** $\sqrt{625}$

GO for Help
Lesson 12-4

What You'll Learn

To solve problems using the Pythagorean Theorem

◀)) **New Vocabulary** legs, hypotenuse, Pythagorean Theorem

Why Learn This?

Suppose you want to take the shortest route from one corner of a rectangular park to the opposite corner. You can use the Pythagorean Theorem to find the shortest distance.

Recall that a right triangle has an angle measuring 90°. In a right triangle, the two shorter sides are called **legs.** The longest side, opposite the right angle, is called the **hypotenuse.**

The Pythagorean Theorem shows the relationship of the side lengths in a right triangle. You usually use the letters *a*, *b*, and *c* to label the unknown lengths of a right triangle.

⬤nline
active math

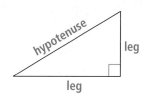

For: Pythagorean Theorem Activity
Use: Interactive Textbook, 12-5

KEY CONCEPTS **Pythagorean Theorem**

In any right triangle, the sum of the squares of the lengths of the legs (*a* and *b*) is equal to the square of the length of the hypotenuse (*c*).

Arithmetic

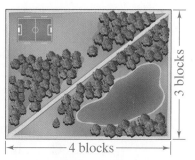

$3^2 + 4^2 = 5^2$

Algebra

$a^2 + b^2 = c^2$

GO Online

Video Tutor Help
Visit: PHSchool.com
Web Code: aqe-0775

EXAMPLE Finding the Length of a Hypotenuse

1 **Multiple Choice** A rectangular park is 12 city blocks long and 9 city blocks wide, as shown below. Find the distance from point A to point B in city blocks.

   Ⓐ 14   Ⓑ 15   Ⓒ 16   Ⓓ 18

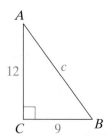

$$a^2 + b^2 = c^2 \quad \leftarrow \text{Write the Pythagorean Theorem.}$$
$$9^2 + 12^2 = c^2 \quad \leftarrow \text{Substitute 9 for } a \text{ and 12 for } b.$$
$$225 = c^2 \quad \leftarrow \text{Square 9 and 12. Then add.}$$
$$\sqrt{225} = \sqrt{c^2} \quad \leftarrow \text{Find the square root of each side.}$$
$$15 = c \quad \leftarrow \text{Simplify.}$$

The shortest distance in city blocks is 15. The correct answer is choice B.

☑ **Quick Check**

1. Find the length of the hypotenuse of a triangle with legs that have lengths of 12 inches and 16 inches.

EXAMPLE Finding the Length of a Leg

2 A ramp forms a right triangle with the ground. How high is the top of the ramp? Round to the nearest tenth.

$$a^2 + b^2 = c^2 \quad \leftarrow \text{Write the Pythagorean Theorem.}$$
$$a^2 + 13^2 = 14^2 \quad \leftarrow \text{Substitute 13 for } b \text{ and 14 for } c.$$
$$a^2 + 169 = 196 \quad \leftarrow \text{Square 13 and 14.}$$
$$a^2 + 169 - 169 = 196 - 169 \quad \leftarrow \text{Subtract 169 from each side.}$$
$$a^2 = 27 \quad \leftarrow \text{Simplify.}$$
$$\sqrt{a^2} = \sqrt{27} \quad \leftarrow \text{Find the square root of each side.}$$
$$a \approx 5.196152423 \quad \leftarrow \text{Simplify.}$$

The top of the ramp is about 5.2 feet high.

☑ **Quick Check**

2. A ramp leading into a truck forms a right triangle with the ground. One leg is 10 feet long. The hypotenuse is 11 feet long. How high is the top of the ramp? Round to the nearest tenth.

1. **Vocabulary** How can you identify the hypotenuse in a right triangle?

2. Fill in the blanks to find the missing side length of the triangle.

$$a^2 + b^2 = c^2$$
$$21^2 + \blacksquare^2 = c^2$$
$$\blacksquare + \blacksquare = c^2$$
$$\sqrt{841} = c$$

3. **Number Sense** Can you use $a = 5$, $b = 12$, and $c = 13$ to form a right triangle? Explain.

4. **Writing in Math** Can a leg of a right triangle ever be longer than the hypotenuse? Explain.

Homework Exercises

For more exercises, see Extra Skills and Word Problems.

GO for Help

For Exercises	See Examples
5–10	1
11–15	2

Find the missing side length. Round to the nearest tenth.

5.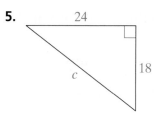

6.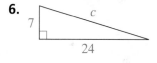

7. $a = 4$, $b = 3$, $c = \blacksquare$

8. $a = 10$, $b = 24$, $c = \blacksquare$

9. $a = 6$, $b = 8$, $c = \blacksquare$

10. $a = 12$, $b = 20$, $c = \blacksquare$

11.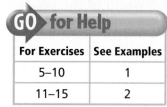

12.

13. $a = \blacksquare$, $b = 7$, $c = 9$

14. $a = 2$, $b = \blacksquare$, $c = 5$

15. A 10-foot ladder leans against a building. The base of the ladder is 6 feet from the building. How high is the point where the ladder touches the building?

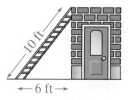

GO Online
Homework Video Tutor
Visit: PHSchool.com
Web Code: aqe-1205

16. Guided Problem Solving A landscaper hammers a stake 9 feet from the base of a tree. A wire goes from the stake to a spot 40 feet up the trunk. How long must the wire be?

- **Make a Plan** Draw a sketch of the triangle. Label the legs and hypotenuse. Find the hypotenuse using $a^2 + b^2 = c^2$.
- **Carry Out the Plan** Solve for c.

In Exercises 17–18, you find the diagonal length in a rectangle. A diagonal of a rectangle connects opposite vertices.

diagonal

17. Framing Corey builds a picture frame. The length of the frame is 24 inches. The width is 10 inches. Corey measures the diagonal to make sure the frame has square corners. What is the length of the diagonal?

18. Television The size of a television screen is based on the diagonal of the screen. You buy a 27-inch television set. The screen has a height of 15 inches. What is the width of the screen, to the nearest inch?

19. (Algebra) Use the Pythagorean Theorem. Write an equation to express the relationship between the legs and the hypotenuse of the triangle.

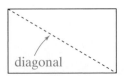

20. Challenge Draw a triangle with hypotenuse $\sqrt{2}$ inches long.

Test Prep and Mixed Review — **Practice**

Multiple Choice

21. The table shows a sequence of terms. Which expression can you use to find the value of a term in the sequence?

Ⓐ $n - 1$ Ⓒ $n + 1$
Ⓑ $n - 5$ Ⓓ $n + 5$

Position, n	Value of Term
10	5
11	6
12	7
n	■

22. Jessica's cat eats about 2 cans of food every 7 days. About how many cans of food does her cat eat in 30 days?

Ⓕ 7 Ⓖ 8 Ⓗ 9 Ⓙ 10

GO for Help

For Exercises	See Lesson
23–26	11-1

Find each value.

23. $|0|$ **24.** $|-3|$ **25.** $|85|$ **26.** $|-84|$

Practice Solving Problems

You can use proportions and the Pythagorean Theorem to solve real-life problems.

Carpentry The slope, or pitch, of the roof in the diagram is $\frac{3}{12}$. The slope indicates that each time the horizontal distance changes by 12 inches, the vertical distance changes by 3 inches. Use the diagram to find the length x.

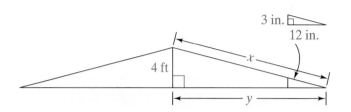

What You Might Think

What do I know?
What do I want to find?

First I will use a proportion to find length y.

Then I will use the Pythagorean Theorem to find length x.

Is the answer reasonable?

What You Might Write

- The legs of the small right triangle are 3 in. and 12 in.
- The triangles are similar. The corresponding sides of the triangles are proportional.
- I want to find length x and length y.

I can change 4 ft to 48 in.

$$\frac{48}{3} = \frac{y}{12}$$

$$\frac{48}{3} \underset{\times 4}{\overset{\times 4}{=}} \frac{y}{12}$$

$$y = 192$$

$$48^2 + y^2 = x^2$$
$$48^2 + 192^2 = x^2$$
$$2{,}304 + 36{,}864 = x^2$$
$$39{,}168 = x^2$$
$$x = \sqrt{39{,}168} \approx 198$$

The length x is about 198 inches, or $16\frac{1}{2}$ feet.

The hypotenuse must be longer than the leg.

Think It Through

1. How can you tell that the two triangles are similar?

2. Explain how you can use the proportion $\frac{4}{3} = \frac{y}{12}$ to find y.

3. Solve the proportion $\frac{4}{3} = \frac{y}{12}$ to find the value of y in feet. Use the Pythagorean Theorem to find x.

Exercises

4. Find the length x shown in the diagram below of the roof.

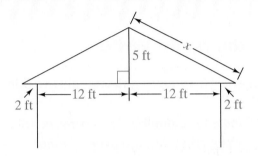

   a. What is the total length of the base of the right triangle?
   b. What formula can you use to find x?

5. As you climb a mountain, the air temperature decreases about 6.5°C for each kilometer you climb.
   a. Assume the air temperature stays the same at the base of a mountain during the day. How many kilometers would you have to climb to feel the temperature decrease 10°C?
   b. How many kilometers would you have to climb to feel the temperature decrease 15°C?

6. The first minute of an international phone call costs $0.25. Each additional minute costs $0.12. What is the greatest number of minutes you can talk without spending more than $15?

7. The minute hand of a clock rotates 360° every hour. The hour hand rotates 360° every 12 hours. What angle do the hands of a clock make at exactly 7:15?

Estimating the Answer

You can use estimation to find an answer, check an answer, or eliminate possible answers from multiple-choice questions.

EXAMPLE

You and a friend owe $4.90 for a taxi ride. The ride costs $1.90 for the first eighth of a mile. Each additional eighth of a mile costs $0.25. About how many miles did you travel?

(A) $\frac{1}{2}$ (B) $1\frac{1}{2}$ (C) 2   (D) $2\frac{1}{2}$

You can estimate the cost by rounding $1.90 to $2.00. You can also round $4.90 to $5.00. Then you can solve a two-step equation using mental math.

$$0.25y + 2 = 5$$ ← Write a rule for finding the taxi fare. Let y be the number of eighths.

$$0.25y + 2 - 2 = 5 - 2$$ ← Subtract 2 from each side to undo the addition.

$$0.25y = 3$$ ← Simplify.

$$\frac{0.25y}{0.25} = \frac{3}{0.25}$$ ← Divide each side by 0.25 to undo the multiplication.

$$y = 12$$ ← Simplify.

$$\frac{1}{8} + \frac{12}{8} = \frac{13}{8}$$ ← Add the number of eighths traveled.

13 eighths is about $1\frac{1}{2}$ miles. The correct answer is choice B.

Exercises

1. Students organize a community clothing drive. They pack 27 boxes of clothes. Each box weighs about 30 pounds. About how many pounds of clothing do they collect?
   (A) 400   (C) 600
   (B) 500   (D) 900

2. Mr. Cortez distributes 4 worksheets to each of his students. He has 116 worksheets. Which equation can be used to find s, the number of students in his class?
   (F) $s = 116 \div 4$ (H) $s = 116 \times 4$
   (G) $s = 116 - 4$ (J) $s = 116 + 4$

Chapter 12 Review

Vocabulary Review

 graph of an inequality
(p. 579)
hypotenuse (p. 591)
inequality (p. 578)
legs (p. 591)

perfect square (p. 588)
Pythagorean Theorem
(p. 591)
rational number (p. 588)

solution of an inequality
(p. 579)
square root (p. 587)
two-step equation (p. 572)

Choose the vocabulary term from the column on the right that best completes each sentence. Not all choices will be used.

1. A(n) _?_ in decimal form terminates or repeats.

2. A(n) _?_ is the square of a whole number.

3. A(n) _?_ is a mathematical sentence using one of the symbols $<, >, \leq, \geq,$ or $\neq$.

4. The inverse of squaring a number is finding the _?_ .

5. The longest side of a right triangle is called the _?_ .

A. hypotenuse
B. inequality
C. leg
D. perfect square
E. rational number
F. square root

Go Online
PHSchool.com
For: Vocabulary quiz
Web Code: aqj-1251

Skills and Concepts

Lesson 12-1
• To solve two-step equations and to use two-step equations to solve problems

A **two-step equation** is an equation containing two operations. To solve many two-step equations, undo the addition or subtraction and then undo the multiplication or division.

Solve each equation. Check the solution.

6. $3h + 6 = 15$
7. $2j - 4 = -2$
8. $\frac{f}{5} + 4 = 29$

Lesson 12-2
• To express and identify solutions of inequalities

An **inequality** compares expressions that are not equal. A **solution of an inequality** is any number that makes the inequality true.

State whether the given number is a solution of $x \leq -4$.

9. 4
10. -4
11. -2
12. -6

Graph each inequality on a number line.

13. $p > -4$
14. $h < 8$
15. $k \geq -5$
16. $g \leq 3$

Lesson 12-3

- To solve inequalities by adding or subtracting

To solve an inequality, get the variable alone on one side of the inequality.

Solve each inequality.

17. $q + 6 < 9$

18. $t - 7 < -2$

19. $v - 4 > 12$

20. $y + 9 \geq -11$

Lesson 12-4

- To find square roots and to identify rational numbers

A **square root** of a number is a number that, when multiplied by itself, equals the given number. A **perfect square** is the square of a whole number.

A **rational number** is a number that can be written as a quotient of two integers, where the divisor is not 0.

Find each square root. Round to the nearest tenth, if necessary.

21. $\sqrt{81}$ **22.** $\sqrt{24}$ **23.** $\sqrt{30}$ **24.** $\sqrt{144}$

Tell which two consecutive whole numbers each square root is between.

25. $\sqrt{6}$ **26.** $\sqrt{12}$ **27.** $\sqrt{21}$ **28.** $\sqrt{31}$

Tell whether each number is rational.

29. $0.\overline{3}$ **30.** $\sqrt{18}$ **31.** 0.123 **32.** $\sqrt{64}$

Lesson 12-5

- To solve problems using the Pythagorean Theorem

The **Pythagorean Theorem** states that, given the triangle at the right, $a^2 + b^2 = c^2$.

Find the missing side length of each right triangle. Round to the nearest tenth, if necessary.

33. $a = 6$, $b = 8$, $c = \blacksquare$

34. $a = 15$, $b = \blacksquare$, $c = 17$

35. $a = 1$, $b = 2$, $c = \blacksquare$

36. $a = \blacksquare$, $b = 6$, $c = 8$

37. For a quilting frame to be rectangular, the diagonals must be the same length. What should the lengths of the diagonals be for a quilting frame 86 inches by 100 inches? Round to the nearest inch.

Go Online For: Online chapter test
PHSchool.com Web Code: aqa-1252

Solve each equation. Check the solution.

1. $4u + 7 = 35$ **2.** $6r - 4 = 20$

3. $\frac{f}{3} + 5 = 20$ **4.** $\frac{n}{8} - 2 = -1$

5. An eraser and five pencils cost $1.20. If the eraser costs $.45, how much does each pencil cost?

6. Write an inequality for each situation.
   a. There are fewer than six hamsters in the cage.
   b. Fifty or more people are at the county fair.

7. Write an inequality for the graph below.

8. Tell whether each number is a solution of $c \le -8$.
   a. 8   **b.** -7 **c.** -8 **d.** -10

Graph each inequality on a number line.

9. $w > -5$ **10.** $x \le 4$

11. $y < 5$ **12.** $z \ge -12$

13. **Writing in Math** Is -9 a solution of the inequality $d \le -9$? Explain.

Solve each inequality.

14. $j + 4 \ge 9$ **15.** $k - 6 < 2$

16. $s - 6 < 42$ **17.** $f + 2 \ge -1$

18. **Bank Fees** You have $59 in a bank account. You need at least $200 to avoid bank fees. Write and solve an inequality to find how much more money you should deposit.

19. To get an A on a four-part test, Dana must score a minimum of 270 points. She scored 240 points on the first three parts of the test. Write and solve an inequality to find what she needs to earn on the fourth part to receive an A.

Find the square root. Round to the nearest tenth, if necessary.

20. $\sqrt{25}$ **21.** $\sqrt{49}$ **22.** $\sqrt{60}$

Tell which two consecutive whole numbers each square root is between.

23. $\sqrt{5}$ **24.** $\sqrt{14}$ **25.** $\sqrt{97}$

Tell whether each number is rational.

26. $\sqrt{14}$ **27.** $5.\overline{5}$ **28.** $\frac{1}{13}$

Find the missing side length.

29.

30.

31. The solution to which inequality is represented by the graph below?

Ⓐ $25 > y + 20$
Ⓑ $y - 5 < -10$
Ⓒ $y - 15 > -20$
Ⓓ $y + 10 \ge -15$

Multiple Choice
Choose the correct letter.

Go Online   **For:** Online end-of-course test
PHSchool.com **Web Code:** aqa-1254

1. What operation would you perform first in the expression $3.9 + 4.1 \times 16 - 6 \div 4.8$?
   - Ⓐ Add 3.9 and 4.1.
   - Ⓑ Multiply 4.1 and 16.
   - Ⓒ Subtract 6 from 16.
   - Ⓓ Divide 10 by 4.8.

2. Four servers at a restaurant equally share $87.44 in tips. How much does each server receive?
   - Ⓕ $20.68
   - Ⓗ $21.86
   - Ⓖ $20.86
   - Ⓙ $22.86

3. Find the next two terms in the pattern: $2, 6, 12, 20, \ldots$
   - Ⓐ 24, 32
   - Ⓒ 30, 42
   - Ⓑ 28, 36
   - Ⓓ 32, 44

4. Solve the equation $0.2x = 46$.
   - Ⓕ 2.3
   - Ⓖ 9.2
   - Ⓗ 23
   - Ⓙ 230

5. Find the quotient $0.317 \div 0.08$.
   - Ⓐ 0.039625
   - Ⓒ 39.625
   - Ⓑ 3.9625
   - Ⓓ 396.25

6. Simplify the expression $4 + 6 \times (-3) - (-10) \div (-2)$.
   - Ⓕ -19
   - Ⓖ -10
   - Ⓗ 10
   - Ⓙ 19

7. Solve the equation $c + 3\frac{2}{3} = 7\frac{4}{5}$.
   - Ⓐ $3\frac{2}{15}$
   - Ⓑ $3\frac{7}{15}$
   - Ⓒ $4\frac{2}{15}$
   - Ⓓ $4\frac{7}{15}$

8. Estimate the product $7\frac{5}{6} \times 5\frac{3}{4}$.
   - Ⓕ 35
   - Ⓖ 40
   - Ⓗ 42
   - Ⓙ 48

9. Find the reciprocal of $4\frac{2}{5}$.
   - Ⓐ $\frac{5}{22}$
   - Ⓑ $\frac{1}{4}$
   - Ⓒ $\frac{5}{2}$
   - Ⓓ $2\frac{4}{5}$

10. What is the ordered pair for P?
    - Ⓕ $(3, 2)$
    - Ⓖ $(-2, -3)$
    - Ⓗ $(2, -2)$
    - Ⓙ $(-3, 2)$

11. Estimate the 8% sales tax for a sweater that costs $29.99.
    - Ⓐ $2.40
    - Ⓒ $24.00
    - Ⓑ $20.40
    - Ⓓ $240.00

12. Which of the following is NOT equivalent to 48%?
    - Ⓕ $\frac{48}{100}$
    - Ⓖ $\frac{24}{50}$
    - Ⓗ 0.048
    - Ⓙ 0.48

13. Which of the following is the most appropriate choice to display your height for each year since your birth?
    - Ⓐ circle graph
    - Ⓒ bar graph
    - Ⓑ line plot
    - Ⓓ frequency table

14. What is the value of cell D3 in the spreadsheet below?

	A	B	C	D	
1	Test A	Test B	Test C	Mean	
2	92	86	80		
3	79	82	82		
4	95	95	95		

   - Ⓕ 81
   - Ⓖ 86
   - Ⓗ 243
   - Ⓙ 285

15. Find the LCM of $20, 35$, and 100.
    - Ⓐ 5
    - Ⓑ 10
    - Ⓒ 100
    - Ⓓ 700

16. You buy tape and seven boxes for $18.55. If the tape costs $2.10, how much is each box?

Ⓕ $.70   Ⓖ $2.35   Ⓗ $2.65   Ⓙ $2.95

17. Solve the proportion $\frac{2m}{21} = \frac{8}{35}$.

Ⓐ $1\frac{3}{5}$ Ⓑ $2\frac{2}{5}$ Ⓒ 7   Ⓓ 12

18. Which drawing shows a rotation of the face below?

Ⓕ   Ⓗ

Ⓖ   Ⓙ

19. Which decimal is equivalent to $\frac{3}{8}$?

Ⓐ 0.037   Ⓑ 0.375   Ⓒ 0.38   Ⓓ 3.75

20. Solve $-9 + w < 12$.

Ⓕ $w < -21$ Ⓗ $w < 21$

Ⓖ $w > -21$ Ⓙ $w > 21$

21. What is 4.3 in words?

Ⓐ four and thirteen hundredths
Ⓑ four hundred and three
Ⓒ forty-three
Ⓓ four and three tenths

22. Which of the following is NOT true about the diagram below?

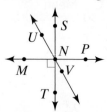

Ⓕ $\angle TNV$ is congruent to $\angle SNU$.
Ⓖ $\angle SNP$ is a right angle.
Ⓗ $\angle UNS$ is congruent to $\angle PNV$.
Ⓙ $\overleftrightarrow{ST}$ is perpendicular to $\overleftrightarrow{NP}$.

23. Which set of numbers is ordered from least to greatest?

Ⓐ $\frac{1}{2}, \frac{3}{4}, \frac{2}{3}, \frac{4}{5}, \frac{9}{10}$ Ⓒ $\frac{1}{3}, \frac{1}{2}, \frac{2}{3}, \frac{9}{10}, \frac{4}{5}$

Ⓑ $\frac{1}{2}, \frac{2}{3}, \frac{3}{4}, \frac{4}{5}, \frac{9}{10}$ Ⓓ $\frac{1}{4}, \frac{3}{10}, \frac{8}{5}, \frac{1}{2}, \frac{2}{3}$

Gridded Response

Record your answer in a grid.

24. A bag contains 1 red marble, 1 yellow marble, and 1 green marble. Your friend chooses the yellow marble. Your turn is next. If the yellow marble is *not* replaced in the bag, find the probability that you will choose the red marble.

25. Out of a sample of 125 CDs, 9 were found to have scratches. In a shipment of 5,000 CDs, how many would you predict will have scratches?

26. Find the surface area in square feet of the figure.

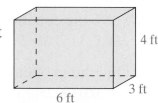

4 ft
3 ft
6 ft

27. The probability of losing a particular game is 55%. Suppose you play this game 20 times. How many times would you expect to win the game?

28. Solve the equation $4j - 8 = 12$ for j.

29. Write 5.6×10^3 in standard form.

30. Simplify the expression $(16 - 8) \times 2 + (10 \div 100)$.

31. Evaluate the expression $j \div 10 + 8.3$ for $j = 11$.

32. Simplify the expression $3 \times 8 - 4 + 5$.

Short Response

33. No more than 12 students volunteered to work at the local food pantry.
  a. Write an inequality for this situation.
  b. Graph the solution on a number line.

34. a. Find $\sqrt{19}$.
  b. Is $\sqrt{19}$ a rational number?

35. The triangles below are congruent. Write two congruences involving corresponding parts of the triangles.

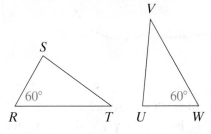

36. Write and then use an equation to find 43% of 87.

37. Sam works at a book store. When he punched in, the time clock read 3:15 P.M. When he punched out, the time clock read 7:45 P.M. He took a 15-minute break. How long did he work?

38. Solve $\frac{b}{2} + 5 = 4$.

39. Solve $n + 9 \geq 17$.

40. Find the prime factorization of 98 by using a factor tree.

41. A map with the scale 5 inches : 325 miles shows two landmarks that are 2 inches apart. How many miles apart are the landmarks?

Extended Response

42. The sum of a number t and 7 is greater than 20.
  a. Write an inequality for this situation.
  b. Solve the inequality.
  c. Graph the solution on a number line.

43. A rectangle measures 5 inches by 7 inches.
  a. What is the area of the rectangle?
  b. A 1 inch-by-1 inch square is cut from each corner of the rectangle. What is the area of the new figure? Explain.

44. An open box is made by folding the sides of the net below.

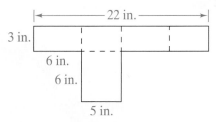

  a. Find the surface area of the open box.
  b. Now find the volume of the box.

45. The cost of your dinner is $18.64. You want to leave a 15% tip for the server.
  a. How much is the tip?
  b. What is the total cost of dinner, excluding any tax?

46. A store sells socks in two colors (gray or white), three sizes (small, medium, or large), and two fabrics (cotton or wool).
  a. Make a tree diagram to find the number of sock choices.
  b. If the store has one of every type of sock, what is the probability you will choose a wool sock at random?

Applying Equations

A Bright Idea Suppose you are changing the light bulbs in your bedroom. Regular (incandescent) light bulbs provide light, but they also get warm. Fluorescent light bulbs stay cool because they convert more energy into light. They cost more than regular bulbs, but they're cheaper to run. Should you replace your regular bulbs with fluorescent bulbs?

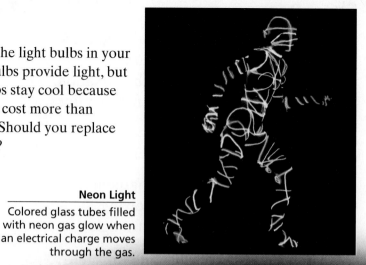

Neon Light

Colored glass tubes filled with neon gas glow when an electrical charge moves through the gas.

Fireflies

Fireflies, or lightning bugs, make light inside their bodies. The light can be any color from pale yellow to reddish green.

Go Online
PHSchool.com
For: Information about energy use
Web Code: aqe-1253

Incandescent light bulb
Cost: $1.80
Power: 100 watts per hour
Duration: 1,000 hours

Electricity costs $.15 per kilowatt-hour.

Fiber-Optic Light

Each hair-thin optical fiber has two layers of glass. Light travels from one end of the fiber to the other by bouncing along the sides of the fiber. A transparent colored disc between the light bulb and the fibers gives the fibers their color.

Fluorescent light bulb
Cost: $15.80
Power: 32 watts per hour
Duration: 10,000 hours

Put It All Together

1. How much more does a fluorescent light bulb cost than an incandescent light bulb?

2. **a.** How much power does each bulb use in 10 hours?
   b. Divide your answers to part (a) by 1,000 to find the number of kilowatt-hours each bulb uses in 10 hours.
   c. What is the cost of electricity for each bulb for 10 hours of use? Round your answer to the nearest cent.

3. Suppose the light is on for 10 hours each day.
   a. How many of each type of bulb would you use in one year? (*Hint:* 1 year = 365 days)
   b. How much would one year's supply of each type of bulb cost?
   c. What is the cost of electricity for each type of bulb for one year? Round your answer to the nearest cent.
   d. Calculate your total cost for each type of bulb for one year.

4. **Writing in Math** Which type of light bulb would you recommend to a friend? Explain.

605

Chapter Projects

Chapter 1 *Whole Numbers and Decimals*

Suppose your class is planning to honor someone special in the community or to congratulate a winning team. You need to decide when and where you will hold the event, how you will decorate, and what entertainment and refreshments you will provide. You may also need to decide how to raise funds for the celebration.

Plan a Celebration Your chapter project is to plan a celebration. You must decide how much it will cost and how much money each member of the class must raise. Your plan should include a list of supplies for the event and their costs.

Go Online
PHSchool.com
For: Information to help you complete your project
Web Code: aqd-0161

ON YOUR OWN TIME

Chapter 2 *Data and Graphs*

RING!!! The last bell of the day has rung. You and your classmates will soon head in different directions. Some of your classmates are on the same team or in the same club as you. Some of them are not. Do you know how much time your classmates spend on their favorite activities? You could guess the answers to the last question, but a more accurate method of finding the answers would be to collect real data.

Conduct a Survey For this chapter project, you will survey 25 of your friends and classmates. You can choose the survey subject, such as how much time your classmates spend on sports. You will organize and graph the data. Then you will present your findings to your class.

Go Online
PHSchool.com
For: Information to help you complete your project
Web Code: aqd-0261

STEPPING STONES

Think about a historic building, such as one of the ancient pyramids or the Eiffel Tower. How many pieces of stone do you think were needed for the bottom of a pyramid compared to the top? Many buildings use mathematical patterns in their designs.

Chapter 3 *Patterns and Variables*

Building a Fort For this project, you will build a model of a simple fort. You will record the amounts of materials needed for each course, or layer of blocks. You will look for patterns and write equations to describe the patterns.

Go Online
PHSchool.com
For: Information to help you complete your project
Web Code: aqd-0361

HOME COURT ADVANTAGE

In Malcolm's daydream, he floats in the air on his way to a slam dunk. In reality, he tosses pieces of paper into a wastebasket. He makes some shots, and he misses others.

Chapter 4 *Number Theory and Fractions*

Compare Basketball Statistics Your project will be to record and compare baskets attempted and baskets made by the players on your own imaginary basketball team. You can shoot baskets with a real basketball on a real court, or you can toss pieces of paper into a wastebasket.

Go Online
PHSchool.com
For: Information to help you complete your project
Web Code: aqd-0461

SEEing is Believing

Have you ever conducted a science experiment? Scientists perform experiments to determine whether an idea is correct or incorrect. You can determine whether something is correct or not in math class, too.

Chapter 5 Adding and Subtracting Fractions

Design a Demonstration You will learn ways to add fractions and mixed numbers with unlike denominators, but can you show that these techniques really work? Your goal is to show that they do by giving several demonstrations.

Go Online
PHSchool.com
For: Information to help you complete your project
Web Code: aqd-0561

CRACK IT and Cook It!

Eating a hearty breakfast is a great way to start any day! You are probably familiar with pouring a bowl of cereal, making toast, or maybe even scrambling eggs. But have you ever made an omelet? An omelet recipe can be simple—eggs, water, and maybe some salt or pepper. However, you can add other ingredients to this basic recipe to suit your taste. A cheese omelet is delicious. So is a bacon-and-tomato omelet. You might also add mushrooms, onions, and peppers.

Chapter 6 Multiplying and Dividing Fractions

Create a Recipe Put on your chef's hat. In this chapter project, you will write and name your own recipe for an omelet. Your final project will be a recipe that can feed everyone in your class.

Go Online
PHSchool.com
For: Information to help you complete your project
Web Code: aqd-0661

When you look up at the stars in the sky, you may not think about how far away they are. Stars appear a lot closer than they really are. The same is true of planets. The huge distances between planets make it impossible for books to show how vast our solar system really is.

Chapter 7 *Ratios, Proportions, and Percents*

Make a Scale Model In this chapter project, you will make scale models of two planets. You will compare their sizes and distances from the sun and calculate the ratios involved in your scale model.

Go Online
PHSchool.com
For: Information to help you complete your project
Web Code: aqd-0761

Puzzling Pictures

Do you remember putting together simple puzzles when you were younger? Puzzles designed for young children are often made of wood and have large pieces. Many of the pieces have corners or straight sides so that a child can put the puzzle together easily.

Chapter 8 *Tools of Geometry*

Create a Puzzle Think about one of your favorite pictures. How would it look as a puzzle? Your project is to make an attractive but challenging puzzle for your classmates. Include as many geometric shapes as you can.

Go Online
PHSchool.com
For: Information to help you complete your project
Web Code: aqd-0861

Go Fish

Have you ever spent time gazing into an aquarium full of fish? You can get lost in thought as you watch the fish through the glass. Many people enjoy having an aquarium because they feel peaceful while observing nature in this miniature environment.

Design an Aquarium In this chapter project, you will design an aquarium for your classroom. You should consider how many fish you want in the aquarium. Also consider the size of each type of fish that you plan to place in the aquarium. As part of your final project, you will create a drawing of your proposed aquarium.

Go Online
PHSchool.com
For: Information to help you complete your project
Web Code: aqd-0961

NOW PLAYING

Suppose you and a friend have to choose among three movies, and you can't make up your minds. Should you flip a coin? You'd probably agree that assigning heads to one movie, tails to the second, and "lands on edge" to the third would not give the third movie much of a chance. What should you do?

Design a Three-Choice System Your project will be to design a device or system that is fair for three different outcomes. You will test your system to make sure each outcome can be expected one third of the time over a large number of trials.

Go Online
PHSchool.com
For: Information to help you complete your project
Web Code: aqd-1061

The TIME of your life

Do you know an older person who has lived an interesting life? That person could probably tell you many stories about his or her life. You can tell stories about your life, too. You may not have lived as long, but there have been important events in your past, and there will be others in your future.

Draw a Timeline Your project will be to build a timeline of your life—past, present, and future. Think about the timelines you have seen in your social studies classes. You will have a chance to apply math concepts such as ratios, measurements, scale drawings, and integers.

Go Online
PHSchool.com
For: Information to help you complete your project
Web Code: aqd-1161

WORKING for a Cause

Chapter 12 Equations and Inequalities

Have you ever participated in a fundraiser? Schools and sports clubs often use fundraisers as a way to pay for such things as equipment, trips, and camps. You have probably purchased candy bars, magazines, or wrapping paper to help a friend or group raise money.

Plan a Fundraiser In this chapter project, you will plan a fundraiser. You will choose a cause or charity, decide how much money you would like to raise, and determine the type of event to hold or the type of product to sell. As part of your final project, you will present a fundraising plan to your class.

Go Online
PHSchool.com
For: Information to help you complete your project
Web Code: aqd-1261

CHAPTER 1

Extra Practice

Skills

● **Lesson 1-1 and Lesson 1-2**   Write each number in words.

1. 854   **2.** 10,059   **3.** 7,302   **4.** 1,205,807

5. 0.26   **6.** 0.3481   **7.** 72.053   **8.** 691.4

Use rounding, front-end estimation, or compatible numbers to estimate each answer.

9. 5.32×2.01 **10.** $15.348 - 7.92$ **11.** $22.961 \div 3.6$ **12.** $728.6 + 36.09$

● **Lesson 1-3**   Tell whether each equation is true or false.

13. $65 = 10 + 65$ **14.** $8 \times 0 = 8$ **15.** $1 \times 9.8 = 9.8$ **16.** $4 + 5 + 7 = 4 + 11$

● **Lesson 1-4**   Find the value of each expression.

17. $2 + 6 \times 3 + 1$ **18.** $(14 + 44) \div 2$ **19.** $3 + 64 \div 4 - 10$ **20.** $144 + 56 \div 4$

● **Lesson 1-5**   Write each number in standard form.

21. two hundred sixteen   **22.** two hundred twenty-two thousandths

● **Lesson 1-6**   Order each set of decimals from least to greatest.

23. 0.2, 0.4, 0.7   **24.** 0.2, 0.02, 0.202, 0.002   **25.** 6.25, 6.05, 6.2, 6.025

● **Lesson 1-7**   First estimate and then find each sum or difference.

26. $1.14 + 9.3$ **27.** $3.541 + 1.333$ **28.** $5.45 - 2.8$ **29.** $4.11 - 2.621$

● **Lesson 1-8**   Find each product.

30. 1.8×4.302 **31.** $0.29(0.43)$ **32.** $7.4(930)$ **33.** $0.617 \cdot 0.09$

● **Lesson 1-9**   Find each quotient.

34. $8 \div 9$ **35.** $23 \div 25$ **36.** $348 \div 60$ **37.** $11 \div 16$

Word Problems

● **Lesson 1-1**

38. **Social Studies** Order the populations in the table at the right from least to greatest.

Population

India	1,080,264,588
China	1,306,313,812
United States	295,734,134

SOURCE: U.S. Census Bureau, 2005

● **Lesson 1-2**

39. You spend $546 on school lunches for the school year. There are about 180 days of school in the school year. About how much do you spend on lunch each day?

● **Lessons 1-3 and 1-4**

40. **Music** What is the total number of instruments in the orchestra shown in the table at the right?

41. A group of 28 students and 3 teachers goes to the theater. Each student pays $12. The school pays an additional $4 per student and $16 per adult. Find the total cost of the trip.

Orchestra

Instrument	Number
Violin	29
Viola	13
Bass	2
Cello	12

● **Lesson 1-5**

42. **Currency** The rupee and the paisa are units of money in India. One paisa is equal to $\frac{1}{100}$ of an Indian rupee. Using decimals, write 256 paisas as a number of rupees.

● **Lesson 1-6**

43. **Animals** The table shows typical weights regularly reached by some adult animals. Order the animals by weight from least to greatest.

Animal	Weight (tons)
American bison	1.5
Anaconda	0.23
Gorilla	0.35
Kodiak bear	0.74
Leatherback turtle	0.8

● **Lesson 1-7**

44. At a bicycle store, an 18-speed bicycle costs $174.99. At another store, the same bicycle costs $222.98. What is the difference in prices?

● **Lessons 1-8 and 1-9**

45. **Money** There are 40 coins in a roll of nickels. Find the value of 25 rolls of nickels.

46. Regular unleaded gasoline costs $2.359 per gallon. You spend $10 on gasoline. About how many gallons do you buy?

Skills

● **Lesson 2-1**   **Find the mean of each data set.**

1. 35, 39, 27, 28   **2.** 253, 277, 249, 279, 265   **3.** 7.5, 3.8, 12.4, 11.7, 12.4

● **Lesson 2-2**   **Find the median and mode of each data set.**

4. 23, 26, 22, 25, 22, 28, 22, 10   **5.** 14.2, 11.3, 12.0, 11.1, 13.0, 13.3 **6.** 36, 42, 58, 29, 45, 63, 57, 29

● **Lesson 2-3**   **Make a frequency table and a line plot for each set of data.**

7. books read each month:
3, 1, 4, 2, 4, 1, 3, 2, 4, 4, 2, 1

8. words typed per minute:
65, 35, 40, 65, 40, 40, 55, 35, 35, 70, 35, 55

● **Lesson 2-4**   **Use the bar graph for Exercises 9–10.**

9. What information is given on each axis?

10. What is the average yearly reading time for books?

Average Yearly Reading by Americans

● **Lesson 2-5**   **The spreadsheet below shows the number of medals the United States won during the 2004 Summer Olympics.**

11. a. What is the value in C2?
  b. What does this number mean?

12. Write the formula for cell E2.

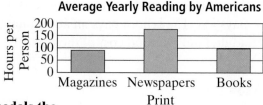

	A	B	C	D	E
1	Country	Gold	Silver	Bronze	Total
2	United States	35	39	29	▪

● **Lesson 2-6**   **Make a stem-and-leaf plot and a box-and whisker plot for the set of data below.**

13. test scores (percents): 86, 76, 72, 85, 69, 85, 78, 91, 77

● **Lesson 2-7**   **Use the line graph at the right.**

14. Explain why the graph is misleading.

15. Use the data to draw a graph that is not misleading.

Daily Total Sales

Word Problems

● **Lessons 2-1 and 2-2**

16. **Biology** The weights, in pounds, of 5 adult coyotes are 36, 25, 28, 39, and 30. What is the mean weight of the adult coyotes?

17. **Weather** The daily high temperatures (°F) for one week are 86°, 78°, 92°, 79°, 87°, 77°, and 91°. Find the median and the mode of the high temperatures.

● **Lesson 2-3**

18. The frequency table at the right shows the number of correct answers each student wrote on a 24-question quiz. What is the range of the number of correct answers?

Number	Tally	Frequency
15	I	1
17	I	1
18	I	1
19	II	2
20	IIII	4
21	II	2
22	II	2
24	I	1

● **Lesson 2-4**

19. **Language** Make a bar graph showing how many different languages are spoken in each country. Use the table.

Languages

Country	Number of Languages
Bolivia	36
Brazil	188
Colombia	80
Mexico	291
Venezuela	40

Source: *Ethnologue: Languages of the World*

● **Lesson 2-5**

20. Write a formula to find the mean score in cell G4 below.

Calories

	A	B	C	D	E	F	G
1	Day	Breakfast	Lunch	Dinner	Snacks	Total	Mean
2	Monday	550	730	920	200		
3	Tuesday	420	660	750	600		
4	Wednesday	250	880	1200	120		

● **Lesson 2-6**

21. **Animals** Make a stem-and-leaf plot for the data in the table at the right showing the speeds of animals.

Animal Speeds

Animal	Miles per hour
Coyote	43
Hyena	40
Rabbit	35
Giraffe	32
Grizzly bear	30
Elephant	25

Source: *World Almanac*

● **Lesson 2-7**

22. **Track and Field** In successive track meets, Andre jumps the following distances.
11 ft 5 in.   11 ft 8 in.   12 ft 1 in.   11 ft 10 in.   12 ft 1 in.
Draw a line graph that appears to show Andre's jumps varying widely. Explain why the graph is misleading.

Skills

● **Lesson 3-1** Write the next three terms and write a rule for each pattern.

1. 1, 4, 16, 64, . . . **2.** 2, 6, 18, 54, . . . **3.** 7, 11, 15, 19, . . . **4.** 80, 74, 68, 62, . . .

● **Lesson 3-2** Evaluate each expression for $n = 9$.

5. $n - 7$ **6.** $3n - 5$ **7.** $22 - 2n$ **8.** $4n \div 6$

● **Lesson 3-3** Write an expression for each word phrase.

9. 1 less than b **10.** p times 2 **11.** 4 more than b **12.** n divided by 2

● **Lesson 3-4** Use mental math to solve each problem.

13. $x + 6 = 8$ **14.** $5x = 40$ **15.** $36 = 36 - x$ **16.** $x + 2 = 8.3$

Use mental math to solve each equation.

17. $20 = y + 1$ **18.** $t - 10 = 24$ **19.** $a \div 3 = 3$ **20.** $178 = 10b$

● **Lessons 3-5 and 3-6** Solve each equation. Then check the solution.

21. $b + 4 = 7.7$ **22.** $c + 3.5 = 7.5$ **23.** $n - 1.7 = 8$ **24.** $8.4 = s - 0.2$

● **Lesson 3-7** Solve each equation.

25. $15t = 600$ **26.** $62 = 2b$ **27.** $x \div 5 = 2.5$ **28.** $a \div 0.05 = 140$

● **Lesson 3-8** Use the Distributive Property to simplify each expression.

29. 7×78 **30.** 3×19 **31.** 6×66 **32.** 4×47

Word Problems

● **Lesson 3-1**

33. Trains The schedule shows the departure times for the Red and Blue Trains. Predict the remaining departure times before 6 P.M. for each train.

Departures

Red Train	Blue Train
12:51 P.M.	12:17 P.M.
1:51 P.M.	1:02 P.M.
2:51 P.M.	1:47 P.M.
3:51 P.M.	2:32 P.M.

● **Lesson 3-2**

34. A company selling T-shirts charges $45 to create a design it will print on shirts. Each T-shirt costs $3. You can use the expression $3x + 45$ to find the cost of an order, where x stands for the number of T-shirts. How much does it cost to order 350 T-shirts?

● **Lesson 3-3**

35. **Boating** A paddleboat rents for $10 plus $8 per hour. How much does it cost to rent a paddleboat for h hours? Draw a model and write an expression for the situation.

● **Lesson 3-4**

36. **Sports** A hockey team spends $75 on chin straps. Each strap costs $5. Solve the equation $5n = 75$ to find how many straps the team buys.

● **Lesson 3-5**

37. **Biology** The height of the female giraffe in a zoo is 14.1 feet. The female is 3.2 feet shorter than the male giraffe. Write and solve an equation to find the male's height.

● **Lesson 3-6**

38. In a class of 26 students, 15 students have birthdays in the first half of the year. Write and solve an equation to find how many students have birthdays in the last half of the year.

● **Lesson 3-7**

39. **Geography** The area of the Pacific Ocean is about 64,000,000 square miles. This area is about twice the area of the Atlantic Ocean. Find the approximate area of the Atlantic Ocean.

● **Lesson 3-8**

40. Your family buys carpeting for the two rooms shown at the right. Write an expression for the total square feet of carpet that your family buys.

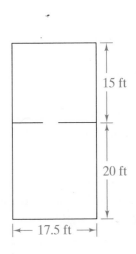

15 ft

20 ft

← 17.5 ft →

Skills

● **Lesson 4-1**   Test each number for divisibility by 2, 3, 5, 9, or 10.

1. 324   **2.** 2,685   **3.** 540   **4.** 114   **5.** 31   **6.** 981

● **Lesson 4-2**   Simplify each expression.

7. $7 + 5^2$ **8.** $(6 - 2)^3 \times 3$ **9.** 8^3 **10.** $9^2 + 2^2$

● **Lesson 4-3**   Tell whether each number is prime or composite.

11. 24   **12.** 49   **13.** 7   **14.** 81   **15.** 37   **16.** 29

● **Lesson 4-4**   Find the GCF of each set of numbers.

17. 10, 30   **18.** 15, 18   **19.** 25, 35   **20.** 28, 36   **21.** 45, 72   **22.** 8, 12, 20

● **Lesson 4-5**   Write each fraction in simplest form.

23. $\frac{6}{60}$ **24.** $\frac{3}{5}$ **25.** $\frac{27}{36}$ **26.** $\frac{40}{50}$ **27.** $\frac{3}{4}$ **28.** $\frac{42}{70}$

● **Lesson 4-6**   Write each mixed number as an improper fraction. Write each improper fraction as a mixed number in simplest form.

29. $1\frac{7}{8}$ **30.** $2\frac{3}{5}$ **31.** $11\frac{1}{9}$ **32.** $\frac{25}{7}$ **33.** $\frac{39}{12}$ **34.** $\frac{12}{5}$

● **Lesson 4-7**   Find the LCM of each set of numbers.

35. 4, 8   **36.** 6, 14   **37.** 15, 25   **38.** 20, 36   **39.** 3, 4, 12   **40.** 8, 10, 15

● **Lesson 4-8**   Order each set of numbers from least to greatest.

41. $\frac{4}{7}, \frac{4}{5}, \frac{4}{9}$ **42.** $\frac{6}{16}, \frac{7}{16}, \frac{5}{16}$ **43.** $\frac{2}{3}, \frac{5}{6}, \frac{7}{12}$ **44.** $\frac{3}{4}, \frac{4}{6}, \frac{7}{9}$ **45.** $2\frac{3}{4}, 2\frac{1}{8}, 2\frac{1}{2}$ **46.** $\frac{5}{8}, \frac{3}{5}, \frac{9}{20}$

● **Lesson 4-9**   Write each decimal as a fraction or mixed number in simplest form.

47. 1.25   **48.** 0.02   **49.** 0.32   **50.** 3.45   **51.** 0.175   **52.** 2.16

Write each fraction or mixed number as a decimal. Use a bar to indicate repeating digits.

53. $\frac{2}{3}$ **54.** $\frac{2}{5}$ **55.** $\frac{1}{4}$ **56.** $7\frac{5}{12}$ **57.** $4\frac{2}{3}$ **58.** $\frac{13}{8}$

Extra Skills and Word Problems

● **Lesson 4-1**

59. You and three friends eat lunch at a restaurant. The bill totals $18.21. Can you and your friends split the bill evenly? Explain.

● **Lessons 4-2 through 4-4**

60. The table shows the number of rectangles you make each time you fold a piece of paper in half. After 6 folds, how many rectangles have you made? Write your answer using an exponent.

61. A photographer arranges 126 students for a class picture. Each row has the same number of students. What numbers of rows can he make?

62. On a field day, 84 girls and 78 boys are divided into teams. Each team has the same number of girls and the same number of boys. At most, how many teams are possible?

Number of Folds	Number of Rectangles
1	2
2	4
3	8
4	16

● **Lessons 4-5 and 4-6**

63. A framer uses an inch ruler marked in sixteenths to measure the frame at the right. What is the measure of the height of the frame to the nearest sixteenth of an inch?

64. A chef uses 2 slices of bread for each of 50 sandwiches. Each loaf of bread has 12 equal slices. Write a mixed number for the number of loaves of bread he uses to make sandwiches.

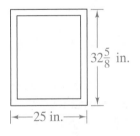

$32\frac{5}{8}$ in.

←—25 in.—→

● **Lessons 4-7 and 4-8**

65. Use the table. Find the least number of folders, stickers, and pens you can buy so that you have the same number of each.

66. What mixed number is halfway between $1\frac{1}{8}$ and $1\frac{3}{8}$? Show your answer on a number line.

Item	Number in Pack
Folders	6
Stickers	10
Pens	12

● **Lesson 4-9**

67. Arrange the side lengths of the triangle in order from least to greatest. Explain your reasoning.

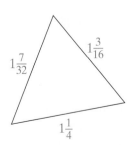

$1\frac{3}{16}$

$1\frac{7}{32}$

$1\frac{1}{4}$

Extra Practice

Skills

● **Lesson 5-1**

Estimate each sum or difference. Use the benchmarks 0, $\frac{1}{2}$, and 1.

1. $\frac{2}{3} + \frac{1}{8}$

2. $\frac{3}{5} + \frac{4}{7}$

3. $\frac{5}{6} - \frac{3}{8}$

4. $\frac{3}{8} - \frac{5}{12}$

Estimate each sum or difference.

5. $12\frac{3}{4} - 7\frac{4}{9}$

6. $5\frac{7}{9} + 9\frac{3}{5}$

7. $2\frac{1}{3} - 1\frac{6}{7}$

8. $6\frac{3}{10} + 4\frac{5}{8}$

● **Lessons 5-2 and 5-3   Find each sum or difference.**

9. $\frac{5}{8} + \frac{1}{8}$

10. $\frac{4}{5} - \frac{2}{5}$

11. $\frac{11}{12} + \frac{5}{12}$

12. $\frac{7}{8} - \frac{3}{8}$

13. $\frac{5}{6} + \frac{2}{3}$

14. $\frac{7}{8} - \frac{3}{4}$

15. $\frac{3}{5} + \frac{5}{8}$

16. $\frac{3}{8} - \frac{1}{12}$

● **Lesson 5-4   Find each sum.**

17. $6\frac{2}{3} + 1\frac{1}{2}$

18. $5\frac{7}{8} + 1\frac{3}{4}$

19. $8\frac{1}{4} + 3\frac{1}{3}$

20. $7\frac{3}{10} + 3\frac{1}{4}$

● **Lesson 5-5   Find each difference.**

21. $7\frac{3}{8} - 1\frac{2}{3}$

22. $11\frac{1}{6} - 2\frac{3}{4}$

23. $7\frac{5}{6} - 2\frac{1}{10}$

24. $6\frac{1}{3} - 2\frac{1}{4}$

● **Lesson 5-6   Solve each equation.**

25. $x + 6\frac{4}{9} = 8\frac{1}{9}$

26. $y + 2\frac{3}{8} = 8\frac{1}{5}$

27. $a + 9 = 12\frac{7}{9}$

28. $4\frac{5}{7} = b - 3\frac{1}{2}$

29. $c - 11\frac{2}{3} = 15$

30. $n + 4\frac{1}{2} = 5$

31. $m - 5\frac{3}{4} = 10\frac{1}{2}$

32. $p - 8\frac{1}{3} = 9\frac{1}{4}$

● **Lesson 5-7   Find the elapsed time in each interval.**

33. from 3:45 P.M. to 5:15 P.M.

34. from 8:10 P.M. to 11:55 P.M.

35. from 11:45 A.M. to 6:23 P.M.

36. from 4:05 A.M. to 4:10 P.M.

37. from 3:25 P.M. to 5:02 P.M.

38. from 8:10 A.M. to 11:55 P.M.

Word Problems

● **Lesson 5-1**

39. You need $1\frac{5}{8}$ yards of solid-colored fabric and $\frac{3}{4}$ yard of print fabric for a quilt. Given the prices in the table at the right, about how much will the fabric cost? Justify your answer.

Fabric Cost

Print	$8.25 per yard
Solid	$7.95 per yard

● **Lesson 5-2**

40. Two scouts explore a cove. One scout explores $\frac{1}{8}$ mile at one end of the cove. The other scout explores $\frac{3}{8}$ mile of the cove at the opposite end. Together, how much of the cove do they explore?

● **Lesson 5-3**

41. You buy two goldfish. One goldfish weighs $\frac{1}{6}$ ounce. The other goldfish weighs $\frac{1}{3}$ ounce. What is the combined weight of the goldfish?

● **Lesson 5-4**

42. Apples You have $1\frac{3}{4}$ pounds of red apples and $2\frac{1}{2}$ pounds of green apples. How many pounds of apples do you have?

● **Lesson 5-5**

43. Science You and a partner are growing bean plants for a science project. The table at the right shows the heights of the plants after one week of growth. Find the difference in the heights of the two plants.

Plant Growth
Height
Bean 1 $7\frac{7}{8}$ in.
Bean 2 $5\frac{15}{16}$ in.

● **Lesson 5-6**

44. You have a rope that is $18\frac{1}{2}$ feet long for a tug-of-war. The team captains agree to shorten the rope by cutting off $1\frac{1}{8}$ feet. How long is the rope after it is cut?

45. A piece of poster board is $2\frac{3}{4}$ feet long. You shorten the length by $\frac{1}{2}$ ft. How long is the shortened poster board?

● **Lesson 5-7**

46. A family reunion begins at 1 P.M. and lasts for 3 hours. It takes 45 minutes to drive from your house to the reunion. How long will you be away from home?

Skills

● **Lesson 6-1** Find each product.

1. $\frac{1}{2}$ of $\frac{2}{3}$

2. $\frac{1}{3}$ of $\frac{1}{5}$

3. $\frac{7}{8} \times \frac{3}{4}$

4. $\frac{7}{6} \times 42$

● **Lesson 6-2** Find each product.

5. $7\frac{1}{2} \times 2\frac{2}{3}$

6. $6\frac{2}{3} \times 7\frac{1}{5}$

7. $5\frac{5}{8} \times 2\frac{1}{3}$

8. $12\frac{1}{4} \times 6\frac{2}{7}$

● **Lesson 6-3** Find each quotient.

9. $2 \div \frac{4}{5}$

10. $\frac{2}{3} \div \frac{2}{5}$

11. $\frac{1}{4} \div \frac{1}{5}$

12. $\frac{4}{11} \div 8$

● **Lesson 6-4** Estimate each quotient.

13. $12 \div 3\frac{1}{5}$

14. $7\frac{3}{7} \div 1\frac{2}{5}$

15. $41\frac{8}{10} \div 6\frac{1}{3}$

16. $36\frac{2}{7} \div 4\frac{3}{9}$

Find each quotient.

17. $2\frac{1}{4} \div \frac{2}{3}$

18. $4\frac{1}{2} \div 3\frac{1}{3}$

19. $2\frac{2}{5} \div \frac{2}{25}$

20. $5\frac{2}{3} \div 1\frac{1}{2}$

● **Lesson 6-5** Solve each equation. Check the solution.

21. $\frac{x}{4} = 8$

22. $\frac{a}{3} = 9$

23. $\frac{c}{7} = 24$

24. $\frac{m}{2} = 14$

25. $\frac{r}{4} = 3.5$

26. $\frac{t}{12} = 3$

27. $\frac{1}{3}y = 15$

28. $\frac{3}{4}w = 12$

● **Lesson 6-6** Choose an appropriate unit for each measurement.

29. capacity of a bathtub

30. weight of a school bus

31. width of a computer monitor

32. weight of a pair of jeans

33. your height

34. capacity of a water pitcher

● **Lesson 6-7** Complete each statement.

35. 4 ft = ■ yd

36. 48 oz = ■ lb

37. 32 qt = ■ gal

38. 8,000 lb = ■ t

39. 10 lb = ■ oz

40. ■ ft = 60 in.

41. 64 c = ■ pt

42. 9 mi = ■ ft

Word Problems

● **Lesson 6-1**

43. To save money, you buy some clothes on sale. You buy a shirt for $\frac{4}{5}$ of the full price, a pair of jeans for $\frac{3}{4}$ of the full price, and a pair of shoes for $\frac{9}{10}$ of the full price. How much money do you save by buying these clothes on sale?

Item	Full Price
Shirt	$21.00
Jeans	$40.00
Shoes	$27.00

● **Lesson 6-2**

44. **Carpentry** A carpenter needs 6 pieces of wood that are $3\frac{1}{2}$ feet long. She has two 10-foot boards. Does she have enough wood? Explain.

● **Lesson 6-3**

45. **Baking** You bake an apple pie. The recipe calls for eight sliced apples. You cut the apples into eighths. How many pieces of apple do you have?

● **Lesson 6-4**

46. **Stock Market** The price of one technology stock rises $71\frac{5}{8}$ points in $7\frac{1}{2}$ hours. Find the number of points gained per hour during that time.

● **Lesson 6-5**

47. Pedro bikes $3\frac{1}{3}$ times as far as Pat, and Pat bikes $\frac{1}{5}$ as far as Jen. If Pedro rides 8 miles a day, how far does Jen ride?

● **Lesson 6-6**

48. **Games** Jai alai is a game played in Cuba, Spain, Mexico, and the United States. The ball, or pelota, weighs $4\frac{1}{2}$ ounces. How many ounces do 16 pelotas weigh?

49. Teresa has 200 yards of ribbon. She needs $1\frac{1}{6}$ yards of ribbon to make a bow. How many bows can she make?

● **Lesson 6-7**

50. **Animals** In parts of Alaska, moose cause traffic jams. An adult moose weighs about 1,000 pounds. How many tons does an adult moose weigh?

51. **Geography** The volcano Aconcagua in Argentina is 22,831 feet high. How many miles high is Aconcagua?

Skills

● **Lesson 7-1** Write two different ratios equal to each ratio.

1. $\frac{30}{60}$ **2.** 5 : 15 **3.** 13 to 52 **4.** 7 : 77 **5.** 18 to 72

● **Lesson 7-2** Find each unit price. Round to the nearest cent. Then determine the better buy.

6. cereal: 12 ounces for $2.99
16 ounces for $3.59

7. rice: 8 ounces for $1.95
15 ounces for $2.99

● **Lesson 7-3** Do the ratios in each pair form a proportion?

8. $\frac{6}{30}, \frac{3}{15}$ **9.** $\frac{9}{12}, \frac{12}{9}$ **10.** $\frac{13}{3}, \frac{26}{6}$ **11.** $\frac{5}{225}, \frac{2}{95}$ **12.** $\frac{64}{130}, \frac{5}{10}$

● **Lesson 7-4** Solve each proportion.

13. $\frac{a}{50} = \frac{3}{75}$ **14.** $\frac{18}{b} = \frac{3}{10}$ **15.** $\frac{51}{17} = \frac{c}{3}$ **16.** $\frac{2}{16} = \frac{d}{24}$ **17.** $\frac{3}{45} = \frac{4}{g}$

● **Lesson 7-5** Find each actual distance. Use a map scale of 1 centimeter : 100 kilometers.

18. 3.5 cm **19.** 1.3 cm **20.** 0.7 cm **21.** 5 cm

● **Lesson 7-6** Write each percent as a decimal and as a fraction in simplest form.

22. 42% **23.** 96% **24.** 80% **25.** 1% **26.** 87% **27.** 88%

● **Lesson 7-7** Find each answer.

28. 20% of 80 **29.** 15% of 22.5 **30.** 50% of 86 **31.** 90% of 100

● **Lesson 7-8** Use the circle graph for Exercises 32–33.

32. What item accounts for the most money in Malinda's budget?

33. About what percent of her budget does Malinda use for rent?

Malinda's Budget

Clothes
Food
Rent
Other
Insurance
Savings
Charity

● **Lesson 7-9** Estimate a 15% tip for each bill amount.

34. $34.90 **35.** $9.54 **36.** $17.50 **37.** $24.80

Word Problems

● **Lessons 7-1 and 7-2**

38. Seven out of 21 students at a school do not like horror movies. Write the ratio, in simplest form, of students who like horror movies to students who dislike horror movies.

39. You baby-sit for four hours and earn $22.00. How much money do you make each hour?

● **Lesson 7-3**

40. The table at the right shows the prices a cable television company and rental store charges for movies. Do the ratios of price to number of movies form a proportion? Explain.

Business	Number of Movies	Price
Movie store	10	$22.50
Cable TV	6	$21.00

● **Lesson 7-4**

41. Each team in the Hopkinton soccer league has 22 players and 3 coaches. How many coaches are needed for 198 players?

● **Lesson 7-5**

42. Aaron builds a model train set. The rails of the model track are 1.5 inches apart. The actual train's rails are 57 inches apart. The actual locomotive is 76 feet long. Write and solve a proportion to find the model locomotive's length.

● **Lessons 7-6 and 7-7**

43. You answer 29 questions correctly on a 40-question test. What percent of your answers are correct?

44. **Basketball** Hector made 80% of his free throws. He attempted 200 free throws. How many free throws did Hector make?

● **Lesson 7-8**

45. **Market Research** A video arcade records the ages of customers over a one-hour period. The results are shown in the line plot at the right. Draw a circle graph.

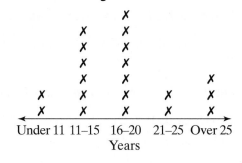

Customer Ages at Video Arcade

● **Lesson 7-9**

46. You buy a camera for 20% off the regular price of $89.99, plus a 7% sales tax. Estimate the cost of the camera.

Extra Practice

Skills

● **Lessons 8-1 and 8-2** Use the diagram at the right for Exercises 1–8. Name each of the following.

1. three collinear points 2. six rays   3. two perpendicular lines

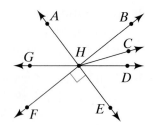

Use a protractor to measure each angle. Classify each angle as *acute, right, obtuse,* or *straight.*

4. ∠BHF   5. ∠FHC   6. ∠FHA   7. ∠CHD   8. ∠AHC

● **Lesson 8-3** Find the complement and the supplement of each angle measure.

9. 28°   10. 13.5°   11. 56.3°   12. 79°   13. 85°

● **Lesson 8-4** Classify each triangle with the given side lengths by its sides.

14. 7 inches, 9 inches, 7 inches   15. 3 feet, 3 feet, 3 feet   16. 18 yards, 16 yards, 5 yards

● **Lesson 8-5** Classify each statement as *true* or *false.*

17. All octagons have eight sides. 18. All rhombuses are squares.   19. All squares are rectangles.

● **Lesson 8-6** Each pair of figures appears to be *similar.* Use proportions to determine whether each pair is similar.

20. 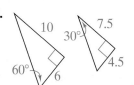   21. 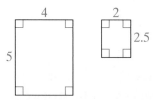   22.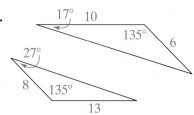

● **Lesson 8-7** Trace the figure at the right.

23. Draw all lines of symmetry in the figure.

● **Lesson 8-8** Copy the figure at the right on graph paper.

24. Draw its reflection over the given line of reflection.

● **Lesson 8-1**

25. Explain why $\overrightarrow{AB}$ represents a ray, and $\overleftrightarrow{AB}$ represents a line.

● **Lessons 8-2 and 8-3**

26. A telescope has a 68° viewing angle. What kind of angle is this angle?

27. Find the complement and the supplement of angle *RST* in the diagram at the right.

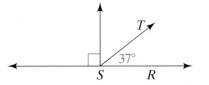

● **Lesson 8-4**

28. A company makes puzzles with triangular pieces. The side lengths of each piece are 2 in., 2 in. and 2 in. What is the type of triangle that the company makes?

● **Lesson 8-5**

29. Give four other names for the shape of a square.

30. **Signs** The shape of some traffic signs in recreation areas and national forests is a trapezoid. What is another name for the shape of a trapezoid?

● **Lesson 8-6**

31. Triangles *QRS* and *MNO* at the right are similar. List the pairs of corresponding sides and corresponding angles.

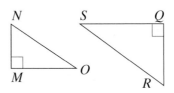

● **Lesson 8-7**

32. The Double Snake Nose Native American basket pattern is shown at the right. How many lines of symmetry does it have? Copy the design and draw the lines of symmetry.

33. How many lines of symmetry does a regular hexagon have? Sketch a regular hexagon and the lines of symmetry to support your answer.

Double Snake Nose

● **Lesson 8-8**

34. A designer makes a logo by copying the shape shown at the right and then drawing its reflection. Draw the shape and its reflection.

Extra Practice

Skills

● **Lesson 9-1** Choose an appropriate metric unit of measure.

1. capacity of a shampoo bottle **2.** mass of a television **3.** length of your shoe

● **Lesson 9-2** Complete each statement.

4. 35 mm = ■ cm   **5.** 10.8 km = ■ m   **6.** ■ L = 2,400 mL   **7.** 1,008 g = ■ kg

● **Lesson 9-3** Estimate the area of each figure. Each square represents 1 square centimeter.

8.   **9.**   **10.**

● **Lessons 9-3 and 9-4** Find the area of each figure.

11.
5.5 ft
9.5 ft

12.
4 m 5 m
6 m

13.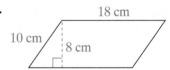
18 cm
10 cm
8 cm

● **Lessons 9-5 and 9-6** Find the circumference and the area of a circle with the given diameter *d* or radius *r*. Use 3.14 for *π* and round to the nearest whole number.

14. $d = 26$ yards   **15.** $d = 10.6$ feet   **16.** $r = 30$ inches   **17.** $r = 11$ miles   **18.** $d = 8.5$ meters

● **Lesson 9-7** Name each figure.

19.   **20.**   **21.**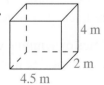
4 m
2 m
4.5 m

● **Lessons 9-8 and 9-9** Find the surface area and the volume of each rectangular prism with the given dimensions.

22. $\ell = 10$ ft, $w = 5$ ft, $h = 8$ ft

23. $\ell = 12$ m, $w = 16$ m, $h = 12$ m

Lessons 9-1 and 9-2

24. The width of a ceiling tile is about $\frac{1}{2}$ meter. How can you estimate the length of a wall that intersects a tiled ceiling?

25. Angel Falls in Venezuela is 0.807 kilometers high. How many meters high is Angel Falls?

Lessons 9-3 and 9-4

26. Construction Find the area of the sheet of plywood in the drawing at the right.

27. A parallelogram has an area of 96 square inches and a base length of 12 inches. What is the height of the parallelogram?

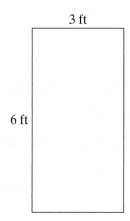

3 ft

6 ft

Lesson 9-5

28. Two cylinders have diameters of 16 and 21 inches. What is the difference in their circumferences? Use 3 for π.

Lesson 9-6

29. Weather Severe thunderstorms are forecast within a 55-mile radius of St. Louis, Missouri. What is the approximate area of the storm region? Use 3 for π.

Lesson 9-7

30. Name the figure at the right. Then find the number of faces, vertices, and edges.

Lessons 9-8 and 9-9

31. Suppose each dimension of a rectangular prism is tripled. How much larger is the surface area of the prism?

32. A packing crate has a length of 8 feet, a width of 6 feet, and a height of 4 feet. What is the volume of the packing crate?

Lesson 9-10

33. A plastic pipe has a radius of 18 in. and a length of 34 in. Find the volume of the pipe. Use 3 for π.

Skills

● **Lesson 10-1** **Draw a tree diagram to find the total number of outcomes.**

  1. You flip a coin three times.

  2. You roll a number cube. Then you toss a coin.

● **Lesson 10-2** **A jar contains 2 red, 4 yellow, 3 green, and 5 blue marbles. You select a marble without looking. Find each probability.**

  3. P(yellow)   **4.** P(green)   **5.** P(red or blue)   **6.** P(red, green, or blue)

● **Lesson 10-3** **Find the experimental probability that each person wins.**

  7. Yelena won 168 of 196 games.

  8. Chang played a game 43 times and did not lose a game.

● **Lesson 10-4** **The probability of winning a game is 80%. How many times should you expect to win if you play the following number of times?**

  9. 4   **10.** 10   **11.** 30

  12. 55   **13.** 125   **14.** 520

  Write and solve a proportion to make the prediction.

  15. In a school of 2,037 students, 500 were asked to name their favorite fruit. Apples were named by 325 students. Predict how many of the 2,037 students would name apples as their favorite fruit.

● **Lesson 10-5** **A bag contains 2 red, 6 blue, and 2 green marbles. Marbles are drawn twice with replacement. Find the probability of each compound event.**

  16. blue, then red   **17.** both blue   **18.** both not green

Word Problems

● **Lesson 10-1**

  19. A car dealership has 9 different models of cars in 6 different colors for you to choose from. How many choices do you have?

● **Lesson 10-2**

20. **Games** A game has a square board divided into 4 equal sections numbered 1 through 4. You win when you toss a chip and it lands on the section numbered 4. What is the probability of winning when a toss lands on the board?

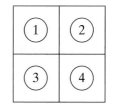

21. **Party** A package of 25 party balloons has 8 red, 6 blue, 6 green, and 5 yellow balloons. Find the probability of selecting a yellow balloon at random. Write your answer as a fraction, a decimal, and a percent.

● **Lesson 10-3**

22. You toss a paper cup 48 times. It lands on its side 36 times. Find the experimental probability that it lands on its side.

23. **Fair Games** The Mandan people played a game in which two players toss a bone disk in a basket. Player A wins if the disk lands in the basket with the decorated side up. Otherwise, Player B wins. In 100 trials, $P(\text{A wins}) = \frac{30}{100}$ and $P(\text{B wins}) = \frac{70}{100}$. Does this seem to be a fair game?

24. The table below shows the number of wins for two players after many games. Find the experimental probability of each player winning.

● **Lesson 10-4**

25. On election day, a pollster surveys 510 people as they leave the voting booths. Two hundred eighty people say they voted for Candidate A. Predict how many votes Candidate A receives if 10,000 people vote.

● **Lesson 10-5**

26. At a soccer game, a referee tosses a coin that comes up heads. At the next game, he tosses a coin and it comes up heads again. Are these two events independent? Explain.

Skills

● **Lesson 11-1   Use an integer to represent each situation.**

1. 1,000 ft above   **2.** in debt \$125   **3.** 17° below 0°C   **4.** gaining 11 lb

● **Lesson 11-2   Order from least to greatest.**

5. 3, −1, 0, −2   **6.** 4, −8, −5, 2   **7.** −6, 8, 7, −8   **8.** −1, −8, 0, 1

● **Lessons 11-3 and 11-4   Find each sum or difference.**

9. −14 + 28   **10.** −72 + (−53)   **11.** −3 − 1   **12.** −27 − (−27)

● **Lessons 11-5 and 11-6   Find each product or quotient.**

13. −8 × 5   **14.** −4 × (−9)   **15.** 93 ÷ (−3)   **16.** −5 ÷ (−2)

● **Lesson 11-7   Solve each equation. Check the solution.**

17. −4 + c = −8   **18.** x − (−6) = 15   **19.** −4y = −68   **20.** p ÷ 3 = −4

● **Lesson 11-8   Use the coordinate grid at the right for Exercises 21–28. Find the coordinates of each point.**

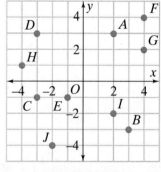

21. A   **22.** B   **23.** C   **24.** D

Name the point with the given coordinates.

25. (4, 2)   **26.** (2, −2)   **27.** (−4, 1)   **28.** (−2, −4)

● **Lesson 11-9   Look at the data for Snazzy Stuff in table at the right. Find the profit or loss for each month.**

29. January   **30.** March   **31.** May

32. Draw a line graph based on the profits and losses for Snazzy Stuff.

● **Lesson 11-10   Make a table and graph each function.**

33. kilometers as a function of meters

34. yards as a function of feet

Snazzy Stuff

Month	Income	Expenses
Jan.	\$9,002	−\$4,000
Feb.	\$8,410	−\$5,113
Mar.	\$7,596	−\$6,333
Apr.	\$7,523	−\$7,641
May	\$7,941	−\$8,027
June	\$8,569	−\$6,299

● **Lessons 11-1 and 11-2**

35. A river has a depth of 6 feet. The water then rises 5 feet. Find the new water level.

36. On a thermometer, the air temperature reads 10°F. It rises 2°F and then falls 13°F. What is the final air temperature?

● **Lessons 11-3 and 11-4**

37. Football A football team gains 6 yards on one play and loses 11 yards on the next play. What is the result of the two plays?

38. Use the table. Find the range of surface temperatures on Mars.

Surface Temperatures on Mars

Low	−125°F
High	23°F

SOURCE: National Aeronautics and Space Administration

● **Lessons 11-5 and 11-6**

39. A fishing line sinks at 4 inches per second. Find the change in depth of the fishing line after 30 seconds.

40. Animals Over five months, a horse loses 15 pounds. Find the rate of change in pounds per month.

● **Lessons 11-7 and 11-8**

41. A diver 100 feet below sea level rises 25 feet per minute. Use an equation to find the time it takes her to reach the surface.

42. Your cousin is at $(-5, -2)$. He walks 3 blocks west and 1 block south to the park. Find the coordinates of the park.

● **Lesson 11-9**

43. The table shows the population growth in the United States. Make a graph of the data and predict the population in 2010.

● **Lesson 11-10**

44. Sales A uniform company sells name patches for uniforms. The company charges $2 per patch plus a handling fee of $5 for each order. The function $p = 2n + 5$ shows how price p relates to the number of patches n. Make a table and graph the function.

Year	Population (in millions)
1900	76
1920	106
1940	132
1960	179
1980	227
2000	281

Extra Practice

Skills

● Lesson 12-1   Solve each equation.

1. $2a + 8 = 26$ **2.** $3c + 2.5 = 29.5$ **3.** $5b - 13 = 17$ **4.** $7.5d - 7 = 53$

5. $4e - 1 = -93$ **6.** $\dfrac{f}{8} + 6 = 8$ **7.** $2 + 8g = 34$ **8.** $-4 + \dfrac{h}{4} = 4$

● Lesson 12-2   Write an inequality for each graph.

9.

```
<+--+--+--○--+--+--+->
 -4 -3 -2 -1  0  1
```

10.

```
<+--+--+--+--●--+--+->
    3  4  5  6  7  8
```

11.

```
<+--+--+--●--+--+--+->
 -1  0  1  2  3  4
```

Write an inequality to represent each situation. Then graph the inequality.

12. The temperature stayed below 0°.

13. You must bring at least $5 to cover the cost of lunch.

14. The paintings for display can be a maximum of 12 inches wide.

● Lesson 12-3   Solve each inequality.

15. $m + 8 < 14$ **16.** $n - 16 \geq 3$ **17.** $p + 9 \leq -5$ **18.** $q - 8 > 7$

● Lesson 12-4   Find each square root.

19. $\sqrt{49}$ **20.** $\sqrt{81}$ **21.** $\sqrt{169}$ **22.** $\sqrt{484}$

● Lesson 12-5   Find the missing side length of each right triangle.

23. $a = 16$, $b = 30$, $c = \blacksquare$ **24.** $a = 21$, $b = \blacksquare$, $c = 35$ **25.** $a = \blacksquare$, $b = 9$, $c = 15$

Word Problems

● Lesson 12-1

26. Your brother buys 4 games. Each game costs the same amount. He uses a coupon for $5 off the total purchase price and owes the cashier $31. How much does each game cost? Use c for the cost of one game. Use the equation $4c - 5 = 31$.

27. You deliver boxes weighing 20 pounds each to a business on the sixth floor of a building. The elevator has a weight limit of 1,500 pounds. Your weight is 180 pounds. How many boxes can you load on the elevator? Use b for the number of boxes. Use the equation $20b + 180 = 1500$.

Lesson 12-2

Use the table on the right.

28. **Careers** Officers in local law enforcement must meet certain requirements at the time of hire. Write and graph an inequality showing the usual age requirement for local law enforcement officers.

29. The requirements for federal law enforcement officers are different from those for local law enforcement officers. Write and graph an inequality showing the maximum age for federal law enforcement officers.

Law Enforcement Hiring Requirements

Level	Federal	Local
U.S. Citizen	Yes	Yes
Age (years) Minimum Maximum	21 36	20 None

Source: *Occupational Outlook Handbook*

Lesson 12-3

30. Angelica sells magazines. She earns $30 a day plus $2 for each magazine subscription sold. Angelica would like to earn a minimum of $65 each day. How many magazine subscriptions must she sell per day to earn the minimum?

Lesson 12-4

31. A square floor has an area of 225 square feet. How long is each side of the floor?

Lesson 12-5

32. **Quilting** To ensure that a quilting frame is exactly rectangular, a quilter measures the diagonals of the frame to be sure they are equal. What should the lengths of the diagonals be for the quilting frame shown in the diagram below? Round your answer to the nearest tenth.

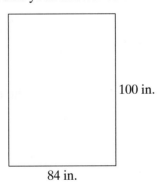

100 in.

84 in.

Place Value of Whole Numbers

The digits in a whole number are grouped into periods. A period has three digits, and each period has a name. Each digit in a whole number has both a place and a value.

Billions Period			Millions Period			Thousands Period			Ones Period		
Hundred billions	Ten billions	Billions	Hundred millions	Ten millions	Millions	Hundred thousands	Ten thousands	Thousands	Hundreds	Tens	Ones
9	5	1	6	3	7	0	4	1	1	8	2

The digit 5 is in the ten billions place. So its value is 5 ten billions, or 50 billion.

EXAMPLE

a. In what place is the digit 7?

millions

b. What is the value of the digit 7?

7 million

Exercises

Use the chart above. Write the place of each digit.

1. the digit 3
2. the digit 4
3. the digit 6
4. the digit 8
5. the digit 9
6. the digit 0

Use the chart above. Write the value of each digit.

7. the digit 3
8. the digit 4
9. the digit 6
10. the digit 8
11. the digit 9
12. the digit 0

Write the value of the digit 6 in each number.

13. 633
14. 761,523
15. 163,500,000
16. 165,417
17. 265
18. 4,396
19. 618,920
20. 204,602
21. 162,450,000,000
22. 7,682
23. 358,026,113
24. 76,030,100
25. 642,379
26. 16,403
27. 45,060
28. 401,601,001

Rounding Whole Numbers

Number lines can help you round numbers. On a number line, 5 is halfway between 0 and 10, 50 is halfway between 0 and 100, and 500 is halfway between 1 and 1,000. The accepted method of rounding is to round 5 up to 10, 50 up to 100, and 500 up to 1,000.

EXAMPLE

1 Round 2,462 to the nearest ten.

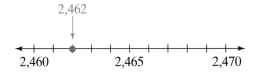

2,462 is closer to 2,460 than to 2,470.

2,462 rounded to the nearest ten is 2,460.

EXAMPLE

2 Round 247,451 to the nearest hundred.

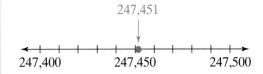

247,451 is closer to 247,500 than to 247,400.

247,451 rounded to the nearest hundred is 247,500.

Exercises

Round each number to the nearest ten.

1. 65 **2.** 832 **3.** 4,437 **4.** 21,024 **5.** 3,545

Round each number to the nearest hundred.

6. 889 **7.** 344 **8.** 2,861 **9.** 1,138 **10.** 50,549

11. 6,411 **12.** 88,894 **13.** 13,735 **14.** 17,459 **15.** 6,059

Round each number to the nearest thousand.

16. 2,400 **17.** 16,218 **18.** 7,430 **19.** 89,375 **20.** 9,821

21. 15,631 **22.** 76,900 **23.** 163,875 **24.** 38,295 **25.** 102,359

26. Describe a situation in which it is helpful to round data.

27. Explain how to round number 17 in the exercises above to the nearest ten thousand.

28. Suppose you round 31 to the nearest hundred. Is 0 the correct response? Explain your answer.

Adding Whole Numbers

When you add, line up the digits in the correct columns. Begin by adding the ones. You may need to regroup from one column to the next.

EXAMPLE

1 Add 463 + 58.

Step 1

$$\begin{array}{r} \overset{1}{} \\ 463 \\ + 58 \\ \hline 1 \end{array}$$

Step 2

$$\begin{array}{r} \overset{11}{} \\ 463 \\ + 58 \\ \hline 21 \end{array}$$

Step 3

$$\begin{array}{r} \overset{11}{} \\ 463 \\ + 58 \\ \hline 521 \end{array}$$

EXAMPLE

2 Find each sum.

a. 962 + 120

$$\begin{array}{r} 962 \\ + 120 \\ \hline 1,082 \end{array}$$

b. 25 + 9 + 143

$$\begin{array}{r} \overset{1}{} \\ 25 \\ 9 \\ + 143 \\ \hline 177 \end{array}$$

c. 3,887 + 1,201

$$\begin{array}{r} \overset{1}{} \\ 3,887 \\ + 1,201 \\ \hline 5,088 \end{array}$$

Exercises

Find each sum.

1. $\begin{array}{r} 45 \\ + 31 \\ \hline \end{array}$

2. $\begin{array}{r} 56 \\ + 80 \\ \hline \end{array}$

3. $\begin{array}{r} 25 \\ + 16 \\ \hline \end{array}$

4. $\begin{array}{r} 43 \\ + 29 \\ \hline \end{array}$

5. $\begin{array}{r} 66 \\ + 78 \\ \hline \end{array}$

6. $\begin{array}{r} 87 \\ + 35 \\ \hline \end{array}$

7. $\begin{array}{r} 81 \\ + 312 \\ \hline \end{array}$

8. $\begin{array}{r} 406 \\ + 123 \\ \hline \end{array}$

9. $\begin{array}{r} 207 \\ + 72 \\ \hline \end{array}$

10. $\begin{array}{r} 480 \\ + 365 \\ \hline \end{array}$

11. $\begin{array}{r} 217 \\ + 347 \\ \hline \end{array}$

12. $\begin{array}{r} 675 \\ + 329 \\ \hline \end{array}$

13. $\begin{array}{r} 2,051 \\ + 843 \\ \hline \end{array}$

14. $\begin{array}{r} 786 \\ + 4,109 \\ \hline \end{array}$

15. $\begin{array}{r} 5,227 \\ + 1,527 \\ \hline \end{array}$

16. $\begin{array}{r} 3,104 \\ + 2,698 \\ \hline \end{array}$

17. $\begin{array}{r} 5,337 \\ + 1,812 \\ \hline \end{array}$

18. $\begin{array}{r} 4,282 \\ + 7,518 \\ \hline \end{array}$

19. 78 + 56

20. 35 + 96

21. 105 + 71

22. 29 + 342

23. 654 + 103

24. 286 + 42

25. 55 + 77

26. 242 + 83

27. 32 + 68

28. 108 + 13

29. 589 + 318

30. 642 + 975

31. 2,308 + 451

32. 976 + 4,035

33. 8,228 + 1,024

34. 5,417 + 2,391

35. 6,470 + 9,828

36. 7,121 + 5,359

Subtracting Whole Numbers

When you subtract, line up the digits in the correct columns. Begin by subtracting the ones. Rename if the bottom digit is greater than the top digit. You may need to rename more than once.

EXAMPLE

1 Subtract 725 − 86.

Step 1
```
  115
 7 2 5
−  8 6
      9
```

Step 2
```
   11
 6 1 15
 7 2 5
 −  8 6
     3 9
```

Step 3
```
   11
 6 1 15
 7 2 5
 −  8 6
   6 3 9
```

EXAMPLE

2 Find each difference.

a. 602 − 174

```
    9
 5 10 12
 6 0 2
 − 1 7 4
   4 2 8
```

b. 625 − 273

```
  5 12
 6 2 5
 − 2 7 3
   3 5 2
```

c. 5,002 − 1,247

```
     9   9
 4 10 10 12
 5, 0 0 2
 − 1, 2 4 7
   3, 7 5 5
```

Exercises

Find each difference.

1. 81 − 37	**2.** 59 − 23	**3.** 41 − 19	**4.** 83 − 25	**5.** 99 − 78	**6.** 87 − 31
7. 707 − 361	**8.** 680 − 47	**9.** 240 − 63	**10.** 881 − 391	**11.** 517 − 287	**12.** 973 − 529
13. 7,411 − 583	**14.** 3,789 − 809	**15.** 6,508 − 2,147	**16.** 8,000 − 5,274	**17.** 3,003 − 1,998	**18.** 8,282 − 4,118

19. 78 − 19 **20.** 231 − 99 **21.** 901 − 65 **22.** 629 − 382 **23.** 918 − 133

24. 800 − 435 **25.** 403 − 122 **26.** 973 − 228 **27.** 721 − 119 **28.** 522 − 146

29. 642 − 223 **30.** 427 − 193 **31.** 444 − 345 **32.** 988 − 489 **33.** 601 − 425

Multiplying Whole Numbers

When you multiply by a one-digit number, multiply the one-digit number by each digit in the other number.

EXAMPLE

1 **Multiply 294 × 7.**

Step 1 Multiply 7 by the ones digit.

$$\begin{array}{r} 2 \\ 294 \\ \times\ 7 \\ \hline 8 \end{array}$$

Step 2 Multiply 7 by the tens digit.

$$\begin{array}{r} 6\,2 \\ 294 \\ \times\ 7 \\ \hline 58 \end{array}$$

Step 3 Multiply 7 by the hundreds digit.

$$\begin{array}{r} 6\,2 \\ 294 \\ \times\ \ \ 7 \\ \hline 2{,}058 \end{array}$$

When you multiply by a two-digit number, first multiply by the ones. Then multiply by the tens. Add the products. Remember, 0 times any number is equal to 0.

EXAMPLE

2 **Multiply 48 × 327.**

Step 1 Multiply the ones.

$$\begin{array}{r} 2\,5 \\ 327 \\ \times\ \ 48 \\ \hline 2{,}616 \end{array}$$

Step 2 Multiply the tens.

$$\begin{array}{r} 1\,2 \\ 327 \\ \times\ \ 48 \\ \hline 2616 \\ +\ 1308 \end{array}$$

Step 3 Add the products.

$$\begin{array}{r} 327 \\ \times\ \ 48 \\ \hline 2616 \\ +\ 1308 \\ \hline 15696 \end{array}$$

Exercises

Find each product.

1. $\begin{array}{r} 81 \\ \times\ 3 \\ \hline \end{array}$	**2.** $\begin{array}{r} 47 \\ \times\ 2 \\ \hline \end{array}$	**3.** $\begin{array}{r} 58 \\ \times\ 6 \\ \hline \end{array}$

4. $\begin{array}{r} 678 \\ \times\ 5 \\ \hline \end{array}$ **5.** $\begin{array}{r} 412 \\ \times\ 7 \\ \hline \end{array}$ **6.** $\begin{array}{r} 326 \\ \times\ 4 \\ \hline \end{array}$

7. 7×45 **8.** 62×3 **9.** 213×4 **10.** 8×177 **11.** 673×9

12. $\begin{array}{r} 25 \\ \times\ 46 \\ \hline \end{array}$ **13.** $\begin{array}{r} 62 \\ \times\ 88 \\ \hline \end{array}$ **14.** $\begin{array}{r} 808 \\ \times\ 60 \\ \hline \end{array}$ **15.** $\begin{array}{r} 409 \\ \times\ 70 \\ \hline \end{array}$ **16.** $\begin{array}{r} 915 \\ \times\ 27 \\ \hline \end{array}$ **17.** $\begin{array}{r} 312 \\ \times\ 53 \\ \hline \end{array}$

18. 415×76 **19.** 500×80 **20.** 320×47 **21.** 562×18 **22.** 946×37

23. 76×103 **24.** 32×558 **25.** 371×84 **26.** 505×40 **27.** 620×19

Multiplying and Dividing Whole Numbers by 10, 100, and 1,000

Basic facts and patterns can help you when multiplying and dividing whole numbers by 10, 100, and 1,000.

$8 \times 1 = 8$	$5,000 \div 1 = 5,000$
$8 \times 10 = 80$	$5,000 \div 10 = 500$
$8 \times 100 = 800$	$5,000 \div 100 = 50$
$8 \times 1,000 = 8,000$	$5,000 \div 1,000 = 5$

Count the number of ending zeros.

The product will have this many zeros.

Count the zeros in the divisor.

If possible, remove this many zeros from the dividend. This number will be the quotient.

EXAMPLE

Multiply or divide.

a. $77 \times 1,000$

    $77,000$ ← **Insert three zeros.**

b. $430 \div 10$

    43 ← **Remove one zero.**

Exercises

Multiply.

1. 85×10	**2.** 85×100	**3.** $85 \times 1,000$	**4.** $420 \times 1,000$	**5.** 420×100
6. 420×10	**7.** 603×100	**8.** 97×10	**9.** 31×100	**10.** 10×17
11. 100×56	**12.** $1,000 \times 4$	**13.** 13×10	**14.** 68×100	**15.** $19 \times 1,000$

Divide.

16. $3,200 \div 10$	**17.** $3,200 \div 100$	**18.** $32,000 \div 1,000$	**19.** $8,000 \div 100$	**20.** $8,000 \div 10$
21. $170 \div 10$	**22.** $45,000 \div 1,000$	**23.** $9,300 \div 10$	**24.** $90 \div 10$	**25.** $6,100 \div 100$
26. $7,900 \div 100$	**27.** $2,400 \div 10$	**28.** $240 \div 10$	**29.** $78,000 \div 1,000$	**30.** $9,900 \div 10$

Multiply or divide.

31. 76×100	**32.** $52 \times 1,000$	**33.** $370 \div 10$	**34.** 505×10	**35.** $6,200 \div 100$
36. $340 \div 10$	**37.** $14,000 \div 1,000$	**38.** 253×100	**39.** $3,700 \div 10$	**40.** 418×10

Dividing Whole Numbers

Division is the opposite of multiplication. So you multiply the divisor by your estimate for each digit in the quotient. Then subtract. You repeat this step until you have a remainder that is less than the divisor.

EXAMPLE

Divide $23\overline{)1,178}$**.**

Step 1 Estimate the quotient.

$$1,178 \div 23 \qquad \leftarrow \text{The dividend is 1,178. The divisor is 23.}$$
$$\downarrow \qquad \downarrow$$
$$1,200 \div 20 = 60 \quad \leftarrow \begin{array}{l}\text{Round 1,178 to the nearest hundred.}\\\text{Round 23 to the nearest ten.}\end{array}$$

Step 2

$$\begin{array}{r} 6 \\ 23\overline{)1178} \\ -138 \end{array} \quad \leftarrow \begin{array}{l} 6 \times 23 = 138 \\ \text{You cannot} \\ \text{subtract, so} \\ 6 \text{ tens is} \\ \text{too much.} \end{array}$$

Step 3

$$\begin{array}{r} 5 \\ 23\overline{)1178} \\ -115 \\ \hline 2 \end{array} \quad \begin{array}{l} \leftarrow \text{Try 5 tens.} \\ \\ \leftarrow 5 \times 23 = 115 \\ \leftarrow \text{Subtract.} \end{array}$$

Step 4

$$\begin{array}{r} 51 \text{ R5} \\ 23\overline{)1178} \\ -115\downarrow \\ \hline 28 \\ -23 \\ \hline 5 \end{array} \quad \begin{array}{l} \\ \\ \leftarrow \text{Bring down 8.} \\ \leftarrow 1 \times 23 = 23 \\ \leftarrow \text{Subtract. The} \\ \text{remainder is 5.} \end{array}$$

Left of Step 2: ← Try 6 tens.

Step 5 Check your answer.

First compare your answer to the estimate. Since 51 R5 is close to 60, the answer is reasonable.

● Then find $51 \times 23 + 5$.

Exercises

Find each quotient. Check your answer.

1. $9\overline{)659}$ **2.** $9\overline{)376}$ **3.** $3\overline{)280}$ **4.** $8\overline{)541}$ **5.** $8\overline{)232}$

6. $1,058 \div 5$ **7.** $3,591 \div 3$ **8.** $5,072 \div 7$ **9.** $1,718 \div 4$ **10.** $3,767 \div 6$

11. $3,872 \div 17$ **12.** $19\overline{)1,373}$ **13.** $27\overline{)1,853}$ **14.** $4,195 \div 59$ **15.** $41\overline{)4,038}$

16. $2,612 \div 31$ **17.** $34\overline{)1,609}$ **18.** $1,937 \div 40$ **19.** $54\overline{)1,350}$ **20.** $1,824 \div 32$

21. **Writing in Math** Describe how to estimate a quotient. Use the words *dividend* and *divisor* in your description.

Zeros in Quotients

When you divide, after you bring down a digit you must write a digit in the quotient. In this example, the second digit in the quotient is 0.

Skills Handbook

EXAMPLE

Find 19)5,823.

Step 1

Estimate the quotient.

$5,823 \div 19$
$\downarrow \qquad \downarrow$
$5,800 \div 20 = 290$

Step 2

$$\begin{array}{r} 3 \\ 19\overline{)5,823} \\ -57 \\ \hline 1 \end{array}$$

Step 3

$$\begin{array}{r} 30 \\ 19\overline{)5,823} \\ -57 \\ \hline 12 \\ -0 \\ \hline 12 \end{array}$$

Step 4

$$\begin{array}{r} 306 \text{ R}9 \\ 19\overline{)5,823} \\ -57 \\ \hline 12 \\ -0 \\ \hline 123 \\ -114 \\ \hline 9 \end{array}$$

Step 5

Check your answer.
Since 306 is close to 290,
the answer is reasonable.
Find $306 \times 19 + 9$.

Exercises

Find each quotient.

1. $7\overline{)212}$
2. $9\overline{)367}$
3. $3\overline{)271}$
4. $8\overline{)485}$
5. $6\overline{)483}$

6. $34\overline{)1,371}$
7. $19\overline{)1,335}$
8. $62\overline{)1,881}$
9. $54\overline{)1,094}$
10. $41\overline{)3,710}$

11. $282 \div 4$
12. $143 \div 7$
13. $181 \div 3$
14. $400 \div 8$
15. $365 \div 9$

16. $1,008 \div 5$
17. $3,018 \div 6$
18. $4,939 \div 7$
19. $1,682 \div 4$
20. $3,647 \div 6$

21. $2,488 \div 31$
22. $3,372 \div 67$
23. $1,937 \div 48$
24. $4,165 \div 59$
25. $1,686 \div 82$

Reading Thermometer Scales

The thermometer at the right shows temperature in degrees Celsius (°C) and degrees Fahrenheit (°F).

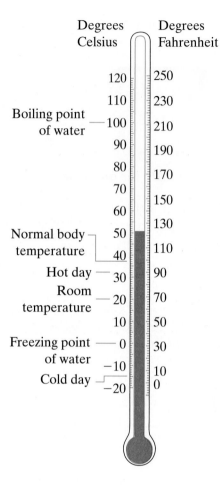

EXAMPLE

1 How do you read point *A* on the Celsius thermometer below?

Each 1-degree interval is divided into 10 smaller intervals of 0.1 degree each. The reading at point *A* is 36.2°C.

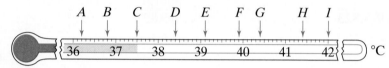

EXAMPLE

2 How do you read point *V* on the Fahrenheit thermometer below?

Each 1-degree interval is divided into 5 smaller intervals. Since 10 ÷ 5 = 2, each smaller interval represents 0.2 degree. Count by 0.2, beginning with 98.0. The reading at point *V* is 98.6°F.

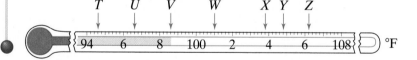

Exercises

Use the thermometers above to write the temperature reading for each point. Tell whether the reading is in degrees Celsius (°C) or degrees Fahrenheit (°F).

1. *B*   **2.** *C*   **3.** *D*   **4.** *T*   **5.** *U*   **6.** *Z*

Use the thermometers above to name the point that relates to each temperature reading.

7. 40.4°C   **8.** 42.0°C   **9.** 39.9°C   **10.** 104.8°F   **11.** 101°F   **12.** 103.8°F

Roman Numerals

The ancient Romans used letters to represent numerals. The table below shows the value of each Roman numeral.

I	V	X	L	C	D	M
1	5	10	50	100	500	1,000

Here are the Roman numerals from 1 to 10.

1	2	3	4	5	6	7	8	9	10
I	II	III	IV	V	VI	VII	VIII	IX	X

Roman numerals are read in groups from left to right.

If the value of the second numeral is the same as or less than the first numeral, add the values. The Roman numerals II, III, VI, VII, and VIII are examples in which you use addition.

If the value of the second numeral is greater than the first numeral, subtract the values. The Roman numerals IV and IX are examples in which you use subtraction.

EXAMPLE

Find the value of each Roman numeral.

a. CD

$500 - 100$

400

b. MXXVI

$1,000 + 10 + 10 + 5 + 1$

1,026

c. XCIV

$(100 - 10) + (5 - 1)$

$90 + 4 = 94$

Exercises

Find the value of each Roman numeral.

1. XI
2. DIII
3. XCV
4. CMX
5. XXIX

6. DLIX
7. MLVI
8. LX
9. CDIV
10. DCV

Write each number as a Roman numeral.

11. 15
12. 35
13. 1,632
14. 222
15. 159

16. 67
17. 92
18. 403
19. 1,990
20. 64

Estimating Lengths Using Nonstandard Units

Jan wanted to find a way to estimate lengths when she did not have any measuring tools. She measured her hand in several ways, the length of her foot, and the length of her walking stride. Then she used these "natural units" as measuring tools.

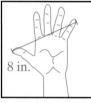

Span

Finger width

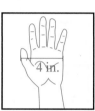

Hand

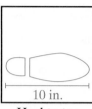

Heel to toe

Stride

EXAMPLE

Jan used strides to measure the length of her room. She counted about 5 strides. What is the approximate length of the room?

$$1 \text{ stride} \approx 32 \text{ in.} \quad \leftarrow \textbf{Write the relationship between strides and inches.}$$
$$5 \times 1 \text{ stride} \approx 5 \times 32 \text{ in.} \quad \leftarrow \textbf{Multiply both sides by 5.}$$
$$5 \text{ strides} \approx 160 \text{ in.} \quad \leftarrow \textbf{Change strides to inches.}$$
$$160 \text{ in.} = (160 \div 12) \text{ ft} \quad \leftarrow \textbf{Change inches to feet.}$$
$$160 \text{ in.} \approx 13 \text{ ft}$$

The approximate length of the room is 13 feet.

Exercises

Measure your "finger width," "hand," "span," and "heel to toe." Use these natural units to find the indicated measure for each object. Then give the approximate measure in inches, feet, or yards.

1. thickness of a math book
2. height of a chair
3. height of a door
4. length of an eraser
5. height of your desk
6. length of a new pencil
7. distance across a room
8. thickness of a door
9. length of a chalkboard

10. **Open-Ended** Measure your stride. Then measure something such as a hallway in strides, and approximate the length in feet or yards. Tell what distance you measured.

Writing Equivalent Times

The standard unit of time is the second (s). You use equivalent units to change from one unit of time to another.

Units of Time
1 minute (min) = 60 s
1 hour (h) = 60 min = 3,600 s
1 day (d) = 24 h = 1,440 min
1 week (wk) = 7 d = 168 h

EXAMPLE

How many seconds are equivalent to 1 minute 20 seconds?

$$1 \text{ minute } 20 \text{ seconds } = 60 \text{ s } + 20 \text{ s} \quad \leftarrow \textbf{One minute is equivalent to 60 seconds.}$$
$$= 80 \text{ s} \quad \leftarrow \textbf{Simplify.}$$

So 1 minute 20 seconds is equivalent to 80 seconds.

Exercises

For each time, write an equivalent time using only the smaller unit.

1. 4 wk 3 days

2. 1 h 30 min

3. 2 min 59 s

4. 8 h 2 min

5. 5 min 36 s

6. 3 wk 5 days

7. 2 days 17 h

8. 2 h 15 min

9. 1 yr 2 wk

10. 12 min 4 s

11. 2 wk 1 day

12. 4 days 14 h

13. 3 yr 14 wk

14. 23 min 32 s

15. 3 h 47 min

16. 7 min 46 s

17. 5 wk 3 days

18. 1 yr 8 wk

19. 12 h 12 min

20. 3 days 4 h

21. 9 min 9 s

22. 5 yr 40 wk

23. 4 h 52 min

24. 7 wk 1 day

Table 1 Measures

Metric	Customary

Length

10 millimeters (mm) = 1 centimeter (cm)
100 cm = 1 meter (m)
1,000 mm = 1 meter
1,000 m = 1 kilometer (km)

Length

12 inches (in.) = 1 foot (ft)
36 in. = 1 yard (yd)
3 ft = 1 yard
5,280 ft = 1 mile (mi)
1,760 yd = 1 mile

Area

100 square millimeters (mm^2) =
  1 square centimeter (cm^2)
10,000 cm^2 = 1 square meter (m^2)

Area

144 square inches ($in.^2$) =
  1 square foot (ft^2)
9 ft^2 = 1 square yard (yd^2)
4,840 yd^2 = 1 acre

Volume

1,000 cubic millimeters (mm^3) =
  1 cubic centimeter (cm^3)
1,000,000 cm^3 = 1 cubic meter (m^3)

Volume

1,728 cubic inches ($in.^3$) =
  1 cubic foot (ft^3)
27 ft^3 = 1 cubic yard (yd^3)

Mass

1,000 milligrams (mg) = 1 gram (g)
1,000 g = 1 kilogram (kg)

Mass

16 ounces (oz) = 1 pound (lb)
2,000 lb = 1 ton (t)

Liquid Capacity

1,000 milliliters (mL) = 1 liter (L)
1,000 L = 1 kiloliter (kL)

Liquid Capacity

8 fluid ounces (fl oz) = 1 cup (c)
2 c = 1 pint (pt)
2 pt = 1 quart (qt)
4 qt = 1 gallon (gal)

Time

60 seconds (s) = 1 minute (min)
60 min = 1 hour (h)
24 h = 1 day
7 days = 1 week (wk)
365 days $\approx$ 52 wk $\approx$ 1 year (yr)

Table 2 Reading Math Symbols

+	plus (addition)	p. 2	P	perimeter	p. 426
−	minus (subtraction)	p. 2	ℓ	length	p. 426
×, ·	times (multiplication)	p. 2	w	width	p. 426
÷, $\overline{)}$	divide (division)	p. 2	A	area	p. 426
=	is equal to	p. 5	s	side	p. 427
>	is greater than	p. 5	b	base	p. 432
<	is less than	p. 5	h	height	p. 432
≈	is approximately equal to	p. 8	C	circumference	p. 439
( )	parentheses for grouping	p. 16	d	diameter	p. 439
*	multiply (in a spreadsheet formula)	p. 81	π	pi; ≈ 3.14	p. 439
			r	radius	p. 439
…	and so on	p. 108	S.A.	surface area	p. 454
≠	is not equal to	p. 124	V	volume	p. 458
$\overset{?}{=}$	Is the statement true?	p. 124	B	area of base	p. 458
3^4	3 to the power 4	p. 162	P(event)	probability of event	p. 482
$\frac{1}{4}$	reciprocal of 4	p. 272	−6	opposite of 6	p. 516
3 : 5	ratio of 3 to 5	p. 306	$|5|$	absolute value of 5	p. 517
%	percent	p. 331	(2, 3)	ordered pair with x-coordinate 2 and y-coordinate 3	p. 548
$\overline{AB}$	segment AB	p. 362			
$\overrightarrow{AB}$	ray AB	p. 362			
$\overleftrightarrow{AB}$	line AB	p. 362	≥	is greater than or equal to	p. 578
∠ABC	angle with sides BA and BC	p. 367	≤	is less than or equal to	p. 578
∠A	angle with vertex A	p. 367	$\sqrt{9}$	square root of 9	p. 578
°	degree(s)	p. 367			
∟	right angle (90°)	p. 368			

Table 3 For Use With Problem Solving Applications

Chapter 2

Highest Peak on Each Continent

Land Mass	Highest Peak	Height (feet)	Height (meters)
Africa	Kilimanjaro	19,340	5,895
Asia	Everest	29,035	8,850
Australia	Kosciusko	7,310	2,228
Antarctica	Vinson Massif	16,066	4,897
Europe	Elbrus	18,510	5,642
North America	McKinley	20,320	6,194
South America	Aconcagua	22,834	6,960

SOURCE: *Time Almanac 2003*

Chapter 5

Top Speeds in Miles per Minute

Animal	Top Speed
Black mamba snake	$\frac{1}{3}$
Cheetah	$\frac{7}{6}$
Chicken	$\frac{3}{20}$
Giant tortoise	$\frac{1}{300}$

Animal	Top Speed
Peregrine falcon	$\frac{10}{3}$
Rabbit	$\frac{3}{5}$
Spider	$\frac{1}{25}$
Whippet	$\frac{71}{120}$

SOURCE: *Natural History Magazine*

Chapter 7
Animal Tracks

Animal	Track	Track Size (inches)	Animal Height (feet)
Beaver		7	2 to $3\frac{3}{5}$
Grizzly bear		12	$5\frac{3}{5}$ to $9\frac{1}{5}$
Moose		$6\frac{1}{4}$	$7\frac{9}{10}$ to $10\frac{1}{5}$
Norway rat		$\frac{5}{8}$	$\frac{3}{10}$ to 1
Striped skunk		$1\frac{1}{2}$	$\frac{9}{10}$ to $1\frac{1}{5}$

SOURCE: *Mammals of the World*

Chapter 11
Selected Earth Temperatures

Location	Temperature (°F)	Elevation (feet)
Vostok Station, Antarctica	−129 (record low)	11,220
Colossal Cave, Arizona	70 (constant)	3,660
El Azizia, Libya	136 (record high)	367
Land surface (average)	47.3	2,559
Sea surface (average)	60.9	0
Upper mantle	932	Above −2,196,480
Lower mantle	3,632	−2,900,000 to −2,196,480
Outer core	9,032	−5,100,000 to −2,900,000
Inner core	12,632	Below −5,100,000

SOURCE: National Oceanic and Atmospheric Administration, *Glossary of Geology*

Formulas and Properties

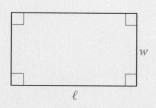

$P = 2\ell + 2w,$ or $P = 2(\ell + w)$
$A = \ell \times w$
Rectangle

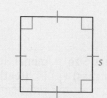

$P = s + s + s + s,$ or $P = 4s$
$A = s \times s,$ or $A = s^2$
Square

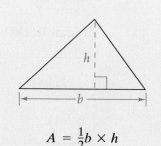

$A = \frac{1}{2}b \times h$
Triangle

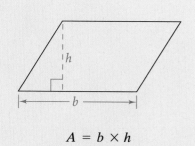

$A = b \times h$
Parallelogram

$C = 2\pi r,$ or $C = \pi d$
$A = \pi r^2$
Circle

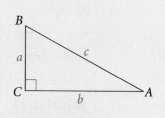

$a^2 + b^2 = c^2$
Pythagorean Theorem

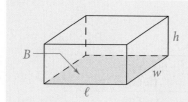

$V = B \times h,$ or $V = \ell \times w \times h$
Surface Area (S.A.) =
$2(\ell \times w) + 2(\ell \times h) + 2(w \times h)$
Rectangular Prism

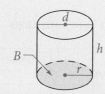

$V = B \times h,$ or $V = \pi r^2 \times h$
Surface Area (S.A.) =
$2\pi r^2 + C \times h$
Cylinder

Properties of Numbers

Unless otherwise stated, the variables a, b, c, and d used in these properties can be replaced with any number represented on a number line.

Associative Properties

Addition $(a + b) + c = a + (b + c)$

Multiplication $(a \cdot b) \cdot c = a \cdot (b \cdot c)$

Commutative Properties

Addition $a + b = b + a$

Multiplication $a \cdot b = b \cdot a$

Identity Properties

Addition $a + 0 = a$ and $0 + a = a$

Multiplication $a \cdot 1 = a$ and $1 \cdot a = a$

Inverse Properties

Addition

$a + (-a) = 0$ and $-a + a = 0$

Multiplication

$a \cdot \frac{1}{a} = 1$ and $\frac{1}{a} \cdot a = 1 (a \neq 0)$

Distributive Properties

$a(b + c) = ab + ac$

$a(b - c) = ab - ac$

Cross Products Property

If $\frac{a}{c} = \frac{b}{d}$, then $ad = bc$ ($c \neq 0$, $d \neq 0$).

Zero-Product Property

If $ab = 0$, then $a = 0$ or $b = 0$.

Properties of Equality

Addition If $a = b$, then $a + c = b + c$.

Subtraction If $a = b$, then $a - c = b - c$.

Multiplication If $a = b$, then $a \cdot c = b \cdot c$.

Division If $a = b$, and $c \neq 0$, then $\frac{a}{c} = \frac{b}{c}$.

Substitution If $a = b$, then b can replace a in any expression.

Reflexive $a = a$

Symmetric If $a = b$, then $b = a$.

Transitive If $a = b$ and $b = c$, then $a = c$.

Properties of Inequality

Addition If $a > b$, then $a + c > b + c$.
If $a < b$, then $a + c < b + c$.

Subtraction If $a > b$, then $a - c > b - c$.
If $a < b$, then $a - c < b - c$.

Multiplication

If $a > b$ and c is positive, then $ac > bc$.

If $a < b$ and c is positive, then $ac < bc$.

Division

If $a > b$ and c is positive, then $\frac{a}{c} > \frac{b}{c}$.

If $a < b$ and c is positive, then $\frac{a}{c} < \frac{b}{c}$.

Note: The Properties of Inequality apply also to $\leq$ and $\geq$.

English/Spanish Illustrated Glossary

EXAMPLES

Absolute value (p. 517) The absolute value of a number is its distance from 0 on a number line.

Valor absoluto (p. 517) El valor absoluto de un número es su distancia del 0 en una recta numérica.

-7 is 7 units from 0, so $|-7| = 7$.

Acute angle (p. 368) An acute angle is an angle with a measure between 0° and 90°.

Ángulo agudo (p. 368) Un ángulo agudo es un ángulo que mide entre 0° y 90°.

0° < measure of ∠1 < 90°

Acute triangle (p. 380) An acute triangle has three acute angles.

Triángulo acutángulo (p. 380) Un triángulo acutángulo tiene tres ángulos agudos.

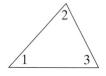

∠1, ∠2, and ∠3 are acute.

Addition Property of Equality (p. 134) The Addition Property of Equality states that if the same value is added to each side of an equation, the results are equal.

Propiedad aditiva de la igualdad (p. 134) La propiedad aditiva de la igualdad establece que si se suma el mismo valor a cada lado de una ecuación, los resultados son iguales.

Since $\frac{20}{2} = 10$, $\frac{20}{2} + 3 = 10 + 3$.
If $a = b$, then $a + c = b + c$.

Algebraic expression (p. 113) An algebraic expression is a mathematical phrase that uses variables, numbers, and operation symbols.

Expresión algebraica (p. 113) Una expresión algebraica es un enunciado matemático que usa variables, números y símbolos de operaciones.

$2x - 5$ is an algebraic expression.

Angle (p. 367) An angle is formed by two rays with a common endpoint called a vertex.

Ángulo (p. 367) Un ángulo está formado por dos rayos que tienen un punto final común llamado vértice.

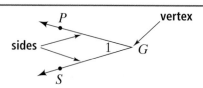

∠1 is made up of $\overrightarrow{GP}$ and $\overrightarrow{GS}$ with common endpoint G.

Angle bisector (p. 373) An angle bisector is a ray that divides an angle into angles of equal measure.

Bisectriz de un ángulo (p. 373) La bisectriz de un ángulo es un rayo que divide un ángulo en ángulos de igual medida.

$\overrightarrow{DB}$ bisects $\angle ADC$, so $\angle 1 \cong \angle 2$.

Area (p. 426) The area of a figure is the number of square units it encloses.

Área (p. 426) El área de una figura es el número de unidades cuadradas que contiene.

Each square equals 1 ft^2. With $\ell = 6$ ft and $w = 4$ ft, the area is 24 ft^2.

Arithmetic sequence (p. 123) In an arithmetic sequence, each term is the result of adding a fixed number (called the common difference) to the previous term.

Progresión aritmética (p. 123) En una progresión aritmética, cada término es el resultado de sumar un número fijo al término anterior.

The sequence 4, 10, 16, 22, 28, . . . is an arithmetic sequence. You add 6 to each term to find the next term.

Associative Property of Addition (pp. 12, 126) The Associative Property of Addition states that changing the grouping of the addends does not change the sum.

Propiedad asociativa de la suma (pp. 12, 126) La propiedad asociativa de la suma establece que cambiar la agrupación de los sumandos no cambia la suma.

$(2 + 3) + 7 = 2 + (3 + 7)$
$(a + b) + c = a + (b + c)$

Associative Property of Multiplication (pp. 13, 126) The Associative Property of Multiplication states that changing the grouping of factors does not change the product.

Propiedad asociativa de la multiplicación (pp. 13, 126) La propiedad asociativa de la multiplicación establece que cambiar la agrupación de los factores no altera el producto.

$(3 \cdot 4) \cdot 5 = 3 \cdot (4 \cdot 5)$
$(a \cdot b) \cdot c = a \cdot (b \cdot c)$

Bar graph (p. 74) A bar graph uses vertical or horizontal bars to display numerical information.

Gráfica de barras (p. 74) Una gráfica de barras usa barras horizontales o verticales para mostrar información numérica.

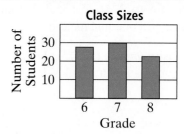

This bar graph represents class sizes for grades 6, 7, and 8.

Base (p. 162) When a number is written in exponential form, the number that is used as a factor is the base.

Base (p. 162) Cuando un número se escribe en forma exponencial, el número que se usa como factor es la base.

$$5^4 = 5 \times 5 \times 5 \times 5$$
$$\text{base}$$

Bases of two-dimensional figures (pp. 432, 433) See *Parallelogram, Triangle,* and *Trapezoid.*

Bases de figuras bidimensionales (pp. 432, 433) Ver *Parallelogram, Triangle* y *Trapezoid.*

Benchmark (p. 212) A benchmark is a convenient number used to replace fractions that are less than 1.

Punto de referencia (p. 212) Un punto de referencia es un número conveniente que se usa para reemplazar fracciones menores que 1.

Using benchmarks, you would estimate $\frac{5}{6} + \frac{4}{9}$ as $1 + \frac{1}{2}$.

Capacity (p. 417) Capacity is a measure of the amount of space an object occupies.

Capacidad (p. 417) La capacidad es una medida de la cantidad de espacio que ocupa un objeto.

A juice bottle has a capacity of about 1 liter.

Cell (p. 80) A cell is a box in a spreadsheet where a row and a column meet.

Celda (p. 80) Una celda es una caja en una hoja de cálculo donde se unen una fila y una columna.

	A	B	C	D	E
1	0.50	0.70	0.60	0.50	2.30
2	1.50	0.50	2.75	2.50	7.25

Column C and row 2 meet at the shaded box, cell C2.

Center of a circle (p. 438)   A circle is named by its center.

Centro de un círculo (p. 438)   Un círculo es denominado por su centro.

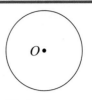

Circle O

Center of rotation (p. 403)   The center of rotation is a fixed point about which a figure is rotated.

Centro de rotación (p. 403)   El centro de rotación es un punto fijo alrededor del cual rota una figura.

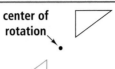

center of rotation

Chord (p. 438)   A chord is a segment that has both endpoints on a circle.

Cuerda (p. 438)   Una cuerda es un segmento que tiene ambos extremos sobre un círculo.

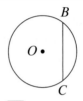

$\overline{CB}$ is a chord of circle O.

Circle (p. 438)   A circle is the set of points in a plane that are all the same distance from a given point called the center.

Círculo (p. 438)   Un círculo es el conjunto de puntos de un plano que están a la misma distancia de un punto dado llamado centro.

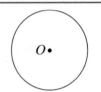

Circle graph (p. 341)   A circle graph is a graph of data in which a circle represents the whole.

Gráfica circular (p. 341)   Una gráfica circular es una gráfica de datos donde un círculo representa el todo.

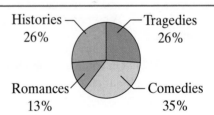

Histories 26%   Tragedies 26%   Romances 13%   Comedies 35%

The circle graph represents the types of plays William Shakespeare wrote.

Circumference (p. 439)   Circumference is the distance around a circle. You calculate the circumference of a circle by multiplying the diameter by π.

Circunferencia (p. 439)   La circunferencia es la distancia alrededor de un círculo. La circunferencia de un círculo se calcula multiplicando el diámetro por π.

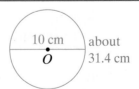

10 cm   about 31.4 cm O

The circumference of a circle with a diameter of 10 cm is approximately 31.4 cm.

Common factor (p. 171)   A factor that two or more numbers share is a common factor.

Factor común (p. 171)   Un número que es factor de dos o más números, es un factor común.

4 is a common factor of 8 and 20.

Common multiple (p. 188)   A multiple shared by two or more numbers is a common multiple.

Múltiplo común (p. 188)   Un número que es múltiplo de dos o más números, es un múltiplo común.

12 is a common multiple of 4 and 6.

Commutative Property of Addition (pp. 12, 126)   The Commutative Property of Addition states that changing the order of the addends does not change the sum.

Propiedad conmutativa de la suma (pp. 12, 126)   La propiedad conmutativa de la suma establece que al cambiar el orden de los sumandos no se altera la suma.

$3 + 1 = 1 + 3$
$a + b = b + a$

Commutative Property of Multiplication (pp. 12, 126)   The Commutative Property of Multiplication states that changing the order of the factors does not change the product.

Propiedad conmutativa de la multiplicación (pp. 12, 126)   La propiedad conmutativa de la multiplicación establece que al cambiar el orden de los factores no se altera el producto.

$6 \cdot 3 = 3 \cdot 6$
$a \cdot b = b \cdot a$

Compass (p. 372)   A compass is a geometric tool used to draw circles or arcs.

Compás (p. 372)   Un compás es una herramienta que se usa en geometría para dibujar círculos o arcos.

Compatible numbers (p. 9)   Compatible numbers are numbers that are easy to compute mentally.

Números compatibles (p. 9)   Los números compatibles son números con los que se puede calcular mentalmente con facilidad.

Estimate $151 \div 14.6$.

$151 \approx 150,\ 14.6 \approx 15$
$150 \div 15 = 10$
$151 \div 14.6 \approx 10$

Complement (p. 483)   The complement of an event is the collection of outcomes not contained in the event.

Complemento (p. 483)   El complemento de un suceso es la colección de resultados que el suceso no incluye.

The event *no rain* is the complement of the event *rain*.

Complementary (p. 374)   Two angles are complementary if the sum of their measures is 90°.

Complementario (p. 374)   Dos ángulos son complementarios si la suma de sus medidas es 90°.

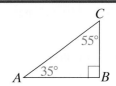

∠*BCA* and ∠*CAB* are complementary angles.

Composite number (p. 166)   A composite number is a whole number greater than 1 with more than two factors.

Número compuesto (p. 166)   Un número compuesto es un número entero mayor que 1, que tiene más de dos factores.

24 is a composite number that has 1, 2, 3, 4, 6, 8, 12, and 24 as factors.

Compound event (p. 501)   A compound event consists of two or more events. When the events are independent, the probability of a compound event is the product of the probabilities of each event.

Suceso compuesto (p. 501)   Un suceso compuesto está formado por dos o más sucesos. Cuando los sucesos son independientes, la probabilidad de un suceso compuesto es el producto de las probabilidades de cada suceso.

Suppose *A* and *B* are independent events. If $P(A) = \frac{1}{3}$ and $P(B) = \frac{1}{2}$, then $P(A \text{ and } B) = \frac{1}{3} \cdot \frac{1}{2} = \frac{1}{6}$.

Cone (p. 450)   A cone is a three-dimensional figure with one circular base and one vertex.

Cono (p. 450)   Un cono es una figura tridimensional con una base circular y un vértice.

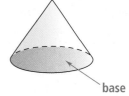

base

Congruent angles (p. 375)   Congruent angles are angles that have the same measure.

Ángulos congruentes (p. 375)   Los ángulos congruentes son ángulos que tienen la misma medida.

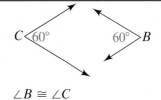

∠*B* ≅ ∠*C*

Congruent figures (p. 392)   Congruent figures are figures with the same size and shape.

Figuras congruentes (p. 392)   Las figuras congruentes son figuras que tienen el mismo tamaño y forma.

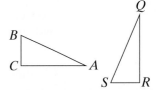

Triangle *ABC* ≅ Triangle *QSR*

English/Spanish Glossary

Congruent segments (p. 381) Segments that have the same length are congruent segments.

Segmentos congruentes (p. 381) Los segmentos que tienen la misma longitud son segmentos congruentes.

A B

W X

$\overline{AB}$ is congruent to $\overline{WX}$.

Conjecture (p. 108) A conjecture is a prediction that suggests what can be expected to happen.

Conjetura (p. 108) Una conjetura es una predicción que sugiere lo que se puede esperar que ocurra.

Every clover has three leaves.

Coordinate plane (p. 548) A coordinate plane is formed by a horizontal number line called the *x*-axis and a vertical number line called the *y*-axis.

Plano de coordenadas (p. 548) Un plano de coordenadas está formado por una recta numérica horizontal llamada eje de *x* y por una recta numérica vertical llamada eje de *y*.

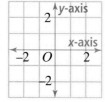

Corresponding parts (p. 393) The matching parts of similar figures are called corresponding parts.

Partes correspondientes (p. 393) Las partes que coinciden de figuras semejantes se llaman partes correspondientes.

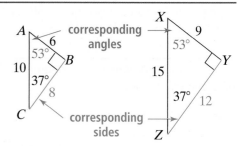

$\overline{BC}$ and $\overline{YZ}$ are corresponding sides.
$\angle A$ and $\angle X$ are corresponding angles.

Counting principle (p. 477) If there are *m* ways of making one choice from a first situation and *n* ways of making a choice from a second situation, then there are $m \times n$ ways to make the first choice followed by the second.

Principio de conteo (p. 477) Si hay *m* maneras de hacer una elección para una primera situación y *n* maneras de hacer una elección para una segunda situación, entonces hay $m \times n$ maneras de hacer la primera elección seguida de la segunda.

Toss a coin and roll a standard number cube. The total number of possible outcomes is $2 \times 6 = 12$.

Cross products (p. 317) For two ratios, the cross products are found by multiplying the denominator of one ratio by the numerator of the other ratio.

Productos cruzados (p. 317) En dos razones, los productos cruzados se hallan al multiplicar el denominador de una razón por el numerador de la otra razón.

In the proportion $\frac{2}{5} = \frac{10}{25}$, the cross products are $2 \cdot 25$ and $5 \cdot 10$.

Cube (p. 449) A cube is a rectangular prism whose faces are all squares.

Cubo (p. 449) Un cubo es un prisma rectangular cuyas caras son todas cuadrados.

Cubic unit (p. 458) A cubic unit is a cube whose edges are one unit long.

Unidad cúbica (p. 458) Una unidad cúbica es un cubo cuyos lados tienen una unidad de longitud.

1 cm

Cylinder (p. 450) A cylinder is a three-dimensional figure with two congruent parallel bases that are circles.

Cilindro (p. 450) Un cilindro es una figura tridimensional con dos bases congruentes paralelas que son círculos.

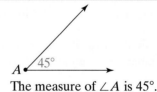

base
height
base

 D

Decagon (p. 386) A decagon is a polygon with 10 sides.

Decágono (p. 386) Un decágono es un polígono que tiene 10 lados.

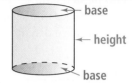

Degrees (p. 367) Angles are measured in units called degrees.

Grados (p. 367) Los ángulos se miden en unidades llamadas grados.

A 45°

The measure of $\angle A$ is 45°.

Diameter (p. 438) A diameter is a segment that passes through the center of a circle and has both endpoints on the circle.

Diámetro (p. 438) Un diámetro es un segmento que pasa por el centro de un círculo y que tiene ambos extremos sobre el círculo.

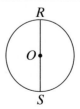

R
O
S

$\overline{RS}$ is a diameter of circle O.

Distributive Property (p. 144) The Distributive Property shows how multiplication affects an addition or subtraction: $a(b + c) = ab + ac$.

$$2\left(3 + \frac{1}{2}\right) = 2 \cdot 3 + 2 \cdot \frac{1}{2}$$
$$8(5 - 3) = 8 \cdot 5 - 8 \cdot 3$$

Propiedad distributiva (p. 144) La propiedad distributiva muestra cómo la multiplicación afecta a una suma o a una resta: $a(b + c) = ab + ac$.

Divisible (p. 158) A whole number is divisible by a second whole number if the first number can be divided by the second number with a remainder of 0.

16 is divisible by 1, 2, 4, 8, and 16.

Divisible (p. 158) Un número entero es divisible por un segundo número entero si el primer número se puede dividir por el segundo número y el residuo es 0.

Division Property of Equality (p. 138) The Division Property of Equality states that if both sides of an equation are divided by the same nonzero number, the sides remain equal.

Since $3(2) = 6$, $3(2) \div 2 = 6 \div 2$. If $a = b$ and $c \neq 0$, then $\frac{a}{c} = \frac{b}{c}$.

Propiedad de división de la igualdad (p. 138) La propiedad de división de la igualdad establece que si ambos lados de una ecuación se dividen por el mismo número distinto de cero, los des lados se mantienen iguales.

Double bar graph (p. 79) A double bar graph is a graph that uses bars to compare two sets of data.

Gráfica de doble barra (p. 79) Una gráfica de doble barra es una gráfica que usa barras para comparar dos conjuntos de datos.

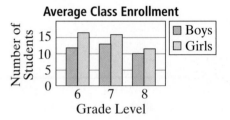

This double bar graph shows class size for grades 6, 7, and 8 for boys and girls.

Double line graph (p. 79) A double line graph is a graph that compares changes over time for two sets of data.

Gráfica de doble línea (p. 79) Una gráfica de doble línea es una gráfica que compara los cambios de dos conjuntos de datos a través del tiempo.

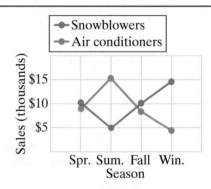

This double line graph represents seasonal air conditioner and snowblower sales for a large department store chain.

Edge (p. 449) An edge is a segment formed by the intersection of two faces of a three-dimensional figure.

Arista (p. 449) Una arista es un segmento formado por la intersección de dos caras de una figura tridimensional.

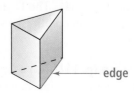

Elapsed time (p. 246)   The time between two events is elapsed time.

Tiempo transcurrido (p. 246)   El tiempo que hay entre dos sucesos es el tiempo transcurrido.

The elapsed time between 8:10 A.M. and 8:45 A.M. is 35 minutes.

Equally likely outcomes (p. 482)   Equally likely outcomes are outcomes that have the same chance of occurring.

Resultados igualmente probables (p. 482)   Los resultados igualmente probables son resultados que tienen la misma posibilidad de ocurrir.

When a number cube is rolled once, the outcomes 1, 2, 3, 4, 5, and 6 are all equally likely outcomes.

Equation (p. 124)   An equation is a mathematical sentence with an equal sign.

Ecuación (p. 124)   Una ecuación es una oración matemática con un signo igual.

$27 \div 9 = 3$ and $x + 10 = 8$ are examples of equations.

Equilateral triangle (p. 381)   An equilateral triangle is a triangle with three congruent sides.

Triángulo equilátero (p. 381)   Un triángulo equilátero es un triángulo que tiene tres lados congruentes.

$\overline{SL} \cong \overline{LW} \cong \overline{WS}$

Equivalent fractions (p. 176)   Equivalent fractions are fractions that name the same amount.

Fracciones equivalentes (p. 176)   Las fracciones equivalentes son fracciones que indican la misma cantidad.

$\frac{1}{2}$ and $\frac{25}{50}$ are equivalent fractions.

Equivalent ratios (p. 307)   Equivalent ratios name the same number. Equivalent ratios written as fractions are equivalent fractions.

Razones equivalentes (p. 307)   Las razones equivalentes indican el mismo número. Las razones equivalentes escritas como fracciones son fracciones equivalentes.

The ratios $\frac{4}{7}$ and $\frac{8}{14}$ are equivalent.

Evaluate an algebraic expression (p. 114)   To evaluate an algebraic expression, replace each variable with a number. Then follow the order of operations.

Evaluación de una expresión algebraica (p. 114)   Para evaluar una expresión algebraica se reemplaza cada variable con un número. Luego se sigue el orden de las operaciones.

To evaluate the expression $3x + 2$ for $x = 4$, substitute 4 for x.
$3x + 2 = 3(4) + 2 = 14$

Even number (p. 159) An even number is any whole number that ends with a 0, 2, 4, 6, or 8.

20 and 534 are even numbers.

Número par (p. 159) Un número par es cualquier número entero que termina en 0, 2, 4, 6 u 8.

Event (p. 476) A collection of possible outcomes is an event.

In a game that includes tossing a coin and rolling a standard number cube, "heads and a 2" is an event.

Suceso (p. 476) Un suceso es un grupo de resultados posibles.

Expanded form (p. 23) The expanded form of a number is the sum that shows the place and value of each digit. See also *Standard form*.

4.85 can be written in expanded form as $4 + 0.8 + 0.05$.

Forma desarrollada (p. 23) La forma desarrollada de un número es la suma que muestra el lugar y valor de cada dígito. Ver también *Standard form*.

Experimental probability (p. 488) For a series of trials, the experimental probability of an event is the ratio of the number of times an event occurs to the total number of trials.

$$P(\text{event}) = \frac{\text{number of times an event occurs}}{\text{total number of trials}}$$

A basketball player makes 15 baskets in 28 attempts. The experimental probability that the player makes a basket is $\frac{15}{28} \approx 54\%$.

Probabilidad experimental (p. 488) En una serie de pruebas, la probabilidad experimental de un suceso es la razón del número de veces que ocurre un suceso al número total de pruebas.

$$P(\text{suceso}) = \frac{\text{número de veces que ocurre un suceso}}{\text{número de pruebas}}$$

Exponent (p. 162) An exponent tells how many times a number, or base, is used as a factor.

exponent

$3^4 = 3 \times 3 \times 3 \times 3$

Read 3^4 as *three to the fourth power*.

Exponente (p. 162) Un exponente dice cuántas veces se usa como factor un número o base.

Expression (p. 16) An expression is a mathematical phrase containing numbers and operation symbols.

The expression $24 - 6 \div 3$ contains two operations.

Expresión (p. 16) Una expresión es un enunciado matemático que contiene números y símbolos de operaciones.

Exterior angles (p. 378) The angles outside two lines that are crossed by a transversal are called exterior angles.

Ángulos exteriores (p. 378) Los ángulos que están fuera de las dos rectas cruzadas por una secante se llaman ángulos exteriores.

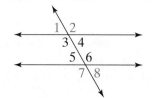

Angles 1, 2, 7, and 8 are exterior angles.

Face (p. 449) A face is a flat, polygon-shaped surface of a three-dimensional figure.

Cara (p. 449) Una cara es una superficie plana de una figura tridimensional que tiene la forma de un polígono.

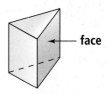

face

Factor (p. 166) A factor is a whole number that divides another whole number with a remainder of 0.

Divisor (p. 166) Un divisor es un número entero que divide a otro número entero y el residuo es 0.

1, 2, 3, 4, 6, 9, 12, 18, and 36 are factors of 36.

Factor tree (p. 167) A factor tree is a diagram that shows how a composite number breaks down into its prime factors.

Árbol de factores (p. 167) Un árbol de factores es un diagrama que muestra cómo se descompone un número compuesto en sus factores primos.

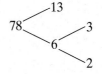

The prime factors of 78 are 2, 3, and 13.

Frequency table (p. 70) A frequency table lists each item in a data set with the number of times the item occurs.

Tabla de frecuencia (p. 70) Una tabla de frecuencia es una tabla que registra todos los elementos de un conjunto de datos y el número de veces que ocurre cada uno.

Household Telephones

Phones	Tally	Frequency
1	ЖШ III	8
2	ЖШ I	6
3	IIII	4

This frequency table shows the number of household telephones for a class of students.

Front-end estimation (p. 32) To use front-end estimation to estimate sums, first add the front-end digits. Then adjust by estimating the sum of the remaining digits. Add the two values.

Estimación de entrada (p. 32) Para estimar usando la estimación de entrada, primero se suman los dígitos de entrada. Luego se ajustan estimando la cantidad de los dígitos restantes. Finalmente, se suman las dos cantidades.

Estimate $3.09 + $2.99.

$$\begin{array}{ll} \$3.09 & \$3.\mathbf{09} \\ + \$2.99 \rightarrow & \$2.\mathbf{99} \\ \hline \$5 & \text{about } \$1 \end{array}$$

So $3.09 + $2.99 ≈ 5 + 1, or $6.

Function (p. 558) A function is a relationship that assigns exactly one output value for each input value.

Función (p. 558) Una función es una relación que asigna exactamente un valor resultante a cada valor inicial.

Earned income i is a function of the number of hours worked h. If you earn $6 per hour, then your income can be expressed by the function $i = 6h$.

English/Spanish Glossary

EXAMPLES

Gram (p. 417) The standard unit of mass in the metric system is the gram.

A paper clip has the mass of about 1 gram.

Gramo (p. 417) La unidad de masa estándar en el sistema métrico es el gramo.

Graph of a function (p. 559) The graph of a function is the graph of all the points whose coordinates are solutions of the equation.

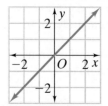

Gráfica de una función (p. 559) La gráfica de una función es la gráfica de todos los puntos cuyas coordenadas son soluciones a la ecuación.

This is the graph of $y = x$.

Graph of an inequality (p. 579) The graph of an inequality shows all solutions that satisfy the inequality.

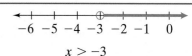

$x > -3$

Gráfica de una desigualdad (p. 579) La gráfica de una desigualdad muestra todas las soluciones que satisfacen la desigualdad.

Greatest common factor (GCF) (p. 171) The greatest common factor of two or more numbers is the greatest factor shared by all of the numbers.

The GCF of 12 and 30 is 6.

Máximo común divisor (MCD) (p. 171) El máximo común divisor de dos o más números es el mayor divisor que comparten todos los números.

Height of two-dimensional figures (pp. 432, 433) See *Parallelogram, Triangle,* and *Trapezoid.*

Altura de figuras bidimensionales (pp. 432, 433) Ver *Parallelogram, Triangle* y *Trapezoid.*

Hexagon (p. 386) A hexagon is a polygon with six sides.

Hexágono (p. 386) Un hexágono es un polígono que tiene seis lados.

Histogram (p. 77) A histogram is a bar graph with no spaces between the bars. The height of each bar shows the frequency of data within that interval.

Histograma (p. 77) Un histograma es una gráfica de barras sin espacio entre las barras. La altura de cada barra muestra la frecuencia de los datos dentro del intervalo.

Board Game Purchases

The histogram gives the frequency of board game purchases at a local toy store.

Hypotenuse (p. 591) In a right triangle, the hypotenuse is the longest side, which is opposite the right angle.

Hipotenusa (p. 591) En un triángulo rectángulo, la hipotenusa es el lado más largo, que es el lado opuesto al ángulo recto.

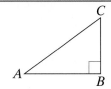

$\overline{AC}$ is the hypotenuse of $\triangle ABC$.

Identity Property of Addition (pp. 12, 126) The Identity Property of Addition states that the sum of 0 and a is a.

Propiedad de identidad de la suma (pp. 12, 126) La propiedad de identidad de la suma establece que la suma de 0 y a es a.

$0 + 7 = 7$
$a + 0 = a$

Identity Property of Multiplication (pp. 13, 126) The Identity Property of Multiplication states that the product of 1 and a is a.

Propiedad de identidad de la multiplicación (pp. 13, 126) La propiedad de identidad de la multiplicación establece que el producto de 1 y a es a.

$1 \cdot 7 = 7$
$a \cdot 1 = a$

Image (p. 402) An image is the result of a transformation of a point, line, or figure.

Imagen (p. 402) Una imagen es el resultado de una transformación de un punto, una recta o una figura.

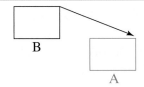

The blue figure is the image of the black figure.

Improper fraction (p. 182) An improper fraction has a numerator that is greater than or equal to its denominator.

Fracción impropia (p. 182) Una fracción impropia tiene un numerador mayor o igual que su denominador.

$\frac{24}{15}$ and $\frac{16}{16}$ are improper fractions.

Independent events (p. 500) Two events are independent events if the occurrence of one event does not affect the probability of the occurrence of the other.

Sucesos independientes (p. 500) Dos sucesos son independientes si el acontecimiento de uno no afecta la probabilidad de que el otro suceso ocurra.

Suppose you draw two marbles one after the other from a bag. If you replace the first marble before drawing the second marble, the events are independent.

Inequality (p. 572) An inequality is a mathematical sentence that contains $<, >, \leq, \geq,$ or $\neq$.

Desigualdad (p. 572) Una desigualdad es una oración matemática que contiene los signos $<, >, \leq, \geq$ o $\neq$.

$x < -5$
$x > 8$
$x \leq 1$
$x \geq -11$
$x \neq 3$

Integers (p. 516) Integers are the set of positive whole numbers, their opposites, and 0.

Enteros (p. 516) Los enteros son el conjunto de números enteros positivos, sus opuestos y el 0.

$\ldots -3, -2, -1, 0, 1, 2, 3, \ldots$

Interior angles (p. 378) The angles between two lines that are crossed by a transversal are called interior angles.

Ángulos interiores (p. 378) Los ángulos que están entre dos rectas, cruzadas por una secante se llaman ángulos interiores.

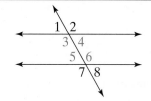

Angles 3, 4, 5, and 6 are interior angles.

Intersecting lines (p. 363) Intersecting lines lie in the same plane and have exactly one point in common.

Rectas que se intersectan (p. 363) Las rectas que se intersectan están en el mismo plano y tienen exactamente un punto en común.

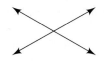

Inverse operations (p. 130) Inverse operations are operations that undo each other.

Operaciones inversas (p. 130) Las operaciones inversas son las operaciones que se anulan entre ellas.

Addition and subtraction are inverse operations.

Irregular polygon (p. 387) An irregular polygon is a polygon with sides that are not all congruent and/or angles that are not all congruent.

Polígono irregular (p. 387) Un polígono irregular es un polígono que tiene lados que no son todos congruentes y/o ángulos que no son todos congruentes.

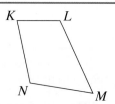

$KLMN$ is an irregular polygon.

Isosceles triangle (p. 381)   An isosceles triangle is a triangle with at least two congruent sides.

Triángulo isósceles (p. 381)   Un triángulo isósceles es un triángulo que tiene al menos dos lados congruentes.

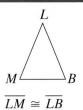

$$\overline{LM} \cong \overline{LB}$$

Least common denominator (LCD) (p. 192)   The least common denominator of two or more fractions is the least common multiple (LCM) of their denominators.

Mínimo común denominador (mcd) (p. 192)   El mínimo común denominador de dos o más fracciones es el mínimo común múltiplo (mcm) de sus denominadores.

The LCD of the fractions $\frac{3}{8}$ and $\frac{7}{10}$ is 40.

Least common multiple (LCM) (p. 188)   The least common multiple of two numbers is the smallest number that is a multiple of both numbers.

Mínimo común múltiplo (mcm) (p. 188)   El mínimo común múltiplo de dos números es el menor número que es múltiplo de ambos números.

The LCM of 15 and 6 is 30.

Legs of a right triangle (p. 591)   The legs of a right triangle are the two shorter sides of the triangle.

Catetos de un triángulo rectángulo (p. 591)   Los catetos de un triángulo rectángulo son los dos lados más cortos del triángulo.

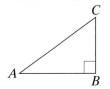

$\overline{AB}$ and $\overline{BC}$ are the legs of triangle ABC.

Line (p. 362)   A line is a series of points that extends in two opposite directions without end.

Recta (p. 362)   Una recta es una serie de puntos que se extiende indefinidamente en dos direcciones opuestas.

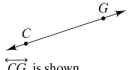

$\overleftrightarrow{CG}$ is shown.

Line graph (p. 75)   A line graph is a graph that uses a series of line segments to show changes in data. Typically, a line graph shows changes over time.

Gráfica lineal (p. 75)   Una gráfica lineal es una gráfica que usa una serie de segmentos de recta para mostrar cambios en los datos. Típicamente, una gráfica lineal muestra cambios a través del tiempo.

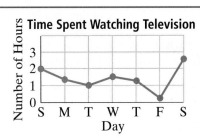

Line of reflection (p. 403) A line of reflection is a line over which a figure is reflected.

Eje de reflexión (p. 403) Un eje de reflexión es una recta sobre la cual se refleja una figura.

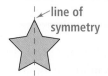

Figure B is a reflection of Figure A.

Line of symmetry (p. 398) A line of symmetry divides a figure into mirror images.

Eje de simetría (p. 398) Un eje de simetría divide una figura en imágenes reflejas.

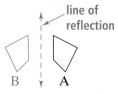

Line plot (p. 71) A line plot is a graph that shows the shape of a data set by stacking ✗'s above each data value on a number line.

Diagrama de puntos (p. 71) Un diagrama de puntos es una gráfica que muestra la forma de un conjunto de datos agrupando ✗ sobre cada valor de una recta numérica.

Pets Owned by Students

```
        ✗
        ✗           ✗
 ✗      ✗    ✗      ✗
 ✗      ✗    ✗      ✗      ✗
 0      1    2      3      4
```

The line plot shows the number of pets owned by each of 12 students.

Liter (p. 417) The liter (L) is the standard unit of capacity in the metric system.

Litro (p. 417) El litro (L) es la unidad de capacidad estándar en el sistema métrico.

A pitcher holds about 2 liters of juice.

Mass (p. 417) Mass is a measure of the amount of matter in an object.

Masa (p. 417) La masa es la medida de la cantidad de materia en un objeto.

A brick has a greater mass than a feather.

Mean (p. 61) The mean of a set of data values is the sum of the data divided by the number of data items.

Media (p. 61) La media de un conjunto de valores de datos es la suma de los datos dividida por el número de datos.

The mean temperature (°F) for the set of temperatures 44, 52, 48, 55, 61, and 67 is

$$\frac{44 + 52 + 48 + 55 + 61 + 67}{6} = 54.5.$$

Median (p. 66) The median of a data set is the middle value when the data are arranged in numerical order. When there is an even number of data values, the median is the mean of the two middle values.

Mediana (p. 66) La mediana de un conjunto de datos es el valor del medio cuando los datos están organizados en orden numérico. Cuando hay un número par de valores de datos, la mediana es la media de los dos valores del medio.

Five temperatures (°F) arranged in order are 44, 48, 52, 55, and 58. The median temperature is 52°F, because it is the middle number in the set of data.

Meter (p. 416) The meter (m) is the standard unit of length in the metric system.

Metro (p. 416) El metro (m) es la unidad de longitud estándar en el sistema métrico.

A doorknob is about 1 meter from the floor.

Metric system (p. 416) The metric system of measurement is a decimal system. Prefixes indicate the relative size of units.

Sistema métrico (p. 416) El sistema métrico de medidas es un sistema decimal. Los prefijos indican el tamaño relativo de las unidades.

1 kilogram $= 1{,}000$ grams

1 centimeter $= \frac{1}{100}$ meter

1 milliliter $= \frac{1}{1{,}000}$ liter

Midpoint (p. 372) The midpoint of a segment is the point that divides the segment into two segments of equal length.

Punto medio (p. 372) El punto medio de un segmento es el punto que divide el segmento en dos segmentos de igual longitud.

$\overset{\bullet}{X} \quad \overset{\bullet}{M} \quad \overset{\bullet}{Y}$

$\overline{XM} = \overline{YM}$. M is the midpoint of $\overline{XY}$.

Mixed number (p. 182) A mixed number is the sum of a whole number and a fraction.

Número mixto (p. 182) Un número mixto es la suma de un número entero y una fracción.

$3\frac{11}{16}$ is a mixed number. $3\frac{11}{16} = 3 + \frac{11}{16}$.

Mode (p. 67) The mode of a data set is the item that occurs with the greatest frequency.

Moda (p. 67) La moda de un conjunto de datos es el dato que sucede con mayor frecuencia.

The mode of the set of prices $2.50, $2.75, $3.60, $2.75, and $3.70 is $2.75.

Multiple (p. 188) A multiple of a number is the product of the number and any nonzero whole number.

Múltiplo (p. 188) Un múltiplo de un número es el producto de ese número y cualquier número entero diferente de cero.

The number 39 is a multiple of 13.

English/Spanish Glossary

Multiplication Property of Equality (p. 139) The Multiplication Property of Equality states that if each side of an equation is multiplied by the same number, the results are equal.

Propiedad multiplicativa de la igualdad (p. 139) La propiedad multiplicativa de la igualdad establece que si cada lado de una ecuación se multiplica por el mismo número, los resultados son iguales.

Since $\frac{12}{2} = 6$, $\frac{12}{2} \cdot 2 = 6 \cdot 2$. If $a = b$, then $a \cdot c = b \cdot c$.

Net (p. 453) A net is a two-dimensional pattern that can be folded to form a three-dimensional figure.

Plantilla (p. 453) Una plantilla es un patrón bidimensional que se puede doblar para formar una figura tridimensional.

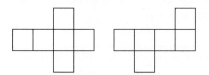

These are nets for a cube.

Numerical expression (p. 113) A numerical expression is an expression with only numbers and operation symbols.

Expresión numérica (p. 113) Una expresión numérica es una expresión que tiene sólo números y símbolos de operaciones.

$2(5 + 7) - 14$ is a numerical expression.

Obtuse angle (p. 368) An obtuse angle is an angle with a measure greater than 90° and less than 180°.

Ángulo obtuso (p. 368) Un ángulo obtuso es un ángulo que mide más de 90° y menos de 180°.

Obtuse triangle (p. 380) An obtuse triangle is a triangle with one obtuse angle.

Triángulo obtusángulo (p. 380) Un triángulo obtusángulo es un triángulo que tiene un ángulo obtuso.

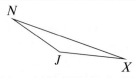

The measure of $\angle J$ is between 90° and 180°. Triangle NJX is an obtuse triangle.

Octagon (p. 386) An octagon is a polygon with eight sides.

Octágono (p. 386) Un octágono es un polígono que tiene ocho lados.

Odd number (p. 159) An odd number is a whole number that ends with a 1, 3, 5, 7, or 9.

43 and 687 are odd numbers.

Número impar (p. 159) Un número impar es un número entero que termina en 1, 3, 5, 7 o 9.

Open sentence (p. 125) An open sentence is an equation with one or more variables.

$b - 7 = 12$

Proposición abierta (p. 125) Una proposición abierta es una ecuación con una o más variables.

Opposites (p. 516) Opposites are two numbers that are the same distance from 0 on a number line, but in opposite directions.

17 and −17 are opposites.

Opuestos (p. 516) Opuestos son dos números que están a la misma distancia del 0 en una recta numérica, pero en direcciones opuestas.

Ordered pair (p. 548) An ordered pair identifies the location of a point. The x-coordinate shows a point's position left or right of the y-axis. The y-coordinate shows a point's position up or down from the x-axis.

Par ordenado (p. 548) Un par ordenado identifica la ubicación de un punto. La coordenada x muestra la posición de un punto a la izquierda o derecha del eje de y. La coordenada y muestra la posición de un punto arriba o abajo del eje de x.

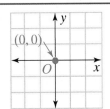

The x-coordinate of the point $(-2, 1)$ is -2, and the y-coordinate is 1.

Order of operations (pp. 16, 163)
1. Work inside grouping symbols.
2. Do all work with exponents.
3. Multiply and divide in order from left to right.
4. Add and subtract in order from left to right.

$2^3(7 - 4) = 2^3 \cdot 3 = 8 \cdot 3 = 24$

Orden de las operaciones (pp. 16, 163)
1. Trabaja dentro de los signos de agrupación.
2. Trabaja con los exponentes.
3. Multiplica y divide en orden de izquierda a derecha.
4. Suma y resta en orden de izquierda a derecha.

Origin (p. 548) The origin is the point of intersection of the x- and y- axes on a coordinate plane.

Origen (p. 548) El origen es el punto de intersección de los ejes de x y de y en un plano de coordenadas.

The ordered pair that describes the origin is $(0, 0)$.

English/Spanish Glossary

Outcome (p. 476)   An outcome is any of the possible results that can occur in an experiment.

The outcomes of rolling a standard number cube are 1, 2, 3, 4, 5, and 6.

Resultado (p. 476)   Un resultado es cualquiera de los posibles desenlaces que pueden ocurrir en un experimento.

Outlier (p. 62)   An outlier is a data item that is much greater or less than the other items in a data set.

The outlier in the data set 6, 7, 9, 10, 11, 12, 14, and 52 is 52.

Valor extremo (p. 62)   Un valor extremo es un dato que es mucho más alto o más bajo que los demás datos de un conjunto de datos.

P

Parallel lines (p. 363)   Parallel lines are lines in the same plane that never intersect.

Rectas paralelas (p. 363)   Las rectas paralelas son rectas en el mismo plano que nunca se intersectan.

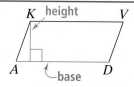

$\overleftrightarrow{EF}$ is parallel to $\overleftrightarrow{HI}$.

Parallelogram (p. 387)   A parallelogram is a quadrilateral with both pairs of opposite sides parallel.

Paralelogramo (p. 387)   Un paralelogramo es un cuadrilátero cuyos pares de lados opuestos son paralelos.

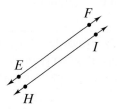

$\overline{KV}$ is parallel to $\overline{AD}$ and $\overline{AK}$ is parallel to $\overline{DV}$, so $KVDA$ is a parallelogram.

Pentagon (p. 386)   A pentagon is a polygon with five sides.

Pentágono (p. 386)   Un pentágono es un polígono que tiene cinco lados.

Percent (p. 331)   A percent is a ratio that compares a number to 100.

Porcentaje (p. 331)   Un porcentaje es una razón que compara un número con 100.

$\frac{25}{100} = 25\%$

Perfect square (p. 588) A perfect square is a number that is the square of an integer.

Since $25 = 5^2$, 25 is a perfect square.

Cuadrado perfecto (p. 588) Un cuadrado perfecto es un número que es el cuadrado de un entero.

Perimeter (p. 426) The perimeter of a figure is the distance around the figure.

Perímetro (p. 426) El perímetro de una figura es la distancia alrededor de la figura.

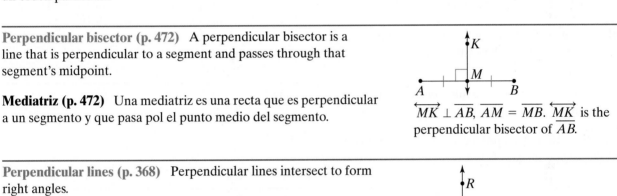

The perimeter of rectangle $ABCD$ is 12 ft.

Permutation (p. 481) A permutation is an arrangement of objects in a particular order.

Permutación (p. 481) Una permutación es un arreglo de objetos en un orden particular.

The permutations of the letters W, A, and X are WAX, WXA, AXW, AWX, XWA, and XAW.

Perpendicular bisector (p. 472) A perpendicular bisector is a line that is perpendicular to a segment and passes through that segment's midpoint.

Mediatriz (p. 472) Una mediatriz es una recta que es perpendicular a un segmento y que pasa pol el punto medio del segmento.

$\overleftrightarrow{MK} \perp \overline{AB}$, $\overline{AM} = \overline{MB}$. $\overleftrightarrow{MK}$ is the perpendicular bisector of $\overline{AB}$.

Perpendicular lines (p. 368) Perpendicular lines intersect to form right angles.

Rectas perpendiculares (p. 368) Las rectas perpendiculares se intersectan para formar ángulos rectos.

$\overleftrightarrow{RS}$ is perpendicular to $\overleftrightarrow{DE}$.

Pi (p. 439) Pi (π) is the ratio of the circumference C of any circle to its diameter d.

Pi (p. 439) Pi (π) es la razón de la circunferencia C de cualquier círculo a su diámetro d.

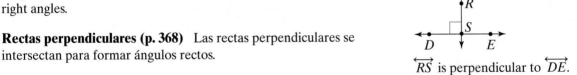

$$C \rightarrow = \frac{C}{d}$$

Place value (p. 4) The place value tells you the value of a digit based on its place in a particular number.

Valor posicional (p. 4) El valor posicional indica el valor de un dígito, basándose en el lugar que ocupa en un número en particular.

In 26, the 6 represents 6 ones, or 6. In 604, the 6 represents 6 hundreds, or 600.

Plane (p. 363)   A plane is a flat surface with no thickness that extends without end in all directions on the surface.

Plano (p. 363)   Un plano es una superficie plana que no tiene grosor, que se extiende indefinidamente en todas las direcciones sobre la superficie.

DEFG is a plane.

Point (p. 362)   A point is a location that has no size.

Punto (p. 362)   Un punto es una ubicación que no tiene tamaño.

•*A*

A is a point.

Polygon (p. 386)   A polygon is a closed figure formed by three or more line segments that do not cross.

Polígono (p. 386)   Un polígono es una figura cerrada que está formada por tres o más segmentos de recta que no se cruzan.

Population (p. 495)   A population is a group of objects or people about which information is wanted.

Población (p. 495)   Una población es un grupo de objectos o personas sobre el que se busca información.

In a survey regarding the hobbies of teenagers, the population would be all people ages 13 through 19.

Power (p. 162)   A power is a number that can be expressed using an exponent.

Potencia (p. 162)   Una potencia es un número que se puede expresar usando un exponente.

3^4, 5^2, and 2^{10} are powers.

Prime factorization (p. 167)   Writing a composite number as the product of prime numbers is the prime factorization of the number.

Factorización en primos (p. 167)   Escribir un número compuesto como el producto de sus factores primos es la factorización en primos del número.

The prime factorization of 12 is $2 \cdot 2 \cdot 3$, or $2^2 \cdot 3$.

Prime number (p. 166)   A prime number is a whole number with exactly two factors, 1 and the number itself.

Número primo (p. 166)   Un número primo es un entero que tiene exactamente dos factores, 1 y el mismo número.

13 is a prime number, because its only factors are 1 and 13.

Prism (p. 449)   A prism is a three-dimensional figure with two parallel and congruent faces that are polygons. These faces are called bases. A prism is named after the shape of its base.

Prisma (p. 449)   Un prisma es una figura tridimensional que tiene dos caras paralelas y congruentes que son polígonos. Estas caras se llaman bases. Un prisma recibe su nombre por la forma de su base.

Rectangular Prism   Triangular Prism

Probability of an event (p. 482) When outcomes are equally likely, the probability of an event is given by this formula:

$$P(\text{event}) = \frac{\text{number of favorable outcomes}}{\text{total number of possible outcomes}}$$

See *Experimental probability*.

Probabilidad de un suceso (p. 482) Cuando los resultados son igualmente posibles, la probabilidad de un suceso se da por esta fórmula:

$$P(\text{suceso}) = \frac{\text{número favorable de resultados}}{\text{número total de resultados posibles}}$$

Ver *Probabilidad experimental*.

Proper fraction (p. 182) A proper fraction has a numerator that is less than its denominator.

$\frac{3}{8}$ and $\frac{11}{12}$ are proper fractions.

Fracción propia (p. 182) Una fracción propia tiene un numerador que es menos que su denominador.

Proportion (p. 316) A proportion is an equation stating that two ratios are equal.

$\frac{3}{12} = \frac{9}{36}$ is a proportion.

Proporción (p. 316) Una proporción es una ecuación que establece que dos razones son iguales.

Pyramid (p. 450) A pyramid is a three-dimensional figure with triangular faces that meet at a vertex. A pyramid's base is a polygon. A pyramid is named after the shape of its base.

Pirámide (p. 450) Una pirámide es una figura tridimensional que tiene caras triangulares que coinciden en un vértice. Su base es un polígono. Una pirámide recibe su nombre por la forma de su base.

Triangular Pyramid   Rectangular Pyramid

Pythagorean Theorem (p. 591) In any right triangle, the sum of the squares of the lengths of the legs (a and b) is equal to the square of the length of the hypotenuse (c): $a^2 + b^2 = c^2$.

Teorema de Pitágoras (p. 591) En cualquier triángulo rectángulo, la suma del cuadrado de la longitud de los catetos (a y b) es igual al cuadrado de la longitud de la hipotenusa (c): $a^2 + b^2 = c^2$.

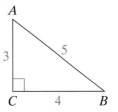

The right triangle has leg lengths 3 and 4 and hypotenuse length 5.

$$3^2 + 4^2 = 5^2$$

Quadrants (p. 548) The *x*- and *y*-axes divide the coordinate plane into four regions called quadrants.

Cuadrantes (p. 548) Los ejes de *x* y de *y* dividen el plano de coordenadas en cuatro regiones llamadas cuadrantes.

The quadrants are labeled I, II, III, and IV.

Quadrilateral (p. 387) A quadrilateral is a polygon with four sides.

Cuadrilátero (p. 387) Un cuadrilátero es un polígono que tiene cuatro lados.

R

Radius (p. 438) A radius of a circle is a segment that connects the center to the circle.

Radio (p. 438) Un radio de un círculo es un segmento que conecta el centro con el círculo.

$\overline{OA}$ is a radius of circle O.

Range (p. 71) The range of a data set is the difference between the greatest and the least values.

Rango (p. 71) El rango de un conjunto de datos es la diferencia entre los valores mayor y menor.

Data set: 62, 109, 234, 35, 96, 49, 201
Range: 201 − 35 = 166

Rate (p. 312) A rate is a ratio that compares two quantities measured in different units.

Tasa (p. 312) Una tasa es una razón que compara dos cantidades medidas en diferentes unidades.

Suppose you read 116 words in 1 minute. Your reading rate is $\frac{116 \text{ words}}{1 \text{ minute}}$.

Ratio (p. 306) A ratio is a comparison of two quantities by division.

Razón (p. 306) Una razón es una comparación de dos cantidades mediante la división.

There are three ways to write a ratio: 9 to 10, 9 : 10, and $\frac{9}{10}$.

Rational number (p. 588)   A rational number is any number that can be written as a quotient of two integers where the denominator is not 0.

$\frac{1}{3}$, -5, 6.4, $0.666\ldots$, $-2\frac{4}{5}$, 0, and $\frac{7}{3}$ are rational numbers.

Número racional (p. 588)   Un número racional es cualquier número que puede ser escrito como cociente de dos enteros, donde el denominador es diferente de 0.

Ray (p. 362)   A ray is part of a line. It has one endpoint and all the points of the line on one side of the endpoint.

Rayo (p. 362)   Un rayo es parte de una recta. Tiene un extremo y todos los puntos de la recta a un lado del extremo.

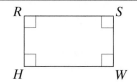

$\overrightarrow{CG}$ represents a ray.

Reciprocal (p. 272)   Two numbers are reciprocals if their product is 1.

Recíproco (p. 272)   Dos números son recíprocos si su producto es 1.

The numbers $\frac{4}{9}$ and $\frac{9}{4}$ are reciprocals.

Rectangle (p. 387)   A rectangle is a parallelogram with four right angles.

Rectángulo (p. 387)   Un rectángulo es un paralelogramo que tiene cuatro ángulos rectos.

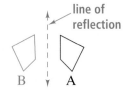

Reflection (p. 403)   A reflection, or flip, is a transformation that flips a figure over a line of reflection.

Refleción (p. 403)   Una refleción es una transformación que voltea una figura sobre un eje de reflexión.

Figure B is a reflection of Figure A.

Regular polygon (p. 387)   A regular polygon is a polygon with all sides congruent and all angles congruent.

Polígono regular (p. 387)   Un polígono regular es un polígono que tiene todos los lados y todos los ángulos congruentes.

$ABDFEC$ is a regular hexagon.

Repeating decimal (p. 198)   A repeating decimal is a decimal that repeats the same digits without end. The repeating block can be one digit or more than one digit.

$0.888\ldots = 0.\overline{8}$
$0.272727\ldots = 0.\overline{27}$

Decimal periódico (p. 198)   Un decimal periódico es un decimal que repite los mismos dígitos interminablemente. El bloque que se repite puede ser un dígito o más de un dígito.

Rhombus (p. 387)   A rhombus is a parallelogram with four congruent sides.

Rombo (p. 387)   Un rombo es un paralelogramo que tiene cuatro lados congruentes.

English/Spanish Glossary

Right angle (p. 368) A right angle is an angle with a measure of 90°.

Ángulo recto (p. 368) Un ángulo recto es un ángulo que mide 90°.

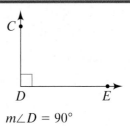

$m\angle D = 90°$

Right triangle (p. 380) A right triangle is a triangle with one right angle.

Triángulo rectángulo (p. 380) Un triángulo rectángulo es un triángulo que tiene un ángulo recto.

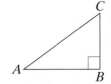

$\triangle ABC$ is a right triangle since $\angle B$ is a right angle.

Rotation (p. 403) A rotation is a transformation that turns a figure about a fixed point called the center of rotation.

Rotación (p. 403) Una rotación es una transformación que gira una figura sobre un punto fijo llamado centro de rotación.

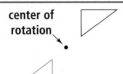

The blue triangle is a rotation of the black triangle.

Sample (p. 495) A sample is a part of a population. You use a sample to make predictions about a population.

Muestra (p. 495) Una muestra es una parte de una población. Se usa una muestra para hacer predicciones acerca de una población.

Suppose 50 students out of the 700 students at a school are surveyed. The 50 students represent a sample population.

Sample space (p. 476) A sample space is the collection of all possible outcomes in a probability experiment.

Espacio muestral (p. 476) El espacio muestral es el total de todos los resultados posibles en un experimento de probabilidad.

The sample space for tossing two coins is HH, HT, TH, and TT.

Scale (p. 326) A scale is the ratio that compares a length in a scale drawing to the corresponding length in the actual object.

Escala (p. 326) Una escala es la razón que compara la longitud en un dibujo con la longitud correspondiente en el objeto real.

A 25-mile road is 1 inch long on a map. The scale can be written three ways:

1 inch : 25 miles, $\frac{1 \text{ inch}}{25 \text{ miles}}$,

1 inch = 25 miles.

Scale drawing (p. 326)   A scale drawing is an enlarged or reduced drawing of an object that is similar to the actual object.

Dibujo a escala (p. 326)   Un dibujo a escala es un dibujo aumentado o reducido de un objeto que es semejante al objeto real.

Maps and floor plans are scale drawings.

Scalene triangle (p. 381)   A scalene triangle is a triangle with no congruent sides.

Triángulo escaleno (p. 381)   Un triángulo escaleno es un triángulo cuyos lados no son congruentes.

Scatter plot (p. 84)   A scatter plot is a graph that relates two sets of data.

Diagrama de dispersión (p. 84)   Un diagrama de dispersión es una gráfica que relaciona dos conjuntos de datos.

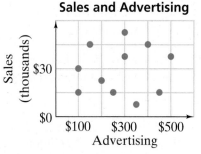

The scatter plot shows amounts spent by several companies on advertising (in dollars) versus product sales (in thousands of dollars).

Segment (p. 362)   A segment is part of a line. It has two endpoints and all the points of the line between the endpoints.

Segmento (p. 362)   Un segmento es parte de una linea. Tiene dos extremos y todos los puntos de la recta entre los puntos extremos.

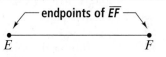

$\overline{EF}$ is a segment.

Sequence (p. 105)   A sequence is a set of numbers that follow a pattern.

Secuencia (p. 105)   Una secuencia es un conjunto de números que sigue un patrón.

$3, 6, 9, 12, 15, \ldots$ is a sequence.

Similar figures (p. 393)   Two figures are similar if their corresponding angles have the same measure and the lengths of their corresponding sides are proportional. The symbol ~ means "is similar to."

Figuras semejantes (p. 393)   Dos figuras son semejantes si sus ángulos correspondientes tienen la misma medida y las longitudes de sus lados correspondientes son proporcionales. El símbolo ~ significa "es semejante a."

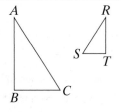

$\triangle ABC \sim \triangle RTS$

Simplest form (p. 177)   A fraction is in simplest form when the numerator and denominator have no common factors other than 1.

The simplest form of $\frac{3}{9}$ is $\frac{1}{3}$.

Mínima expresión(p. 177)   Una fracción está en su minima expresión cuando el numerador y el denominador no tienen otro factor común más que el uno.

Simulation (p. 498)   A simulation of a real-world situation is a model used to find experimental probabilities.

A baseball team has equal chances of winning or losing the next game. You can use a coin to simulate the outcome.

Simulación (p. 498)   Una simulación de una situación real es un modelo que se usa para hallar probabilidades experimentales.

Skew lines (p. 363)   Skew lines are neither parallel nor intersecting. They lie in different planes.

Rectas cruzadas (p. 363)   Las rectas cruzadas no son paralelas ni se intersecan. Están en planos diferentes.

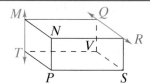

$\overleftrightarrow{MT}$ and $\overleftrightarrow{QR}$ are skew lines.

Solution (pp. 125, 579)   A solution is any value or values that makes an equation or inequality true.

4 is the solution of $x + 5 = 9$.
7 is a solution of $x < 15$.

Solución (pp. 125, 579)   Una solución es cualquier valor o valores que hacen que una ecuación o una desigualdad sea verdadera.

Sphere (p. 450)   A sphere is the set of all points in space that are the same distance from a center point.

Esfera (p. 450)   Una esfera es el conjunto de todos los puntos en el espacio que están a la misma distancia de un punto central.

Spreadsheet (p. 80)   A spreadsheet is a tool used for organizing and analyzing data. Spreadsheets are arranged in numbered rows and lettered columns.

	A	B	C	D	E
1	0.50	0.70	0.60	0.50	2.30
2	1.50	0.50	2.75	2.50	7.25

Column C and row 2 meet at cell C2.

Hoja de cálculo (p. 80)   Una hoja de cálculo es una herramienta que se usa para organizar y analizar datos. Las hojas de cálculo se organizan en filas numeradas y columnas en orden alfabético.

Square (p. 387)   A square is a parallelogram with four right angles and four congruent sides.

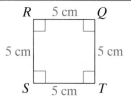

Cuadrado (p. 387)   Una cuadrado es un paralelógramo que tiene cuatro ángulos rectos y cuatro lados congruentes.

$QRST$ is a square. $\angle Q$, $\angle R$, $\angle S$, and $\angle T$ are right angles, and $\overline{QR} \cong \overline{RS} \cong \overline{ST} \cong \overline{QT}$.

Square root (p. 587) Finding the square root of a number is the inverse of squaring a number.

$\sqrt{9} = 3$ because $3^2 = 9$.

Raíz cuadrada (p. 587) Hallar la raíz cuadrada de un número es el inverso de elevar un número al cuadrado.

Standard form (p. 4) A number written using digits and place value is in standard form. See also *Expanded form*.

2,174 is in standard form.

Forma normal (p. 4) Un número escrito usando dígitos y valor posicional está escrito en forma normal. Ver también *Expanded form*.

Stem-and-leaf plot (p. 86) A stem-and-leaf plot is a graph that uses the digits of each number to show the shape of the data. Each data value is broken into a "stem" (digit or digits on the left) and a "leaf" (digit or digits on the right).

Diagrama de tallo y hojas (p. 86) Un diagrama de tallo y hojas es una gráfica en la que se usan los dígitos de cada número para mostrar la forma de los datos. Cada valor de los datos se divide en "tallo" (dígito o dígitos a la izquierda) y "hojas" (dígito o dígitos a la derecha).

stem	leaves
27	7
28	5 6 8
29	6 9
30	8

Key: 27 | 7 means 27.7

This stem-and-leaf plot displays recorded times in a race. The stems represent whole numbers of seconds. The leaves represent tenths of a second.

Straight angle (p. 368) A straight angle is an angle with a measure of 180°.

The measure of $\angle TPL$ is 180°.

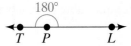

Ángulo llano (p. 368) Un ángulo llano es un ángulo que mide 180°.

Subtraction Property of Equality (p. 131) The Subtraction Property of Equality states that if the same number is subtracted from each side of an equation, the results are equal.

Since $\frac{20}{2} = 10$, $\frac{20}{2} - 3 = 10 - 3$.
If $a = b$, then $a - c = b - c$.

Propiedad sustractiva de la igualdad (p. 131) La propiedad sustractiva de la igualdad establece que si se resta el mismo número a cada lado de una ecuación, los resultados son iguales.

Supplementary (p. 374) Two angles are supplementary if the sum of their measures is 180°.

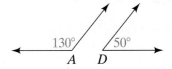

Suplementario (p. 374) Dos ángulos son suplementarios si la suma de sus medidas es 180°.

$\angle A$ and $\angle D$ are supplementary angles.

English/Spanish Glossary

Surface area of a three-dimensional figure (p. 454) The surface area of a three-dimensional figure is the sum of the areas of all the surfaces.

Área total de una figura tridimensional (p. 454) El área total de una figura tridimensional es la suma de las áreas de todas sus superficies.

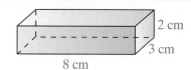

Term (p. 108) A term is a number in a pattern.

Término (p. 108) Un término es un número en un patrón.

6, 12, 24, 48, . . . The third term in this pattern is 24.

Terminating decimal (p. 198) A terminating decimal is a decimal that stops, or terminates.

Decimal finito (p. 198) Un decimal finito es un decimal que termina.

Both 0.6 and 0.7265 are terminating decimals.

Tessellation (p. 406) A tessellation is a repeating pattern of congruent shapes that completely covers a plane without gaps or overlaps.

Teselación (p. 406) Una teselación es un patrón repetido de formas congruentes que cubre completamente un plano, sin espacios o sobreposiciones.

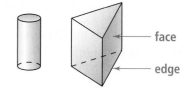

This tessellation consists of small and large squares.

Three-dimensional figure (p. 449) Three-dimensional figures are figures that have length, width, and height.

Figura tridimensional (p. 449) Las figuras tridimensionales son figuras que tienen longitud, anchura y altura.

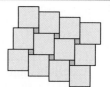

Transformation (p. 402) A transformation is a change in position, shape, or size of a figure. Three types of transformations that change position only are translations, reflections, and rotations.

Transformación (p. 402) Una transformación es un cambio de posición, forma o tamaño de una figura. Tres tipos de transformaciones que cambian la posición son las traslaciones, las reflexiónes y las rotaciones.

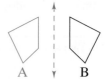

Figure A is a reflection, or flip, of Figure B.

Translation (p. 402) A translation is a transformation that slides each point of a figure the same distance and in the same direction.

Traslación (p. 402) Una traslación es una transformación que desliza cada punto de una figura la misma distancia y en la misma dirección.

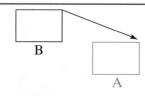

Figure A is a translation of Figure B.

Transversal (p. 378) A line that intersects two or more lines is called a transversal.

Secante (p. 378) Una recta que interseca a dos o más rectas se llama secante.

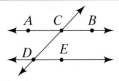

$\overleftrightarrow{CD}$ is a transversal.

Trapezoid (p. 387) A trapezoid is a quadrilateral with exactly one pair of parallel sides.

Trapecio (p. 387) Un trapecio es un cuadrilátero que tiene exactamente un par de lados paralelos.

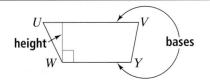

$\overline{UV}$ is parallel to $\overline{WY}$.

Tree diagram (p. 477) A tree diagram is an organized list of all possible combinations of items.

Diagrama en árbol (p. 477) Un diagrama en árbol es una lista organizada de todas las combinaciones posibles de los elementos.

```
        H
    H <
        T
        H
    T <
        T
```

There are four possible outcomes for tossing two coins: HH, HT, TH, and TT.

Triangle (p. 380) A triangle is a polygon with three sides.

Triángulo (p. 380) Un triángulo es un polígono que tiene tres lados.

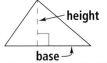

Two-step equation (p. 572) A two-step equation is an equation containing two operations.

Ecuación de dos pasos (p. 572) Una ecuación de dos pasos es una ecuación que contiene dos operaciones.

$2x + 3 = 10$

Unit cost (p. 313) A unit cost is a unit rate that gives the cost of one item.

Costo unitario (p. 313) Un costo unitario es una tasa unitaria que da el costo de un artículo.

$$\frac{\$5.98}{10.2 \text{ fluid ounces}} = \$.59/\text{fluid ounce}$$

Unit rate (p. 312) The rate for one unit of a given quantity is called the unit rate.

If you drive 130 miles in 2 hours, your unit rate is $\frac{65 \text{ miles}}{1 \text{ hour}}$ or 65 mi/h.

Tasa unitaria (p. 312) La tasa para una unidad de una cantidad dada se llama tasa unitaria.

Variable (p. 113) A variable is a letter that stands for a number. The value of an algebraic expression varies, or changes, depending upon the value given to the variable.

x is a variable in the equation $9 + x = 7$.

Variable (p. 113) Una variable es una letra que representa un número. El valor de una expresión algebraica varía, o cambia, dependiendo del valor que se le dé a la variable.

Vertex of an angle (p. 367) The vertex of an angle is the point of intersection of two sides of an angle or figure.

Vértice de un ángulo (p. 367) El vértice de un ángulo es el punto de intersección de dos lados de un ángulo o figura.

vertex

Vertical angles (p. 375) Vertical angles are formed by two intersecting lines. Vertical angles have equal measures.

Ángulos verticales (p. 375) Los ángulos verticales están formados por dos rectas que se intersecan. Los ángulos verticales tienen la misma medida.

$\angle 1$ and $\angle 2$ are vertical angles, as are $\angle 3$ and $\angle 4$.

Volume (p. 458) The volume of a three-dimensional figure is the number of cubic units needed to fill the space inside the figure.

Volumen (p. 458) El volumen de una figura tridimensional es el número de unidades cúbicas que se necesitan para llenar el espacio dentro de la figura.

The volume of the rectangular prism is 36 cubic units.

x-axis (p. 548) The *x*-axis is the horizontal number line that, together with the *y*-axis, forms the coordinate plane.

Eje de *x* (p. 548) El eje de *x* es la recta numérica horizontal que, junto con el eje de *y*, forma el plano de coordenadas.

***x*-coordinate (p. 548)** The *x*-coordinate is the first number in an ordered pair. It tells the number of horizontal units a point is from 0.

Coordenada *x* (p. 548) La coordenada *x* es el primer número en un par ordenado. Indica el número de unidades horizontales a las que un punto está del cero.

The *x*-coordinate is −2 for the ordered pair (−2, 1). The *x*-coordinate is 2 units to the left of the *y*-axis.

***y*-axis (p. 548)** The *y*-axis is the vertical number line that, together with the *x*-axis, forms the coordinate plane.

Eje de *y* (p. 548) El eje de *y* es la recta numérica vertical que, junto con el eje de *x*, forma el plano de coordenadas.

***y*-coordinate (p. 548)** The *y*-coordinate is the second number in an ordered pair. It tells the number of vertical units a point is from 0.

Coordenada *y* (p. 548) La coordenada *y* es el segundo número en un par ordenado. Indica el número de unidades verticales a las que un punto está del cero.

The *y*-coordinate is 1 for the ordered pair (−2, 1). The *y*-coordinate is 1 unit up from the *x*-axis.

Zero pair (p. 523) The pairing of one "+" chip with one "−" chip is called a zero pair.

Par cero (p. 523) El emparejamiento de una ficha "+" con una ficha "−" se llama par cero.

⊕ ⊖ ⟵ a zero pair

English/Spanish Glossary

✓ Answers to Instant Check System™

Chapter 1

Check Your Readiness   p. 2

1. 310 **2.** 7,530 **3.** 40 **4.** 60 **5.** 700 **6.** 1,990
7. 175 **8.** 145 **9.** 14,192 **10.** 3,027 **11.** 10,000
12. 1,392 **13.** 747 **14.** 4,544 **15.** 43,700 **16.** 462
17. 5 **18.** 17 **19.** 32 **20.** 72

Lesson 1-1   pp. 4–5

Check Skills You'll Need 1. Answers may vary. Sample:
8, 3.5 **2.** 2 tens or 20 **3.** 2 ones or 2
4. 2 thousands or 2,000 **5.** 2 hundreds or 200

Quick Check 1. twenty-six billion, two hundred
thirty-six million, eight hundred forty-eight
thousand, eighty dollars. **2.** < **3.** 978; 9,897;
9,987

Lesson 1-2   pp. 8–9

Check Skills You'll Need 1. hundreds **2.** 50 **3.** 60
4. 140 **5.** 490

Quick Check 1a. about 170 **b.** about 20 **2a.** about
320 **b.** about 14 **3.** about 30

Lesson 1-3   pp. 12–13

Check Skills You'll Need 1. addition **2.** 150 **3.** 90
4. 350

Quick Check 1. 95 **2.** 600

Lesson 1-4   pp. 16–20

Check Skills You'll Need 1. Comm. Prop. of Add. **2.** 57
3. 30 **4.** 175

Quick Check 1a. 27 **b.** 16 **2.** $43

Checkpoint Quiz 1 1. > **2.** < **3.** > **4.** about 200
5. about 9,000 **6.** about 2 **7.** 57 **8.** 38 **9.** 1,000
10. 0 **11.** 70 **12.** $70 **13.** about 1,200 feet
14. 6,893,000; 7,134,000; 7,283,000; 7,293,000

Lesson 1-5   pp. 22–23

Check Skills You'll Need 1. 1,321 **2.** twenty-eight
3. eight thousand, six hundred seventy-two
4. six hundred twelve thousand, nine hundred
eighty **5.** fifty-eight thousand, twenty-six

Quick Check 1a. sixty-seven and three tenths **b.** six
and seven hundred thirty-four thousandths
c. sixty-seven hundredths **2.** 0.15; 0.1 + 0.05
3a. 2.34 **b.** 0.1735 **c.** 9.1

Lesson 1-6   pp. 26–27

Check Skills You'll Need 1. Answers may vary. Sample:
Compare the digits, starting with the greatest
place value. **2.** > **3.** <

Quick Check 1. Model may vary. Sample:

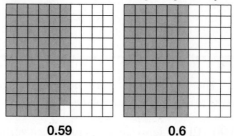

0.6 is greater. **2.** > **3.** 3.059, 3.46, 3.64

Lesson 1-7   pp. 32–33

Check Skills You'll Need 1. Rounding **2.** 70 **3.** 110
4. 100 **5.** 3,200

Quick Check 1. about 6; 6.16 **2.** about $22
3. 2.72 m

Lesson 1-8   pp. 38–43

Check Skills You'll Need 1. Yes; 130 is easy to divide by
5 mentally. **2.** about 600 **3.** about 180 **4.** about
100 **5.** about 10

Quick Check 1a. 0.78 **b.** 21.85 **2a.** 0.06 **b.** 10.108
c. 0.126 **3.** $3.55

Checkpoint Quiz 2 1. twelve and thirty-five
thousandths **2.** 8.0; 8.05; 8.7; 9; 9.31 **3.** 7.8
4. 8.0 **5.** 17.1 **6.** 7.32 **7.** 8.26 **8.** 32.76 **9.** 1.42
10. 1.65 lb

Lesson 1-9   pp. 44–45

Check Skills You'll Need 1. A dividend is the number
being divided. A divisor is the number that
divides. **2.** 187 **3.** 37 **4.** 53

Quick Check 1a. 48.2 **b.** 1.52 **2.** 11 trading cards

Chapter 2

Check Your Readiness   p. 58

1. 0.12, 0.13, 0.21, 0.35, 0.45 **2.** 44.0, 45.01, 45.1,
46.01 **3.** 63.1 **4.** 423.9 **5.** 105.82 **6.** 25.87
7. 20.21 **8.** 1.06 **9.** 1.8 **10.** 14.203 **11.** 22.6
12. 4.03

Lesson 2-1   pp. 61–62

Check Skills You'll Need 1. quotient **2.** 27.5 **3.** 42.75 **4.** 59.35

Quick Check 1. 4 **2.** 20 **3.** The outlier increases the value of the mean.

Lesson 2-2   pp. 66–67

Check Skills You'll Need 1. 5 **2.** 20 **3.** 22.4 **4.** 57

Quick Check 1. 28 **2.** 2 **3.** Answers may vary. Sample: The median is the best measure, as 288.75 is an outlier that affects the mean, and there is no mode.

Lesson 2-3   pp. 70–71

Check Skills You'll Need 1. The mode is the data item(s) that appear(s) most often. **2.** 5.25; 5; 4 **3.** about 2.29; 1.5; 0

Quick Check 1.

Initial	Tally	Frequency
A	|	1
B	|	1
C	|	1
D	||	2
J	|	1
K	||	2
L	|||	3
P	|	1
S	|	1
T	|	1
V	|	1

2.

Number of Sales Calls

```
X
X                       X
X  X                    X
X  X              X  X
X  X  X  X        X  X  X  X
0  1  2  3  4  5  6  7  8  9
        Sales Calls
```

Answers may vary. Sample: Either a low number of sales calls were made each hour (0–3), or a high number (6–9).
3. 32

Lesson 2-4   pp. 74–75

Check Skills You'll Need 1. The range is the difference between the least and greatest values.

2.
```
X   X   X   X
X   X   X   X
5   6   7   8
```

3.
```
                    X
X       X           X           X
10 11 12 13 14 15 16 17 18 19 20 21
```

Quick Check 1. 380 mg **2.** Less than; it is decreasing. **3.** Line graph; it shows change over time.

Lesson 2-5   pp. 80–85

Check Skills You'll Need 1. usually **2.** 159 **3.** 814

Quick Check 1. 30; the minutes of country music on disc 3 **2.** = D2 + D3 + D4

Checkpoint Quiz 1 1. 21.07; 21; 21 **2.** 9 **3.** Yes; 26 is much higher than the majority of the data.
4. Answers may vary. Sample: The mode represents which high temperature occurred the most.

5.

Grams of Fat	Tally	Frequency
0	ⅢⅢ III	8
1	ⅢⅢ III	8
2	ⅢⅢ	5
3	III	3

6. L = B2 + B3 + B4 + B5
7. $800
8.

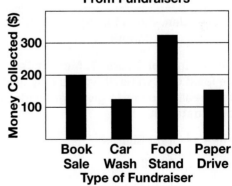

Money Collected From Fundraisers

9.

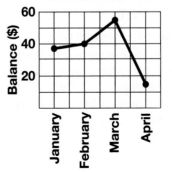

Account Balance

Lesson 2-6

pp. 86–87

Check Skills You'll Need 1. The median of a data set is the middle value when the data are arranged in numerical order. **2.** 32 **3.** 15 **4.** 5.2

Quick Check 1. 35 **2.**

```
12 | 1 3 4 5 5 6 7
13 | 0 2 3 6 7 8 8
14 | 0 1 4 5
15 | 0 5
16 |
17 |
18 | 1
```
Key: 12|3 means 123

Lesson 2-7

pp. 93–98

Check Skills You'll Need 1. The mean of a set of data values is the sum of the data divided by the number of data values. **2.** 55.5 **3.** 13.5 **4.** 131

Quick Check 1.

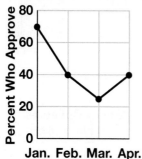

Mayor's Performance

2a. It's twice as tall. **b.** 3 cars **3.** Median; the mode is the least data value. It occurs only twice, so its value is really too low to give a good idea of what a typical data value is.

Checkpoint Quiz 2 1. Test Scores

```
6 | 4 8
7 | 6
8 | 1 4 4 5 5 6 9
9 | 1 2 5 7
```
Key: 6 | 4 means 64%

2. 15 years **3.** 8 **4.** 36 **5.** Answers may vary. Sample: Median; an outlier affects the mean.
6. Answers may vary. Sample: Starting a graph at 60 ft³ on the vertical axis will make the differences in cars seem very large.

Chapter 3

Check Your Readiness

p. 106

1. 29 **2.** 39 **3.** 18 **4.** 30 **5.** about 42; 42.15
6. about 9; 9.5 **7.** about 5; 5.1 **8.** about 2; 2.16
9. about 2; 2.27 **10.** about 15; 14.36 **11.** 18.95
12. 19.456 **13.** 310.27 **14.** 3.3 **15.** 170 **16.** 0.71

Lesson 3-1

pp. 108–109

Check Skills You'll Need 1. value **2.** 3.1, 3.31, 3.331
3. 0.0105, 0.105, 10.5

Quick Check 1. 22 tiles **2a.** 90, 75, 60, 45, 30, 15
b. 1, 3, 9, 27, 81, 243 **3a.** Start with 1.5 and multiply by 3 repeatedly; 121.5, 364.5, 1,093.5.
b. Start with 256 and divide by 2 repeatedly; 32, 16, 8.

Lesson 3-2

pp. 113–114

Check Skills You'll Need 1. A mathematical expression is a phrase containing numbers, variables, and operation symbols. **2.** 32 **3.** 19 **4.** 441

Quick Check 1. 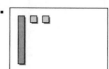 **2a.** 36 **b.** 5 **c.** 28 **3.** $255

Lesson 3-3

pp. 118–119

Check Skills You'll Need 1. To evaluate an expression means to replace a variable with a number and simplify it. **2.** 10 **3.** 30 **4.** 48 **5.** 11

Quick Check 1. $x + 2$ **2.** Let b = Brandon's age; $b + 28$ **3.** $n + 4$

Lesson 3-4

pp. 124–129

Check Skills You'll Need 1. Add the whole dollars first and then estimate when adding the cents.
2. about 6; 6.37 **3.** about 4; 3.7 **4.** about 2; 1.7

Quick Check 1a. true **b.** false **c.** false **2a.** 9 **b.** 80 **c.** 1.2 **3.** 43

Checkpoint Quiz 1 1. Start with 1 and multiply by 6 repeatedly; 1,296; 7,776; 46,656. **2.** Start with 285 and subtract 15 repeatedly; 225, 210, 195.
3. Start with 50 and divide by 10 repeatedly; 0.005, 0.0005, 0.00005. **4.** 56 **5.** 9 **6.** 70 **7.** $17 - d$
8. ae **9.** $14 \div q$

Lesson 3-5 — pp. 130–131

Check Skills You'll Need **1.** It has one or more variables. **2.** 1 **3.** 70 **4.** 14

Quick Check **1.** 4.8 **2.** w = the cat's weight last year; $1.8 + w = 11.6$; 9.8 lb

Lesson 3-6 — pp. 134–137

Check Skills You'll Need **1.** It makes the equation true. **2.** 14 **3.** 11 **4.** 10

Quick Check **1a.** 81 **b.** 55 **2.** Let t = temperature at 7 P.M.; $t - 9 = 54$; $t = 63$.

Checkpoint Quiz 1 **1.** 60 **2.** 18.2 **3.** 2.2 **4.** 7.6 **5.** 10.8 **6.** 26.6 **7.** 7 **8.** 38.4 **9.** x = change received; $x + 5.73 = 10.00$; $x = \$4.27$

Lesson 3-7 — pp. 138–139

Check Skills You'll Need **1.** Answers may vary. Sample: Equations contain equal signs, and expressions do not. **2.** 9 **3.** 2 **4.** 9 **5.** 3

Quick Check **1.** 40 **2.** 865 cards **3.** 15

Lesson 3-8 — pp. 144–145

Check Skills You'll Need **1.** Answers may vary. Sample: The Associative Property changes the grouping of numbers and the Commutative Property changes the order of the numbers. **2.** 58 **3.** 173 **4.** 183

Quick Check **1.** $5 \times (70 - 2) = (5 \times 70) - (5 \times 2) = 350 - 10 = 340$ **2.** $14.00

Chapter 4

Check Your Readiness — p. 156

1. four tenths **2.** thirty-seven hundredths **3.** one and eight tenths **4.** two hundred five thousandths **5.** twenty and eighty-eight hundredths **6.** one hundred fifty thousandths **7.** 4.02, 4.2, 4.21 **8.** 0.033, 0.3, 0.33 **9.** 6.032, 6.203, 6.302 **10.** 9.013, 9.031, 9.103 **11.** 0.8 **12.** 0.55 **13.** 19 **14.** 36.3 **15.** 132 **16.** 53

Lesson 4-1 — pp. 158–159

Check Skills You'll Need **1.** division **2.** 49 **3.** 41 **4.** 50

Quick Check **1a.** no **b.** yes **2a.** divisible by 2, 3, 5, and 10 **b.** divisible by none of these **c.** divisible by 2 and 3 **3.** yes

Lesson 4-2 — pp. 162–163

Check Skills You'll Need **1.** expression **2.** 25 **3.** 0 **4.** 2

Quick Check **1a.** 3.94^2; 3.94; 2 **b.** 7^4; 7; 4 **c.** x^3; x; 3 **2.** 27 **3a.** 6 **b.** 14

Lesson 4-3 — pp. 166–170

Check Skills You'll Need **1.** No; 25 is divisible by 5 but not divisible by 10. **2.** 2, 3, 5, 9, 10 **3.** divisible by none of these **4.** 2, 5, and 10 **5.** 2, 5, and 10

Quick Check **1.** 1×24, 2×12, 3×8, 4×6 **2a.** composite; $39 = 3 \times 13$ **b.** Prime; it has only two factors, 1 and 47. **c.** composite; $63 = 3 \times 21$ or $63 = 7 \times 9$ **3.** 3^3

Checkpoint Quiz 1 **1.** 3, 5 **2.** 2 **3.** 2, 3, 5, 10 **4.** 64 **5.** 10 **6.** 3,125 **7.** 64 **8.** $2 \times 3 \times 7$ **9.** $2^4 \times 5$ **10.** $2^3 \times 5^3$ **11.** 1×105, 3×35, 5×21, 7×15

Lesson 4-4 — pp. 171–172

Check Skills You'll Need **1.** Answers may vary. Sample: Multiply two factors together to find the product. **2.** $3^2 \times 5$ **3.** 3×7 **4.** $3^2 \times 11$

Quick Check **1 a.** factors of 6: 1, 2, 3, 6; factors of 21: 1, 3, 7, 21; GCF of 6 and 21: 3 **b.** factors of 18: 1, 2, 3, 6, 9, 18; factors of 49: 1, 7, 49; GCF of 18 and 49: 1 **c.** factors of 14: 1, 2, 7, 14; factors of 28: 1, 2, 4, 7, 14, 28; GCF of 14 and 28: 14 **2.** 6 in. **3 a.** GCF = 16 **b.** GCF = 12

Lesson 4-5 — pp. 176–177

Check Skills You'll Need **1.** The GCF is the largest number in the set of common factors. **2.** 5 **3.** 6 **4.** 1

Quick Check **1a–b.** Answers may vary. Samples are given. **1a.** $\frac{2}{5}$, $\frac{8}{20}$ **b.** $\frac{10}{16}$, $\frac{15}{24}$ **2.** $\frac{3}{4}$ **3.** $\frac{7}{20}$

Lesson 4-6 — pp. 182–187

Check Skills You'll Need **1.** when the only common factor of the numerator and denominator is 1 **2.** $\frac{1}{3}$ **3.** $\frac{2}{3}$ **4.** $\frac{5}{16}$

Quick Check **1.** $\frac{25}{7}$ **2.** 9 qt **3a.** $4\frac{4}{9}$ **b.** $5\frac{1}{3}$ **c.** $5\frac{3}{4}$

Checkpoint Quiz 1 **1.** 5 **2.** 24 **3.** 3 **4.** 6 **5.** $\frac{16}{5}$ **6.** $1\frac{5}{8}$ **7.** $\frac{8}{3}$ **8.** 2 toys, 6 balloons, 12 bags of peanuts

Lesson 4-7 — pp. 188–189

Check Skills You'll Need **1.** A factor tree helps you write a number as a product of prime factors. **2.** $2^4 \times 5$ **3.** 2^5 **4.** $2^4 \times 13$ **5.** $2^2 \times 5^3$

Quick Check **1 a.** 60 **b.** 70 **2.** 24

Lesson 4-8 — pp. 192–193

Check Skills You'll Need **1.** When you write a fraction in simplest form, you are writing an equivalent fraction using division. **2–5.** Answers may vary. Samples are given.

2. $\frac{1}{3}, \frac{21}{63}$ **3.** $\frac{1}{5}, \frac{2}{10}$ **4.** $\frac{4}{6}, \frac{20}{30}$ **5.** $\frac{1}{6}, \frac{5}{30}$

Quick Check **1.** < **2.** Yes; $\frac{7}{8} = \frac{28}{32}$, and $\frac{28}{32} > \frac{27}{32}$. So $6\frac{7}{8} > 6\frac{27}{32}$. **3.** $\frac{1}{3}, \frac{3}{8}, 1\frac{2}{3}, 2\frac{4}{5}, 2\frac{5}{6}$

Lesson 4-9 — pp. 198–199

Check Skills You'll Need **1.** 3; 12 **2.** 1.5 **3.** $0.\overline{6}$ **4.** 1.6 **5.** 0.3

Quick Check **1.** $5\frac{2}{25}$ **2.** you **3.** $1.8, 2\frac{2}{3}, 2.7, 3\frac{1}{5}$

Chapter 5

Check Your Readiness — p. 210

1. 2.59 **2.** 1.99 **3.** 6.22 **4.** 7.65 **5.** $\frac{1}{2}$ **6.** $\frac{2}{5}$ **7.** $\frac{3}{4}$ **8.** $9\frac{2}{3}$ **9.** $5\frac{1}{4}$ **10.** $7\frac{1}{2}$ **11.** 72 **12.** 80 **13.** 210

Lesson 5-1 — pp. 212–213

Check Skills You'll Need **1.** Compatible numbers are numbers that are easy to compute mentally. **2.** 60 **3.** 150 **4.** 900 **5.** 1,230

Quick Check **1.** 1 **2 a.** $1\frac{1}{2}$ **b.** 1 **3.** about 5 h

Lesson 5-2 — pp. 217–218

Check Skills You'll Need **1.** A fraction is in simplest form when the GCF of the numerator and denominator is 1. **2.** $\frac{1}{4}$ **3.** $\frac{1}{3}$ **4.** $\frac{5}{6}$ **5.** $\frac{3}{7}$

Quick Check **1 a.** $\frac{1}{3}$ **b.** $\frac{2}{3}$ **2 a.** $1\frac{1}{8}$ **b.** $1\frac{2}{5}$ **3.** $\frac{1}{3}$ foot

Lesson 5-3 — pp. 222–226

Check Skills You'll Need **1.** Answers may vary. Sample: Write the prime factorization for each number. **2.** 18 **3.** 120 **4.** 150 **5.** 60

Quick Check **1.** $\frac{7}{10}$ **2.** $\frac{5}{6}$ h **3.** $\frac{1}{6}$ yd

Checkpoint Quiz 1 **1.** $1\frac{1}{2}$ **2.** 1 **3.** $1\frac{1}{2}$ **4.** 0 **5.** $1\frac{1}{5}$ **6.** $\frac{1}{2}$ **7.** $1\frac{1}{4}$ **8.** $\frac{17}{30}$ **9.** $\frac{1}{2}$ **10.** $\frac{7}{10}$ **11.** $\frac{11}{18}$ of the class **12.** $1\frac{1}{6}$ c **13.** $\frac{3}{8}$ gal

Lesson 5-4 — pp. 228–229

Check Skills You'll Need **1.** The numerator is greater than the denominator. **2.** $1\frac{1}{3}$ **3.** $2\frac{1}{2}$ **4.** $1\frac{3}{4}$ **5.** $2\frac{1}{2}$

Quick Check **1.** $5\frac{5}{6}$ yd **2 a.** $9\frac{3}{4}$ **b.** $21\frac{4}{15}$ **3.** $4\frac{1}{8}$ in.

Lesson 5-5 — pp. 232–238

Check Skills You'll Need **1.** Answers may vary. Sample: Write multiples of 6 until a multiple is divisible by 4. 12 is divisible by both 6 and 4. **2.** $\frac{3}{5}, \frac{13}{20}, \frac{7}{10}$ **3.** $2\frac{7}{32}, 2\frac{1}{4}, 2\frac{5}{16}, 2\frac{3}{8}$

Quick Check **1.** $7\frac{3}{16}$ in. **2 a.** $1\frac{1}{3}$ **b.** $5\frac{3}{4}$ **3.** $2\frac{1}{12}$ ft

Checkpoint Quiz 2 **1.** $5\frac{5}{8}$ **2.** $4\frac{3}{4}$ **3.** $14\frac{5}{6}$ **4.** $5\frac{8}{9}$ **5.** $5\frac{5}{6}$ **6.** $\frac{4}{9}$ **7.** $9\frac{7}{8}$ **8.** $4\frac{1}{6}$ **9.** $4\frac{1}{4}$ hours **10.** $\frac{11}{20}$ mile

Lesson 5-6 — pp. 240–241

Check Skills You'll Need **1.** subtraction **2.** 26 **3.** 3.8 **4.** 18.9

Quick Check **1 a.** $2\frac{3}{4}$ **b.** $11\frac{1}{4}$ **c.** $3\frac{2}{3}$ **2 a.** $\frac{7}{12}$ **b.** $\frac{1}{4}$ **3.** $1\frac{3}{4}$ in.

Lesson 5-7 — pp. 246–248

Check Skills You'll Need **1.** Answers may vary. Sample: seconds, hours, days, weeks **2.** 482 min **3.** 123 hours **4.** 26 days

Quick Check **1.** 1 h 26 min **2.** 4 h **3.** 9 h 15 min **4.** 6:20 P.M.

Chapter 6

Check Your Readiness — p. 258

1. 4 **2.** 5 **3.** 12 **4.** 112 **5.** 100 **6.** 0.6 **7.** 12 **8.** 7 **9.** 3 **10.** 20 **11.** 6 **12.** 21 **13.** $\frac{3}{7}$ **14.** $\frac{2}{3}$ **15.** $\frac{1}{3}$ **16.** $\frac{3}{8}$ **17.** $\frac{1}{4}$ **18.** $\frac{3}{7}$

Lesson 6-1   pp. 261–262

Check Skills You'll Need   **1. Answers may vary. Sample:** $\frac{2}{5}$ and $\frac{4}{10}$ **2.** $\frac{1}{2}$ **3.** $\frac{3}{5}$ **4.** $\frac{2}{3}$ **5.** $\frac{9}{10}$

Quick Check   **1a.** $\frac{3}{20}$ **b.** $\frac{10}{63}$ **2.** 10 ft

Lesson 6-2   pp. 266–267

Check Skills You'll Need   **1. A proper fraction has a numerator that is less than the denominator. An improper fraction has a denominator that is less than or equal to the numerator.**
2. $\frac{27}{7}$ **3.** $\frac{17}{3}$ **4.** $\frac{47}{4}$ **5.** $\frac{79}{9}$

Quick Check   **1a.** 36   **b.** 56   **2a.** $28\frac{3}{16}$ **b.** $27\frac{1}{2}$
3. $2\frac{5}{8}$ mi

Lesson 6-3   pp. 272–273

Check Skills You'll Need   **1. List the factors of 4 and 15. Choose the largest number that is a factor of both 4 and 15. 2.** 6   **3.** $\frac{1}{5}$ **4.** $\frac{1}{7}$ **5.** $\frac{4}{11}$

Quick Check   **1a.** $\frac{4}{3}$ or $1\frac{1}{3}$ **b.** $\frac{1}{7}$ **2a.** $\frac{3}{4}$ **b.** $2\frac{2}{5}$
3. $\frac{1}{6}$ yard

Lesson 6-4   pp. 276–281

Check Skills You'll Need   **1. The product of the fractions is not 1. 2.** 28   **3.** $\frac{7}{24}$ **4.** $\frac{1}{6}$ **5.** $2\frac{8}{11}$

Quick Check   **1a.** about 7   **b.** about 5   **2.** $1\frac{1}{4}$ cups
3a. 6   **b.** $2\frac{1}{20}$

Checkpoint Quiz 1   **1.** 15   **2.** $23\frac{5}{8}$ **3.** 64   **4.** $\frac{1}{6}$ **5.** $1\frac{11}{21}$
6. $\frac{3}{5}$ **7.** $16\frac{1}{3}$ **8.** $2\frac{7}{30}$ **9.** 34   **10.** $4\frac{1}{2}$ **11.** $2\frac{1}{5}$
12. $15\frac{1}{2}$ **13.** 39 ft **14.** 24 cookies   **15.** about 13

Lesson 6-5   pp. 282–283

Check Skills You'll Need   **1. Divide each side by 4.**

2. $\frac{7}{30}$ **3.** $\frac{3}{11}$ **4.** $\frac{2}{5}$ **5.** $\frac{9}{25}$

Quick Check   **1 a.** 30   **b.** 72   **2.** 48   **3.** 20 flags

Lesson 6-6   pp. 288–289

Check Skills You'll Need   **1. Answers may vary. Sample: Find the least common denominator of 4 and 12 and write equivalent fractions using the LCD to compare. 2.** > **3.** > **4.** >

Quick Check   **1–3. Answers may vary. Samples are given.**

**1a. Inches; pencils are shorter than a foot.
b. Feet or yards; small whales are twice as long as a man. 2. Pounds; a refrigerator weighs less than a piano. 3a. Gallons; a tanker truck holds more gasoline than can fit in a small bucket.
b. Fluid ounces or cups; a container of yogurt is usually less than a pint.**

Lesson 6-7   pp. 292–296

Check Skills You'll Need   **1. An improper fraction has a numerator greater than the denominator. A mixed number is the sum of an integer and a proper fraction.**
2. $1\frac{1}{6}$ **3.** $\frac{7}{12}$ **4.** $\frac{3}{20}$ **5.** $1\frac{7}{9}$

Quick Check   **1.** 4,000 lb   **2.** $1\frac{1}{4}$ qt   **3.** 8 lb 1 oz

Checkpoint Quiz 2   **1.** $10\frac{1}{2}$ **2.** $\frac{2}{5}$ **3.** 46   **4.** $\frac{8}{5}$ or $1\frac{3}{5}$
5. mile   6. pound   7. 51 markers

Chapter 7

Check Your Readiness   p. 304

1. 48 **2.** 42 **3.** 24 **4.** 9 **5.** $\frac{2}{5}$ **6.** $\frac{5}{11}$ **7.** $\frac{2}{3}$ **8.** $\frac{1}{3}$ **9.** >
10. > **11.** < **12.** = **13.** $\frac{8}{21}$ **14.** $\frac{1}{2}$ **15.** $3\frac{8}{9}$ **16.** $4\frac{1}{8}$

Lesson 7-1   pp. 306–307

Check Skills You'll Need   **1. A fraction is in simplest form when the numerator and denominator have only a common factor of 1. 2.** $\frac{1}{3}$ **3.** $\frac{2}{3}$ **4.** $\frac{2}{9}$ **5.** $\frac{1}{16}$

Quick Check   **1a.** 2 to 4, 2 : 4, $\frac{2}{4}$ **b.** 2 to 6, 2 : 6, $\frac{2}{6}$
2a–c. Answers may vary. Samples are given.
2a. 2 to 7, 4 to 14   **b.** 4 to 1, 8 to 2   **c.** 4 to 11, 12 to 33   **3.** 1 : 8

Lesson 7-2   pp. 312–313

Check Skills You'll Need   **1. division 2.** 4 **3.** 4 **4.** 5
5. 6

Quick Check   **1.** 79 cents per pound   **2.** 11¢ per ounce; 9¢ per ounce; the 32 ounce container
3a. $\frac{\$5}{1 \text{ hour}} = \frac{\$25}{5 \text{ hours}}$ **b.** $\frac{25 \text{ words}}{1 \text{ minute}} = \frac{250 \text{ words}}{10 \text{ minutes}}$

Lesson 7-3   pp. 316–317

Check Skills You'll Need   **1. You see whether the two fractions are equal or whether one is greater.**
2. < **3.** = **4.** < **5.** <

Quick Check   **1. No;** $\frac{36}{20}$ cannot reduce to $\frac{8}{5}$. **2. No;** $\frac{1}{12}$ and $\frac{3}{26}$ are not equal.

Lesson 7-4
pp. 320–325

Check Skills You'll Need **1.** Answers may vary. Sample: The ratios do not form a proportion, because their cross products are not equal. **2.** yes **3.** no

Quick Check **1.** 15 **2a.** 15 **b.** 4 **3.** $4.71

Checkpoint Quiz 1 **1.** 18 to 40, $\frac{18}{40}$ **2.** $2.85 **3.** $37.50 **4.** no **5.** no **6.** yes **7.** 12 **8.** 78 **9.** $16.20 **10.** $7.92

Lesson 7-5
pp. 326–327

Check Skills You'll Need **1.** Answers may vary. Sample: You could rewrite the ratios so the numerators or the denominators are equal. **2.** 25 **3.** 2

Quick Check **1.** 1 in. : 14 in. **2.** about 100 mi **3.** 17 in.

Lesson 7-6
pp. 331–335

Check Skills You'll Need **1.** No; $\frac{10}{12}$ in simplest form equals $\frac{5}{6}$, which is larger than $\frac{3}{4}$. **2.** $\frac{6}{25}$ **3.** $\frac{2}{5}$ **4.** $\frac{3}{4}$ **5.** $\frac{1}{3}$

Quick Check **1a.** $\frac{11}{20}$ **b.** $\frac{1}{25}$ **2a.** 0.25 **b.** 0.02 **3 a.** 52% **b.** 5% **c.** 50% **4.** 5%

Checkpoint Quiz 2 **1.** 0.74, $\frac{37}{50}$ **2.** 0.06, $\frac{3}{50}$ **3.** 0.6, $\frac{3}{5}$ **4.** 84% **5.** 70% **6.** 5% **7.** about 268 mi **8.** about 587 mi **9.** about 570 mi **10.** 1 in. : 3 ft

Lesson 7-7
pp. 336–337

Check Skills You'll Need **1.** Answers may vary. Sample: You can set the cross products equal to each other to write and solve an equation. **2.** 8 **3.** 15 **4.** 78 **5.** 230

Quick Check **1.** $8 **2a.** 10.92 **b.** 21.78 **3.** 9

Lesson 7-8
pp. 341–342

Check Skills You'll Need **1.** Answers may vary. Sample: You can write a proportion by setting the ratio equal to $\frac{x}{100}$. Solve the proportion and write the solution with a percent sign. **2.** 98 **3.** 104 **4.** 96

Quick Check **1.** They are processed.
2. processed; 39% > 13%
3. Lunches for 50 Students

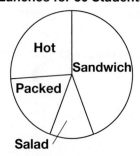

Lesson 7-9
pp. 348–349

Check Skills You'll Need **1.** Write 98 as 100 − 2 and multiply by 3; 3(100 − 2). **2.** 5,015 **3.** 40.8

Quick Check **1.** about $10.60 **2.** about $6 **3.** about $24

Chapter 8

Check Your Readiness
p. 360

1. 9 **2.** 9 **3.** 4 **4.** 10 **5.** 1.27 **6.** 59.5 **7.** 27.1 **8.** 17.5 **9.** 33.3 **10.** 12.07 **11.** yes **12.** no **13.** no **14.** yes **15.** no **16.** yes

Lesson 8-1
pp. 362–363

Check Skills You'll Need **1.** Answers may vary. Sample: Numbers are ordered from smallest to largest as you move from left to right on a number line. **2.** 1.03, 1.06, 1.3, 1.6 **3.** 0.2, 0.4, 0.6, 0.9 **4.** 1.04, 1.3, 1.4, 1.5

Quick Check **1 a.** Answers may vary. Samples are given. $\overleftrightarrow{VP}, \overleftarrow{MV}$ **b.** $\overline{VM}, \overline{VP}, \overline{MP}$ **2.** Answers may vary. Samples are given. **a.** NE 4th St. and NE 2nd St. **b.** N. Miami Ave. and NE 2nd St.

Lesson 8-2
pp. 367–368

Check Skills You'll Need **1.** A line continues in opposite directions without end. A ray has one endpoint and continues in one direction without end. **2.** Answers may vary. Samples are given. $\overleftrightarrow{AC}, \overrightarrow{BE}, \overline{DB}$ **3.** Answers may vary. Sample: $\overleftrightarrow{EB}, \overrightarrow{BD}$

Quick Check **1.** 125° **2.** about 60°; acute **3a.** acute **b.** right **c.** right

Lesson 8-3
pp. 374–379

Check Skills You'll Need **1.** Check students' work.

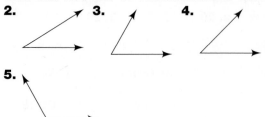

2. **3.** **4.**

5.

Quick Check **1.** 37° **2.** 35° **3.** 38°; 142°

Checkpoint Quiz 1 1–10. Answers may vary. Samples are given.
1. $\overleftrightarrow{LM}$ and $\overleftrightarrow{KN}$ **2.** $\overrightarrow{JP}$ and $\overrightarrow{NK}$ **3.** ∠PJM **4.** ∠PJK **5.** ∠PJN **6.** ∠LJM **7.** ∠KJL and ∠MJN **8.** ∠KJL **9.** ∠PJK and ∠KJL

10. ∠*LJN* and ∠*NJM*

Check Skills You'll Need 1. No; an obtuse angle itself is already larger than 90°. **2.** acute **3.** obtuse **4.** right **5.** straight

Quick Check 1. right triangle **2.** 50°. **3.** isosceles triangle; two sides are congruent

Check Skills You'll Need 1. No; skew lines are not in the same plane. **2.** Answers may vary. Sample: $\overline{CB}$ and $\overline{GH}$

Quick Check 1a. quadrilateral **b.** hexagon **c.** octagon **2a.** irregular **b.** irregular **3.** Parallelogram, rectangle; rectangle; answers may vary. Sample: a rectangle has four right angles and two pairs of parallel lines. **4.** 56°

Checkpoint Quiz 2 1. obtuse **2.** right **3.** acute **4.** isosceles **5.** scalene **6.** equilateral **7.** 4 m **8.** pentagon **9.** octagon **10.** quadrilateral **11.** trapezoid; trapezoid **12.** parallelogram, rhombus; rhombus **13.** parallelogram, rectangle; rectangle

Check Skills You'll Need 1. They have the same measure. **2.** isosceles **3.** scalene

Quick Check 1a. no **b.** yes **2.** yes; $\frac{17}{20} = \frac{34}{40}$ **3.** 15

Check Skills You'll Need 1. Answers may vary. Sample:

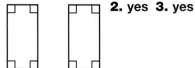

2. yes **3.** yes

Quick Check 1. No; if you fold the figure along the line, the two parts do not match.
2 a. 1

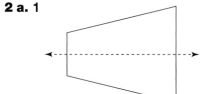

b. 4

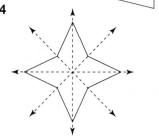

Check Skills You'll Need 1. See if the two sides match when the paper is folded.

2.   **3.**

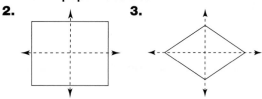

Quick Check 1. no **2.**
3 a. no **b.** yes **c.** no

Chapter 9

1. pounds **2.** miles **3.** 144 **4.** $3\frac{5}{6}$ **5.** $3\frac{5}{8}$ **6.** >
7. < **8.** > **9.** rhombus **10.** isosceles triangle
11. trapezoid

Check Skills You'll Need 1. Answers may vary. Sample: ft, lb, fl oz **2.** Feet (yards would also be appropriate). **3.** Pints (cups or fluid ounces would also be appropriate).

Quick Check 1. meters **2a.** kilograms **b.** kilograms **c.** milligrams **3a.** liters **b.** kiloliters **c.** milliliters

Check Skills You'll Need 1. multiplication **2.** 144 **3.** 16 **4.** 2

Quick Check 1a. 150 mm **b.** 837,000 m **2.** 60 km **3a.** 0.015 **b.** 0.386 **c.** 0.082

Check Skills You'll Need 1. base: 3; exponent: 2 **2.** 16 **3.** 36 **4.** 29.16 **5.** 2.56

Quick Check 1. $P = 26$ ft, $A = 40$ ft^2 **2.** 49 in.^{2}

Check Skills You'll Need 1. square
2. $P = 20$ in.; $A = 24$ in.^{2}
3. $P = 34$ m; $A = 60$ m^2

Quick Check 1. 70 m^2 **2.** 259.5 m^2 **3.** 16 m^2

Checkpoint Quiz 1 **1.** cm **2.** kg **3.** 0.062 L
4. 4,300 g **5.** 1.78 m **6.** 0.0031 g **7.** 500 L
8. 0.083 g **9.** $P = 34$ cm, $A = 72.25$ cm^2
10. $P = 26$ mi, $A = 36$ mi^2 **11.** 193.6 ft^2
12. 70.65 cm^2 **13.** 30.5 in.^{2}

Lesson 9-5 pp. 438–440

Check Skills You'll Need **1.** product **2.** 6 **3.** 24 **4.** 210
5. 60

Quick Check **1.** $\overline{AC}, \overline{BD}$ **2.** 4 cm **3.** 22π **4.** 18 cm

Lesson 9-6 pp. 444–445

Check Skills You'll Need **1.** $2^3 \cdot 3^2$ **2.** 144 **3.** 16
4. 100 **5.** 18

Quick Check **1a.** about 452.16 km^2 **b.** about
28.26 in.^{2} **c.** about 50.24 yd.^{2} **2.** 154 in.^{2}

Lesson 9-7 pp. 449–450

Check Skills You'll Need **1.** A rectangle that is not a
square is a 4-sided polygon with 4 right angles
and with the length different from the width.
2. hexagon **3.** triangle

Quick Check **1a.** pentagonal prism **b.** rectangular
prism **c.** triangular prism **2.** rectangular prism

Lesson 9-8 pp. 453–454

Check Skills You'll Need **1.** The area of a piece of paper
is the two-dimensional space a rectangle of the
same dimensions as the paper encloses.
2. 21 m^2 **3.** 60 m^2

Quick Check **1.** Answers may vary. Sample:
2. 1,728 m^2

Lesson 9-9 pp. 458–461

Check Skills You'll Need **1.** base **2.** 110.5 **3.** 2.7

Quick Check **1.** 36 units^3 **2.** 560 m^3

Checkpoint Quiz 2 **1.** 346.8 ft^2 **2.** triangular pyramid
3. cone **4.** pentagonal pyramid **5.** hexagonal
prism **6.** 62 cm^2 **7.** 30 cm^3

Lesson 9-10 pp. 462–464

Check Skills You'll Need **1.** The radius of a circle is the
distance from the center to the edge of the circle.
2. 200.96 m^2 **3.** 12.56 yd^2

Quick Check **1.** 96.6 in.^{2} **2.** 452 in.^{3}

Chapter 10

Check Your Readiness p. 474

1. 0.68 **2.** 0.92 **3.** 0.4 **4.** 0.766 **5.** $\frac{3}{5}$ **6.** $\frac{2}{3}$ **7.** $\frac{7}{8}$ **8.** $\frac{3}{5}$
9. $\frac{5}{12}$ **10.** $\frac{2}{3}$ **11.** $\frac{1}{4}$ **12.** $\frac{16}{27}$ **13.** 0.25; 25%
14. $0.\overline{3}$; $\approx$ 33% **15.** 0.8; 80% **16.** 0.7; 70%

Lesson 10-1 pp. 476–477

Check Skills You'll Need **1.** Associative **2.** 50
3. 2,000 **4.** 12,000

Quick Check **1.** 9 outcomes
2. Pants   Shirts **3.** 48 desserts

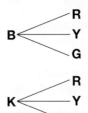

6 outcomes

Lesson 10-2 pp. 482–487

Check Skills You'll Need **1.** A percent is a ratio that
compares a number to 100. **2.** 32% **3.** 36%
4. 40% **5.** 2%

Quick Check **1.** $\frac{1}{3}$ **2.** $\frac{5}{6}$ **3.** 0.6

Checkpoint Quiz 1 **1.** shirt 1, jeans 1; shirt 1, jeans 2;
shirt 2, jeans 1; shirt 2, jeans 2; shirt 3, jeans 1;
shirt 3, jeans 2
2. Roll   Toss **3.** 48 desserts **4.** $\frac{2}{6}$ or $\frac{1}{3}$ **5.** 0

6. $\frac{2}{6}$ or $\frac{1}{3}$ **7.** $\frac{3}{8}$ **8.** $\frac{3}{8}$ **9.** $\frac{1}{8}$
10. $\frac{2}{8}$ or $\frac{1}{4}$ **11.** $\frac{7}{8}$ **12.** $\frac{1}{8}$
13. 60 hairdos

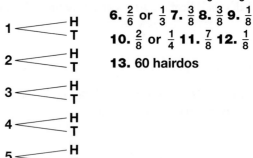

12 outcomes

Lesson 10-3 pp. 488–489

Check Skills You'll Need **1.** You can write a ratio as a
fraction, as a phrase using "to," or as an
expression using a colon. **2.** $\frac{3}{5}$ **3.** $\frac{3}{5}$ **4.** $\frac{4}{15}$ **5.** $\frac{13}{20}$

Quick Check 1. $\frac{11}{20}$ 2. Yes; the probabilities are about the same.

Lesson 10-4 pp. 494–499

Check Skills You'll Need 1. A proportion must be an equality. 2. 6 3. 2 4. 3

Quick Check 1. 6 times 2. 1,080 toy robots

Checkpoint Quiz 2 1. $\frac{4}{20}$ or $\frac{1}{5}$ 2. $\frac{3}{20}$ 3. $\frac{12}{20}$ or $\frac{3}{5}$ 4. $\frac{8}{20}$ or $\frac{2}{5}$ 5. $\frac{8}{20}$ or $\frac{2}{5}$ 6. 28,000 men

7. 315 customers 8. 750 hats

Lesson 10-5 pp. 500–501

Check Skills You'll Need 1. no 2. $\frac{9}{16}$ 3. $\frac{2}{21}$ 4. $\frac{2}{9}$ 5. $\frac{1}{4}$

Quick Check 1. Not independent; after selecting the first card, there is one card fewer from which to choose. The first selection affects the second selection. 2. $\frac{4}{25}$ 3. $\frac{1}{16}$

Chapter 11

Check Your Readiness p. 514

1. 79 2. 31 3. 39 4. 31 5. 0.6 6. 66 7. 41
8. 72 9. 15 10. 252 11. < 12. > 13. =
14. $\frac{1}{12}, \frac{1}{8}, \frac{1}{3}$ 15. $\frac{4}{9}, \frac{7}{12}, \frac{5}{6}$ 16. $\frac{1}{4}, \frac{1}{2}, \frac{6}{7}$

Lesson 11-1 pp. 516–517

Check Skills You'll Need 1. The Identity Property of Addition states that the sum of any number and 0 is that number. The Identity Property of Multiplication states that the product of any number and 1 is that number. 2. 9 3. 10 4. 0

Quick Check 1. −8 2. 5 3a. 1 b. 7

Lesson 11-2 pp. 520–521

Check Skills You'll Need 1. less than; greater than
2. < 3. = 4. >

Quick Check 1a. > b. < 2. −50, −25, 75, 100

Lesson 11-3 pp. 524–528

Check Skills You'll Need 1. −6, 6 2. 15 3. 12 4. 8
5. 8

Quick Check 1. −4 2. −3 3. −21 4. −7

Checkpoint Quiz 1 1. 13 2. 64 3. −3 4. −12
5. −32 6. −17, −15, −14, 16, 18 7. 12°F

Lesson 11-4 pp. 530–531

Check Skills You'll Need 1. −6 2. 10 3. −5 4. −11
5. 14

Quick Check 1a. 6 b. −6 2. −4 3. 622 ft; closer

Lesson 11-5 pp. 534–535

Check Skills You'll Need 1. negative 2. −8 3. 64
4. −28 5. −90

Quick Check 1a. −12 b. 12 2a. 27 b. −15 3. −20

Lesson 11-6 pp. 540–541

Check Skills You'll Need 1. positive 2. 16 3. 1,024
4. 196 5. 2,025

Quick Check 1a. −4 b. 18 c. −4 2. −$4/day

Lesson 11-7 pp. 543–544

Check Skills You'll Need 1. addition and subtraction, multiplication and division 2. 17 3. 25 4. 14
5. 64

Quick Check 1a. 10 b. 28 c. −6 2. $20

Lesson 11-8 pp. 548–552

Check Skills You'll Need 1. 0 2.
3.

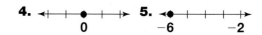

4. 5.

Quick Check 1a. $B(-3, 2)$ b. $D(-2, -3)$ c. $E(2, -2)$
2a–c.

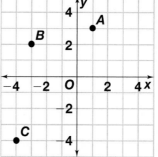

3a. City Hall
b. $(3, -1)$

Checkpoint Quiz 2 1. −2 2. −12 3. −36 4. −16
5. −7 6. 7 7. −13 8. 8 9. −4
10. $t - 15 = -2$; 13°F 11. $(2, -4)$ 12. $(1.5, 1.5)$
13. $(-2, -1.5)$ 14. $(-3.5, 2)$ 15. $(0.5, 0)$

Lesson 11-9 pp. 554–555

Check Skills You'll Need 1. Answers may vary. Sample: If the signs of both integers are the same, add their absolute values and use the same sign. If the integers' signs are different, subtract their absolute values and use the sign of the integer with the greatest absolute value. 2. 38 3. 9
4. −13 5. −29

Quick Check 1. −$2,886; $821 **2.** Mar., Apr., June, July, Aug., Nov., Dec.

Check Skills You'll Need 1. An expression does not have an equal sign. **2.** 11 **3.** 6 **4.** 12 **5.** 18

Quick Check 1a. 4, −6, 9 **b.** −14, −9, −4

2.

x	−2	0	2	6
y	−5	−3	−1	3

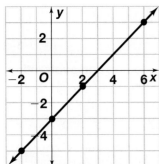

3.

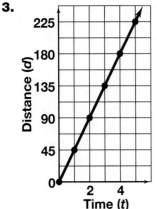

t	d
0	0
1	45
2	90
3	135
4	180
5	225

Chapter 12

1. 25 **2.** −13 **3.** 43 **4.** 10 **5.** 13 **6.** 7 **7.** 19 **8.** 64 **9.** 63 **10.** 125 **11.** 4^3; 4; 3 **12.** 2^2; 2; 2 **13.** 1^4; 1; 4 **14.** < **15.** < **16.** >

Check Skills You'll Need 1. = **2.** 20 **3.** 48 **4.** 21 **5.** 192

Quick Check 1a. 3 **b.** 9 **2.** $42

Check Skills You'll Need 1. A number line shows integers from least to greatest. A number to the left of another number on a number line is less than the other number. **2.** > **3.** > **4.** < **5.** <

Quick Check 1. Let a represent the altitude from which most skydivers jump. $a \leq 14,500$ **2.** Let t represent the number of hours you spend studying. $t \geq 2$. **3.** no

Check Skills You'll Need 1. If you subtract the same value from each side of an equation, the two sides remain equal. **2.** −9 **3.** 15

Quick Check 1. $u \leq 9$ **2.** $z > 9$ **3.** Let $p =$ the number of additional people the restaurant can serve; $p + 97 \leq 115$, $p \leq 18$; the restaurant can serve at most 18 more people.

Checkpoint Quiz 1 1. 8 **2.** 8 **3.** 13
4. $p < -5$
5. $n \geq -12$
6. $d \leq 4$

Check Skills You'll Need 1. multiplication **2.** 4^5 **3.** 999^3 **4.** 3.6^2

Quick Check 1. 10 **2.** 3.2 **3.** No; the decimal does not terminate or repeat.

Check Skills You'll Need 1. Answers may vary. Sample: 36; 25; 16 **2.** 3 **3.** 8 **4.** 5 **5.** 6 **6.** 11 **7.** 25

Quick Check 1. 20 in. **2.** 4.6 ft

Selected Answers

Chapter 1

Lesson 1-1 — pp. 6–7

EXERCISES 1. 1,273 **3.** hundred; two **5.** <
9. one hundred forty-five thousand, six hundred
seventy-five **11.** seven million, three hundred
forty-seven thousand, two hundred **15.** > **17.** >
21. 901; 910; 990 **23.** 17,414; 17,444; 17,671
33. 2,129

Lesson 1-2 — pp. 10–11

EXERCISES 1. Yes; 60 can be divided by 6
mentally. **3.** 40 **5.** 70 **7.** 10; 10 **9.** 600; 20
11. about 300 **13.** about 190 **19.** about 8,000
21. about 10 **31a.** about $9 **b.** Compatible
numbers make division easy to compute mentally.
33. about 1,300 **41.** 4,541; 4,567; 4,678; 4,687

Lesson 1-3 — pp. 14–15

EXERCISES 1. Comm. Prop. of Add. **5.** 50 **7.** 61
9. 66 **17.** 470 **19.** 1,300 **27.** = **33.** $360

Lesson 1-4 — pp. 18–19

EXERCISES 1. expression **3.** multiplication
7. > **9.** 15 **11.** 19 **19.** $60 **21.** $91
29. $(1 + 2) \times (15 - 4) = 33$ **31.** 76 g

Lesson 1-5 — pp. 24–25

EXERCISES 1. 5; it is in the hundredths place. 7 is
in the thousandths place. **3.** 3 tenths **5.** 3
thousandths **7.** $1 + 0.2$ **9.** $7 + 0.5 + 0.02$
11. two and three tenths **13.** six thousandths
21. 40.009; $40 + 0.009$ **23.** 0.700; 0.7 **27.** 2.7
29. 10.96 **35.** B: $0.9 million; $900,000 C: $1.6
million; $1,600,000 **37.** 4 tenths, or 0.4 **39.** 4
ten-thousandths, or 0.0004 **49.** 70

Lesson 1-6 — pp. 29–30

EXERCISES 1. Answers may vary. Sample: I
would compare the values of numbers in similar
places. In the hundredths place, 1.697 has
9 hundredths. 1.697 > 1.679 **3.** 0.57 **5.** 0.575

7.

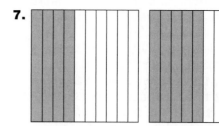

0.4   0.5

0.5 is greater.
11. = **13.** < **17.** 13.7, 17.1, 17.7 **19.** 9.02,
9.024, 9.2, 9.209 **23.** *The Top* . . .: 031.02; *Going
to* . . .: 370.973; *How Music* . . .: 398.2; *The
Night* . . .: 398.9; *Art of* . . .: 709.52; *France*: 944;
Japan: 952 **25.** 0.6595, 0.6095, 0.62 **33.** 26

Lesson 1-7 — pp. 34–35

EXERCISES 1. The decimal points were not lined
up before subtracting. $5.8 - 2 = 3.8$. **3.** 1.38
5. $9 **9.** about 6; 6.644 **11.** about 21; 21.516
15. about $15 **17.** about $48 **19.** about 3; 2.83
21. about 3; 3.05 **27.** $47.99 **29.** < **31.** >
33. 1.26 million **41.** 800 **43.** 1,400

Lesson 1-8 — pp. 40–41

EXERCISES 1. 7; there are 3 decimal places in the
first number and 4 decimal places in the second
number. So $3 + 4 = 7$. **7.** 262.0 **9.** 56.414
11. 17.1 **13.** 2.34 **19.** 0.32 **21.** 0.63 **37.** 40;
Methods may vary. Sample: paper and pencil
41. 483.48 million mi **47.** 11.61

Lesson 1-9 — pp. 46–47

EXERCISES 1. quotient
3.

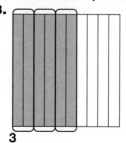

3
5. 3; 3 **7.** 25.25 **9.** 7.2 **15.** 73.75 **17.** 3.31
23a. 90 pieces **b.** yes **25.** $7.65 **27.** 4.40
29. 33.16 **37.** 8.03, 8.035, 8.3, 8.308

1. Ident. Prop. of Add. 2. compatible numbers
3. standard form 4. expression 5. Assoc. Prop. of Add. 6. five million, twenty-five 7. five thousand, twenty-five 8. 1,001; 1,010; 1,100; 1,101 9. 2,232; 2,322; 2,323; 2,332 10. about 8,000 11. about 180 12. about 400 13. about 3,000 14. about 1,000 15. about 60 16. 350 17. 130 18. 30 19. 37 20. 0 21. 42 22. five hundred twenty-five and five tenths 23. five thousand, two hundred fifty-five ten-thousandths 24. five and twenty-five thousandths 25. fifty and twenty-five ten-thousandths 26. 45.2 27. 98.6 28. 5.13 29. 1.25 30. 0.06; 0.14; 0.4; 0.52 31. 23; 23.03; 23.2; 23.25

32–37. Answers may vary. Samples are given.

32. about 357; 357.48 33. about 1; 0.931
34. about 3; 3.4 35. about 2; 1.7 36. about 4; 3.867 37. about 7; 7.4 38. 35.4 39. 2.02
40. 480 41. 9.18 42. 6.94 43. 31.458 44. 10.4
45. 170

Chapter 2

EXERCISES 1. Answers may vary. Sample: Add the data and divide the sum by 5. 3. 6 5. 5
7. 10 15. 50; increases 18. Check students' work. 19. 10.2 23. 91 29. 19.341

EXERCISES 1. median 3. 8; 8 5. Answers may vary. Sample: 60, 100. 7. 0.5 9. 475 13. 8
19. 13.2; 13.5; 13.5 21. 45 25a. mean: 6,172.75 m; median: 6,044.5 m b. They both increase. The mean becomes 6,708.2 m. The median becomes 6,194 m. 31. 15

EXERCISES 1. Answers may vary. Sample: Both the line plot and frequency table show the data grouped in an easy-to-read way.
3.
```
        X
        X   X
    X   X   X
    X   X   X   X
    ─────────────
    5   6   7   8
```

5. Answers may vary. Sample: A line plot immediately shows the mode.

7.

Type of Car	Tally	Frequency
Compact	IIII	4
Mid-size	III	3
SUV	II	2
Wagon	I	1
Pick-up	II	2

compact
9. Word Lengths in a Sentence
```
  X X          X X
  X X X X    X X X X X
  ──────────────────────
  1 2 3 4 5 6 7 8 9 10
  Word Lengths (letters)
```
There are very few words with fewer than 3 letters. 11. 1.7 m 13. 25 mph 15. the number of organisms in a sample 17. Answers may vary. Sample: Data items 3 and 4 did not occur often but will affect the mean. 23. 60

EXERCISES 1. line 3. Number of days
5.

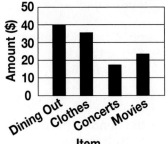

Planned Monthly Budget

11.

Prime Ministers' Years in Office

13. Hours of Battery Life 17. <

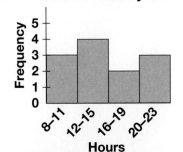

EXERCISES 1. A cell is a box in a spreadsheet where a specific row and column meet. **3.** B
7. F2, F3, F4, F5 **11.** 80
15. = (B4 + C4 + D4)/3 or = E4/3 **19.** 5
25. = C8 ÷ 6 **29.** 7

EXERCISES 1. stem-and-leaf **3.** 4 **7.** 3 entries
9. Heights of Tomato Plants (inches)

```
2 | 6 7 9
3 | 0 1 3 3 5 6 6
4 | 0 1
```

Key: 2|6 means 26 in.

13a. Ages of People

```
0 | 9
1 | 1 2 2 2 2 3 3 5 5 6 9
2 | 0 1 3 4
3 | 5
4 | 0
```

Key: 2 | 6 means 26 years old

Ages of Eighteen People

```
X
X
XX  X
X  XXX  XX    XXX  XX        X      X
10   15   20   25   30   35   40
            Years
```

b. Stem-and-leaf plot; explanations may vary. Sample: The data with a stem of 1 and a leaf of 3 or more represent the teenagers. **21.** 13

EXERCISES 1. It looks like there was a dramatic decrease in sales. **3.** 3 more sales **5.** The graph is misleading because the intervals on the vertical axis are unequal; it appears there was a greater increase in January than there actually was.

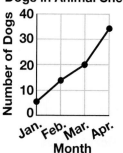

Dogs in Animal Shelter

9. Candidate A: graph I, Candidate B: graph II; the candidate would present a graph to make the results look more favorable. **11.** Graphs may vary. Samples:

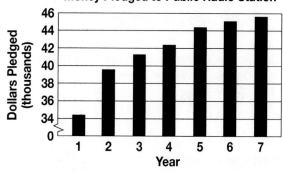

Money Pledged to Public Radio Station

1. C **2.** A **3.** G **4.** F **5.** E **6.** 45, 49, 50 **7.** 6, 7, 9
8.

	Number of Times Vowels Occur	
Vowels	Tally	Frequency
A	||||| ||||| ||||| |||	18
E	||||| ||||| ||||| |||	18
I	||||| |||||	10
O	|||||	5
U	|||||	5
Y	|||	3

9. Number of Times Listed Words Appear

```
        X
        X
        X
 X      X
 X      X    X
─────────────────
the    and   a   of
Times Words Appear
```

10.

Ticket Prices

11.

Ticket Prices

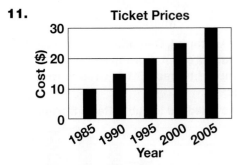

12. Line graph; it shows changes over time.
13. B2, B3 **14.** 75 **15.** = B2 + C2 + D2

16.
```
3 | 01 41 67 79 88 99
4 | 65 79 79 83
5 | 07 12 43 48
```
Key: 4|65 means 465

17. mean or median, since they are the same
18. median or mode **19.** mode **20.** median
21. Answers may vary. Sample: Start the vertical axis at zero and use intervals of 10.

Chapter 3

Lesson 3-1   pp. 110–111

EXERCISES 1. conjecture **3.** Start with 53 and subtract 4 repeatedly. **5.** 18, 22 **11.** 512, 256, 128, 64, 32, 16 **13.** Start with 0.12 and multiply by 10 repeatedly; 1,200; 12,000. **17.** 48; 60
21.

25. about 12; 12.7

Lesson 3-2   pp. 115–116

EXERCISES 1. Answers may vary. Sample: A numerical expression is a mathematical phrase with only numbers and operation symbols. An algebraic expression is a mathematical expression with one or more variables. **3.** 20
5. 16

7. 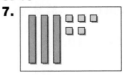   **9.**

15. 8 **17.** 193
21.

x	$x + 6$
1	7
4	10
7	13

25. 75 **27.** 4,620 bricks **29.** 10 hits; 15 misses
33. 29.16

Lesson 3-3   pp. 120–122

EXERCISES 1. Answers may vary. Sample: Your grandfather is 50 years older than you. The expression $y + 50$ relates his age to yours.
3. $m + 4$ **5.** $6 \times z$ **7.** $k - 34$ **9.** $50 + d$
17. $n - 3$ **19.** $n + 2$ **25.** $m \div n - 5$ **27.** $h + 2$
29. $(20 + 0.75n)t$ **33.** 14.505

Lesson 3-4   pp. 126–127

EXERCISES 1. The value(s) of the variable(s) that make(s) the equation true is (are) unknown.
3. 15 **5.** 3 **7.** false **9.** true **11.** false **13.** true
15. 2 **17.** 4.3 **29.** 3.3 lb

Lesson 3-5   pp. 132–133

EXERCISES 1. subtracting 6 **3.** 18 **5.** 2.7
7. 48 **9.** 39
19. y = the year Mozart was born;
    $y + 6 = 1762$; $y = 1756$
21. m = number of minutes of music before adding song;
    $m + 4 = 120$; $m = 116$
23. 10 minutes **25.** 8.2 **27.** 0.29 **29.** 5.5 **33.** 37, 40, 43, 46, 49

Lesson 3-6   pp. 135–136

EXERCISES 1. She subtracted 4 from each side instead of adding 4 to each side. **3.** C **5.** B
7. 4.2 **9.** 108 **21.** 12 **25.** 0

Lesson 3-7
pp. 140–141

EXERCISES 1. The Multiplication Property of Equality states that you can multiply each side of an equation by the same nonzero number and the equation will be the same. The Division Property states the same is true for division. **3.** B **5.** A **7.** 14 **9.** 9.5 **11.** 18 **19.** 441 **21.** 51,772 **29.** about 8.25 feet **31.** 0.2 **33.** 3.42 **41.** =

Lesson 3-8
pp. 146–147

EXERCISES 1. C **3.** J **5.** 72
7. $5 \times (60 + 3) = 5 \times 60 + 5 \times 3 = 300 + 15 = 315$
9. $6 \times (100 - 1) = 6 \times 100 - 6 \times 1 = 600 - 6 = 594$
19. y **21.** $23.20 **23.** C **27.** false

Chapter Review
pp. 150–151

1. term **2.** algebraic expression **3.** solution **4.** variable **5.** equation **6.** Start with 2 and multiply by 3 repeatedly; 162; 486; 1,458. **7.** Start with 7 and add 12 repeatedly; 55, 67, 79. **8.** Start with 7 and multiply by 2 repeatedly; 112, 224, 448. **9.** 8 **10.** 49 **11.** 42 **12.** $x \div 12$ **13.** $2b$ **14.** $h + k$ **15.** false **16.** true **17.** false **18.** 5 **19.** 8 **20.** 8 **21.** 5,640 **22.** 7 **23.** 1.4 **24.** 6.06 **25.** 129.7 lb **26.** 56 **27.** 128 **28.** 2.5 **29.** 10.8 **30.** 60.8 **31.** 0.9 **32.** $16.68
33. $7(20 + 8) = 140 + 56 = 196$
34. $5(3 + 0.4) = 15 + 2.0 = 17$
35. $(10 + 1)57 = 570 + 57 = 627$

Chapter 4

Lesson 4-1
pp. 160–161

EXERCISES 1. If the number is divisible by 2, then the number is even; otherwise, the number is odd. **3.** C **5.** A **7.** no **11.** 3 and 5 **13.** 2 and 3 **23.** no **27.** 4 **29.** 4 **31.** Yes; $5 + 6 + 6 + 1 = 18$ and 18 is divisible by 9, so 5661 or $56.61, is divisible by 9. **33.** $1.00 **39.** 36

Lesson 4-2
pp. 164–165

EXERCISES 1. The exponent tells how many times the base is used as a factor. **3.** 3^2 **5.** 9^3 **7.** 2, 2, 2 **9.** 29^1; 29; 1 **11.** 25^3; 25; 3 **19.** 64 **21.** 25 **29.** 64 **31.** 40 **33.** 2^8 cells **35.** 5 and 6

39.

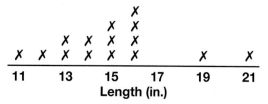

Length of Lake Trout

Lesson 4-3
pp. 168–169

EXERCISES 1. A prime number has exactly two factors and a composite number has more than two factors. **3.** 7; 7 has just two factors, 1 and 7. **5.** 1, 2, 4, 7, 14, 28 **7.** 1, 17 **15.** Prime; the only factors are 1 and 67. **19.** $2 \times 3 \times 7$ **21.** $2^4 \times 5^2$ **27.** 1,001 **29.** 9 rows **31.** If $p > 2$ and prime, then p is always odd. So $p + 1$ is even and always composite. **33.** 3, 5; 5, 7; 11, 13; 17, 19; 29, 31; 41, 43; 59, 61; 71, 73 **37.** >

Lesson 4-4
pp. 173–174

EXERCISES 1. When two numbers have 1 as their only common factor, then the GCF = 1. **3.** B **5.** A **7.** factors of 24: 1, 2, 3, 4, 6, 8, 12, 24; factors of 45: 1, 3, 5, 9, 15, 45; GCF of 24 and 45: 3 **9.** factors of 30: 1, 2, 3, 5, 6, 10, 15, 30; factors of 35: 1, 5, 7, 35; GCF of 30 and 35: 5

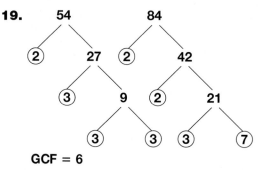

GCF = 6

21.

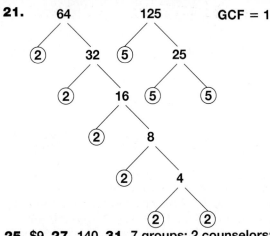

GCF = 1

25. $9 **27.** 140 **31.** 7 groups; 2 counselors; 11 campers **33.** 2

Lesson 4-5 pp. 178–179

EXERCISES 1. simplest form **3.** A **5.** B

7. $\frac{12}{14}$, $\frac{24}{28}$ **9.** $\frac{6}{32}$, $\frac{9}{48}$ **15.** $\frac{2}{7}$ **17.** $\frac{4}{5}$ **25.** yes **27.** no; $\frac{1}{3}$ **29.** $\frac{1}{2}$ **31a.** $\frac{2}{3}$, $\frac{4}{6}$, $\frac{10}{15}$, $\frac{20}{30}$ **b.** $\frac{2}{3}$; when you divide the numerator and the denominator by the common factor a, the result is in simplest form.

35. 8

Lesson 4-6 pp. 184–185

EXERCISES 1. C **3.** B **5.** $3\frac{1}{4}$; $\frac{13}{4}$ **7.** $\frac{22}{7}$ **9.** $\frac{11}{2}$

15. $3\frac{2}{5}$ **17.** $2\frac{1}{4}$ **25.** $\frac{7}{5}$; $1\frac{2}{5}$ **27.** $\frac{13}{5}$; $2\frac{3}{5}$

31. 9 boxes; $1,350

33. $1\frac{5}{8}$ in.; $1\frac{13}{16}$ in. **35.** 374 squares **39.** true

Lesson 4-7 pp. 190–191

EXERCISES 1. Answers may vary. Sample: One number has many multiples. **3.** 16, 24, 32, 40 **5.** 48 **7.** 30 **9.** 80 **19.** 72 **21.** 56 **29.** 120th customer **31.** 48 **33 a.** 2, 4, 5 **b.** 40 **35.** $2x$ **37.** $200xy$

41.

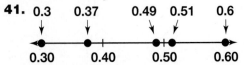

0.3 0.37 0.49 0.51 0.6

0.30 0.40 0.50 0.60

Lesson 4-8 pp. 194–195

EXERCISES 1. It is the LCM of the denominators. **3.** 8 **5.** > **7.** > **9.** > **11.** = **25.** $3\frac{2}{5}$, $3\frac{7}{15}$, $3\frac{2}{3}$ **27.** $\frac{3}{12}$, $\frac{1}{2}$, $2\frac{2}{3}$, $3\frac{1}{4}$ **31.** >; the numerators are equal, so the fraction with the lesser denominator is larger. **33.** >; the numerators are equal, so the fraction with the lesser denominator is larger.

35a. $\frac{1}{2}$, $\frac{1}{4}$, $\frac{1}{8}$, $\frac{1}{16}$ **b.**

The note symbol that is "open" has the greatest value, and for the other symbols, the more flags there are, the less the value of the note.
43. $\frac{4}{9}$

Lesson 4-9 pp. 200–201

EXERCISES 1. $\frac{3}{10}$ **3.** $\frac{3}{4}$

5. $2\frac{3}{4} = 2 + \frac{3}{4} = 2 + 0.75 = 2.75$

7. A **9.** 1.6, $1\frac{3}{4}$, 2.3 **11.** 3.1, $3\frac{3}{8}$, $4\frac{3}{5}$ **13.** $\frac{17}{100}$

15. $5\frac{1}{2}$ **21.** $0.4\overline{6}$ **23.** $1.\overline{1}$ **31.** A **33.** B

37. $6.625, $8.50 **39.** $5\frac{7}{8}$ in., 5.875 in. **45.** 612

Chapter Review pp. 204–205

1. equivalent fractions **2.** mixed number **3.** prime factorization **4.** 3 and 9 **5.** 3, 5, and 9 **6.** 2, 3, and 9 **7.** 2, 3, 5, 9, and 10 **8.** 17 **9.** 5 **10.** $2^2 \times 7$ **11.** 3×17 **12.** $2^2 \times 5^2$ **13.** 2×5^3 **14.** 2 **15.** 2 **16.** 5 **17.** 8 **18.** No; $\frac{1}{4}$; answers may vary. Sample: $\frac{2}{8}$, $\frac{3}{12}$, $\frac{10}{40}$ **19.** No; $\frac{2}{3}$; answers may vary. Sample: $\frac{10}{15}$, $\frac{8}{12}$, $\frac{20}{30}$ **20.** Yes; answers may vary. Sample: $\frac{2}{6}$, $\frac{3}{9}$, $\frac{4}{12}$ **21.** Yes; answers may vary. Sample: $\frac{4}{18}$, $\frac{6}{27}$, $\frac{8}{36}$ **22.** $\frac{14}{3}$ **23.** $\frac{41}{5}$ **24.** $4\frac{1}{3}$ **25.** $9\frac{2}{3}$ **26.** 132 **27.** 140 **28.** $\frac{1}{6}$, $\frac{1}{4}$, $\frac{1}{2}$ **29.** $2\frac{4}{15}$, $2\frac{1}{3}$, $2\frac{2}{5}$ **30.** $\frac{5}{16}$, $\frac{7}{20}$, $\frac{17}{40}$ **31.** 0.1875 **32.** $6.208\overline{3}$ **33.** $\frac{3}{50}$ **34.** $4\frac{13}{25}$

Chapter 5

Lesson 5-1 pp. 214–215

EXERCISES 1. Benchmarks are whole numbers or fractions that are easy to use, such as 0, $\frac{1}{2}$, or 1. Rounding uses place value to find approximate values for numbers. **3.** 0 **5.** 1 **7.** 0 **9.** 1 **13.** $\frac{1}{2}$ **15.** $1\frac{1}{2}$ **27.** about $3\frac{1}{2}$ in. **31.** < **35.** 0.047 **37.** 0.006

Lesson 5-2 pp. 219–220

EXERCISES 1. $\frac{3}{5}$; you do not add the denominators when adding two or more fractions. **3.** $\frac{2}{6} + \frac{3}{6} = \frac{5}{6}$ **5.** $\frac{1}{2}$ **7.** $\frac{2}{3}$ **13.** $\frac{2}{3}$ **15.** $\frac{1}{5}$ **25.** $\frac{71}{100}$ **27.** $\frac{1}{2}$ in. **31.** 5 **35.** Answer may vary. Sample: $\frac{6}{16}$, $\frac{9}{24}$

Lesson 5-3   pp. 224–225

EXERCISES 1. $\frac{9}{10}$ **3.** $\frac{1}{2}$ **5.** $\frac{1}{2}$ **7.** $1\frac{13}{18}$ **15.** $\frac{9}{20}$
17. $\frac{2}{3}$ **23.** $1\frac{7}{8}$ **27a.** $1\frac{1}{2}$ in. **b.** $1\frac{7}{40}$ in. **29.** greater
than 1 mi **35.** 11

Lesson 5-4   pp. 230–231

EXERCISES 1. Answers may vary. Sample:
$1\frac{1}{4} + 3\frac{3}{4}$ **3.** $6\frac{2}{3}$ **5.** $11\frac{3}{5}$ **7.** $11\frac{1}{2}$ **9.** $6\frac{7}{10}$ **21.** >
23a. $7\frac{2}{3}$ ft **b.** $8\frac{1}{4}$ ft **25.** 13 yd **27.** $8\frac{1}{18}$ **31.** 77

Lesson 5-5   pp. 234–236

EXERCISES 1. C **3.** $1\frac{1}{4}$ **5.** $1\frac{7}{20}$ **7.** $5\frac{8}{15}$ **15.** $3\frac{3}{8}$
17. $6\frac{7}{10}$ **25.** $\frac{11}{12}$ ft **27.** 6 in. **29.** 1 ft $4\frac{1}{4}$ in.
33. $\frac{3}{5}$

Lesson 5-6   pp. 242–243

EXERCISES 1. C **3.** D **5.** $11\frac{1}{6}$ ft **7.** $14\frac{1}{3}$ **9.** $5\frac{1}{5}$
13. $\frac{13}{45}$ **15.** $\frac{1}{8}$ **31.** n has the greater value.
35. $\frac{3}{10}, \frac{1}{2}, \frac{4}{7}, \frac{2}{3}$

Lesson 5-7   pp. 248–250

EXERCISES 1. elapsed time
3.

5. 1 h 25 min **7.** 1 h 17 min **11.** 7 h **15.** 1 h 39 min
19. 29 min **23.** 2:00 P.M. **25.** $x + 3$
27.

Activity	Start Time	End Time
1st show	10:00 A.M.	10:45 A.M.
Break	10:45 A.M.	11:45 A.M.
2nd show	11:45 A.M.	12:30 P.M.
Break	12:30 P.M.	1:30 P.M.
3rd show	1:30 P.M.	2:15 P.M.

31. 39

Chapter Review   pp. 252–253

1. benchmark **2.** elapsed time

3–10. Answers may vary. Samples are given.

3. $1\frac{1}{2}$ **4.** 0 **5.** 1 **6.** 0 **7.** 14 **8.** 10 **9.** 15 **10.** 6
11. about 6 c **12.** $1\frac{2}{5}$ **13.** $\frac{1}{2}$ **14.** $\frac{3}{5}$ **15.** $\frac{5}{9}$ **16.** $\frac{7}{8}$
17. $\frac{1}{2}$ **18.** $\frac{1}{8}$ **19.** $1\frac{7}{30}$ **20.** $\frac{13}{15}$ mi **21.** $7\frac{1}{8}$ **22.** $17\frac{1}{3}$
23. $63\frac{9}{10}$ **24.** about $59\frac{7}{12}$ in. **25.** $3\frac{3}{5}$ **26.** $6\frac{3}{8}$

27. $16\frac{7}{9}$ **28.** $\frac{3}{7}$ **29.** $\frac{1}{8}$ **30.** $1\frac{1}{9}$ **31.** $3\frac{1}{3}$ **32.** $11\frac{1}{18}$
33. $6\frac{2}{5}$ **34.** 3 h 41 min **35.** 8 h 48 min
36. 8:10 P.M.

Chapter 6

Lesson 6-1   pp. 263–264

EXERCISES 1. Greater; you are multiplying by a
greater number. **3.** B **5.** C **7.** $\frac{10}{77}$ **9.** $\frac{1}{9}$ **25.** 1
31. 65 **35.** $\frac{7}{6}$ or $1\frac{1}{6}$

Lesson 6-2   pp. 269–270

EXERCISES 1. $3 \times 3\frac{1}{2}$; $3\frac{1}{2}$ is greater than 3.
3. $\frac{10}{3}$ **5.** $\frac{1}{2}$ **7.** $3\frac{1}{8}$ **9.** 75 **11.** 80 **15.** 65 **17.** $10\frac{1}{2}$
25. 14 **29.** $2\frac{1}{3}$ ft by $2\frac{1}{6}$ ft **37.** 4

Lesson 6-3   pp. 274–275

EXERCISES 1. 1 **3.** Answers may vary. Sample:
$\frac{2}{3}, \frac{3}{2}$ **5.** 2 **7.** 7 **11.** $11\frac{2}{3}$ **13.** 15 **27.** 2
31. about $1\frac{3}{10}$ times more **33.** 4 **37.** 2, 3

Lesson 6-4   pp. 278–279

EXERCISES 1. about 3 **3.** Annie; Jocelyn
incorrectly renamed $4\frac{1}{2}$ as $\frac{8}{2}$. **5.** about 7 **9.** $1\frac{7}{12}$
13. 4 **15.** $2\frac{2}{9}$ **19.** $1\frac{1}{25}$ **23.** $4.55 **25.** 30 books
31. 2×7^2

Lesson 6-5   pp. 284–285

EXERCISES 1. Answers may vary. Sample: Let
$b = 8$. Since $\frac{8}{4} = 2$, b must be greater than 8.
3. $\frac{5}{2}$ **5.** 44 **7.** 10 **9.** 56 **11.** 45 **23.** $4\frac{1}{6}$
27. $\frac{d}{12} = 14\frac{1}{2}$; 174 mi **29.** 4 **33.** $2\frac{1}{4}$

Lesson 6-6   pp. 290–291

EXERCISES 3. cups

5–13. Answers may vary. Samples are given.

5. Feet; lots are usually measured in feet.
9. Pounds; one orange weighs less than a pound,
so a bag of oranges would weigh more than a
pound. **13.** Fluid ounces; a sample size bottle of
shampoo holds less than a cup. **19.** <
23. 960 grains **27.** 1 h 59 min

Lesson 6-7 — pp. 294–295

EXERCISES

1. 3 ft

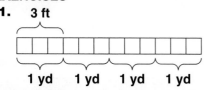

1 yd 1 yd 1 yd 1 yd

3. divide **5.** false; 6 ft = 2 yd **7.** false;
$2\frac{1}{2}$ t = 5,000 lb **9.** 15,840 **11.** 9 **21.** 11 gal
27. > **31.** Yes. You have 192 cups of punch and
you need 180. **35.** A: $5\frac{1}{2}$ lb; B: 9 lb; C: 15 lb
39. $5\frac{3}{14}$

Chapter Review — pp. 298–299

1. 12 **2.** 12 **3.** 80 **4.** 84 **5.** $\frac{3}{10}$ **6.** $\frac{2}{39}$ **7.** $\frac{2}{5}$
8. 15 **9.** $17\frac{1}{2}$ **10.** $3\frac{7}{8}$ **11.** $6\frac{14}{15}$ **12.** $20\frac{15}{22}$
13. $\frac{1}{3}$ c **14.** 16 **15.** $5\frac{2}{3}$ **16.** $\frac{5}{11}$ **17.** $\frac{8}{9}$ **18.** $1\frac{3}{7}$
19. $\frac{2}{25}$ **20.** $4\frac{17}{52}$ **21.** $12\frac{3}{7}$ **22.** 20 buckets
23. 1; $\frac{33}{35}$ **24.** 3; $2\frac{76}{105}$ **25.** 3; $3\frac{51}{112}$ **26.** 2; $1\frac{11}{13}$
27. about 19 appointments **28.** 96 **29.** 25 **30.** 2
31. $\frac{3}{4}$ **32.** 4 **33.** 2 **34.** $7\frac{1}{5}$ **35.** $\frac{13}{50}$ **36.** tons
37. fluid ounces **38.** $73\frac{1}{3}$ **39.** 40 **40.** 6
41. 150 ft

Chapter 7

Lesson 7-1 — pp. 308–309

EXERCISES 1. $\frac{9}{5}$ is a comparison of two numbers
by division; $1\frac{4}{5}$ is not. **3.** D **5.** C
7. 35 to 24, 35 : 24, $\frac{35}{24}$ **11.** $\frac{2}{7}$, $\frac{16}{56}$, $\frac{28}{98}$ **15.** 4 : 3
17. $\frac{1}{3}$ **23.** 2 **25.** 64 **29.** 5 : 7 **31.** Yes; 14 to 20 is
equivalent to $\frac{7}{10}$. **33.** 1 : 2 **37.** $\frac{6}{35}$

Lesson 7-2 — pp. 314–315

EXERCISES 1. $\frac{12 \text{ inches}}{1 \text{ foot}}$ is a unit rate because it
has 1 in the denominator. **3.** C **5.** D **7.** 23 desks
per classroom **11.** 15¢ per oz; 16¢ per oz; 16 oz
for $2.39 **19.** 208 words in 8 min **21.** 132 points
in 12 games **23.** About 28.6 miles per gallon;
answers may vary. Sample: I divided 279.9 by 9.8.
25. 0.15 mi/s

Lesson 7-3 — pp. 318–319

EXERCISES 1. The cross products are equal.
3. Answers may vary. Sample: $\frac{2}{5}$, $\frac{4}{10}$, $\frac{24}{60}$ **5.** yes
7. no **25.** yes **29.** no **31.** No; answers may vary.
Sample: If two ratios are equivalent, a third ratio
must be equivalent to both of them or neither of
them. **37.** $1\frac{8}{9}$

Lesson 7-4 — pp. 322–324

EXERCISES 1. Answers may vary. Sample: You
could determine whether their cross products are
equal or put each ratio in simplest form and see if
they are equivalent. **7.** 84 **9.** 5 **25.** 33 in.
27. $6.40 **31.** 16 teachers **33.** x = 2; y = 21
37. 5

Lesson 7-5 — pp. 328–329

EXERCISES 1. One inch on the map represents
an actual distance of 50 miles. **3.** approximate;
Explanations may vary. Sample: It's very difficult
to get exact measurements using a ruler.
5. 1 ft : 20 ft **7.** 47 mi **11.** 4 in. **17.** 1.25 cm
19. 1.7 cm **21 a.** Reduce. The map is 4 cm wide
and 3 cm high. For each centimeter on the map, I
would draw 0.5 centimeter on my drawing. My
drawing would measure 2 cm wide and 1.5 cm
high.
b.

27. $7\frac{1}{2}$

Lesson 7-6 — pp. 332–334

EXERCISES 1. The ratio does not compare a
number to 100. **3.** Answers may vary. Samples: $\frac{5}{6}$
and 0.85. **5.** $\frac{7}{10}$ **7.** $\frac{1}{20}$ **15.** 0.15 **17.** 0.82
27. 8% **31.** 95% **33.** 25% **39.** C
43. $\frac{1}{5}$, 22%, 0.24, $\frac{1}{4}$ **45.** $\frac{17}{20}$, $\frac{22}{25}$, 0.9, 95%
49. 75% **51.** 25%

Lesson 7-7
pp. 338–339

EXERCISES 1. 5 **3.** 3 **5.** 30 **7.** 16.8 **9.** 66
19. 36 **25.** 6 **27.** 152 **29.** No; 50% off is half the
price. The 10%-off coupon is applied to a price
that is less than $60. **31.** $120 **35.** Store B has a
better rate; $\frac{2}{3}$ is equal to $66\frac{2}{3}$%, which is greater
than 60%. **39.** $\frac{2}{5}$

Lesson 7-8
pp. 342–344

EXERCISES 1. whole **3.** The sum of the
fractions is not 1. **5.** basketball
9.   **13.**

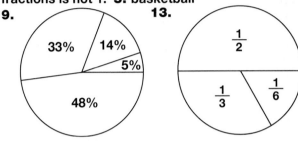

19. $57.05 **23.** $1\frac{1}{2}$

Lesson 7-9
pp. 350–351

EXERCISES 1. about $55 **3.** $20 × 0.09
5. $40 × 0.05 **7.** $1.96, $29.96 **11.** $6.30
15. $24 **23.** 36, underestimate **25.** $31.85
27. Florida: $3.90, $68.90 Georgia: $2.60, $67.60
Massachusetts: $3.25, $68.25 Tennessee: $4.55,
$69.55 **29.** 5 ft 6 in. **33.** 75

Chapter Review
pp. 354–355

1. B **2.** D **3.** C **4.** A **5.** 15 to 23, 15 : 23, $\frac{15}{23}$
6. 15 to 8, 15 : 8, $\frac{15}{8}$ **7.** 23 to 8, 23 : 8, $\frac{23}{8}$
8. 15 to 46, 15 : 46, $\frac{15}{46}$ **9.** 1 to 4 **10.** $\frac{3}{5}$
11. 3 ft : 1 yd **12.** $\frac{5 \text{ boys}}{6 \text{ girls}}$ **13.** 40 min
14. $12.50 **15.** $.10 per oz, $.06 per oz, A 24-oz
loaf is the better buy. **16.** no **17.** yes **18.** yes
19. no **20.** 354 marbles **21.** 99 ft **22.** 148.5 in.
23. 132 in. **24.** $\frac{3}{10}$, 0.3 **25.** $\frac{1}{4}$, 0.25
26. $\frac{14}{25}$, 0.56 **27.** $\frac{3}{25}$, 0.12 **28.** 60 students
29. 60%

30.

Favorite Types
of Books

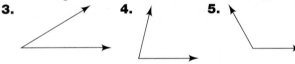

Fiction
55%

Humor
10%

Biographies
13%

Mysteries
22%

31. 10 **32.** $1.20 **33.** $6.00

Chapter 8

Lesson 8-1
pp. 364–365

EXERCISES 1. C **3.** A **5.** C **7.** $\overrightarrow{KJ}$ **9.** $\overrightarrow{QP}$
17. always **23.** Answers may vary. Sample: $\overline{DH}$
29. 7

Lesson 8-2
pp. 370–371

EXERCISES 1. A right angle measures 90°; an
obtuse angle measures between 90° and 180°.
3.   **4.**   **5.**

7. 60° **9.** acute **13.** obtuse **21.** 20° **25.** acute
29. 165°

Lesson 8-3
pp. 376–377

EXERCISES 1. Complementary angles have a
sum of 90°; supplementary angles add to 180°.
3. C **5.** B **7.** 45° **11.** 90° **15.** 62° **21.** never
23. 20° **25.** An obtuse angle does not have a
complement. **29.** 5

Lesson 8-4
pp. 382–383

EXERCISES 1. right, scalene **3.** acute, scalene
5. right **9.** 65° **11.** scalene **15.** scalene
19. right **21.** right; right
25. $3x = 180$ or
 $x + x + x = 180$
27. $180° - 2x$ **31.** 50 people

Lesson 8-5 — pp. 389–390

EXERCISES 1. All four sides will be congruent.
5. decagon **7.** irregular **11.** rectangle, parallelogram **13.** 14°

17. 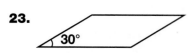 **19.**

23.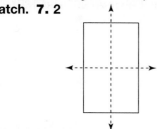

30°

25. All **27.** All **31.** 36%

Lesson 8-6 — pp. 394–395

EXERCISES 1. congruent **3.** A **5.** B **7.** no
9. no **13.** 63° **17a.** ∠MNO and ∠PQR,
∠MON and ∠PRQ,
∠OMN and ∠RPQ

b. 3 : 4 : 5 = 12 : 16 : 20 **19.** 149 **21.** 4, 5

Lesson 8-7 — pp. 399–401

EXERCISES 1. yes **5.** No; the two sides do not match. **7.** 2

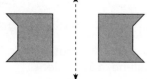

11. no **15.** 3
23. Answers may vary. Sample: $\overrightarrow{AC}, \overrightarrow{BC}, \overrightarrow{AD}$

Lesson 8-8 — pp. 404–405

EXERCISES 1. C **3.** B **5.** no
10.

11. no **17.** Answers may vary. Sample:

19. Answers may vary. Sample: directly left, directly right, up and slightly to the right
21. reflection or 180° rotation **27.** $9\frac{1}{9}$

Chapter Review — pp. 408–409

1. obtuse **2.** equilateral **3.** perpendicular
4. rectangle **5.** line **6.** Answers may vary.
Sample: $\overleftrightarrow{EF}$ and $\overrightarrow{AB}$ **7.** Answers may vary.
Sample: $\overrightarrow{BC}, \overrightarrow{BA}$ **8.** ∠DEG and ∠BEF **9.** ∠FEG
10. ∠ABE and ∠EBC **11.** ∠DEG **12.** rectangle
13. hexagon **14.** pentagon **15.** similar
16. congruent **17.** Answers may vary. Sample:

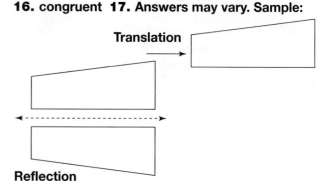

Translation

Reflection

Chapter 9

Lesson 9-1 — pp. 418–419

EXERCISES 1a. mass **3.** Answers may vary.
Sample: pencil, finger **5.** true **7.** false;
1 L = 1,000 mL **9.** meters **11.** centimeters
15. grams **17.** kilograms **21.** liters
23. kiloliters **29.** 0.001 **33.** No; a ladybug would be measured in grams or milligrams. **35.** Less;
8 × 12 = 96, so 96 cm < 1 m. **41.** 46°; 136°

Lesson 9-2 — pp. 423–424

EXERCISES 1. 5 m; 5 m = 5,000 mm **3.** divide
5. divide **7.** 600,000 cm **9.** 20,000,000 cm
15. 3.07 **17.** 610 **25.** about 299,792.458 km (or about 300,000 km) **27.** 7 g **29.** 340 m
35. 519 m **41.** right isosceles triangle

Lesson 9-3 — pp. 429–430

EXERCISES 1. Perimeter is the distance around a figure. Area is the two-dimensional space the figure takes up. **3.** $P = 26$ ft, $A = 36$ ft^2
5. $P = 38$ in., $A = 84$ in.^{2}
7. $P = 44$ in., $A = 117$ in.^{2} **15.** 25 m^2

19. There are 3 ft × 3 ft, or 9 ft², in 1 yd².

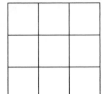

21. $P = 70$ mm; $A = 294$ mm² **23.** 84 ft²

Lesson 9-4	pp. 434–435

EXERCISES 1. The height of a triangle is the length of the perpendicular segment from a vertex to the base opposite that vertex. **3.** The triangle's area is half of the rectangle's area. **5.** 16 m²
7. 31.5 m² **11.** 10 ft² **15.** 157.5 in.²
17. 220.5 ft² **19.** 13.2 in. **21.** 6 ft **25.** 246

Lesson 9-5	pp. 440–441

EXERCISES 1. Yes; a chord that does not pass through the center is not a diameter.
3. $\overline{QR}, \overline{QS}, \overline{QT}$ **7.** 70 mi **13.** 15.7 in.
15. 87.92 mi **19.** 30.6 ft **25.** about 6.3 ft **29.** 7.5

Lesson 9-6	pp. 446–447

EXERCISES 1. 616 cm² **3.** 12 in.² **5.** 1,200 cm²
7. 200.96 mm² **11.** 379.94 yd² **13.** $17\frac{1}{9}$ mm²
19. 4.5 cm² **23.** 38.28 ft² **25.** 30.96 cm²
29. When the diameter is tripled, the area becomes 9 times greater.
33. four

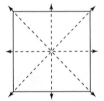

Lesson 9-7	pp. 451–452

EXERCISES 1. Answers may vary. Sample: They are both three-dimensional shapes. A prism has two parallel and congruent bases, but a pyramid has only one base. **3.** cone **5.** cylinder
7. hexagonal prism **9.** pentagonal prism
13. pyramid **17.** trapezoidal prism; 6 faces, 8 vertices, 12 edges
19. Answers may vary. Sample:

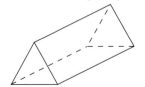

Lesson 9-8	pp. 454–456

EXERCISES 1. A net lets you see a 3-dimensional object in 2 dimensions. **3.** 24 cm²
5.

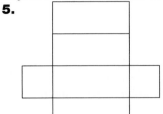

7. 78 cm² **9.** 216 ft² **17.** 3 in. **19.** 243.8 in.²
21. 4 times larger; 9 times larger; 16 times larger
27. milliliters

Lesson 9-9	pp. 459–460

EXERCISES 1. Volume is the measure of an object's capacity. Area is the measure of the number of square units on the surface of the figure. **3.** 264 m³ **5.** 192 cubic units **9.** 5,940 m³
13. Answers may vary. Sample: 5 feet by 4 feet by 4 feet **15.** 480,000 bottles **19.** 36 ft²

Lesson 9-10	pp. 464–466

EXERCISES 1. $2\pi r^2$ represents the area of the two circular bases and $C \times h$ represents the area of the rectangle; their sum represents the total surface area. **3.** 200.48 in.² **5.** 351.68 cm²
9. 706.5 m³ **15.** 71.3 cm²; 44.2 cm³
17. 824.06 cm³ **21.** 2,574,466.7 m³

Chapter Review	pp. 468–469

1. faces **2.** pyramid or cone **3.** radius **4.** 300
5. 1.5 **6.** 5.7 **7.** 30 ft; 48 ft² **8.** 68.9 m; 187.72 m²
9. 64 in.; 240 in.² **10.** $\overline{XV}, \overline{YW}, \overline{VW}$ **11.** $\overline{XV}$
12. $\overline{OV}, \overline{OX}, \overline{OY}$ **13.** 31.4 in. **14.** 79 in.²
15. triangular prism **16.** rectangular pyramid
17. cylinder **18.** 40 in.²; 16 in.³ **19.** 122 m²; 84 m³ **20.** 715.92 ft²; 1,469.52 ft³

Chapter 10

Lesson 10-1	pp. 479–480

EXERCISES 1. sample space **3.** Answers may vary. Sample: You can use the counting principle to multiply 5×6 and find 30 different ways.

5. 9 outcomes

7. Flip 1   Flip 2 4 outcomes

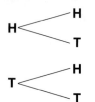

9. 8 outcomes **13.** 6 colors **15.** 500 four-digit numbers **17.** tons

Lesson 10-2	pp. 484–486

EXERCISES 1. The sum of the probability of an event and the probability of its complement always equals 1. **5.** B **7.** $\frac{4}{10}$ or $\frac{2}{5}$ **13.** 0.2 **19.** $\frac{2}{6}$ or $\frac{1}{3}$ **21.** $\frac{3}{6}$ or $\frac{1}{2}$ **23.** Answers may vary. Sample: 0.55 **25.** Answers may vary. Sample: 0.65 **27.** $\frac{3}{4}$ **33.** $5\frac{2}{3}$

Lesson 10-3	pp. 490–491

EXERCISES 1. Experimental probability is found by conducting an experiment. **3.** $\frac{20}{50}$ or $\frac{2}{5}$ **5.** $\frac{8}{50}$ or $\frac{4}{25}$ **7.** $\frac{7}{15}$ **9.** 0 **11.** No; the experimental probability of rolling an even number is $\frac{27}{80}$. **15.** $\frac{2}{3}$ **23.** $\frac{13}{20}$; $\frac{7}{20}$ **25.** 24 in.² **29.** congruent

Lesson 10-4	pp. 495–497

EXERCISES 1. A sample is a part of a population. **3.** B **5.** 2 **7.** 6 **13.** 450 pairs of socks **19.** 4,650 gadgets **21.** $\frac{16}{20}$ or $\frac{4}{5}$ **23.** 48 red marbles **27.** 10.5

Lesson 10-5	pp. 502–503

EXERCISES 1. are **5.** Independent; none of the rolls has an effect on another. **7.** $\frac{9}{100}$ **9.** $\frac{25}{100}$ or $\frac{1}{4}$ **13.** $\frac{1}{8}$ **19.** $\frac{1}{48}$ **21.** $\frac{1}{4}$ **23.** Yes; the first spin has no effect on the second spin. **25.** $\frac{1}{2}$ **29.** 48 cm³

Chapter Review	pp. 508–509

1. C **2.** B **3.** A **4.** D **5.** 24 ways **6.** $\frac{1}{6}$ **7.** $\frac{3}{6}$ or $\frac{1}{2}$ **8.** $\frac{2}{6}$ or $\frac{1}{3}$ **9.** Kayla: $\frac{1}{3}$; Noel: $\frac{2}{3}$ **10.** $\frac{1}{4}$ **11.** $\frac{1}{3}$ **12.** $\frac{7}{12}$ **13.** 2,200 defective computers

14. Check students' work. **15.** Independent; the first roll does not affect the fourth roll. **16.** Not independent; after drawing the first cube, there is one cube fewer in the bag. **17.** $\frac{9}{81}$ or $\frac{1}{9}$ **18.** $\frac{6}{81}$ or $\frac{2}{27}$ **19.** $\frac{8}{81}$

Chapter 11

Lesson 11-1	pp. 517–519

EXERCISES 1. Answers may vary. Sample: Some integers are −1, 0, 1, 2, and 3; −5.7, 0.3, 2.92, and 10.5 are not integers. **3.** M **5.** P **7.** 100 **9.** −12 **13.** 10 **15.** −14 **21.** 38 **23.** 9 **31.** Janet **33.** −6 **35.** 5 **37.** −3; 3 **39.** −101; 101 **41.** negative **47.** Dudhsagar Falls

Lesson 11-2	pp. 521–522

EXERCISES 1. C **5.** < **7.** < **17.** −5, −2, 0, 2, 5 **21.** −62°F, −54°F, −34°F, −22°F, 85°F, 86°F, 90°F, 96°F

23. 9 **25 a.** < **b.** > **29.** 15 yd²

Lesson 11-3	pp. 526–527

EXERCISES 1. always **3.** sometimes **5.** −8 **7.** −4 **13.** −3 **15.** −47 **25.** 45°F **27.** −3 **32.** Placement of numbers may vary. Sample:

3	−4	1
−2	0	2
−1	4	−3

37. $\overline{CF}$, $\overline{DG}$, $\overline{EH}$

Lesson 11-4	pp. 532–533

EXERCISES 1. −3 − (−2) **3.** −10 + (−3) **5.** −1 + 3 **7.** 9 **9.** −7 **13.** −5 **15.** −16 **23.** −1,250 ft **25.** −43 **27.** 26 **29.** Answers may vary. Sample: 3 − 7 = −4, 7 − 3 = 4, −4 ≠ 4. **33.** Answers may vary. Sample: $\overrightarrow{AB}$, $\overrightarrow{DC}$, $\overrightarrow{DE}$

Lesson 11-5   pp. 536–537

EXERCISES 1. Start at 0. Make 5 groups of −2 on the number line. **3.** negative **5.** negative **7.** 8 **9.** −8 **13.** −22 **15.** 54 **25.** 144 **27.** −126 **29.** −940 **31.** −3; 1 − 2 + 3 − 4 × 5 − 6 **35.** 318 m²

Lesson 11-6   pp. 541–542

EXERCISES 1. Zarita; the quotient of 2 negative numbers is always positive. **3.** −2°/hour **5.** negative **7.** 8 **9.** 6 **15.** 18 stairs/min **19.** −$6/day **21.** Yes; fresh water evaporates at 125 mL/day. Salt water evaporates at 120 mL/day. **25.** 40°; 130°

Lesson 11-7   pp. 544–545

EXERCISES 3. 4 min **5.** B **7.** C **9.** −3 **11.** −5 **23.** $80 **25.** 5 hours **29.** 64

Lesson 11-8   pp. 550–551

EXERCISES 1. Answers may vary. Sample: The first coordinate tells how far to move left or right. The second coordinate tells how far to move up or down. **3.** B **5.** (−1, 1) **9.** *P* **19.** (2, −1) **23.** III **25.** *y*-axis **27.** *x*-axis **29.** *x*-axis **31.** (−3, 0) **33a.** Africa **b.** Europe **35.** (−1, 2), (7, 2), (5, 8)

Lesson 11-9   pp. 555–557

EXERCISES 1a. negative **b.** positive **c.** negative **d.** positive **3.** −$2,256 **7.** Monday: $9; Tuesday: $18; Wednesday: −$9; Thursday: $17; Friday: −$12; Saturday: −$1 **11.** 120 bottles **15.** 30 **17.** Weeks 1 and 3

19.

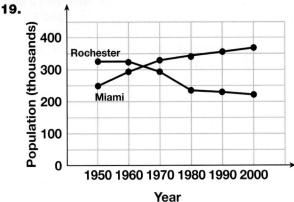

21. Rochester **25.** obtuse **27.** right

Lesson 11-10   pp. 561–562

EXERCISES 1. *x* **3.** multiply **5.** −1; 12; 35

7.

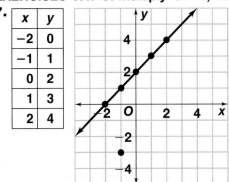

x	y
−2	0
−1	1
0	2
1	3
2	4

9.

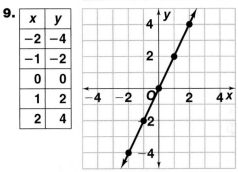

x	y
−2	−4
−1	−2
0	0
1	2
2	4

17. 5; 6; divide by 5. **19.** Linear; the graph is a line. **21.** Not linear; the graph is not a line. **25.** 9:00 A.M.

Chapter Review   pp. 564–565

1. function **2.** integers **3.** quadrants **4.** opposites **5.** −14 **6.** > **7.** < **8.** < **9.** > **10.** −2, −1, 1, 2 **11.** −6, −4, 0, 5 **12.** −7, −3, 5, 9 **13.** 11 **14.** −4 **15.** −2 **16.** −13 **17.** 8 **18.** 8 **19.** −11 **20.** −8 **21.** 36 **22.** −21 **23.** −10 **24.** 48 **25.** 4 **26.** −5 **27.** 7 **28.** −4 **29.** −15 **30.** −9 **31.** −4 **32.** −36 **33–36.**

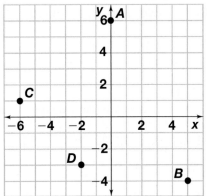

37. $26,286 **38.** profit

39.

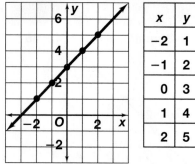

x	y
-2	1
-1	2
0	3
1	4
2	5

40.

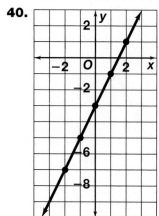

x	y
-2	-7
-1	-5
0	-3
1	-1
2	1

41.

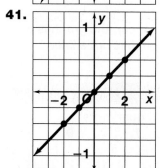

x	y
-2	-0.5
-1	-0.25
0	0
1	0.25
2	0.5

Chapter 12

Lesson 12-1 pp. 574–576

EXERCISES 1. two-step **3.** two-step
5. $2b + 4 = 12$;
$\quad 2b + 4 - 4 = 12 - 4$;
$\quad 2b \div 2 = 8 \div 2$;
$\quad b = 4$

7. -5 **9.** 8 **19.** 5
21. 5 **25.** The error is dividing by 5 instead of multiplying by 5. **27.** A; $2,000 **29.** Rule: Multiply by 2 and then add 3. 19; 33 **31.** $9\frac{1}{3}$ **35.** $\frac{1}{4}$ in.

Lesson 12-2 pp. 580–581

EXERCISES 1. solutions **3.** $x < -1$ **5.** $\ell > 15$
7. $p \le 4$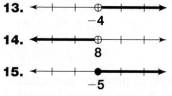

13. true **15.** true
19.

Lesson 12-3 pp. 583–584

EXERCISES 1. addition **3.** subtraction
5. $c \le 10$ **7.** $z < 5$ **9.** $j > -7$
21. $a + 2,500 < 32,000$;
$\quad a < 29,500$ ft
27. rectangular prism

Lesson 12-4 pp. 589–590

EXERCISES 1. Yes. $\sqrt{4} = 2$; 2 is an integer, and integers are rational numbers. **3.** 2.6 **5.** 1 **7.** 9
13. 4.6 **15.** 7.1 **19.** rational **21.** rational **31.** 2
33. 3 **35.** Yes; no; explanations may vary. Sample: Since $\sqrt{1} = 1$, $\sqrt{2}$ must be greater than 1. Since $\sqrt{4} = 2$, $\sqrt{2}$ must be less than 2.
37. 230 m **45.** 12.6 ft^2

Lesson 12-5 pp. 593–594

EXERCISES 1. It is the longest side and opposite the right angle. **3.** yes; $5^2 + 12^2 = 13^2$ **5.** 30
7. 5 **17.** 26 in. **19.** $r^2 + s^2 = t^2$ **23.** 0

Chapter Review pp. 598–599

1. E **2.** D **3.** B **4.** F **5.** A **6.** 3 **7.** 1 **8.** 125
9. no **10.** yes **11.** no **12.** yes
13.

14.

15.

16.

17. $q < 3$ **18.** $t < 5$ **19.** $v > 16$ **20.** $y \ge -20$
21. 9 **22.** 4.9 **23.** 5.5 **24.** 12 **25.** between 2 and 3 **26.** between 3 and 4 **27.** between 4 and 5
28. between 5 and 6 **29.** rational **30.** not rational **31.** rational **32.** rational **33.** 10 **34.** 8
35. 2.2 **36.** 5.3 **37.** 132 in.

Index

Index

circumference of, 437, 439–441, 469, 470, 551
defined, 438, 469
diameter of, 437, 438, 439, 469, 527, 576
dividing, 342
exploring, 437
identifying parts of, 438
radius of, 438, 439, 441, 462, 469, 527, 576
segments of, 112
semicircle, 447

Circle graphs, 340–345, 355, 383, 401, 456

Circumference, 437, 439–441, 469, 470, 551

Classification
of angles, 368, 370, 380–383
of polygons, 386–390, 414
of quadrilaterals, 388, 409
of triangles, 380–383, 391, 392, 409, 414, 424

Clockwise rotation, 403, 404

Common denominator. *See* Least common denominator (LCD)

Common factor. *See* Factor(s)

Common multiple, 188, 205

Communication. *See* Error Analysis; Reasoning; Vocabulary; Writing in Math

Commutative Property
of Addition, 12, 13, 52, 126, 144, 148
of Multiplication, 13, 52, 126

Comparing
area, 431
decimals, 26–30, 156
equations and expressions, 138, 558
fractions, 192–195, 266, 288, 292, 304, 316, 514, 520
integers, 520–522, 564, 570, 578
mixed numbers, 193
standard form and expanded form, 22
symbols for, 5
unit price, 313, 314
whole numbers, 5

Compass, 370, 372, 373

Compatible numbers, 9, 10, 38, 52, 212

Complement of an event, 483–484, 485

Complementary angles, 374–377, 380, 409, 410, 419, 542

Complex figures, area of, 433, 434, 435

Composite numbers, 166–167, 169, 204

Compound event, 501, 509

Computer(s)
exercises, 7, 509
geometry software, 379
spreadsheets, 80–83, 85, 101, 498
See also Technology

Concept maps, 425

Cone, 450, 451

Congruent angles, 375, 392, 409

Congruent figures, 392–395
corresponding parts in, 392

defined, 392, 409
identifying, 392, 394–395

Congruent rectangles, 398

Congruent triangles, 392, 395, 409

Conjecture, 108, 150, 379, 385

Connections. *See* Interdisciplinary Connections; Real-World Applications

Connections to math strands. *See* Algebra; Data Analysis; Geometry; Measurement; Pattern(s); Probability

Constant rate of change, 108, 109, 110, 111, 112, 115, 123, 152

Construction
of angle bisectors, 373
of angles, 368, 371
of circle graphs, 383
of perpendicular bisectors, 372

Conversions
of decimals to fractions, 198, 200
of decimals to percents, 332, 333, 482
of fractions to decimals, 199, 200, 201, 474
of fractions to percents, 332, 333, 474, 482
of improper fractions to mixed numbers, 183, 187, 205, 210, 218, 228
to larger units, 293–295, 422, 423
of mixed numbers to improper fractions, 182, 184, 185, 187, 205, 233, 266, 267–269
of percents to decimals, 331, 333–334, 352, 355
of percents to fractions, 331, 333–334, 355
of ratios as percents, 341, 343
to smaller units, 292, 294, 421, 423–424
of units in customary system, 292–295, 414
of units in metric system, 421–424, 436

Coordinate
map, 549, 550, 551
naming, 548, 552
x-coordinate, 548, 553
y-coordinate, 548, 553

Coordinate plane, 363, 566
defined, 548, 565
graphing points on, 547, 548–551, 565
reflections in, 553
x-axis, 548, 553, 565
y-axis, 548, 553, 565

Corresponding parts, 392

Cost, estimating, 348

Counting Principle, 477, 478, 479, 508

Critical thinking. *See* Reasoning

Cross-curriculum exercises. *See* Interdisciplinary Connections

Cross products
defined, 317
solving proportions using, 321, 336
using, 317

Cube(s), 449, 450
surface area of, 454
volume of, 163, 165, 459

Cubic unit, 458

Cumulative Reviews. *See* Assessment, Test Prep Cumulative Review

Customary system of measurement
for capacity (volume), 288, 289, 290, 414, 416, 421
choosing appropriate units of measure in, 289, 299, 414, 416
conversions in, 292–295, 414
for length, 288, 289, 290, 291, 296, 414, 416
for weight (mass), 288, 289, 290, 291, 414, 416, 417, 418, 419, 421, 422, 424

Cylinder(s), 451
defined, 450, 461
exploring, 461
surface area of, 462–465
volume of, 464–466, 469

D

Data
analyzing. *See* Data Analysis
interpreting, 507, 539
making predictions from, 494–497
organizing in spreadsheet, 80–83, 85, 101

Data Analysis
Applying Inequalities, 585
bar graph, 74, 76–79, 94–96, 98, 101, 507, 539, 585
circle graph, 340–344, 383
Conducting a Survey, 97, 202, 401
frequency table, 70, 72, 73, 88, 100
histogram, 77
line graph, 75–77, 79, 101, 395, 555
mean, median, and mode, 60–70, 86, 93, 95, 96, 98, 99, 100, 101, 365, 441
misleading graphs and statistics, 93–96
Reading a Table, 48
Reporting Survey Results, 345
spreadsheet, 80–84, 85, 101
stem-and-leaf plot, 86–90, 98, 99, 101, 102, 405
Using Decimals, 48
Using Pictographs, 239
See also Statistics; Table(s)

Data Collection, 64, 77, 90, 97, 202, 343, 345, 437, 491, 492

Data Updates. *See* Internet links

Decimal(s)
adding, 31, 32–35, 58, 106, 122
changing mixed numbers to, 232
comparing, 26–30, 156
dividing, 42, 44–47, 53, 58, 106, 156
estimating with, 30, 32–33, 34, 106, 210, 350, 441
modeling, 21, 26, 29, 31, 37, 38, 45, 46
multiplying, 37, 38–42, 53, 106, 438, 476

ordering, 26–30, 53, 58, 108, 156, 191, 362
place value and, 25, 28
repeating, 280
rounding, 8, 23, 32, 53, 210, 280
subtracting, 31, 33–35, 58, 106, 474
writing, 22–25, 156
writing as fractions, 198, 200
writing as percents, 332, 333, 482
writing fractions as, 199, 200, 201, 474
writing in expanded form, 23–25, 53
writing in standard form, 23–25, 53
writing percents as, 331, 352, 355
Decimal points, aligning, 32
Decision making. *See* Choose a Method
Deductive reasoning. *See* Reasoning
Degree, 367
Denominator. *See* Fraction(s)
Dependent event, 504
Diagonal, 390, 599
Diagrams
modeling with, 131, 367
for problem solving, 131, 286
tree, 477, 478, 479, 481, 487
Diameter, 527
circumference and, 437
defined, 438, 469
finding, 439, 576
Difference. *See* Subtraction
Direction words, 65, 128, 311, 384, 493
Discrete mathematics
counting principle, 477, 478, 479, 508
permutation, 481
tree diagram, 477, 478, 479, 481, 487
Distributive Property
defined, 144
using, 144–147, 151, 201, 348
Dividend, 44
Divisibility tests, 158–161, 166, 170, 204, 275
Divisible, 158, 166
Division
of decimals, 42, 44–47, 53, 58, 106, 156
estimating quotients, 276, 277, 278, 279, 298
of fractions, 271–275, 276, 298, 304
of integers, 540–542, 565
Mental Math for, 42
of mixed numbers, 276–279, 298
modeling, 45, 46, 271, 272
signs and, 540, 541, 542
solving equations using, 137–141, 258, 514
of whole numbers, 2, 641, 642
by zero, 138, 643
Division equations, solving, 138–141, 258, 282–285, 299, 514
Division ladder, 167, 172, 173
Division Property of Equality, 138, 151, 321
Divisor, 44
Double bar graph, 79

Draw a Picture or Diagram **Problem Solving Strategy,** xxxiv, 121, 131, 149, 178, 214, 230, 262, 263, 269, 274, 286, 294, 323, 333, 347, 389, 407, 429

E

Edge, 449
Elapsed time
calculating, 247, 253
defined, 246, 253
estimating, 247, 249
measuring, 246–250, 253, 291
Enrichment. *See* Challenge; Extension; Stretch Your Thinking
Equality
Addition Property of, 134, 151
Division Property of, 138, 151, 321
Multiplication Property of, 139, 151, 282, 317
properties of, to solve equations, 543, 565
Subtraction Property of, 131, 151, 582
understanding, 265
writing from number line, 579, 580
Equally likely outcomes, 482
Equation(s)
addition, 130–133, 142
comparing with expressions, 138, 558
defined, 124, 151
division, 138–141, 514
estimating solutions of, 125
multiplication, 138–141, 514
one-step. *See* One-step equations
solution of, 125, 151. *See also* Solving equations
subtraction, 134–136
two-step. *See* Two-step equations
writing to solve problems, lvii, 132, 136, 142–143, 284
Equilateral triangle, 381–383, 401, 409, 410
Equivalent fractions, 176–179, 192, 205, 210, 258, 261, 322
Equivalent ratios, 307, 354
Equivalent times, 246, 647
Error Analysis, 10, 15, 18, 34, 40, 135, 146, 219, 274, 278, 541, 575
Estimation
of area, 445, 446
circumference of a circle, 437
with compatible numbers, 9, 10, 38, 52
of cost, 348
with decimals, 30, 32–33, 34, 106, 210, 350, 441
of differences, 33, 111, 124, 213, 214, 226, 252
drawing pictures and, 214
of elapsed time, 247, 249
examples that use, 39, 125, 213, 228, 247, 277, 349
exercises that use, 10, 19, 20, 34, 50, 52, 53, 54, 111, 215, 225, 226, 227, 231, 249, 252, 254, 269, 278, 287, 298, 300,

315, 350, 351, 419, 441, 486, 566, 589, 590
with fractions, 213, 214, 228, 252
front-end, 32–33, 34, 53
of length using nonstandard units, 646
with mixed numbers, 213, 227, 228, 266, 276
with percents, 348–351, 355
of differences, 212–216
of probability, 486
of products, 39, 266, 267, 269, 298, 300
of quotients, 276, 277, 278, 279, 298
of radius, 441
of reasonable solution, 32, 33, 39, 41, 53, 125, 267, 277, 445, 446
by rounding, 8, 9, 10, 32, 125, 210
of sale price, 349
of sales tax, 348, 350, 351
of solutions to equations, 125
of sums, 32, 33, 111, 212–216, 226, 252
of tip, 349
using, 597
with whole numbers, 8–11
Evaluating
defined, 114, 150
expressions, 114–116, 118, 165, 264, 270, 274, 275, 344, 497, 558
Even number, 159, 499
Event
complement of, 483–484, 485
compound, 501, 509
defined, 476, 508
dependent, 504
independent, 500–503, 509
probability of, 476, 482–486, 500–503, 508. *See also* Probability
simulating, 490, 498, 509
Expanded form, 22–25, 53
Expenses, 554, 556, 565
Experimental probability, 492, 498
analyzing, 489
defined, 488, 509
finding, 488–491, 509, 581
formula for, 488, 509
trial, 488, 490
Exponents
defined, 162, 204
identifying, 426
using, 162–165, 204, 444
writing, 570, 587
Expressions
comparing with equations, 138, 558
defined, 16, 53
evaluating, 17, 18, 53, 114–116, 118, 165, 264, 270, 274, 275, 344, 497, 558
modeling, 117
numerical, 113, 150
patterns and, 112
simplifying, 44, 163, 164, 170, 426, 444
value of, 113, 162
variables and, 113–116, 150
writing using exponents, 587
See also Algebraic expressions

Index

Index

Index

equivalent units of, 246, 647
interpreting, 538
reading and using schedules, 189, 248, 249, 250
Real-World Applications, 161
units of, 246

Time zones, 250, 533
Timeline, 519
Transformations, 402–405, 410
Translation (slide), 402, 404, 405, 410, 452
Transversal, 378
Trapezoid, 181, 406, 419, 434
Tree diagram
    defined, 477
    using, 477, 478, 479, 481, 487
Trial, 488, 490
Triangle(s)
    acute, 380–383, 409, 410
    angles in, 379, 380–383, 576
    area of, 431, 433, 434, 435, 458, 468
    base of, 433, 434
    classifying, 380–383, 391, 392, 409, 414, 424
    congruent, 392, 395, 409
    equilateral, 381–383, 401, 409, 410
    height of, 433
    hypotenuse of, 591–592, 593, 594
    isosceles, 381–383, 401, 407, 409, 410
    legs of, 591–592, 593, 594, 599
    measures of angles in, 381
    obtuse, 380–383, 409, 410
    perimeter of, 468
    right. *See* Right triangle
    scalene, 381–383, 401, 409, 410
    similar, 393–395
Triangular prism, 449, 453
Triominoes, 382
Turn (rotation), 403, 404
Two-dimensional figures, 380–383, 386–390
Two-step equations
    defined, 572, 598
    solving, 572–576, 598

U

UNIT key, of fraction calculator, 237
Unit cost, 313, 314, 354
Unit rate
    defined, 312
    finding, 312–315
    using, 312–315, 320, 322
Units of measurement
    for capacity, 288, 289, 290, 414, 416, 417, 418, 419, 421, 422, 430
    changing, 414
    choosing, 289, 299, 414, 416–420
    converting, 292–295, 414, 421–424, 436
    for length, 288, 289, 290, 291, 414, 416–419, 420, 421, 422, 646
    for mass, 288, 289, 290, 291, 417, 418, 419, 421, 422, 424

metric. *See* Metric units
    for volume, 288, 289, 417, 418, 419, 420
    for weight, 288, 289, 290, 291, 414, 416, 421
    See also Customary system of measurement
Unlike denominators, 221, 222–225, 243

V

Value
    absolute. *See* Absolute value
    of expressions, 113, 162
    place, 4–5, 8, 25, 28, 636
    in sequences, 383
Variable(s)
    defined, 113, 150
    using, 113–116, 150, 240, 563, 579
Variable expressions. *See* Algebraic expressions
Vertex, 367, 449
Vertical angle, 375, 376, 409
Video Tutor Help Online, 32, 39, 67, 131, 159, 163, 222, 229, 272, 277, 306, 342, 368, 381, 483, 489, 531, 535, 592
Views, of three-dimensional figures, 448, 450
Visual thinking. *See* Spatial visualization
Vocabulary exercises, 6, 10, 14, 18, 63, 68, 72, 76, 81, 89, 110, 115, 126, 132, 140, 146, 160, 164, 168, 173, 178, 184, 190, 194, 214, 248, 274, 308, 314, 318, 328, 332, 342, 364, 370, 376, 382, 389, 394, 399, 404, 418, 429, 434, 440, 451, 454, 459, 479, 484, 490, 495, 502, 517, 550, 555, 561, 574, 580, 589, 593
    Key Vocabulary, 3, 59, 107, 157, 211, 259, 305, 361, 415, 475, 515, 571
    New Vocabulary, 4, 8, 12, 16, 22, 32, 61, 66, 70, 74, 80, 86, 108, 113, 124, 130, 134, 138, 144, 158, 162, 166, 171, 176, 182, 188, 192, 198, 212, 246, 272, 306, 312, 316, 326, 331, 341, 362, 367, 374, 380, 386, 392, 398, 402, 416, 426, 432, 438, 449, 453, 458, 476, 482, 488, 494, 500, 516, 548, 558, 572, 578, 587, 591
    Vocabulary Builder, 36, 55, 65, 103, 128, 153, 187, 207, 255, 301, 311, 357, 384, 411, 425, 471, 493, 511, 567
    Vocabulary Review, 4, 8, 12, 16, 22, 26, 32, 38, 44, 52, 61, 66, 70, 74, 80, 86, 93, 100, 108, 113, 118, 124, 130, 134, 138, 144, 150, 158, 162, 166, 171, 176, 182, 188, 192, 198, 204, 212, 217, 222, 228, 232, 240, 246, 252, 261, 266, 272, 276, 282, 288, 292, 298, 312, 316, 320, 326, 331, 336, 341, 348, 354, 362, 367, 374, 380, 386, 392, 398, 402, 408, 416, 421, 426, 432, 438, 444, 449, 453, 458, 462, 468, 476, 482, 494, 500, 508, 516, 520, 524, 530, 534, 540, 543, 548, 554, 558, 564, 572, 578, 582, 587, 591, 598
    Vocabulary Tips, 5, 8, 13, 44, 68, 74, 124, 126, 162, 185, 198, 212, 217, 262,

290, 292, 327, 337, 341, 362, 375, 403, 426, 438, 447, 449, 483, 486, 501, 530, 548, 559, 588
    High-Use Academic Words, 36, 65, 311, 384, 493
    Making Word Lists, 187
    Use Academic Words, 128
    Using Concept Maps, 425
Volume
    of cube, 163, 165, 459
    customary units of, 288
    of cylinder, 464–466, 469
    defined, 458, 469
    formulas for. *See* Formulas
    metric units of, 418, 466
    of prism, 457, 458–460, 469, 503
    of pyramid, 466
    units of measurement for, 288, 289, 417, 418, 419, 420
    See also Capacity

W

Wedges, 366
Weight
    customary units of, 288, 289, 290, 291
    metric units of, 417, 418, 419, 422, 424
Whole numbers
    adding, 2, 80, 253, 638
    comparing, 5
    dividing, 2, 641, 642
    divisibility of, 158, 160, 166
    estimating with, 8–11
    multiplying, 2, 12, 640, 641
    ordering, 5, 232
    place value of, 4–5, 8, 636
    renaming, 233
    rounding, 2, 32, 212, 637
    standard form of, 4
    subtracting, 2, 639
    writing as fractions, 313
    writing in words, 4
    See also Integers; Mixed numbers
Why Learn This?, 4, 8, 12, 16, 22, 26, 32, 38, 44, 61, 66, 70, 74, 80, 86, 93, 108, 113, 118, 124, 130, 134, 138, 144, 158, 162, 166, 171, 176, 182, 188, 192, 198, 212, 217, 222, 228, 232, 240, 246, 261, 266, 272, 276, 282, 288, 292, 306, 312, 316, 320, 326, 331, 336, 341, 348, 362, 367, 374, 380, 386, 392, 398, 402, 416, 421, 426, 432, 438, 444, 449, 453, 458, 462, 476, 482, 488, 494, 500, 516, 520, 524, 530, 534, 540, 543, 548, 554, 558, 572, 578, 582, 587, 591
Wilson, Blaine, 23
Word(s)
    academic, 36, 65, 128, 311, 384, 493
    direction, 65, 128, 311, 384, 493
Word knowledge, 36, 65, 128, 311, 384, 493
Word lists, 187
***Work Backward* Problem Solving Strategy,** xl, 353

X

Y

Z

Acknowledgments

Staff Credits

The people who make up the **Prentice Hall Math** team—representing design services, editorial, editorial services, educational technology, marketing, market research, photo research and art development, production services, publishing processes, and rights & permissions—are listed below. Bold type denotes core team members.

Dan Anderson, Carolyn Artin, Nick Blake, **Stephanie Bradley**, Kyla Brown, Patrick Culleton, Kathleen J. Dempsey, **Frederick Fellows**, **Suzanne Finn**, Paul Frisoli, Ellen Granter, **Richard Heater**, Betsy Krieble, Lisa LaVallee, Christine Lee, Kendra Lee, Cheryl Mahan, **Carolyn McGuire**, Eve Melnechuk, Terri Mitchell, Jeffrey Paulhus, Mark Roop-Kharasch, Marcy Rose, Rashid Ross, Irene Rubin, Siri Schwartzman, Vicky Shen, **Dennis Slattery**, Elaine Soares, Dan Tanguay, Tiffany Taylor, Mark Tricca, Paula Vergith, Kristin Winters, Helen Young

Additional Credits

Paul Astwood, Sarah J. Aubry, Jonathan Ashford, Peter Chipman, Patty Fagan, Tom Greene, Kevin Keane, Mary Landry, Jon Kier, Dan Pritchard, Sara Shelton, Jewel Simmons, Ted Smykal, Steve Thomas, Michael Torocsik, Maria Torti

TE Design

Susan Gerould/Perspectives

Illustration

Additional artwork: Rich McMahon; Ted Smykal

Kenneth Batelman: **186, 267, 257**
Joel Dubin: **263, 306**
John Edwards, Inc.: **307, 477**
Trevor Johnston: **264, 341, 342**
Precision Graphics: **77**
XNR Productions, Inc.: **249, 250, 285, 327, 328**
Wilkinson Studios: **289**

Photography

Front cover: Wolfgang Kaehler/CORBIS
Back cover: Ian Cartwright/Getty Images.

Title page: tl, Bob Daemmrich Photography; **tr,** Williamson Edwards/The Image Bank; **bl,** David Muench; **br,** Bob Daemmrich Photography.

Front matter: Page x, David Young-Wolff/PhotoEdit, Inc.; **xi,** STUDIO CARLO DANI/Animals Animals; **xii,** ThinkStock/SuperStock; **xiii,** Tony Freeman/Photo Edit; **xiv,** Faidley/Agliolo/International Stock/Grant Heilman Photography, Inc., **xv,** David Young-Wolff/Photo Edit, Inc.; **xvi,** AP Photo/The Grand Rapids Press, Lance Wynn; **xvii,** Raphael Gaillarde/Liaison/Getty Images, Inc.; **xviii,** Theo Allofs/Corbis; **xix,** Pearson Education; **xx,** 2004 Jay Wade, www.JayWade.com; **xxi,** AFP Photo/Don Emmert/Corbis; **xlviii & xlix,** Richard Haynes; **l,** PhotoEdit; **lii,** Bob Daemmrich/Stock Boston; **liii,** Getty Images; **liv,** Ryan McVay/Getty Images, Inc., **lv,** Owaki-Kulla/Corbis; **lvi,** Russell Illig/Getty Images, Inc., **lvii,** Michael Spingler/AP Wide World Photos

Chapter 1: Page 3, Andrew Leyerle/Dorling Kindersley; **4,** Prentice Hall School; **7,** www.SellPhotos.CA; **8,** Mary Kate Denny/PhotoEdit Inc.; **9,** Nancy Richmond/The Image Works; **11,** Stockdisc Classic/Getty Images; **12,** Mitch Kezar/Getty Images, Inc.; **13 bl,** Richard Haynes; **15,** Jonathan Nourok/PhotoEdit Inc.; **16,** Lori Adamski Peek/Getty Images, Inc.; **18,** John Moore; **19,** Nathan Benn/Corbis; **21 tr,** Richard Haynes; **22,** ©Syracuse Newspapers/Dick Blume/The Image Works; **23,** AP Photo/Tom Gannam; **24,** Royalty-Free/Getty Images, Inc. **26,** David Young-Wolff/PhotoEdit Inc.; **28 mr & bl,** Richard Haynes; **30 bl,** L. Clarke/Corbis; **31,** Richard Haynes; **32,** David Young-Wolff/PhotoEdit Inc.; **32 bl,** PictureQuest **33** Bob Daemmrich/The Image Works; **34,** Royalty-Free/Corbis; **36 tr,** Richard Haynes; **37,** Tony Freeman/PhotoEdit; **38,** Marc Romanelli/Alamy; **39 tl,** Richard Haynes; **42,** David Young-Wolff/PhotoEdit; **44,** Chad Slattery/Getty Images, Inc.; **45,** John Moore; **47,** Toyofumi Mori/Getty Images; **56 t,** The British Museum/Dorling Kindersley; **56 bl,** The Science Museum/Dorling Kindersley; **56 br,** Russ Lappa; **57 tl,** The Science Museum/Dorling Kindersley; **57 tr,** Steve Gorton/Dorling Kindersley; **57 br,** Alistair Duncan/Dorling Kindersley

Chapter 2: Page 59, Mark Newman/Alamy; **59 bl,** Gianni Dagli Orti/Corbis; **60,** Richard Haynes; **61,** Bob Daemmrich/Stock Boston; **62,** STUDIO CARLO DANI/Animals Animals; **64,** Gary Braasch/Getty Images, Inc.; **65,** Richard Haynes; **66,** Dick Blume/Syracuse Newspaper/The Image Works; **67,** Richard Haynes; **68,** RO-MA Stock/Omni-Photo Communications; **69,** Photo Courtesy of Adidas America, Public Relations Office; **71,** Craig Lovell/Corbis; **73,** Nancy Sheehan/PhotoEdit **77 t1,** AP/Wide World Photos; **77 t4,** Pascal Volery/Reuters/Corbis; **77 t2,** Eddie Adams/Getty Images, Inc.; **77 t3,** Homer Sykes/Woodfin Camp & Associates; **80,** ROB & SAS/Corbis; **82,** Bob Daemmrich/Stock Boston; **83,** Myrleen Ferguson Cate/Photo Edit; **85,** Jeff Greenberg/The Image Works; **86,** Mary Kate Denny/Photo Edit; **87,** Syracuse Newspapers/The Image Works; **88 tl & mr,** Richard Haynes; **89,** Jim Sugar/Getty Images; **93,** Jon Riley/Stone/Getty Images, Inc.; **94,** NBAE/Getty Images; **105 br,** David Robbins/Getty Images, Inc.

Chapter 3: Page 107, Vanessa Vick/Photo Researchers, Inc.; **108,** Michael Rosenfeld/Getty Images, Inc.; **110,** Gunter Marx Photography/Corbis; **110,** Russ Lappa; **111,** Jerry Lodriguss/Photo Researchers, Inc.; **112 tr,** Richard Haynes; **113,** Tom Prettyman/PhotoEdit; **114,** Index Stock Imagery, Inc.; **116,** ThinkStock/SuperStock; **118,** Getty Images; **120 tl,** Richard Haynes; **120 mr,** Richard Haynes; **122,** NASA; **124** Peter Beck/Corbis; **124,** Park Street/Photo Edit; **125,** Russ Lappa; **128 tr,** Richard Haynes; **129,** Richard Haynes; **131,** Image Source/SuperStock, Inc.; **131 bl,** Richard Haynes; **133,** National Geographic Society; **134,** David Young-Wolff/Photo Edit; **137,** Richard Haynes; **138,** Digital Vision/Getty Images; **140,** RubberBall Productions/IndexStock; **141,** Dianna Blell/Peter Arnold, Inc.; **144,** Spencer Grant/Photo Edit; **154–155 b,** Carlyn Iverson/Absolute Science; **154 tr,** Julian Baum/Dorling Kindersley; **154 ml,** R. P. Meleski; **155 t,** Grace Davies/Omni-Photo Communications, Inc.

Chapter 4: Page 157, Blair Seitz/Photo Researchers, Inc.; **158,** Scott Payne/FoodPix; **159 bl,** Wally McNamee/Corbis; **159 tl,** Richard Haynes; **160,** Prentice Hall; **161,** Bob Daemmrich/Photo Edit; **162,** Frank Zullo/Photo Researchers; **163 bl,** Richard Haynes; **164,** Terry W. Eggers; **165,** Prof. G. Schatten/ Science Photo Library/Photo Researchers, Inc.; **166,** Tom Carter/ PhotoEdit; **169,** Jeremy Horner/Corbis; **170,** Richard Haynes; **171,** Osterreichische Post AG; **172,** Rhoda Sidney/PhotoEdit; **173,** Steve Cole/Getty Images; **174,** Jeff Greenberg/PhotoEdit; **175 tr,** Richard Haynes; **177,** TSI Pictures/Getty Images, Inc.; **179,** David Young-Wolff/PhotoEdit; **181,** Richard Haynes; **182,** Mark Burnett/Stock Boston; **183,** Chris Salvo/Getty Images, Inc.; **183 mr,** Russ Lappa; **184,** Jeff Greenberg/Photo Edit; **186 bl,** Russ Lappa; **186 bc,** Russ Lappa; **186 br,** Russ Lappa; **186 tr,** Richard Haynes; **187 tr,** Richard Haynes; **188,** Tom Stewart/ Corbis; **189 mr,** Richard Haynes; **189 ml,** Russ Lappa; **191,** Tony Freeman/Photo Edit; **192,** David Young-Wolff/Photo Edit; **193,** Bloom Productions/Getty Images; **195,** Tim Ridley/DK Picture Library; **198,** Bill Miles/Corbis; **200,** Joseph D. Poellot/Index Stock; **201 t,** Alan Schein Photography/Corbis; **201 b,** Alan Schein Photography/Corbis; **208 tr,** Geoff Brightling/Dorling Kindersley; **208 br,** S. Wanke/Getty Images, Inc.; **209 t,** Dorling Kindersley; **209 br,** Richard Megna/Fundamental Photographs

Chapter 5: Page 211, Mark C. Burnett/Photo Researchers, Inc.; **212,** David Young-Wolff/PhotoEdit, Inc.; **214,** Adrian Sherratt/ Alamy; **214 m,** Russ Lappa; **215,** Russ Lappa; **216 tr,** Richard Haynes; **217,** Todd Powell/Index Stock; **218,** SuperStock; **220,** NIBSC/Science Photo Library-Photo Researchers, Inc.; **222 tr,** Spencer Grant/PhotoEdit; **222 ml,** Richard Haynes; **223,** Bob Daemmrich/Stock Boston; **225,** Faidley/Agliolo/International Stock/Grant Heilman Photography, Inc.; **226,** Dave Bartruff/ Corbis; **227 tr,** Richard Haynes; **228 mr,** Michael S. Yamashita/ Corbis; **228 bl,** Ronn Maratea/Image State; **229 tl,** Richard Haynes; **231,** Tony Freeman/PhotoEdit; **232,** Michael Rosenfeld/ Getty Images; **233,** Renee Lynn/Corbis; **234 tl & mr,** Richard Haynes; **236,** Tony Freeman/PhotoEdit; **238 mr,** John Moore; **238 br,** Richard Haynes; **240,** Adam Smith/Getty Images, Inc.; **243,** Frozen Images/The Image Works; **246,** Dave Bartruff/ Corbis; **248,** Royalty-Free/Corbis; **250,** Vicki Silbert/PhotoEdit; **256 ml,** AFP/Corbis; **256 tr,** Al Grillo/AP/Wide World Photos; **257 m,** Robert Laberge/Getty Images, Inc.; **257 br,** Jerome Delay/AP/Wide World Photos

Chapter 6: Page 259, Frank Siteman/IndexStock; **260,** Richard Haynes; **261,** age fotostock/SuperStock; **262,** Silver Burdett & Ginn/Pearson Education; **264,** Brian Parker/Tom Stack & Associates, Inc.; **266,** Guinness World Records, Ltd.; **268 tl,** Richard Haynes; **268 br,** Richard Haynes; **270,** John Moore; **271,** Richard Haynes; **272,** Dan McCoy/Rainbow; **272 bl,** Richard Haynes; **273,** Alan Linda Detrick/Grant Heilman Photography, Inc.; **275,** Prentice Hall; **277 tl,** Russ Lappa; **277 bl,** Richard Haynes; **279,** Ariel Skelley/Corbis; **281,** Richard Haynes; **282,** Richard Cummings/SuperStock; **284,** Joseph Nettis/Photo Researchers, Inc.; **289,** David Young-Wolff/Photo Edit, Inc.; **290,** Past /Project Exploration; **292,** Russ Lappa; **293,** Bettmann/ Corbis; **295,** AP/Wide World Photos; **296,** Richard Haynes; **302 tr,** James Muldowney/Getty Images, Inc.; **302 bl,** Annabelle Halls/Dorling Kindersley; **303 b,** Mike Powell/Getty Images, Inc.; **303 tm tl & tr,** James Jackson/Dorling Kindersley

Chapter 7: Page 317 tl, Jeffrey Sylvester/Getty Images, Inc.; **305** Mack Henley/Visuals Unlimited; **306 bl,** Richard Haynes; **308,** Russ Lappa; **309,** LWA-Dann Tardif/CORBIS; **310 tr,** Richard Haynes; **311 tr,** Richard Haynes; **312,** Michael Newman/ PhotoEdit; **315,** AP Photo/The Grand Rapids Press, Lance Wynn; **316,** SW Production/Index Stock Imagery, Inc.; **317,** Andersen/Ross/Brand X Pictures/Getty Images; **319,** Fotopic/ Omni-Photo Communications, Inc.; **320,** American Honda Motor Co., Inc.; **321,** Ken O'Donoghue; **322, ml & mr,** Richard Haynes; **324,** AP/Wide World Photos; **325 tr,** Richard Haynes; **326,** David Young-Wolff/PhotoEdit, Inc.; **330 tr,** Richard Haynes/PhotoEdit; **332,** David Hanover/Getty Images, Inc; **334,** The Academy of Natural Science/Corbis; **335,** SuperStock, Inc.; **336,** Dennis MacDonald/PhotoEdit; **340 tr,** Richard Haynes; **342 tl,** Richard Haynes; **351 & 352,** Russ Lappa; **358 tr,** Royal Tyrrell Museum/Alberta Community Development/Dorling Kindersley; **359 tl,** Jeffrey Sylvester/Getty Images, Inc.; **359 mr,** Andy Crawford/Dorling Kindersley; **359 br,** Prentice Hall; **359 m,** John Paul Endress/Silver Burdett Ginn/Pearson Education

Chapter 8: Page 361, Joseph Nettis/Photo Researchers, Inc.; **362,** Dennis Di Cicco/Peter Arnold, Inc.; **366 tr,** Richard Haynes; **367,** David Brooks/Corbis; **368 bl,** Richard Haynes; **369 tl,** Richard Haynes; **369 br,** Richard Haynes; **371,** Howie Garber/Animals Animals/Earth Scenes; **374,** Alvis Upitis/SuperStock; **375,** Peter Menzel/Stock Boston; **376,** ©Charles C. Benton; **377,** Corbis; **378 br,** Shadows & Light/The Image Works; **378 tr,** Richard Haynes; **380,** W. Cody/Corbis; **381 bl,** Richard Haynes; **382,** Russ Lappa **383,** Rob Crandall/Stock Boston; **384 & 385 tr,** Richard Haynes; **386 bl,** S. Wanke/PhotoDisc/Getty Images, Inc.; **386 bm,** Ryan McVay/Getty Images, Inc.; **386 br,** Russel Illig/Getty Images, Inc.; **390,** Raphael Gaillarde/Liaison/Getty Images, Inc.; **391,** AP/Wide World Photos; **392,** age fotostock/Superstock; **393,** AP/Wide World Photos; **398,** Corel Corporation; **400 ml,** Siede Preis/Getty Images, Inc.; **400 bl,** Andrew J. Martinez/Photo Researchers, Inc.; **400 br,** Rod Planck/Photo Researchers, Inc.; **402,** Corbis; **405 tl,** Dallas & John Heaton/Stock Boston; **405,** Russ Lappa; **406,** Richard Haynes; **412 tr,** Tony Freeman/ PhotoEdit; **412 bl,** Paul Barton/Corbis; **413 Bkgd,** David Jeffrey/ Getty Images, Inc.; **413 mr,** PhotoEdit; **413 tr,** Jim Hiss/Hispanic Business Inc.

Chapter 9: Page 415, Jeff Greenberg/Peter Arnold, Inc.; **416,** Ken O'Donoghue; **417 tl,** Russ Lappa; **417 ml,** Russ Lappa; **419,** Topham/The Image Works; **421,** Theo Allofs/Corbis; **422,** NASA/ Goddard Flight Center; **423,** Audrey Gibson/Gibson Stock Photography; **424,** Warren Bolster/Getty Images, Inc.; **425,** Richard Haynes; **426,** Evan Sklar/Botanica/PictureQuest; **428 mr & tl,** Richard Haynes; **429,** George McLean/ CardinalSpellman Philatelic Museum; **430,** Digital Vision/Getty Images; **431,** Richard Haynes; **432,** Tim Thompson/Getty Images, Inc.; **435,** Tony Hopewell/Getty Images, Inc.; **436,** Stephen Simpson/Getty Images, Inc.; **438,** L. Clarke/Corbis; **439,** Tony Freeman/PhotoEdit; **441,** Digital Vision/Getty Images, Inc.; **444,** Craig Aurness/Corbis; **445,** Russ Lappa; **446,** Photo Researchers, Inc.; **448 ml, mm, mr, & tr,** Russ Lappa; **449,** Royalty Free/ Corbis; **450,** Sara Karulwich/NYT Pictures; **451 ml,** Tony Freeman/PhotoEdit; **451 mr,** R. M. Arakaki/International Stock; **451 bl,** Tony Freeman/PhotoEdit; **451 br,** John Elk III/Stock Boston; **453,** Alan Klehr/Getty Images, Inc.; **457,** Richard Haynes; **458,** Zigmund Leszcynski/Animals Animals; **461,** Richard Haynes; **462,** David Young-Wolff/PhotoEdit, Inc.; **472–73 b,** Elfi Kluck/Index Stock Imagery, Inc.; **472 tr,** Kim Sayer/Dorling Kindersley; **472 ml,** Photo Courtesy of Northland College, Ashland, Wisconsin; **473 mr,** Neil Setchfield/Dorling Kindersley

Chapter 10: Page 475, Robert Llewellyn/ImageState/Alamy; **476,** Bob Daemmrich/The Image Works; **478 tl & br,** Richard Haynes; **480,** EyeWire/Getty Images, Inc.; **482,** Cleo Photography; **483,** Richard Haynes; **484,** David Young-Wolff/ PhotoEdit, Inc.; **487,** Courtesy of Milton Bradley Co.; **488,** Tony Di Zinno/See Jane Run; **489,** Richard Haynes; **491,** Corbis; **492 ml,** Pearson Education; **492 mr,** Pearson Education; **493,** Richard Haynes; **494,** Anthea Sieveking/Petit Format/Photo Researchers, Inc.; **495,** HARUYOSHI YAMAGUCHI/CORBIS SYGMA; **497,** Pearson Education; **499,** Richard Haynes; **501,** Randi Anglin/Syracuse Newspaper/The Image Works; **503,** Ken Ross/ Taxi/Getty Images, Inc.; **503,** Russ Lappa; **512 tr,** C Squared Studios/Getty Images, Inc.; **512 ml,** Al Francekevich/Corbis; **513,** MMI Flash! Light/Stock Boston

Chapter 11: Page 515, Science VU/Visuals Unlimited; **516,** Neal Preston/Corbis; **518,** Rene Frederick/Getty Images; **519,** Corbis; **520,** Tom Carter/PhotoEdit; **523,** Richard Haynes; **525,** Michael Yelman/SuperStock; **526,** Norbert Wu/Minden Pictures; **527,** Walter Bibikow/Index Stock Imagery/PictureQuest; **528 & 529,** Richard Haynes; **530,** 2005 Jay Wade, www.JayWade.com; **531,** Richard Haynes; **533,** Judith Canty/Stock Boston; **534,** Tom Sanders/Corbis; **535,** Richard Haynes; **537,** Bob Daemmrich Photo, Inc.; **540,** Newsmakers/Getty Images, Inc.; **541,** Michael Schwartz/The Image Works; **543,** David Young-Wolff/PhotoEdit, Inc.; **549,** Myrleen Ferguson Cate/PhotoEdit; **552,** Jack Kurtz/ The Image Works; **554,** Ariel Skelley/Masterfile; **555,** Tom Stewart/Corbis; **560 tl & br,** Richard Haynes; **562,** Sally & Derk Kuper; **568 t,** Art Wolfe, Inc.; **568 b,** Harald Sund/Getty Images, Inc.; **568-569 bkgrd,** Planetary Visions, Ltd.; **568 tl,** Gery Randall/Getty Images, Inc.; **569 tr,** Peter Gridley/Getty Images, Inc.; **569 ml,** Jeff Greenberg/Omni-Photo Communications, Inc.; **569 mr,** Getty Images/Eyewire, Inc.; **569 bl,** David Muench/ Getty Images, Inc.; **569 br,** Harvey Lloyd/Getty Images, Inc.

Chapter 12: Pages 571, Andrea Wells/Getty Images; **572,** Pete Saloutos/Corbis; **573,** Gary Conner/PhotoEdit; **574 tl,** Richard Haynes; **574 mr,** Richard Haynes; **576,** T. Krüsselmann/Zefa/ Masterfile; **578,** 1986 James Mayo/Chicago Tribune; **579,** Tony Freeman/PhotoEdit; **581,** Mike Dobel/Masterfile; **582,** AFP Photo/Don Emmert/Corbis; **586 tm,** Russ Lappa; **586 mr,** Russ Lappa; **586,** Richard Haynes; **587,** Photodisc/Getty Images; **590,** Roger Wood/Corbis; **592 bl,** Zigy Kaluzny/Getty Images, Inc.; **592 tl,** Richard Haynes; **594,** Ron Fehling/Masterfile; **604 tr,** Tim Flach/Getty Images, Inc.; **604 tl,** Chris Bjornberg/Photo Researchers, Inc.; **604-605 b,** Amanda Friedman/Getty Images, Inc.; **605 tm,** Davies & Starr/Getty Images, Inc.; **605 mr,** General Electric Lighting